ZAM

SAFARI

LUANGWA

LOWER ZAMBEZI • VICTORIA FALLS

CHRIS McINTYRE & SUSIE McINTYRE

www.bradtguides.com

Bradt Guides Ltd, UK
The Globe Pequot Press Inc, USA

Bradt GUIDES
TRAVEL TAKEN SERIOUSLY

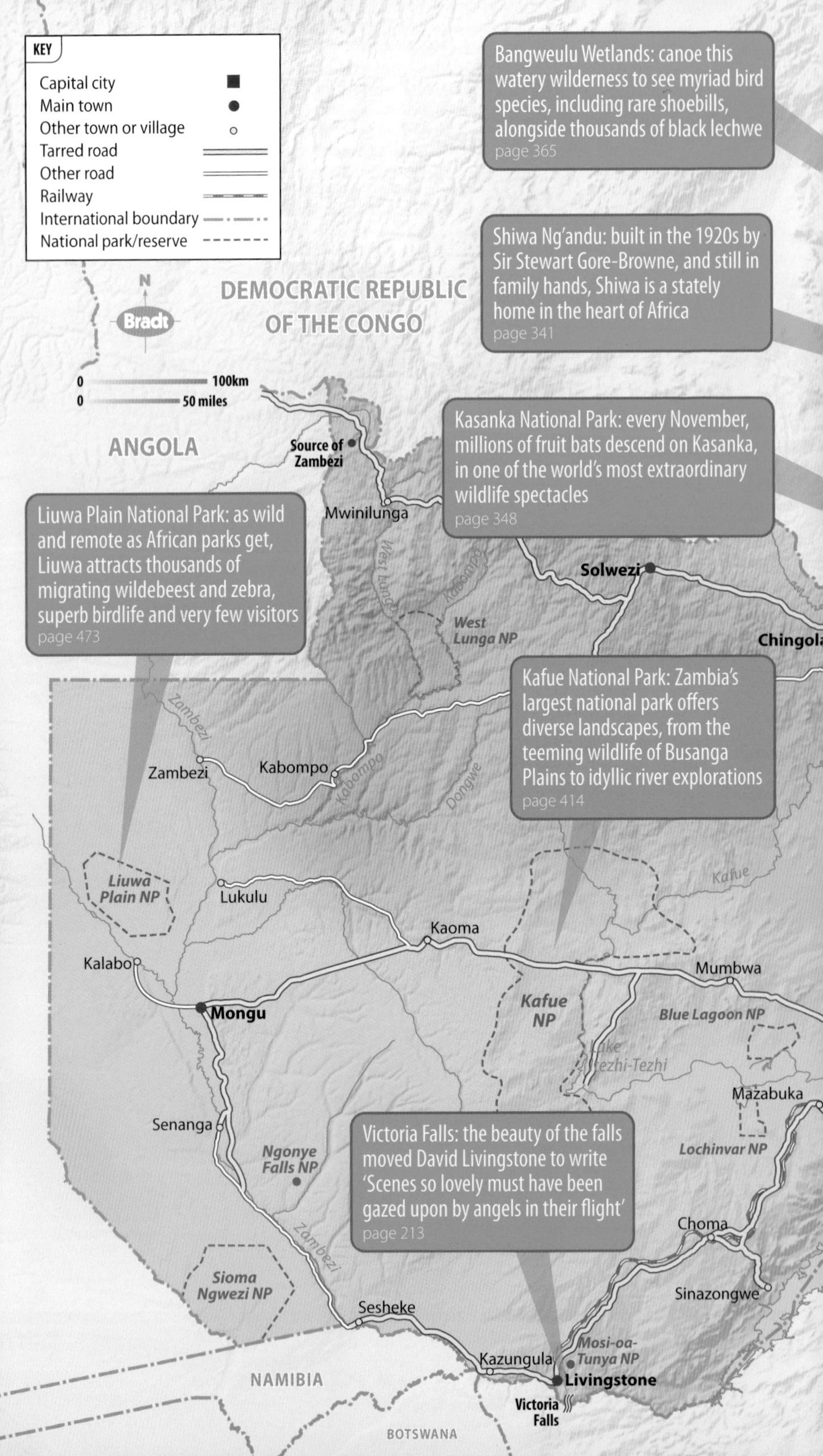

KEY
Capital city
Main town
Other town or village
Tarred road
Other road
Railway
International boundary
National park/reserve
N
Bradt
0 100km
0 50 miles
DEMOCRATIC REPUBLIC OF THE CONGO
ANGOLA
NAMIBIA
BOTSWANA
Bangweulu Wetlands: canoe this watery wilderness to see myriad bird species, including rare shoebills, alongside thousands of black lechwe
page 365
Shiwa Ng'andu: built in the 1920s by Sir Stewart Gore-Browne, and still in family hands, Shiwa is a stately home in the heart of Africa
page 341
Kasanka National Park: every November, millions of fruit bats descend on Kasanka, in one of the world's most extraordinary wildlife spectacles
page 348
Liuwa Plain National Park: as wild and remote as African parks get, Liuwa attracts thousands of migrating wildebeest and zebra, superb birdlife and very few visitors
page 473
Kafue National Park: Zambia's largest national park offers diverse landscapes, from the teeming wildlife of Busanga Plains to idyllic river explorations
page 414
Victoria Falls: the beauty of the falls moved David Livingstone to write 'Scenes so lovely must have been gazed upon by angels in their flight'
page 213
Source of Zambezi
Mwinilunga
West Lunga
Kabompo
West Lunga NP
Solwezi
Chingola
Zambezi
Kabompo
Dongwe
Liuwa Plain NP
Lukulu
Kafue
Kaoma
Kalabo
Mongu
Mumbwa
Kafue NP
Blue Lagoon NP
Lake Itezhi-Tezhi
Mazabuka
Senanga
Ngonye Falls NP
Lochinvar NP
Choma
Sioma Ngwezi NP
Sinazongwe
Sesheke
Mosi-oa-Tunya NP
Kazungula
Livingstone
Victoria Falls

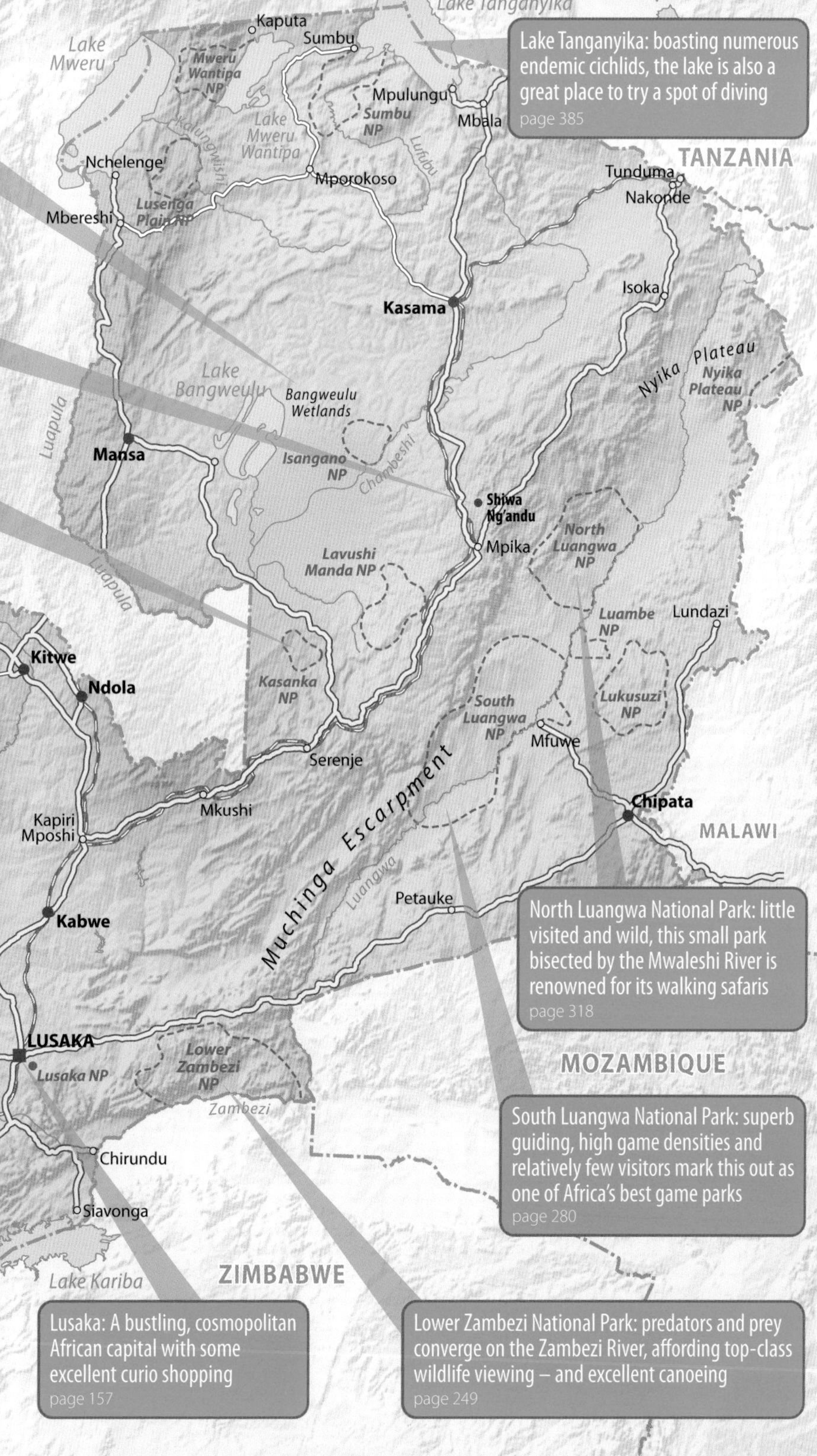
Lake Tanganyika
Lake Tanganyika: boasting numerous endemic cichlids, the lake is also a great place to try a spot of diving
page 385
Lake Mweru
Kaputa
Sumbu
Mweru Wantipa NP
Mpulungu
Sumbu NP
Mbala
Lake Mweru Wantipa
Kalungwishi
Lufubu
TANZANIA
Nchelenge
Mporokoso
Tunduma
Nakonde
Lusenga Plain NP
Mbereshi
Isoka
Kasama
Nyika Plateau
Nyika Plateau NP
Lake Bangweulu
Bangweulu Wetlands
Luapula
Mansa
Isangano NP
Chambeshi
Shiwa Ng'andu
North Luangwa NP
Mpika
Lavushi Manda NP
Luapula
Luambe NP
Lundazi
Kitwe
Ndola
Kasanka NP
South Luangwa NP
Lukusuzi NP
Mfuwe
Serenje
Muchinga Escarpment
Chipata
Mkushi
Kapiri Mposhi
MALAWI
Luangwa
Petauke
Kabwe
North Luangwa National Park: little visited and wild, this small park bisected by the Mwaleshi River is renowned for its walking safaris
page 318
LUSAKA
Lusaka NP
Lower Zambezi NP
MOZAMBIQUE
Zambezi
South Luangwa National Park: superb guiding, high game densities and relatively few visitors mark this out as one of Africa's best game parks
page 280
Chirundu
Siavonga
Lake Kariba
ZIMBABWE
Lusaka: A bustling, cosmopolitan African capital with some excellent curio shopping
page 157
Lower Zambezi National Park: predators and prey converge on the Zambezi River, affording top-class wildlife viewing – and excellent canoeing
page 249

ZAMBIA
DON'T MISS...

BIRDLIFE
With 734 species from southern, central and east Africa, Zambia's diverse habitats offer superb birdwatching PAGE 77
(SS)

VICTORIA FALLS
The spectacular Victoria Falls are 1,688m wide and average just over 100m in height PAGE 213
(SS)

NATIONAL PARKS

National parks and conservation areas cover 30% of Zambia; Luangwa (pictured), Lower Zambezi and Kafue are among Africa's finest for wildlife and experience PAGE 35

(PF/S)

CULTURE

Zambia is home to tribes with many important cultural celebrations. The annual Kuomboka Ceremony for the Lozi king is especially spectacular PAGE 25

(TT)

WILDLIFE

Zambia is home to classic African wildlife, with phenomenal leopard and herds of elephant, as well as endemic subspecies of giraffe, zebra and lechwe PAGE 39

(CS)

ZAMBIA
IN COLOUR

above (CS) — The most peaceful safari activity: a spectacular sunrise canoe trip through Lower Zambezi National Park PAGE 249

below (SS) — Zambia's largest port, Mpulungu, is a vibrant, bustling fishing harbour and the access point for Lake Tanganyika's secluded beach lodges PAGE 388

Artisan crafts make perfect souvenirs. Visit Collective, Tribal Textiles and Mulberry Mongoose for some of Zambia's best PAGES 174 & 279

above left (MMG) & above right (C)

The Royal Livingstone Express offers an unusual vantage point for spotting wildlife in Mosi-oa-Tunya National Park PAGE 217

right (AG/D)

Livingstone's superb curio market is the perfect souvenir stop: from intricate basketry and carved animals to stone sculptures and vibrant kangas PAGE 218

below (M50/D)

AUTHORS

Chris McIntyre went to Africa in 1987, after reading physics at The Queen's College, Oxford. He taught with VSO in Zimbabwe and travelled extensively, before co-authoring the UK's first guide to Namibia and Botswana for Bradt Guides. He now has three Bradt guides to his name: *Namibia*, *Botswana* and *Zambia Safari Guide*, and co-authors three others: *Tanzania Safari Guide*, *Northern Tanzania Safari Guide* and *Zanzibar*. Chris is also the managing director of Expert Africa, the leading tour operator to Zambia. His award-winning company creates tailor-made safaris across southern and eastern Africa for travellers from across the world.

Chris maintains a keen interest in development and conservation issues, acting as professional advisor to various organisations. He is a Fellow of the Royal Geographical Society, and writes and photographs for magazines and newspapers. Chris lives in the UK with his wife and co-author, Susie, and their two bush-savvy children. Chris can be contacted on e chris.mcintyre@expert.africa or through his website w expert.africa.

Susie McIntyre had an adventurous childhood in Zambia and Saudi Arabia, enjoying numerous family adventures to Kafue, Kariba and Luangwa. She has since spent decades promoting responsible global travel, both as a PR and marketing consultant, and as an author and journalist. She is passionate about Africa: its people, wildlife and diversity. From Indian Ocean diving to cutting-edge conservation, community development to off-grid adventures, Susie is dedicated to spreading the word on the wonders of Africa. While focused on ensuring that the continent's complexities are accurately represented, she is both candid and enthusiastic about travel. Susie spends a significant amount of time each year in sub-Saharan Africa to stay abreast of developments and the latest safari camp openings, all of which she meticulously writes about. Susie can be contacted by email on e susie.mcintyre@expert.africa.

AUTHORS' STORY

Between us, we have approaching 75 years of history with Zambia. Susie grew up in Zambia's Copperbelt from the late 1970s, relishing carefree childhood explorations to the Luangwa Valley, messing around in boats on the Kafue River, swimming in glittering pyrite lakes and bouncing around in the back of a pick-up to wild camp with friends near and far. Everything in Zambia at the time was home-grown, homemade or fashioned from something no longer needed. Everyday challenges could be tough, but people were unfailingly warm, the sense of community real, and the scenery simply stunning. To the outside world, however, the problems were often all that was known.

And so it was for Chris in 1995 when he first crossed the Zambezi River with trepidation. Leaving behind prosperous Zimbabwe, where he'd lived for several years, Zambia was very much the unknown. With little information about the country's attractions available, and numerous problems anticipated, he pressed on. In the unfolding reality, he encountered nothing but joy and kindness while backpacking around the country. In fact, marvelling at the Victoria Falls, venturing into national parks, canoeing on the Zambezi and dining under the stars all led to the creation of the first travel guide to Zambia – the first edition of this book.

Years later, having met over a shared love of Zambia, and married, Chris and Susie embarked on uncovering some of the country's most remote corners and returning to familiar haunts together. On backpacking trips, long 4x4 camping expeditions to the country's Western Provinces and far northern reaches, and more decadent fly-in trips to the country's main safari destinations, they travelled extensively across Zambia. Exploring further, they discovered myriad hidden waterfalls and private reserves, the colonial extravagance of Shiwa Ng'andu, and the superb birding of Liuwa's expansive plains. Talking to conservationists, safari operators and community leaders, and plotting and drafting maps of key national parks, and working consistently to showcase the country's ever-improving safari scene has been an ongoing obsession.

Over the years, our love of the country has simply grown. We've been lucky enough to share it with our children and family, and also with the many wonderful travellers sent by Expert Africa. This seventh edition of the guide is now a dedicated safari companion, and our hope is that its readers will find Zambia's incredible wilderness and communities just as spectacular and enchanting as we do.

Contents

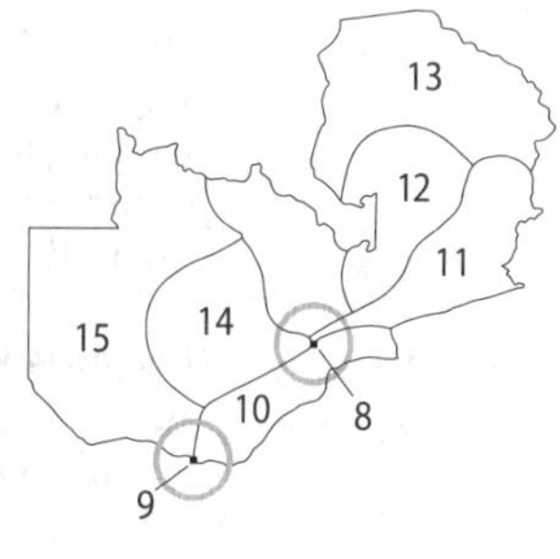

Introduction

Zambia may be increasingly well known as a safari destination, yet the country retains an authentic sense of wilderness: wild, beautiful and slightly unpredictable. It is to these remote, scarcely touched areas that, along with the glories of the Victoria Falls, most visitors are drawn. For that reason, this seventh edition focuses squarely on the country's superb wildlife and wilderness offerings. It is a guide with safari, in all its forms, at its heart.

For afficionados, Zambia remains *the* place for walking safaris in Africa. In its three main national parks – the Luangwa Valley, the Lower Zambezi and Kafue – you'll find first-class, owner-run camps, superb game and some of the continent's best guides. In all of these places you'll see few other visitors too; most Zambian camps remain intimate and remote, a luxury in an increasingly urban world. You'll travel around using small, open-sided 4x4s, seeing few, if any, other vehicles. Throughout Africa there are khaki-uniformed chauffeurs who can drive through the bush, but here, you'll find expert guides to enthrall, enlighten and entrust with your life.

In 1999, the second edition of this guide noted that Zambia was a country for the cognoscenti – it wasn't a place for everyone. You needed to be prepared to rough it a bit and accept last-minute changes without thought. The situation today is radically different. An enormous amount has changed in the intervening years and the options for visitors have broadened immensely. Zambia now offers much more than simply superb bushcamps – though the smallest camps still often remain our favourites. There is increasing diversity in the accommodation and activities on offer, with cultural interactions, family-friendly safaris and several luxury lodges to compete with the very best in the world. Transport has become much easier: internal flights have made virtually all areas accessible, while old Africa hands continue to enjoy mini-expeditions in self-contained 4x4s, along better roads and with easier border crossings. National parks that had been written off from historic poaching are coming back to life, as partnerships with African Parks and established conservation groups invest millions of dollars into improving infrastructure, community development and wildlife protection. Pioneers have opened up super camps in offbeat areas and innovators have introduced new technologies to keep the whole industry progressing. Silent safaris in electric 4x4s and boats are transformative, solar farms power safari camps and mobile phones have transformed communications. Levels of quality and choice have increased phenomenally, and yet not at a rate as to detract from that all-important sense of wilderness and escapism.

Gradually, the whole of this huge country (twice the size of Zimbabwe) is being opened up, and its less famous, but no less wonderful, attractions are starting to share more of the limelight. North Luangwa National Park has been globally recognised for its incredible success in community-backed, black rhino conservation. The wild dogs in Kafue National Park are doing so well that the population is now used to feed into other parks. Cheetah have been reintroduced into Liuwa Plains and the team at Bangweulu Wetlands has launched a global-first scheme to hand-rear critically endangered shoebill storks. Lusaka has transformed into a hip African city with boutique hotels and funky restaurants; Livingstone continues to trailblaze adrenalin sports, and everywhere individuals strive to improve the communities around them through conservation and tourism-backed initiatives.

Zambia is a truly amazing country. Its government encourages tourism, and foreign exchange is desperately needed to alleviate the poverty of many of its people and to ensure that its national parks continue to be preserved and protected. It is for that reason that this guide was first written. Many would prefer Zambia to stay as it is – a favourite place to visit, with superb wildlife, fascinating culture, few other visitors, and Zambians who still treat travellers with kindness and hospitality. So having committed many of Zambia's wild secrets to paper, we ask those who use this guide to do so with respect. Travelling in the wilderness requires great care to ensure its protection. Local cultures are easily eroded by a visitor's lack of sensitivity, and hospitality once abused is seldom offered again. There is immense good that comes from venturing into Zambia's national parks and beyond, and oh

ACCOMMODATION AND RESTAURANT PRICE CODES

Rates at places to stay in this guide have been coded. For urban establishments, and others offering B&B accommodation, rates are based on the cost of a double room with breakfast. Single supplements average around 20%, but may be significantly higher. VAT may be charged extra.

B&B double

$$$$$	£165+; US$250+; K1,875+
$$$$	£100–165; US$150–250; K1,125–1,875
$$$	£50–100; US$80–150; K600–1,125
$$	£25–50; US$40–80; K300–600
$	up to £25; up to US$40; up to K300

For **all-inclusive** places, such as safari lodges and camps, rates are based on a double room including full board and activities (FBA).

♛♛♛♛♛	US$2,000+; £1,330+
♛♛♛♛	US$1,300–2,000; £865–1,330
♛♛♛	US$600–1,300; £400–865
♛♛	US$250–600; £165–400
♛	up to US$250; up to £165

Restaurant price codes are based on the average cost of a main course, which usually exclude VAT (currently 16%) and service of around 10%. For specialities such as seafood, you can expect to pay considerably more.

$$$$$	£9+; US$13+; K100+
$$$$	£7–9; US$10.50–13; K80–100
$$$	£5.50–7; US$8–10.50; K60–80
$$	£3.50–5.50; US$5–8; K40–60
$	up to £3.50; up to US$5; up to K40

so much to enjoy! Please be a thoughtful visitor, for the whole country's sake; the rewards will be greater than you can imagine.

USEFUL INFORMATION

NOTE ON DATUM FOR GPS CO-ORDINATES For all the GPS co-ordinates in this book, note that the datum used is WGS 84 – and you must set your receiver accordingly before copying in any of these co-ordinates.

All GPS co-ordinates in this book have been expressed as degrees, minutes, and decimal fractions of a minute. For further details see page 104.

NOTE ON ACCOMMODATION LISTINGS Where a small group of lodges or hotels come under the same umbrella organisation within a similar area, these have been grouped together. For ease of recognition, the typography used for the 'parent' lodge is as for other lodges, but subsidiaries within the group are noted in small capital letters, with a grey symbol. For example:

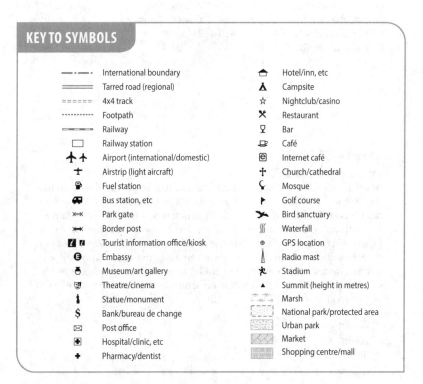

KEY TO SYMBOLS

- International boundary
- Tarred road (regional)
- 4x4 track
- Footpath
- Railway
- Railway station
- Airport (international/domestic)
- Airstrip (light aircraft)
- Fuel station
- Bus station, etc
- Park gate
- Border post
- Tourist information office/kiosk
- Embassy
- Museum/art gallery
- Theatre/cinema
- Statue/monument
- Bank/bureau de change
- Post office
- Hospital/clinic, etc
- Pharmacy/dentist
- Hotel/inn, etc
- Campsite
- Nightclub/casino
- Restaurant
- Bar
- Café
- Internet café
- Church/cathedral
- Mosque
- Golf course
- Bird sanctuary
- Waterfall
- GPS location
- Radio mast
- Stadium
- Summit (height in metres)
- Marsh
- National park/protected area
- Urban park
- Market
- Shopping centre/mall

LIST OF MAPS

FEEDBACK REQUEST

At Bradt Guides we're aware that guidebooks start to go out of date on the day they're published – and that you, our readers, are out there in the field doing research of your own. You'll find out before us when a fine new family-run hotel opens or a favourite restaurant changes hands and goes downhill. So why not tell us about your experiences? Contact us on 01753 893444 or e info@bradtguides.com. We will forward emails to the author who may post updates on the Bradt website at w bradtguides.com/updates. Alternatively, you can add a review of the book to Amazon, or share your adventures with us on social:

BradtGuides
BradtGuides
BradtGuides, ExpertAfrica & Africaphile

HOW TO USE THIS GUIDE

AUTHORS' FAVOURITES Finding genuinely characterful accommodation or that unmissable off-the-beaten-track café can be difficult, so the authors have chosen a few of their favourite places throughout the country to point you in the right direction. These 'authors' favourites' are marked with a ✱.

MAPS

Keys and symbols Maps include alphabetical keys covering the locations of those places to stay, eat or drink that are featured in the book. Note that regional maps may not show all hotels and restaurants in the area: other establishments may be located in towns shown on the map.

Grids and grid references Several maps use gridlines to allow easy location of sites. Map grid references are listed in square brackets after the name of the place or sight of interest in the text, with page number followed by grid number, eg: [158 C3].

Landmarks On occasion, hotels or restaurants that are not listed in the guide (but which might serve as alternative options if required or serve as useful landmarks to aid navigation) are also included on the maps; these are marked with accommodation or restaurant symbols.

WEBSITES Although all third-party websites were working at the time of going to print, some may cease to function during this edition's lifetime. If a website doesn't work, you might want to check back at another time as they often function intermittently. Alternatively, you can let us know of any website issues by emailing e info@bradtguides.com.

EXCHANGE RATES Where sterling and US dollar equivalents are given in this guide, I have assumed a notional rate of around £1 for ZMK23, or US$1 for ZMK18, corresponding to rates that prevailed at the time of research. Despite fluctuations in the value of the kwacha, US dollar prices remain relatively constant, making them a more stable gauge for visitors than the local currency.

Part One

GENERAL INFORMATION

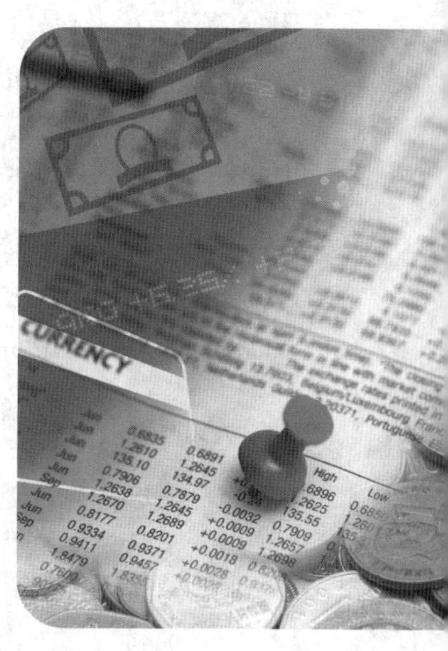

ZAMBIA AT A GLANCE

Location Landlocked in the tropics at the northern edge of the region referred to as 'southern Africa'
Size 752,610km^2
Climate December–April hot and wet, with torrential downpours in the afternoon; May–August dry, and fairly cool; September–November dry, but progressively hotter.
Status Republic
Population 19,610,769 (2022 census)
Population growth per year 2.8% (2022)
Life expectancy at birth Male 60 years; female 65 years (2020, World Bank)
Capital Lusaka; provincial population 3,079,964 (2022 census)
Other main towns Livingstone, Kitwe, Ndola, Kabwe, Chipata, Kasama
Economy Minerals (principally copper and cobalt), agriculture, hydro-electricity, tourism
Natural resources Copper, cobalt, gemstones
GDP US$22.15 billion (2021, World Bank)
GDP growth rate 4.5% annually (2023, World Bank)
Currency Kwacha (K)
Rate of exchange £1 = KMZ23.55, US$1 = KMZ18.23, €1 = KMZ20.07, ZAR1 = KMZ0.97 (July 2023)
Language English, numerous ethnic languages
Religion Christianity, Islam, indigenous beliefs
International telephone code +260
Time GMT +2
Electricity 220v, delivered at 50Hz; British-style plugs with three square pins
Weights and measures Metric
Flag Bright green background; panel lower right of three vertical bands of red, black and orange, surmounted by an orange fish eagle in flight.
Motto 'One Zambia, One Nation'
Public holidays 1 January, Women's Day (8 March), Youth Day (12 March), Kenneth Kaunda Day (28 April), Good Friday, Holy Saturday, Labour Day (1 May), African Unity Day (25 May), Heroes' Day (1st Mon of July), Unity Day (July), Farmers' Day (1st Mon of August), National Prayer Day (18 October), Independence Day (24 October), Christmas (25–26 December). See page 90.
Tourist board w zambiatourism.com

1

History, Politics and Economy

HISTORY

ZAMBIA'S EARLIEST INHABITANTS Palaeontologists looking for evidence of the first ancestors of the human race have excavated a number of sites in Zambia. The earliest remains yet identified are stone tools dated to about 2 million years ago recovered from gravel deposits in the Luangwa Valley and probably also from Victoria Falls. It is thought that these probably belong to the *Homo erectus* species, whose hand-axes in Ethiopia have been dated to 1.75 million years. These were hunter-gatherer people, who could use fire, make tools, and had probably developed some simple speech.

Experts divide the Stone Age into the middle, early and late Stone Ages. The transition from early to middle Stone-Age technology – which is indicated by a larger range of stone tools often adapted for particular uses, and signs that these people had a greater mastery of their environment – was probably in progress around 300,000 years ago in Zambia, based on recent excavations near Lusaka and at Kalambo Falls near Mbala.

The famous 'Broken Hill Man' lived around this time. His skull and other bones and stone artefacts were unearthed from about 20m underground during mining operations near Kabwe in 1921. He has been described as being from a species called *Homo rhodesiensis*, but is more generally attributed to *Homo heidelbergensis*, the common ancestor of *Homo sapiens* in Africa, and of the Neanderthals in Europe. (His name comes from the fact that Kabwe's old name was Broken Hill.)

The late Stone Age in Zambia is normally characterised by a distinctive tradition of geometric rock art; by the use of composite tools, those made of wood and/or bone and/or stone used together; and by the presence of a revolutionary invention: the bow and arrow. This first appeared in Zambia about 25,000 years ago. Skeletons found around the Kafue Flats area indicate that some of these late Stone-Age hunters had a close physical resemblance to the modern San/Bushmen people, whose culture, relying on a late Stone-Age level of technology, survived intact in the Kalahari Desert until the middle of the 20th century.

THE IRON AGE Around 3000BC, late Stone-Age hunter-gatherer groups in Ethiopia, and elsewhere in north and west Africa, started to keep domestic animals, sow seeds and harvest the produce: they were among the world's first farmers.

By around 1000BC these new pastoral practices had spread south into the equatorial forests of what is now the Democratic Republic of Congo (DRC), to around Lake Victoria, and into the northern area of the Great Rift Valley, in northern Tanzania. However, agriculture did not spread south into the rest of central/southern Africa immediately. Only when the technology, and the tools, of iron-working became known did the practices start their relentless expansion southwards.

The spread of agriculture and Iron-Age culture seems to have been rapid. It was brought south by Africans who were taller and heavier than the existing small inhabitants. The ancestors of the San/Bushmen people, with their simple Stone-Age technology and hunter-gatherer existence, just could not compete with these Iron-Age farmers, who became the ancestors of virtually all the modern black Africans in southern Africa.

This major migration occurred around the first few centuries AD, and since then the San/Bushmen of southern Africa have gradually been either assimilated into the migrant groups, or effectively pushed into areas which could not be farmed. Thus the older Stone-Age cultures persisted in the forests of the north and east of Zambia – which were more difficult to cultivate – much longer than they survived in the south of the country.

MORE IMMIGRANTS By the 4th or 5th century AD, Iron-Age farmers had settled throughout much of southern Africa. As well as iron-working technology, they brought with them pottery, the remains of which are used by archaeologists to work out the migrations of various different groups of these Bantu settlers. These migrations continued, and the distribution of pottery styles suggests that the groups moved around within the subcontinent: this was much more complex than a simple north–south influx.

THE ORIGINS OF TRADE In burial sites dating from the latter half of the first millennium, occasional 'foreign' objects start to occur: the odd cowrie shell, or copper bangles in an area where there is no copper. This indicates that some small-scale bartering with neighbouring villages was beginning to take place.

In the first half of the second millennium, the pace and extent of this trade increased significantly. Gold objects appear (as well as the more common copper, iron and ivory) and shells from the Indian Ocean. The frequency of these indicates that trade was gradually developing. We know from European historical sources that Muslim traders (of Arab or possibly African origin) were venturing into the heart of Africa by around AD1400, and thus trade routes were being established.

As trade started, so the second millennium also saw the development of wealth and social structures within the tribes. The evidence for this is a number of burial sites that stand out for the quantity and quality of the goods that were buried with the dead person. One famous site, at Ngombe Ilede, near the confluence of the Lusitu and Zambezi rivers, was occupied regularly over many centuries. There is evidence that its inhabitants traded from the 14th century with people further south, in Zimbabwe, exporting gold down the Zambezi via traders coming from the Indian Ocean. Indications of cotton-weaving have also been found there, and several copper crosses unearthed are so similar that they may have been used as a simple form of currency – valuable to both the local people and traders from outside.

By the middle of the second millennium, a number of separate cultures seem to have formed in Zambia. Many practised trade, and a few clearly excelled at it. Most were starting to develop social structures within the group, with some enjoying more status and wealth than others.

THE CHIEFS From around the middle of the second millennium, there is little good archaeological evidence that can be accurately dated. However, sources for the events of this period in Zambia's history are the oral histories of Zambia's people, as well as their current languages and social traditions. The similarities and differences between the modern Zambian languages can be extrapolated by linguistic experts to point to the existence of about nine different root languages, which probably existed in Zambia in the 15th century.

The latter half of the second millennium AD saw the first chiefs, and hence kingdoms, emerge from Zambia's dispersed clans. The title 'chief' can be applied to anyone from a village headman to a god-like king. However, this was an era of increasing trade, when the groups with the largest resources and armies dominated local disputes. Thus it made sense for various clans to group together into tribes, under the rule of a single individual, or chief.

One of the oldest groups is thought to have been that of the Chewa people, led by the Undi, who came to the Luangwa area from the southern side of Lake Malawi in the 16th century. By the end of that century the Ng'andu clan (clan of the crocodile) established a kingdom among the Bemba people. These lived mostly in woodland areas, practising simple slash-and-burn types of agriculture. Perhaps because of the poverty of their lifestyle, they later earned a reputation as warriors for their raids on neighbouring tribes.

In the latter part of the 17th century the first recorded Lozi king (or Litunga, as he is known) is thought to have settled near Kalabo, in the west of Zambia, starting a powerful dynasty which lasts to the present day. Early in the 18th century Mwata Kazemba established a kingdom around the southern end of Lake Mweru in the Luapula Valley.

THE GROWTH OF TRADE As various cohesive kingdoms developed, their courts served as centres of trade, and their chiefs had the resources to initiate trade with other communities. Foodstuffs, iron, copper, salt, cotton, cloth, tobacco, baskets, pottery and many other items were traded within Zambia, between the various tribes.

From around the 14th century, Zambia had a trickle of trade with non-Africans: mostly Muslims exporting gold through the east coast of Africa. (This trade had started as early as the 10th century on the Limpopo River, south of Zimbabwe's gold fields.) However, by the early 17th century the Muslims had been supplanted by the Portuguese, and by the latter half of the 17th century these Portuguese merchants were operating out of Mozambique, trading gold, ivory and copper with Zambia.

Trade with the outside world escalated during the 18th century, as more and more tribes became involved, and more foreigners came to the table. Some chiefs started to barter their commodities for weapons, in attempts to gain advantage over their neighbours. Those vanquished in local conflicts were certainly used as sources of slaves – an increasingly valuable trading commodity. These and other factors increased the pressure on Zambians to trade, and the influx of foreign traders made the picture more complex still.

By the early 19th century, both traders and slavers were visiting Zambia with increasing frequency. These were responding to the increasing consumer demands of newly industrialised Europe and America. More trade routes were opening up, not just through Mozambique and Angola, but also to the north and south. Internal conflicts were increasing, as both the means to conduct these, and the incentives for victory, grew.

WESTERN REQUIREMENTS During the 19th century, the West (western Europe and North America) had traded with the native Africans to obtain what they wanted – commodities and slave labour – without having to go to the trouble of ruling parts of the continent. However, as the century progressed, and the West became more industrialised, it needed these things in greater quantities than the existing tribal structures in Africa could supply. Further, there was demand for materials that could be produced in Africa, like cotton and rubber, but which required Western production methods.

Given that the West wanted a wider range and greater quantity of cheaper raw materials, the obvious solution was to control the means of supply. African political organisation was widely regarded as primitive, and not capable of providing complex and sustained trade. Inward investment would also be needed, but would be forthcoming only if white enterprises were safe from African interference. Hence the solution to Western requirements was to bring Africa, and the Africans, under European rule.

Another reason for considering the acquisition of African territory was that the world was shrinking. There were no inhabitable continents left to discover. Staking a nation's claim to large chunks of Africa seemed prudent to most of the Western powers of the time, and growing competition for these areas meant they could always be traded for one another at a later date.

LIVINGSTONE'S CONTRIBUTION David Livingstone's *Missionary Travels and Researches in South Africa* excited great interest in England. This account of his journeys across southern Africa in the 1840s and '50s had all the appeal that undersea or space exploration has for us now. Further, it captured the imagination of the British public, allowing them to take pride in their country's exploration of Africa, based on the exploits of an explorer who seemed to be the epitome of bravery and righteous religious zeal.

Livingstone had set out with the conviction that if Africans could see their material and physical well-being improved – probably by learning European ways, and earning a living from export crops – then they would be ripe for conversion to Christianity. He was strongly opposed to slavery, but sure that this would disappear when Africans became more self-sufficient through trade.

In fact Livingstone was almost totally unsuccessful in his own aims, failing to set up any successful trading missions, or even to convert many Africans permanently to Christianity. However, his travels opened up areas north of the Limpopo for later British missionaries, and by 1887 British mission stations were established in Zambia and southern Malawi.

THE SCRAMBLE FOR AFRICA British foreign policy in southern Africa had always revolved around the Cape Colony, which was seen as vital to British interests in India and the Indian Ocean. Africa to the north of the Cape Colony had largely been ignored. The Boers were on the whole left to their farming in the Transvaal area, and posed no threat to the colony.

However, Germany annexed South West Africa (now Namibia) in 1884, prompting British fears that they might try to link up with the Boers. Thus, to drive a wedge through the middle of these territories, the British negotiated an alliance with Khama, a powerful Tswana king, and proclaimed as theirs the Protectorate of Bechuanaland – the forerunner of modern Botswana.

Soon after, in 1886, the Boers discovered large gold deposits in the Witwatersrand (around Johannesburg). The influx of money from this boosted the Boer farmers, who expanded their interests to the north, making a treaty with Khama's enemy, the powerful Lobengula. This in turn prompted the British to look beyond the Limpopo, and to back the territorial aspirations of a millionaire British businessman, Cecil Rhodes. By 1888 Rhodes, a partner in the De Beers consortium, had control of the lucrative diamond-mining industry in Kimberley, South Africa. He was hungry for power, and dreamt of linking the Cape to Cairo with land under British control.

His wealth enabled Rhodes to buy sole rights to mine minerals in Lobengula's territory. Thence he persuaded the British government to grant his company – the British South Africa Company – the licence to stake claims to African territory with the authority of the British government. In 1889 Rhodes sent out several expeditions to the chiefs in the area now comprising Zimbabwe, Zambia and Malawi, to make treaties. These granted British 'protection and aid' in return for sole rights to minerals in the chiefs' territories, and assurances that they would not make treaties with any other foreign powers. This effective strategy was greatly helped by the existing British influence from the missions, which were already established in many of the regions. By 1891 the British had secured these areas (through Rhodes's British South Africa Company) from the other European powers, and confirmed their boundaries in treaties with the neighbouring colonial powers.

By the closing years of the 19th century, Zambia – or Northern Rhodesia as it was called – was clearly under British rule. However, this had little impact until local administrations were set up, and taxes started to be collected.

THE MINES In the early years of the 20th century, Rhodes's British South Africa Company did little in Northern Rhodesia. Its minerals were not nearly as accessible or valuable as those in Southern Rhodesia, and little protection or aid actually materialised. It became viewed by the colonials as a source of cheap labour for the mines of South Africa and Southern Rhodesia.

To facilitate this, taxes were introduced for the local people, which effectively forced them to come into the cash economy. Virtually the only way for them to do this was to find work in one of the mines further south. By 1910 a railway linked the mine at Kimberley, in South Africa, with Victoria Falls and beyond, making long-distance travel in the subcontinent more practical.

Meanwhile the cost of administering and defending the company's interests was rising, and in 1923 Southern Rhodesia became self-governing. In 1924 the British Colonial Office took over administration of Northern Rhodesia from the British South Africa Company, though the mining rights remained with the Company. The Colonial Office then set up a legislative council to advise on the government of the province, though only a few of its members came from outside the administration.

Shortly afterwards, in 1928, huge deposits of copper were located below the basin of the upper Kafue, under what is now known as the Copperbelt. Over the next decade or so these were developed into a number of large copper mines, working rich, deep deposits of copper. World War II demanded increased production of base metals, and by 1945 Northern Rhodesia was producing 12% of the non-communist world's copper. This scale of production required large labour forces. The skilled workers were mostly of European origin, often from South Africa's mines, while the unskilled workers came from all over Northern Rhodesia.

Wages and conditions were very poor for the unskilled miners, who were treated as migrant workers and expected to go home to their permanent villages every year or so to 'recover'. Death rates among them were high. Further, the drain of men to work the mines inevitably destabilised the villages, and poverty and malnutrition were common in the rural areas.

WELFARE ASSOCIATIONS As early as 1929 welfare associations had formed in several of the territory's southern towns, aimed at giving black Africans a voice and trying to defend their interests. These associations were often started by teachers or clerks, the more educated members of the communities. They were small at first, far too small to mount any effective challenge to the establishment, but they did succeed in raising awareness among the Africans, all of whom were being exploited.

In 1935 the African mineworkers first organised themselves to strike over their pay and conditions. By 1942 the towns of the African labourers in the Copperbelt were forming their own welfare associations, and by 1949 some of these had joined together as the Northern Rhodesian African Mineworkers' Union. This had been officially recognised by the colonial government as being the equal of any union for white workers. In 1952 the union showed its muscle with a successful and peaceful three-week strike, resulting in substantial wage increases.

The unions remain a force in Zambia, especially in the state sector. In February 2004, a coalition of unions organised the country's first national strike in 16 years, protesting against tax hikes and wage freezes which were being imposed on government employees.

CENTRAL AFRICAN FEDERATION The tiny European population in Northern Rhodesia was, on the whole, worried by the growth of the power of black African mineworkers. Most of the white people wanted to break free from colonial rule, so that they could control the pace and direction of political change. They also resented the loss of vast revenues from the mines, which went directly to the British government and the British South Africa Company, without much benefit for Northern Rhodesia.

During the 1930s and 1940s the settlers' representation on Northern Rhodesia's Legislative Council was gradually increased, and calls for self-rule became more insistent. As early as 1936 Stewart Gore-Browne (founder of Shiwa Ng'andu; page 341) had proposed a scheme for a Central African Federation, with an eye to Britain's future (or lack of one) in Africa. This view gained ground in London, where the government was increasingly anxious to distance itself from African problems.

In 1948 the South African Nationalist Party came to power in South Africa, on a tide of Afrikaner support. The historical enmity between the Afrikaners and the British in South Africa led the British colonials in Southern and Northern Rhodesia to look to themselves for their own future, rather than their neighbours in South Africa. In 1953 their pressure was rewarded and Southern and Northern Rhodesia were formally joined with Nyasaland (which is now Malawi), to become the independent Central African Federation.

The formation of the Federation did little to help the whites in Northern Rhodesia, though it was strongly opposed by the blacks, who feared that they would then lose more of their land to white settlers. Earlier, in 1948, the Federation of African Societies – an umbrella group of welfare associations – changed its name at an annual general meeting into an overtly political Northern Rhodesian Congress. This had branches in the mining towns and the rural areas, and provided a base upon which a black political culture could be based. A few years later, it was renamed as the Northern Rhodesia African National Congress.

INDEPENDENCE Despite the Federation, Northern Rhodesia actually remained under the control of the Colonial Office. Further, the administration of the Federation was so biased towards Southern Rhodesia that the revenues from its mines simply flowed there, instead of to Britain. Thus though the Federation promised much, it delivered few of the settlers' wishes in Northern Rhodesia.

A small core of increasingly skilled African mineworkers gained better pay and conditions, while poverty was rife in the rest of the country. By the 1950s small improvements were being made in the provision of education for black Zambians, but widespread neglect had demonstrated to most that whites did not want blacks as their political or social equals. Thus black politics began to focus on another goal: independence.

In 1958 elections were held, and about 25,000 blacks were allowed to vote. The Northern Rhodesia African National Congress was divided about whether to participate or not, and eventually this issue split the party. Kenneth Kaunda, the radical secretary general, and others founded the Zambia African National Congress (ZANC). This was soon banned, and Kaunda was jailed during a state of emergency.

Finally, in 1960, Kaunda was released from jail, and greeted as a national hero. He took control of a splinter party, the United National Independence Party (UNIP), and after a short campaign of civil disobedience forced the Colonial Office to hold universal elections. In October of 1962, these confirmed a large majority for UNIP. In 1963 the Federation broke up, and in 1964 elections based on universal adult suffrage gave UNIP a commanding majority. On 24 October 1964 Zambia became independent, with Kenneth Kaunda as its president.

ZAMBIA UNDER KAUNDA President Kenneth Kaunda (usually known as just 'KK') took over a country whose income was controlled by the state of the world copper market, and whose trade routes were entirely dependent upon Southern Rhodesia, South Africa and Mozambique. He also inherited a 50 million kwacha national debt from the colonial era, and a populace which was largely unskilled and uneducated. (At independence, there were fewer than one hundred Zambians with university degrees, and fewer than a thousand who had completed secondary school.)

In 1965, shortly after Zambia's independence, Southern Rhodesia made a Unilateral Declaration of Independence (UDI). This propelled Zambia's southern neighbour further along the path of white rule that South Africa had adopted. Sanctions were then applied to Rhodesia by the rest of the world. Given that most of Zambia's trade passed through Rhodesia, these had very negative effects on the country's economy.

As the black people of Rhodesia, South Africa and South West Africa (Namibia) started their liberation struggles, Kaunda naturally wanted to support them. Zambia became a haven for political refugees, and a base for black independence movements. However ideologically sound this approach was, it was costly and did not endear Zambia to its economically dominant white-ruled neighbours. As the apartheid government in South Africa began a policy of destabilising the black-ruled countries around the subcontinent, so civil wars and unrest became the norm in Mozambique and Angola, squeezing Zambia's trade routes further.

The late 1960s and early 1970s saw Zambia try to drastically reduce its trade with the south. Simultaneously it worked to increase its links with Tanzania – which was largely beyond the reach of South Africa's efforts to destabilise. With the help of China, Tanzania and Zambia built excellent road and rail links from the heart of Zambia to Dar es Salaam, on the Indian Ocean. However, as a trading partner Tanzania was no match for the efficiency of South Africa, and Zambia's economy remained sluggish.

During these difficult years Zambia's debt grew steadily. The government's large revenues from copper were used in efforts to reduce the country's dependence on its southern neighbours, and to improve standards of living for the majority of Zambians. Education was expanded on a large scale, government departments were enlarged to provide employment, and food subsidies maintained the peace of the large urban population. Kaunda followed Julius Nyerere's example in Tanzania in many ways, with a number of socialist policies woven into his own (much promoted) philosophy of 'humanism'.

In retrospect, perhaps Kaunda's biggest mistake was that he failed to use the large revenues from copper either to reduce the national debt, or to diversify Zambia's export base – but his choices were not easy.

By 1969, the Zambian government was receiving about three-quarters of the profits made by the mining industries in taxes and duties. Because of this, they were reluctant to invest further. With the stated aim of encouraging expansion in the industry and investment in new mines, the government started to reform the ownership of the copper mines. A referendum was held on the subject and the government took control of mining rights throughout the country. It then bought a 51% share in each of the mines, which was paid for out of the government's own dividends in the companies over the coming years. Thus began ZCCM (Zambia Consolidated Copper Mines).

In the early 1970s, the world copper price fell dramatically. Simultaneously the cost of imports (especially oil) rose, the world economy slumped and the interest rates on Zambia's debt increased. These factors highlighted the fundamental weaknesses of Zambia's economy, which had been established to suit the colonial powers rather than the country's citizens.

The drop in the price of copper crippled Zambia's economy. Efforts to stabilise the world copper price – through a cartel of copper-producing countries, similar to the oil-producing OPEC countries – failed. The government borrowed more money, betting on a recovery in copper prices that never materialised.

In the 1970s and 1980s Kaunda's government became increasingly intertwined with the International Monetary Fund (IMF) in the search for a solution to the country's debt. None was found. Short-term fixes just made things worse, and the country's finances deteriorated. The West did give Zambia aid, but mostly for specific projects that usually had strings attached. What Zambia most needed was help with the enormous interest payments that it was required to make to the West.

Various recovery plans, often instituted by the IMF, were tried. In 1986 food subsidies were sharply withdrawn, starting with breakfast meal, one of the country's staple foods. This hit the poor hardest, and major riots broke out before subsidies were hastily reintroduced to restore calm. In 1988 Zambia applied to the United Nations for the status of 'least-developed nation' in the hope of obtaining greater international assistance. It was rejected. By the end of the decade Zambia's economy was in tatters. The official exchange rate bore little relation to the currency's actual worth, and inflation was rampant. Zambia was one of the world's poorest countries, with a chronic debt problem, a weak currency and at times very high inflation. A reputation for corruption, reaching to the highest levels of the government, did little to encourage help from richer nations.

Despite Kaunda's many failures with the economy, his policies did encourage the development of some home-grown industries to produce goods which could replace previously imported items. It also created systems for mass education, which were almost entirely absent when he came to power.

ZAMBIA UNDER CHILUBA These economic problems, and the lack of obvious material benefits for the majority of Zambians, gradually fomented opposition. UNIP's tendency to become authoritarian in its demands for unity also led to unrest. Kaunda's rule was finally challenged successfully by the capitalist Movement for Multiparty Democracy (MMD) led by Frederick Chiluba. This received widespread support during the late 1980s, on a platform of liberalisation and anti-corruption measures.

Kaunda agreed to an election, apparently certain that he would win. In the event, UNIP was resoundingly defeated by the MMD (16% to 84%), and Chiluba became Zambia's second elected president, in November 1991. Kaunda accepted the results, at least at face value. However, he later claimed that the elections were unfair because many of Zambia's older people, whom he regarded as his natural constituency, didn't vote. He continued to head UNIP until 2000, and lived in Zambia until his death in 2021 – which, in itself, is a rare and encouraging co-existence in the volatile world of modern African politics.

When elected, Frederick Chiluba faced enormous economic problems, which he attempted to tackle. He succeeded in liberalising and privatising much of the economy, resulting in a freely floating market for the kwacha, and policies to attract inward investment. However, in 1995 the country's debt stood at US$6.25 billion, and debt service payments were some 40% of the gross national product – equivalent to about US$600/£400 per capita per annum. Zambia owed US$3.1 billion to the World Bank and the IMF alone.

Initially Chiluba gained the confidence of Western donors when he came to power in 1991. However, his reforms were long term, and much of their success depended on the continued willingness of international donors to help him. Many allege that corruption grew during his time in power.

Certainly the general attitude of Zambians towards visitors changed under Chiluba: Zambia became a more welcoming country than it was under Kaunda's reign. Tourism began to be recognised as a direct and helpful source of jobs and foreign currency, and the climate of suspicion prevailing in Kaunda's Zambia was replaced with a warmer welcome.

LATE 20TH CENTURY Presidential elections were held in 1996. However, using his enormous majority, Chiluba changed the constitution to include a clause that 'no person born of non-Zambian parents can be president'. Kenneth Kaunda, as is well known, was born of Malawian parents, and so this was a clear move to exclude him from running for the office. It was not the only such move, and caused endless furore.

As head of UNIP, KK called for all UNIP candidates to boycott the elections, believing that they could not be fair. In the event, several UNIP candidates split off and stood as independent candidates, but the overall result was another resounding win for Chiluba. (MMD won about 132 of 150 seats.) It's widely thought that he would have won anyhow, even in a fair election, so it seems a pity that he resorted to dubious tactics to achieve the victory.

With poetic justice, it later transpired that Chiluba himself was of illegitimate birth and uncertain national origin. *The Post* newspaper claimed to have researched and verified that his own parents were of DRC/Zairean descent, which led to a long-running persecution of the paper by the government for 'being disrespectful' and 'insulting' the president – both of which are punishable offences in Zambia. (Travellers take note!)

THE COUP At the end of October 1997, a small group of soldiers briefly took over the state-run radio station. They were led by Stephen Lungu, the self-styled 'Captain Solo', who claimed to represent the 'National Redemption Council'. (Neither he nor the council had been heard of before.) He announced that the group had launched 'Operation Born-again' and ousted the MMD government and Chiluba, saying later in a short broadcast that he had seen 'an angel and the message was that the government had to be overthrown'.

Although this group transpired to have been little more than a few drunken soldiers, Chiluba used the incident as an excuse to institute a state of emergency for five months. He detained more than 70 civilians and soldiers, including opposition leaders and the former president, KK. Some detainees claimed that torture was used during interrogations, allegations which were later substantiated by the government's own human rights commission headed by Supreme Court judge, Lombe Chibesakunda. The clampdown by the state attracted heavy criticism from human rights groups and affected the international donor community's willingness to release funds for debt relief.

A year later the case against many was dropped for lack of evidence, and some sued the state for wrongful arrest. Nevertheless, 44 were convicted and sentenced to death, although within months their sentences were commuted by the president to between ten and 20 years of hard labour.

THE END OF CHILUBA'S REGIME Many regarded President Chiluba's presidency as a disappointment, yet looking at conditions in neighbouring Zaire and Zimbabwe, most agreed that the situation in Zambia could have been much worse. Chiluba avoided any military involvement in the conflict in neighbouring Democratic Republic of Congo (DRC) – which had already sucked in Zimbabwe, Angola, Namibia, Chad, Uganda and Rwanda – and instead played a high-profile role in brokering various peace talks.

However, he continued KK's habit of regularly reshuffling ministers (thus ensuring that none developed their own power base), was slow to take decisions and proved unable to control corruption. Despite vowing that he would stand by the constitution, he tried his best to arrange a third term for himself. It was only tremendous pressure from the people, and from within the MMD, that forced him to step down in 2001.

THE 21ST CENTURY In 2001 the MMD's candidate and Chiluba's chosen successor, Levy Patrick Mwanawasa, was narrowly declared the victor with just 29% of the vote, but the elections were criticised by international observers, and three of the opposition parties challenged the results in the High Court.

A lawyer by profession, Mwanawasa was almost universally respected for his integrity. With his mandate of 'Continuity with Change', he launched an anti-corruption campaign which resulted in the prosecution of Chiluba, and many of the ex-president's supporters. Yet despite the allegations of misappropriating some US$500,000 of government funds, Chiluba was finally cleared of all charges in 2009. He died on 18 June 2011.

Mwanawasa himself was re-elected in 2006 with a rather more convincing 43% of the vote, but he died from a stroke in 2008. His vice-president, Rupiah Banda, took over the reins – albeit with a similarly shaky mandate – but it was not to last. In September 2011, following a fiercely contested and at times violent election, the MMD met defeat at the hands of the Patriotic Front (PF), led by the charismatic Michael Sata. The 74-year-old Sata, nicknamed King Cobra, had significant experience, having served with both UNIP and the MMD before setting up the PF in 2001. Indeed, he was only narrowly defeated in the 2008 presidential by-election. The failure of the MMD to hold on to power was in part due to Sata himself, a more colourful character than his presidential adversary, but other factors included a public reaction against the state-controlled section of the media, and increasing concern at the perceived lack of benefit to Zambia from the privatised mining industry.

Once again, however, fate intervened. The new president was already rumoured to be suffering from ill health when he was sworn in, and following medical treatment in several countries, he died in the UK on 28 October 2014. His deputy, Guy Scott, stepped into the breach as interim president, but the 70-year-old white Zambian was ineligible to run for president as the constitution bars candidates whose parents were not born in Zambia. Following a by-election on 20 January 2015, Sata's Patriotic Front colleague, Edgar Chagwa Lungu, was voted into office, winning by the narrowest of margins: just 1.66%.

Described on his website as 'officer, gentleman, lawyer and politician', Lungu held ministerial roles in the areas of home affairs and defence during the Sata administration. He was also secretary-general of the PF, a position from which he was notably ousted by Scott, albeit for just one day. Although the early days of Lungu's presidency were also marked by ill health, he was, at 58, considerably younger than his predecessor. His promise of lower interest rates and promotion of human rights spoke of a liberal approach, as did his appointment of a female vice-president.

In August 2016, Lungu was re-elected for a full five-year term as president. There was some worrying evidence at the time that PF hardliners, desperate to hold onto power, were utilising very undemocratic strategies, notably violence, intimidation and curbs on press freedom (the independent newspaper, *The Post*, was forced to suspend operations by government order). The hardliners' admiration for Robert Mugabe's one-party state was no secret and Zambia's influential Chinese backers certainly value stability above democracy. However, international observers from the EU, US and African Union did agree that, in spite of the unbalanced nature of the state media, the elections were free, transparent and peaceful. That's very impressive in post-independence southern Africa.

Lunga's time as president came to an end in August 2021 when he was defeated by Hakainde Hichilema of the liberal United Party for National Development. The elections were deemed to be free and transparent by observers but, once again, criticism was levelled at the one-sided state media. However, the transition was peaceful with Lunga issuing a televised congratulatory message to his successor. Hichilema, a wealthy, well-educated cattle rancher from Monze, came to power promising economic reform, fiscal responsibility and corruption-free politics, having led his party since 2006.

From his appointment of a 'New Dawn' cabinet with representatives from all of Zambia's provinces, it was clear that Hichilema was seeking to restore ethnic balance to the government's key positions, and away from the predominantly Bemba-speaking rule under PF. Sadly, however, only four of the 25 cabinet ministers are female, a somewhat retrograde step, which alongside the dissolution of the Ministry of Gender, does not appear in line with the UPND's election promise to strive for gender equality in all positions of government. That said, the appointment of a respected chief justice and experienced economist as finance minister do herald the way for the promised reforms.

Hichilema has also made positive moves to restore press freedom, and at his first national budget allocated funds to recruit 30,000 teachers and over 11,000 health professionals. Alongside this, he has made decisive moves to decentralise the budget and move significant financial resources into the provinces to encourage local – especially rural – development. Significantly, he has also abolished all fees for primary and secondary public education.

At the time of writing, approaching two years of Hichilema's presidency, there is a positivity towards this government, both nationally and internationally, and a sense that freedom, stability and democracy are tangibly stronger. Many, especially Zambia's youth, have high hopes for their future under his leadership.

GOVERNMENT AND ADMINISTRATION

The chief of state and the head of government is the president, who appoints cabinet ministers from members of the National Assembly, a chamber of 156 elected representatives, plus a further eight nominated by the president and three ex-officio members: the Speaker, First Deputy Speaker and the Vice President. Elections are held every five years, with all Zambian citizens of 18 years and over eligible to vote in a first-past-the-post system.

The country is divided into ten provinces for administrative purposes: Central, Copperbelt, Eastern, Luapula, Lusaka, Muchinga, Northern, North-Western, Southern and Western.

The judicial system was set up according to a British model, based on English common law and customary law. Legislative acts receive judicial review in an ad hoc constitutional council.

ECONOMY

Zambia's economy is totally dependent upon its mining sector, and particularly its copper mines, although agriculture, industry and tourism all make their contribution, and the government is committed to diversification. The country's high, well-watered plateau means that it has about 40% of southern Africa's water resources. Hydro-electric schemes, which provide most of the country's power, make it self-sufficient in energy, and Zambia already exports power to neighbouring countries.

Despite recent improvements in the economy and the write-off of most external debt, Zambia remains among the world's poorest countries. While its mineral wealth has brought considerable economic dividends over the years, heavy reliance on that sector also serves to make the country very vulnerable to fluctuations in world markets. In the last few years, world growth and the continued rise in demand for consumer electronics and electric cars has driven up demand for raw materials such as copper and cobalt, with direct benefits to Zambia.

RECENT ECONOMIC HISTORY Zambia's recent economic history has been a bumpy ride. In the mid 1990s, prospects looked good. GDP growth was about 6.5%; inflation was down to 24% (from 187% in 1993); a decline in manufacturing had been reversed; non-traditional exports were expanding at a rate of 33% a year; and the privatisation programme was being hailed as one of Africa's most successful. Even the kwacha had been stabilised and a surge in foreign investment was being reported.

By 1998, however, the reversal of Zambia's economic fortunes was stark. GDP growth was minimal, manufacturing output was again in a downturn, and inflation was slowly rising. While the breakdown in the privatisation of Zambia Consolidated Copper Mines (ZCCM) was a major cause of this reversal (page 17), part of the problem stemmed from the coup attempt in late 1997. On both counts, Western donors withheld aid to Zambia.

A year later, when the signs improved, aid and debt relief were again forthcoming, and there was optimism that Zambia's economy could continue to improve. Privatisation of the government-owned copper mines relieved the government from covering mammoth losses generated by the industry and greatly improved the chances for copper mining to return to profitability and spur economic growth.

THE BURDEN OF DEBT For years, Zambia was visibly crippled by its burden of debt. At around US$500 per person, the country had one of the highest levels of per-capita debt in the world, but a GNI (gross national income) of only around US$340 per capita. About two-thirds of all Zambians lived on less than US$1 per day, a figure that remains largely unchanged.

For most of the 1990s, Zambia followed a programme of economic reforms largely dictated by the IMF and World Bank. This scheme, known as the Enhanced Structural Adjustment Facility (ESAF), allowed the world's poorest nations to pay lower interest rates on the money that they owed. In 1995, with assistance from ESAF, Zambia embarked on a series of far-reaching reforms. These centred on trade liberalisation, deregulation and exchange-rate reform. Pivotal to the whole programme was a greater role for the private sector, and the sale of state-owned enterprises, thus encouraging direct foreign investment. The Zambia Privatisation Agency (ZPA), now the Zambia Development Agency, was set up to oversee privatisation.

Having largely followed the dictates of the IMF and World Bank, Zambia found itself in the 'good books' of its donors. However the social consequences were onerous: rising unemployment, increased prices for basic necessities (including the staple mealie-meal) and cuts in health care and education. All of these tended to foster an increase in social unrest.

By the late 1990s, Zambia's annual debt repayments were equivalent to about a third of the value of its exports of goods and services. To put this in perspective, Zambia was spending five times more on its interest repayments than it did on education, and three times as much as on health care. The consequences were clear: literacy declined and the percentage of infant deaths doubled from 1992 to 1999.

Despite this, Zambia managed to remain current on its debt-service payments and even to clear some of its arrears – although such commitments were clearly a major constraint on economic development. Zambia relied on foreign donors for 35% of its budget, but for every dollar Zambia received in aid, it repaid US$3 to service its debt.

Debt write-offs and HIPC status In 1999, the Finnish government announced that it was writing off US$7.5 million of Zambia's debt, and the IMF gave Zambia a much-needed boost with US$14 million of its new US$349 million ESAF loan. Also, the World Bank promised US$65 million, despite continuing problems in selling the mines. These were crucial signals to other donors, and on 16 April of the same year the Paris Club agreed to write off US$670 million of Zambian debt, and restructure the repayments of about US$330 million of the rest. Another major step towards helping the country was to confer on Zambia the status of highly indebted poor country (HIPC), which would open the door to the World Bank and other donors relieving more of the debt.

Optimists hoped that these payments would mark the start of concerted efforts by the international community to alleviate Zambia's crippling debt, and that moves to liberalise Zambia's economy would bear fruit. However this optimism was tempered with more realism. Though Zambia had taken most of the economic medicine prescribed for it, trade liberalisation was tough on the country in the short term. A report by the World Development Movement, *Zambia: Condemned to Debt* (page 511), accused the IMF-backed reforms of being undemocratic and unfair and of undermining development – as well as of being counter-productive and unsuccessful. In 2003 the donors' 'Balance of Payment support' was frozen, on account of the country's weak fiscal management and inability to institute a new Poverty Reduction and Growth Facility strategy (PRGF) proposed by the IMF. Successful implementation of this PRGF strategy was one of the crucial milestone indicators needed by the IMF and World Bank before Zambia could reach the 'completion point' under the HIPC initiative that would trigger debt relief. Meanwhile, Zambia's debt repayments continued to cripple the economy.

In 2005, it was agreed at the G8 summit to write off US$40 billion of debt owed by 18 of the worlds HIPCs, of which Zambia was one. Following a write-off of US$7 billion, the country was left with a residual external debt of US$500 million. The Zambian government pledged to invest the proceeds in health and education, and in 2006 restored free health care to those living in rural areas.

In 2020, Zambia defaulted on its sovereign debt, and its new government began aggressively pursuing debt restructuring. Chinese creditors account for almost US$6 billion of the country's debt and, in early 2023, Zambia was in direct discussion with them to complete the restructuring. The IMF has also agreed a US$1.3 billion, three-year loan programme to assist in the restructuring programme. Borrowing continues, however: Zambia's external public debt reached US$14.87 billion at the end of June 2022.

THE ECONOMY TODAY Like most nations, the Covid-19 pandemic had a significant impact on the Zambian economy. In 2020, the country's economic growth was reduced to 2.8%, though it has since rebounded, hitting real GDP growth of 4.6% in 2021. The effects of the war in Ukraine and falling copper prices, alongside debt restructuring, which triggered a 30% depreciation of the kwacha in the first quarter of 2023, has placed additional pressure on official reserves. However, at the time of writing, Zambia's recovery is expected to strengthen with a projected GDP growth rate of 4.5% anticipated for 2023–25. Positive market confidence in the aftermath of the 2021 elections and the new government's economic management remains, while the stabilisation of the kwacha, increasing demand from China for copper and cobalt, and the sustained growth of the construction and service sector bode well for private-sector investment, growth and fiscal stability.

Zambia's mining industry Mining as a whole accounts for around 80% of Zambia's export earnings and about 12% of its GDP. Investment in recent years from countries as diverse as Brazil, South Africa and – most importantly – China has resulted from a combination of high copper prices and changes in regulations that have attracted considerable overseas interest in the sector. However, the slowdown in China's growth, which has been instrumental in the declining value of copper since 2011, has combined with a recent increase in governmental taxation to put heavy pressure on the industry.

Copper is easily the country's most important natural resource, with cobalt second; it also has small but significant reserves of gold and other minerals and gemstones.

Copper Zambia has large, high-quality deposits of copper ore, and is the world's eighth-largest producer of copper. In 2013, production totalled 790,007 tonnes, a marginal increase on the previous year, and 12.3% up on 2012 figures. While the opening of several new mines in the last few years has contributed to a boom in Zambia's industrial heartland, the Copperbelt region, the impact of the more recent fall in prices has in turn created big problems both for business and the workforce.

Before 2000, all the mines were controlled by the parastatal Zambia Consolidated Copper Mines (ZCCM), which had long been viewed as the jewel of Zambia's economic crown. Of these, Nchanga and Nkana mines alone accounted for 65% of Zambia's total copper production. However, disuse and mismanagement caused Zambia's mines to degenerate, and by the late 1990s they were recording losses of around US$15–20 million per month. In 2000 they were eventually privatised, and bought by a consortium led by Anglo American – which, ironically, owned the mines before they were nationalised. Today, the country's mining base has expanded beyond the Copperbelt into the Northwestern Province, with a third large mine in that area, Kalumbila, coming on-stream in 2015 to join the Kansanshi and Lumwana mines. A subsidiary of ZCCM retains a holding share of between 10 and 20% in most large mines.

Cobalt Cobalt is a valuable, strategic metal, usually produced as a by-product of copper or nickel mines. Zambia is currently the world's 13th-largest producer of the metal, having fallen in the rankings from second, largely as a result of cobalt production ceasing when international processing collapsed a decade ago. However, the rise in popularity of electric cars and consumer electronics has altered the market, as cobalt is used in the manufacture of lithium-ion batteries. This economic opportunity has resulted in the resumption of cobalt processing in the country, so Zambia may once again rise in the global cobalt market.

Coal Zambia's largest coal mine is the former state-owned, open-pit mine at Maamba, near Lake Kariba, which opened in 1967. In 2009, a controlling share (65%) in the mine was bought by a Singapore-based company, who constructed a thermal power plant at the site (supplying just over 10% of the national grid electricity) and increased coal production to hit almost 670,000 tonnes in 2022. Total combined reserves of low- and high-grade coal are estimated at more than 190 million tonnes.

A NOTE ON 'TRIBES'

The people of Africa are often viewed, from abroad, as belonging to a multitude of culturally and linguistically distinct tribes – which are often portrayed as being at odds with each other. While there is certainly an enormous variety of different ethnic groups in Africa, most are closely related to their neighbours in terms of language, beliefs and way of life. Modern historians eschew the simplistic tag of 'tribes', noting that such groupings change with time.

Sometimes the word 'tribe' is used to describe a group of people who all speak the same language; it may be used to mean those who follow a particular leader or to refer to all the inhabitants of a certain area at a given time. In any case, 'tribe' is a vague word which is used differently for different purposes. The term 'clan' (blood relations) is a smaller, more precisely defined, unit – though rather too precise for our broad discussions here.

Certainly, at any given time, groups of people or clans who share similar language and cultural beliefs do band together and often, in time, develop 'tribal' identities. However, it is wrong to then extrapolate and assume that their ancestors will have had the same groupings and allegiances centuries ago.

In Africa, as elsewhere in the world, history is recorded by the winners. Here the winners, the ruling class, may be the descendants of a small group of intruders who achieved dominance over a larger, long-established community. Over the years, the history of that ruling class usually becomes regarded as the history of the whole community, or tribe. Two 'tribes' have thus become one, with one history – which will reflect the origins of that small group of intruders, and not the ancestors of the majority of the current tribe.

Zambia is typical of a large African country. Currently historians and linguistics experts can identify at least 16 major cultural groupings, and more than 72 different languages and dialects are spoken in the country. As you will see, there are cultural differences between the people in different parts of the country. However, these are no more pronounced than those between the states of the USA, or the different regions of the (relatively tiny) UK.

There continues to be lots of intermarriage and mixing of these peoples and cultures – perhaps more so than in the past, due to the efficiency of modern transport systems. Generally, there is very little friction between these communities (whose boundaries, as we have said, are indistinct) and Zambia's various peoples live peacefully together.

Other mineral resources Zambia has natural resources of amethyst, fluorite, feldspar, gypsum, aquamarine, lead, zinc, tin and gold – as well as a variety of gemstones. All are on a small scale, and few are being commercially exploited. An exception is emeralds, which are said to be among the highest quality in the world. These are being mined to the order of about US$200 million per year, with the Kagem Emerald Mine – the world's largest emerald mine – in the Copperbelt responsible for about half the country's gems, or 25% of global production. Despite millions of carats being mined annually, data suggests that significant numbers of emeralds, rubies and other gemstones are being smuggled out of the country, so the true production amounts remain uncertain.

Other industrial sectors Zambia's manufacturing industry is focused primarily on construction, chemicals, textiles and fertiliser production, with steel and cement coming to the fore in recent years. The domestic market is small though, and high costs mean that it isn't very competitive regionally.

Agriculture Agriculture represents 3.4% of Zambia's GDP, but employs perhaps 50% of its workforce. Although most farming (90%) is still done by small-scale subsistence farmers, large commercial farms are becoming more important, often financed by private investors. The country's varied topography encourages a wide diversity in the crops cultivated. The main commercial crops are maize (the staple food for most people), sugar, tobacco, cotton and coffee, with sorghum, rice, peanuts, soya beans, sunflowers and cassava also grown, and cattle, goats, beef, poultry and eggs produced. Maize is Zambia's most important crop and the country is currently the leading supplier of the crop in Africa. In 2022, Zambia produced 3.6 million tonnes – the largest maize crop on record. The land given over to maize production has increased considerably over time, and production has nearly doubled over the last 20 years thanks to generally good harvests. It's a staple food for the population – eaten as *nshima* porridge for most meals – and is exported to several neighbouring countries.

In 2022, the National Development Plan set out a five-year blueprint to diversify the economy, which laid out plans to increase agricultural production, mechanisation and support for the sector. The government hopes to increase agricultural growth by more than 10% a year until 2026, increasing exports to US$2 billion from its 2021 level of US$756.2 million.

Tourism Zambia has the (arguable) benefit of a late-developing tourism industry, which should allow it to learn from the mistakes of others. Hopes for the development of tourism lie firmly with the private sector, and the government is happy for private investors to buy into the industry. Since the mid 1990s tourism has been expanding very steadily – which is by far the best way for a tourism industry to move if it is to stay on a sustainable basis – and increasingly there is a focus on the development that tourism can bring to local communities.

Until around 2000, Zambia's annual visitor influx could still probably have been counted in the low thousands. Then came political turmoil in Zimbabwe, which resulted in the rapid demise of that country's tourism industry. Livingstone, meanwhile, experienced significant developments in its tourist infrastructure (albeit not without considerable pressure for unsustainable development from some sectors). As a result, the town for many years took on the mantle of regional tourism capital, formerly held by its neighbour, the Zimbabwean town of Victoria Falls. Although the situation is now more balanced, Livingstone remains a big focus for Falls tourism, and makes a significant contribution to Zambia's tourist industry.

While tourism remains one of Zambia's least-developed sectors, generating in total an estimated 7.7% of GDP in 2019, it continues to grow. In 2021, the industry supported 489,700 jobs (World Travel & Tourism Council, 2021). It is estimated that in 2019, the country welcomed 1.27 million tourists, generating around US$820 million.

The praises of Zambia's national parks are sung elsewhere in this book, but here it's worth noting that the country's best camps command prices (and standards) to match their equivalents in Tanzania, Zimbabwe or Botswana. What's more, Zambia still has vast tracts of pristine wilderness, which is exactly what is needed for new safari destinations. Most importantly, visitors to Africa realise that top wildlife guides, like those found in Zambia, are few and far between.

2

People and Culture

POPULATION OVERVIEW

Zambia's 2022 census puts the country's population at just over 19.6 million, a number that has quadrupled since 1969. Almost two-thirds of the people live below the poverty line, with 40% surviving on less than US$1.25 a day. The vast majority of people are of black African (Bantu) descent, though there are significant communities whose ancestors came from Europe and India. Zambia is a large country, and its population density – around 25 people per square kilometre – is relatively low: just over half that of Zimbabwe, or about a quarter of the population density of Kenya.

Zambia's urban population is increasing and is currently about 45% of the total, with the capital, Lusaka, home to some 3.08 million people, and a further 2.8 million or so residing in the Copperbelt Province. Conversely, rural areas generally have a low population density, and the country retains large tracts of wilderness.

Statistics indicate that 43% of the population is under 14 years of age, and the population growth rate is about 3% per annum. Infant mortality continues a slow decline, while the average life expectancy for a Zambian at birth has risen to 62 years. This marks a significant increase over recent years, and at least in part reflects the decline in incidence of HIV/AIDS: it is estimated that the number of people between the ages of 15 and 49 who are affected by AIDS has declined to 11%, thanks to political commitment and the continued efforts of international development partners.

However, the statistics say nothing of the warmth that the sensitive visitor can encounter. If you venture into the rural areas, take a local bus, or try to hitchhike with the locals, you will often find that Zambians are curious about you. Chat to them openly, as fellow travellers, and you will find most Zambians to be delightful. They will be pleased to assist you where they can, and as keen to help you learn about them and their country as they are interested in your lifestyle and what brings you to Zambia.

ETHNIC GROUPS

AFRICAN LANGUAGE GROUPS English is the official language in Zambia, and most urban Zambians speak it fluently. In rural areas it is used less, though only in truly remote settlements will you encounter any problems communicating in English.

The main vernacular languages are Bemba, Kaonde, Lozi, Lunda, Luvale, Nyanja and Tonga – though more than 72 different languages and dialects are spoken in the country. When the colonial powers carved up Africa, the divisions between the countries bore only a passing resemblance to the traditional areas of these various ethnic groups. Thus, many of the groups here span several countries.

Below are detailed some of the major language groups, arranged alphabetically. This is only a rough guide to the languages and dialects of Zambia's people. Although

these different language groupings do loosely correspond to what many describe as Zambia's tribes, the distinctions are blurred further by the natural linguistic ability of most Zambians. While it is normal to speak English plus one local language, many Zambians will speak a number of local languages fluently.

That said, some of the less prevalent tribal languages are becoming endangered these days, as the more commonly spoken languages dominate and younger people, especially those with access to education and ambition, increasingly view minority tribal languages as redundant in economic and social value. For most Zambians and visitors alike, the most widely recognised and understood languages are Nyanja and Bemba and it's worth learning a few basic words and phrases to raise a smile on your travels (page 508).

Bemba According to the 2022 census, Bemba is now the first or second language of 33.4% of the population. It is spoken in the rural areas of northern Zambia, from the Luapula River eastwards to Mpika, Kasama and beyond. People from these areas were the original workers in the mines of the Copperbelt and Bemba subsequently achieved the status of *lingua franca* in the major urban areas of the Copperbelt and Lusaka.

It is recognised for administration and education purposes within Zambia, while outside its borders Bemba is also spoken by people in the Democratic Republic of Congo, and in Tanzania.

Kaonde A Bantu language, Kaonde-speakers live mostly around the northern side of Kafue National Park, centring on the area around Kasempa, and extending southeast as far as Mumbwa. They are one of Zambia's larger language groups, and probably number about 360,000 (1.8% of the population).

Lozi There are just over 1 million people speaking Lozi as their first language (5.5% of the population), largely concentrated in the Western and Southern provinces, around Barotseland and Livingstone, where it's the first language of over 70% of the regional population. The centre of Lozi culture is the rich agricultural floodplain around the Upper Zambezi River near Mongu – and it is here that the spectacular Kuomboka (page 25) takes place each year.

Luchazi This language has only a small number of speakers in the west of Zambia – less than 1% of the country's population – and is found in similar numbers in eastern-central Angola.

Lunda Not to be confused with Luunda, which is a dialect of Bemba, Lunda is the first language of 36% of Zambian's living in the country's northwest (380,000 Zambians), areas of the Copperbelt and into neighbouring DRC and Angola. It is officially taught in primary schools, and can occasionally be heard on the radio or seen in newspapers in these areas.

Luvale Luvale is an important language in Angola, where it is spoken by almost 1 million people. In Zambia there are fewer than 300,000 people whose first language is Luvale, and they live in the North-Western and Western provinces.

Luyana The Luyana-speaking people are a small group, likely numbering fewer than 100,000 in total, found almost exclusively in Zambia's Western Province. Also spoken in Angola, Namibia and along the Okavango River in Botswana, the language has not been well documented.

Mambwe-Lungu These are other languages that need further study – so far they appear to differ from each other only slightly, as dialects would. In total about 300,000 Zambians, largely based in the northeast of the Northern Province, south of Lake Tanganyika, count them as their first language. As you might expect, they are also spoken in Tanzania.

Mashi Mashi is spoken by fewer than 100,000 Zambians from a largely nomadic tribe in a southwestern area of the Western Province. Little has been documented about this language – though it has been noted that virtually all the native speakers of Mashi follow traditional spiritual practices, rather than the introduced Christian beliefs.

Mbunda The first language of about 130,000 Zambians, Mbunda is spoken in the north of Barotseland and the northern side of western Zambia – as well as in Angola.

Nkoya-Mbwela Nkoya and Mbwela are two closely related languages. Mbwela is often referred to as a dialect of Nkoya, though here we have grouped them together as equals. They have only a tiny, dwindling number of speakers, who are found around the Mankoya area, in Zambia's Western and Southern provinces, with evidence showing that the people, especially the youth, here are increasingly speaking Lozi instead.

Nsenga There are thought to be over 580,000 people speaking Nsenga as their first language in Zambia (2.9% of the population). They are clustered around Petauke in the east of the country – close to the borders with Zimbabwe, Mozambique and Malawi, where the language is spoken in small numbers.

Nyanja Nyanja is the Bantu language most often encountered by visitors in Zambia. It is widely used in much of the country, including the key cities of Lusaka and Livingstone. Nyanja is sometimes described as not being a language *per se*, but rather a common skill enabling people of varying tribes living in eastern, central and southern parts of Zambia and Malawi to communicate without following the strict grammar of specific local languages. In other words, like Swahili and other 'universal' languages, Nyanja is something of a *lingua franca* for Zambia.

Nyanja is certainly the official language of the police, and is widely used for administrative and educational purposes. About 3 million Zambians use Nyanja (nearly 15% of the population) – mostly in the eastern and central areas of the country – and it is currently the most widely spoken language in Malawi, where it is known as Chewa. Nyanja-speakers can also be found in Zimbabwe and Mozambique, with around 5 million people in the subcontinent speaking Nyanja as their first language.

Nyika Also known as Nyiha, or more precisely as Chi-Nyika, Nyika is spoken most widely in Tanzania, and also in Malawi. In Zambia it is used around the Isoka and Chama areas, across to the Malawi border. (It is closely related to the language known as Ichi-Lambya in Tanzania and Malawi.)

Tonga Tonga is the language of a small minority of Zimbabweans, many of whom were displaced south by the creation of Lake Kariba (page 238). However, in Zambia it is the first language of around 2.3 million people, about 11.4% of the country's population, and is widely used in the media. Tonga is distributed throughout the south of the country, with its highest concentration in the middle Zambezi Valley.

Tumbuka Zambia has about 500,000 people who speak Tumbuka as a first language, mostly living on the eastern side of the country. Outside Zambia many Tumbuka-speakers live in Malawi and Tanzania, bringing the total number to about 2 million.

OTHER ETHNIC GROUPS

White Zambians There are a small number of white Zambians (around 1.1% of the population) who have European origins but hold Zambian citizenship. These people are very different from the expat community (page 24) who are often white but simply working in the country on a temporary basis. Many white Zambians will trace their families back to colonial immigrants who came over during British rule, but most will regard themselves as Zambian rather than, say, British. This is generally an affluent group of people, and many of the country's businesses and especially the safari companies, are owned and run by white Zambians.

Asian Zambians Like the white Zambians, many people of Asian origin came here during the colonial period. When the British ruled African colonies like Zambia as well as India, there was movement of labour from Asia to Africa. Now, like the white Zambians, this is generally an affluent group. On the whole, Zambians of Asian descent retain a very strong sense of Asian identity and culture, and many are traders or own small shops.

Expatriates Distinct from Zambians, there is a large expat community in Zambia. These foreigners usually come to Zambia for two or three years, to work on short-term contracts, often for either multi-national companies or aid agencies. Most are highly skilled individuals who come to share their knowledge with Zambian colleagues – often teaching skills that are in short supply in Zambia.

In the 1990s there was a migration of trained Zambian teachers and lecturers to neighbouring countries, where they are paid better, but this has now stabilised.

RELIGION

It has been estimated that there are some 200 different Christian churches in Zambia, of which the most active in the community is considered to be the Catholic Church. However, as in many other sub-Saharan African countries, many people will also subscribe to some traditional African religious practices and beliefs.

EDUCATION

Zambia's literacy rates have fluctuated over recent years, with some 87% of adult Zambians (aged over 15) currently considered literate. The figure masks variation in terms of age and sex. For adult men, the literacy rate rises to 90%, whereas for women in the same age group, it's closer to 83% (UNESCO).

In January 2022, President Hichilema abolished all public school fees in a landmark decision that will undoubtedly benefit the poorest children. Although primary education had been theoretically free to all children in Zambia from 2002, in practice this was only half the story. Parents were still required to pay for school uniform, books and pencils, and an annual 'fee' was not unusual: around US$10.50/£7 for each primary-age child and US$42/£28 for secondary level. These necessities were a crippling burden to impoverished Zambian families so their complete removal is an immensely positive step.

Typically, primary schools are run on a shift pattern, with children spending 3 hours in the classroom each day; the first are in school at 07.00, finishing at 10.00, when the next group starts. The secondary school day normally runs from 07.00 to 13.00. There are also 'basic' schools, which serve a wider age range than primary in areas where there is no secondary school. Class sizes are large, frequently exceeding the expected norm of 45 children, and lessons are often disrupted by strike action on the part of the teachers.

Zambia's first university, the University of Zambia, was established in Lusaka as recently as 1966, shortly after independence. It has since been joined by several more in both the public and private sectors.

FESTIVALS

Zambia has several major cultural festivals which, on the whole, are rarely seen by visitors. If you can get to any, then you will find them to be very genuine occasions, where ceremonies are performed for the benefit of the local people and the participants, and not for the odd tourist who is watching.

Cultural celebrations were strongly encouraged during Kenneth Kaunda's reign, as he favoured people being aware of their cultural origins. 'A country without culture is like a body without a head', was one of his phrases. Thus during the 1980s one group after another 'discovered' old traditional festivals. Most are now large local events, partly cultural but also part political rally, religious gathering and sports event.

Bear in mind that, like most celebrations worldwide, these are often accompanied by the large-scale consumption of alcohol. To see these festivals properly, and to appreciate them, you will need a good guide: someone who understands the rituals, can explain their significance, and can instruct you on how you should behave. After all, how would you feel about a passing Zambian traveller who arrives, with curiosity, at your sibling's wedding (a small festival), in the hope of being invited to the private reception?

Photographers will find superb opportunities at such colourful events, but should behave with sensitivity. *Before* you brandish your camera, remember to ask permission from anyone who might take offence.

FEBRUARY: THE NC'WALA On 24 February there is a festival at Mutenguleni village, near Chipata to celebrate the first fruit. This large celebration was recently revived, after 80 years of not being practised. It consists of two parts. First the chief tastes the first fruit of the land – usually sugarcane, maize and pumpkins. Then there is the ritual rebirth of the king (involving the king being locked up in his house) and the blessing of the fruit – which consists of a fairly gory spearing of a black bull whose blood the king has to drink. It's all accompanied by traditional dancing and beer-drinking.

EASTER: THE KUOMBOKA The most famous of Zambia's ceremonies takes place in the Western Province. It used to be around February or March, often on a Thursday, just before full moon. The precise date would be known only a week or so in advance, as it was decided upon by the Lozi king. Now that the ceremony attracts more visitors, it is usually held at Easter, though if water levels are not high enough, it will not take place at all.

The Lozi kingdom is closely associated with the fertile plains around the Upper Zambezi River. When dry, this well-defined area affords good grazing for livestock, and its rich alluvial soil is ideal for cultivation. It contrasts with the sparse surrounding woodland, growing on poor soil typical of the rest of western Zambia. So for much of the year, these plains support a dense population of subsistence farms.

However, towards the end of the rains, the Zambezi's water levels rise. The plains then become floodplains, and the settlements gradually become islands. The people must leave them for the higher ground, at the margins of the floodplain. This retreat from the advancing waters – known as the Kuomboka – is traditionally led by the king himself, the Litunga, from his dry-season abode at Lealui, in the middle of the plain. He retreats with his court to his high-water residence, at Limulunga, on the eastern margins of the floodplain.

The Litunga's departure is heralded by the beating of three huge old royal war drums – Mundili, Munanga and Kanaono. These continue to summon the people from miles around until the drums themselves are loaded aboard the royal barge, the *nalikwanda*, a very large wooden canoe built around the turn of the century and painted with vertical black-and-white stripes. The royal barge is then paddled and punted along by 96 polers, each sporting a skirt of animal skins and a white vest. Their scarlet hats are surmounted by tufts of fur taken from the mane of unfortunate lions.

The royal barge is guided by a couple of 'scout' barges, painted white, which search out the right channels for the royal barge. Behind it comes the Litunga's wife, the Moyo, in her own barge, followed by local dignitaries, various attendants, many of the Litunga's subjects, and the odd visitor lucky enough to be in the area at the right time. The journey takes most of the day, and the flotilla is accompanied by an impromptu orchestra of local musicians.

John Reader's excellent book, *Africa: A Biography of the Continent* (page 511), comments:

> When the Litunga boards the *nalikwanda* at Lealui he customarily wears a light European-style suit, a pearl-grey frock coat and a trilby hat; when he leaves the barge at Limulunga he is dressed in a splendid uniform of dark-blue serge ornately embroidered with gold braid, with matching cockade hat complete with a white plume of egret feathers.

In fact, Chapter 47 of this book contains the fascinating story of some of the first Europeans to see the original Kuomboka, and the sad narration of the gradual European subjugation of the Lozi kingdom. It also includes details of the Litunga's trip to London, in 1902, for the coronation of King Edward VII. It was here that the problem arose of what the Litunga should wear. Reader reports:

> By happy coincidence, the king [Edward VII] took a particular interest in uniforms; he was an expert on the subject and is even said to have made a hobby of designing uniforms. Doubtless the king had approved the design of the new uniforms with which Britain's ambassadors had recently been issued. Certainly he was aware that the introduction of these new outfits had created a redundant stock of the old style, which were richly adorned with gold braid. Lewanika [the Litunga] should be attired in one of those, the king ordained. And thus the Litunga acquired the uniform which has become part of the Kuomboka tradition. Not an admiral's uniform, as is often reported, but a surplus dress uniform of a Victorian ambassador; not a gift from Queen Victoria, but the suggestion of her son…

When the royal barge finally arrives at Limulunga, the Litunga steps ashore in the ambassador's uniform to spend an evening of feasting and celebrations, with much eating, drinking, music and traditional dancing.

JULY: MUTOMBOKO (also Umutomboko) This is nothing to do with the Kuomboka, described on page 25. It is an annual two-day celebration, performed during the last weekend of July, whereby the paramount chief celebrates the arrival of the Lunda people, the 'crossing of the river'. It is held in a specially prepared arena, close to the Ng'ona River, at Mwansabombwe.

On the first day the chief, covered in white powder, receives tributes of food and drink from his subjects – the cause for much feasting and celebration by all. On the second day an animal (often a goat) is slaughtered and the highlight is the chief's dance with his sword. See also page 402.

AUGUST: LIKUMBI LYA MIZE The Luvale people of western Zambia have an annual 'fair' type of celebration, which takes place for four or five days towards the end of August. '*Likumbi Lya Mize*' means 'Mize day' and the event is held at the palace of the senior chief – at Mize, about 7km west of Zambezi. This provides an opportunity for the people to see their senior chief, watch the popular Makishi dancers, and generally have a good time. There is also lots of eating and drinking, plus people in traditional dress, displays of local crafts, and singing.

SEPTEMBER/OCTOBER: SHIMUNENGA This traditional gathering is held on the weekend of a full moon, in September or October, at Maala on the Kafue Flats –

about 40km west of Namwala. Then the Ila people (whose language is closely related to Tonga) gather together, driving cattle across the Kafue River to higher ground. It used to be a lechwe hunt, but that is now forbidden.

OTHER FESTIVALS The list of festivals described from page 24 is by no means exhaustive; others include:

February: Lwiindi A ceremony celebrated by Chief Mokuni, of the Toka Leya people near Livingstone, around February. The people honour their ancestors and offer sacrifices for rain.

May: Kufukwila A celebration led by the chief of the Kaonde people, held in the Solwezi area of northwestern Zambia.

July: Malaila A ceremony to honour past chiefs, held by the Kunda people. It is currently celebrated by Chieftainess Nsefu, near Mfuwe in the Luangwa Valley.

August: Kulamba Also a thanksgiving ceremony for the Chewa people. It's held in the Katete Province, in eastern Zambia, and here you'll be able to see lots of fascinating Nyao (secret society) dancers.

August: Lukuni Luzwa Buuka A celebration of past conquests by the Toka people in the Southern Province, usually held in August.

October: Tuwimba A thanksgiving festival for the Nsenga people.

3

The Natural Environment

PHYSICAL ENVIRONMENT

TOPOGRAPHY Zambia lies landlocked between the Tropic of Capricorn and the Equator, far from both the Atlantic and the Pacific oceans. It is at the northern edge of the region referred to as 'southern Africa', while sharing many similarities with its neighbours in east and central Africa. Shaped like a giant butterfly, it covers about 752,610km^2, slightly smaller than the UK and France combined, and slightly larger than California plus Nevada. In comparison with its neighbours, it is almost double the size of Zimbabwe, but only two-thirds that of South Africa.

Most of the country is part of the high, undulating plateau that forms the backbone of the African continent. Typically, it has an altitude of between 1,000m and 1,600m, deeply incised by the great valleys of the Zambezi, the Kafue, the Luangwa and the Luapula that lie below 500m.

There are several large lakes on Zambia's borders: Tanganyika and Mweru in the north, and the manmade Kariba in the south. Lake Bangweulu, and its swamps and floodplain, dominate a large area of the interior.

GEOLOGY Zambia's oldest rocks, known as the Basement Complex, were laid down at an early stage in the pre-Cambrian era – as long as 2,000 million years ago. These were extensively eroded and covered by sediments which now form the Katanga system of rocks, dating from around 1,000 to 620 million years ago. These are what we now see near the surface in most of northeast and central Zambia, and they contain the important mineral deposits of the Copperbelt. Later still, from about 300 to 150 million years ago, the karoo system of sedimentary rocks was deposited: sandstones, mudstones, conglomerates and even coal. Towards the end of this era, molten rock seeped up through cracks in the crust, and covered areas of western Zambia in layers of basalt – the rock that is seen cut away by the Zambezi River in the gorges below Victoria Falls.

About 150 million years ago, during the Jurassic era of the dinosaurs, Africa was still part of Gondwana – a super-continent which included South America, India, Australasia and Antarctica. Since then Zambia's highlands have been eroded down from an original altitude of over 1,800m (Nyika Plateau is still at this altitude) to their present lower levels.

Very recently, perhaps only a few million years ago, the subcontinent had a dry phase. Then the sands from the Kalahari Desert blew far across southern Africa, covering much of western Zambia with a layer of Kalahari sand – as becomes abundantly clear the moment you try to drive in the region.

CLIMATE Situated squarely in the tropics, Zambia gets a lot of strong sunlight, though the intense heat normally associated with the tropics is moderated in most

CLIMATE STATISTICS: LUSAKA

	Temp °C		Temp °F		Humidity %		Rainfall
	max	min	max	min	am	pm	mm
Jan	25	18	77	64	84	71	264
Feb	25	18	77	64	85	80	235
Mar	25	18	77	64	83	56	130
Apr	24	16	76	60	71	47	48
May	24	14	75	56	59	37	4
Jun	22	12	71	53	56	32	0
Jul	22	11	71	52	54	28	0
Aug	25	13	77	56	46	26	0
Sep	29	17	84	62	41	19	1
Oct	31	19	87	67	39	23	16
Nov	29	19	84	67	57	46	102
Dec	26	18	79	65	76	61	275

places by the country's altitude and its rainfall. The climate is generally moderate; only in the great valleys does it feel oppressive. It can be summarised broadly into three periods: from December to April it is hot and wet, with torrential downpours often in the late afternoon; from May to August it is dry, and becomes increasingly cool; and from September to November it remains dry, but gets progressively hotter.

This follows a similar pattern to that in most of southern Africa, with rainfall when the sun is near its zenith from November to April. The precise timing and

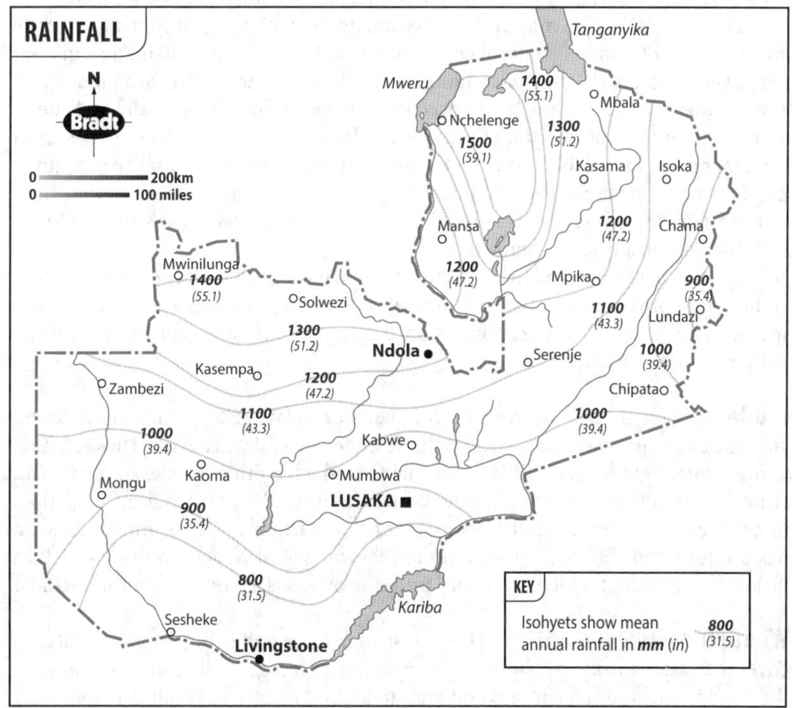

duration of this is determined by the interplay of three airstreams: the moist 'Congo' air mass, the northeastern monsoon winds, and the southeastern trade winds. The water-bearing air is the Congo air mass, which normally brings rain when it moves south into Zambia from central Africa. This means that the northern areas, around Lakes Tanganyika and Mweru, receive the first rainfall – often in late October or November. This belt of rain will then work south, arriving in southern Zambia by the end of November or the start of December.

As the sun's intensity reduces, the Congo air mass moves back north, leaving southern Zambia dry by around late March, and the north by late April or May. Most areas receive their heaviest rainfall in January, though some of the most northerly have two peaks: one in December and one in March. This twin-peak cycle is more characteristic of central and eastern Africa. The heaviest total rainfall is found in the north, and the lightest in the south. It's worth adding a caveat here. Zambia, as elsewhere, is experiencing fluctuations in its traditional weather patterns, so while the traditional pattern remains a good guide, be prepared for variations from the norm.

Lusaka's climate statistics (page 29) are typical of the pleasant climate found in the higher areas of southern and central Zambia. The lower-lying valleys, including the Luangwa and Lower Zambezi, follow the same broad pattern but are considerably hotter throughout the year. In October, which is universally the hottest month, temperatures there often reach over 45°C in the shade.

FLORA AND FAUNA

Zambia has many large national parks and game management areas (GMAs) where conservation and sustainable utilisation of the native wildlife are encouraged.

Miombo woodland – a mixture of grassland dotted with trees and shrubs – makes up about 70% of Zambia's natural environment, with *mopane* woodland dominating the lower-lying areas. The native fauna is classic big game found throughout east and southern Africa. Among the predators, leopard do exceptionally well here; lion are common but cheetah are not. Wild dog are uncommon, though seem to have increased in numbers in recent years, and there are many smaller predators. Zambia's antelope are especially interesting for the range of subspecies that have evolved. Giraffe, wildebeest, waterbuck and, especially, lechwe are notable for this – each having subspecies endemic to the country.

With rich vegetation and lots of water, Zambia has a great variety of both resident and migrant birds, over 850 species in total. Wetland and swamp areas attract some specialised waterfowl, and Zambia is on the edge of the range for both southern African and east African species.

FLORA As with animals, each species of plant has its favourite conditions. External factors determine where each species thrives, and where it will perish. These include temperature, light, water, soil type, nutrients, and what other species of plants and animals live in the same area. Species with similar needs are often found together, in communities which are characteristic of that particular environment. Zambia has a number of different such communities, or typical 'vegetation types', within its borders – each of which is distinct from the others. The more common include:

Woodlands Where they haven't been destroyed or degraded by people, woodlands cover the vast majority of Zambia, with miombo being especially common. Because the canopies of the trees in a woodland area don't interlock, you'll generally find them lighter and more open than the country's relatively few forested areas. The main types of woodland are:

Miombo woodland Without human intervention, the natural vegetation of most of Zambia (about 70%) is miombo woodland and its associated *dambos* (page 32). This exists on Zambia's main plateau and its adjacent escarpments, where the acid soils are not particularly fertile and have often been leached of minerals by the water run-off.

Miombo woodland consists of a mosaic of large wooded areas and smaller, more open spaces dotted with clumps of trees and shrubs. The woodland is broadleafed and deciduous (though just how deciduous depends on the available water), and the tree canopies generally don't interlock. The dominant trees are *Brachystegia*, *Julbernardia* and *Isoberlinia* species – most of which are at least partially fire-resistant. There is more variation of species in miombo than in mopane woodland, but despite this it is often known simply as 'brachystegia woodland'. The ground cover is also generally less sparse here than in mopane areas.

Mopane woodland The dominant tree here is the remarkably adaptable mopane (*Colophospermum mopane*), which is sometimes known as the butterfly tree because of the shape of its leaves. It is very tolerant of poorly drained or alkaline soils, and those with a high clay content. This tolerance results in the mopane having a wide range of distribution throughout southern Africa; in Zambia it occurs mainly in the hotter, drier, lower parts of the country, including the Luangwa and Zambezi valleys.

Mopane trees can attain a height of 25m, especially if growing on rich, alluvial soils. These are often called cathedral mopane, for their height and the graceful arch of their branches. However, shorter trees are more common in areas that are poor in nutrients, or have suffered extensive fire damage. Stunted mopane will form a low scrub, perhaps only 5m tall. All mopane trees are semi-deciduous. The leaves turn beautiful shades of yellow and red before falling between August and October, depending on their proximity to water (the closer the water, the later the leaves fall). Fresh new leaves start unfurling from late October.

Ground cover in mopane woodland is usually sparse, just thin grasses, herbs and the occasional bush. The trees themselves are an important source of food for game, as the leaves have a high nutritional value – rich in protein and phosphorus – which is favoured by browsers and is retained even after they have fallen from the trees. Mopane forests support large populations of rodents, including tree squirrels (*Peraxerus cepapi*), which are so typical of these areas that they are known as 'mopane squirrels'.

Munga woodland The word 'munga' means thorn, and this is the thorny woodland which occurs when open grassland has been invaded by trees and shrubs – normally because of some disturbance like cultivation, fire or overgrazing. *Acacia*, *Terminalia* (bearing single-winged seeds) and *Combretum* (bearing seeds with four or five wings) are the dominant species, but many others can be present. Munga occurs mainly in the southern parts of Zambia.

Forests In most equatorial areas further north in Africa, where rainfall is higher, forests are the norm. However, there are a few specific ecological niches in Zambia where you will find forests – distinguished from woodlands by their interlocking canopy. These are:

Teak forest In a few areas of western and southwestern Zambia (including the southern part of Kafue National Park), the Zambezi teak (*Baikaea plurijuga*), forms dry semi-evergreen forests on a base of Kalahari sand. This species is not fire-resistant, so these stands occur only where slash-and-burn cultivation methods have never been used. Below the tall teak is normally a dense, deciduous thicket of vegetation usually referred to as *mutemwa*, interspersed with sparse grasses and herbs in the shadier spots of the forest floor.

Moist evergreen forest In areas of higher rainfall (mostly in the north of Zambia), and near rivers, streams, lakes and swamps, where a tree's roots have permanent access to water, dense evergreen forests are found. Many species occur, and this lush vegetation is characterised by having three levels: a canopy of tall trees, a sub-level of smaller trees and bushes, and a variety of ground-level vegetation. In effect, the environment is so good for plants that they have adapted to exploit the light from every sunbeam.

This type of forest is prevalent in the far north of the country, especially in the Mwinilunga area. However, three more localised environments can give rise to moist evergreen forests in other areas of the country.

Riparian forests (often called riverine forests) are very common. They line many of Zambia's major rivers and are found in most of the national parks. Typical trees and shrubs here include ebony (*Diospyros mespiliformis*), mangosteen (*Garcinia livingstonei*), wild gardenia (*Gardenia volkensii*), sausage tree (*Kigelia africana*), Natal mahogany (*Trichilia emetica*) and various species of figs. But walk away from the river, and you'll find riparian species thinning out rapidly.

Montane forests are found on the lower slopes of mountains, where the rainfall is high. The Zambian slopes of Nyika Plateau are probably the best example of this kind of vegetation.

Finally *swamp* forest occurs near to some of Zambia's permanent swamps. Kasanka National Park probably has the country's best, and most accessible, examples of this.

Grasslands and open areas

Dambo A 'dambo' is a shallow grass depression, or small valley, that is either permanently or seasonally waterlogged. It corresponds closely to what is known as a 'vlei' in other parts of the subcontinent. These open, verdant dips in the landscape often appear in the midst of miombo woodlands and support no bushes or trees. In higher valleys among hills, they sometimes form the sources of streams and rivers. Because of their permanent dampness, they are rich in species of grasses, herbs and flowering plants, like orchids – and are excellent grazing (if a little exposed) for antelope. Their margins are usually thickly vegetated by grasses, herbs and smaller shrubs.

Pan Though not an environment for rich vegetation, a pan is a shallow, seasonal pool of water with no permanent streams leading into or out of it. The bush is full of small pans in the rainy season, most of which will dry up soon after the rains cease. Sometimes there's only a fine distinction between a pan and a dambo.

Floodplain Floodplains are the low-lying grasslands on the edges of rivers, streams, lakes and swamps that are seasonally inundated by floods. Zambia has some huge areas of floodplain, most obviously beside the Kafue River, in the Barotseland area around the Zambezi, and south of the permanent Bangweulu Swamps. These often contain no trees or bushes, just a low carpet of grass species that can tolerate being submerged for part of the year. In the midst of some floodplains, like the Busanga Plains, you'll find isolated small 'islands' of trees and bushes, slightly raised above the surrounding grasslands.

Montane grassland More common in other areas of Africa, montane grassland occurs on mountain slopes at higher altitudes where the precipitation is heavy and the climate cool. Zambia's best examples of this are on Nyika Plateau, and here you'll find many species of flora and fauna that occur nowhere else in Zambia.

FAUNA See page 39, for an introductory field guide to some of Zambia's larger mammals, birds and reptiles.

FIELD GUIDES Finding good, detailed field guides to plants, animals and birds in Zambia is becoming much easier. There are now very comprehensive guides on the flora and fauna of southern Africa, which remain invaluable in Zambia. For total coverage there are also many smaller guides, published in Zambia by the Wildlife and Environmental Conservation Society of Zambia (page 98), covering snakes, trees, wild flowers, birds and the like, and ideal for general game viewing and birdwatching. There's even a guide to the Zambian bird species that have been excluded from the southern Africa guides, and – at the other end of the scale – a heavy but very comprehensive guide to the birds of sub-Saharan Africa. See page 512 for more details.

CONSERVATION

A great deal has been written about the conservation of animals in Africa, much of it over-simplistic and intentionally emotive. As an informed visitor you are in the unique position of being able to see some of the issues at first hand, and to appreciate the perspectives of local people. So abandon your preconceptions, and start by considering the complexities of the issues involved. Here I shall try to develop a few ideas common to most current thinking on conservation, ideas to which the rest of the book only briefly alludes.

First, conservation must be taken within its widest sense if it is to have meaning. Saving animals is of minimal use if the whole environment is degraded, so we must consider conserving whole areas and ecosystems, not just the odd isolated species.

Observe that land is regarded as an asset by most societies in Africa, as it is elsewhere. To 'save' the land for the animals, and use it merely for the recreation of a few privileged foreign tourists, is a recipe for huge social problems – especially if the local people remain excluded from benefit and in poverty. Local people have hunted animals for food for centuries. They have always killed game that threatened them, or ruined their crops. If we now try to protect animals in populated areas without addressing the concerns of the people, then our efforts will fail.

The only pragmatic way to conserve Zambia's wild areas is to see the development of the local people, and the conservation of the animals and the environment, as interlinked goals.

In the long term, one will not work without the other. Conservation without development leads to resentful locals who will happily, and frequently, shoot, trap and kill animals. Development without conservation will simply repeat the mistakes that most developed countries have already made: it will lay waste a beautiful land and kill off its natural heritage. Look at the tiny areas of undisturbed natural vegetation that survive in the UK, the USA or Japan. See how unsuccessful we in the northern hemisphere have been at long-term conservation over the past 500 years.

As an aside, the local people in Zambia are sometimes wrongly accused of being the only agents of degradation. Many would like to see 'poachers' shot on sight, and slash-and-burn agriculture banned. But observe the importation of tropical hardwoods by the West to see the problems that our demands place on the natural environment in the developing world.

In conserving some of Zambia's natural areas and assisting the development of its people, the international community has a vital role to play. It could effectively encourage the Zambian government to practise sustainable long-term strategies, rather than grasping for the short-term fixes which politicians seem universally to prefer. But such solutions must have the backing of the people themselves, or they will fall apart when the foreign-aid budgets eventually wane.

In practice, to get this backing from the local communities it is not enough for a conservation strategy to be compatible with development. Most Zambians are more concerned about where they live, what they can eat and how they will survive, than they are about the lives of small, obscure species of antelope that taste good when roasted.

To succeed in Africa, conservation must not only be compatible with development, it must actually promote it. It must actively help the local people to improve their own standard of living. If that situation can be reached, then local communities can be mobilised behind long-term conservation initiatives.

Governments are the same. As Luangwa's late conservationist Norman Carr once commented, 'governments won't conserve an impala just because it is pretty'. But they will work to save it if they can see that it is worth more to them alive than dead.'

The best strategies tried so far on the continent attempt to find lucrative and sustainable ways to use the land. They then plough much of the revenue back into the surrounding local communities. Once the local communities see revenue from conservation being used to help them improve their lives – to build houses, clinics and schools, and to offer paid employment – then such schemes rapidly get their backing and support.

Carefully planned, sustainable tourism is one solution that can work effectively. For success, the local communities must see that the visitors pay because they want the wildlife. Thus, they reason that the existence of wildlife directly improves their income, and they will strive to conserve it.

It isn't enough for people to see that the wildlife helps the government to get richer; that won't dissuade a local hunter from shooting a duiker for dinner. However, if he is directly benefitting from the visitors, who come to see the animals, then he has a vested interest in saving that duiker.

It matters little to the Zambian people, or ultimately to wildlife species, whether these visitors come to shoot the wildlife with a camera or with a gun. The vital issue is whether the hunting is done on a sustainable basis (ie: only a few of the oldest 'trophy' animals are shot each year, so that the size of the animal population remains largely unaffected).

Photographers may claim the moral high ground, but should remember that hunters pay far more for their privileges. Hunting operations generate large revenues from few guests, who demand minimal infrastructure and so cause little impact on the land. Photographic operations need more visitors to generate the same revenue, and so generally cause greater negative effects on the country.

Conservation of Zambian wildlife and the environment falls within the remit of the Ministry of Tourism (page 36), whereas the body responsible for heritage conservation is the National Heritage Conservation Commission (NHCC; Old

Lusaka Boys' School, Dedan Kimathi Rd, Lusaka). The commission publishes a biannual magazine, *Zambia Heritage.*

A considerable area of Zambia – about 30% – is protected by national parks and game management areas. Of these, the most recent to be gazetted is Lusaka National Park, close to the capital, which opened in June 2015, creating further protection in a more urban area. These parks are designated for photographic visitors; here no hunting is allowed. Around the parks are large areas designated as game management areas (GMAs). Within these are villages and hence small-scale farms, and hunting is (at least in theory) controlled and practised sustainably. Both local and overseas hunters use the GMAs, and the latter usually pay handsomely for the privilege.

Integral to this model is that the GMAs provide a buffer between the pristine national park and the land outside where uncontrolled hunting is allowed. This should serve to protect the national park's animals from incursions by poachers, while the park acts as a large gene pool and species reservoir for the GMA.

The theory of GMAs is good, but their administration has many practical difficulties. In some of them hunting by the local people has been uncontrolled, and in a few much of the game has been wiped out – resulting in no income from the wildlife, and so more pressure to hunt unsustainably. Many have projects that aim to reverse this trend, to regenerate their game resources and then set the communities off on a sustainable path. However, much more work needs to be done if a long-term effect is to be felt across the country.

There are also community partnership parks (CPPs), the first of which is in the Bangweulu Wetlands. In broad terms, these parks are owned by the local

FIRE! *Tricia Hayne*

Somewhere – at any given time of the year – part of Zambia burns. Sometimes these are forest fires, spontaneously setting the bush alight as they have for millennia. Often, however, they are set deliberately. The reasons for this are many and varied, and not all are negative; fire is considered a mixed blessing by both agriculturalists and conservationists.

At worst, fires are set by poachers, or even traditional hunters, to drive animals out into the open. Subsistence farmers, too, employ destructive slash-and-burn techniques in order to create new plots of agricultural land from scrub or forest. More positively, fire is an important tool in the conservation armoury. Burning off the old grass before it is totally dry, for example, encourages the growth of new sweet shoots, which in turn attract grazers such as wildebeest. At a more local level, villagers will often set fire to long grass to create an open space around houses or to clear paths, thus discouraging rats and snakes. And sometimes controlled fires may be used to clear an area in order to create a firebreak as an insurance against greater damage.

Many of the tree species that make up the classic miombo woodland which covers large tracts of Zambia have evolved over time to become at least partially fire-resistant – and this in turn may help to explain their dominance in areas where fires are a regular part of the annual cycle. Other miombo species, however, as well as numerous indigenous trees such as mopane and teak, exhibit no such resistance. Thus, while the benefits are there, the risk of fire resulting in long-term environmental damage is a real threat.

community, and are managed by a partner within the private sector in co-operation with the state.

In 2015, responsibility for both national parks and GMAs was removed from the semi-independent Zambia Wildlife Authority (ZAWA), to be incorporated back into a government department - the Department of National Parks and Wildlife (DNPW) - within the Ministry of Tourism. ZAWA had more autonomy and greater financial independence, and there was concern that the move would result in greater political interference, especially on environmental issues. Some long-standing Zambian safari operators feel this concern has proven to be well founded, with many decisions being politicised. Park financing is of significant concern; in Luangwa, for example, operators have commented that all revenue derived from the national park (around US$3 million per annum) now finds itself in Treasury coffers while budgets within DNPW are being severely constrained (one recent year as little as US$60,000 was allocated to South Luangwa Management Unit). The implications of this for conservation efforts and infrastructure are significant. However, there are hopes that the government under President Hakainde Hichilema will be more positive and forward thinking in approach. In addition, the long-term partnership work with African Parks (page 476) in supporting and developing key Zambian national parks – Liuwa Plain and Kafue – bodes incredibly well for long-term conservation efforts around the country.

TOURISM Zambia lies in the heart of sub-Saharan Africa. To the northeast lie the 'original' safari areas of east Africa: Kenya and Tanzania. Some of their best parks are now rather crowded, though their wildlife spectacles are still on a grand scale. South of Zambia are the more subtle attractions of Zimbabwe, Botswana and Namibia. Each country draws its own type of wildlife enthusiasts, and all have an element of wilderness that can seem difficult to find in east Africa today.

All have embraced tourism in different ways. Zambia is fortunate in having addressed this question later than the others, with the chance to learn from the mistakes of its neighbours. It is hoped that sustainable tourism can be a saviour of Zambia's economy as well as its wildlife, though there is a long way to go before tourism contributes a sizeable slice of the country's revenue.

Nevertheless, tourism is helping Zambia – both in economic terms and with conservation. It is providing employment and bringing foreign exchange into the country, which gives the politicians a reason to support the preservation of the parks. Increasingly Zambia's small-scale safari operators have mobilised themselves behind local development objectives, and in recent years we're seeing very positive initiatives for tourism to help development and sustainable land use, both inside and outside of Zambia's national parks.

The visitor on an expensive safari is generally, by his or her mere presence, making a financial contribution to development and conservation in Zambia. When on safari, one very simple thing that you can do to help is to ask your safari operator:

- Besides employment, how do local people benefit from this camp?
- How much of this camp's revenue goes directly back to the local people?
- What are you doing to help the people living near this reserve?
- How much control do the local people have over what goes on in the area where these safaris operate?

If more visitors did this, it would make a huge difference. That said, most operators do have programmes to help their local communities. They've already realised that

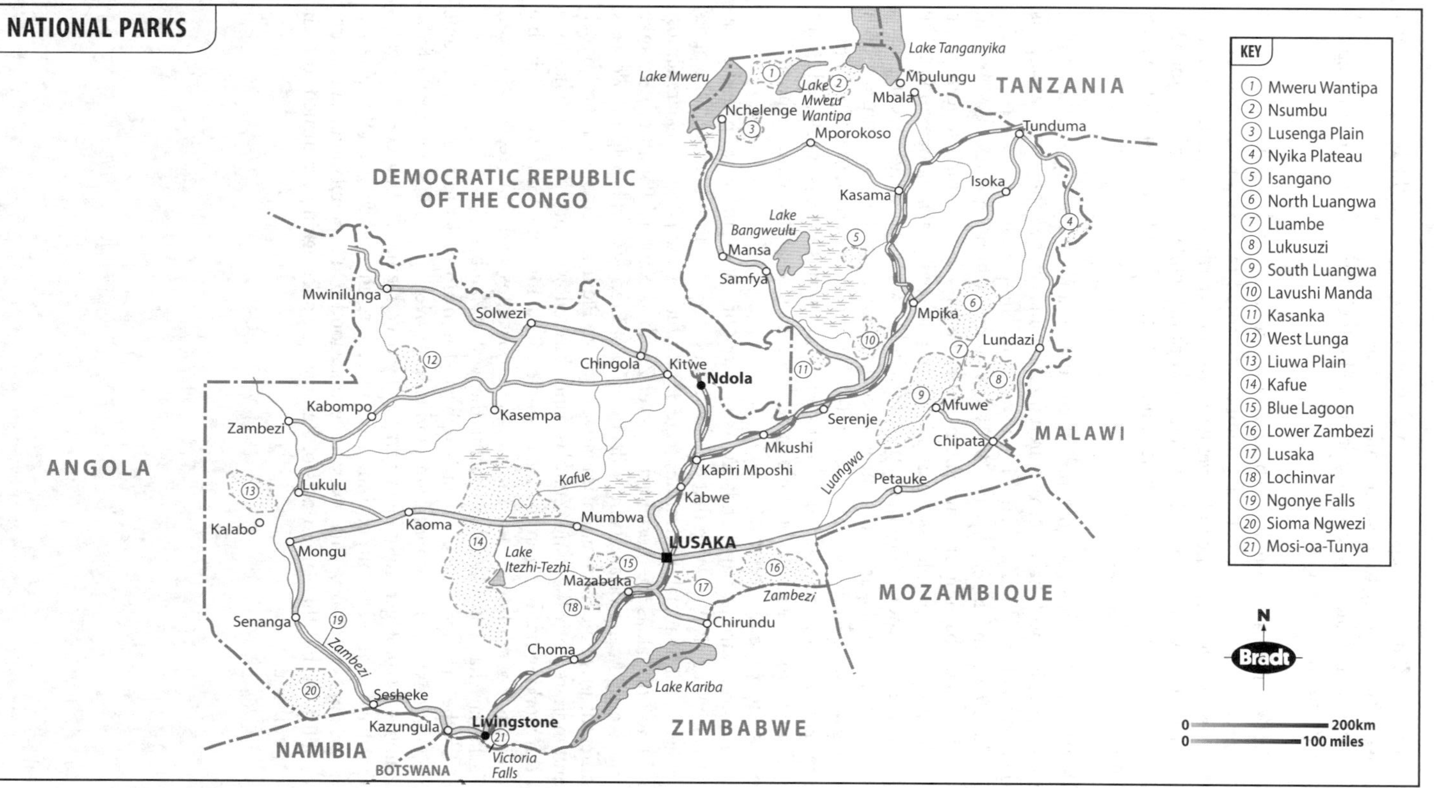

NATIONAL PARKS
KEY
1 Mweru Wantipa
2 Nsumbu
3 Lusenga Plain
4 Nyika Plateau
5 Isangano
6 North Luangwa
7 Luambe
8 Lukusuzi
9 South Luangwa
10 Lavushi Manda
11 Kasanka
12 West Lunga
13 Liuwa Plain
14 Kafue
15 Blue Lagoon
16 Lower Zambezi
17 Lusaka
18 Lochinvar
19 Ngonye Falls
20 Sioma Ngwezi
21 Mosi-oa-Tunya
DEMOCRATIC REPUBLIC OF THE CONGO
TANZANIA
MALAWI
MOZAMBIQUE
ZIMBABWE
NAMIBIA
BOTSWANA
ANGOLA
Lake Tanganyika
Lake Mweru
Lake Mweru Wantipa
Lake Bangweulu
Lake Itezhi-Tezhi
Lake Kariba
Victoria Falls
Mpulungu
Mbala
Nchelenge
Mporokoso
Tunduma
Isoka
Kasama
Mansa
Samfya
Mpika
Lundazi
Mfuwe
Chipata
Serenje
Mkushi
Petauke
Luangwa
Mwinilunga
Solwezi
Chingola
Kitwe
Ndola
Kabompo
Kasempa
Zambezi
Kapiri Mposhi
Kabwe
Kafue
Lukulu
Kalabo
Kaoma
Mumbwa
LUSAKA
Mongu
Mazabuka
Chirundu
Senanga
Choma
Sesheke
Kazungula
Livingstone
N
Bradt
0 200km
0 100 miles

the mass of Zambian people must benefit more (and more directly) from tourism if conservation is going to be successful in Zambia.

For ways in which you can support small local charities which directly help the people of Zambia, see page 124.

HUNTING Big-game hunting, where visiting hunters pay large amounts to kill trophy animals, is practised on a number of private ranches and hunting areas. It is also a valuable source of revenue in the long term for people living in the country's GMAs. In some this is already working, while in others development agencies, including the World Wide Fund for Nature (WWF), are working to start up sustainable schemes.

Poaching After tales of government corruption and complicity with poachers, those travellers who have not ventured into Zambia can be forgiven for asking, 'Is there any game left in Zambia?' The answer is a definitive 'Yes'.

The 1970s and especially the 1980s saw rampant hunting in the GMAs, and considerable poaching in Zambia's national parks – partly small-scale hunting for food by local people, and partly large commercial poaching operations. The government reaction to this was a mixture of indifference and, allegedly, complicity. The only national park with an appreciable number of foreign visitors, South Luangwa, was effectively defended from all but the most persistent infiltrations of specialist rhino-poachers. Other parks were, to various extents, neglected. Most still suffer from the results of that past neglect even now, and in some of the smaller parks, the battle can feel lost.

However, various parks and GMAs are now firmly on the way up, and a real attraction for visitors. With that development comes a reason to protect the parks (as well as a financial motivation; page 33). Kafue's game populations are almost back to normal, as are those in the Lower Zambezi National Park. Both Kasanka and North Luangwa are being effectively protected with the help of two very different private conservation initiatives, Liuwa Plain has embraced that model, and more recently the Bangweulu Wetlands has followed suit. The WWF has long been working hard to help the local people earn an income from the sustainable utilisation of wildlife around the Bangweulu Swamps, and more recently African Parks have had considerable impact in the west of Zambia.

So the message from Zambia is upbeat. The main parks have excellent game populations and many more are gradually recovering. Unlike much of Africa, Zambia has not generally been ravaged by overgrazing, and so even the parks that have suffered from poaching have usually retained their natural vegetation in pristine condition. This gives hope that good game populations can be re-established, and that large tracts of Zambia will once again be returned to their natural state.

4

Zambia Wildlife Guide

This wildlife guide is designed in a manner that should allow you to identify most **large mammals** that you'll see on safari in Zambia. Less common species are featured under the heading *Similar species* beneath the animal to which they are most closely allied, or bear the strongest resemblance. The **birdlife** covers some of the most compelling and colourful species found around the country.

MAMMALS

Zambia's large mammals are typical of the savannah areas of east and (especially) southern Africa. The large predators here are lion, leopard, cheetah, wild dog and spotted hyena, although cheetah and wild dog are relatively uncommon.

Elephant and buffalo occur in large herds in protected national parks, and in small, furtive family groups where poaching is a problem. Black rhino were, sadly, probably extinct in Zambia until they were re-introduced into North Luangwa National Park in 2003. There are also white rhino in the small, well-protected Mosi-oa-Tunya National Park at Livingstone, re-introduced from South Africa.

Antelope are well represented, with puku and impala numerically dominant in the drier areas. There are several interesting, endemic subspecies found in Zambia, including the Angolan and Thornicroft's giraffes, Cookson's wildebeest, Crawshay's zebra and two unusual subspecies of lechwe – the black and the Kafue lechwe – which occur in very large numbers in some of the country's bigger marshy areas.

Cheetah, Kafue National Park

SS

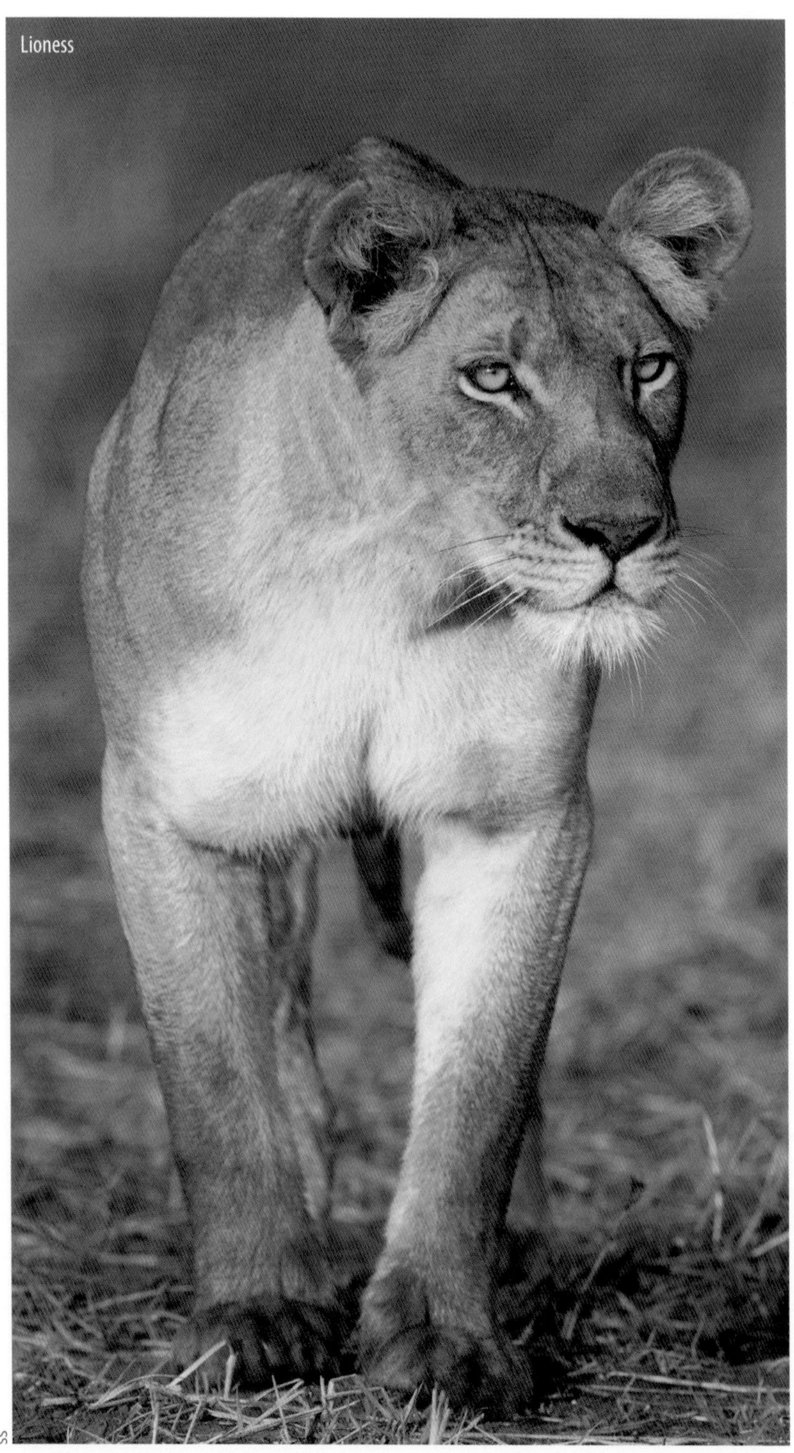

SS

Because Zambia is a wet country, with numerous marshy areas, its natural vegetation is lush and capable of supporting a high density of game. The country has a natural advantage over drier areas, and this accounts for the sheer volume of big game to be found in its better parks.

CATS AND DOGS

Lion (*Panthera leo;* shoulder height 100–120cm, weight 150–220kg) Africa's largest predator, the lion is the animal that everybody hopes to see on safari. It is a sociable creature, living in prides of five to ten animals and defending a territory of 20–200km^2. Lions often hunt at night, and their favoured prey is large or medium antelope such as wildebeest and impala. Most of the hunting is done by females, but dominant males normally feed first after a kill. Rivalry between males is intense and takeover battles are frequently fought to the death, so two or more males often form a coalition. Young males are forced out of their home pride at three years of age, and cubs are usually killed after a successful takeover.

When not feeding or fighting, lions are remarkably indolent – they spend up to 23 hours of any given day at rest – so the anticipation of a lion sighting is often more exciting than the real thing. Lions naturally occur in any habitat, except desert or rainforest. They once ranged across much of the Old World, but these days they are all but restricted to the larger conservation areas in sub-Saharan Africa (one residual population exists in India).

Lions occur throughout Zambia, and are very common in the larger parks with better game densities – Luangwa (north and south), Kafue and Lower Zambezi. Spend a week in any of these with a good guide and you'd be unlucky not to see at least some lion! They occur in smaller numbers in the more marginal parks and game management areas (GMAs), and more sparsely in areas with more human population.

Leopard (*Panthera pardus;* shoulder height 70cm, weight 60–80kg) The powerful leopard is the most solitary and secretive of Africa's big cats. It hunts at night, using stealth and power, often getting to within 5m of its intended prey before pouncing. If there are hyenas and lions around then leopards habitually move their kills up into trees to safeguard them. The leopard can be distinguished from the cheetah

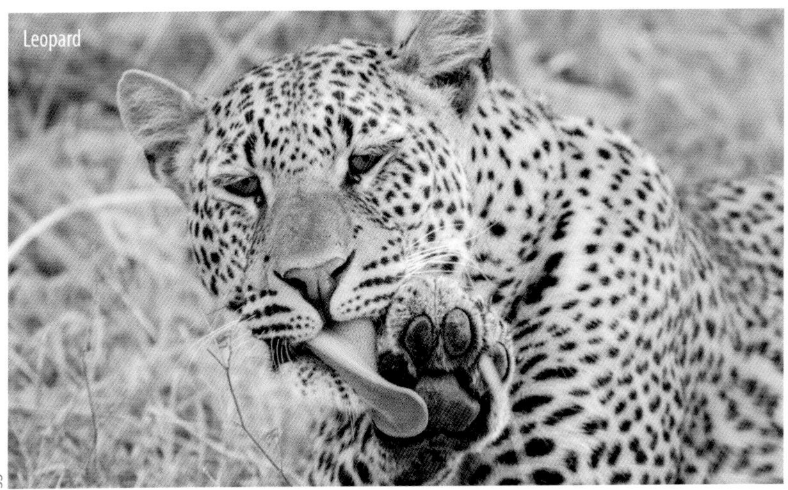
Leopard

SS

by its rosette-like spots, lack of black 'tearmarks' and more compact, low-slung, powerful build.

The leopard is the most common of Africa's large felines. Zambia's bush is perfect for leopard, which are prevalent throughout the country, as they favour habitats with plenty of cover, like riverine woodlands. Despite this, a good sighting in the wild during the day is unusual. In fact there are many records of individuals living for years, undetected, in close proximity to humans. Sightings at night are a different story and, because Zambia's national parks allow night drives, it's probably Africa's best country for seeking leopard.

South Luangwa National Park was chosen by the BBC for the filming of their remarkable documentary *Night of the Leopard* and acclaimed wildlife documentary *Leopard Legacy*. The same documentary team is currently resident in the park working on further updates of both the park's leopards and lions. Leopard sightings often become the main goal of night drives there. Your chances of spotting them are equally good in the Lower Zambezi, while consistently first-class sightings are also reported from the Lufupa area in Kafue. Remarkably they usually seem unperturbed by the presence of a vehicle and spotlight, and will often continue whatever they are doing regardless of an audience. Watching a leopard stalk is captivating viewing.

Cheetah (*Acynonix jubatus*; shoulder height 70–80cm, weight 50–60kg) This remarkable spotted cat has a greyhound-like build, and is capable of running at over 70km/h in bursts, making it the world's fastest land animal. Despite superficial similarities, you can easily tell a cheetah from a leopard by the former's simple spots, disproportionately small head, streamlined build, diagnostic black 'tearmarks' and preference for relatively open habitats. It is often seen pacing the plains restlessly, either on its own or in a small family group consisting of a mother and her offspring. Diurnal hunters, cheetah favour the cooler hours of the day to hunt smaller antelope like steenbok and duiker, and small mammals like scrub hares.

Zambia has a small but growing population of cheetah, centred on Kafue National Park and Liuwa Plain, which was featured in the wonderful BBC wildlife series *Dynasties II*. Cheetahs have had a historical presence in the Luangwa, although they are likely now absent from the area. Re-introduction attempts were made in the Lower Zambezi, but these were unsuccessful.

Similar species The **serval** (*Felis serval*) is smaller than a cheetah (shoulder height 55cm) but has a similar build and black-on-gold spots giving way to streaking near the head. Seldom seen, it is widespread and quite common in moist grassland, reed beds and riverine habitats throughout Africa, including Zambia. It does particularly well in some of the swampier areas. Servals prey on mice, rats and small mammals, but will sometimes take the young of small antelope.

Caracal (*Felis caracal*; shoulder height 40cm, weight 15–20kg) The caracal resembles the European lynx with its uniform tan coat and tufted ears. It is a solitary and mainly nocturnal hunter, feeding on birds, small antelope and young livestock. Found throughout the subcontinent, it easily adapts to a variety of environments and even occurs in some of Zambia's populated areas. Despite this, it is rarely seen due to being nocturnal. Caracals normally stalk their prey as closely as possible, before springing with surprise.

Similar species The smaller **African wild cat** (*Felis sylvestris*) is found from the Mediterranean to the Cape of Good Hope, and is similar in appearance to the

Cheetah
NWD/S

Serval
AKS/S

African wild cat
SS

Caracal
SP/S

SS

CF/S

MM/S

domestic tabby cat, though a little larger. It has an unspotted torso, a ringed tail and a reddish-brown tinge to the back of its ears. Wild cats are generally solitary and nocturnal, often utilising burrows or termite mounds as daytime shelters. They prey on reptiles, amphibians and birds, as well as small mammals.

African wild dog (*Lycaon pictus;* shoulder height 70cm, weight 25kg) Also known as the painted hunting dog, the wild dog is distinguished from other African dogs by its large size and mottled black, brown and cream coat. Highly sociable, living in packs of up to 20 animals, wild dogs are ferocious hunters that literally tear apart their prey on the run. They are now threatened with extinction, the most endangered of Africa's great predators. This is the result of relentless persecution by farmers, who often view the dogs as dangerous vermin, and their susceptibility to diseases spread by domestic dogs. Wild dogs are now extinct in many areas where they were formerly abundant, like the Serengeti, and they are common nowhere. The global population of fewer than 3,000 is concentrated in southern Tanzania, Zambia, Zimbabwe, Botswana, South Africa and Namibia.

Wild dogs prefer open savannah with only sparse tree cover, if any, and packs have enormous territories, typically covering 400km^2 or more. They travel huge distances in search of prey and so few parks are large enough to contain them. In Zambia wild dogs have their strongest base in Kafue, closely followed by the Luangwa, and they are being seen with increasing frequency and in growing pack sizes. They are sometimes seen in Liuwa and Nsumbu areas, and a super-sized pack in Lower Zambezi National Park is currently being filmed by wildlife documentary makers. Elsewhere their existence is less certain.

Side-striped jackal (*Canis adustus*; shoulder height 35–40cm, weight 8–12kg) Despite its prevalence in other areas of Africa, the side-striped jackal is common nowhere in Zambia, although it occurs throughout the country. It is greyish in colour and has an indistinct pale horizontal stripe on each flank and often a white-tipped tail. These jackals are most often seen singly or in pairs at dusk or dawn. They are opportunistic feeders, taking rats, mice, birds, insects, wild fruits and even termites. The side-striped jackal is Zambia's only species of jackal.

Spotted hyena (*Crocuta crocuta*; shoulder height 85cm, weight 70kg) Hyenas are characterised by their bulky build, sloping back, rough brownish coat, powerful jaws and dog-like expression. Contrary to popular myth, spotted hyenas are not exclusively scavengers; they are also adept hunters, which hunt in groups and kill animals as large as wildebeests. Nor are they hermaphroditic, an ancient belief that stems from the false scrotum and penis covering the female hyena's vagina. Sociable animals, hyenas live in loosely structured clans of about ten animals, led by females who are stronger and larger than males, based in a communal den.

Hyenas utilise their kills far better than most predators, digesting the bones, skin and even teeth of antelope. This results in the distinctive white colour of their faeces – which is an easily identified sign of them living in an area.

The spotted hyena is the largest hyena, identified by its light brown, blotchily spotted coat. It is found throughout Zambia, though is increasingly restricted to the national parks and GMAs. Although mainly nocturnal, spotted hyenas can often be seen around dusk and dawn in the Luangwa, Kafue and Lower Zambezi, with particularly large clans being found in Liuwa. Their distinctive, whooping calls are a spine-chilling sound of the African night. Note that neither of the spotted hyena's close relatives, the brown hyena and aardwolf, are thought to occur in Zambia.

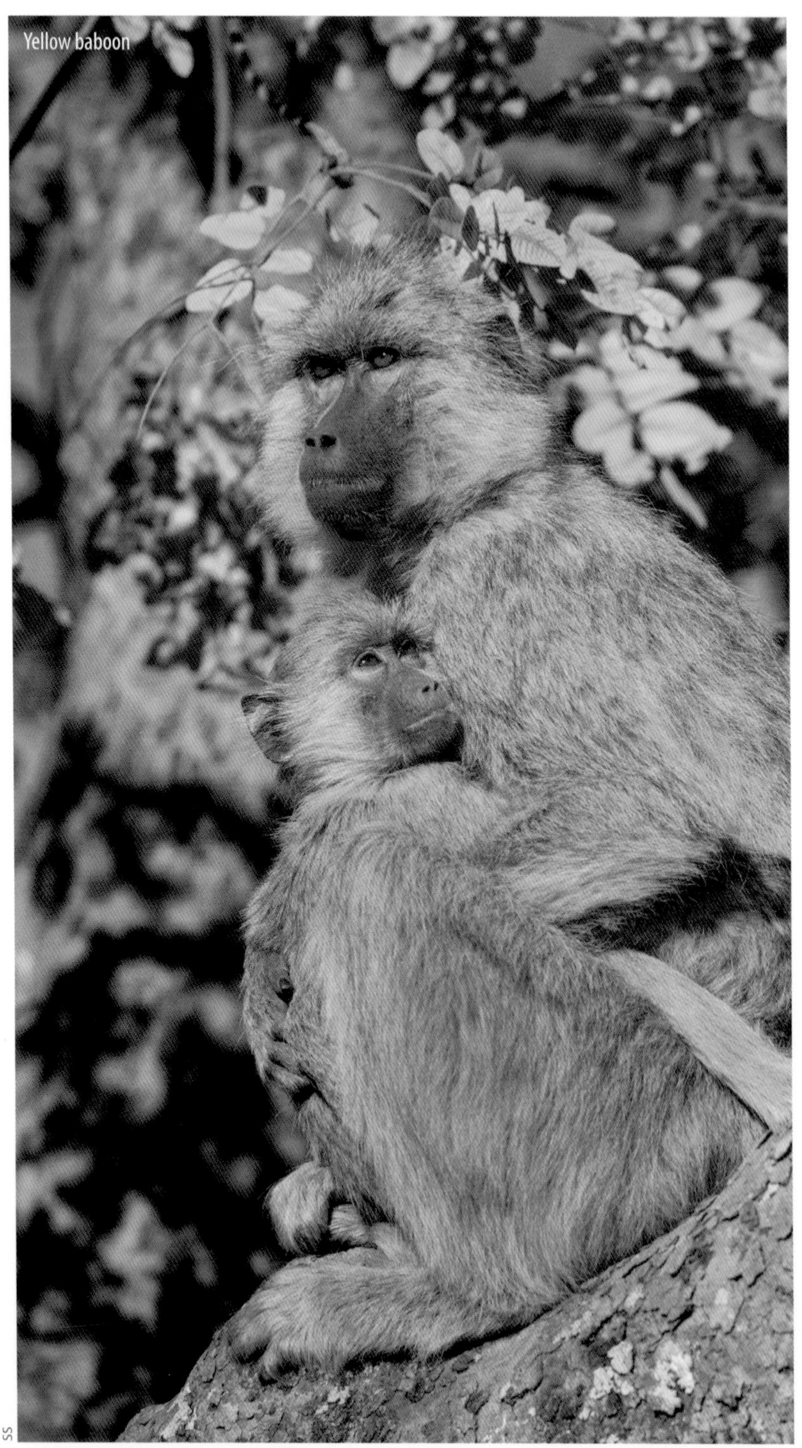

Yellow baboon

SS

PRIMATES

Baboon (*Papio cynocephalus*; shoulder height 50–75cm approx, weight male 16–29kg, female 10–16kg) This powerful terrestrial primate, distinguished from any other monkey by its much larger size, inverted U-shaped tail and distinctive canines, is fascinating to watch from a behavioural perspective. It lives in large troops that boast a complex, rigid social structure characterised by a matriarchal lineage and plenty of inter-troop movement by males seeking social dominance. Omnivorous and at home in almost any habitat, the baboon is the most widespread primate in Africa, frequently seen in most game reserves. With their highly organised defence system, the only predator that seriously affects baboons is the leopard, which will try to pick them off at night while they are roosting in trees.

There are as many as nine types of baboon ranging in Africa and Saudi Arabia, of which three species live in Zambia: the **yellow baboon** (*Papio cynocephalus*) in the east, the grey-footed **chacma baboon** (*Papio ursinus*) in the south and the **Kinda baboon** (*Papio kindae*) in the north – which some consider to be a subspecies of the yellow baboon (hence *Papio cynocephalus kindae*). Both yellow and chacma baboons have large ranges in Africa. More of a rarity is the Kinda baboon, which is found only in northern Zambia, Angola and parts of the DRC. In Zambia, it is readily seen in Kasanka National Park, Lavushi Manda and the Kafue. Smaller than other baboons, Kindas have softer coats and are generally lighter in colour. Socially, research by the Kasanka Baboon Project (w kasankababoonproject.com) suggests that Kinda males and females have stronger bonds with each other than females have with other females, which is strikingly different to other baboon species.

Vervet monkey (*Cercopithecus aethiops*; length (excluding tail) 40–55cm, weight 4–6kg) Also known as the green or grivet monkey, the vervet is probably the world's most numerous monkey and certainly the most common and widespread representative of the *Cercopithecus* guenons, a taxonomically controversial genus associated with African forests. An atypical guenon in that it inhabits savannah and woodland rather than true forest, the vervet spends a high proportion of its time on the ground. It occurs throughout Zambia, preferring belts of tall trees and thicker vegetation within easy reach of water.

Chacma baboon

TB/S

Kinda baboon

SS

The vervet's light-grey coat, black face and white forehead band are distinctive – as are the male's garish blue genitals. Vervets live in troops averaging about 25 animals; they are active during the day and roost in trees at night. They eat mainly fruit and vegetables, though are opportunistic and will take insects and young birds, and even raid tents at campsites (usually where ill-informed visitors have previously tempted them into human contact by offering food).

Blue monkey (*Cercopithecus mitis*; length (excluding tail) 50–60cm, weight 5–8kg) The blue monkey is known also as Moloney's monkey in Zambia, the samango monkey throughout southern Africa, the golden monkey in southwest Uganda, Sykes' monkey in Kenya and the diademed or white-throated guenon in some field guides. This most variable monkey is divided by some authorities into several species. It is unlikely to be confused with the vervet monkey, as blue monkeys have a dark, blue-grey coat, which becomes reddish towards its tail. Its underside is lighter, especially its throat.

These monkeys live in troops of up to ten animals and associate with other primates where their ranges overlap. They live in evergreen forests, and so are most likely to be seen around the Copperbelt and North Western Provinces, or north of Kasanka. However, they occur as far south as the Lower Zambezi National Park and are resident along the Luangwa's Muchinga Escarpment.

Angola black-and-white colobus monkey (*Colobus angolensis;* length (excluding tail) 65cm, weight 12kg) This beautiful jet-black monkey has bold white facial markings, a long white tail and white sides and shoulders. Almost exclusively arboreal, it is capable of jumping up to 30m, a spectacular sight with its white tail streaming behind. Several races have been described, and most authorities recognise this Angolan variety as a distinct species. In Zambia they are very rare, but have been reported from the forests north of Mwinilunga.

Bushbaby (*Galago crassicaudatus*; length (excluding tail) 35cm, weight 1–1.5kg) The bushbaby is Zambia's commonest member of a group of small and generally indistinguishable nocturnal primates, distantly related to the lemurs of Madagascar. In Zambia they occur throughout the country, though are very seldom seen during the day. At night their wide, endearing eyes are often caught in the spotlight during night drives.

Bushbabies are nocturnal and even around safari camps they can sometimes be seen by tracing a cry to a tree and shining a torch into the branches; their eyes reflect as two red dots. These eyes are designed to function in what we would describe as total darkness, and they feed on insects – some of which are caught in the air by jumping – and also by eating sap from trees, especially acacia gum.

They inhabit wooded areas, and prefer acacia trees or riverine forests. I remember once being startled, while lighting a barbecue, by a small family of bushbabies. They raced through the trees above us, bouncing from branch to branch while chattering and screaming out of all proportion to their modest size.

Similar species The **lesser bushbaby** (*Galago senegalensis;* length (excluding tail) 17cm, weight 150g), also known as the night ape, is half the size of the bushbaby and seems to be less common than its larger cousin. Where it is found, it is often among acacia or terminalia vegetation, rather than mopane or miombo bush (page 31).

Vervet monkey
SS

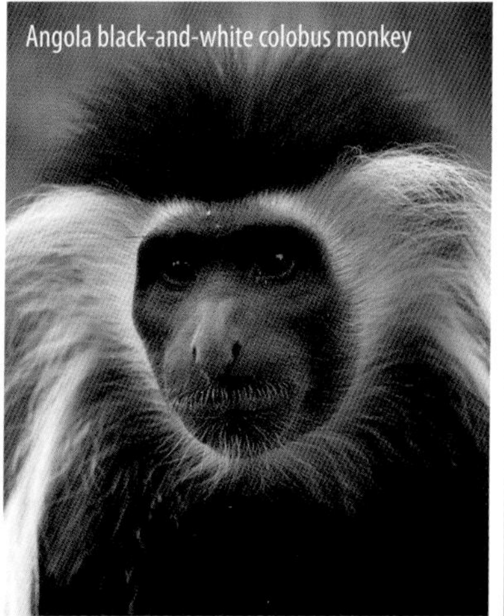
Angola black-and-white colobus monkey
SS

Blue monkey
SS

Bushbaby
CW/S

Lesser bushbaby
SS

LARGE ANTELOPE

Sable antelope (*Hippotragus niger*; shoulder height 135cm, weight 230kg) The striking male sable is jet black with a distinct white face, underbelly and rump, and long decurved horns – a strong contender for the title of Africa's most beautiful antelope. The female is chestnut brown and has shorter horns, while the young are a lighter red-brown colour. Sable are found throughout the wetter areas of southern and east Africa.

They are not common in Zambia. However, Kafue is probably the best park for sable, with Kasanka also worthy of note. In the Luangwa, they're confined to the foothills of the Muchinga Escarpment, so very rarely seen by visitors. Nsumbu has a small population, and there have been reports of sable in Sioma Ngwezi and West Lunga.

Sable are normally seen in small herds: either bachelor herds of males, or breeding herds of females and young which are often accompanied by the dominant male in that territory. The breeding females give birth around February or March; the calves remain hidden, away from the herd, for their first few weeks. Sable are mostly grazers, though will browse, especially when food is scarce. They need to drink at least every other day, and seem especially fond of low-lying dewy vleis in wetter areas.

Roan antelope (*Hippotragus equinus;* shoulder height 120–150cm, weight 250–300kg) This handsome horse-like antelope is uniform fawn-grey with a pale belly, short decurved horns and a light mane. It could be mistaken for the female sable antelope, but this has a well-defined white belly, and lacks the roan's distinctive black-and-white facial markings. The roan is a relatively rare antelope, common almost nowhere in Africa (the Nyika Plateau being one obvious exception to this rule). In Zambia small groups of roan are found in South Luangwa, Kafue, Kasanka, Nsumbu, Liuwa Plains and (probably) Sioma Ngwezi.

Roan need lots of space if they are to thrive and breed; they don't generally do well where game densities are high. Game farms prize them as one of the most valuable antelope (hence expensive to buy). They need access to drinking water, but are adapted to subsist on relatively high plateaux with poor soils.

Roan antelope

CM

Sable antelope

SHO

Common waterbuck female with young

NWD/S

Defassa waterbuck

GTW/S

Blue wildebeest

SS

Lichtenstein's hartebeest

DL/S

Tsessebe

SS

Waterbuck (*Kobus ellipsiprymnus;* shoulder height 130cm, weight 250–270kg) The waterbuck is easily recognised by its shaggy brown coat and the male's large, lyre-shaped horns. The common race of southern Africa (*K. e. ellipsiprymnus)* and areas east of the Rift Valley has a distinctive white ring around its rump. The defassa race (known as *K. e. defassa* or *K. e. crawshayi*) of the Rift Valley and areas further west has a full white rump.

In Zambia, the common waterbuck populates the Luangwa and Lower Zambezi valleys, while the defassa race occurs throughout most of the rest of the country, including Kafue National Park. They need to drink very regularly, so usually stay within a few kilometres of water, where they like to graze on short, nutritious grasses. At night they may take cover in adjacent woodlands. It is often asserted that waterbuck flesh is oily and smelly, which may discourage predators.

Blue wildebeest (*Connochaetes taurinus*; shoulder height 130–150cm, weight 180–250kg) This ungainly antelope, also called the brindled gnu, is easily identified by its dark coat and bovine appearance. The superficially similar buffalo is far more heavily built. When they have enough space, blue wildebeest can form immense herds – as perhaps a million do for their annual migration from Tanzania's Serengeti Plains into Kenya's Masai Mara. In Zambia, one such gathering occurs on the Liuwa Plains around November, when tens of thousands of animals congregate here as the rains arrive.

Elsewhere, wildebeest naturally occur from around the Kafue National Park area westwards, to Angola. There's also a subspecies, Cookson's wildebeest (*Connochaetes taurinus cooksoni)*, which is endemic to the Luangwa Valley. It's found commonly on the north side, in North Luangwa, but only rarely further south. It differs from the main species by having cleaner colours, including slightly reddish bands, and being a little smaller and more compact.

Lichtenstein's hartebeest (*Alcelaphus lichtensteini*; shoulder height 125cm, weight 120–150kg) Hartebeests are awkward antelopes, readily identified by the combination of large shoulders, a sloping back, a smooth coat and smallish horns in both sexes. Numerous subspecies are recognised, all of which are generally seen in small family groups in reasonably open country. Though once hartebeest were found from the Mediterranean to the Cape, only isolated populations still survive. Hartebeests are almost exclusively grazers and they like access to water.

The only one native to Zambia is Lichtenstein's hartebeest, which used to be found throughout the country, except for the extreme south and west. They are seen frequently in Kafue, and also occur in Nsumbu and Kasanka. The Luangwa has a good population, but they generally stay away from the river, and so remain out of view for most visitors.

Similar species The **tsessebe** (*Damaliscus lunatus*) is basically a darker version of the hartebeest with striking yellow lower legs. (A closely related subspecies is known as *topi* in east Africa.) These are very sparsely distributed in Zambia, occurring in the Kasanka–Bangweulu area, and to the far west of the Zambezi, in Liuwa and Sioma Ngwezi. Its favourite habitat is open grassland, where it is a selective grazer, eating the younger, more nutritious grasses. The tsessebe is one of the fastest antelope species, and jumps very well.

Kudu (*Tragelaphus strepsiceros*; shoulder height 140–155cm, weight 180–250kg) The kudu (or, more properly, the greater kudu) is the most frequently observed member of the genus Tragelaphus. These medium-size to large antelopes are characterised by their grey-brown coats and up to ten stripes on each side. The male has magnificent double-spiralled corkscrew horns. Occurring throughout Mozambique, Zimbabwe, Zambia, Botswana and Namibia, kudu are widespread and common, though not in dense forests or open grasslands. They are normally associated with well-wooded habitats. These browsers thrive in areas with mixed tree savannah and thickets, and the males will sometimes use their horns to pull down the lower branches of trees to eat, with mahogany (*Trichelia emetica)* being a particular favourite.

In Zambia they occur throughout the country except for the far northern areas. Normally they're seen in small herds, consisting of a couple of females and their offspring, sometimes accompanied by a male. Otherwise the males occur either singly, or in small bachelor groups.

Eland (*Taurotragus oryx*; shoulder height 150–175cm, weight 450–900kg) Africa's largest antelope, the eland is light brown in colour, sometimes with a few faint white vertical stripes. Relatively short horns and a large dewlap accentuate its somewhat bovine appearance. It was once widely distributed in east and southern Africa, though the population has now been severely depleted. Small herds of eland frequent grasslands and light woodlands, often fleeing at the slightest provocation. (They have long been hunted for their excellent meat, so perhaps this is not surprising.)

Eland are opportunist browsers and grazers, eating fruit, berries, seed pods and leaves as well as green grass after the rains, and roots and tubers when times are lean. They run slowly, though can trot for great distances and jump exceedingly well. In Zambia they occur widely but sparsely, and are largely confined to the country's protected areas.

MEDIUM AND SMALL ANTELOPE

Bushbuck (*Tragelaphus scriptus*; shoulder height 70–80cm, weight 30–45kg) This attractive antelope, a member of the same genus as the kudu, is widespread throughout Africa and shows great regional variation in its colouring. It occurs in forest and riverine woodland, where it is normally seen singly or in pairs. The male is dark brown or chestnut, while the much smaller female is generally a pale reddish brown. The male has relatively small, straight horns and both sexes are marked with white spots and sometimes stripes, though the stripes are often indistinct.

Bushbuck tend to be secretive and very skittish, except when used to people. They depend on cover and camouflage to avoid predators, and are often found in the thick, herby vegetation around rivers. They will freeze if disturbed, before dashing off into the undergrowth. Bushbuck are both browsers and grazers, choosing the more succulent grass shoots, fruit and flowers. In Zambia they are very widely distributed and fairly common.

Impala (*Aepeceros melampus*; shoulder height 90cm, weight 45kg) This slender, handsome antelope is superficially similar to the springbok, but in fact belongs to its own separate family. Chestnut in colour, and lighter underneath than above, the impala has diagnostic black-and-white stripes running down its rump and tail, and the male has large, lyre-shaped horns. One of the most widespread and successful antelope species in east and southern Africa, the impala is normally seen in large herds in wooded savannah habitats. It is the most common antelope in the Luangwa Valley, and throughout much of the central and southern areas of Zambia. However, in more northerly areas, puku are sometimes more common. As expected of such a successful species, it both grazes and browses, depending on what fodder is available.

Greater kudu

AVZ

Impala

TR/S

Eland

SS

Bushbuck

CM

Reedbuck
KM/S

Klipspringer
TW/S

Lechwe
SS

Red lechwe
EP/S

Black lechwe
SS

Reedbuck (*Redunca arundinum*; shoulder height 80–90cm, weight 45–65kg) Sometimes referred to as the southern reedbuck (as distinct from mountain and Bohor reedbucks, found further east), these delicate antelope are uniformly fawn or grey in colour, and lighter below than above. They are generally found in reedbeds and tall grasslands, often beside rivers, and are easily identified by their loud, whistling alarm call and distinctive bounding running style. In Zambia they occur widely, though seem absent from the very bottom of the Zambezi and Luangwa valley floors. (They do occur in both Luangwa and Lower Zambezi national parks, but usually on slightly higher ground, away from the rivers.)

Klipspringer (*Oreotragus oreotragus*; shoulder height 60cm, weight 13kg) The klipspringer is a strongly built little antelope, normally seen in pairs, and easily identified by its dark, bristly grey-yellow coat, slightly speckled appearance and unique habitat preference. Klipspringer means 'rock jumper' in Afrikaans and it is an apt name for an antelope which occurs exclusively in mountainous areas and rocky outcrops from Cape Town to the Red Sea.

They occur throughout most of Zambia, except for the extreme western areas, but only where rocky hills or kopjes are found. Given Zambia's generally rolling topography, this means only the odd isolated population exists. They are seen occasionally on the escarpments of the main valleys, but usually away from the main game areas. Klipspringers are mainly browsers, though they do eat a little new grass. When spotted they will freeze, or bound at great speed across the steepest of slopes.

Lechwe (*Kobus leche*; shoulder height 90–100cm, weight 80–100kg) Lechwe are sturdy, shaggy antelope with beautiful lyre-shaped horns, adapted to favour the seasonal floodplains that border lakes and rivers. They need dry land on which to rest, but otherwise will spend much of their time grazing on grasses and sedges, standing in water if necessary. Their hooves are splayed, adapted to bounding through their muddy environment when fleeing from the lion, hyena and wild dog that hunt them, making them the most aquatic of antelope after sitatunga.

Lechwe are found in the DRC, Angola, northern Botswana and Namibia's Caprivi Strip, but their stronghold is Zambia. Wherever they occur, the males are generally larger and darker than the females, and in Zambia there are three subspecies (though none occurs in the Luangwa or Lower Zambezi valleys).

The **red lechwe** (*K. l. leche*) is the most widespread subspecies. It's the only one found outside Zambia and has a chestnut-reddish coat, darker on the back and much lighter (almost white) underneath. Its legs have black markings, as does the tip of its tail. Inside Zambia red lechwe are found in large numbers (about 5,000 probably) on the Busanga Plains, with smaller populations in the Western Province and the Lukanga Swamps.

The **Kafue lechwe** (*K. l. kafuensis*) are slightly larger animals, with bigger horns, and are restricted to the Kafue Flats area, between Lake Itezhi-Tezhi and Lusaka. This race is more light brown than red, with black patches on their shoulders that run into the black on their legs. Most of the 40,000–50,000 that remain are confined to the Lochinvar and Blue Lagoon national parks.

The **black lechwe** (*K. l. smithemani*) used to occur in huge numbers, perhaps as many as half a million animals, centred on the plains to the south of the Bangweulu Wetlands. They are now restricted to about 30,000–40,000 animals in the same area, and a small population has been re-introduced into the Nashinga Swamps to the west of Chinsali. Black lechwe are much darker and the older males have almost black backs and brownish undersides.

Puku (*Kobus vardoni*; shoulder height 80cm; weight 60–75kg) Unless you see them beside each other, puku can be hard to distinguish from red lechwe – though the adults are generally slightly smaller than the lechwe. They are also stocky, orangey-red antelope with shaggy coats. Male pukus have stout, ribbed horns which curve forwards at the tips, though are shorter and spread out less than a lechwe's horns.

Puku are grazers, typically inhabiting open plains adjacent to rivers or marshes, or woodland fringes. They are always found close to water, although are not as fond of completely flooded areas as lechwe. Puku usually feed early or late in the day, and will often lie down in the shade when the sun is at its highest.

They are one of Zambia's most common antelope, found throughout western and northern Zambia and the Luangwa Valley, although they are noticeably absent from the Lower Zambezi Valley. In the south of Zambia, puku are exceedingly rare, occurring only in one small corner of northern Chobe; to the north they are native to areas of Malawi and the DRC, and common in Tanzania.

Young males form bachelor groups, from which prime animals break away to form territories. The more dominant the buck, the more appealing are the feeding resources within these territories, into which they attract females. Breeding takes place between April and July and thus calves are born in the green season when food resources are abundant.

Sitatunga (*Tragelaphus spekei*; shoulder height 85–90cm, weight 105–115kg) The semi-aquatic antelope is a widespread but infrequently observed inhabitant of west and central African papyrus swamps from the Okavango in Botswana to the Sudd in Sudan. In Zambia sitatunga are very widespread. Good populations are found in Bangweulu, the Busanga Swamps, Nsumbu and Kasanka.

Because of its preferred habitat, the sitatunga is very elusive and seldom seen, even in areas where it is relatively common. They are also less easy to hunt/poach than many other species, although they are exceedingly vulnerable to habitat destruction. Kasanka National Park is one of Africa's very best places to see these antelope; its tree hide provides more agile visitors with a superb vantage point above a small section of papyrus swamp, where sightings are virtually guaranteed in the early morning or late afternoon. Sitatunga are noted for an ability to submerse themselves completely, with just their nostrils showing, when pursued by a predator.

Steenbok (*Raphicerus campestris*; shoulder height 50cm, weight 11kg) This rather nondescript small antelope has red-brown upper parts and clear white underparts, and the male has short, straight horns. It is very common south of the Zambezi, but only occurs in southwestern Zambia (Mazabuka seems to be about the limit of their distribution). They like grasslands and open country with a scattering of cover, and seem to do very well in the drier areas. Like most other small antelopes, the steenbok is normally encountered singly or in pairs and tends to freeze when disturbed, before taking flight.

Similar species **Sharpe's grysbok** (*Raphicerus sharpei*) is similar in size and appearance, though it has a distinctive white-flecked coat. It occurs widely throughout Zambia, and appears to be absent only from the far northwest (Liuwa/Mwinilunga area). It is almost entirely nocturnal in its habits and so very seldom seen.

The **oribi** (*Ourebia ourebi*) is also a widespread but generally uncommon antelope. It is usually found only in large, open stretches of dry grassland, with the termitaria zones of the Busanga Plains, Lochinvar and Bangweulu area standing

Puku

CM

Steenbok

E/S

Sitatunga

C/S

Sharpe's grysbok

ET/S

Oribi

CM

out as good places to spot them. It looks much like a steenbok but stands about 10cm higher at the shoulder and has an altogether more upright bearing.

Common duiker (*Sylvicapra grimmia*; shoulder height 50cm, weight 20kg) This anomalous duiker holds itself more like a steenbok or grysbok and is the only member of its (large) family to occur outside of forests. Generally grey in colour, the common duiker can most easily be separated from other small antelopes by the black tuft of hair that sticks up between its horns. They occur throughout Zambia, and tolerate most habitats except for true forest and very open country. They are even found near human settlements, where shooting and trapping is a problem, and are usually mainly nocturnal. Duikers are opportunistic feeders, taking fruit, seeds and leaves, as well as crops, small reptiles and amphibians.

LARGE UNGULATES

Black rhinoceros (*Diceros bicornis*; shoulder height 160cm, weight 1,000kg) This is the more widespread of Africa's two rhino species, and is an imposing and rather temperamental creature. (White rhino are not thought to have been native to Zambia.) In the 1960s, the black rhino was recorded in the Kafue, Luangwa and Lower Zambezi and in the far north around Nsumbu and Mweru Wantipa. However, by the late 1990s it had probably been poached to extinction in Zambia, while becoming highly endangered in many of the other countries within its range. (There were a handful of reports of isolated individual animals existing in very remote areas; none was ever confirmed.) However, re-introductions established a breeding population in a subsection of North Luangwa National Park, with the population standing at 34 in 2015. Today, protection protocol means that specific population numbers are not disclosed, but the black rhino population in the park has more than doubled, making it one of continental significance, and it continues to demonstrate one of the fastest growth rates in Africa – a testament to those involved in ongoing conservation work.

Black rhinos exploit a range of habitats from woodland to open grassland, and are generally solitary. They can survive without drinking for four to five days. However, their territorial behaviour and regular patterns of movement make them an easy target for poachers. Black rhinos can be very aggressive when disturbed and will charge with minimal provocation. Their hearing and sense of smell are acute, while their eyesight is poor (so they often miss if you keep a low profile and don't move).

Hippopotamus (*Hippopotamus amphibius*; shoulder height 150cm, weight 2,000kg) Characteristic of Africa's large rivers and lakes, this large, lumbering animal spends most of the day submerged but emerges at night to graze. Strongly territorial, herds of ten or more animals are presided over by a dominant male who will readily defend his patriarchy to the death. Hippos are abundant in most protected rivers and water bodies and are still quite common outside of reserves.

Hippos are widely credited with killing more people than any other African mammal, but I know of no statistics to support this. John Coppinger (one of the Luangwa Valley's most experienced guides) suggests that crocodile, elephant and lion all account for more deaths in that area than hippos – despite the valley having one of Africa's highest concentrations of hippos. So while undoubtedly dangerous, perhaps they don't quite deserve their reputation.

In Zambia they are exceptionally common in most of the larger rivers, where hunting is not a problem. The Kafue, the Luangwa and the Zambezi all have large hippo populations.

Common duiker
CH/S

Black rhinoceros
BM/S

Hippopotamus
DLS/S

TR/S

PF/S

SHS

Buffalo (*Syncerus caffer*; shoulder height 140cm, weight 700kg) Frequently and erroneously referred to as a water buffalo (an Asian species), the African, or Cape, buffalo is a distinctive, highly social ox-like animal that lives as part of a herd. It prefers well-watered savannah, though also occurs in forested areas. Common and widespread in sub-Saharan Africa, it is widely distributed in Zambia. The Luangwa, and especially the north park, seems to have some particularly large herds, hundreds of animals strong. Buffalo are primarily grazers and need regular access to water, where they swim readily. They smell and hear well, and it's often claimed that they have poor eyesight. This isn't true, though when encountered during a walking safari, they won't be able to discern your presence if you keep still and the wind is right.

Huge herds are generally fairly peaceful, and experienced guides will often walk straight through them on walking safaris. However, small bachelor herds, or even single old bulls (known in the Luangwa as *kakuli*), can be very nervous and aggressive. They have a reputation for charging at the slightest provocation, often in the midst of thick bush, and are exceedingly dangerous if wounded. Lion often follow herds of buffalo, their favourite prey.

Giraffe (*Giraffa camelopardis*; shoulder height 250–350cm, weight 1,000–1,400kg) The world's tallest and longest-necked land animal, a fully grown giraffe can measure up to 5.5m high. Quite unmistakable, giraffe live in loosely structured herds of up to 15, though herd members often disperse, when they may be seen singly or in smaller groups. Formerly distributed throughout east and southern Africa, these great browsers are now found only on the southern side of the Luangwa Valley and in the far southwest of Zambia.

About eight subspecies of giraffe have been identified in Africa, and the Luangwa Valley contains one such distinct population, **Thornicroft's giraffe** (*G. c. thornicroftii*). These are generally regarded as having dark body patches and lighter neck patches than the normal 'southern' race of giraffe, and their colour patches don't normally extend below the knees, leaving their lower legs almost white. Their faces are also light or white. The vast majority of these live on the east side of the Luangwa River, in the GMA outside the park. They have been protected from hunting by a local taboo.

Much further west, the pocket of giraffe which are thought to still survive around the Sioma Ngwezi National Park are **Angolan giraffe** (*G. c. angolensis*), although so little is known of what survives in Sioma Ngwezi that their current status there is uncertain.

Plains zebra (*Equus quagga*; shoulder height 130cm, weight 300–340kg) Also known as common zebra, this attractive striped horse is widespread throughout most of east and southern Africa, where it is often seen in large herds alongside wildebeest. It is common in most conservation areas from northern South Africa all the way up to the southeast of Ethiopia.

Most southern races, although not those found in Zambia, have paler brownish 'shadow-stripes' between their bold black stripes. In Zambia, the subspecies in the Luangwa Valley is **Crawshay's zebra** (*E. q. crawshaii*), which also occurs on Nyika Plateau and possibly in Malawi's Vwaza Marsh. Norman Carr comments in his book on the Luangwa's wildlife (page 512) that the zebra found to the west of the Muchinga Escarpment belong to the *E. q. zambeziensis* subspecies. In the Kafue's Busanga Plains, the subspecies is known as **Grant's** or **Boehm's zebra** (*Equus q. boehmii*).

Regardless of these minor taxonomic differences, zebra are widely distributed throughout Zambia, though they tend to be restricted by human activity to the more remote or protected areas. They lack the brown shadow-stripes of their cousins further south, but otherwise are very similar.

Warthog (*Phacochoerus aethiopicus*; shoulder height 60–70cm, weight up to 100kg) This widespread and often conspicuously abundant resident of the African savannah is grey in colour with a thin covering of hairs, wart-like bumps on its face and rather large upward-curving tusks. Africa's only diurnal swine, the warthog is often seen in family groups, trotting around with its tail raised stiffly (a diagnostic trait) and a determinedly nonchalant air. They occur in most areas of Zambia, except in the extreme northwest, and are very common in most of the national parks. They don't usually fare well near settlements, as they are very susceptible to subsistence hunting/poaching. Wherever they occur, you'll often see them grazing beside the road, on bended knee, with their tails held high in the air as soon as they trot away.

Similar species Bulkier, hairier and browner, the **bushpig** (*Potomochoerus larvatus*) is known to occur throughout Zambia, and even in the vicinity of cultivated land where it can do considerable damage to crops. However, it is very rarely seen due to its nocturnal habits and preference for dense vegetation.

AFRICAN ELEPHANT (*Loxodonta africana*; shoulder height 2.3–3.4m, weight up to 6,000kg) The world's largest land animal, the African elephant is intelligent, social and often very entertaining to watch. Female elephants live in close-knit clans in which the eldest female plays matriarch over her sisters, daughters and granddaughters. Their lifespans are comparable to those of humans, and mother–daughter bonds are strong and may last for up to 50 years. Males generally leave the family group at around 12 years to roam singly or form bachelor herds. Under normal circumstances, elephants range widely in search of food and water, but when concentrated populations are forced to live in conservation areas their habit of uprooting trees can cause serious environmental damage.

Elephants are widespread and common in habitats ranging from desert to rainforest. In Zambia they were common everywhere except for the Upper Zambezi's floodplains, but have now become more restricted by human expansion. However, individuals often wander widely, turning up in locations from which they have been absent for years.

Zambia's strongest population is in the Luangwa, where there are now about 15,000. As recently as 1973 estimates put the Luangwa's population at more than 100,000, but the late 1970s and '80s saw huge commercial poaching for ivory, which wiped out a large proportion of this. Outside of a small, protected area in South Luangwa National Park, Zambia's elephants fared even worse. The populations in Kafue and even North Luangwa are still small, and the individuals are very nervous and skittish near people. (The exception here is possibly the Lower Zambezi, where the elephants regularly swim between Zimbabwe and Zambia, because the Zimbabwean parks were, on the whole, better protected from poaching than the Zambian parks. Hence the Lower Zambezi's elephant population is also fairly relaxed and numerous.)

SMALL MAMMALS

African civet (*Civettictis civetta*; shoulder height 40cm, weight 10–15kg) This bulky, long-haired, rather feline creature of the African night is primarily carnivorous, feeding on small animals and carrion, but will also eat fruit. It has a

Warthog

CM

Bushpig

SP/S

African elephant

SS

similar-coloured coat to a leopard: densely blotched with large black spots becoming stripes towards the head. Civets are widespread and common throughout Zambia in many habitats, and make frequent cameo appearances on night drives. Though occasionally called 'civet cats', this is misleading because they are far more closely related to mongooses than felines.

Similar species The smaller, more slender **tree civet** (*Nandinia binotata*) is an arboreal forest animal with a dark brown coat marked with black spots. It is really a resident of the equatorial forests, although is found in a few mountain areas on Zambia's Malawi border (including Nyika) as well as north of Mwinilunga. It is nocturnal, solitary and largely arboreal – and so is very seldom seen.

The **small-spotted genet** (*Genetta genetta*), **large-spotted genet** (*Genetta tigrina*) and **rusty-spotted genet** (*Genetta rubignosa*) are the most widespread members in Zambia of a large group of similar small predators (which even the experts often can't tell apart without examining their skins by hand). All the genets are slender and rather feline in appearance (though they are not cats), with a grey to gold-brown coat marked with black spots (perhaps combining into short bars) and a long ringed tail.

You're most likely to see them on nocturnal game drives or occasionally scavenging around game reserve lodges. They are found all over Zambia, even in urban areas if there is a plentiful supply of rodents. They are excellent climbers and opportunists, eating fruit, small birds, termites and even scorpions.

Banded mongoose (*Mungos mungo*; shoulder height 20cm, weight around 1kg) The banded mongoose is probably the most commonly observed member of a group of small, slender, terrestrial carnivores. Uniform dark grey-brown except for a dozen black stripes across its back, it is a diurnal mongoose occurring in playful family groups, or troops, in most habitats throughout Zambia. It feeds on insects, scorpions, amphibians, reptiles and even carrion and bird's eggs, and can move through the bush at quite a pace.

Similar species Another eight or so mongoose species occur in Zambia; some are social and gather in troops, others are solitary. Several are too scarce and nocturnal to be seen by casual visitors. Of the rest, the **water** or **marsh mongoose** (*Atilax paludinosus*) is large, normally solitary and has a very scruffy brown coat; it's widespread in the wetter areas. The **white-tailed mongoose** (*Ichneumia albicauda*), or white-tailed ichneumon, is a solitary, large brown mongoose with long, coarse, woolly hair. It is nocturnal and easily identified by its bushy white tail if seen crossing roads at night. It's not uncommon in cattle-ranching areas, where it eats the beetle-grubs found in the manure.

The **slender mongoose** (*Galerella sanguinea*) is as widespread and also solitary, but it is very much smaller (shoulder height 10cm) and has a uniform brown or reddish coat and blackish tail tip. Its tail is held up when it runs, and it is common throughout Zambia where there is lots of cover for it. The **dwarf mongoose** (*Helogate parvula*) is a diminutive (shoulder height 7cm), highly sociable light-brown mongoose often seen in the vicinity of the termite mounds where it nests. This is Africa's smallest carnivore, occurring in a higher density than any other, and is widespread throughout Zambia. Groups of 20 to 30 are not unknown, consisting of a breeding pair and subordinate others. These inquisitive little animals can be very entertaining to watch.

The **large grey mongoose** (*Herpestes ichneumon*), also called the Egyptian mongoose, is a large mongoose with coarse, grey-speckled body hair, black lower

S/D
EP/S
SS
SS
OP/S
SS

legs and feet, and a black tip to its tail. It's found all over Zambia, but is common nowhere, is generally diurnal and is solitary or lives in pairs. It eats small rodents, reptiles, birds and also snakes – generally killing rather than scavenging. The **bushy-tailed mongoose** (*Bdeogale crassicaude*) is a small, predominantly nocturnal species that looks mainly black, especially its legs and tail. It is found throughout Zambia, though appears relatively uncommon south of the Zambezi.

Meller's mongoose (*Rhynchogale melleri*) is a variable shaggy, grey colour with dark legs and a large muzzle. Its distribution is patchy and somewhat uncertain, but it is thought to occur throughout western Zambia and the Luangwa, but not north of the Serenje–Mbala road. It is solitary and nocturnal, eating a large proportion of termites as well as reptiles, amphibians and fruit. **Selous's mongoose** (*Paracynictis selousi*) is smaller, with fine, speckled grey fur, and a white tip at the end of its tail. It likes open country and woodlands, occurring in many areas of southern and western Zambia, even including the Luangwa. It is nocturnal and solitary, eating mainly insects, grubs, small reptiles and amphibians – it seems especially fond of the larvae of dung beetles, and so is sometimes found in cattle country.

BC/S

MS/S

TR/S

AVZ

SS

Honey badger (*Mellivora capensis*; shoulder height 30cm, weight 12kg) Also known as the ratel, the honey badger is black with a puppyish face and grey-white back. It is an opportunistic feeder best known for its allegedly symbiotic relationship with a bird called the honeyguide which leads it to a beehive, waits for it to tear it open, then feeds on the scraps. The honey badger is among the most widespread of African carnivores, and also among the most powerful and aggressive for its size; it occurs all over Zambia. However, it is thinly distributed and infrequently seen, except when it has lost its fear of people and started to scavenge from safari camps.

Similar species Several other mustelids occur in the region, including the **striped polecat** (*Ictonyx striatus*), a widely distributed but rarely seen nocturnal creature which has black underparts and a bushy white back, and the similar but much scarcer **striped weasel** (*Poecilogale albincha*). This has been reported from several locations in Zambia, but only rarely.

The **Cape clawless otter** (*Aonyx capensis*) is a brown freshwater mustelid with a white collar, while the smaller **spotted-necked otter** (*Lutra maculicollis*) is darker with light white spots on its throat. Both occur fairly commonly throughout the rivers, swamps and lakes of Zambia.

Aardvark (*Orycteropus afer*; shoulder height 60cm, weight up to 70kg) This singularly bizarre nocturnal insectivore is unmistakable with its long snout, huge ears and powerful legs, adapted to dig up the nests of termites, on which it feeds. Aardvarks occur throughout southern Africa, except the driest western areas of the Namib. Though their distinctive three-toed tracks are often seen, and they are not uncommon animals, sightings of them are rare.

Aardvarks prefer areas of grassland and sparse scrub, rather than dense woodlands. They are absent from Zambia's floodplains and marshes, but otherwise occur throughout the country where termites are found.

Pangolin (*Manis temmincki*; total length 70–100cm, weight 8–15kg) Sharing the aardvaak's diet of termites and ants, the pangolin is another very unusual nocturnal insectivore – with distinctive armour plating and a tendency to roll up in a ball when disturbed. (Then it can swipe its tail from side to side, inflicting serious damage on its aggressor.) Sometimes known as **Temminck's pangolins**, or **scaly anteaters**, these strange animals walk on their hindlegs, using their tail and front legs for balance. They are both nocturnal and rare – so sightings are exceedingly unusual and their distribution is uncertain. However, they are thought to occur in Kafue National Park and southern Zambia, as well as in the Luangwa Valley. (Evidence of their occurrence in the Luangwa is limited to about two sightings over the last few decades.)

In some areas further south, particularly Zimbabwe, local custom is to make a present of any pangolin found to the paramount chief (often taken to mean the president). This has caused great damage to their population.

Porcupine (*Hystrix africaeaustralis*; total length 80–100cm, weight 15–25kg) This is the largest rodent found in the region, and occurs throughout Zambia and all over southern Africa. It is easily identified by its black-and-white-striped quills, generally black hair and shambling gait. If heard in the dark, then the slight rattle of its quills augments the rustle of its foraging. These quills drop off fairly regularly, and are often found in the bush.

The porcupine's diet is varied, and they are fairly opportunistic when it comes to food. Roots and tubers are favourites, as is the bark of certain trees; they will also eat meat and small reptiles or birds if they have the chance.

Similar species Also spiky, the **southern African hedgehog** (*Erinaceus frontalis*) has been recorded in a few locations in Zambia, including the Lusaka, Mumbwa and Chipata areas. It's likely to occur elsewhere, though is small and nocturnal, so rarely seen even where it does occur. Hedgehogs are about 20cm long (much smaller than porcupines), omnivorous and uncommon.

Yellow-spotted rock hyrax (*Heterohyrax brucei*; length 35–50cm, weight 2.5–3.5kg) Rodent-like in appearance, hyraxes (also known as **dassies**) are claimed to be the closest living relative of elephants. Yellow-spotted rock hyraxes are often seen sunning themselves in rocky habitats, and become tame when used to people.

They are social animals, living in large groups, and largely herbivores, eating leaves, grasses and fruits. Where you see lots of dassies, watch out for black eagles and other raptors which prey extensively on them.

Similar species Very similar, the **tree hyrax** (*Dendrohyrax arboreus*) has been recorded in a few locations on the eastern side of the country, including South Luangwa.

Scrub hare (*Lepus saxatilis*; shoulder height 45–60cm, weight 1–4.5kg) This is the largest and commonest African hare, occurring throughout Zambia. In some areas a short walk or drive at dusk or after nightfall might reveal three or four scrub hares. They tend to freeze when disturbed.

Tree squirrel (*Paraxerus cepapi*; total length 35cm, weight 100–250g) This common rodent is a uniform grey or buff colour, with a long tail that is furry but not bushy. It's widely distributed all over southern and east Africa, and occurs throughout Zambia in most woodland habitats, although not wet evergreen or montane forests. It's often so common in mopane woodlands that it can be difficult to avoid seeing it, hence its other common name – the mopane squirrel.

Tree squirrels can live alone, in pairs or in small family groups, usually nesting in a drey of dry leaves, in a hole in a tree. They are diurnal and venture down to the ground to feed on seeds, fruit, nuts, vegetable matter and small insects. When alarmed they will usually bolt up the nearest tree, keeping on the side of the trunk away from the threat and so out of sight as much as possible. If they can attain a safe vantage point with a view of the threat, then they'll sometimes make a loud clicking alarm call.

Similar species The **sun squirrel** (*Heliosciurus rufobrachium*) is the largest of Zambia's squirrels, and is found everywhere north of a rough line between Kabwe and Lukulu. It has similar habits to those of the more common tree squirrel, though will lie in the sun more often. Its colour varies considerably between individuals and also seasons, from light fawn to greyish brown, though its long bushy tail is consistently crossed by numerous whitish, longitudinal stripes.

The **red-and-black squirrel** (*Heliosciurus lucifer*) is a very pretty species with flame-red upper parts, a black patch in the middle of its back, and whitish underside. It occurs only in montane forest and in Zambia is thought to be restricted to the Nyika Plateau.

Boehm's squirrel (*Paraxerus boehmi*) has a similar size, shape and greyish colouring to the tree squirrel. However, it has two very distinct white stripes, bordered by black, down the side of its back from nape to tail. It inhabits riverine evergreen forest, and has a limited distribution in Zambia, restricted to the country's far north, around the Nsumbu and Lusenga Plain areas.

The **flying squirrel** (*Anomalurus derbianus*) is quite unmistakable as there's a membrane of skin linking the fore and hind legs, and also the base of the tail. It uses this to glide with, when jumping from a higher branch to a lower one. It's a solitary, arboreal species that prefers miombo woodlands. It occurs from the Liuwa area east across Mwinilunga and the Copperbelt, and into the western side of northern Zambia, but is seldom seen.

REPTILES

Zambia's varied habitats provide suitable environments for 192 documented reptile species, including snakes, lizards, tortoises and crocodiles.

Reptiles are a group of cold-blooded vertebrates (animals with a backbone) belonging to the class Reptilia and are characterised by several distinct features. They are ectothermic animals, meaning their body temperature is regulated by external sources such as the sun; they cannot generate their own body heat internally. Their dry skin is made up of keratinised scales or scutes, which provide protection and help prevent water loss through the skin. They inhabit a variety of habitats, with some, like snakes and lizards, being primarily terrestrial, while others, like crocodiles, are adapted to aquatic environments. Regardless of habitat, all reptiles have lungs and breathe air, though they have developed various lung structures to facilitate efficient oxygen absorption, and most reproduce by laying amniotic eggs, which have a protective shell and provide a self-contained environment for the developing embryo.

Reptiles play important ecological roles as predators, prey and contributors to ecosystem balance. While reptiles share some characteristics, they exhibit a wide diversity in their physical features, behaviours and favoured habitats. It's important to note that some reptiles, such as crocodiles and venomous snakes, should be observed from a safe distance to ensure personal safety.

NILE CROCODILE *Mike Unwin*

(*Crocodylus niloticus*; length over 5m, weight over 1,000kg) Few visitors to Zambia's mighty rivers will want to miss the opportunity to see this antediluvian creature. With its powerful serrated tail, horny plated skin and up to 100 peg-like teeth crammed into a long, sinister smile, the Nile crocodile is the stuff of nightmares and action movies. Contrary to the more lurid myths, crocodiles generally avoid

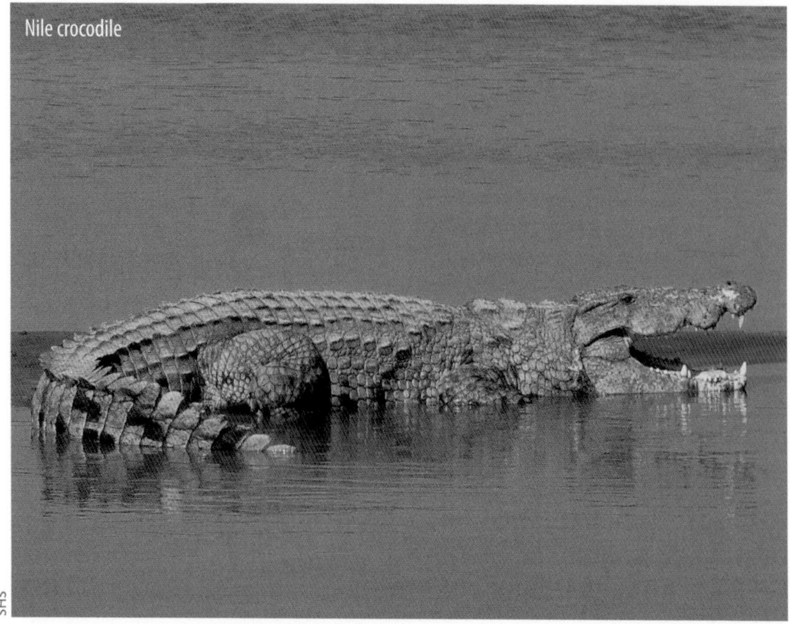

Nile crocodile

SHS

SS

people (understandably, given the slaughter they have suffered). Yet while they will not usually launch themselves into boats or come galloping after you on land, humans are still potential prey for a big one, and tragedies do occasionally occur. When in crocodile country, it is sensible to keep your distance from the water's edge.

Crocodiles can live up to 100 years, but reach sexual maturity at 12–15 years. They inhabit lakes, rivers and swamps. Whereas youngsters are boldly marked in black and green, adults are generally a muddy grey-brown colour – usually lighter in rivers than in lagoons. Theirs is an amphibious life: basking on land, jaws agape to lose heat, or cruising the waters, raised eyes and nostrils allowing them to see and breathe undetected. As well as eating fish such as bream and barbel, adult crocs will ambush mammals up to the size of buffalo, grabbing them with an explosive sideways lunge from the water, before dragging them under to drown. Large numbers of crocodiles gather to scavenge big carcasses, churning up the water as they thrash and spin to dislodge chunks of flesh. They will even leave the water to steal a nearby lion kill.

Similar species The endangered **slender-snouted crocodile** (*Crocodylus cataphractus* or *Mecistops cataphractus*) occurs in Zambia only in isolated instances. In Lake Tanganyika, it is largely confined to the quieter sections of the lake around Nsumbu National Park. Historically it is also said to occur in the upper streams of the Congo basin around Kasanka, although there have been no reliable sightings reported for many years.

LIZARDS, CHAMELEONS, GECKOS AND SKINKS The **Nile monitor lizard** or water monitor (*Varanus niloticus*) is a large lizard species found in Zambia. Known for their impressive size, reaching lengths of up to 2.5m, Nile monitors are both excellent swimmers and climbers. A fast-moving monitor lizard splashing into the water is easily mistaken for a small crocodile, though the monitor's lighter, yellow markings and smoother skin quickly distinguish them after the initial flurry of activity. The **Kafue round-snouted worm lizard** (*Zygaspis kafuensis*) and the blue-headed **Bill's tree agama** (*Acanthocercus branchi*) are both endemic lizards.

Zambia is home to five chameleon species, including the **smooth chameleon** (*Chamaeleo laevigatus*) and the **flap-necked chameleon** (*Chamaeleo dilepis*), which is the only one commonly seen. Famed for their fascinating ability to change colour, independently moving eyes and their tongue projection mechanism to capture prey, chameleons are arboreal reptiles with a specialised grip that allows them to cling to branches and twigs. In traditional folklore, chameleons are believed to possess magical powers and carry great symbolism; for some people they remain a bad omen and for others they're the root of stories on wisdom and adaptability. Zambia has several gecko species, including **Turner's gecko** (*Chondrodactylus turneri*) and the **tropical house gecko** (*Hemidactylus mabouia*). Geckos are small to medium-sized lizards known for their adhesive toe pads, which enable them to climb walls and ceilings. They are primarily nocturnal and feed on insects. Equally numerous are smooth-skinned **skinks**, some of which have the ability to shed their tails as a defence mechanism, and one of which, a **legless skink** (*Acontias schmitzi*), is endemic to Zambia's Western Province.

SNAKES There are 102 known snake species in Zambia, forming an integral part of the country's diverse ecosystems. They are middle-level predators that eat prey, from small antelope to termites, and are an important food source for raptors, ground hornbills and mongooses among others. Generally shy, snakes are keen to avoid human contact and most will silently slither away unnoticed. The majority of Zambia's snakes pose no threat to humans, though 16 species are considered deadly, such as the black mamba, cobras and puff adders, and 16 are capable of inflicting extremely painful bites, including pythons and stiletto snakes. In the unlikely event of a snakebite, seek immediate medical attention (**Snakebite Emergency**: +260 974 248 144).

The venomous snake most likely encountered in Zambia is the **puff adder** (*Bitis arietans*). A viper subspecies, puff adders are ambush predators, relying on their excellent camouflage to lie in wait for prey to pass by, and as a result are unusually confrontational if encountered by walkers. Identified by their stout, heavy body, broad triangular head and a series of dark, zigzag patterns on their back, they produce a distinctive hissing sound and 'puff' up aggressively in defence when threatened. Puff adders strike very quickly, possess long fangs and potent venom and are responsible for a significant number of snakebite incidents in Africa.

The **Southern African python** (*Python natalensis*) by contrast is a non-venomous snake. The largest snake species in Africa, with some individuals 5.5m in length, they are powerful constrictors and target a range of prey, including small to medium-sized mammals and birds, swallowing prey whole and laying low while they digest. The **black mamba** (*Dendroaspis polylepis*) is Africa's longest venomous snake, growing up to 4.5m in length, and remains one of the continent's most feared, while the **black-necked** (*Naja nigricollis*) and **Mozambique spitting cobras** (*Naja mossambica*) live up to their names and squirt venom from their fangs in self-defence. Both are commonly seen in Lusaka, South Luangwa and the Lower Zambezi. **Rasmussen's night adder** (*Causus rasmusseni*) and the **Zambian sand snake** (*Psammophis zambiensis*) are Zambia's two endemic snakes.

For most travellers on safari, if they're lucky enough to see a snake at all, it is likely to be a harmless, vibrant green **spotted bush snake** (*Philothamnus semivariegatus*) or a timid **brown house snake** (*Boaedon capensis*) on the hunt for mice.

Nile monitor lizard
JM
Bill's tree agama
DH/S
Puff adder
MVD/HHISS
Black mamba
MVD/HHISS
Black-necked spitting cobra
MVD/HHISS
Southern African python
MVD/HHISS
Brown house snake
MVD/HHISS
Spotted bush snake
WVZ/S

Leopard tortoise

EP/S

Serrated turtle

KE/S

TORTOISES AND TERRAPINS The most commonly encountered tortoise in Zambia is the **leopard tortoise** (*Stigmochelys pardalis*). Known for their distinctive appearance, they have a large, dome-shaped carapace (shell) that can reach up to 45–60cm in length, which is patterned with unique yellow and black markings, resembling the spots of a leopard. They also have long legs and a long neck, which allows them to browse on vegetation, feeding on various grasses, succulent plants, leaves and occasionally fruits. The **pancake tortoise** (*Malacochersus tornieri*), noted for its thin, flattened shell, is also found in the rocky outcrops of northeastern Zambia. They are protected as a vulnerable species under CITES.

There are six turtle and terrapin species in Zambia, found in the country's many rivers, dams and freshwater lakes: the **Zambezi soft-shelled turtle** (*Cycloderma frenatum*), **dwarf hinged terrapin** (*Pelusios nanus*), **Mashona hinged terrapin** (*Pelusios rhodesianus*), **black-bellied hinged terrapin** (*Pelusios subniger*), **Okavango mud turtle** (*Pelusios bechuanicus*) and the **serrated turtle** (*Pelusios sinuatus*). Keep an eye out for them basking on rocks beside calm rivers.

Much of Zambia is still covered by original, undisturbed natural vegetation, and hunting is not a significant factor for most of the country's birds. Thus, with a range of verdant and natural habitats, Zambia is a superb birding destination, with 734 different species recorded by 2022. BirdWatch Zambia (formerly the Zambian Ornithological Society), in partnership with BirdLife International, has designated a total of 42 'Important Bird & Biodiversity areas' (IBAs), covering 14% of the country. For details, see Peter Leonard's *Important Bird Areas in Zambia* (page 512).

While the animal species differ only occasionally from the 'normal' species found in southern Africa, the birds are a much more varied mix of those species found in southern, eastern and even central Africa. The obvious celebrity is the ungainly shoebill stork, which breeds in the Bangweulu Wetlands, and only one or two other places in central Africa. A lesser-known attraction is the Zambian or Chaplin's barbet, Zambia's only endemic bird species, found in southern Zambia around the south side of Kafue National Park. However, there are many other unusual, rare and beautifully coloured species that attract enthusiasts to Zambia, from the collared barbet to the black-cheeked lovebird, Heuglin's robin and Schalow's turaco.

In addition to its resident bird species, Zambia receives many migrants. In September and October the Palaearctic migrants (those that come from the northern hemisphere – normally Europe) appear, and they remain until around April or May. This is also the peak time to see the intra-African migrants, which come from further north in Africa.

The rains from December to April see an explosion in the availability of most birds' food: seeds, fruits and insects. Hence this is the prime time for birds to nest, even if it is also the most difficult time to visit the more remote areas of the country.

Lesser masked weavers

SS

FOREST AND BUSH BIRDS

1 The delightful emerald-green **little bee-eater** (*Merops pusillusi*), with its canary yellow throat and turquoise brow, is often seen hawking for flying insects from low perches, before returning to beat its prey on a branch before feeding. **2** Zambia's only endemic bird, the cackling **Chaplin's barbet** (*Lybius chaplini*) is a small white bird with a distinctive red ring around its eye, black tail and heavy bill. Breeding only in established sycamore figs, they're classed as Vulnerable due to deforestation. **3** Named for its rolling aerobatics, the photogenic **lilac-breasted roller** (*Coracias caudatus*) poses perfectly on high perches to scan for prey. Monogamous and territorial, these vibrant birds are a firm favourite. **4** The forest-dwelling, green-and-yellow **collared sunbird** (*Hedydipna collaris*) is a tiny, iridescent bird known to feed on nectar by piercing the base of flowers. The male has a narrow purple collar. **5** Found in small, noisy flocks, the **common bulbul** (*Pycnonotus barbatus*) is a forest-living species. **6** With dazzling yellow eyes, the dark, glossy green and violet plumage of the **greater blue-eared starling** (*Lamprotornis chalybaeus*) is a common sighting. **7** Spectacular, raspberry-coloured **southern carmine bee-eaters** (*Merops nubicoides*) nest in large colonies along the sandy riverbanks of the Luangwa and Lower Zambezi rivers. Visit in September and October to guarantee sightings. **8** Dining on insects and arthropods, **Heuglin's robin** (*Cossypha heuglini*) – aka white-browed robin-chat – is an accomplished mimic with a with a melodious, crescendo song. **Page 77** As with all aptly named weavers, the **lesser masked weavers** (*Ploceus intermedius*) are master nest-builders.

JM

PWH

JM

ME/S

TR/S

WH/D

TR/S

CN/S

CM

PWH

PJ/D

OP/S

ME/S

DD/S

9 Standing 40–45cm tall, the **giant kingfisher** (*Megaceryle maxima*) is Africa's largest kingfisher, notable for its shaggy, monochrome crest, huge bill and harsh call. **10** Perching low to the water, the small **malachite kingfisher** (*Alcedo cristata*) lies in wait for aquatic prey. Sudden vertical dives into the water are successful, with fish eaten headfirst on return to their perch. Look out for low, colourful flights along rivers. **11** A gregarious bird, the **pied kingfisher** (*Ceryle rudis*) is often seen hovering and diving over rivers. During breeding season, they excavate long, narrow tunnels in vertical riverbanks to nest, and cooperatively raise chicks. **12** Jade-coloured and crested, beautiful **Schalow's turaco** (*Tauraco schalowi*) is tricky to spot, liking to bounce around in dense woodland along the upper Zambezi. Largely frugivorous, they feed in flocks but breed in solitary, monogamous pairs. **13** With a bright red face and throat, and namesake black collar, the plump **black-collared barbet** (*Lybius torquatus*) sings a notable duet with its mate and bows in greeting. **14 Red-throated twinspot** (*Hypargos niveoguttatus*) is small and secretive, with a crimson face and pure white spots on its belly. Its call is a grasshopper-like trill. **15** The glossy dark purple plumage of **Lady Ross's turaco** (*Musophaga rossae*) is complemented by a striking yellow bill and crimson primary feathers and crest. This frugivorous forest resident and adept canopy climber rarely strays far from its birthplace. **16** The largely monochrome **trumpeter hornbill** (*Bycanistes bucinator*) is found in small flocks in thickets and riverine forest, where it feeds in the canopy of large fruit trees. Distinguished by a grey casque on its upper bill and loud baby-like cry in flight.

WR/D

SS

WATERBIRDS

1 A tall, black-and-white stork with a distinctive yellow 'saddle' on its bill, the **saddle-billed stork** (*Ephippiorhynchus senegalensis*) is a wading bird, known to stab its prey. **2** Found in large flocks, the long-necked **white-faced whistling ducks** (*Dendrocygna viduata*) have a distinctive three-note whistle and feed at night. **3** The grey, stocky **black-crowned night heron** (*Nycticorax nycticorax*) is found in communal, waterside roosts by day, flying out at dusk to hunt fish and frogs. **4** A wading, bald-headed bird with a curved bill, the **African sacred ibis** (*Threskiornis aethiopicus*) was considered the incarnation of Thoth, the Ancient Egyptian god of knowledge and wisdom. **5** Flocks of rare **wattled cranes** (*Bugeranus carunculatus*) are found in Liuwa and Bangweulu. They are monogamous and perform elaborate courtship dances. **6** Sometimes called the 'snakebird', thanks to its long, S-shape neck protruding from the water as it swims, the **African darter** (*Anhinga rufa*) does not have waterproof oil on its feathers, making it a super diver. Often seen with wings outstretched, drying its feathers. **7** Bangweulu Wetlands is home to the endangered, prehistoric-looking **shoebill stork** (*Balaeniceps rex*). An ingenuous chick-rearing initiative is underway to boost numbers (page 368). **8 Yellow-billed storks** (*Mycteria ibis*) have a marvellous breeding colony in South Luangwa. Every May–June, over 1,000 birds nest in a stand of large ebony trees, surrounded by water. **9 Pelicans** (*Pelecanus onocrotalus*) are a spectacle whether fishing cooperatively in 'parties' or soaring high seeking new waterholes.

SS

SS

S/D

C/D

5

AVZ

6

SS

7

©1975 Peter W. Hills (all rights reserved)

PWH

8

CM

9

CM

PWH

RK/D

SS

PWH

SS

BIRDS OF PREY

1 The largest eagle in Africa, the **martial eagle** (*Polemaetus bellicosus*) is a ferocious predator. With keen eyesight, it hunts on the wing, spotting prey from up to 5km away, stooping sharply and killing on impact. **2** With a seagull-like call, the **African fish eagle** (*Haliaeetus vocifer*) is a monogamous bird, often seen in pairs along rivers, catching fish with a shallow dip into the water's surface. **3** A ginger, barred owl, **Pel's fishing owl** (*Scotopelia peli*) is shy and a relatively uncommon sighting. Roosting in riverine forest by day, it hunts fish and frogs at night. **4** One of Africa's smallest owls, the round-faced, speckled **pearl-spotted owlet** (*Glaucidium perlatum*) is active by day and will often respond to a good mimic call from a guide. **5** A common raptor between July and March, with distinctive fork tail, the **yellow-billed kite** (*Milvus aegyptius*) is a scavenger. **6** With a large head, yellow eyes, and barred wings visible in flight, the **black-chested snake eagle** (*Circaetus pectoralis*) hunts snakes and reptiles, occasionally hovering briefly before diving. Snakes are swallowed whole in flight. **7** At 58–66cm tall, **Verreaux's (giant) eagle-owl** (*Bubo lacteus*) is Africa's largest owl, with pale grey plumage and distinctive pink eyelids. **8** Easily identified by its low, gliding flight and tendency to rock in a stiff, side-to-side motion, the **bateleur** (*Terathopius ecaudatus*) is a territorial, short-tailed eagle. They are known to react aggressively if their nests are approached.

6
PWH

7
SM

8
PWH

GROUND BIRDS Although grouped as 'ground birds', all of the birds in this category can, and do, fly. They are, however, all largely terrestrial and many also nest on the ground, like the guineafowl and spurfowl, which create a hidden scrap in the ground, only occasionally lined with grass and twigs. The ground hornbill will look for large, natural tree cavities in which to nest, but spends two-thirds of its day walking, while the secretary bird is in fact a largely terrestrial raptor, pacing across large areas from dawn to dusk, when it returns to its, often thorny, treetop nest.

1 Helmeted guineafowl (*Numida meleagris*) are commonly sighted in noisy, skittish flocks. They have attractive black-and-white, spotted feathers and a small, naked blue-and-red head, topped with the distinctive casque that gives them their name. **2** Increasingly rare, the large black **southern ground hornbill** (*Bucorvus leadbeateri*) has a distinctive red face and throat pouch and a decurved bill. Usually seen in family groups walking slowing through grasslands, foraging for reptiles, insects and small animals. A monogamous, dominant pair breed, with the family cooperatively raising any chicks, which can live for up to 50–60 years. Listen out for their deep grunting and booming early-morning breeding duet. **3** Common, chicken-like birds, the **red-necked spurfowl** (*Pternistis afer*) is found across Zambia. **4** The tall, crane-like **secretary bird** (*Sagittarius serpentarius*) derives its name from its quill-like crest of feathers, lending it the appearance of a secretary tucking pens behind their ears. Striding purposefully at an impressive 2.5–3km/h, it hunts daily for reptiles, insects and small mammals, which it kills with powerful blows from its feet.

1

SS

2

PWH

3

PWH

4

MP/S

5

Planning and Preparation

Tourists generally come to Zambia in small numbers, and for the most part restrict themselves to a few of the main towns and national parks. Away from these centres, visitors are regarded with mild curiosity and often shown great warmth and hospitality. Zambia is a genuinely friendly country which (perhaps Lusaka excepted) has not yet had enough bad experiences of visitors to lower its opinion of them.

Zambia's attitude to tourism has changed considerably over the past decade, and visitors are now generally seen as good for the country because they spend valuable foreign currency and create employment. Tourism is helping both Zambia's economy and – by making a major contribution to the preservation of the national parks – its conservation policy.

WHEN TO GO AND HIGHLIGHTS

WEATHER See page 28 for a detailed description of the weather that can be expected, and note that Zambia's rainy season occurs around December to April (slightly different every year).

Dry season Most of Zambia's tourists come during the dry season, with the peak being August to early October. Zambia's small camps and lodges ensure that it never feels busy, even when everywhere is full. Others visit early or late in the season – May to July or November – because the camps are quieter and often costs are lower. The dry season (May to November), when you are unlikely to meet rain and can expect clear blue skies, is certainly the easiest time to travel and is ideal if this is your first trip to Africa, or if seeing lots of big game is top of your wish list.

June to August are the coolest months, then from September onwards the heat gradually builds up. Note, though, that where the altitude is relatively low – like the Luangwa, the Lower Zambezi Valley or Lake Tanganyika – the temperature is always higher. These places, especially, can get very hot towards the end of October, and occasions of over 40°C in the shade in the middle of the day have earned October the tag of 'suicide month' among the locals.

November is a variable month, but many days can be cooler than October, as the gathering clouds shield the earth from the sun. On some days these bring welcome showers; on others they simply build, and with them come tension and humidity. It's always an interesting month.

Wet season A small but increasing number of visitors come during what's known as the 'emerald season', from December to April. While the likelihood of rain means that this isn't for everybody, it remains a fascinating time of year to visit. The camps that open then will often be quiet for days. Their rates can be much lower, and they're often far more flexible about bringing children on safari.

At this time of year, the days can vary enormously from one to the next. Even within a day, skies will often change from sunny to cloudy within minutes and then back again. Downpours are usually heavy and short, and often in the late afternoon. Even in the lower valleys, temperatures are pleasant, rising to only around 30°C, and the nights only slightly cooler (typically down to perhaps 15°C). You will need a good waterproof for the rainy season, but it seldom rains for long enough to really stop you doing anything. Except travelling on bush roads…

TRAVELLING Travelling around Zambia in the dry season often has its challenges – but in the wet season it's a totally different game. Most untarred roads become quagmires; many are completely impassable. The rivers swell to bursting, often beyond, as their surging brown waters undermine trees and carry them downstream like Pooh-sticks. Streams that were ankle-deep in October become potential rafting challenges. Many rural areas are cut off for a few months, so getting anywhere away from the main routes can be tricky.

However, if you are planning to fly into a national park for a safari, you'll find that only a few camps remain open. The South Luangwa has a network of all-weather roads for driving safaris. If you've often been to Africa in the dry season, then this is a fascinating time to visit – like being introduced to a different side of an old friend.

VEGETATION During the wet season, the foliage runs wild. The distinctive oxbow lagoons of the Luangwa and Lower Zambezi fill, while trees everywhere are deeply green. The open sandy plains become verdant meadows, often with shallow pools of water. It's a time of renewal, when a gentler light dapples Zambia's huge forests and areas of bush.

When the rains end, the leaves gradually dry and many eventually drop. More greys and browns appear, and good shade becomes harder to find. Eventually, by late September and October, most plants look dry and parched, coloured from straw-yellow to shrivelled brown.

GAME From the point of view of most herbivores, the wet season is a much more pleasant time to visit. Those in national parks live in enormous salad bowls, with convenient pools of water nearby. It's a good time to have their young and eat themselves into good condition. Val and Bob Leyland were the first visitors for whom I ever organised a trip during the rains. On returning, they commented that 'having [previously] visited Africa last dry season, there's something special about seeing all the animals when they aren't struggling with thirst and a lack of vegetation…It gives a sense of luxuriance which isn't there in the dry season.'

Visiting South Luangwa in the wet season you will see game, but probably less of it. On my last trip during the rains I went on two night drives. On the first we saw a good range of antelope (including some wonderful sightings of young animals), a few elephant and buffalo and a leopard at the end of the evening. The next we found a hyena on a kill, and later followed three lionesses hunting for several hours. The birding was consistently phenomenal, far better than during the dry season.

However, if game viewing is your priority, or this is one of your first trips to Africa, then the animals are much easier to spot when it's dry, as no thick vegetation obscures the view. Further, they are forced to congregate at well-known water points, like rivers, where they can be observed. Many more tracks are navigable in the bush, and so more areas can be explored by vehicle. So if you want to see large numbers of animals, then do come to Zambia in the dry season – and later rather than earlier if possible.

A few specific animal highlights include:

- **February–May** Most of the herbivores are in their best condition, having fed well on the lush vegetation.
- **May–August** Leopard are generally easier to see, as they come out more during the twilight hours. Later in the year they often come out later in the evening, waiting until it is cool.
- **September–October** Buffalo groups tend to amalgamate into larger, more spectacular herds. (They splinter again just before the rains.) Lion sightings become more frequent, as they spend more time near the limited remaining water sources.
- **October–December** Crocodiles are nesting, so are found on or near exposed sandbanks.
- **November** The great wildebeest gathering masses on Liuwa Plain, in western Zambia. It's still accessible by 4x4 at this time of year, but you'll need a small expedition to witness it.
- **November–March** Baby warthogs and impala start to appear in November, followed by most of the mammals that calve sometime during the rainy season.

BIRDLIFE The birdlife in Zambia is certainly best when the foliage is most dense, and the insects are thriving: in the wet season. Then many resident birds are nesting and in their bright, breeding plumage. This coincides to a large extent with the 'summer' period, from around October to March, when the Palaearctic migrants from the northern hemisphere are seen. Certainly in terms of water birds – storks, herons, ducks, geese and the smaller waders – the rainy season (and just after) is an infinitely better time to visit.

The birding calendar's highlights include:

- **March–July** Large breeding colonies of storks and herons gather to breed. The only sites I know are in the Nsefu Sector of the South Luangwa National Park.
- **August–October** 'Fishing parties' of herons, egrets and storks will arrive at pools as they dry up, to feed on the stranded fish.
- **September–November** Carmine bee-eaters form large nesting colonies in the soft sand of vertical riverbanks.
- **October–November** Pennant-winged nightjars are in resplendent breeding plumage.
- **November–April** Most of the weavers are in breeding plumage.
- **February–April** Fire-crowned bishop birds, yellow-billed storks and the spectacular paradise whydahs have their breeding plumage on display.
- **April–June** Resident African skimmers are nesting.

Birdwatching novices and experts alike might consider downloading the excellent Birds of Zambia App (£19.99) before travel to allow instant identification, comparison and recording of the species spotted on their travels. If you are planning a birding safari to Zambia and are looking for a specialist guide, Frank Willems (0978 430655; e birdingzambia@gmail.com; w birdingzambia.com) is the country's leading ornithologist and runs scheduled tours, as well as bespoke private guiding trips, across the country: a super experience for bird enthusiasts.

PHOTOGRAPHY I find the light clearest and most spectacular during the rainy season. Then the rains have washed the dust from the air, and the bright sunlight can contrast wonderfully with dark storm clouds. The vegetation's also greener and brighter, and the animals and birds often in better condition. However, it will rain occasionally when you're trying to take shots, and the long periods of flat, grey light through clouds can be very disappointing. Sometimes it can seem as if you're waiting for the gods to grant you just a few minutes of stunning light, between the clouds.

A more practical time is probably just after the rains, around April to June, when at least you are less likely to be interrupted by a shower.

The dry season's light is reliably good, if not quite as inspirational as that found during the rains. You are unlikely to encounter any clouds, and will get better sightings of game to photograph. Try to shoot in the first and last few hours of the day, when the sun is low in the sky. Otherwise, use a filter (perhaps a polariser) to guard against the strength of the light leaving you with a camera full of washed-out shots.

WALKING SAFARIS For safe and interesting walking, you need the foliage to be low so that you can see through the surrounding bush as easily as possible. This means that the dry season is certainly the best time for walking. Walking in the wet season, through shoulder-high grass, is possible – but I'd only go with a very experienced guide and it is harder than during the dry season. My favourite months for walking are June to September, as October can get hot on longer walks.

FISHING The best times to fish in Zambia depend on the area. In the north, on Lake Tanganyika, the rainy season is ideal, between November and March, but in most other areas of the country much of that period is off limits for fishing. On Zambia's great rivers, such as the Zambezi, Kafue and Luangwa, fishing is at its best when the waters are clear. This usually happens from around May to June and lasts until the end of November. Although it is cold during those months the fish are there and will usually fall to bait and spinner, and even fly.

There is a ban on fishing during the months of December to February in all Zambian waters, with the exception of Lake Tanganyika, Lake Kariba, and private dams.

TOURIST INFORMATION

The Zambia Tourism Board (☎ 0211 229087; **e** ztb@zambiatourism.org.zm, info@zambiatourism.org.zm; **w** zambiatourism.com) offers consumer and general information, and visa advice to potential travellers. It has a good website, and three offices overseas, listed here. For details of other websites offering tourist information, see page 515.

South Africa 570 Ziervogel St, Arcadia, Pretoria; ☎ +27 12 3261854; **e** tourism@zambiapretoria.net, zambiatourism@iburst.co.za

UK 2 Palace Gate, London W8 5NG; ☎ 020 7589 6655; **e** info@zambiahc.org.uk

USA 2200R St, Washington, DC 20008; ☎ +1 202 234 4009; **e** embzambia@aol.com

PUBLIC HOLIDAYS

Aside from the private lodges and large hotels, much of Zambia effectively shuts down on public holidays. Independent travellers in particular may need to plan ahead, especially in terms of changing money and finding fuel.

New Year's Day	1 January
Women's Day	8 March

Youth Day	12 March
Good Friday	around March/April
Holy Saturday	day following Good Friday
Kenneth Kaunda Day	28 April
Labour Day	1 May
African Unity Day	25 May
Heroes' Day	first Monday of July
Unity Day	first Tuesday of July
Farmers' Day	first Monday of August
National Prayer Day	18 October
Independence Day	24 October
Christmas Day	25 December
Boxing Day	26 December

ORGANISING A SAFARI

Most visitors who come to Zambia for a few weeks' safari stay at some of the small safari camps. Combinations of time in the Kafue, the Luangwa Valley, the Lower Zambezi and a few days around Victoria Falls would be typical.

WHEN TO BOOK If you have favourite camps, or a tight schedule, then book as far ahead as you can; eight months to a year in advance is perfect. Bear in mind that most camps are small, and thus easily filled. They organise their logistics with military precision and so finding space at short notice, especially in the busier months, can be tricky. (The exception to this rule is usually the rainy season.)

If you are looking to travel in the next few months, then one or two of your chosen camps may be full; you'll have to accept alternatives.

HOW MUCH? Safaris in Zambia are not cheap. Expect to pay US$4,400–11,000/£3,500–9,000 per person sharing per week, plus international airfares. This would include a few of your internal transfers or flights, camp transfers, meals, activities, laundry, park fees and even drinks.

HOW TO BOOK It's best to arrange everything together, using a reliable, independent tour operator. Many operators sell trips to Zambia, but few know the country well. Insist on dealing directly with someone who does. Zambia is changing fast, so up-to-date local knowledge is vital in putting together a trip that runs smoothly and suits you. Make sure that whoever you book with is bonded, so your money is protected if they go broke. If you're unsure, pay with a credit card. Never book a trip from someone who hasn't spent time there – you are asking for problems. Ask the person you're dealing with specifically, 'Have you been to this camp or place?'

Booking directly with most Zambian camps is easily possible; the camps are the easy bit. Once they are organised, you need to piece together the jigsaw puzzle of transfers, internal flights and stopovers to link them into your trip. Without local knowledge, this can be tricky – and you will have little recourse if anything goes wrong.

European, US and local operators usually work on commission for the trips that they sell, which is deducted from the basic cost that the visitor pays. Thus you should end up paying the same whether you book through an overseas operator, or talk directly to a camp in Zambia.

Perhaps because of the UK's historical links, or the high number of British safari-goers, there seems to be more competition among UK tour operators than elsewhere. Hence they've a reputation for being generally cheaper than US operators for the same trips.

TOUR OPERATORS Zambia is something of a touchstone for tour operators to southern Africa: those who know Zambia well are the small core of Africa specialists. Most operators can send you to Cape Town with ease. But ask them where to visit in Zambia, and you'll rapidly sort those that know southern Africa from those that haven't got a clue.

Don't let anyone convince you that there are only three first-class safari camps in Zambia, as it's rubbish. If your operator doesn't know most of the camps in this book – and offer a wide choice to suit you – then use one that does.

Here we must, as the authors, admit a personal interest in the tour-operating business. Chris runs Expert Africa (page 268), which is currently the leading operator to Zambia. With offices in London, New Zealand, Windhoek and Cape Town, we organise trips to Zambia for travellers from all over the world. Our website has detailed original maps, the widest choice of Zambian lodges and camps, and extensive reviews from many of our travellers. Booking your trip with a tour operator like us will always cost you the same as or less than if you contacted Zambia's camps directly – plus you get independent advice, full financial protection, and experts to organise it for you. Our safaris are completely flexible; they cost from about US$5,600/£4,500 per person for a week, including accommodation, meals and game activities, and excluding international flights.

For a fair comparison, international tour operators featuring Zambia include the following. (Tour operators based in Zambia are listed in the relevant chapters.)

UK

Aardvark Safaris w aardvarksafaris.com. Small, reliable upmarket safari specialist to Africa, Mauritius & Seychelles. Also has US office.

Abercrombie & Kent w abercrombiekent.co.uk. Worldwide individual & group holidays to upmarket destinations with upmarket price tags.

Acacia Adventure Holidays w acacia-africa.com. Small group adventure holidays & overland/camping safaris throughout Africa.

Africa Explorer w africa-explorer.co.uk. Tiny but knowledgeable company run by the jovial John Haycock.

Africa Travel w africatravel.co.uk. General operator offering trips across Africa & the Indian Ocean.

Audley Travel w audleytravel.com. Large tailor-made operator offering trips worldwide from Burma to New Zealand, including Africa.

Cazenove & Loyd w cazloyd.com. Top-end tailor-made operator with worldwide options, including Africa.

Exodus w exodus.co.uk. Worldwide guided group specialists, with safari & canoe trips in Zambia.

Expert Africa w expertafrica.com. Africa specialists with the most comprehensive website on Zambia safaris & a very wide range of options. Run by this book's author.

Extraordinary Africa w extraordinary-africa.com. New, small tailor-made operator featuring East and southern Africa, inc Zambia, plus Seychelles & Mauritius.

Gane & Marshall w ganeandmarshall.com. Tailor-made operator with worldwide destinations that include Africa.

Hartley's Safaris w hartleys-safaris.co.uk. Long-established tailor-made specialists to east & southern Africa & Indian Ocean islands.

Journeys by Design w journeysbydesign.com. Small tailor-made operator (ground arrangements only) featuring east & southern Africa.

Okavango Tours & Safaris w okavango.com. Tailor-made specialists to Africa & Indian Ocean islands, with a good knowledge of Zambia.

Original Travel w originaltravel.co.uk. Upmarket holidays including to Africa.

Rainbow Tours w rainbowtours.co.uk. Once pure Africa specialists, now part of the larger ITC travel group.

Safari Consultants w safari-consultants.com. Long-established tailor-made specialists to East & southern Africa, & Indian Ocean islands, with a good knowledge of Zambia.
Safari Drive w safaridrive.com. Specialising in self-drive 4x4 trips across southern & East Africa.
Scott Dunn World w scottdunn.com. Worldwide coverage, with itineraries & tailor-made trips to Zambia.
Steppes Africa w steppestravel.com. Upmarket tailor-made operators to destinations worldwide.
Tribes Travel w tribes.co.uk. Worldwide travel on fair-trade principles; particularly strong on cultural trips.
Wildlife Worldwide w wildlifeworldwide.com. Worldwide operator offering tailor-made & small-group wildlife holidays.
Yellow Zebra w yellowzebra.com. Tailor-made safari company that merged with Wilderness Safaris in 2021, offering trips to Africa and the Indian Ocean.

France

Makila Voyages w makila.fr

Africa

Land & Lake Safaris ☎ +265 (0)175 7120; e info@landlake.net; w landlake.net. Based in Lilongwe, this operator focuses on Malawi, with some trips to Zambia.
Pulse Africa ☎ +27 (0)11 325 2290; e info@pulseafrica.com; w pulseafrica.com. Long-standing, reputable & highly bespoke operator based in South Africa, run by knowledgeable Sandy Wood. Offers East & southern Africa.

North America

Africa Adventure Company 2601 E Oakland Park Bd, Suite 600, Fort Lauderdale, FL 33306; ☎ 954 491 8877, 1 800 882 9453; e safari@africanadventure.com; w africa-adventure.com
Geographic Expeditions 1008 General Kennedy Av, San Francisco, CA 94129-0902; ☎ 888 570 7108; w geoex.com
OAT ☎ 1 800 955 1925; w oattravel.com. Typically OAT takes over entire camps for a minimum of a year. They appeal to more mature US-based clients with highly structured activities at low prices.

Australasia

The Classic Safari Company 124A Queen St, Woollahra, NSW 2025, Australia; ☎ 1300 130 218; w classicsafaricompany.com.au
Expert Africa 11 Brightwater Cres, Totara Park, Upper Hutt 5018, New Zealand; ☎ 04 976 7585; e info@expertafrica.com; w expertafrica.com

SUGGESTED ITINERARIES Those backpacking and driving themselves around Zambia need time but have great flexibility, and part of the adventure of such a trip is having no itinerary. However, most visitors have a much shorter time available.

Fly-in trips If you're flying in, then getting your itinerary right and arranging it carefully in advance is important. For most visitors to Zambia, the four main areas of attraction are the Luangwa Valley, Kafue National Park, the Lower Zambezi Valley and Livingstone. All these parks are worth visiting for a week (less than three nights in a park is really too short), and there's often a slight saving if you spend at least a week exclusively with one operator. For most people, a visit to Livingstone takes two to three nights.

When designing a trip, bear in mind that:

- Keen walkers would usually include the Luangwa, and some of the smaller 'walking bushcamps' in their trip.
- Visit the Lower Zambezi or the Kafue for water-based activities.
- If you want to visit North Luangwa, then first spend a few days in the South Park, then perhaps 3–5 nights in North Luangwa.
- Shiwa Ng'andu works really well for 3–4 nights, ideally as part of a trip that passes through South Luangwa (the closest place for flights is Mfuwe).
- Kasanka, Bangweulu and Shiwa Ng'andu work well together, usually in that sequence.

NOTES FOR TRAVELLERS WITH LIMITED MOBILITY

Although Zambia's tourism infrastructure is developing fast, proper facilities for people with limited mobility are still rare. But don't let this put you off; depending on your ability and sense of adventure, most obstacles are surmountable and Africans are used to finding solutions for practical problems: if you need help, you will receive it.

The UK's **gov.uk** website (w gov.uk/government/publications/disabled-travellers/disability-and-travel-abroad) has a downloadable guide giving general advice and practical information for travellers with a disability (and their companions) preparing for overseas travel. The **Society for Accessible Travel and Hospitality** (w sath.org) also provides some general information about travelling with medical conditions or disabilities, although no specific details on safari travel. The best advice and most relaxing travel will come from open discussions with a knowledgeable tour operator who can ensure safari camps and transfer operators are fully aware of your requirements in advance.

PLANNING AND BOOKING Most mainstream operators listed in this guide (page 92) will listen to your needs and try to create an itinerary suitable for you. In Zambia, there are two operators that specialise in catering to travellers with a disability (see opposite). For the more independent traveller, it is possible to limit potential surprises by contacting local operators and establishments by email in advance.

ACCOMMODATION Some of Zambia's international-standard hotels have adapted rooms, including the Radisson Blu and the Southern Sun Ridgeway in Lusaka, and Livingstone's Avani Victoria Falls Resort and Royal Livingstone. We have yet to hear of completely accessible accommodation in any of Zambia's national parks, but many lodges are making efforts to improve access for those with limited mobility, including the provision of level paths, and ramps rather than steps. At Chisa Busanga (page 425), there is a lift in one of the incredible accommodation 'nests'.

TRANSPORT

Air travel Both Lusaka and Livingstone international airports have assistance, wheelchairs and aisle chairs for those who need help entering or leaving the aircraft. Livingstone also has accessible toilets and this feature is part of the plan for Lusaka's airport, too.

Buses and trains There is no effective legislation in Zambia to facilitate journeys by public transport for travellers with limited mobility; therefore, if you cannot walk at all then both of these options are going to be difficult. You will need to ask for

Some combinations that work well are:

Short trips

- 7 nights South Luangwa, or Lower Zambezi, or Kafue
- 2–3 nights Livingstone plus 5–6 nights Kafue, or vice versa

Slightly longer trips

- 5–6 nights South Luangwa plus 4 nights North Luangwa
- 5–6 nights South Luangwa plus 3–4 nights Shiwa Ng'andu

help from fellow passengers to lift you to your seat, it will often be crowded and it is unlikely that there will be an accessible toilet.

By car Distances are great and roads are often bumpy, so if you are prone to skin damage you need to take extra care. Place your own pressure-relieving cushion on top of (or instead of) the original car seat and if necessary, pad around knees and elbows. If you're not sticking to the main roads, you will need to use a 4x4 vehicle, which will be higher than a normal car making transfers more difficult. Drivers/guides are normally happy to help, but are not trained in this skill, so you must thoroughly explain your needs and always stay in control of the situation. In Livingstone, Hemingways (page 190) can provide wheelchair-accessible transfers.

HEALTH AND INSURANCE Doctors will know about 'everyday' illnesses, but you must understand and be able to explain your own particular medical requirements. Zambian hospitals and pharmacies are often basic, so it is wise to take as much essential medication and equipment as possible with you, and it is advisable to pack this in your hand luggage during flights in case your main luggage gets lost. Zambia can be hot; if this is a problem for you then try to book accommodation with fans or air conditioning. A useful cooling aid is a plant-spray bottle.

Most insurance companies will insure travellers with a disability, but it is essential that they are made aware of your disability. In the UK, both Age UK (☎ 0800 389 4852; w ageuk.org.uk) and Free Spirit (☎ 02392 419 080; w free-spirit.com) offer travel insurance for people with pre-existing medical conditions.

SECURITY For anyone following the usual safety precautions (page 134), the chances of robbery are greatly reduced. In fact, as someone with a disability I often feel more 'noticed' when in public places, and therefore a less attractive target for thieves. But the opposite may also apply, so do stay aware of where your bags are and who is around you, especially during car transfers and similar activities.

SPECIALIST OPERATORS

Endeavour Safaris 23 Lark Cres, Table View, 7441 Cape Town, South Africa; ☎ +27 (0)21 556 6114; m +27 (0)73 206 7733; e info@endeavour-safaris.com; w endeavour-safaris.com. Specialists in Botswana, South Africa & Namibia who also cover Livingstone.

Hemingways ☎ +260 0213 323097; m +260 977 866492/870232; e info@hemingwayszambia.com; w hemingwayszambia.com. Livingstone-based operator offering transfers using wheelchair-accessible vehicle. See page 190.

- 5–6 nights Kafue plus 4 nights Lower Zambezi
- 5–6 nights Kafue or Lower Zambezi or South Luangwa, plus 2–3 nights Livingstone

Two weeks If you've got about two weeks, the obvious option is to devote a week each to two of the main three parks. For something a bit more offbeat, consider:

- 3 nights Kasanka, 3 nights Bangweulu (especially green season), 4 nights Shiwa Ng'andu, 4 nights South Luangwa

TAKING CHILDREN ON SAFARI

Ten years ago, taking children on safari in Zambia might have been considered unusual, but things are changing, and the country's lodges and camps haven't been slow to pick up on the trend.

The idea of taking a child on safari might at first seem obvious. You'll be out in a wilderness environment, with plenty of animals to watch, and seemingly non-stop entertainment. But that, of course, is part of the problem. The 'entertainment' cannot be guaranteed, so during a typical three-hour game drive, there's often time when things that might fascinate you – colourful birds, the construction of a termite mound, last night's hyena tracks, even a(nother) herd of puku – will be of little interest to a child. And when big game is spotted, instead of being able to leap up and down with excitement, your child is expected to be absolutely quiet and still. Then there's the often unspoken concern of a sensitive child witnessing a kill.

Add to this the rather exclusive make-up of many safari camps, the safety issues within camp (wildlife, high walkways, rivers and unguarded pools being just a few), and the lack of opportunity for letting off steam, and the considerations mount up.

So how can it work? Although many lodges still maintain a very adult atmosphere, designating a high minimum age for children, several offer some form of 'family' accommodation. Sometimes that's simply a room with an extra bed or two, rather than anything particularly child friendly; at others, it's a suite of rooms, either sharing a bathroom or with each of them en suite, and occasionally with their own lounge area. More specifically, a handful of places have built entirely separate houses that are exceptionally well suited to families – including Chongwe River House and Kasaka's Hippo Pod in the Lower Zambezi, Robin's House and Luangwa Safari House in the South Luangwa, and Tangala House in Livingstone

4x4 trips If you're an experienced Africa hand, driving in your own self-contained vehicle in the dry season, then the choices are much wider. All such trips are long; they're effectively mini-expeditions. The country is your oyster, but there are two obvious routes, and a third that's rather more offbeat, each taking at least three weeks:

Western circuit Livingstone – Upper Zambezi – Mongu – Liuwa Plain – Mongu – Lukulu – Kafue (from northern tip right through to southern tip) – Livingstone

Eastern circuit Lusaka – Kasanka – Lake Waka Waka – Bangweulu – Mutinondo Wilderness – Shiwa Ng'andu – transit through North Luangwa – Luambe – South Luangwa – Lusaka

Northern circuit This suggestion, perhaps for those who have already visited some of the country's highlights, could take you north, visiting some of the lesser-known waterfalls and the Lake Tanganyika area: Lusaka – Kasanka – Bangweulu – Luapula River – Nsumbu National Park – Kasama – Shiwa Ng'andu – Mutinondo Wilderness – Lusaka.

NATIONAL PARKS

Head office Since 2015, almost all Zambia's national parks have fallen under the control of the government-run Department of National Parks and Wildlife (DNPW;

– with space to run around, and your own chef so that you can eat at times that suit your family rather than other guests. Mealtimes in many lodges can be a trial for children, though some will prepare meals early, so that you can dine with the other guests while a member of staff (not a qualified childminder) babysits for you.

One further option would be to base yourself in a family-friendly hotel in Livingstone, where you'll be rewarded with the Victoria Falls, as well as wildlife in the Mosi-oa-Tunya National Park and boat trips on the Zambezi River, without feeling cooped up the rest of the time.

When lodges do accept families, many insist that those with children under, say, eight years old reserve a private vehicle and guide. If this at first seems draconian, consider too that this is for the benefit of the children, as well as for other guests. With your own guide, you select where you stop and spend time, and if your children want to ask questions, that's fine.

In accordance with national parks' regulations, children under the age of 12 cannot go on canoe safaris or bush walks, for very good safety reasons. Some camps have imposed their own, higher, age limits, such as 14 at Musekese in the Kafue, and 16 at Lion Camp in the South Luangwa. However, all camps and guides will assess the maturity of individual children before embarking on these activities. Some camps, among them Kafunta River Lodge in the South Luangwa, and Kasaka River Lodge in the Lower Zambezi, will offer a member of staff to look after your children while you do these activities, perhaps taking them fishing, or on a short nature walk around the camp grounds.

Whatever your decision, be aware that if you opt for a conventional safari trip, you will need to take plenty to occupy your children when in camp. Bored children are likely to be the bane of everyone's life on safari, including yours.

Private Bag 1, Chilanga; ☎ 0211 278482; e info.dnpw@mota.gov.zm) – formerly the Zambia Wildlife Authority. They set the rules and administer the parks. If you want to do anything other than simple photographic safaris, such as filming or some form of research, you first approach the staff at Chilanga or, failing that, contact the Zambia Tourism Board (page 90).

Park entry fees Most organised trips include park entry fees in their costs, but if you are travelling on your own then you must pay these directly, either at one of the DNPW offices or at the park gates – or, very occasionally, at individual lodges. Park offices are normally open 06.00 to 18.00. When paying your fees, you will need to state the gate from which you will be leaving the park. This is ostensibly for security reasons – though don't bank on anyone coming to find you if you come unstuck.

Park fees are officially payable per day (06.00–18.00), rather than per 24 hours, but the DNPW head office acknowledges that those staying overnight have until 08.00 the following morning to leave the park without paying that day's park fees. However, if you are staying overnight and leaving any later than that, then you will have to pay for two days, as well as the overnight levy. There is a scale of entry fees, with additional charges for taking a vehicle into the parks, and for staying overnight. Fees vary, not just between parks, but according to the visitor, with international visitors paying significantly higher rates than those from southern Africa (SADC), who in turn pay more than Zambian citizens. In 2023, national park fees for international visitors were as follows, per person, per day:

South Luangwa	US$25 (self-drive vehicle US$30/day)
Lower Zambezi	US$25 (self-drive vehicle US$30/day)
North Luangwa	US$20 (self-drive vehicle US$25/day)
Kafue	US$20 (self-drive vehicle US$15/day)
Liuwa Plain	US$40 (self-drive vehicle US$15/day)
Luambe	US$15
Mosi-oa-Tunya	US$10 (self-drive US$15)
Blue Lagoon, Kasanka, Lochinvar, Nsumbu, Lavushi Manda	US$10
Other parks	US$5

In addition to park fees, self-drivers will need to pay a nominal fee for their **vehicle** (up to 3 tonnes/50hp). This varies between US$15 and US$30 per day for internationally registered vehicles, or K25.50 a day (around $1.50) for a Zambian-registered vehicle (which includes local hire cars). In most parks, an additional bed levy of around US$20–50 is charged per person per night, a fee that is almost always included in the rates at individual lodges. For campers, however, there is a camping levy of US$5 that is payable at the park gate, on top of any campsite rates.

All park fees are payable in cash – US dollars or kwacha – and you are strongly advised to have the correct money as change can be a problem. Do check the documentation carefully, and retain all receipts as these may be required both at lodges and at your exit gate.

Guides For more adventurous trips to remote parks, hire a game scout from the nearest camp to act as your guide – or, better, arrange this in advance through DNPW. For around US$35 per day, this can be an inexpensive way to get a local guide who may be able to add a whole new dimension to your trip. It can also save wasted driving time, and probably personal anguish over navigational puzzles. Nowadays, guides normally have their own tents and food.

WECSZ The Wildlife and Environmental Conservation Society of Zambia (4435 Kumoyo Rd, off Los Angeles Bd, Lusaka; ☎ 0211 251630; e wecsz@coppernet.zm; w conservationzambia.org; ⏱ 08.00–17.00 Mon–Fri; international membership K275/year) supports environmental education and awareness in Zambia. It sponsors various conservation activities, organises monthly talks for Lusaka members, and runs innovative children's clubs, like the Chongololo and Chipembele conservation clubs, and the related Chongololo Club of the Air (broadcast on Radio 2 each Sunday). It also publishes a number of good, inexpensive field guides specific to Zambia (page 512).

The WECSZ owns three very simple camps in the national parks: Kafwala and Chibila camps in Kafue, and the Wildlife Camp at Mfuwe, as well as Chembe Bird Sanctuary in the Copperbelt. They are managed by others, but some of the revenue still comes back to the society. All are for members only, and may be booked either in writing or in person at the Lusaka office. The society's books can also be bought in Lusaka or at one of the bookshops in town.

RED TAPE

VISAS AND ENTRY REQUIREMENTS In 2022, Zambia changed its visa requirements, dropping the need for an entry visa for many overseas nationals, including travellers from the UK, US, much of Europe, Australia and New Zealand. A full list of nationalities who benefit from this change is published on the Zambian immigration website (w zambiaimmigration.gov.zm/nationals-who-dont-require-visa) and it's always worth double-checking before travelling.

For travellers who require a visa, this can be obtained on arrival at border posts on payment of the correct fee in US dollars cash, online from w evisa.zambiaimmigration.gov.zm, or overseas from your local Zambian diplomatic mission. You must have at least six months left on your passport, and at least three blank pages. You may also be asked to show an onward ticket, or at least demonstrate that you can support yourself as you pass through the country (credit cards are invaluable), but this is unusual.

Visa extensions Visas can be extended by personal application to the Immigration Office in Lusaka (Kent Bldg, Haile Selassie Rd; ☎ 0211 251725/252669; m 0955 659493, 0962 172550, 0971 718499; e zambiavisa@zambiaimmigration.gov.zm; w zambiaimmigration.gov.zm). You'll need two completed application forms (each with a passport photo), a valid passport and proof of sufficient funds to cover your stay. If it's a business application then you'll also need an explanatory letter with some good reasons. Your application will take at least three working days to process.

ZAMBIA'S DIPLOMATIC MISSIONS ABROAD A complete list of Zambia's embassies and high commissions abroad can be found at w zambiaimmigration.gov.zm/zambia-missions-abroad. For foreign embassies in Zambia, see page 175.

GETTING THERE

BY AIR However you get to the subcontinent, if you don't fly directly to Lusaka then do book your flight to Africa and any scheduled internal links between countries (eg: Nairobi–Lusaka or Johannesburg–Lusaka flights) at the same time. Booking the whole trip together is almost certain to save you money. Sometimes the airline taking you to Africa will have cheap regional flights within Africa; for example Johannesburg–Lusaka with South African Airways is usually much cheaper if booked with an SAA flight from London to Johannesburg, than it is if booked alone. At other times the tour operator you book through will have special deals if you book all the flights with them. And most importantly, if you book all your flights together then you'll be sure to get connecting ones, so you have the best schedule possible.

A US$25 **departure tax** is levied on all international flights. While this is almost always prepaid on your ticket nowadays, it might be wise to ensure that you have sufficient US dollars in cash as a precaution; credit cards are not accepted.

From Europe There are currently no direct flights from western Europe to Zambia. Passengers must transit through one of the major African hubs, usually Nairobi, Addis Ababa or Johannesburg, or via Dubai in the Middle East.

Finding cheap tickets on any of these is usually difficult (if not impossible). Expect to pay about £700–1,200/US$900–1,500 for a return flight. Tour operators (page 92) can sometimes have access to slightly cheaper seats, especially if you're booking very early (around 11 months before departure). However, you will only be able to buy these as part of a complete holiday package. Last-minute bargains are increasingly rare and invariably only available in the low season.

From the Middle East **Emirates** (w emirates.com) have daily flights to and from Dubai from a wide variety of destinations in Europe, North America, India and Asia, with connections from Dubai to Zambia.

From within Africa The only Zambian airline operating within the region is **Proflight** (w proflight-zambia.com), which has three direct flights per day between Lusaka and Johannesburg, three direct flights per week between Ndola and Johannesburg and, as at the time of writing, is about to launch a twice-weekly flight to Cape Town (Tuesdays and Saturdays).

Several operators have regular flights linking regional cities with both Lusaka and other Zambian towns. From Johannesburg (JNB), **South African Airways** (SAA; w flysaa.com) flies into Lusaka (LUN), and **Airlink** (w flyairlink.com) flies direct to Lusaka (LUN), Livingstone (LVI) and Ndola (NLA).

Among other airlines servicing Lusaka directly, **Kenya Airways** (w kenya-airways.com) has daily flights from Nairobi (NBO). **Ethiopian Airlines** (w ethiopianairlines.com) has daily flights to Addis Ababa (ADD). Both have excellent feeder connections from Europe and the US, and it's worth noting that Ethiopia is one of the few African countries from which the US government allows direct flights to and from the USA.

From North America If you are coming from the US, you will probably need to stop in Addis Ababa, Nairobi, Johannesburg or Dubai to make connections to Zambia. There are no direct flights. Booking everything in the US may not save you money; investigate the flight prices in comparison with those available in London. Increasingly visitors from America are discovering that UK operators offer better-value safaris than their competitors in America. So consider buying a cheap ticket across the Atlantic, and then organising your Zambian trip through a reliable UK operator.

OVERLAND Most overland border posts open from about 06.00 to 18.00, although this is less rigidly adhered to at the smaller, more remote posts. The paperwork required can be lengthy and time consuming, so allow plenty of time – and in some cases, such as at Kazungula on the border with Botswana, several hours.

To/from South Africa or Namibia The South African Intercape Mainliner (w intercape.co.za) has a regular bus between Windhoek and Livingstone/Victoria Falls.

CR Holdings (t 0211 288425; m 0978 960517, 621148; e crholdingslimited@gmail.com) operates a service between Lusaka and Johannesburg every Monday, Wednesday and Friday.

For self-drivers, there is a high-level bridge across the Zambezi at Sesheke (page 460).

To/from Zimbabwe Zambia's greatest flow of visitors comes from Zimbabwe, over the Livingstone–Victoria Falls border. Many visitors come for just a day trip and locals come to shop, so this is usually a very relaxed and swift border crossing. The crossings over the Kariba Dam and at Chirundu are also straightforward, and the latter is especially good for hitchhiking on long-distance lorries, which ply the route from Harare to Lusaka.

To/from Botswana Despite their territories only meeting at a point, Botswana does have a border crossing with Zambia, across a new super-bridge (923m long) at Kazungula, which opened in 2022 (page 460). This elegant US$260 million bridge is an efficient one-stop border post, replacing the once-chaotic pontoon ferry crossing.

To/from Angola Parts of northern Angola are still not regarded as safe to visit, so do check with the Foreign and Commonwealth Office (w fco.gov.uk) if you're planning to use this route. The easiest border post with Angola is near Chavuma, northwest of Zambezi town. Elsewhere in western Zambia there is a danger of accidentally wandering into Angola, as the border has few markings.

To/from Democratic Republic of Congo There are numerous crossings between Zambia and the DRC, especially around the Copperbelt. Otherwise there is a good track leading into DRC reached via Mwinilunga and Ikelenge. However, the DRC remains an unstable and potentially dangerous place to visit; you should check on the latest security situations before crossing the border, and be careful not to stray across by accident if you're in the Copperbelt region or heading east near Mkushi.

To/from Tanzania Many visitors from Tanzania enter Zambia by ferryboat across Lake Tanganyika into Mpulungu. The main alternative is the land border, either by road crossing or by Tanzania Zambia Railway Authority (TAZARA) train, crossing east of Tunduma. See page 162 for more details of TAZARA's important rail link between Zambia and Dar es Salaam. There should also be good hitchhiking opportunities as there are plenty of long-distance lorries plying the route, as well as Zambian drivers picking up Japanese cars in Dar es Salaam.

To/from Malawi The main crossing between Zambia and Malawi is east of Chipata. This would also be the swiftest way to reach the Nyika Plateau, as the roads in Malawi are better than those to Nyika in Zambia.

To/from Mozambique There is a land crossing between Zambia and Mozambique south of Katete, which itself is southwest of Chipata, though this is not often used. A more common route would be via Malawi or Zimbabwe.

WHAT TO TAKE

This depends on how you intend to travel and exactly where you are going. If you are flying in for a short safari holiday then you need not pack too ruthlessly – provided that you stay within your weight allowance. However, note that smaller, privately chartered planes may specify a maximum weight of 10–12kg for hold luggage, which must be packed in a soft, squashable bag. Once you see the stowage spaces in a small charter plane, you'll understand the importance of not bringing along large or solid suitcases.

If you are backpacking then weight becomes much more important, and minimising it becomes an art form. Each extra item must be questioned: is its benefit worth its weight?

If you have your own vehicle then neither weight nor bulk will be as vital, and you will have a lot more freedom to bring what you like. Here are some general guidelines.

CLOTHING For most days all you will want is light, loose-fitting cotton clothing. Pure cotton, or at least a cotton-rich mix, is cooler and more absorbent than synthetic materials, making it more comfortable in the heat. A squashable hat and a robust pair of sunglasses with a high UV-absorption are essential.

No matter what your plans, you'll need something warmer, such as a thick fleece, for evenings during the cooler winter months – roughly from April until August. And in the rainy season, don't forget an umbrella if you want to avoid getting drenched; a waterproof jacket, while occasionally useful, is rarely up to the task.

Zambia's dress code is generally conservative. For men, shorts (not too short) are fine in the bush, but long trousers are more socially acceptable in towns and villages. (You will rarely see a respectable black Zambian man wearing shorts outside a safari camp.) For women, a knee-length skirt, culottes or loose trousers are ideal. A woman wearing revealing clothing in town implies that she is a woman of ill repute, while untidy clothing suggests a poor person, of low social standing.

These rules are redundant at safari camps, where dress is casual, and designed to keep you cool and protect skin from the sun. Green, khaki and dust-brown cotton is *de rigueur* at the more serious camps (especially those offering walking trips) and among visitors out to demonstrate how well they know the ropes. The same cognoscenti are usually to be found wearing old and well-worn items, rather than anything straight out of the box; charity shops in the UK can be a great source of safari wear! At the less serious camps you'll see a smattering of brighter-coloured clothes among many dull bush colours, the former usually worn by first-time visitors who are less familiar with the bush. On a practical note, women may want to consider a sports bra for safaris in bumpy game-drive vehicles.

Note that washing is done daily at virtually all safari camps, so few changes of clothes are necessary.

FOOTWEAR If you plan to do much walking, either on safari or with a backpack, then lightweight walking boots (with ankle support if possible) are essential. This is mainly because the bush is not always smooth and even, and anything that minimises the chance of a twisted ankle is worthwhile. Secondly, for the nervous, it will reduce still further the minute chance of being bitten by a snake, or other creepy-crawly, while walking.

Because of the heat, take the lightest pair of boots you can find – preferably canvas, or a breathable material such as Gore-Tex. Leather boots are too hot in October, but thin single-skin leather is bearable for walking in July and August. Never bring a new pair, or boots that aren't completely worn in. Always pack several pairs of thin socks – two thin pairs of socks are more comfortable than one thick pair, and will help to prevent blisters.

CAMPING EQUIPMENT If you are on an organised safari, then even a simple bushcamp will mean walk-in chalets with linen, mosquito nets and probably an en-suite shower and toilet. However, if you're planning any camping, then note that little equipment is available outside of Lusaka; see page 146 for ideas of what to take.

ELECTRICAL ITEMS The local voltage is 220V, delivered at 50Hz. Sockets fit plugs with three square pins, like the current design in the UK. Even the most remote safari camp nowadays can usually arrange for you to charge a camera battery, but if this is important, do make sure to check facilities in advance.

OTHER USEFUL ITEMS Obviously no list is comprehensive; only travelling will teach you what you need, and what you can do without. Here are a few of my own favourites and essentials, just to jog your memory.

For visitors embarking on an organised safari, camps will have most things but useful items include:

- Sunblock and lipsalve – for vital protection from the sun
- Binoculars – totally essential for game viewing
- A small pocket torch (page 147)

- 'Leatherman' tool – never go into the bush without one, but always pack it in your check-in bag; never in your hand luggage
- A small water bottle, especially on flights (page 147)
- Electrical insulating tape – remarkably useful for general repairs
- Camera – long lenses are vital for good shots of animals
- Basic sewing kit – with at least some really strong thread for repairs
- Cheap waterproof watch (leave expensive ones, and jewellery, at home)
- Couple of paperback novels
- Large plastic 'bin-liner' (garbage) bags, for protecting luggage from dust
- Simple medical kit (page 128) and insect repellent

And for those driving or backpacking, useful extras are:

- Concentrated, biodegradable washing powder
- Long-life candles (Zambian candles are often soft, and burn quickly)
- Nylon 'paracord' – bring at least 20m for emergencies and washing lines
- Hand-held GPS navigation system, for expeditions to remote areas
- Good compass and a whistle
- More comprehensive medical kit

WHAT NOT TO TAKE There are several things worth leaving behind. In particular, avoid anything which looks military; wearing camouflage patterns anywhere in Africa is asking for trouble. You are very likely to be stopped by the genuine military, or at least the police, who may assume that you are a member of some militia – and question exactly what you are doing in Zambia. Few will believe that this is a fashion statement elsewhere in the world.

Even if you're going on the most expensive of safaris, leave any jewellery that you don't usually wear all day, every day, at home. It'll take a load off your mind not to have to worry about its security.

MAPS AND NAVIGATION

MAPS Many overland travellers with a GPS (page 104) would be lost – sometimes quite literally – without **Tracks4Africa** (w tracks4africa.co.za), a digital mapping software package that covers the whole continent. The maps and information are clear, reliable and up to date, and we'd highly recommend purchasing the GPS map if you plan on any self-driving in the country. Note: Do not mistake their phone app for the GPS map though – the app is a static guide only, not a navigational tool. With accurate, annotated maps, the Tracks4Africa GPS system can prove invaluable in unknown bush territory or during night-time travel. They do also publish a 1:1,000,000 waterproof traditional map, titled *Zambia Travellers Map*, with insets on Lusaka, Kafue, South Luangwa and Liuwa Plain. More prescriptively, **Open Africa** (w openafrica.org) is a non-profit organisation linking a network of tourism routes across the continent, including several in Zambia, with the aim of encouraging visitors to explore further afield and to benefit local communities.

For general purposes, there are several reasonable road maps of Zambia, of which the best is currently the 1:1,500,000 sheet published in Germany by Ilona HupeVerlag, and available at bookshops in Lusaka. In addition to good road and topographical detail, it features fuel stations, campsites and GPS co-ordinates – though the last (and the distances) aren't always entirely reliable. There are also inset overview maps of Lusaka and Livingstone, and the major national parks.

Other commercially produced maps, available both in Zambia and overseas, include those published by International Travel Maps, Globetrotter (New Holland), both at 1:1,500,000, and Macmillan (1:2,200,000). The **International Travel Map** shows contours and the parks, with surrounding text boxes covering topics from wildlife to Zambia's history and geography. Road detail is good, with many of the pontoons (flat, open-sided ferryboats) carefully marked, though coverage of the main points of tourist interest is less detailed. The illustrated **Globetrotter** map incorporates several regional and national park maps at a larger scale, as well as town plans of Livingstone and Lusaka, and climate charts. The smaller-scale **Macmillan** map is less detailed, but better at marking the points of interest for visitors, and on the reverse are many excellent 'inset' maps of the main parks, plus plans of Lusaka and Livingstone.

For **more detail**, Zambia has an excellent range of 'Ordnance Survey'-type maps available cheaply in Lusaka, from the Ministry of Lands in Mulungushi House (page 163). A wide range of maps is kept here, including the useful 1:250,000 series, a number of town plans, some 'tourist' maps of the parks – including an excellent 1989 map of South Luangwa's landscape and vegetation – and many more detailed maps of selected areas. Some are always out of print, and many are out of date – but you can usually find at least some sort of map to cover most areas. If you are planning to drive yourself around, then buy the maps for your trip at the start.

Navigation by any of these maps becomes more difficult as your location becomes more remote, when expecting any of them to be entirely accurate is unrealistic. Thus if you're heading into the wilds, get what maps you can and compare them with reality as you go.

GPS SYSTEMS If you are heading into one of the more remote parks in your own vehicle, then invest in a GPS (global positioning system). These can fix your latitude, longitude and elevation to within about 10m, using a network of satellites that constantly pass in the skies overhead. They will work anywhere on the globe.

What to buy As is usual with high-tech equipment, prices are continually falling and the number and efficiency of features are expanding.

Whatever make you buy, you don't need a top-of-the-range machine, but you do need something sturdy and reliable. Your GPS should enable you to store 'waypoints' and build a simple electronic picture of an area, as well as working out basic latitude, longitude and elevation. So, for example, you can store the position of your campsite and the nearest road, making it easier to be reasonably sure of navigating back without simply retracing your steps. This can be invaluable in remote areas with lots of bush and no signposts, but it comes with a warning: a GPS takes no account of bends in the road, or indeed of natural hazards, so both directional arrows and distances may appear misleading in the bush.

Although a GPS may help you to recognise your minor errors before they are amplified into major problems, note that it is no substitute for good map work and navigation. Try not to rely on technology entirely, or you will be unable to cope if it fails, and always have a back-up plan in case it stops working. Note, too, that all these units use lots of battery power, so bring spares with you and/or a cigarette-lighter adaptor.

GPS positions in this book You'll note that we've given almost all of the GPS locations in this book a six-letter name. These were simply the names that were assigned to them in our system, as we recorded them, and we've used them throughout for ease of reference. All GPS co-ordinates have been expressed as degrees, minutes, and decimal fractions of a minute.

We hope that their inclusion may enable more adventurous and experienced readers to venture safely out to Zambia's lesser-known corners, although my points don't remove the need to take up-to-date local advice on safety and conditions.

Important note: For all the GPS co-ordinates in this book, note that the datum used is WGS 84; you must set your receiver accordingly before copying in any of these co-ordinates. Many maps in Zambia used the ARC 1950 datum – so you should expect a slight discrepancy between points estimated from such maps, and your GPS unit.

PHOTOGRAPHY AND OPTICS

Don't expect to find any reasonably priced or reasonably available optical equipment in Zambia – so bring everything that you will need with you.

Pictures taken around dawn and dusk will have the richest, deepest colours, while those taken in the middle of the day, when the sun is high, will seem pale and washed-out by comparison. Beware of the very deep shadows and high contrast that are typical of tropical countries – cameras just cannot capture the range of colours and shades that our eyes can. If you want to take pictures in full daylight, and capture details in the shadows, then you will need a good camera, and to spend some time learning how to use it fully. By restricting your photography to mornings, evenings and simple shots you will get better pictures and encounter fewer problems.

The bush is very dusty, so bring plenty of lens-cleaning cloths, and a blow-brush. Take great care not to get dust into the back of any camera, as a single grain on the back-plate can be enough to make a long scratch which ruins every frame taken.

CAMERA INSURANCE Most travel insurance policies are poor at covering valuables, including cameras. If you are taking valuable camera equipment abroad, then include it in your house insurance policy, or cover it separately with a specialist.

BINOCULARS For a safari holiday, especially if you are doing much walking, a good pair of binoculars is essential. They will bring you far more enjoyment than a camera, as they make the difference between merely seeing an animal or bird at a distance, and being able to observe its markings, movements and moods closely. Do bring one pair per person; one between two is just not enough.

There are two styles: the small 'pocket' binoculars, perhaps 10–12cm long, which account for most modern sales, and the larger, heavier styles, double or triple that size, which have been manufactured for years. Both styles vary widely in cost and quality. If you are buying a pair, then consider getting the larger style. The smaller ones are fine for spotting animals, but are difficult to hold steady, and very tiring to use for extensive periods. You will only realise this when you are out on safari, by which time it is too late.

Around 8 x 30 is an ideal size for field observations, as most people need some form of rest, or tripod, to hold the larger 10 x 50 models steady. Get the best-quality ones you can for your money. If you use binoculars regularly, as against for just one holiday, then try to stretch your budget above the £500/US$900 barrier. Once you do this, makes like Swarovski, Zeiss and Leica, which are considerably better than cheaper models, come within reach – and will hugely enhance your experience of viewing wildlife.

MONEY AND BUDGETING

CURRENCY Zambia's unit of currency is the kwacha (K), which is divided into 100 ngwee. Most currency comes in the form of notes, and there are three coins, in denominations of one kwacha, 50 ngwee and 10 ngwee.

EXCHANGE RATES Payments made in Zambia, except to tourism providers, will most likely be made in kwacha. Thus prices in this guide are generally given in kwacha, with those quoted in US dollars usually for lodges and operators whose clientele comes primarily from overseas and pays in one of the international currencies.

Where foreign currency rates are used in this guidebook, we have used the rates at the time of writing in early 2023, when the exchange rates against the kwacha were:

£1 = KMZ23.20	€1 = KMZ20.43
US$1 = KMZ18.73	ZAR1 = KMZ1.10

BUDGETING Zambia is not a cheap country to visit, especially if you want to see some of the national parks. This isn't because of high park fees: on the contrary, with all the parks charging US$5–40/£4–32 per person per day, it's reasonable by African standards. Rather, costs are high because most safari camps are small and seasonal, and their supply logistics are difficult and costly. However, you do generally get what you pay for: camps in remote locations and pristine environments tend to set very high standards.

To make up a trip using such camps, which are the easiest and most practical way for visitors to Zambia, budget for an all-inclusive cost of about US$400–1,500/£320–1,200 per person per day when staying in a camp. Internal flights cost varying amounts, but US$250/£200 per leg would be a good approximation.

At the other end of the spectrum, if you travel through Zambia on local buses, camping and staying in the occasional local (sometimes seedy) resthouse, then Zambia is not expensive. A budget of US$40–70/£32–56 per day for food, accommodation and transport would suffice. However, most backpackers who undertake such trips are simply 'in transit' between Malawi and Zimbabwe. They see little of Zambia's wildlife or its national parks, missing out on even its cheaper attractions.

If you have your own rugged 4x4 with equipment *and* the experience to use it, then you will be able to camp and cook for yourself, which can cut costs for four people down to around US$50-70/£40–56 per person per day including camping and park fees, but excluding fuel (which is expensive in Zambia). However, to hire a 4x4 vehicle would cost upwards of another US$195–235/£155–188 per day, plus fuel.

The cost of food depends heavily on where you buy it, as well as what you buy. If you can shop in Lusaka or one of the bigger towns for your camping supplies then you will save money and have a wider choice than elsewhere. Imported foods are inevitably more expensive than locally produced items. If you are sensible, then US$12–30/£10–24 per day would provide the supplies for a good, varied diet, including the odd treat. In any event, it will be cheaper than eating out.

In Lusaka and the main cities the bigger hotels are about US$200–350/£160–280 for a double room, while a good guesthouse will cost around US$65–120/£52–95. Camping at organised sites on the outskirts of the cities is, again, a good bet if you have the equipment and transport. It will cost from around US$10–12/£8–10 per person per night.

Restaurant meals in the towns are still relatively inexpensive, although costs have risen in recent years as the quality and variety of cuisine has improved: US$20–50/£16–40 for a good evening meal, including a beer or glass of wine. Imported beers are more expensive than local beer (which is perfectly adequate), and South African wines are more costly again.

European wines and spirits, as you might expect, fetch a high price: a decent bottle of champagne or Scotch whisky will be well over US$100, and so make excellent gifts if you are visiting someone here! But there's an excellent range of South African wines for around US$10 per bottle, and African beers are readily available.

Finally, do be aware that prices in Zambia – as anywhere else – can and do rise, as can VAT (which is currently 16%). Rates quoted in this guide were correct at the time of research in 2023, but many will change during the life of the guide, so please do be sensitive to any increases.

HOW TO TAKE YOUR MONEY Although both US dollars and UK pounds sterling are easily changed at a bank, in practice US dollars are far more useful to the visitor. You will normally need to have US dollars in cash to pay for visas at the border, and for any tax due at the airport, and they're usually required for national parks' fees, too. Occasionally you may be able to pay for the larger hotels and other services in US dollars (small-denomination notes) too, although this becomes less common away from the bigger towns, so don't rely on it.

If you're going to more offbeat locations, kwacha are essential – although in case of need, some places will accept cash in low denominations of US dollars. If you're driving yourself, however, it is crucial that you allow sufficient cash (in kwacha) to pay for fuel; with only one or two notable exceptions in Lusaka, credit cards will not be accepted, and neither will US dollars.

In addition to kwacha, we travel with mostly US$1, US$5, US$10 and US$20 bills (and a few £10 or £20 notes). Because of the risk of forgeries, people are sometimes suspicious of larger-denomination notes; conversely, some places offer a lower exchange rate for smaller-denomination notes. US$100 and even US$50 bills are often rejected in shops and even some banks.

In the Western Province near the Namibian border, South African rand may occasionally be accepted; elsewhere they're virtually useless.

Most of the larger hotels and shops, and some safari camps, accept the major **credit and debit cards** (Visa and MasterCard), but bear in mind that a 3–5% commission may be levied, so be sure to enquire, prior to using your card, about any charges. Don't expect to be able to pay park fees, or for fuel, by card. It is advisable to take at least two cards, ideally a Visa and a MasterCard, though note that many banks – with the notable exception of Stanbic – will accept Visa but not MasterCard. Do remember to notify your bank of your travel plans in advance of departure, in case of any attempted fraud (and thus a block on your account) while you're travelling.

CHANGING MONEY AND BANKING Almost all banks will exchange US dollars, but to change foreign currency, receive bank drafts, or do any other relatively complex financial transactions, then banks in the larger cities (ideally Lusaka) are your best option. Typically, banking hours are around 08.30–15.30, Monday to Friday, although in smaller towns they may close earlier, or – crucially – be open only on certain days. A few of the bigger banks also open around 09.00–11.00 on Saturdays.

ATMs are widely available in the major towns, but are not the norm elsewhere. Even where they do exist, they are not entirely reliable, so carry plenty of cash as a backup. At a number of banks, you can use European debit cards bearing the Maestro or Visa logo to withdraw cash, up to around K2,000 per day.

If you are changing money at one of the main banks, in Lusaka or Livingstone, there is minimal difference in the rates between travellers' cheques and pounds sterling or US dollars in cash. At a bureau de change, however, you'll usually get better rates for cash.

TIPPING Tipping is a difficult and contentious topic – worth thinking about carefully. Read page 154, and realise that thoughtlessly tipping too much is just as bad as tipping too little.

Faced with rising concern over wages, the Zambian government has introduced a compulsory 10% service charge to be added to all bills in tourism-related service industries, including lodges, hotels and restaurants. Elsewhere, ask locally what's appropriate; here I can give only rough guidance. Helpers with baggage might expect K15–20/US$1 and someone looking after your car around K30–40/US$2, depending on the time you're away. Given that restaurants must now add a 10% service charge to the bill, it is difficult to decide whether or not you should add anything further. Certainly for the most part it would not be the norm. Tipping a taxi driver is not normally expected.

At safari camps, tipping is not obligatory, despite the assumption from some visitors that it is. If a guide has given you really good service then a tip of about US$10 per day per guest would be a good reflection of this. If the service hasn't been that good, then don't tip. Similarly, a tip to the general camp staff of about US$10 per day per guest would reflect a good stay.

Always tip at the end of your stay, not at the end of each day or activity. Do not tip after every game drive. This leads to the guides only trying hard when they know there's a tip at the end of the morning. Such camps aren't pleasant to visit and this isn't the way to encourage top-quality guiding. It's best to wait until the end of your stay, and then give what you feel is appropriate in one lump sum.

However, before you do this find out if tips go into one box for all of the camp staff, or if the guides are treated differently. Ask the managers as you're about to leave. Then ensure that your tip reflects this – with perhaps as much again divided between the rest of the staff.

GETTING AROUND

BY AIR For those who want to fly internally in Zambia, the number of possibilities is increasing. Although only Proflight operates a scheduled service, offering internet booking with payment by credit card, several other local companies provide very reliable charter flights. Aside from Proflight, none of the other companies features on any of the global flight reservations systems, so outside of Zambia (and even inside sometimes) most travel agents won't have a clue about the intricacies of Zambia's internal flights. You are strongly advised to book your internal flights through an experienced tour operator who uses them regularly. (As an aside, this means that, if the airline goes bust, the tour operator loses money; you don't.) If you want to arrange something while you are in Zambia, or need to get in touch with an airline in a hurry, see the contact details opposite.

The services that we have encountered are high-quality operations, so you need have few worries about safety. On the whole, the smaller charter operations are very reliable, and more flexible for individual passengers, than the larger airlines.

ONE-WAY FLYING DISTANCES (KM)

	Bangweulu	Kafue	Kalabo	Kasanka	Livingstone	Zambezi	Lusaka	Mfuwe	Nchila	Shiwa Ng'andu
Bangweulu		490	885	70	810	410	435	235	650	185
Kafue (Lunga)	490		405	465	410	385	255	610	400	670
Kalabo	885	405		865	455	750	610	1,015	450	1,070
Kasanka	70	465	865		760	350	380	195	670	220
Livingstone	810	410	455	760		480	390	840	750	980
Zambezi (Jeki)	410	385	750	350	480		140	365	750	545
Lusaka	435	255	610	380	390	140		455	635	600
Mfuwe	235	610	1,015	195	840	365	455		860	230
Nchila	650	400	450	670	750	750	635	860		810
Shiwa Ng'andu	185	670	1,070	220	980	545	600	230	810	

However, if you book an internal flight a long time in advance, be aware that its timings (and indeed existence) may change. Cancellation at short notice is unlikely, though taking a philosophical attitude towards this possibility would be wise. A good operator will always be able to make a backup plan for you, and most will try extremely hard to do so.

Note that internal flights are subject to a US$16 **departure tax**. This cost is included in the ticket price for scheduled flights with Proflight, but will need to be paid in cash upon departure for any other company.

There are an increasing number of scheduled internal flights offered by Proflight (see below), but for other destinations you will have to **charter** your own plane. This isn't for the backpacker's budget, but if you plan to stay at private safari camps then short charters may be within your price range.

It's possible to charter planes seating from three passengers up to 29. Costs vary according to the size of plane, and the rates fluctuate significantly according to the route travelled, the individual companies and the (increasingly high) price of fuel. When considering flight options do remember that tour operators who book these trips every day will be given much better rates than individuals interested in a one-off charter. And if you do decide to charter, it's important to be aware that on most flights there is a maximum luggage allowance of 12kg per person (15kg on Proflight, or 20kg on a 12-passenger Caravan), to be carried in soft bags only.

Scheduled airlines

Proflight m 0971 246950; e reservations@proflight-zambia.com; w proflight-zambia.com. Proflight has regular scheduled flights linking Lusaka with Livingstone, Mfuwe, Solwezi, Ndola, Mansa &, in season, the Lower Zambezi & Liuwa Plains. Internationally, flights connect Lusaka & Mansa with Johannesburg.

Charter airlines

Proflight In addition to its scheduled service, Proflight (page 100) operates charter flights nationwide.

Royal Air Charters m 0969 783 128; e reservations@royalaircharters.com; w royalaircharters.com. With a fleet of 8-, 12-, 30- & even 50-seater planes, Royal Air operate charters countrywide from Lusaka.

Sky Trails m 0967 867848; e reservations@skytrailszambia.com; w skytrailszambia.com. Founded in 2003, Sky Trails operates throughout Zambia & neighbouring countries from its bases in Lusaka & Kasanka NP (May & November). Their fleet of planes seat between 3 & 8 passengers, & include a great Piper PA31-350 Chieftain that allows passengers to face each other with a little more legroom. They also have a helicopter available for charter. As experts in wildlife aerial surveys & anti-poaching work, they have high-wing aircraft that offer good views, a real boon for scenic flights.

Wilderness Air ☎ 0213 321578–80; m 0966 770485; e reservations@wilderness-air.com; w wilderness-air.com. Operates all of Wilderness Safaris' flights & private charters into various lodges across Zambia.

BY RAIL There are two totally separate rail systems in Zambia: ordinary trains and TAZARA (Tanzania Zambia Railway Authority) trains. Zambia's **ordinary rail network** was privatised in 2003 and is now run by RSZ (Railway Systems of Zambia). Passenger trains run on only one line, linking Livingstone with Lusaka; the journey north to the Copperbelt has for now been discontinued. Once painfully slow, and rarely used by travellers – one local described the journey as 'like signing a death warrant' – it is now a weekly overnight service and is relatively competitive with buses on the same route. For details, see page 162.

In contrast, the **TAZARA** service has long been very popular with backpackers. It connects Kapiri Mposhi with the Indian Ocean, at Dar es Salaam in Tanzania. This is a reliable international transport link which normally runs to time and is by far the fastest way between Zambia and Tanzania with the exception of flying. See page 162, for details of this useful service.

For rail afficionados, there's an occasional third option in the form of the luxury train operated by the South African Rovos Rail (☎ +27 12 315 8242; e reservations@rovos.co.za; w rovos.com) between Cape Town and Dar es Salaam. It's a 15-day journey, which operates three times a year (usually Jan, Jun/Jul & Sep), crossing into Zambia at the Victoria Falls Bridge near Livingstone, and joining the TAZARA line at Kapiri Mposhi before entering Tanzania. At the time of writing, prices start from around US$14,950 per person/sharing.

BY BUS AND COACH Zambia's **local buses** are cheap, frequent and a great way to meet local people, although they can also be crowded, uncomfortable and noisy. In other words they are similar to any other local buses in Africa, and travel on them has both its joys and its frustrations. In the main bus stations, there are essentially two different kinds: the smaller minibuses, and the longer, larger 'normal' buses. Both will serve the same destinations, but the smaller ones tend to go faster and stop less. They may also be a little more comfortable. Their larger relatives will take longer to fill up before they leave the bus station (because few buses ever leave before they are full), and then go slower and stop at more places. For the smaller, faster buses there is usually a premium of about 20% on top of the price. Be aware, too, that even buses said to be running to a timetable may not depart until they are full, so check carefully what service you can expect – and ideally take a look at the bus on which you'll be travelling too. A broken windscreen hints at poor overall maintenance.

Then there are a few **postbuses** which operate between the post offices in the main towns, taking both mailbags and passengers as they go. These conform to a more fixed schedule, and standards have improved in recent years. Tickets are booked in advance at the nearest post office (page 121).

Various luxury **coach services** connect most major towns and the smaller towns in between. See individual chapters for details of those that are running at the time of writing.

BY TAXI Taxis are common and very convenient in Lusaka, Livingstone and the main towns of the Copperbelt, and are starting to appear in smaller towns; Tom Kok reports that even Kaoma has several taxis. (Elsewhere they are uncommon or don't formally exist.) They can be hailed in the street, though foreign travellers may be best advised to book one through a reliable source or through your hotel. Meters are non-existent, but all drivers should have typed sheets of the 'minimum' rates to and from various local places – though charges can be higher if their customers appear affluent. Rates should always be agreed before getting into the vehicle. If you are unsure of the route then rates per kilometre, or per hour, are easy to negotiate.

BY POSTBOAT Rather like the postbuses, postboats used to operate on the Upper Zambezi and the waters of Lake Bangweulu during the rainy season, transporting cargo, passengers and even vehicles. However, this service has now been subcontracted, with information sketchy and none too reliable, even at the individual ports themselves. For the most part it's best to ask advice locally.

DRIVING Driving in Zambia is on the left, based on the UK's model. However, the standard of driving is generally poor, matched only by the quality of the roads. Most roads in the cities, and the major arteries connecting these, are tar. These vary from silky-smooth recently laid roads, to pot-holed routes that test the driver's skill at negotiating a 'slalom course' of deep holes, while avoiding the oncoming traffic that's doing the same. Inconveniently, the smooth kind of road often changes into the holed variety without warning, so speeding on even the good tar is a dangerous occupation. Hitting a pot-hole at 40–60km/h will probably just blow a tyre; any faster and you risk damaging the suspension, or even rolling the vehicle.

As an additional hazard, even the tar roads are narrow by Western standards, often with steep sides designed to drain off water during the rains. As a result, it's all too easy, faced with a sharp bend or an oncoming lorry, to veer off the road, a fact borne out by the regular sight of a truck lying on its side in the ditch, or to damage the sump of the vehicle. Finally, watch out for speed humps that may occur without warning, even on major roads. You often find these at the entrance and exit of a town (Kapiri Mposhi, for example), but also sometimes as you approach a level crossing.

Away from the main arteries the roads are gravel or just dirt and usually badly maintained. During the dry season these will often need a high-clearance vehicle: a 4x4 is useful here, but not vital. (The exceptions are areas of western Zambia standing on Kalahari sand, which always require 4x4.) During the wet season Zambia's gravel roads are less forgiving, and they vary from being strictly for 4x4s to being impassable for any form of vehicle. Travel on anything except the tar roads is very difficult during the rains. For more details, and particularly if you intend to hire a vehicle, read the important section on driving from page 139.

Most overseas visitors may drive on a national licence for up to 90 days. Speed limits are 120km/h on main roads and 50km/h in towns, but there are significant local variations, particularly in the approach roads to Lusaka, where they tend to be strictly enforced. Beware of speed humps, often without warning, at the approach to a town or school, in both directions.

All vehicles should carry two warning triangles for use in case of an accident or breakdown (although you'll often see brushwood laid out on the road at strategic intervals for the same purpose). They should also display reflective tape: white at the front, and red at the rear. Failure to comply with these regulations may result in a fine.

DISTANCE CHART

Distances in kilometres (approx)
Note that distances between towns are only one part of the equation when calculating travelling times. More important are the type of road (tar, gravel, dirt), and the conditions, both of which must be taken into consideration.

	Chipata	Chirundu	Kapiri Mposhi	Kasama	Kitwe	Livingstone	**Lusaka**	Mansa	Mbereshi	Mongu	Mpika	Mporokoso	Mpulungu	Mwinilunga	Sesheke	Solwezi	Zambezi
Chipata																	
Chirundu	695																
Kapiri Mposhi	780	346															
Kasama	1475	996	644														
Kitwe	990	498	150	796													
Livingstone	1080	608	682	1332	834												
Lusaka	**560**	**136**	**210**	**860**	**362**	**472**											
Mansa	1400	926	650	350	800	1262	**790**										
Mbereshi	1600	1126	850	386	1000	1462	**990**	200									
Mongu	1210	760	834	1484	986	525	**624**	1414	1614								
Mpika	1269	839	493	221	643	1175	**703**	559	759	1327							
Mporokoso	1635	1156	804	160	954	1492	**1020**	307	181	1644	381						
Mpulungu	1679	1210	864	210	1014	1576	**1074**	517	560	1698	431	370					
Mwinilunga	1470	1020	674	1324	501	1356	**884**	1324	1524	780	1167	1478	1538				
Sesheke	1260	741	872	1522	1024	190	**662**	1452	1652	335	1311	1682	1736	1115			
Solwezi	1210	744	398	1042	225	1080	**608**	1048	1248	896	891	1202	1262	292	1231		
Zambezi	1650	1156	810	1454	658	1150	**1020**	1460	1660	625	1303	1614	1674	396	960	515	

Police (and immigration) roadblocks are an occupational hazard of driving, and you can expect to be stopped regularly. They are usually indicated in advance by oil drums or traffic cones placed in the middle of the road, but some are very poorly marked, so keep an eye out for them, and do stop! Note that driving using a mobile phone when at the wheel is illegal, and infringement of the drink-driving laws now incurs a mandatory prison sentence. For more on this subject, see page 114.

Fuel Availability of fuel can be a problem, so it is important to top up whenever you can rather than to let the tank run low. Fuel stations may be prominent in towns and cities, but they're thin on the ground outside major centres, and supplies can be erratic, especially in outlying areas.

The price of fuel is high by southern African standards, which is largely a reflection of high government taxes. Despite the country's distance from the nearest port, transportation is less of an issue: crude oil is brought by pipeline from Dar es Salaam to Ndola, where it is refined then distributed both within Zambia and to the DRC. In the past, the cost of transporting the oil was reflected in widely varying prices, but the price that you'll pay at the pumps is now fixed by the Energy Regulation Authority. In mid 2023, thanks to high international oil prices, charges were increased and petrol cost K27.59/US$1.54 a litre, with diesel at K26.28/US$1.48. That said, in parts of the country, such as the Western Province, where supplies at the pumps often run dry, you could well find yourself paying far more to fill your tank on the black market.

Vehicle hire With difficult roads, which seem to vanish completely in some of the more remote areas, driving around Zambia away from the main arteries is not easy. The big car-hire firms do have franchises in Lusaka, but most concentrate on businesspeople who need transport around the city. Even now, some will insist that foreigners hiring cars also hire a chauffeur, and only the specialists are geared up for visitors in search of recreation.

Hiring a 2WD A mid-range model like a Ford Focus from, say, Europcar (**w** europcarzambia.com) will cost around US$116/£77 per day with fully comprehensive insurance, 100km 'free' per day, and a 35¢/24p charge per kilometre after that. While this is an improvement on rates even a few years ago, just add up the distances on a map and you'll realise that it still isn't viable for most trips. Further, a standard saloon vehicle just wouldn't stand up to the pot-holes found on most of the main highways, never mind the state of the dirt tracks beyond, so for exploring beyond the major towns you'll be needing either a high-clearance 2WD or – better – a 4x4.

See the car hire sections in Lusaka (page 163) and Livingstone (page 190) for contact details of the various car-hire agencies.

Hiring a 4x4 Until recently, it wasn't possible to hire reliable 4x4 vehicles in Zambia so the only option was to bring them in from outside, or arrange for a safari company to take you around on a mobile safari. While this has changed, and there are now a few options within Zambia itself, it may still be cheaper to organise a vehicle through one of the specialists in South Africa or Namibia such as Britz (**w** britz.co.za) or Kwenda Safari (**w** kwendasafari.co.za).

That said, it's important to realise that self-drive trips around Zambia are not for the inexperienced; I think that they're suitable only for those who have previously taken several in Africa, including at least one self-drive 4x4 trip (a 4x4 trip around

MOTORING ACCIDENTS

If you drive carefully in Zambia, during the day, and stick to the speed limits and sensible speeds (maximum 100–120km/h on good tar, much less on gravel or pot-holed tar), then you should never have an accident here. However, traffic – especially around Lusaka – is increasing fast, and animals and people (especially cyclists) on the road can be a nightmare, so don't be shy about using your horn a lot, and well in advance, particularly in busy towns.

If you're unfortunate enough to be involved in an accident, you need to think clearly. If you've hit a dog, a goat or a chicken, then you do not have to stop. It would be courteous to compensate the owner – although you may end up in a heated situation which becomes very difficult. If you hit a wild animal, you should report it to the local ZAWA office, or police station. Always check the vehicle, too; if you have hit a goat, for example, the impact could damage the coolant system and cause a leak.

If you hit a person, then the accident must be reported. Your natural instinct will be to stop – but most Zambians will tell you that you should not do so, for fear of being seriously assaulted by friends or relatives of the injured person. That said, if the person is injured then you may be able to help to get him or her to hospital. I've never had to make this choice, and hope I never have to. (Should you be in this situation, and decide to help, do remember to wear plastic gloves and glasses to minimise the risk of HIV infection, and don't attempt mouth-to-mouth resuscitation without a protective mask.) In any case, you must go directly to the nearest police station, or police roadblock. If a death has occurred then you will be expected to hand over your passport to the police.

In order to make an insurance claim in Zambia you will need to obtain a police report, for which you'll be expected to pay.

Botswana makes a perfect precursor). And if you have any doubts, see page 296, then think hard about what you're planning. Bear in mind, too, that self-drive trips are expensive; it can often be cheaper to fly between major cities before collecting a vehicle. There are a few obvious candidates for hiring a 4x4; the best choice depends on the route you're taking.

Hemingways See page 190.

Limo Hire Zambia m 0977 743145; e limohirezambia@gmail.com, info@limohire-zambia.com; w limohire-zambia.com. From its base south of Lusaka, this company offers a wide range of vehicles, including 4x4 Toyota Land Cruisers with rooftop tents and all the necessary equipment for bush camping.

Voyagers 4015 Lagos Road, Lusaka; ☎ 0211 375700; e DMC@voyagerszambia.com; w zambiadmc.com. This professional operation hires a range of 2WD and 4x4 vehicles, both Ford and Toyota.

Dangers of drink driving Unfortunately, drinking and driving is common in Zambia. It is more frequent in the afternoon/evening, and towards the end of the month when people are paid. Accepting a lift with someone who is drunk, or drinking and (simultaneously) driving, is foolish. Occasionally your driver will start drinking on the way, in which case you would be wise to start working out how to disembark politely.

An excuse for an exit, which I used on one occasion, was to claim that some close family member was killed while being driven by someone who had been drinking. Thus I had a real problem with the whole idea, and had even promised a surviving relative that I would never do the same…hence my overriding need to leave at the next reasonable town/village/stop. This gave me an opportunity to encourage the driver not to drink any more; and when that failed (which it did), it provided an excuse for me to disembark swiftly. Putting the blame on my own psychological problems avoided blaming the driver too much, which might have caused a difficult scene.

Hitchhiking and safety Notwithstanding the occasional drunk driver, Zambia is generally a safe place to hitchhike for a robust male traveller, or a couple travelling together, and there's no question it allows you the opportunity to talk to a whole variety of people, especially in remote areas. It is safer than in the UK, and considerably safer than the USA; but hitchhiking still cannot be recommended, especially for single women, or women travelling together. This is not because of any known horror stories, but because non-Zambian women, especially white women, hitching would evoke intense curiosity among the local people. Local people might view their hitching as asking for trouble, while some would associate them with the 'promiscuous' behaviour of white women seen on imported films and television programmes. The risk seems too high. Stick to buses.

ACCOMMODATION

Zambia boasts the full range of accommodation, from top-class safari lodges and international hotels to simple guesthouses and campsites, with an equally diverse range of standards and prices. Pricing can appear complex at first, since many of the better establishments have a two- or even three-tier structure. Typically, there will be two rates: one for local visitors, the other for international guests. In some cases, the 'local' rate will be further divided into Zambian citizens and Zambian residents; in others, these two may be lumped together, but a further category introduced: visitors from within southern Africa.

Prices quoted in this guide are for the most part international rates – those payable by visitors from Europe, America and other Western countries. While prices were correct at the time of research, inevitably many will rise during the life of the guide.

HOTELS Traditionally, hotels in Zambia tended to fall into two categories, all geared to the business market: large concrete blocks with pretensions to an 'international' standard, or small, run-down places catering to some of the less discerning local market. They were a very uninspiring bunch on the whole, and most visitors spent as little time in them as possible. Things first began to change in 2001 when Sun International opened two hotels focused on the tourism sector, just beside Victoria Falls. Other investors have since seized the initiative and the industry has blossomed, with original, pleasant properties, and even some stylish boutique hotels, now found across the country.

The larger hotels are found mostly in Lusaka, Livingstone and the Copperbelt. They generally have clean, modern rooms, good communications, a reasonable restaurant and all the usual facilities that international travellers expect. Their prices (increasingly dynamic) reflect this, at around US$200–350/£160–280 for a double room.

Zambia's smaller and cheaper hotels vary tremendously, but very few are good and many seem overpriced.

ACCOMMODATION PRICE CODES

Rates at places to stay in this guide have been coded. For urban establishments, and others offering **B&B accommodation**, rates are based on the cost of a double room with breakfast. Single supplements average around 20%, but may be significantly higher. VAT may be charged extra.

B&B double	
$$$$$	£165+; US$250+; K1,875+
$$$$	£100–165; US$150–250; K1,125–1,875
$$$	£50–100; US$80–150; K600–1,125
$$	£25–50; US$40–80; K300–600
$	up to £25; up to US$40; up to K300

For **all-inclusive** places, such as safari lodges and camps, rates are based on a double room including full board and activities (FBA).

♛♛♛♛♛	US$2,000+; £1,330+
♛♛♛♛	US$1,300–2,000; £865–1,330
♛♛♛	US$600–1,300; £400–865
♛♛	US$250–600; £165–400
♛	up to US$250; up to £165

GUESTHOUSES As tourism has grown, Zambia's larger towns – and especially Lusaka – have seen a proliferation of small guesthouses of varying quality spring up throughout the more spacious suburbs. These are not very practical if you need a courtesy bus to the airport, room service, or a telephone beside your bed – but they are often full of character and can be good value. Expect them to cost US$65–120/£52–95 for a double room, with rates typically including a continental breakfast, which is usually just a roll or a couple of slices of bread and a cup of tea, but could be a substantial meal complete with eggs.

GOVERNMENT RESTHOUSES These are dotted around the country in virtually every small town: a very useful option for the stranded backpacker. The town or district council usually runs them and, although a few have degenerated into brothels, others are adequate for a brief overnight stop. Most have rooms with private facilities that are normally clean (as are the sheets), though rarely spotless or in mint condition.

LODGES AND BUSHCAMPS Zambia's lodges and bushcamps are some of the best in Africa. As befits a destination for visitors who take their game viewing and birdwatching seriously, the camps are invariably original in design and extremely comfortable, with an increasing level of luxury available, even in the most rustic. En-suite showers and toilets are almost universal, the accommodation is generally thoughtful and spacious, the organisation smooth and home-cooked food invariably good to excellent. The best camps remember though that their reputations are won and lost by the standards of their individual guides.

Aside from a few larger lodges, you can usually expect a maximum of ten to 18 guests, and close personal care. But beware: if you seek a safari for its image, wanting to sleep late and then be pampered in the bush; or expect to dine from silverware and sip from cut-glass goblets…there are only a couple of spots in Zambia that will meet your expectations.

FOOD AND DRINK

FOOD Zambia's native cuisine is based on *nshima,* a cooked porridge made from ground maize. (In Zimbabwe this is called *sadza,* in South Africa *mealie-pap.*) Nshima is usually made thin, perhaps with sugar, for breakfast, then eaten thicker – the consistency of mashed potatoes – for lunch and dinner. For these main meals it will normally be accompanied by some spicy relish, perhaps made of meat and tomatoes, or dried fish. Do taste this at some stage when visiting. Safari camps will often prepare it if requested, and it is always available in small restaurants in the towns. Often these will have only three items on the menu: nshima and chicken; nshima and meat; and nshima and fish – and they can be very good.

Camps, hotels and lodges that cater to overseas visitors serve a very international fare, and the quality of food prepared in the most remote bushcamps amazes visitors. Coming to Zambia on safari, your biggest problem with food is likely to be the temptation to eat too much.

If you are driving yourself around and plan to cook, it makes sense to stock up at a supermarket in Lusaka or one of the larger towns, where you'll find pretty well all that you will need. While supermarkets are beginning to put in an appearance in the smaller towns, supplies here may be limited to products that are popular locally. These include bread, flour, rice, soups and various tinned vegetables, meats and fish, though locally grown produce such as tomatoes, bananas, watermelon or sweet potatoes will be available in season. This is fine for nutrition, but you may get bored with the selection in a week or two.

DRINK

Alcohol Like most countries in the region, Zambia has two distinct beer types: clear and opaque. Most visitors and more affluent Zambians drink the **clear beers,** which are similar to European lagers and best served chilled. Mosi, Castle and Carling Black Label are the lagers brewed by South African Breweries' Zambian subsidiaries. They are widely available and usually good.

Note that most beer produced in Zambia has a deposit on its bottles, like those of soft drinks. If you want to avoid this, buy non-returnable bottles or cans instead. The contents will cost about US$0.80/K14 from a supermarket, or around double in a hotel bar or restaurant (US$1.70/K30). Imported lagers such as Windhoek, Holsten and Amstel may cost considerably more than this.

RESTAURANT PRICE CODES

Price codes are based on the average cost of a main course, which usually exclude VAT (currently 16%) and service of around 10%. For specialities such as seafood, you can expect to pay considerably more.

$$$$$	£9+; US$13+; K100+
$$$$	£7–9; US$10.50–13; K80–100
$$$	£5.50–7; US$8–10.50; K60–80
$$	£3.50–5.50; US$5–8; K40–60
$	up to £3.50; up to US$5; up to K40

RECIPE FOR FRIED TERMITES *Judi Helmholz*

November typically marks the beginning of the rainy season in Zambia. The first rains bring vast swarms of termites out of their nests to find mates and reproduce. Termites are a once-a-year delicacy not to be missed for culinary adventurers. And capturing them is half the fun!

Termites are attracted to light, so it's easiest to catch them when they are swarming around in the evening. Get a large bowl and fill it with water. Catch live termites with your hand as they fly around and drop them into the water (which keeps them from flying or crawling out). Or you can wait until the morning and collect them off the ground after they have dropped their wings (then you don't have to pull the wings off yourself). Gather as many as you need, live ones only.

PREPARATION Remove any wings from termites and throw wings away. Place wingless termites in a colander or bowl and rinse them under running water. Heat a frying pan with a dash of cooking oil until sizzling temperature. Drop in live termites and sauté until they are crisp and golden brown (about 1 minute). Add salt to taste. Serve in a bowl as you would peanuts. *Bon appétit*!

Less-affluent Zambians usually opt for some form of the **opaque beer** (sometimes called *chibuku*, after the market-leading brand). This is a commercial version of traditional beer, usually brewed from maize and/or sorghum. It's a sour, porridge-like brew, an acquired taste, and is much cheaper than lager. Locals will sometimes buy a bucket of it, and then pass this around a circle of drinkers. It would be unusual for a visitor to drink this, so try some and amuse your Zambian companions. Remember, though, that traditional opaque beer changes flavour as it ferments and you can often ask for 'fresh beer' or 'strong beer'. If you aren't sure about the bar's hygiene standards, stick to the pre-packaged brands of opaque beer like Chibuku, Chinika, Golden, Chipolopolo or Mukango.

A word of caution: if you're planning to drive, stay well clear of alcohol. Aside from the obvious safety reasons, drink-driving in Zambia carries a mandatory jail sentence.

Soft drinks Soft drinks are available everywhere, which is fortunate when the temperatures are high. Choices are often limited, though the ubiquitous Coca-Cola is usually there at around US$1/K17 – perhaps a little cheaper in a supermarket, and a little more in a decent café. Diet drinks are rarely seen in the rural areas – which is no surprise for a country where malnutrition is a problem.

Until recently, all soft drinks were sold in glass bottles, though increasingly plastic bottles are in use. If you're faced with glass, try to buy up at least one actual bottle (per person) in a city before you go travelling: it will be invaluable. Because of the cost of bottle production, and the deposit system (typically around US$0.05/K1 per 330ml bottle or K15 for a 24-bottle crate), you will often be unable to buy full bottles of soft drinks in rural areas without swapping them for empty ones in return. The alternative is to stand and drink the contents where you buy a drink, and leave the empty behind you. This is fine, but can be inconvenient if you have just dashed in for a drink while your bus stops for a few minutes.

Water Water in the main towns is usually purified, provided there are no shortages of chlorine, breakdowns or other mishaps. The locals drink it, and are used to the relatively innocuous bugs that it may harbour. If you are in the country for a long time, then it may be worth acclimatising yourself to it – though be prepared for some days spent near a toilet. However, if you are in Zambia for just a few weeks, then try to drink only bottled, boiled or treated water in town – otherwise you will get stomach upsets. Bottled water can be bought almost anywhere, although if you want it cold you may often find it's frozen! Expect to pay around US$0.28/K5 for a 750ml in a supermarket, more in a smaller outlet or garage.

Out in the bush, most of the camps and lodges use water from boreholes. These underground sources vary in quality, but are normally free from bugs so the water is perfectly safe to drink. Sometimes it is sweet, at other times a little alkaline or salty. Ask locally if it is suitable for an unacclimatised visitor to drink, then take their advice.

SHOPPING

CURIOS Zambia's best souvenirs are handicrafts: carvings and baskets made locally. The curio stall near Victoria Falls close to the Zimbabwean border has a good selection, but prices are lower if you buy away from tourist areas; in Lusaka try the rondavels at Kabwata Cultural Village (page 178), the Sunday craft market or even the roadside stalls.

Wherever you buy handicrafts, don't be afraid to bargain gently. Expect an eventual reduction of about a quarter of the original asking price and always be polite and good-humoured. After all, a few cents will probably make more difference to the person with whom you are bargaining than it will mean to you.

Note that you will often see carvings on sale in the larger stalls which have been imported from Kenya, Tanzania, DRC and Zimbabwe. Assume that they would be cheaper if purchased in their countries of origin, and try to buy something Zambian as a memento of your trip.

Occasionally you will be offered 'precious' stones to buy – rough diamonds, emeralds and the like. Expert geologists may spot the occasional genuine article among hoards of fakes, but most mere mortals will end up being conned. Stick to the carvings if you want a bargain.

ABOUT CIGARETTES AND BEER

Willard Nakutonga and Judi Helmholz

There are several types of beer or *mooba* ('beer' in Nyanja) produced in Zambia. If you're after a bottle of the standard lager, such as Rhino, you can ask for it in Nyanja by saying '*Nifuna mooba wa Rhino*' – 'I want Rhino beer'. The cheaper opaque beer or *chibuku* is a favourite among more traditional Zambians. It is also known as Shake-Shake – appropriate since it resembles an alcoholic milkshake.

Don't confuse this with the main illicit beer, *kachusu* – akin to 'moonshine'. It is brewed in villages or at shebeens, and best avoided. Not only is it illegal, so you may be arrested just for drinking it, but it may also damage your liver and kidneys.

Cigarettes, or *fwaka* in Nyanja, can be purchased almost anywhere. In local markets, you can find big bins of raw tobacco, or tobacco shavings, for those who like to roll their own. The most popular cigarette brand available is Peter Stuyvesant, affectionately referred to as 'Peters'. Don't even think about trying *mbanje* or *dagga* (marijuana); if you're arrested there is no bail, and the penalty is five years in prison with hard labour.

For a more practical and much cheaper souvenir get a *chitenje* for about K80–160/US$3.50–7 in a fabric shop (price depends on whether it is cotton or polyester), though you're likely to pick one up considerably cheaper in a local market. You'll find them for sale in even the smallest of towns and will see these 2m-long sections of brightly patterned cotton cloth everywhere, often wrapped around local women. While travelling use them as towels, sarongs, picnic mats or – as the locals do – simply swathed over your normal clothes to keep them clean. When back home, you can turn the material into clothes, cushion covers or tablecloths. Either way, you will have brought a splash of truly African colour back home with you.

Imports and exports There is no problem in exporting normal curios, but you will need an official export permit from the Department of National Parks to take out any game trophies. Visitors are urged to support the letter and the spirit of the CITES bans on endangered species, including the ban on the international trade in ivory. This has certainly helped to reduce ivory poaching, so don't undermine it by buying ivory souvenirs here. In any case, you will probably have big problems when you try to import them back into your home country.

SUPPLIES Since 1996, Zambia's shops have emerged from a retailing time warp, where cramped corner shops had the monopoly. Until then, most of the country's residents were innocent of consumer-friendly hypermarkets where wide, ergonomically designed aisles are lined with endless choice. Then, in 1996, Shoprite/Checkers arrived, promoting a largely alien practice of high-volume, low-margin superstores using good levels of pay to reward honest employees. This rocked Lusaka's existing, mainly Asian, shop-owning community who had always gone for the high-margin corner-shop approach. Rumours were rife of the ways in which Shoprite's arrival was resisted, and even blocked by the capital's existing business community. Now, though, Shoprite has found a very solid footing, with stores in most of Zambia's major towns, and some smaller ones, and they are normally the best and most reliable places to shop for supplies.

However, all is not rosy. To many it seems that while the state is dismantling many of its own monopolies, the private sector is being allowed to generate new ones. Several aggressive South African companies, such as Shoprite and Game, have moved into Zambia and their increasing dominance causes resentment from local businesspeople, who fear that they are losing out. Critics say the success of these is down to South Africa's policy of lucrative tax breaks, which effectively subsidise exports. They point to the import bills generated by such stores, which often source more of their stock from outside Zambia than from inside. However, supporters cite the increased availability of goods, and the small Zambian businesses that are improving their standards and starting to supply these stores.

Whatever the arguments, you can now buy most things in Zambia (and in kwacha) at a price, and if you have the money then this will seem like a good thing. Perhaps the best advice for the careful visitor is to try to buy Zambian products wherever possible, for the sake of the local economy, and accept that some items may only be available in the bigger stores.

COMMUNICATIONS AND MEDIA

POST The post is neither cheap nor fast, though it is fairly reliable for letters and postcards. It's worth noting that Zambia has some lovely stamps for sale, a favourite of stamp collectors.

The best way to send mail quickly within Zambia is via EMS (Expedited Mail Service), a reasonably priced service where letters are hand delivered (no postbox mail). It is also available to overseas destinations and is generally less expensive than a courier company. For express mail services, there are several choices, some of which also offer phone and internet as well. With any you can send letters, parcels and small packets to destinations within Zambia and worldwide. This is costly but reliable. If you need important documents sent from overseas, couriers such as DHL or FedEx (pages 175 and 209 for contact details in Lusaka and Livingstone) are the quickest way to be assured of them reaching you safely. Packages take about a week from Europe or the USA.

Post offices in large towns are normally open Monday to Friday, 08.00–17.00, Saturday 08.00–12.30, but you can expect shorter hours in more out-of-the-way places.

TELEPHONE The Zambian telephone system, operated by Zamtel, is overloaded and has difficulty coping, despite an overhaul in 2007 and its more recent privatisation. It is still common for companies to have several different numbers, although increasingly both business and personal users rely on mobile phones.

The old payphones may have given way to cardphones, but these too are increasingly hard to find, and those that remain are none too reliable. In theory, phonecards are available from Zamtel offices and other outlets from around K10. You can dial internationally from these, and there is no time limit placed on their use.

Telephone codes To dial into the country from abroad, the international access code for Zambia is +260. From inside Zambia, you dial 00 to get an international line, then the country's access code (eg: 44 for the UK, or 1 for the USA). All regional codes have been prefixed with the numbers 021 though increasingly mobile phones, particularly via WhatsApp, are used.

Mobile phones The use of mobile phones, or 'cells' as they're usually called in Zambia, has grown very rapidly to counter the problems with the country's still-unreliable landline network. Coverage is surprisingly widespread, although in rural areas you can expect it to be patchy at best, or non-existent. The major networks are Airtel (which has the widest coverage) and MTN, as well as the state-owned Zamtel. All Zambian mobile-phone numbers are prefaced 09, and consist of ten digits.

Top-up cards for each of the mobile networks are available in even the smallest towns, or from touts at major road junctions. If you're in the Livingstone area, be careful of picking up Zimbabwean networks, as prices may be based on official Zimbabwean exchange rates, and hence be much more expensive than their Zambian equivalents.

If you're planning to use your own mobile phone in Zambia, it's almost certainly going to be cheaper to buy a local SIM card for the duration of your visit. Note, however, that for security reasons, all SIM cards must now be registered, so allow plenty of time for this, and make sure you take along some form of ID, such as a passport (making the MTN kiosk at Lusaka airport a good place to make your purchase on arrival). With prices fairly consistent across all the main operators (MTN, Airtel & Zamtel), expect to pay around US$5 for a prepaid SIM card with a week's unlimited messaging or US$8 for a 10GB data bundle. There are myriad bundles on offer for using your phone with particular apps or at certain times of the day. As elsewhere, there are numerous packages, so do ask before you buy. Whatever you select, call charges to other Zambian mobiles are exceptionally reasonable by Western standards, and international texts shouldn't break the bank either.

EMAIL AND THE INTERNET Wi-Fi access is broadening rapidly, even in the most remote safari camp, and despite ongoing issues with speed and outdated hardware. Yet while the email community in Zambia is quite large, far fewer people have access to the internet. If you're emailing someone in Zambia and don't get a reply within 48 hours, it would be wise to resend the email. There are fairly reliable and high-speed internet cafés in Lusaka and many of the bigger towns.

MEDIA

The press The main daily papers are the *Times of Zambia* (**w** times.co.zm) and the *Zambia Daily Mail*, both of which are State owned. The *Financial Mail* is part of the *Daily Mail*, as are the *Sunday Mail* and the *Sunday Times*. It's well worth having a look at the various websites before you go; some of the stories can be fascinating. For an online digest, consider also **w** lusakatimes.com, which is free to access.

There are also several weekly papers, including the *National Mirror*, *Monitor* and *Mail & Guardian*, which despite its independent status tends to be strongly pro-government.

Zambia claims to have a free press, most issues are debated openly, and the current president does appear to be rolling back some of the restrictions imposed by the previous administration, which certainly bodes well for open media discussions.

Perhaps the most interesting glossy magazine for visitors to the country is *Nkwazi* (**w** nkwazimagazine.com), the inflight magazine of Proflight and which you'll also find in many hotels and lodges. Full of interesting articles and features on everything from newly opened restaurants to national park adventures and sustainability and conservation initiatives, it's an attractive, engaging read.

Radio and television Radio is limited, as Zambia National Broadcasting Corporation (ZNBC) runs three channels which are all used as government communication tools: Radio 1, Radio 2 and Radio 4. (Radio 4 used to be the rather fun Radio Mulungushi, until it was swallowed up.)

There is some good news though, as in the cities – especially Lusaka – you'll find smaller commercial stations. The obvious one is Radio Phoenix, which broadcasts popular music and Zambian news, though it's worth scanning the airwaves for others. Outside of the large cities, you'll find little, although those with short-wave radios can always seek the BBC World Service, the Voice of America and Radio Canada.

Four public television stations are also run by **ZNBC**, with more channels planned. TV1, as their first channel is known, is the main news channel (broadcasting in English and several local languages), while TV4 is devoted to education with programmes on specific topics and subjects. There's also **Muvi TV** (**w** muvitv.com), a privately owned station that tends to focus on local productions. Most hotels with in-room televisions subscribe to satellite channels such as DSTV, often including BBC World, CNN and/or the South African cable network, M-Net, with its multitude of sports and movie channels.

CULTURAL GUIDELINES

Comments here are intended to be a general guide, just a few examples of how to travel more sensitively. They should not be viewed as blueprints for perfect Zambian etiquette. Cultural sensitivity is a state of mind, not a checklist of behaviour – so here we can only hope to give the sensitive traveller a few pointers in the right direction.

When we travel, we are all in danger of leaving negative impressions with local people. It is easily done – by snapping that picture quickly, while the subject is not looking; by dressing scantily, offending local sensitivities; by just brushing aside the feelings of local people, with the high-handed superiority of a rich Westerner. These things are easy to do, in the click of a shutter, or flash of a dollar bill.

You will get the most representative view of Zambia if you cause as little disturbance to the local people as possible. You will never blend in perfectly when you travel – your mere presence there, as an observer, will always change the local events slightly. However, if you try to fit in and show respect for local culture and attitudes, then you may manage to leave positive feelings behind you.

One of the easiest, and most important, ways to do this is with **greetings**. African societies are rarely as rushed as Western ones. When you first talk to someone, you should greet them leisurely.

So, for example, if you enter a bus station and want some help, do not just ask outright, 'Where is the bus to…' That would be rude. Instead you will have a better reception (and better chance of good advice) by saying:

Traveller: 'Good afternoon.'
Zambian: 'Good afternoon.'
Traveller: 'How are you?'
Zambian: 'I am fine, how are you?'
Traveller: 'I am fine, thank you.' *(Pause)* 'Do you know where the bus to…'

This goes for approaching anyone – always greet them first. For a better reception still, learn these phrases of greeting in the local language (page 508). English-speakers are often lazy about learning languages, and, while most Zambians understand English, a greeting given in an appropriate local language will be received with delight. It implies that you are making an effort to learn a little of their language and culture, which is always appreciated.

Occasionally, in the town or city, you may be approached by someone who doesn't greet you. Instead s/he tries immediately to sell you something, or even hassle you in some way. These people have learned that foreigners aren't used to greetings, and so have adapted their approach accordingly. An effective way to dodge their attentions is to reply to their questions with a formal greeting, and then politely – but firmly – refuse their offer. This is surprisingly effective.

Another part of the normal greeting ritual is **handshaking**. As elsewhere, you would not normally shake a shop-owner's hand, but you would shake hands with someone to whom you are introduced. Get some practice when you arrive; there is a gentle, three-part handshake used in southern Africa which is easily learnt.

Your **clothing** is an area that can easily give offence. Most Zambians frown upon skimpy or revealing clothing, especially when worn by women. Shorts are fine for walking safaris, otherwise dress conservatively and avoid short shorts, especially in the more rural areas. Respectable locals will wear long trousers (men) or long skirts (women).

Homosexuality is illegal in Zambia, although no-one – as far as I know – has ever been prosecuted, and same-sex relationships have never been a problem for guests in safari camps. While it's not at all unusual in traditional societies to see two men – or two women – casually holding hands, public **displays of affection** between two people (gay or straight) may create tension and are best avoided.

Photography is a tricky business. Most Zambians will be only too happy to be photographed – provided you ask their permission first. Sign language is fine for this question: just point at your camera, shrug your shoulders, and look quizzical. The problem is that then everyone will smile for you, producing the type of 'posed' photograph that you may not want. However, stay around and chat for 5 or 10 minutes more, and people will get used to your presence, stop posing, and you will get more natural shots of them (a camera with a quiet shutter is a help). Note that special care is needed with photography near government buildings, bridges and similar sites of strategic importance. You must ask permission before photographing anything here, or you risk people thinking that you are a spy.

If you're **seeking directions**, don't be afraid to stop and ask. Most people will be polite and keen to help – so keen that some will answer 'Yes' to questions if they think that this is what you want to hear. So try to avoid asking leading questions. For example, 'Yes' would often be the typical answer to the question, 'Does this road lead to…?' And in a sense the respondent is probably correct – it will get you there. It's just that it may not be the quickest or shortest way. To avoid misunderstandings, it is often better to ask open-ended questions like, 'Where does this road go to?' or 'How do I drive to…?'

The specific examples above can only be taken so far – they are general by their very nature. But wherever you find yourself, if you are polite and considerate to the Zambians you meet, then you will rarely encounter any cultural problems. Watch how they behave and, if you have any doubts about how you should act, then ask someone quietly. They will seldom tell you outright that you are being rude, but they will usually give you good advice on how to make your behaviour more acceptable.

TRAVELLING POSITIVELY

If you ask locally you'll often find projects that need your support. Many lodges and camps also assist with community or wildlife projects, and will be able to suggest a good use for donations. Alternatively, there are several ideas below. All welcome donations – so make a resolution now to help at least one of them as an integral part of the cost of your trip.

HELPING ZAMBIA'S POORER COMMUNITIES Visiting Zambia, especially the rural agricultural areas and the towns, many visitors are struck by the poverty and wish to help. Giving to beggars and those in need on the street is one way. It will alleviate your feelings of guilt, and perhaps some of the immediate suffering, but it is not a long-term solution.

There are ways in which you can make a positive contribution, but they require more effort than throwing a few coins to someone on the street.

Habitat for Humanity Zambia (HFHZ) 9696 Munali Rd, Lusaka; ☎ 0211 251087; **e** hfhzam@habitatzam.org.zm; **w** habitatforhumanityzambia.org. Part of a wider Christian NGO, not-for-profit HFHZ works towards solving the housing problems of the poor. Since 1984, they have worked across the country to build more than 4,000 houses, installed 68 water stations, trained over 100 financial savings groups & advocated for systems & policy change to ensure access to land & shelter. Using largely volunteer labour, some from overseas, they have effected real change.

Project Luangwa Mfuwe Rd, Mfuwe; **w** projectluangwa.org. Myriad excellent community projects are continually being established by this charitable organisation (page 279) on the edge of South Luangwa National Park.

ZOCS (Zambia Open Community Schools) 20 Tito Rd, Lusaka; ☎ 0211 253841/3; **e** info@zocs.org.zm; **w** zocs.org.zm. A wonderful project,

ZOCS provides a basic education to orphaned & vulnerable young Zambians, especially girls & those with special needs, who would not otherwise be able to go to school. Education is vital for Zambia's future, while in the present it gives children some hope. Deaths from AIDS have left increasing numbers of orphans, many of whom end up on the streets. This project is making a difference on a local level, currently supporting over 1,000 schools in 76 districts across Zambia – that's over 170,000 pupils.

ENVIRONMENT AND WILDLIFE Of the numerous worthwhile conservation initiatives in Zambia, these two are involved in areas most visited by tourists – so seem particularly apt. Both are committed to working with the local community and wildlife authorities to promote the conservation and sustainable use of the area's natural resources through a programme of environmental protection, education and community development. They have excellent and informative websites, and produce interesting newsletters if you're keen to keep abreast of developments after your safari.

Conservation Lower Zambezi (CLZ)
e info@conservationlowerzambezi.org; w conservationlowerzambezi.org; page 252.

Conservation South Luangwa (CSL)
w cslzambia.org; page 288.

VOLUNTEERING Zambia, like many African countries, hasn't been slow to take advantage of the upsurge in volunteering holidays. To set the ball rolling, contact **The Book Bus** (11 The Orchard, Montpelier Rd, London W5 2QW, UK; ☎ 020 8099 9280; e info@thebookbus.org; w thebookbus.org), which takes volunteers to help operate their mobile library and reader mentoring service in Livingstone, Mfuwe and Kitwe.

Meanwhile there are many pitfalls for unwary volunteers, so be sure to do your homework – especially if you are trying to get involved with a local community. An excellent place to start is w ethicalvolunteering.org, which also has a downloadable pamphlet entitled *The Ethical Volunteering Guide*. Some of the many issues to consider include:

- For every bona fide organisation there will be others who are willing to take your cash without delivering on their side of the deal.
- Try to be realistic about what your skills are; they will probably define what you can usefully contribute. Zambian communities don't need unskilled hobbyists; they need professionals. To teach skills properly takes years of volunteering, not weeks. (How long did *you* take to learn those skills?) So, for example, if you're not a qualified teacher or builder in your home country, then don't expect to be let loose to do any teaching or building in Zambia.
- Most volunteers will learn much more than the members of the communities that they come to 'help'; be aware of this when you describe who is helping whom.
- Make sure that what you are doing isn't effectively taking away a job from a local person.

Time in Zambia will do you lots of good; make sure it's not to the detriment of your hosts.

6

Health and Safety

There is always great danger in writing about health and safety for the uninitiated visitor. It is all too easy to become paranoid about exotic diseases that you may catch, and all too easy to start distrusting everybody you meet as a potential thief – falling into an unjustified us-and-them attitude towards the people of the country you are visiting.

As a comparison, imagine an equivalent section in a guidebook to a Western country – there would be a list of possible diseases and advice on the risk of theft and mugging. Many Western cities are very dangerous, but with time we learn how to assess the risks, accepting almost subconsciously what we can and cannot do.

It is important to strike the right balance: to avoid being either excessively cautious or too relaxed about your health and your safety. With experience, you will find the balance that best fits you and the country you are visiting.

HEALTH *with Dr Daniel Campion*

Zambia, like most parts of Africa, is home to several tropical diseases unfamiliar to people living in more temperate and sanitary climates. However, with adequate preparation, and a sensible attitude to malaria prevention, the chances of serious mishap are small. To put this in perspective, your greatest concern after malaria should not be the combined exotica of venomous snakes, stampeding wildlife, trigger-happy soldiers or the Ebola virus, but something altogether more mundane: a road accident.

PREPARATIONS Sensible preparation will go a long way to ensuring your trip goes smoothly. Particularly for first-time visitors to Africa, this includes a visit to a travel clinic to discuss matters such as vaccinations and malaria prevention. A full list of current travel clinic websites worldwide is available on w istm.org. For other journey preparation information, consult w travelhealthpro.org.uk (UK) or w wwwnc.cdc.gov/travel (USA). All advice found online should be used in conjunction with expert advice received prior to or during travel. The following summary points are worth emphasising:

- Don't travel without comprehensive medical **travel insurance** that will fly you home or to another country in an emergency.
- Make sure all your **immunisations** are up to date. On the whole Zambia is no longer considered a yellow fever endemic area, although there remains a very low risk of the disease in the northwest of the country. Vaccination may therefore be recommended for travellers to that part of the country. Otherwise, under International Health Regulations (2005), a certificate of yellow fever vaccination is required from travellers over nine months of age arriving from countries with a risk of yellow fever transmission and for travellers having

transited for more than 12 hours through an airport of a country with a risk of yellow fever transmission. Like most countries, Zambia considers that the yellow fever vaccine lasts for life. South Africa is no longer asking for a yellow fever certificate from Zambia as they do not consider Zambia to be a yellow fever endemic country. Please take advice from a Yellow Fever Registered Centre.

- It is unwise to travel in the tropics without being up to date with immunisation against measles, mumps and rubella (MMR), tetanus, polio and diphtheria (now given as an all-in-one vaccine), hepatitis A and typhoid. Immunisation against rabies, hepatitis B, and possibly TB may also be recommended.
- The biggest health threat is **malaria**, carried by nocturnal mosquitoes. There is currently no vaccine available for travellers, but a variety of preventative drugs is available, including mefloquine, atovaquone/proguanil (often known by its trademark Malarone) and the antibiotic doxycycline. Atovaquone/proguanil and doxycycline need only be started two days before entering Zambia, but mefloquine should be started two to three weeks before. Doxycycline and mefloquine need to be taken for four weeks after the trip and atovaquone/proguanil for seven days. It is as important to complete the course, as it is to take it before and during the trip. The most suitable choice of drug varies depending on the individual (their health and age) and the countries in which they are travelling, so visit your GP or a specialist travel clinic for medical advice. If you will be spending a long time in Africa, and be visiting remote areas, consider taking an emergency treatment kit in addition to prophylaxis. It is also worth noting that no homeopathic prophylactic for malaria exists, nor can any traveller acquire effective 'natural immunity' to malaria after infection. Those who don't make use of preventative drugs risk their life in a manner that is both foolish and unnecessary.
- Though an advisable precaution for all travellers, a **pre-exposure rabies vaccination**, involving three doses taken over a minimum of 21 days, is particularly important if you intend to have contact with animals, or are likely to be 24 hours away from medical help. If you have not had this then you will almost certainly need to evacuate for medical treatment, as it is possible that Zambia will not have all the necessary treatment.
- Anybody travelling away from major centres should carry a **personal first-aid kit**. Contents might include an antiseptic such as iodine or chlorhexidine, plasters, suncream, insect repellent, aspirin or paracetamol, antifungal cream (eg: Canesten), antibiotics such as azithromycin (if recommended by a doctor for severe diarrhoea in high-risk travellers), antibiotic eye drops, tweezers, condoms or femidoms, a digital thermometer and a needle-and-syringe kit with accompanying letter from health-care professional.
- Bring any **drugs or devices relating to known medical conditions** with you. That applies both to those who are on medication prior to departure, and those who are, for instance, allergic to bee stings, or are prone to attacks of asthma. However, always check with the Zambia Medical Regulatory Authority (w zamra.co.zm) who can identify any restricted medications. Allow plenty of time in case you need to apply for a licence to import your medication into Zambia. Carry a copy of your prescription and a letter from your GP explaining why you need the medication.
- Prolonged immobility on long-haul flights can result in **deep-vein thrombosis** (DVT), which can be dangerous if the clot travels to the lungs to cause pulmonary embolus. The risk increases with age, and is higher in obese or

pregnant travellers, heavy smokers, those taller than 6ft/1.8m or shorter than 5ft/1.5m, and anybody with a history of clots, recent major operation or varicose veins surgery, cancer, a stroke or heart disease. If any of these criteria apply, consult a doctor before you travel.

COMMON MEDICAL PROBLEMS

Malaria This potentially fatal disease occurs throughout Zambia all year round. Since no malaria prophylactic is 100% effective, one should take all reasonable precautions against being bitten by the nocturnal *Anopheles* mosquitoes that transmit the disease (page 132). Malaria usually manifests within two weeks of transmission, but it can be as little as seven days and anything up to a year. Any fever occurring after seven days should be considered as malaria until proven otherwise. These typically include a rapid rise in temperature (over 38°C), and any combination of a headache, flu-like aches and pains, a general sense of disorientation, and possibly even nausea and diarrhoea. The earlier malaria is detected, the better it usually responds to treatment. So if you display possible symptoms, *get to a doctor or clinic immediately.* (In the UK go to accident and emergency and say that you have been to Africa.) A simple test, available at even the most rural clinic in Africa, is usually adequate to determine whether you have malaria. You need three negative tests to be sure it is not malaria. While experts differ on the question of self-diagnosis and self-treatment, the reality is that if you think you have malaria and are not within easy reach of a doctor, it would be wisest to start treatment. If you use a self-treatment kit, you should still seek medical assistance as soon as possible, for definitive diagnosis and treatment.

Travellers' diarrhoea Many visitors to unfamiliar destinations suffer a dose of travellers' diarrhoea, usually as a result of imbibing contaminated food or water. Rule one in avoiding diarrhoea and other sanitation-related diseases is arguably to wash your hands regularly, particularly before snacks and meals. As for what food you can safely eat, a useful maxim is: PEEL IT, BOIL IT, COOK IT OR FORGET IT. This means that fruit you have washed and peeled yourself should be safe, as should hot cooked foods. However, raw foods, cold cooked foods, salads, fruit salads prepared by others, ice cream and ice are all risky. It is rarer to get sick from drinking contaminated water but it can happen. Bottled water is safe and widely available; to limit plastic waste, consider buying your own filter bottle such as Aquapure.

If you suffer a bout of diarrhoea, it is dehydration that makes you feel awful, so drink lots of water and other clear fluids. These can be infused with sachets of oral rehydration salts, though any dilute mixture of sugar and salt in water will do you good, for instance a bottled soda with a pinch of salt. If diarrhoea persists beyond a couple of days, it is possible it is a symptom of a more serious sanitation-related illness (typhoid, cholera, hepatitis, dysentery, worms, etc), so you should see a doctor. You should also seek medical advice immediately if you develop a fever, notice blood or mucus in your stool or experience symptoms such as confusion, severe abdominal pain, jaundice or a rash. If the diarrhoea is greasy and bulky, and is accompanied by sulphurous (eggy) burps, one likely cause is the parasite *Giardia*, which can cause persistent symptoms but is treatable. Again, seek medical advice if you suspect this.

Bilharzia Also known as schistosomiasis, bilharzia is an unpleasant parasitic disease transmitted by freshwater snails most often associated with reedy shores where there is lots of water weed. It cannot be caught in hotel swimming pools or the ocean, but should be assumed to be present in any freshwater river pond, lake or similar habitat, even those advertised as 'bilharzia free'. The most risky shores will be within 200m of villages or other places where infected people use water, wash clothes, etc. Ideally, however, you should avoid swimming in any fresh water other than an artificial pool. Drying off vigorously with a towel after a brief water exposure may help to prevent the *Schistosoma* parasite from penetrating the skin, but should not be relied upon. Bilharzia is often asymptomatic in its early stages, but some people experience an intense immune reaction, including fever, cough, abdominal pain and an itching rash, around four to six weeks after infection. Later symptoms vary but often include a general feeling of lethargy. Bilharzia can be tested for at specialist travel or tropical medicine clinics, ideally at least six weeks after likely exposure. Fortunately, it is easy to treat at present.

Rabies This deadly disease can be carried by any mammal and is usually transmitted to humans via a bite, a scratch that breaks the skin and saliva on broken skin or other mucous membranes such as eyes, nose or mouth. Beware village dogs and monkeys, but assume that *any* mammal can carry rabies, even if it looks healthy. First, scrub the affected area with soap under a running tap for a good 10–15 minutes, or while pouring water from a jug, then pour on a disinfectant such as iodine or alcohol solution, which will guard against infections and might reduce the risk of the rabies virus entering the body. Whether or not you underwent pre-exposure vaccination, it is vital to obtain post-exposure prophylaxis as soon as possible after the incident. Don't wait until you are back in your home country. Those who have not been immunised will need a full course of four or five vaccinations as well as rabies immunoglobulin (RIG), but this product is expensive and may not be available, so you may need to be evacuated to another country – another reason why pre-exposure vaccination should be encouraged. If you have been vaccinated before exposure, then you should not usually need the RIG, just further doses of vaccine. It is important to tell the doctor if you have had the pre-exposure vaccine – so be sure to carry your vaccine record with you. Treatment may differ if your immune system is weakened, eg: if you take immunosuppressant medication. Do take rabies seriously – death from rabies is probably one of the worst ways to go, and once you show symptoms it is too late to do anything. The mortality rate is close to 100%.

Tetanus Tetanus is caught through deep dirty wounds, including animal bites, so ensure that such wounds are thoroughly cleaned. Immunisation protects for ten years, provided you don't have an overwhelming number of tetanus bacteria on board. If you haven't had a tetanus shot in ten years, or you are unsure, get a booster immediately.

HIV/AIDS Rates of HIV infection are high in most parts of Africa, and other sexually transmitted diseases are common. Condoms (or femidoms) greatly reduce the risk of transmission.

Tick bites Ticks in Africa are not the rampant disease transmitters that they are in the Americas, but they may spread tickbite fever along with a few dangerous rarities. Ticks should ideally be removed whole, and as soon as possible, to reduce the chance of infection. You can use special tick tweezers, which can be bought in good travel shops; or failing this, with your fingernails, grasp the tick as close to your body as possible, and pull it away steadily and firmly at right angles to your skin without jerking or twisting. Applying irritants (eg: Olbas oil) or lit cigarettes is to be discouraged as a means of removal since they can cause the ticks to regurgitate and therefore increase the risk of disease. Once the tick is removed, if possible douse the wound with alcohol (any spirit will do), soap and water, or iodine. If you are travelling with small children, remember to check their heads, and particularly behind the ears, for ticks. Spreading redness around the bite and/or fever and/or aching joints after a tick bite imply that you have an infection that requires antibiotic treatment. In this case seek medical advice.

Skin infections Any mosquito bite or small nick is an opportunity for a skin infection in warm humid climates, so clean and cover the slightest wound in a quick-drying liquid antiseptic such as dilute iodine, potassium permanganate or crystal (or gentian) violet. Prickly heat is a fine pimply rash that can be alleviated by cool showers, dabbing (not rubbing) dry and talc, and sleeping naked under a fan or in an air-conditioned room. Fungal infections also get a hold easily in hot moist climates so wear 100%-cotton socks and underwear and shower frequently.

Eye problems Bacterial conjunctivitis (pink eye) is a common infection in Africa, particularly for contact-lens wearers. Symptoms are sore, gritty eyelids that often stick closed in the morning. They will need treatment with antibiotic drops or ointment. Lesser eye irritation should settle with bathing in salt water and keeping the eyes shaded. If an insect flies into your eye, extract it with great care, ensuring you do not crush or damage it, otherwise you may get a nastily inflamed eye from toxins secreted by the creature.

Sunstroke and dehydration Overexposure to the sun can lead to short-term sunburn or sunstroke, and increases the long-term risk of skin cancer. Wear a T-shirt and waterproof sunscreen when swimming. On safari or walking in the direct sun, cover up with long, loose clothes, wear a hat, and use sunscreen. The glare and the dust can be hard on the eyes, so bring UV-protecting sunglasses. A less direct effect of the tropical heat is dehydration, so drink more fluids than you would at home.

Other insect-borne diseases Although malaria is the insect-borne disease that attracts the most attention in Africa, and rightly so, there are others, most too uncommon to be a significant concern to short-stay travellers. These include dengue fever and other arboviruses (spread by day-biting mosquitoes), sleeping sickness (tsetse flies), and river blindness (blackflies). Bearing this in mind, however, it is clearly sensible, and makes for a more pleasant trip, to avoid insect bites as far as possible (page 132). Two nasty (though ultimately relatively harmless) flesh-eating insects associated with tropical Africa are *tumbu* or *putsi* flies, which lay eggs, often on drying laundry, that hatch and bury themselves under the skin when they come into contact with humans, and jiggers, which latch on to bare feet and set up home, usually at the side of a toenail, where they cause a painful boil-like swelling. Drying laundry indoors and wearing shoes are the best way to deter this pair of flesh-eaters.

Tsetse flies are slightly larger than a housefly and have pointed mouth-parts designed for sucking blood; they hurt when they bite. They thrive in broad-leaved woodland across Zambia but are highly localised. They are also said to be attracted to the colour blue and moving vehicles. Locals will advise on where they are a problem and where they transmit sleeping sickness. Bites are nasty, and the vast majority will swell up and turn red – that is a normal allergic reaction to any bite. However, if the bite develops into a boil-like swelling after five or more days, and a fever starts two or three weeks later, then seek immediate medical treatment. The name 'sleeping sickness' refers to a daytime drowsiness which is characteristic of the later stages of the disease. It can cause permanent damage to your central nervous system.

AVOIDING MOSQUITO AND INSECT BITES

The *Anopheles* mosquitoes that spread malaria are active at dusk and after dark. Most bites can thus be avoided by covering up at night. This means donning a long-sleeved shirt, trousers and socks from around 30 minutes before dusk until you retire to bed, and applying a DEET-based insect repellent to any exposed flesh. It is best to sleep under a net, or in an air-conditioned room, though burning a mosquito coil and/or sleeping under a fan will also reduce (though not entirely eliminate) bites. Travel clinics usually sell a good range of nets and repellents, as well as Permethrin treatment kits. These will render even the tattiest net a lot more protective, and help prevent mosquitoes from biting through a net when you roll against it. These measures will also do much to reduce exposure to other nocturnal biters. Bear in mind, too, that most flying insects are attracted to light: leaving a lamp standing near a tent opening or a light on in a poorly screened hotel room will greatly increase the insect presence in your sleeping quarters.

It is also advisable to think about avoiding bites when walking in the countryside by day, especially in wetland habitats, which often teem with day-biting mosquitoes. Wear a long, loose shirt and trousers, preferably 100% cotton, as well as sturdy walking or hiking shoes with heavy socks (the ankle is particularly vulnerable to bites), and apply a DEET-based insect repellent to any exposed skin.

WILD ANIMALS Don't confuse habituation with domestication. Most wildlife in Africa is genuinely wild, and widespread species such as hippo or hyena might attack a person given the right set of circumstances. Such attacks are rare, however, and they almost always stem from a combination of poor judgement and poorer luck. A few rules of thumb: never approach potentially dangerous wildlife on foot except in the company of a trustworthy guide; never swim in lakes or rivers without first seeking local advice about the presence of crocodiles or hippos; never get between a hippo and water; and never leave food (particularly meat or fruit) in the tent where you'll sleep. For further information, see page 148.

SNAKE AND OTHER BITES *With Marcel Van Driel, Helping Hands in Snake Safety (HHISS)*

Snakes are very secretive and bites are a genuine rarity, but certain spiders and scorpions can also deliver venomous bites and stings. In all cases, the risk is minimised by wearing closed shoes and trousers when walking in the bush, and watching where you put your hands and feet, especially in rocky areas or when gathering firewood. Only 10% of Zambian snakes have a type of venom strong enough to be life-threatening, but it is important to keep the victim calm and inactive, and to seek urgent medical attention; head to the nearest farm, camp or town.

Seventy per cent of Zambia's snakes are harmless. If bitten, you are unlikely to have received deadly venom. Many 'traditional' first-aid techniques do more harm than good: tourniquets are dangerous; and suction and electrical inactivation devices do not work. The only treatment for a life-threatening snakebite is antivenom.

If you receive a bite that you fear may have been from a venomous snake:

- Try to keep calm – it is likely that mild venom or no venom (a dry bite) has been dispensed.

- Stay very still – prevent movement of the bitten limb by applying a splint.
- Remove any jewellery or tight-fitting clothes from the bitten limb (most dangerous snakebites cause severe swelling).
- Do not attempt to dress or bandage the wound unless trained to do so. Most venomous bites cause localised tissue damage and swelling, and a dressing which becomes too tight could make matters worse.
- A pressure bandage is only advisable in the case of bites from mambas and non-spitting cobras, but they are complicated to apply and their correct use requires training.
- Call the National Helpline on +260 974 248144 for immediate advice and evacuate to a hospital.

And remember:

- Never give aspirin or ibuprofen, which may exacerbate bleeding (paracetamol is safe).
- Never cut or suck the wound.
- Do not apply ice packs or electric current.
- Do not apply a tourniquet.
- Do not try to capture or kill the snake, as this may result in further bites.

CAR ACCIDENTS Dangerous driving is probably the biggest threat to life and limb in most parts of Africa. On a chauffeured tour, don't be afraid to tell the driver to slow or calm down if you think they are driving too fast or being reckless. See page 111 for information on driving.

ASSISTANCE

Hospitals and dentists Zambia's public-health system is overstretched and under-funded, presenting a risk of coming away with something worse than you had when you arrived. In the main cities – Lusaka, Livingstone and the Copperbelt – there are better-funded private hospitals that cater for both affluent Zambians and expats/diplomatic staff. These are much better, and will accept payment from genuine travel health insurance schemes.

For situations that are more serious, and may require immediate evacuation, **Specialty Emergency Services (SES)** (m 0962 740300, 0977 770302; e Lusaka-clinic@ses-unisure.com; w ses-zambia.com) operates throughout Zambia, with bases in Lusaka and Kitwe. It offers ambulances and in-patient care, as well as emergency cover. SES can also arrange short-term insurance cover for visitors, either prior to arriving in Zambia or at their local offices. Most tour operators, and many lodges, include SES cover in their rates, but it's important to have good travel insurance – costs for evacuation are extremely high.

Pharmacies Pharmacies in main towns have a basic range of medicines, often at considerably lower prices than in their Western counterparts; they also stock malaria-test kits. That said, not all of these outlets are reliable, so stick to one that has been recommended locally.

As you might expect, specific brands are often unavailable, so bring with you all that you will need, as well as a repeat prescription for anything that you might run out of. Outside of the main centres, you will be lucky to find anything other than very basic medical supplies. Thus you should carry a very comprehensive medical kit if you are planning to head off independently into the wilds.

STAYING HEALTHY Rural Zambia is often not a healthy place to be. However, visitors using the better hotels, lodges and camps are unlikely to encounter any serious problems. The standards of hygiene in even the most remote bushcamps are generally at least as good as you will find at home.

The major dangers in Zambia are car accidents (page 114) and sunburn. Both can also be very serious, yet both are within the power of the visitor to avoid.

The following is general advice, applicable to travelling anywhere, including Zambia.

Food and storage Throughout the world, most health problems encountered by travellers are contracted by eating contaminated food or drinking unclean water. If you are staying in safari camps or lodges, or eating in restaurants, then you are unlikely to have problems in Zambia.

However, if you are backpacking and cooking for yourself, or relying on local food, then you need to take more care. Tins, packets and fresh green vegetables (when you can find them) are least likely to cause problems – provided that clean water has been used in preparing the meal. In Zambia's hot climate, keeping meat or animal products unrefrigerated for more than a few hours is asking for trouble.

Water and purification While piped water in the major towns is unlikely to harbour any serious pathogens, it will almost certainly cause upset stomachs for overseas visitors. In more rural areas, the water will generally have had less treatment, and therefore will be even more likely to cause problems. Hence, as a general rule, ensure that all water used for drinking or washing food in Zambia is purified.

To purify water yourself, first filter out any suspended solids, perhaps passing the water through a piece of closely woven cloth, or something similar. Then bring it to the boil, or sterilise it chemically. Boiling is much more effective, provided that you have the fuel available. Tablets sold for purification are based on chlorine dioxide. Iodine is no longer recommended for use and is not sold in the UK and the rest of Europe as there have been concerns over its safety. Reusable water bottles with a built-in filter are also available.

Returning home Many tropical diseases have a long incubation period, and it is possible to develop symptoms weeks after returning home (this is why it is important to keep taking anti-malaria prophylaxis for the prescribed duration after you leave a malarial zone). If you do get ill after you return home, be certain to tell your doctor where you have been.

SAFETY

Zambia is not a dangerous country. If you are travelling on an all-inclusive trip and staying at lodges and hotels, then problems of personal safety are exceedingly rare. There will always be someone on hand to help you. Even if you are travelling on local transport, perhaps on a low budget, you will not be attacked randomly just for the sake of it. A difficult situation is most likely to occur if you have made yourself an obvious target for thieves, perhaps by walking around, or driving an expensive 4x4, in town at night. The answer then is to capitulate completely and give them what they want, and cash in on your travel insurance. Heroics are not a good idea.

The British Foreign and Commonwealth Office currently advises caution when travelling in rural parts of the country bordering the Democratic Republic of Congo (DRC), especially after dark, a reflection of ongoing cross-border raids. The advice does not relate to main roads, or to towns along the routes, including

SAFETY FOR WOMEN TRAVELLERS

Janice Booth

When attention becomes intrusive, it can help if you are wearing a wedding ring and have photos of 'your' husband and children, even if they are someone else's. A good reason to give for not being with them is that you have to travel in connection with your job – biology, zoology, geography, or whatever. (But not journalism – that's risky.)

Pay attention to local etiquette, and to speaking, dressing and moving reasonably decorously. Look at how the local women dress, and try not to expose parts of yourself that they keep covered. Think about body language. In much of southern Africa direct eye contact with a man will be seen as a 'come-on'; sunglasses are helpful here.

Don't be afraid to explain clearly – but pleasantly rather than as a put-down – that you aren't in the market for whatever distractions are on offer. Remember that you are probably as much of a novelty to the local people as they are to you; and the fact that you are travelling abroad alone gives them the message that you are free and adventurous. But don't imagine that a Lothario lurks under every bush: many approaches stem from genuine friendliness or curiosity, and a brush-off in such cases doesn't do much for the image of travellers in general.

Take sensible precautions against theft and attack – try to cover all the risks before you encounter them – and then relax and enjoy your trip. You'll meet far more kindness than villainy.

those between Kapiri Mposhi and Serenje, Serenje and Mansa, and the main routes through the Copperbelt. However, those proposing to travel north from Ndola to Mufulira should be cautious.

For women travellers, especially those travelling alone, it is doubly important to learn the local attitudes, and how to behave acceptably. This takes some practice, and a certain confidence. You will often be the centre of attention but, by developing conversational techniques to avert over-enthusiastic male attention, you should be perfectly safe. Making friends of the local women is one way to help avoid such problems.

THEFT Theft is a problem in Zambia's urban areas. Given that a large section of the population is living below the poverty line and without any paid work, it is surprising that the problem is not worse. Despite Lusaka's reputation, in our experience theft is no more of an issue here than it is in Harare – while the centre of Johannesburg is significantly more dangerous than either. However, car-jacking does occasionally occur, usually at night, so it is wise to take sensible precautions to protect your vehicle, and yourself, such as keeping car doors locked, windows up, and being vigilant when entering or exiting a car after dark.

How to avoid it Thieves in the bigger cities usually work in groups – choosing their targets carefully. These will be people who look vulnerable and who have items worth stealing. To avoid being robbed, try not to fit into either category – and certainly not into both. Observing a few basic rules, especially during your first few weeks in Zambia's cities, will drastically reduce your chances of becoming a target. After that you should have learnt your own way of assessing the risks, and avoiding thefts. Until then:

- Try not to carry anything of value around with you.
- If you must carry cash, then use a concealed money-belt for your main supply – keeping smaller change separately and to hand.
- Try not to walk around alone. Move in groups. Take taxis instead.
- Try not to look too foreign. Blend in to the local scene as well as you can. Act like a streetwise expat rather than a tourist, if you can. (Conspicuously carrying a local newspaper may help with this.)
- Rucksacks and large, new bags are bad. If you must carry a bag, choose an old battered one. Around town, a local plastic carrier bag is ideal.
- Move confidently and look as if you know exactly what you are doing, and where you are going. Lost foreigners make the easiest targets.
- Never walk around at night – that is asking for trouble.

If you have a vehicle then don't leave anything in it, and avoid leaving it parked outside in a city. One person should always stay with it, as vehicle thefts are common, even in broad daylight. Armed gangs doing American-style vehicle hijacks are on the increase, though still rare – and their most likely targets are new 4x4 vehicles. When driving in urban areas, and especially at night, keep the doors locked, and ensure that you're not using a mobile phone within easy reach of a passer-by. Scams to get you to stop include faking an accident, so be on the alert. And if you are held up then just surrender: you have little choice if you want to live.

Reporting thefts to the police If you are the victim of a theft then report it to the police – they ought to know. Also try to get a copy of the report, or at least a reference number on an official-looking piece of paper, as this will help you to claim on your insurance policy when you return home. Some insurance companies won't act without it. But remember that reporting anything in a police station can take a long time, and do not expect any speedy arrests for a small case of pickpocketing.

ARREST To get arrested in Zambia, a foreigner will normally have to try quite hard. During the Kaunda regime, when the state was paranoid about spies, every tourist's camera became a reason for suspicion and arrest. Fortunately that attitude has now vanished, though as a precaution you should still ask for permission to photograph near bridges or military installations. This simple courtesy costs you nothing, and may avoid a problem later.

One excellent way to get arrested in Zambia is to try to smuggle drugs across its borders, or to try to buy them from 'pushers'. Drug offences carry penalties at least as stiff as those you will find at home – and the jails are a lot less pleasant. Zambia's police are not forbidden to use entrapment techniques or 'sting' operations to catch criminals. Buying, selling or using drugs in Zambia is just not worth the risk.

Failing this, arguing with any policeman or army official – and getting angry into the bargain – is a sure way to get arrested. It is essential to control your temper and stay relaxed when dealing with Zambia's officials. Not only will you gain respect, and hence help your cause, but also you will avoid being forced to cool off for a night in the cells.

If you are careless enough to be arrested, you will often only be asked a few questions. If the police are suspicious of you, then how you handle the situation will determine whether you are kept for a matter of hours or for days. Be patient, helpful, good-humoured and as truthful as possible. Never lose your temper; it will only aggravate the situation. Avoid any hint of arrogance. If things are going badly after half a day or so, then start firmly, but politely, to insist on seeing someone in higher authority. As a last resort you do, at least in theory, have the right to contact your embassy or consulate, though the finer points of your civil liberties may be overlooked by an irate local police chief.

BRIBERY Bribery is a fact of life in Zambia, though it is a difficult subject to write about. If you're visiting on an organised holiday, then it's unlikely to become an issue – you'll not come across any expectation of bribes. However, independent travellers ought to think about the issue before they arrive, as they are more likely to encounter the problem, and there are many different points of view on how to deal with it.

Some argue that it is present already, as an unavoidable way of life, and so must be accepted by the practical traveller. They view using bribery as simply practising one of the local customs. Others regard paying bribes as an unacceptable step towards condoning an immoral practice; thus any bribe should be flatly refused, and requests to make them never acceded to.

Whichever school of thought you favour, bribery is an issue in Zambia that you may need to consider. It is not as widespread, or on the same scale, as countries further north – but on a low level is not uncommon. A large 'tip' is often expected for a favour, and acceptance of small fines from police for traffic offences often avoids proceedings which may appear deliberately time-consuming. Many pragmatic travellers will only use a bribe as a very last resort, and only then when it has been asked for repeatedly.

Never attempt to bribe someone unsubtly, or use the word 'bribe'. If the person involved hasn't already dropped numerous broad hints to you that money is required, then offering it would be a great insult. Further, even if bribes are being asked for, an eagerness to offer will encourage any person you are dealing with to increase their price.

Never simply say, 'Here's some dollars, now will you do it?' Better is to agree, reluctantly, to pay the 'on-the-spot-fine' that was requested; or to gradually accept the need for the extra 'administration fee' that was demanded; or to finally agree to help to cover the 'time and trouble' involved…provided that the problem can be overcome.

7

In the Wilds

DRIVING

Driving around Zambia isn't for the novice, or the unprepared. Long stretches of the tarred roads are extensively pot-holed, most of the secondary gravel roads are in very poor repair, and many areas rely on bush tracks maintained only by the passage of vehicles. If you plan on exploring in the more rural areas, and remote parks, then you will need at least two sturdy, fully equipped 4x4 vehicles. It says something of the roads in general that until very recently most of Zambia's car-hire companies would rent vehicles only if you took a local driver – and even then only for use in towns.

Those planning to drive themselves around Zambia should read this section in conjunction with the general details on driving on page 111.

EQUIPMENT AND PREPARATIONS

Fuel and fuel consumption Petrol and diesel are available in most of the towns (page 113), but elsewhere diesel is generally more widely available. Although shortages are relatively rare these days, they do still occur – especially in the more remote west – and you'll need to be prepared for them. For travel into the bush in particular you will need long-range fuel tanks, and/or a large stock of filled jerrycans. It is essential to plan your fuel requirements well in advance, and to carry more than you expect to need.

Remember that using the vehicle's 4x4 capability, especially in low-ratio gears, will significantly increase your fuel consumption. Similarly, the cool comfort of a vehicle's air conditioning will burn your fuel reserves swiftly.

Spares Zambia's garages do not generally have a comprehensive stock of vehicle spares – though bush mechanics can effect the most amazing short-term repairs, with remarkably basic tools and raw materials. Spares for the more common makes are easiest to find, so most basic Land Rover and Toyota 4x4 parts are available somewhere in Lusaka, at a price. If you are arriving in Zambia with a foreign vehicle, it is best to bring as many spares as you can, though be aware that you could be charged import duty. Spares for Ford, Mercedes and Jeep are available in Lusaka, and general parts can be found at branches of Autoworld in several major cities.

Navigation See page 104, for detailed comments. You should absolutely have a good GPS system and suitable navigation software (we recommend Tracks4Africa) if you are heading off the main roads in the more remote areas of the country. Paper maps remain useful backups and planning references, and we've included GPS points in the maps and text throughout this guide. In addition, there are good

– if old – survey maps available from the Surveyor General's office in Mulungushi House, Lusaka (0211 252323; e info@mlnr.gov.zm).

COPING WITH ZAMBIA'S ROADS

Tar roads Many of Zambia's tar roads are excellent, and a programme of tarring is gradually extending these good sections. However, within them there are occasional patches of pot-holes. These often occur in small groups, making some short stretches of tar very slow going indeed. If you are unlucky, or foolish, enough to hit one of these sections after speeding along a smooth stretch of tar, then you are likely to blow at least one tyre and in danger of a serious accident. For this reason, if for no other, even tar roads that look good are worth treating with caution. It is wiser never to exceed about 80km/h.

If you're coming into a town, or approaching a roadblock, or near a school, you're likely to come across some form of traffic-calming measure. Typically these take the form of speed humps of varying degrees of efficacy and height, and some can do considerable damage to a vehicle if hit at even a modicum of speed. They can also slow traffic down to a crawl, which can be immensely frustrating.

POLICE ROADBLOCKS

Often in Zambia you'll come across a police or immigration roadblock. You'll find them on all the main roads around the larger towns, and randomly placed on other tar roads and arteries also. It's vital that you stop for them, and it'll speed your journey if you know how to deal with them. I usually slow down on my approach, turn off any music or air conditioning, take off my sunglasses and roll down my window. Then greet the officer with a broad smile and a traditional greeting, or at least a polite 'Good morning, how are you?' (See page 508, for more on these.)

Foreigners will often be waved through. Sometimes you'll be asked a few questions – typically about where you are going and what you are doing. Keep your answers simple, honest and clear. You may be asked to test your lights, or indicators, or to show your insurance or identification, so it's important to have your passport, driving licence and vehicle documentation to hand. Answer politely with good humour and keep cool.

Like any country, Zambia has occasional radar traps, and there are rules of the road; if you contravene these, then you may be fined. If so, then it's best to fill out the official forms, pay the official fine as swiftly as possible, and keep the receipt. Fines vary from K300 for driving without a seatbelt or with a defective tyre to K450 for using a hand-held mobile phone.

SPURIOUS CHARGES The vast majority of roadblocks are fair and friendly, but occasionally you may find one where the officers are really looking to levy a fine. This is rare, but it happens! Then the officers will either find a problem, or make one up, to try to get you to pay an on-the-spot fine – and they won't be using official forms.

Some of their favourite excuses may be the finer, real or fictitious, points of the law of the road. These might include claiming that you haven't got two six-inch white strips of reflective tape on your front bumper, or two in red on the back bumper; or that you should have two steel triangles that are easy to get at (a favourite is to fine people with plastic ones!); or that your reversing lights don't

At the beginning of the rainy season, in October and November, take particular care. During the dry season there can be a considerable build-up of diesel and oil on tar roads, so after the first rains water tends to lie on this layer and can create a surface akin to black ice.

Strip roads Occasionally there are roads where the sealed tar surface is only wide enough for one vehicle. This becomes a problem when you meet another vehicle travelling in the opposite direction…on the same stretch of tar. Then local practice is to wait until the last possible moment before you steer left, driving with two wheels on the gravel adjacent to the tar, and two on the tar. Usually, the vehicle coming in the opposite direction will do the same, and after passing each other both vehicles veer back on to the tar. If you are unused to this, then slow right down before you steer on to the gravel.

Gravel roads Gravel (or dirt) roads can be very deceptive. Even when they appear smooth, flat and fast (which is not often), they still do not give vehicles much traction. You will frequently put the car into small skids, and with practice at slower

work. Another ploy is to charge a fine, but one that's lower than it should be – if you're asked for, say, K25 for driving without a seatbelt, the likelihood is that no receipt will be forthcoming.

Whatever the charge, however unreasonable, it's vital that you keep your cool, take your time, and don't appear at all bothered. Act as if you've all the time in the world, keep smiling and stay helpful and cheerful. Never get angry; always keep it amiable. However, do politely insist on a few of Zambia's basic road laws:

- You should always, very pleasantly and politely, record the officer's name and number – I'd be casual about this – but make it clear that you have done it.
- Note that higher police officers and authorities try hard to stamp out this sort of corrupt behaviour. For this reason you should always find a way to report dodgy behaviour to a higher officer at the local station, though obviously don't imply that the officer(s) in question is doing anything wrong.
- You never need to give your car keys or licence to a police officer; they have the right to see your licence – but not to take it off you.
- If you are charged with anything, then you have the right to insist that the officer accompanies you to the local police station, to discuss the charge with his superior. So, basically, you say politely that you're happy to pay the fine… but you wish to do so at the local police station.
- Never threaten to 'report' an officer – but instead you might innocently insist that you need a receipt with a stamp – and you'll have to take it to the station for one, even after they let you go.
- Finally, I'd never admit to being late, or having to be anywhere too quickly; it's tantamount to admitting that you'll be willing to pay a bribe to get away faster.
- If you willingly pay bribes then your corruptness is perpetuating the practice. Don't do it.

Stick to these rules, take your time, remain patient and they'll eventually let you go – or at least the price of the 'fine' will reduce to being insignificant!

speeds you will learn how to deal with them. Gravel is a less forgiving surface on which to drive than tar. The rules and techniques for driving well are the same for both, but on tar you can get away with sloppy braking and cornering which would prove fatal on gravel.

Further, in Zambia you must always be prepared for the unexpected: an animal wandering onto the road, a rash of huge pot-holes, or an unexpected corner. So it is verging on insane to drive over about 60km/h on any of Zambia's gravel roads. Other basic driving hints include:

Slowing down If in any doubt about what lies ahead, always slow down. Road surfaces can vary enormously, so keep a constant lookout for pot-holes, ruts or patches of soft sand which could put you into an unexpected slide. If you do find the vehicle wandering having hit a corrugated section, always steer into the direction in which you are travelling.

Passing vehicles When passing other vehicles travelling in the opposite direction, always slow down to minimise both the damage that stone chippings will do to your windscreen, and the danger in driving through the other vehicle's dust cloud.

Using your gears In normal driving, a lower gear will give you more control over the car – so keep out of high 'cruising' gears. Rather stick with third or fourth, and accept that your revs will be slightly higher than they normally are.

Cornering and braking Under ideal conditions, the brakes should only be applied when the car is travelling in a straight line. Braking while negotiating a corner is dangerous, so it is vital to slow down before you reach corners. Equally, it is better to slow down gradually, using a combination of gears and brakes, than to use the brakes alone. You are less likely to skid.

DRIVING AT NIGHT Never drive at night unless you have to. Both wild and domestic animals frequently spend the night by the side of busy roads, and will actually sleep on quieter ones. Tar roads are especially bad as the surface absorbs all the sun's heat by day, and then radiates it at night – making it a warm bed for passing animals. A high-speed collision with any animal, even a small one like a goat, will not only kill the animal, but also cause very severe damage to a vehicle, with potentially fatal consequences. A word of caution about other road users, too: there's a prevalence for both drivers and pedestrians to be under the influence of alcohol at night. Finally, watch out for drivers with poorly maintained vehicles, who tend to drive between dawn and dusk to avoid contact with the police.

4X4 DRIVING TECHNIQUES You will need a high-clearance 4x4 to get anywhere in Zambia that's away from the main arteries. However, no vehicle can make up for an inexperienced driver – so ensure that you are confident of your vehicle's capabilities before you venture into the wilds with it. You really need extensive practice, with an expert on hand to advise you, before you'll have the first idea how to handle such a vehicle in difficult terrain. Finally, driving in convoy (preferably with some reasonably strong people) is an essential precaution in the more remote areas, in case one vehicle gets stuck or breaks down. Some of the more relevant techniques include:

Driving in sand If you're in a 4x4 and are really struggling in deep sand, then stop on the next fairly solid area that you come to. Lower your tyre pressure until there is a small bulge in the tyre walls (having first made sure that you have the means to re-inflate them when you reach solid roads again). A lower pressure will help your traction greatly, but increase the wear on your tyres. Pump them up again before you drive on a hard surface at speed, or the tyres will be badly damaged.

Where there are clear, deep-rutted tracks in the sand, don't fight the steering wheel – just relax and let your vehicle steer itself. Driving in the cool of the morning is easier than later in the day because when sand is cool it compacts better and is firmer. (When hot, the pockets of air between the sand grains expand and the sand becomes looser.)

If you do get stuck, despite these precautions, don't panic. Don't just rev the engine and spin the wheels – you'll only dig deeper. Instead stop. Relax and assess the situation. Now dig shallow ramps in front of all the wheels, reinforcing them with pieces of wood, vegetation, stones, material or anything else which will give the wheels better traction. Lighten the vehicle load (passengers out) and push. Don't let the engine revs die as you engage your lowest-ratio gear. That probably means using '4x4 low' rather than '4x4 high'. Use the clutch to ensure that the wheels don't spin wildly and dig themselves further into the sand.

Sometimes rocking the vehicle backwards and forwards will build up momentum to break you free. This can be done by the driver intermittently applying the clutch and/or by getting helpers who can push and pull the vehicle at the same frequency. Once the vehicle is moving, the golden rule of sand driving is to keep up the momentum: if you pause, you will sink and stop.

Navigation note Remember that your fuel consumption when driving in sand is much higher than on harder surfaces. Also, when navigating on sandy roads observe that your wheels slip and spin, and so your milometer will register a much greater distance than you have actually travelled. I've generally used a GPS to track distances for this book – not a vehicle's milometer.

Driving through high grass After the rains, many of Zambia's tracks are often knee-high in seeding grass. As your vehicle drives through, stems and especially seeds can build up in front of and inside the radiator, and get trapped in crevices underneath the chassis. This is a major problem in the less-visited areas of Kalahari sand. It's at its worst in March to June, after the rains, and in western Zambia and Kafue.

This causes a real danger of overheating (page 144) and fire. First, the build-up of seeds and stems over the radiator insulates it. Thus, if you aren't watching your gauges, the engine's temperature can rocket. It will swiftly seize up and catch fire. Secondly, the grass build-up itself, if allowed to become too big, can catch fire due to its contact with the hot exhaust system, underneath the vehicle.

In addition to the obvious precaution of carrying a fire extinguisher, there are several strategies to minimise these dangers; best apply them all. Firstly, before you set out, buy a few square metres of the tightly woven window-meshing gauze material used in the windows of safari tents. Fix one large panel of this on the vehicle's bull-bars, well in front of the radiator grill. Fix another much closer to it, but still outside of the engine compartment. This should vastly reduce the number of seeds reaching your radiator.

Secondly, watch your vehicle's engine-temperature gauge like a hawk when you're travelling through areas of grassland.

Thirdly, stop every 10km or so (yes, really, that often) and check the radiator and the undercarriage for pockets of stems and seeds. Pay special attention to the hot areas of the exhaust pipe; you should not allow a build-up of flammable material there. Use a stick or piece of wire to clean these seeds and stems out before you set off.

When driving through the grass, take particular care to avoid hidden obstacles, which can inflict considerable damage to your vehicle. Watch out too, for bush fires, which can move rapidly and make some roads impassable for a while.

Driving in mud This is difficult, though the theory is the same as for sand: keep going and don't stop. That said, even the most experienced drivers get stuck. Many areas of Zambia (like large stretches of the Kafue, Luangwa and Lower Zambezi valleys) have very fine soil known as 'black-cotton' soil, which becomes impassable when wet. This is why many of the camps close down for the rains, as the only way to get there would be to walk.

Mud can also have the same overheating effect as grass seed, so it's important to wash it away from the radiator once you stop.

Push-starting when stuck If you are unlucky enough to need to push-start your vehicle while it is stuck in sand or mud, there is a remedy. Raise up the drive wheels, and take off one of the tyres. Then wrap a length of rope around the hub and treat it like a spinning top: one person (or more) pulls the rope to make the axle spin, while the driver lifts the clutch, turns the ignition on, and engages a low gear to turn the engine over. This is a very difficult equivalent of a push-start, but it may be your only option.

On rocky terrain Have your tyre pressure higher than normal and move very slowly. If necessary, passengers should get out and guide you along the track to avoid scraping the undercarriage on the ground. This can be a very slow business, but often applies in some of Zambia's mountainous areas.

Crossing rivers The first thing to do is to stop and check the river. You must assess its depth, its substrate (type of riverbed) and its current flow; and determine the best route to drive across it. This is best done by wading across the river (while watching for hippos and crocodiles, if necessary). Beware of water that's too deep for your vehicle, or the very real possibility of being swept away by a fast current and a slippery substrate.

If everything is OK, then select your lowest gear ratio and drive through the water at a slow but steady rate. Your vehicle's air intake must be above the level of the water to avoid your engine filling with water. It's not worth taking risks, so remember that a flooded river may subside to safer levels by the next morning.

Many rivers in Zambia have pontoon crossings capable of ferrying vehicles across. Traditionally these are hand-operated wooden platforms tied on top of buoyant empty oil cans and kept in line by steel cables stretched across the river. Nowadays, on the busier crossings, such structures are often motorised, with a steel superstructure, but in many cases the cables remain. The pontoons are usually manned by local people for either a large official charge (K56 per vehicle is fairly average) or – occasionally – a handsome tip. You need to take great care (everybody out, use first gear) when driving on and off these, and make sure that the pontoon is held tightly next to the bank on both occasions.

Overheating If the engine has overheated then the only option is to stop and turn it off. Don't open the radiator cap to refill it until the radiator is no longer hot to the touch. Even then, keep the engine running and the water circulating while you refill the radiator – otherwise you run the risk of cracking the hot metal by suddenly cooling it. Flicking droplets of water onto the outside of a running engine will cool it. And see *Driving through high grass* above.

DRIVING NEAR BIG GAME The only animals which are likely to pose a threat to vehicles are elephants – and generally only elephants which are familiar with vehicles. So, treat them with the greatest respect and don't 'push' them by trying to move ever closer. Letting them approach you is much safer, and they will feel far less threatened and more relaxed. Then, if the animals are calm, you can safely turn the engine off, sit quietly, and watch as they pass you by.

If you are unlucky, or foolish, enough to unexpectedly drive into the middle of a herd, then don't panic. Keep your movements, and those of the vehicle, slow and measured. Back off steadily. Don't be panicked, or overly intimidated, by a mock charge – this is just their way of frightening you away. Professionals will sometimes switch their engines off, but this is not for the faint-hearted.

BUSH CAMPING

Many 'boy scout'-type manuals have been written on survival in the bush, usually by military veterans. If you are stranded with a convenient multi-purpose knife, then these useful tomes will describe how you can build a shelter from branches, catch passing animals for food, and signal to the inevitable rescue planes which are combing the globe looking for you – while avoiding the attentions of hostile forces.

In Zambia, bush camping is usually less about survival than comfort. You're likely to have much more than the knife: probably at least a bulging backpack, if not a loaded 4x4. Thus the challenge is not to camp and survive, it is to camp and be as comfortable as possible. With practice you'll learn how, but a few hints may be useful for the less experienced.

WHERE YOU CAN CAMP In frequently visited national parks, there are designated campsites that you should use, as directed by the local game scouts. Elsewhere the rules are less obvious, though it is normal to ask the scouts, and get their permission, for any site that you have in mind.

Outside of the parks, you should ask the local landowner, or village head, if they are happy for you to camp on their property. If you explain patiently and politely what you want, then you are unlikely to meet anything but warm hospitality from most rural Zambians. They will normally be as fascinated with your way of life as you are with theirs. Company by your campfire is virtually assured.

CHOOSING A SITE Only experience will teach you how to choose a good site for pitching a tent, but a few points may help you avoid a lot of problems:

- Avoid camping on what looks like a path through the bush, however indistinct. It may be a well-used game trail.
- Beware of camping in dry riverbeds: dangerous flash floods can arrive with little or no warning.
- In marshy areas camp on higher ground to avoid cold, damp mists in the morning and evening.
- Camp a reasonable distance from water: near enough to walk to it, but far enough to avoid animals which arrive to drink.

- If a lightning storm is likely, make sure that your tent is not the highest thing around.
- Finally, choose a site which is as flat as possible – you will find sleeping much easier.

CAMPFIRES Campfires can create a great atmosphere and warm you on a cold evening, but they can also be damaging to the environment and leave unsightly piles of ash and blackened stones. Deforestation is a major concern in much of the developing world, including parts of Zambia, so if you do light a fire then use wood as the locals do: sparingly. If you have a vehicle, consider buying firewood in advance from people who sell it at the roadside.

If you collect it yourself, then take only dead wood, nothing living. Never just pick up a log: always roll it over first, checking carefully for snakes or scorpions.

Experienced campers build small, highly efficient fires by using a few large stones to absorb, contain and reflect the heat, and gradually feeding just a few thick logs into the centre to burn. Cooking pots can be balanced on the stones, or at the point where the logs meet and burn. Other campers will use a small trench, lined with rocks, to similar effect. Either technique takes practice, but is worth perfecting. Whichever you do, bury the ashes, take any rubbish with you when you leave, and make the site look as if you had never been there.

Don't expect an unattended fire to frighten away wild animals – that works in Hollywood, but not in Africa. A campfire may help your feelings of insecurity, but lion and hyena will disregard it with stupefying nonchalance.

Finally, do be hospitable to any locals who appear. Despite your efforts to seek permission for your camp, you may effectively be staying in their back gardens.

USING A TENT (OR NOT) Whether to use a tent or to sleep in the open is a personal choice, dependent upon where you are. In an area where there are predators around (specifically lion and hyena) then you should use a tent – and sleep *completely* inside it, as a protruding leg may seem like a tasty takeaway to a hungry hyena. This is especially true at organised campsites, where the local animals are so used to humans that they have lost much of their inherent fear of man.

Outside game areas, you will be fine sleeping in the open, or preferably under a mosquito net, with just the stars of the African sky above you. On the practical side, sleeping under a tree will reduce the morning dew that settles on your sleeping bag. If your vehicle has a large, flat roof then sleeping on this will provide you with peace of mind, and a star-filled outlook. (Hiring a vehicle with a built-in rooftop tent would seem like a perfect solution, until you want to take a drive while leaving your camp intact.)

CAMPING EQUIPMENT If you are taking an organised safari, you will not need any camping equipment at all. However, for those travelling independently very little kit is available in Zambia. So buy high-quality equipment beforehand as it will save you a lot of time and trouble once you arrive. Here are a few comments on various essentials.

Tent During the rains a good tent is essential in order to stay dry. Even during the dry season one is useful if there are lion or hyena around. If backpacking, invest in a high-quality, lightweight tent. Mosquito-netting ventilation panels, allowing a good flow of air, are essential. (Just a corner of mesh at the top of the tent is not enough for comfort.) Don't go for a tent that's small; it may feel cosy at home, but will be hot and claustrophobic in the heat. Mesh doors and windows allow for a welcome breeze to circulate. The alternative to a good tent is a mosquito net, which is fine unless it is raining or you are in a big game area.

Sleeping bag A lightweight, 'three-season' sleeping bag is ideal for Zambia, unless you are heading up to the Nyika Plateau in winter where the nights freeze. Down is preferable to synthetic fillings for most of the year, as it packs smaller, is lighter, and feels more luxurious to sleep in. However, when down gets wet it loses its efficiency, so bring a good synthetic bag if you are likely to encounter much rain.

Ground mat A ground mat of some sort is essential. It keeps you warm and comfortable, and it protects the tent's groundsheet from rough or stony ground. (Do put it underneath the tent!) Closed cell foam mats are widely available outside Zambia, so buy one before you arrive. The better mats cost double or treble the price of the cheaper ones, but are stronger, thicker and warmer – well worth the investment.

Sheet sleeping bag Thin, pure-cotton sheet sleeping bags are small, light and very useful. They are easily washed and so are normally used like a sheet, inside a sleeping bag, to keep it clean. They can, of course, be used on their own when your main sleeping bag is too hot.

Stove 'Trangia'-type stoves, which burn methylated spirits, are simple to use, light, and cheap to run. They come complete with a set of light aluminium pans and a very useful all-purpose handle. Often you'll be able to cook on a fire with the pans, but it's nice to have the option of making a brew in a few minutes while you set up camp. Methylated spirits is cheap and widely available, even in the rural areas, but bring a tough (purpose-made) fuel container with you as the bottles in which it is sold will soon crack and spill all over your belongings.

Petrol- and kerosene-burning stoves are undoubtedly efficient on fuel and powerful – but invariably temperamental and messy. Gas stoves use pressurised canisters, which are not allowed on aircraft and are difficult to buy in Zambia.

Torch (flashlight) This should be on every visitor's packing list – whether you're staying in upmarket camps or backpacking. Find one that's small and tough, and preferably water- and dust-proof. Headtorches leave your hands free (useful when cooking or mending the car) and the latest designs are light and comfortable to wear. Consider one of the new generation of super-bright LED torches; the LED Lenser range is excellent.

Water containers For everyday use, a small two-litre water bottle is invaluable, however you are travelling. If you're thinking of camping, you should also consider a strong, collapsible water-bag – perhaps 5–10 litres in size – which will reduce the number of trips that you need to make from your camp to the water source. (Ten litres of water weighs 10kg.) Drivers will want to carry a number of large containers of water, especially if venturing into the Kalahari sand in western Zambia, where good surface water is not common.

See page 102, for a memory-jogging list of other useful items to pack.

ANIMAL DANGERS FOR CAMPERS Camping in Africa is really very safe, though you may not think so from reading this. If you have a major problem while camping, it will probably be because you did something stupid, or because you forgot to take a few simple precautions. Here are a few general basics, applicable to anywhere in Africa and not just Zambia.

Large animals Big game will not bother you if you are in a tent – provided that you do not attract its attention, or panic it. Elephants will gently tiptoe through your guy ropes while you sleep, without even nudging your tent. However, if you wake up and make a noise, startling them, they are far more likely to panic and step on your tent. Similarly, scavengers will quietly wander round, smelling your evening meal in the air, without any intention of harming you. Bear the following precautions in mind:

- Remember to use the toilet before going to bed, and avoid getting up in the night if possible.
- Scrupulously clean everything used for food that might smell good to scavengers. Put these utensils in a vehicle if possible, suspend them from a tree, or pack them away in a rucksack inside the tent.
- Do not keep any smelly foodstuffs, like meat or citrus fruit, in your tent. Their smells will likely attract unwanted attention.
- Do not leave anything outside that could be picked up – like bags, pots, pans, etc. Hyenas, among others, will take anything. (They have been known to crunch a camera's lens, and eat it.)
- If you are likely to wake in the night, then leave the tent's zips a few centimetres open at the top, enabling you to take a quiet peek outside.

Creepy-crawlies As you set up camp, clear stones or logs out of your way with great caution: underneath will be great hiding places for snakes and scorpions. Long moist grass is ideal territory for snakes, and dry, dusty, rocky places are classic sites for scorpions.

If you are sleeping in the open, it is not unknown to wake and find a snake lying next to you in the morning. Don't panic: your warmth has just attracted it to you. You will not be bitten if you gently edge away without making any sudden movements. (This is one good argument for using at least a mosquito net!)

Before you put on your shoes, shake them out. Similarly, check the back of your backpack before you slip it on. Just a curious spider, in either, could inflict a painful bite.

WALKING IN THE BUSH

Walking in the African bush is a totally different sensation from driving through it. You may start off a little unready – perhaps even sleepy – for an early morning walk, but swiftly your mind will awake. There are no noises except the wildlife, and you. So every noise that isn't caused by you must be an animal, or a bird, or an insect. Every smell and every rustle has a story to tell, if you can understand it.

With time, patience and a good guide you can learn to smell the presence of elephants, and hear when a predator alarms impala. You can use oxpeckers to lead you to buffalo, or vultures to help you locate a kill. Tracks will record the passage of animals in the sand, telling what passed by, how long ago and in which direction.

Eventually your gaze becomes alert to the slightest movement, your ears aware of every sound. This is safari at its best: a live, sharp, spine-tingling experience that's hard to beat and very addictive. Be careful: watching game from a vehicle will never be the same again for you.

WALKING TRAILS AND SAFARIS One of Zambia's biggest attractions is its walking safaris, which can justly claim to be among the best in Africa. The concept was pioneered here, in the Luangwa Valley, by the late Norman Carr. He also founded Nsefu Camp and Kapani Lodge, and trained several of the valley's best guides. It was he who first operated walking safaris for photographic guests, as opposed to hunters. The Luangwa still has a strong tradition of walking – which, in itself, fosters excellent walking guides. Several of the camps are dedicated to walking safaris, and guiding standards are generally very high.

One of the reasons behind the valley's success is the stringent tests that a guide must pass before he, or she, will be allowed to take clients into the bush. Walking guides have the hardest tests to pass; there is a less demanding exam for guides who conduct safaris from vehicles.

The second major reason for excellence is Zambia's policy of having a safari guide and an armed game scout accompany every walking safari. These groups are limited (by park rules) to a maximum of seven guests, and there's normally a tea-bearer (carrying drinks and refreshments) as well as the guide and armed scout.

If a problem arises with an aggressive animal, then the guide looks after the visitors – telling them exactly what to do – while the scout keeps his sights trained on the animal, just in case a shot is necessary. Fortunately such drastic measures are needed only rarely. This system of two guides means that Zambia's walks are very safe. Few shots are ever fired, and I can't remember hearing of an animal (or a person) ever being injured.

Contrast this with other African countries where a single guide (who may, or may not, be armed) watches out for the game *and* takes care of the visitors at the same time. The Zambian way is far better.

Etiquette for walking safaris If you plan to walk then avoid wearing any bright, unnatural colours, especially white. Dark, muted shades are best; greens, browns and khaki are ideal. Hats are essential, as is sunblock. Even a short walk will last for 2 hours, and there's no vehicle to which you can retreat if you get too hot.

Binoculars should be immediately accessible – one pair per person – ideally in dust-proof cases strapped to your belt or around your neck. Cameras too, if you decide to bring any, as they are of little use buried at the bottom of a camera bag. Heavy tripods or long lenses are a nightmare to lug around, so leave them behind if you can (and accept, philosophically, that you may miss shots).

Walkers see the most when walking in silent single file. This doesn't mean that you can't stop to whisper a question to the guide; just that idle chatter will reduce your powers of observation, and make you even more visible to the animals (who will usually flee when they sense you).

With regard to safety, your guide will always brief you in detail before you set off. S/he will outline possible dangers, and what to do in the unlikely event of them materialising. Listen carefully: this is vital.

Face-to-face animal encounters Whether you are on an organised walking safari, on your own hike, or just walking from the car to your tent in the bush, it is not unlikely that you will come across some of Africa's larger animals at close quarters. Invariably, the danger is much less than you imagine, and a few basic guidelines will enable you to cope effectively with most situations.

First of all, don't panic. Console yourself with the fact that animals are not normally interested in people. You are not their normal food, or their predator. If you do not annoy or threaten them, you will be left alone.

If you are walking to look for animals, then remember that this is their environment and not yours. Animals have evolved in the bush, and their senses are far better attuned to it than yours. To be on less unequal terms, remain alert and try to spot them from a distance. This gives you the option of approaching carefully, or staying well clear.

Finally, the advice of a good guide is far more valuable than the simplistic comments noted here. Animals, like people, are all different. So while we can generalise here and say how the 'average' animal will behave, the one that's glaring at you over a small bush may have had a really bad day, and be feeling much grumpier than normal.

That said, here are a few general comments on how to deal with some potentially dangerous situations.

Buffalo This is probably the continent's most dangerous animal to hikers, but there is a difference between the old males, often encountered on their own or in small groups, and large breeding herds.

The former are easily surprised. If they hear or smell something amiss, they will charge without provocation – motivated by a fear that something is sneaking up on them. Buffalo have an excellent sense of smell, but fortunately they are short-sighted. Avoid a charge by quickly climbing the nearest tree, or by side-stepping at the last minute. If adopting the latter, more risky, technique then stand motionless until the last possible moment, as the buffalo may well miss you anyhow.

The large breeding herds can be treated in a totally different manner. If you approach them in the open, they will often flee. Sometimes though, in areas often used for walking safaris, they will stand and watch, moving aside to allow you to pass through the middle of the herd.

Neither encounter is for the faint-hearted or inexperienced, so steer clear of these dangerous animals wherever possible.

Black rhino If you are both exceptionally lucky to find a black rhino, and then unlucky enough to be charged by it, use the same tactics as you would for a buffalo: tree climbing or dodging at the last second. (It is amazing how even the least athletic walker will swiftly scale the nearest tree when faced with a charging rhino.)

Elephant Normally elephants are a problem only if you disturb a mother with a calf, or approach a male in musth (state of arousal). So keep well away from these. Lone bulls can usually be approached quite closely when feeding. If you get too close to any elephant it will scare you off with a 'mock charge': head up, perhaps shaking – ears flapping – trumpeting. Lots of sound and fury. This is intended to be frightening, and it is. But it is just a warning and no cause for panic. Just freeze to assess the elephant's intentions, then back off slowly.

When elephants really mean business, they will put their ears back, their head down, and charge directly at you without stopping. This is known as a 'full charge'. There is no easy way to avoid the charge of an angry elephant, so take a hint from the warning and back off very slowly as soon as you encounter a mock charge. Don't run. If you are the object of a full charge, then you have no choice but to run – preferably round an anthill, up a tall tree, or wherever.

Lion Tracking lion can be one of the most exhilarating parts of a walking safari. Sadly, they will normally flee before you even get close to them. However, it can be a problem if you come across a large pride unexpectedly. Lion are well camouflaged; it is easy to find yourself next to one before you realise it. If you had been listening, you would probably have heard a warning growl about 20m ago. Now it is too late.

The best plan is to stop, and back off slowly, but confidently. If you are in a small group, then stick together. *Never* run from a big cat. First, they are always faster than you are. Secondly, running will just convince them that you are frightened prey, and worth chasing. As a last resort, if they seem too inquisitive and follow as you back off, then stop. Call their bluff. Pretend that you are not afraid and make loud, deep, confident noises: shout at them, bang something. But do not run.

John Coppinger, one of Luangwa's most experienced guides, adds that every single compromising experience that he has had with lion on foot has been either with a female with cubs, or with a mating pair, when the males can get very aggressive. You have been warned.

Leopard Leopard are very seldom seen, and would normally flee from the most timid of lone hikers. However, if injured, or surprised, then they are very powerful, dangerous cats. Conventional wisdom is scarce, but never stare straight into the leopard's eyes, or it will regard this as a threat display. (The same is said, by some, to be true with lion.) Better to look away slightly, at a nearby bush, or even at its tail. Then back off slowly, facing the direction of the cat and showing as little terror as you can. As with lion – loud, deep, confident noises are a last line of defence. Never run from a leopard.

Hippo Hippo are fabled to account for more deaths in Africa than any other animal (ignoring the mosquito). Having been attacked and capsized by a hippo while in a dugout canoe, I find this very easy to believe, but see page 60 for an alternative comment on this. Visitors are most likely to encounter hippo in the water, when paddling a canoe (see below) or fishing. However, as they spend half their time grazing on land, they will sometimes be encountered out of the water. Away from the water, out of their comforting lagoons, hippos are even more dangerous. If they see you, they will flee towards the water – so the golden rule is never to get between a hippo and its escape route to deep water. Given that a hippo will outrun you on land, standing motionless is probably your best line of defence.

Snakes These are really not the great danger that people imagine. Most flee when they feel the vibrations of footsteps; only a few will stay still. The puff adder is responsible for more cases of snakebite than any other venomous snake in Zambia because, when approached, it will simply puff itself up and hiss as a warning, rather than slither away. This makes it essential to always watch where you place your feet when walking in the bush.

Similarly, there are a couple of arboreal (tree-dwelling) species which may be taken by surprise if you carelessly grab vegetation as you walk. So don't.

Spitting cobras are also encountered occasionally, which will aim for your eyes and spit with accuracy. If one of these rears up in front of you, then turn away and avert your eyes. If the spittle reaches your eyes, you must wash them out *immediately* and thoroughly with whatever liquid comes to hand: water, milk, even urine if that's the only liquid that you can quickly produce.

CANOEING

The Zambezi – both above the Victoria Falls and from Kariba to Mozambique – is in constant use for canoeing trips. Paddling along this beautiful, tropical river is as much a part of Zambia's safari scene in the Lower Zambezi as are open-top Land Rovers. Generally you either canoe along the river for a set number of days, stopping each night at a different place, or paddle for a short stretch from one of the camps – as an alternative activity to a walk or a game drive.

Rather than traditional *mekoro* (dugout canoes, singular *mokoro*), most operators use large, two- or three-person Canadian-style fibreglass canoes. Three-person canoes usually have a guide in the back of each, while two-person canoes are often paddled in 'convoy' with a guide in just one of the boats. Less confident (or lazier) paddlers might prefer to have a guide in their own canoe, while the more energetic usually want to have the boat to themselves.

ZAMBEZI CANOE GUIDES Most of the Zambezi's specialist canoeing operations are run by large companies on a very commercial basis. On these you can expect to join a party of about seven canoes, one of which will contain a guide. S/he should know the stretch of river well and will canoe along it regularly. The actual distances completed on the two-/three-night trips are quite short. All the trips run downstream and a day's canoeing could actually be completed in just 3 hours with a modicum of fitness and technique.

Like other guides, the 'river guides' must possess a professional licence in order to be allowed to take paying guests canoeing. Note that only a few of the best river guides also hold licences as general professional guides (ie: are licensed to lead walking safaris). These all-rounders generally have a far deeper understanding of the environment and the game than those who are only 'river guides'.

However, their greater skill commands a higher wage – and so they are usually found in the smaller, more upmarket operations. Given the inexperience of some of the river guides, I would always be willing to pay the extra. Although the safety record of river trips is good, accidents do happen occasionally.

THE MAIN DANGERS

Hippo Hippos are strictly vegetarians, and will usually attack a canoe only if they feel threatened. The standard avoidance technique is first of all to let them know that you are there. If in doubt, bang your paddle on the side of the canoe a few times (most novice canoeists will do this constantly anyhow).

During the day, hippopotami will congregate in the deeper areas of the river. The odd ones in shallow water – where they feel less secure – will head for the deeper places as soon as they are aware of a nearby canoe. Avoiding hippos then becomes a fairly simple case of steering around the deeper areas, where the pods will make their presence obvious. This is where experience, and knowing every bend of the river, becomes useful. Problems arise when canoes inadvertently stray over a pod of hippos, or when a canoe cuts a hippo off from its path of retreat into deeper water. Either is dangerous, as hippos will overturn canoes without a second thought, biting them and their occupants. Once in this situation, there are no easy remedies. So – avoid it in the first place.

Crocodiles Crocodiles may have sharp teeth and look prehistoric, but are rarely a danger to a canoeist while in the boat, although the larger, wilier animals can pose a serious threat. If you find yourself in the water, the situation is considerably worse. Then the more you struggle and the more waves you create, the more you will attract their unwelcome attentions. There is a major problem when canoes are overturned by hippos – then you must get out of the water as soon as possible, either into another canoe or onto the bank.

When a crocodile attacks an animal, it will try to disable it, normally by getting a firm, biting grip, submerging, and performing a long, fast barrel-roll. This will disorient the prey, drown it, and probably twist off the limb that has been bitten. In this dire situation, your best line of defence is probably to stab the reptile in its eyes with anything sharp that you have. Alternatively, if you can lift up its tongue and let the water into its lungs while it is underwater, then a crocodile will start to drown and will release its prey.

Jo Pope reports that a man survived an attack in the Zambezi when a crocodile grabbed his arm and started to spin backwards into deep water. The man wrapped his legs around the crocodile, to spin with it and avoid having his arm twisted off. As this happened, he tried to poke his thumb into its eyes, but with no effect. Finally he put his free arm into the crocodile's mouth, and opened up the beast's throat. This worked. The crocodile left him and he survived with only a damaged arm. Understandably, anecdotes about tried and tested methods of escape are rare.

MINIMUM IMPACT

When you visit, drive through, or camp in an area and have 'minimum impact' this means that that area is left in the same condition as – or better than – when you entered it. While most visitors view minimum impact as being desirable, spend time to consider the ways in which we contribute to environmental degradation, and how these can be avoided.

DRIVING Use your vehicle responsibly. If there's a road, or a track, then don't go off it – the environment will suffer. Driving off-road can leave a multitude of tracks that detract from the 'wilderness' feeling for subsequent visitors. Equally, don't speed through towns or villages: remember the danger to local children, and the amount of dust you'll cause.

HYGIENE Use toilets if they are provided, even if they are basic longdrop loos with questionable cleanliness. If there are no toilets, then human excrement should always be buried well away from paths, or groundwater, and any tissue used should be burnt and then buried.

If you use rivers or lakes to wash, then soap yourself near the bank, using a pan for scooping water from the river – making sure that no soap finds its way back into the water. Use biodegradable soap. Sand makes an excellent pan-scrub, even if you have no water to spare.

RUBBISH Biodegradable rubbish can be burnt and buried with the campfire ashes. Don't just leave it lying around: it will look very unsightly and spoil the place for those who come after you.

Bring along some bags with which to remove the remainder of your rubbish, and dispose of it at the next town. Items that will not burn, like tin cans, are best cleaned and squashed for easy carrying. If there are bins, then use them, but also consider when they will next be emptied, and also if local animals are likely to rummage through them first. Carrying out all your own rubbish may still be the sensible option.

HOST COMMUNITIES While the rules for reducing impact on the environment have been understood and followed by responsible travellers for years, the effects of tourism on local people have only recently been considered. Many tourists believe it is their right, for example, to take intrusive photos of local people – and even become angry if the local people object. They refer to higher prices being charged to tourists as a rip-off, without considering the hand-to-mouth existence of those selling these products or services. They deplore child beggars, then hand out sweets or pens to local children with outstretched hands.

Our behaviour towards 'the locals' needs to be considered in terms of their culture, with the knowledge that we are the uninvited visitors. We visit to enjoy ourselves, but this should not be at the expense of local people. Read *Cultural guidelines*, page 122, and aim to leave the local communities better off after your visit.

LOCAL PAYMENTS If you spend time with any of Zambia's poorer local people, perhaps camping in the bush or getting involved with one of the community-run projects, then take great care with any payments that you make.

First, note that most people like to spend their earnings on what *they* choose. This means that trying to pay for services with beads, food, old clothes or anything else instead of money isn't appreciated. Ask yourself how you'd like to be paid, and you'll understand this point.

Second, find out the normal cost of what you are buying. Most community campsites will have a standard price for a pitch and, if applicable, an hour's guided activity, or whatever. Find this out before you sleep there, or accept the offer of a walk. It is then important that you pay about that amount for the service rendered – no less, and not too much more.

As most people realise, if you try to pay less you'll get into trouble – as you would at home. However, many do not realise that if they generously pay a lot more, this can be equally damaging. Local rates of pay in rural areas can be very low, and a careless visitor can easily pay disproportionately large sums. Where this happens, local jobs can lose their value overnight. Imagine working hard to become a game scout, only to learn that a tourist has given your friend the equivalent of your whole month's wages for just a few hours guiding. What incentive is there for you to carry on with your regular job?

If you want to give more – for good service, a super guide, or just because you want to help – then either buy some locally made produce (at the going rate) or donate money to one of the organisations working to improve the lot of Zambia's most disadvantaged (page 124).

Part Two

THE GUIDE

8

Lusaka

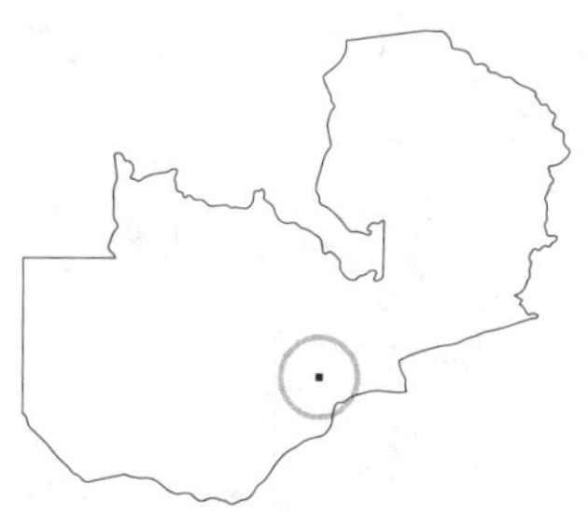

For many safari-goers, Lusaka is a necessary staging post to the country's many national parks. Despite the assertions of the tourist board, it's simply not high on Zambia's list of major attractions. Yet its wide, tree-lined boulevards can be pleasant and, like cities the world over, it holds a fascination because it is unmistakably cosmopolitan and buzzing. Home to almost one in five of Zambia's people, the capital has a discernible heartbeat. The traffic is chaotic and many of the suburbs are sprawling, but it is vibrant, boasts a few great hotels and has a booming restaurant scene. Lusaka is far and away the best place in the country to meet a cross-section of people and soak up modern African city life.

HISTORY

Lusaka is a relatively young capital city, dating only from 1935. Until then, the capital of Northern Rhodesia was Livingstone in the south of the country. As Zambia's mines were developed it was felt that the town was too far away from The Copperbelt, the country's industrial heartland.

The new capital was chosen for its central location, high plateau situation and relatively cooler climate. Lusaka was already a permanent settlement here, established as a camp for workers constructing the railway at the beginning of the 20th century. The new state buildings, however, were built on the ridge a couple of kilometres to the east of the railway on account of the frequency with which the lower-lying land was flooded during the annual rains. While it was anticipated that Lusaka's heart would eventually shift east, the capital remained firmly divided, with its spacious new administrative area contrasting with the bustle of the business area focused on Cairo Road. Now commercial developments and increasing levels of affluence have shifted the focus once again – blurring the traditional divide and opening up new areas both close to the centre and out towards the burgeoning suburbs.

LUSAKA *Orientation*

For listings, see from page 164

Where to stay

1 Latitude 15 .... G6
2 Radisson Blu E3
3 Shakespeare Court Serviced Apartments H7

Off map

Chaminuka Lodge H2
Ciêla Resort & Spa H2
Eureka Camping Park B7
Lilayi Lodge B7
Pioneer Lodge & Camp H2
Protea Hotel Safari Lodge B1
Wayside Guesthouse A7

Where to eat and drink

4 Bombay Lounge E3
5 Cantina H7
Chang Thai (see Acacia Park) E3
Latitude 15 .... (see 1)
Mint Café (see Arcades) E3
Mint Lounge (see Acacia Park) E3
Royal Dil (see Acacia Park) E3
6 Taste Tea Room & Brew Bar D3

Off map

Hana Saku H7
Il Portico H7
Sugarbush Café H7

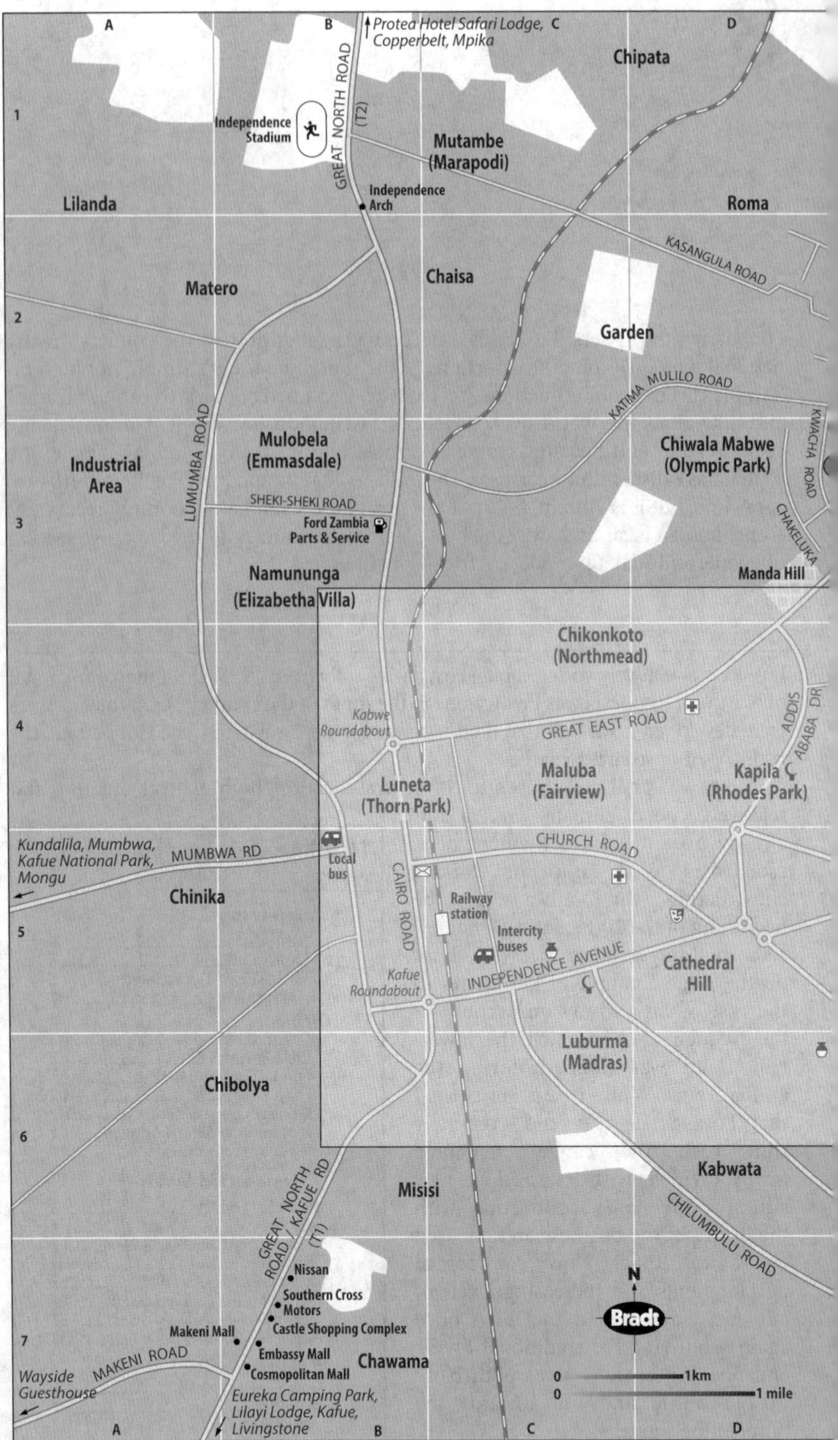

A
B
C
D
Protea Hotel Safari Lodge, Copperbelt, Mpika
Chipata
GREAT NORTH ROAD
(T2)
Independence Stadium
Mutambe (Marapodi)
Independence Arch
Lilanda
Roma
KASANGULA ROAD
Matero
Chaisa
Garden
KATIMA MULILO ROAD
LUMUMBA ROAD
Mulobela (Emmasdale)
Industrial Area
Chiwala Mabwe (Olympic Park)
KWACHA ROAD
SHEKI-SHEKI ROAD
Ford Zambia Parts & Service
CHAKELUKA
Namununga (Elizabetha Villa)
Manda Hill
Chikonkoto (Northmead)
Kabwe Roundabout
GREAT EAST ROAD
ADDIS ABABA DR
Maluba (Fairview)
Kapila (Rhodes Park)
Luneta (Thorn Park)
Kundalila, Mumbwa, Kafue National Park, Mongu
MUMBWA RD
Local bus
CHURCH ROAD
CAIRO ROAD
Chinika
Railway station
Intercity buses
INDEPENDENCE AVENUE
Cathedral Hill
Kafue Roundabout
Luburma (Madras)
Chibolya
Kabwata
Misisi
GREAT NORTH ROAD / KAFUE RD
(T1)
CHILUMBULU ROAD
Nissan
Southern Cross Motors
Castle Shopping Complex
Makeni Mall
Embassy Mall
Cosmopolitan Mall
Chawama
MAKENI ROAD
Wayside Guesthouse
Eureka Camping Park, Lilayi Lodge, Kafue, Livingstone
N
Bradt
0
1km
0
1 mile
1
2
3
4
5
6
7

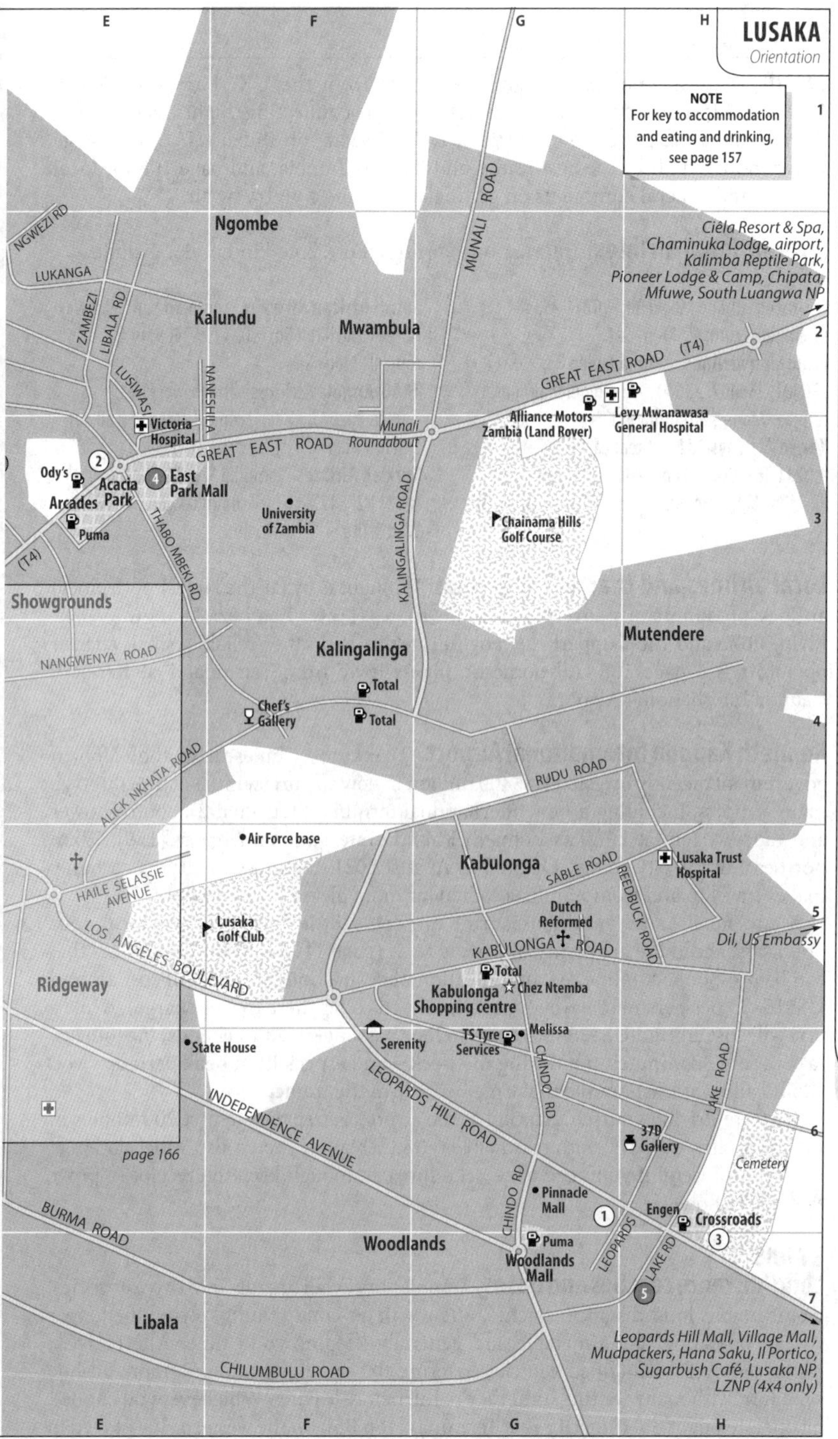
LUSAKA
Orientation
NOTE
For key to accommodation and eating and drinking, see page 157
Ngombe
Kalundu
Mwambula
Ciêla Resort & Spa, Chaminuka Lodge, airport, Kalimba Reptile Park, Pioneer Lodge & Camp, Chipata, Mfuwe, South Luangwa NP
GREAT EAST ROAD (T4)
MUNALI ROAD
NGWEZI RD
LUKANGA
ZAMBEZI
LIBALA RD
LUSIWASI
NANESHILA
Victoria Hospital
Munali Roundabout
Alliance Motors Zambia (Land Rover)
Levy Mwanawasa General Hospital
Ody's
Acacia Park
Arcades
Puma
East Park Mall
GREAT EAST ROAD
University of Zambia
THABO MBEKI RD
KALINGALINGA ROAD
Chainama Hills Golf Course
(T4)
Showgrounds
NANGWENYA ROAD
Kalingalinga
Mutendere
Total
Chef's Gallery
Total
ALICK NKHATA ROAD
RUDU ROAD
Air Force base
Kabulonga
SABLE ROAD
Lusaka Trust Hospital
REEDBUCK ROAD
HAILE SELASSIE AVENUE
Lusaka Golf Club
LOS ANGELES BOULEVARD
Dutch Reformed
KABULONGA ROAD
Dil, US Embassy
Ridgeway
Total
Kabulonga Shopping centre
Chez Ntemba
State House
Serenity
TS Tyre Services
Melissa
CHINDO RD
LAKE ROAD
LEOPARDS HILL ROAD
INDEPENDENCE AVENUE
37D Gallery
Cemetery
page 166
Pinnacle Mall
CHINDO RD
Engen
Crossroads
BURMA ROAD
Woodlands
Puma
Woodlands Mall
LEOPARDS
LAKE RD
Libala
Leopards Hill Mall, Village Mall, Mudpackers, Hana Saku, Il Portico, Sugarbush Café, Lusaka NP, LZNP (4x4 only)
CHILUMBULU ROAD
E
F
G
H
1
2
3
4
5
6
7

GETTING THERE AND AWAY

BY AIR There are no direct flights to Lusaka from the UK, Europe or North America. Most visitors from these regions use connecting flights via Nairobi (Kenya), Johannesburg (South Africa), Doha (Qatar) or Dubai (UAE). See page 99 for more details of the best routes and fares to Zambia, and page 108 for local airlines, and general comments on getting around the country by air.

International airlines

International airlines represented in Lusaka include:

Emirates Thabo Mbeki Rd; ☎ 0211 258484; **w** emirates.com; ⏲ Mon–Sat
Ethiopian Airlines Katima Mulilo Rd; ☎ 0211 236401, 236402, 236403; **w** ethiopianairlines.com; ⏲ Mon–Sat mornings
Kenya Airways/KLM Great East Rd; ☎ 0211 367200; **w** kenya-airways.com; ⏲ Mon–Sat mornings
South African Airways Southern Sun Ridgeway Hotel, Church Hill Rd; ☎ 0211 252409; **w** flysaa.com; ⏲ Mon–Sat
TAAG-Angola Airlines Thabo Mbeki Rd; ☎ 0978 402013; **w** taag.com; ⏲ Mon–Fri all day, Sun morning
Turkish Airlines Terminal 1, KKIA Airport; ☎ 0211 271127; **w** turkishairlines.com; ⏲ Mon, Wed & Thu

Local airlines and charter companies

Proflight is by far the largest of the local airlines, predominantly covering domestic routes (Lower Zambezi, Luangwa Valley, Livingstone and the Copperbelt). For full details and other reliable, small charter operators, see page 108. All domestic flights leave from Terminal 1 at Kenneth Kaunda International Airport.

Kenneth Kaunda International Airport

Thanks to a Chinese loan, the Zambian government recently invested US$400 million in new airport facilities at the country's main airports, including a new international terminal (Terminal 2), control tower and radar system at Lusaka's Kenneth Kaunda International Airport [159], 27km northeast of the city centre. Opened in August 2021, the modern airport certainly makes travel to and from Zambia's capital far more pleasant and efficient.

Many hotels and guesthouses run airport shuttle buses, as do local tour operators, and there are plenty of private taxis (page 111) and shuttle services that can be pre-booked online. As an indication of cost, a hotel shuttle will cost around US$15–35 per person one way (only a few hotels offer these free of charge), while a taxi will cost around US$25–50 for up to four passengers. At weekends, the journey takes about 30 minutes, but during the week – and especially at peak periods – you should allow at least double that time because of the traffic.

If you're driving yourself, parking at the airport is free for the first 20 minutes in the short-term car park, with reasonable rates thereafter. There's also a fuel station at the airport, useful if you need to refuel a hire car, though keep the receipt to prove that you've done so.

BY BUS

Long-distance coaches and buses

Zambia's buses fall broadly into two categories. Comfortable, long-distance coaches, often with air conditioning, plying the longer routes, operating to a timetable and generally keeping good time. Alternatively, rather less well-maintained vehicles covering the same ground, on a more ad-hoc schedule, with many waiting until they're full before leaving. Whichever you choose, all operate out of the **Intercity Bus Terminal** [166 B5], on the western side of Dedan

Kimathi Road, near the railway station. It's a noisy, bustling place, sheltering under a large purpose-built roof, and is *the* place to catch a bus to virtually any of Zambia's provincial or district capitals, even those that are quite isolated.

Locals are paranoid about thieves who frequent the area, so expect warnings about safety. Although it's best avoided at night, if you keep your wits about you, avoid showing valuables and keep a firm eye on your belongings, then you should have no problems. Be aware, though, that ticket touts can be quite aggressive in their bid for your custom, so be firm.

Despite the apparent confusion that greets you, there is some order to the terminal's chaos. The buses sitting in bays are grouped roughly by their eventual destinations, as indicated on the boards displayed next to the driver. If you can't see the name you want, then ask someone – most people will go out of their way to help, and the staff on the 24-hour information desk (☎ 0211 226676), something of an oasis in the centre of the terminal, are usually very helpful. While in theory you can phone for details of buses, in practice it's far better to turn up in person or book online in advance.

Coach operators Intercity bus travel is popular; there are several established operators –and always a few newcomers – so it's worth asking around and talking to the city's travel agents before booking anything. Reliable operators include:

CR Holdings m 0978 621148, 960517
Euro-Africa m 0977 772025, 311565
Juldan Motors m 0955 776315, 0965 732016; e info@juldanmotors.com
Mazhandu Family Bus Service m 0977 805064

Tickets It is best to buy **tickets** in advance, either at the terminus or online. There are often different prices, depending on the bus company, standard of the bus, and speed of service. Expect about a 20% premium for the better companies. Tickets are on sale at the bus station the day beforehand and at branches of PostNet Arcades, Manda Hill and Kabulonga malls. Some routes can be purchased online (w zambia.quickbus.com) or through mobile apps such as ZAMGO and Tafika Tickets.

Schedules The larger companies and Postbuses (page 110) run their buses to a timetable, but those operated by smaller companies may not leave until they are full, which can take hours. If this is the case, try to avoid paying until the bus has started on its way, as you may want to swap buses if another appears to be filling faster and hence is likely to depart earlier.

Buses to some destinations leave frequently, others weekly, according to demand; the best way to find out is to go to the bus station and ask. There are regular services between Lusaka and Livingstone (8hrs; US$9). The first departures tend to be early in the morning, around 05.00, and are fairly punctual. It's advisable to be there half an hour ahead of any listed departure time.

Postbus The Zambian Postal Service operates a reliable, scheduled passenger bus service that combines mail delivery with select intercity transport. Stopping only at post offices, the Postbuses run high-quality vehicles to a fixed timetable, so are generally quicker than the normal buses, and they tend to be less crowded too.

Tickets can usually be bought on the day of departure, but they're available up to seven days ahead, and it's advisable to pre-book by phone (m 0974 557764, 0976 118024) or in person. The ticket office in Lusaka is tucked behind the main post office on Cairo Road [166 B4] (🕘 05.00–17.00 Mon–Fri, 06.00–14.00 Sat–Sun), and tickets are also available at post offices along the various routes. Boarding starts half an hour prior to departure.

BY TRAIN Lusaka's railway station [166 B4] (Dedan Kimathi Rd) is just north of the bus station. The rail network is run by Zambia Railways and ordinary passenger trains have for many years been far too slow and totally impractical for travellers, but the Lusaka to Livingstone *Zambezi* train (formerly the *Golden Jubilee Express*) is the possible exception if time is relaxed and budgets limited. The *Zambezi*'s red carriages – refurbished from a past-life in South Africa – ply the intercity route once a week, with everything from clean economy seats to air-conditioned four-berth sleeper cabins, and an adequate restaurant car serving drinks and traditional Zambian food.

It's worth double-checking train times locally but at the time of writing the *Zambezi* leaves Lusaka on a Saturday morning around 07.30, arriving in Livingstone at an antisocial 02.00 the next morning. The return train departs Livingstone on Monday evening at 20.00, reaching Lusaka the following day around 13.30. One-way fares in different classes are K70, K80, K90 and – for a sleeper – K135. All tickets must be purchased at the station; there is no online-booking facility at the moment.

The regular TAZARA (Tanzania-Zambia Railway Authority) trains to Dar es Salaam, Tanzania have long been more efficient. Take note though, these trains depart from New Kapiri Mposhi station, 200km north of Lusaka. The 48-hour journey aboard their Mukuba Express Train departs Kapiri Mposhi at 16.00 every Tuesday, while the Ordinary Passenger train departs every Friday at 14.00. It's better to buy your TAZARA tickets (Express Service US$16/first class; US$13/second class) in Lusaka at Tazara House [166 B5] (Independence Av – entrance gate on Dedan Kimathi Road; **w** tazarasite.com; 🕘 07.30–16.30 Mon–Fri), before travelling to Kapiri Mposhi's hectic station. There's frequent public transport to Kapiri Mposhi from Lusaka as regular minibus and intercity buses pass through its centre on their way to the Copperbelt.

DRIVING FROM LIVINGSTONE For details of getting to Lusaka by road from Livingstone, see page 233.

ORIENTATION

Lusaka is a large, sprawling city. Its business heart was once the axis of Cairo Road, which runs roughly north–south: 4km long, about six lanes of traffic wide, and with a tree-lined island running like a spine down its centre. Parallel to Cairo Road, to the west, is Chachacha Road – a terminus for numerous local minibuses and home to the lively Central Market, while west again, on Lumumba Road, is the larger New City Market.

As the west of the city has become increasingly congested, many businesses have upped sticks and moved their head offices 4km east, clustering around the single-storey shopping mall, Arcades. Centred on Cathedral Hill and Ridgeway, this area is home to various government departments and international embassies, with the quiet and official air you find in the diplomatic and administrative districts of capitals around the world.

MAPS The abundance of smartphones with accurate navigation apps has reduced the need to purchase paper maps, especially if you're just passing though Lusaka en route to a safari. If you'll be using your smartphone to navigate, it's worth purchasing a local

SIM card and data bundle to avoid eye-watering bills; navigation apps use fantastic amounts of data very quickly!

If you're planning on doing any significant driving, we'd also recommend taking a traditional paper map and purchasing the excellent Tracks4Africa GPS map (w tracks4africa.co.za; page 103).

A limited selection of Zambia's most commonly used maps can often be found in one of the city's bookshops (page 173), or ordered online in advance of travel, while detailed maps covering the whole of Zambia can be bought from the main government map office at the Ministry of Lands (basement of Mulungushi Hse, cnr Independence Av & Nationalist Rd; 0211 250827/4; 08.00–17.00 Mon–Fri). To see what's in stock, browse through the maps in the entrance area before choosing. If you do not opt for the Tracks4Africa GPS map and are planning trips beyond Lusaka, and particularly off the main roads, we'd recommend that you buy a selection of the 1:250,000 series, or for serious expeditions, the more detailed 1:50,000 sheets. They're generally very good, though their information is inevitably dated.

GETTING AROUND

If you don't have your own vehicle, you'll need to use taxis or, for a distinctly local experience, the small minibuses operating between the outer suburbs and the centre. It's also possible to hire a car with a driver for a few hours or even the whole day; a hassle-free option that also allows the driver to act as a convenient guide for a short trip and gives flexibility to see the city and know your ride is always to hand. As the number of vehicles on the road has increased, traffic congestion has become a major problem in central Lusaka, especially in the mornings and evenings, so pick your journey times carefully.

BY TAXI Lusaka's legal, licenced taxis are light blue and white in colour, with a large number painted on their side. There are designated ranks at the city's major shopping malls. The vehicles are not metered but should have a rate sheet – you should ***always*** agree a rate for the journey before you get into the vehicle.

Dial-a-Cab (m 0966 222222, 0977 773937) is an established company offering a 24-hour, metered taxi service that can be booked by phone. There are now a couple of reliable, Uber-esque companies in Lusaka too, offering trackable, advanced booking of taxis from mobile Apps (IOS or Android): Ulendo Taxi (m 0976 692365) and Palm Ride Taxi (m 0978 916492).

BY MINIBUS These are the packed transport used by Lusaka's poorer commuters to travel between the outer, satellite suburbs and the city centre. Coloured blue with prominent orange side stripes, these minibuses weave through the traffic scene, fanning out from their bases at City Market [166 A4], the Kulima Tower on Freedom Way [166 A4], and Downtown, by the Kafue roundabout [166 B5]. The buses are all privately owned, and cover many different routes, so competition between them is fierce. Fares are low (exact change in kwacha only) reflecting the cramped seating and general lack of timetable – for the most part, buses leave town only when they are full. Minibuses do have regular stops – look for the roadside queues – but can sometimes just be flagged down if they're not full.

CAR HIRE The majority of Lusaka's car-hire companies cater to businesspeople visiting the city rather than tourists. Some offer only chauffeur-driven vehicles, with only time-and-mileage rates, which may be practical if you're in the city for a few days and want to avoid taxis. The larger companies and a handful of specialists offer quality 4x4 vehicle hire, which is absolutely essential for any travel in Zambia outside of the city.

Avis Airport Terminal 1, KKIA Airport; 0211 271020; m 0971 251448; e reservation@avis.co.za; w avis.co.za; 08.00–18.30 Sun–Fri, 09.00–14.00 Sat

Juls Africa 5507 Libala Rd, Kalundu; 0211 292942, 293972; e res@julstravel.co.zm; w julstravelzambia.com; 08.30–17.00 Mon–Fri, 08.30–14.00 Sat. Family-owned, Zambian company offering everything from saloon cars to 4x4s, either self-drive or chauffeur-driven.

Limo Car Hire 21 Lilayi Rd; 0211 278628; m 0977 743145; e limohirezambia@gmail.com; w limohire-zambia.com; 07.00–17.00 Mon–Fri, 08.30–noon Sat. Established, reliable company hiring saloon cars & 4x4s with roof tents, full camping kit & driver options.

Voyagers/Europcar 4015 Lagos Rd; 0211 375700, 253084; e rentals@voyagerszambia.com; w voyagerszambia.com, europcarzambia.com; 08.00–17.00 Mon–Fri, 08.00–11.00 Sat. Reliable Europcar franchise. 2WD & 4x4 vehicles, with or without a driver.

DRIVING YOURSELF Traffic in and around Lusaka can be chaotic and accidents are not infrequent. Speed limits on the roads around the city are strictly enforced, with an on-the-spot fine for infringements. The general speed limit is 50km/h in Lusaka and 100km/h outside the city limits, but do look out for variable speed limits and speed traps.

Parking on the streets is not a good idea unless you leave someone trustworthy in charge of the vehicle. Far more sensible is to use one of the guarded private car parks. Most hotels have secure, free parking, as do many restaurants and shopping complexes, including Levy Park, Manda Hill and the Arcades.

It is not advisable to drive at night in or around the city. Aside from pot-holes and the risk of car-jackings, you're likely to encounter vehicles without lights (especially around the time of the full moon), and, alarmingly, even people sleeping on the warm tarmac, a hazard that's said to be particularly common on the Great North Road.

There are numerous fuel stations throughout the city and more springing up on every corner, many with ATMs.

WHERE TO STAY

From large, international chain hotels to backpacker hostels, quaint lodges beyond the city suburbs to campsites for 4x4 self-drivers, and much more in between, Lusaka offers the raft of accommodation options. If budget allows, the pick of the bunch for city vibes is the funky boutique hotel Latitude 15.

Some visitors prefer the space and tranquillity offered by properties out of town – Lilayi, Pioneer, and Chaminuka (page 168) – and accept that these come with additional transport costs, while others are simply in Lusaka for a stopover between international flights and one of the national parks, in which case Ciêla Resort & Spa (page 165) is perfectly placed near the airport.

Those on a tight budget should choose their lodgings with care. Price is often a poor guide and the quality of the budget hotels and guesthouses varies considerably. Lusaka's cheap hotels and hostels are often seedy so you'll likely be better at one of the established backpackers' hostels or campsites listed.

If you're self-driving, the larger hotels in the city will offer secure overnight parking; alternatively, there are a couple of attractive options for those with tents who want to camp on the outskirts of town.

If you've more than a night and want somewhere to relax away from city bustle, then it's well worth seeking out one of the lovely lodges just outside of the city. With lush surrounds, often with gentle game wandering around, and plenty of space, they make a great spot to ease into a safari holiday or simply to chill before departing Zambia.

TOP END

✷ **Ciêla Resort & Spa** [159 H2] (249 rooms) Ngwerere Rd; 0211 433250; e reservations@cielaresort.com; w cielaresort.com. A super spot for late-night international arrivals, Ciêla is only 9km from the airport. Set on the lush Bonanza Estate, this contemporary Marriott resort offers well-equipped, minimalist rooms, efficient service & a host of on-site facilities: 4 restaurants, a pool, 18-hole golf course & spa. **$$$$$**

✷ **Latitude 15** [159 G6] 35F Leopards Ln, Kabulonga; 0211 268802–4; e 15@thelatitudehotels.com; w thelatitudehotels.com. Latitude 15's functional, Corbusier-style building gives no hint of what to expect inside: classy, contemporary & colourful, it's a feast for the eyes & very much the place to be seen. The 35 air-conditioned rooms & suites, some with pool-view balconies, are airy & light, their pale grey décor enlivened by plush soft furnishings & vibrant artwork. In the communal areas, African artefacts jostle for space with creative modern pieces, old Zanzibari doors do service as coffee tables, & sofas lie inside & out by a proper pool in tree-shaded gardens. At the cool bar, they'll mix you up a cocktail as fast as pouring you a beer, & the restaurant (page 170) is in a class of its own. The suburban location is quiet, yet the drive to the international airport takes only 30mins along back roads. **$$$$$**

Taj Pamodzi Hotel [167 E4] Addis Ababa Dr; 0211 254455; e pamodzi.lusaka@tajhotels.com; w tajhotels.com. The long-standing Taj Pamodzi offers a great level of comfort & service in the heart of the city. Its 193 rooms, some with balconies, have all the standard mod cons & those on the top floors have fine views. There's a swimming pool under pretty jacarda trees, a well-equipped fitness centre & spa, two restaurants & a consistently courteous staff. **$$$$$**

Radisson Blu Hotel [159 E3] (142 rooms) 19029 Great East Rd; 0211 368900; e info.lusaka@radissonblu.com; w radissonblu.com/hotel-lusaka. Light, contemporary & spacious, the Radisson is well positioned opposite the Arcades shopping mall (page 172), so close to shops, restaurants & cafés & the weekend curio market. Low-rise blocks of well-appointed rooms, along with a superb terraced pool, fitness centre with spa, secure parking for self drivers & excellent service make this a great city-centre choice. **$$$–$$$$$**

MID-RANGE

Southern Sun Ridgeway [167 E4] (155 rooms) Cnr Independence Av & Church Rd; 0211 251666; e res@southernsun.co.zm; w tsogosunhotels.com. The rooms here are comfortable, the service friendly & the atmosphere relaxed. There's an inviting garden swimming pool, an impressive masked weaver bird colony & a few small crocs resident in the central courtyard, & two dining spots: the more formal Musuku restaurant & the casual pub & terrace serving salads & 'pub grub' against a backdrop of TV sport. **$$$**

Stayeasy [166 B3] (130 rooms) Church Rd; 0211 372000; e res@stayeasylusaka.co.zm; w southernsun.com. Alongside Levy Park Mall, so convenient for the west of the city, Stayeasy is a budget-friendly bolthole offering clean, compact twin & dbl rooms, with contemporary bathrooms & standard mod cons. Outside, there's a small pool with lawns & shaded tables. **$$$**

LUSAKA *Centre*
For listings, see from page 164

Where to stay

1 Lusaka Backpackers.......................C3
2 Southern Sun Ridgeway................E4
3 Stayeasy...B3
4 Taj Pamodzi Hotel..........................E4

Where to eat and drink

5 3 Trees...F2
6 Marlin...G4
7 Rhapsody's.......................................G1
Vasilis (see Manda Hill Mall)..........F1
8 The Zambean Coffee Co................F2
Zoran Café (see Levy Park)............B3

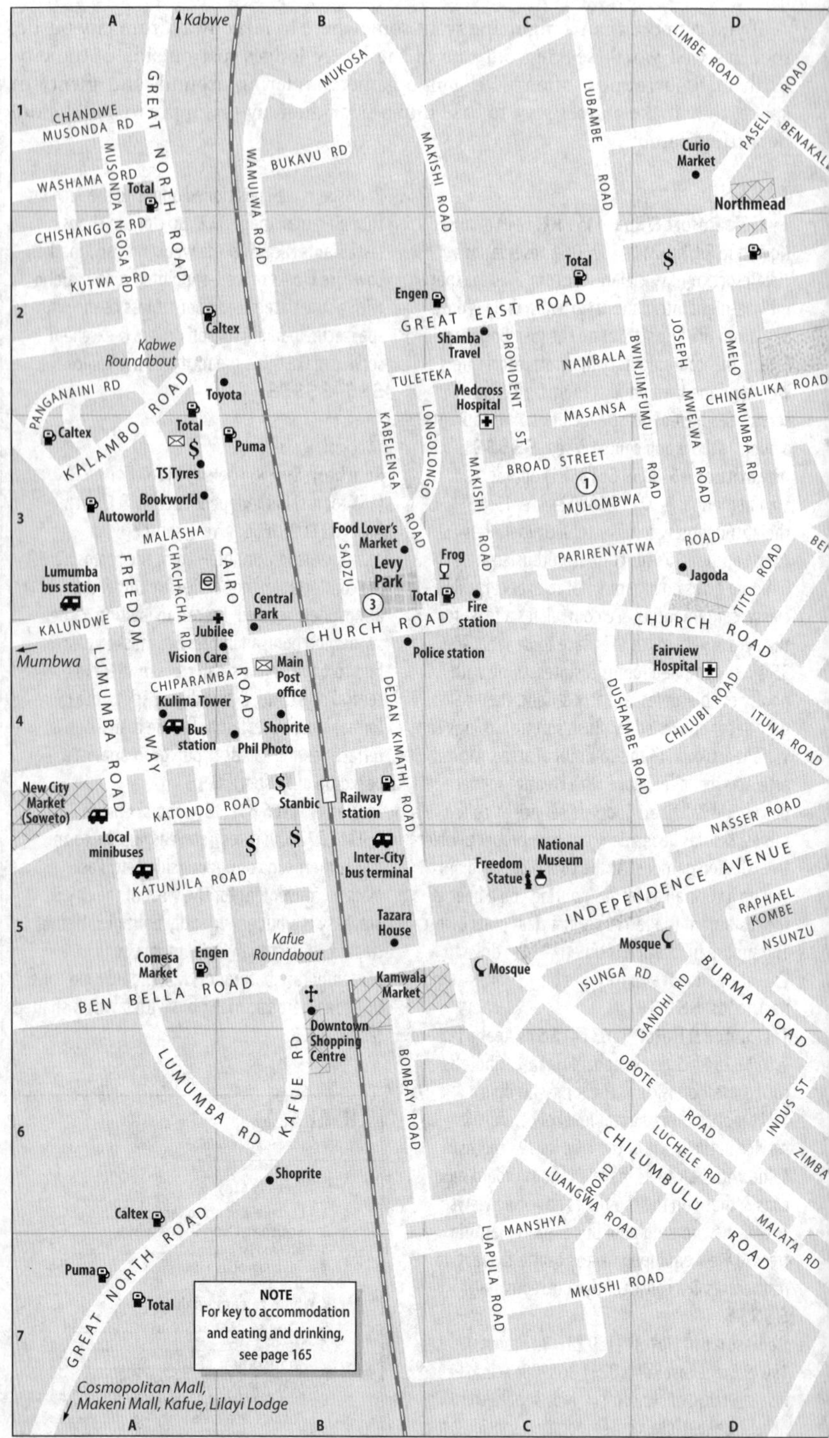
Kabwe
Mumbwa
Cosmopolitan Mall, Makeni Mall, Kafue, Lilayi Lodge
GREAT NORTH ROAD
GREAT EAST ROAD
CHURCH ROAD
INDEPENDENCE AVENUE
BEN BELLA ROAD
CAIRO ROAD
FREEDOM WAY
LUMUMBA ROAD
LUMUMBA RD
KAFUE RD
KALAMBO ROAD
Kabwe Roundabout
Kafue Roundabout
Curio Market
Northmead
Caltex
Toyota
Total
Puma
TS Tyres
Bookworld
Autoworld
Engen
Shamba Travel
Medcross Hospital
Food Lover's Market
Levy Park
Frog
Fire station
Police station
Central Park
Lumumba bus station
Jubilee
Vision Care
Main Post office
Kulima Tower
Bus station
Shoprite
Phil Photo
New City Market (Soweto)
Local minibuses
Stanbic
Railway station
Inter-City bus terminal
Freedom Statue
National Museum
Tazara House
Comesa Market
Kamwala Market
Downtown Shopping Centre
Mosque
Jagoda
Fairview Hospital
NOTE
For key to accommodation and eating and drinking, see page 165

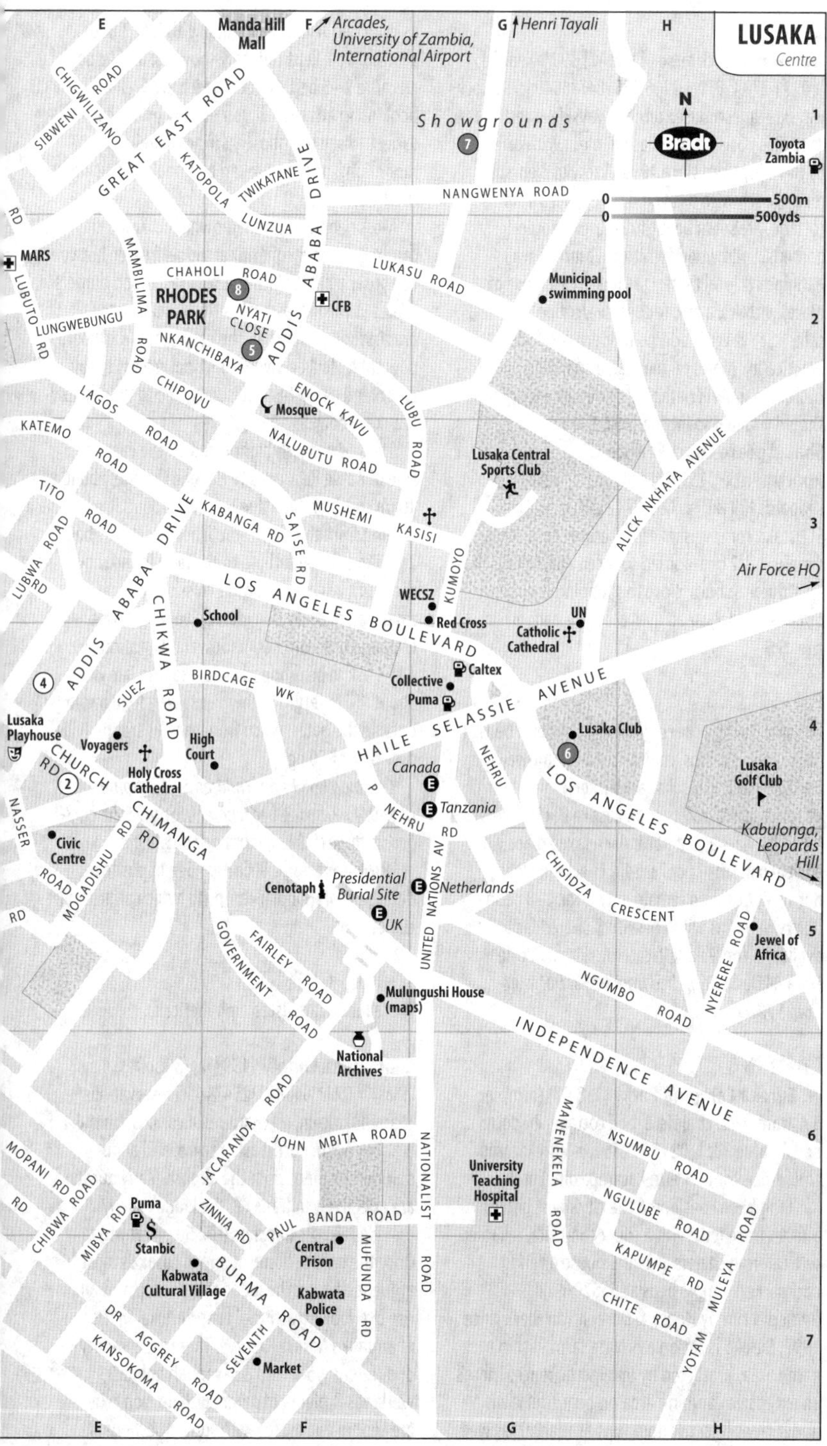
LUSAKA
Centre
Manda Hill Mall
Arcades, University of Zambia, International Airport
Henri Tayali
Showgrounds
Bradt
N
Toyota Zambia
0 500m
0 500yds
E
F
G
H
1
2
3
4
5
6
7
CHIGWILIZANO ROAD
SIBWENI
GREAT EAST ROAD
KATOPOLA
TWIKATANE
LUNZUA
ADDIS ABABA DRIVE
NANGWENYA ROAD
LUKASU ROAD
Municipal swimming pool
MARS
LUBUTO RD
MAMBILIMA ROAD
CHAHOLI ROAD
RHODES PARK
NYATI CLOSE
LUNGWEBUNGU
NKANCHIBAYA
CFB
CHIPOVU
Mosque
ENOCK KAVU
LUBU ROAD
LAGOS ROAD
KATEMO ROAD
NALUBUTU ROAD
Lusaka Central Sports Club
ALICK NKHATA AVENUE
TITO ROAD
KABANGA RD
SAISE RD
MUSHEMI
KASISI
KUMOYO
LUBWA RD
LOS ANGELES BOULEVARD
WECSZ
Red Cross
UN
Catholic Cathedral
Air Force HQ
School
CHIKWA ROAD
BIRDCAGE WK
Caltex
Collective
Puma
HAILE SELASSIE AVENUE
SUEZ
Lusaka Club
Lusaka Playhouse
Voyagers
Holy Cross Cathedral
High Court
NEHRU
Canada
Tanzania
P NEHRU RD
Lusaka Golf Club
CHURCH RD
CHIMANGA RD
NASSER RD
Civic Centre
MOGADISHU RD
ROAD
Kabulonga, Leopards Hill
CHISIDZA CRESCENT
Cenotaph
Presidential Burial Site
Netherlands
UK
UNITED NATIONS AV
Jewel of Africa
NYERERE ROAD
GOVERNMENT ROAD
FAIRLEY ROAD
NGUMBO ROAD
Mulungushi House (maps)
INDEPENDENCE AVENUE
National Archives
JACARANDA ROAD
JOHN MBITA ROAD
NATIONALIST ROAD
University Teaching Hospital
MANENEKELA ROAD
NSUMBU ROAD
MOPANI RD
CHIBWA ROAD
RD
Puma
Stanbic
MIBYA RD
ZINNIA RD
PAUL BANDA ROAD
NGULUBE ROAD
Central Prison
MUFUNDA RD
KAPUMPE RD
MULEYA ROAD
Kabwata Cultural Village
BURMA ROAD
Kabwata Police
CHITE ROAD
DR AGGREY ROAD
KANSOKOMA ROAD
SEVENTH
Market
YOTAM

BUDGET

Wayside Guesthouse [158 A7] 39 Makeni Rd; ☎ 0211 273439; m 0966 765184/860494; e info@wayside-guesthouse.com; w wayside-guesthouse.com. This oasis of calm has been run with care by Beverley Horn since 1998. A row of 8 en-suite rooms, each with a covered porch, & a 3-room cottage, are set in beautiful, mature tropical gardens. Solid wood furniture, Zambian wall-hangings & local fabric curtains give a sense of place, with AC, a fan, fridges, tea/coffee facilities, safe, DSTV & Wi-Fi adding modern comfort & practicality. Meals on request, a sparkling pool & tranquil parkland paths big enough for jogging should you feel so inclined. **$$$**

Shakespeare Court Serviced Apartments [159 H7] (24 rooms) 22882 Leopards Hill Rd; m 0979 742537; e Stay@SCLusaka.com; w shakespearecourt.com. Neat, simple, 1 & 2 bedroomed serviced apartments in an affluent suburb, close to shopping & dining options. A pool, small gym & secure parking on site. **$$**

HOSTELS

Lusaka Backpackers [166 C3] (26 dorm beds, 4 dbl rooms, 2 cabins, chalet) 161 Mulombwa Cl; m 0977 805483; e lusakabackpackers@gmail.com; w lusakabackpackers.com. Lusaka Backpackers (aka Chachacha) is a naturally relaxed place with a lively bar, small pool & 24hr check-in. Clean dorms – including female only – for 4–8 people, dbl/twin rooms with en-suite & shared facilities available. There's a self-catering kitchen, café & travel desk. *Dorm bed from US$8; Dbl room from $18.*

CAMPING

✷ **Eureka Camping Park** [158 B7] (camping, 4 A-frames, 13 chalets, 5-bed cottage, 26 dorm beds) Kafue Rd; ☎ 0211 272351; e eurekacamp.zm@gmail.com; w eurekacamp.com. Eureka has long been considered the city's best bet for budget travellers, with a super campsite, reliable self-catering chalets & a bunkhouse offering backpackers simple beds at US$20/night. Owned & run by Henry & Doreen van Blerk since 1992, Eureka is set on a private farm within a game area, protected by an electric fence. There's an extensive camping area on beautiful lawn under trees (electric hook-ups available), as well as thatched A-frame chalets, with 2 or 3 beds, sharing well-kept toilets & showers, and larger en-suite 2–5 bed chalets, which are well worth booking in advance. If you do stay under canvas, expect to see the ghostly stripes of zebra by moonlight, or to be woken by impala browsing the trees.

Most people bring their own food, using the camp's kitchen & communal fridge/freezer, but you can order a hearty farmhouse b/fast, good burgers & pies at the bar, as well as fresh meat for the *braai*, wood & charcoal. The easy chairs, dartboard, pool table, fenced swimming pool & a volleyball court lend a laid-back, leisurely vibe to this reliably low-key spot.

The site is clearly signposted on the eastern side of Kafue Rd, opposite Baobab College, about 10km south of the Kafue Rd roundabout. If you're coming from the south, you'll need to drive about 2km beyond the turning to the next roundabout, then turn back, as you can't cross the central reservation. If you don't have a vehicle, take a Chilanga bus from Kulima Tower bus station [166 A4] & ask to be dropped at Eureka; the fare is about K5. To return to town, just wait for a minibus outside the gates. A taxi from the bus station will cost about K50 pp.

Camping US$14 pp (children $7); A-frame US$40/45 2-bed/3-bed; chalet US$60/75 2-bed/3-bed; cottage US$125; dorm bed US$20 pp.

✷ **Pioneer Lodge & Camp** See opposite for details of this popular campsite, which offers smart chalets, too.

LODGES OUTSIDE TOWN

These lodges are listed alphabetically.

Chaminuka Lodge [159 H2] (30 suites; 4 villas) ☎ 0211 840883/254146; e reservations@chaminuka.com; w chaminuka.com. Chaminuka is about 50km northeast of town, and about half that distance from the airport. Many guests are effectively in transit & the lodge usually provides airport transfers (US$50 pp return). Once the private home of one of Lusaka's most affluent citizens, the lodge stands atop a small rise overlooking artificial Lake Chitoka, in the Chaminuka Nature Reserve. There are a variety of different woodland & savannah habitats, wetlands & plenty of game. Buffalo, lion & hyena are kept in enclosures with some questionable opportunities for guests to feed the lions through the fence wires.

Chaminuka is said to house the country's largest collection of traditional & contemporary Zambian art, alongside a small spa, 3 conference centres & plenty of leisure facilities and activities. Accommodation is in square, red-brick chalets & 4 self-contained villas. ♛♛

✷ **Lilayi Lodge** [158 B7] (12 chalets) ☎ 0211 840435/6; m 0971 002010; e reservations@lilayi.com; w lilayi.com. Situated on a 650ha farm criss-crossed with game-viewing roads, Lilayi is one of the most pleasant of the more upmarket options close to Lusaka, though you'll need your own transport to get there.

Lilayi means 'place of rest', & the name is apt: cool green lawns are dotted with comfortable, well-furnished brick chalets. 10 of these are suites, with a bedroom, spacious lounge, & en-suite bath, shower & toilet; the others have 2 en-suite bedrooms off a small, shared lounge. The main building has a good-sized bar & restaurant overlooking a large pool, plus an upstairs lounge. The à-la-carte menu ($$$$) includes daily specials such as venison, & is sometimes complemented by an outdoor braai and there's a new wine-tasting experience on offer, featuring Lilayi's own-label bottles from Stellenbosch, South Africa.

The farm has been well stocked with most of Zambia's antelope, including some of the less common species like roan, defassa waterbuck, tsessebe & giraffe, & boasts a good range of bird species. So if you failed to sight something in one of the parks, walk around here for a few hours or ask to be taken on a game drive, guided walk or even a run on the purpose-made trails. **$$$$$**, ♛♛♛

✷ **Pioneer Lodge & Camp** [159 H2] (11 chalets, 2 tents, cottage, camping) Palabana Rd; m 0966 432700; e mail@pioneercampzambia.com; w pioneercampzambia.com. Run by owner Paul Barnes, Pioneer is located in a wooded area just outside Lusaka, only 20mins' drive from the airport. The accommodation at Pioneer is closer to that of a safari lodge than the city hotels, with 2 safari-style walk-in tents with a thatch covering, 2 basic chalets, a couple of 3-bed thatched chalets sharing a toilet & shower; 2 family chalets of a similar standard with their own facilities; a large, self-contained 2-bedroom cottage sleeping up to 6; & 7 twin 'luxury' chalets, located on the edge of the site & facing east to catch the sunrise. These last are a cut above the others: spacious & well designed, each with an en-suite bathroom; one is built of natural stone under high thatch, cool & dark, with a toilet & stone bath discreetly tucked behind a solid screen of the same material. Campers remain welcome, with a large shady campsite with a clean ablution block, & a small, fenced pool – all in about 12ha of woodland surrounded by a discreet electric fence, beyond which is a 6km walking trail. The camp's rural location means that you'll wake to the sound of Heugelin's robin rather than the blare of a horn.

The large, thatched bar area is the focus for a real mix of travellers, which makes for plenty of interesting conversation. There are comfy chairs aplenty, & a small sat TV. Snacks & meals are on hand, with a full b/fast (*around US$5*), & dinner (*US$10*), with the huge steaks being a speciality. Fridge/freezer space is available, as are laundry facilities. With its rural location close to the airport, Pioneer is a good choice for the first or last night of a safari holiday. *'Safari' chalet US$60 pp sharing B&B, or US$160 dinner, B&B, inc airport transfers; 3-bed chalet US$80 pp B&B. Cottage US$200 (6 people, exc b/fast). Camping US$10 pp.* **$$**

Protea Hotel Safari Lodge [158 B1] (60 rooms) Chisamba; ☎ 0211 252384; e reservations@phsafarilodge.co.zm; w proteahotels.com. This safari-style Protea stands in a 12km² private game reserve of rolling bush about 45km north of Lusaka.

A large, thatched roof shelters the lounge, bar & Mutete restaurant, which extends out onto a large terrace overlooking the gardens. The food is good, popular among Lusaka's more affluent residents for the buffet Sun lunch.

The original, high-ceilinged bedrooms are with views across the lawns from a private veranda. They're well kitted out & all have en-suite bathrooms with marble tops, bath & a separate (powerful) shower. Larger suites or family rooms are constructed in pairs, each with 2 bunks in a separate area & the option of interlinking rooms. Outside, beautiful herbaceous borders surround a patio & swimming pool area with plentiful sunloungers, as well as a network of lawns. Beyond lies a wilderness area, including a lake (in the rainy season), which is home to a wide range of wildlife. I've watched a memorable flock of Abdim's stork during the wet season here, but the grass was too high (& lunch too good) to go out searching for game, though you'd expect to find zebra, warthogs, reedbuck, puku, kudu & impala among other common game. More surprising is the presence of Lichtenstein's hartebeest, tsessebe, oribi, sable, Kafue lechwe, eland & sitatunga. Clearly it's worth exploring during the dry season, either on a game drive (*US$16 pp*) or by quad bike (*US$25 pp*), or on one of 2 short walking trails. A lion enclosure houses 2 resident lions, a male & a female, while even more prominent are various hand-reared antelope, including a bushbuck. **$$$$**

WHERE TO EAT AND DRINK

Like cities the world over, Lusaka has its fair share of dining highlights these days. Chic restaurants serve global cuisine from tacos to fillet steak and it's now possible to pick between French fine dining and family-run Italian trattorias. For something more casual, cool, organic cafés and ubiquitous fast food chains have appeared in abundance across the city over recent years, with many of the former being a real delight.

If you're on a tight budget or catering for yourself, see page 172 for details of the various shopping options.

RESTAURANTS Almost every ethnic cuisine is catered for (frequently in the same venue) and with a range of standards to match. If you're looking for somewhere special, then informed opinion gives Lusaka's top spots for foodies as Marlin and Latitude 15. Many of the better hotels have decent food and good service, making them an easy option for visitors, but it's fair to say that there are often more interesting alternatives within relatively easy reach and taxis are easily arranged by every hotel.

The restaurants listed here can get very busy – especially on Friday and Saturday nights – so it's wise to book in advance.

Bombay Lounge [159 E3] East Park Mall, Great East Rd & Thabo Mbeki Rd; m 0960 942164; ⌚ noon–22.30 daily. In addition to its original restaurant base in East Park Mall, this family-run Indian also has outlets in the city's Woodlands & Pinnacle shopping centres. Serving authentic coal-fired tandoori kebabs, beaten copper bowls of pilau, spicy masalas & mango lassi. **$$$**

Cantina [159 H7] 8818 Lake Rd, Woodlands; m 0972 949900; e ronishjoory@icloud.com; w cantinalsk.com; ⌚ noon–14.30 & 15.00–22.00 Tue–Sat. A Mexican gem! Tasty tacos loaded with fresh flavours, homemade tortillas with fresh guacamole & salsa, tempting sharing plates of crayfish ceviche & ginger-fried chicken, decent cocktails & chocolatey churros. **$$–$$$$**

✷ **Latitude 15** [159 G6] See page 165; ⌚ 06.00–10.30, noon–15.00, 18.00–22.00 daily. The restaurant at Latitude 15 shares some of the whackiness of the hotel – check out the dreadlock light fittings! – but the menu is altogether more serious. From tables inside & out on tree-shaded lawns, indulge in the likes of spice-rubbed pork fillet with tzatziki, romesco sauce, roast potatoes & seasonal veg. There are plenty of innovative salads, too, some home grown, as well as cosmopolitan takes on fish, steak & chicken, & options such as Thai jungle curry. Service is friendly, if rather erratic. **$$$$–$$$$$**

Rhapsody's [167 G1] The Showgrounds, Nangwenya Rd; ☎ 0211 256705; e lusaka@rhapsody.co.za; w rhapsodys.co.za; ⌚ 08.00–22.00 daily. With its large semi-circular bar, varnished brickwork, & open girders, Rhapsody's is often buzzing – especially on Fri nights. The restaurant serves steaks, salads, sushi & popular chicken *espetadas* on hanging skewers. **$$$–$$$$$**

Chang Thai [159 E3] Acacia Park; ☎ 0211 258425; m 0975 835999; ⌚ noon–22.30 Sun–Thu, noon–23.00 Fri/Sat. An unlikely find in Lusaka, Chang Thai is at its best in the evening when soft lighting & candles illuminate the warmth of the interior. The food is surprisingly good, the staff efficient & friendly, & there's a take-away service too. $$$–$$$$

✷ **Marlin** [167 G4] Lusaka Club, nr cnr of Los Angeles Bd & Haile Selassie Av, Longacres; ☎ 0211 252206; m 0966 765462, 0979 627546; ⌚ noon–14.30, 18.30–22.00 Mon–Sat. At the back of the old sports club, this apparently uninspiring place serves some of the best (& best-value) food in town. The sizeable pepper steaks are renowned (ask for a 'lady's steak' if you're not up for it), or try the superb crab tom yam soup. Salads, chow meins & stir fries are always good, & the service is professional & discreet. Booking strongly advised. $$$–$$$$

Royal Dil [159 E3] Acacia Park; ☎ 0211 841015; m 0974 566878; ⌚ noon–23.00 daily. Central & welcoming, serving fresh & tasty Indian dishes. The veranda area is favoured for comfort. $$$–$$$$

Zoran Café [166 B3] Levy Park; m 0966 060347, 0979 060374; ⌚ 10.00–22.00 daily. Upstairs in Levy Park, with more tables on the balcony, the Karaleic family brings Serbian cuisine to a cosmopolitan menu. Daily specials such as Serbian *muchkalica* (slow-cooked pork) & psychedelic-coloured cocktails. $$$

Il Portico [159 H7] Leopards Hill Rd; m 0977 700468. A little out of town in 'The Village Mall', expats & locals alike head here for the excellent wood-fired pizzas, lasagne & steaks. It gets busy at the weekend so it's worth booking, & there's live music on Wed & at the w/end. $$–$$$

Mint Lounge [159 E3] Acacia Park; ☎ 0978 507030; e mint.lounge.cafe@gmail.com; f MintLoungFood; ⌚ 08.00–21.30 daily. Lusaka's buzzword for healthy eating, Mint Lounge is a great lunchtime venue & a good spot for sundowners. Informal, cool & with inside & outside seating, it's a must for burgers, salads, wraps, cakes or a late b/fast. $$–$$$

CAFÉS, PUBS AND LIGHT MEALS Café culture has produced a flurry of hip, laid-back places to eat around Lusaka, with new places opening frequently. Reasonably priced, freshly made, wholesome food is easy to come by, with all the places listed here worth a visit.

✷ **3 Trees** [167 F2] 4 Nkanchibaya Rd; m 0978 728652; ⌚ 07.30-17.00. Behind sage green walls & neat palms, 3 Trees is a great city-centre hideaway. A bustling garden café, with laid-back music, animated chatter & umbrella-shaded tables under beautiful frangipani & jacaranda trees. From all-day breakfasts to salads, burgers & even sushi, it's casual, consistent & reasonably priced. A fine line in homemade cakes & freshly squeezed juices are on offer: try the caramel velvet gateau. Halal meat; no alcohol served. $$–$$$$

Hana Saku [158 H7] Leopards Hill Rd; m 0955 402617; e hanasaku.arigato@gmail.com; f SushiSakeSalmonSouzaiYa; ⌚ noon–17.00 Mon–Fri, 08.00–15.00 Sat. Run by a gracious Japanese owner, Yuka, this small, low-key restaurant serves up authentic sushi & sake at long timber tables. Take-away bento boxes available. $$$

Mint Café [159 E3] Arcades; m 0965 900800; ⌚ 08.00–21.00 Sun–Thu, 08.00–21.30 Fri/Sat. This stylish little café is modern & minimalist. Stop for light meals – salads, wraps & sandwiches – smoothies & fresh juices – or head for its more grown-up sibling, Mint Lounge, at Acacia Park. $$

✷ **Sugarbush Café** [159 H7] Leopards Hill Rd; m 0967 648761; ⌚ 08.00–17.00 Tue–Sun. One of the new generation of out-of-town cafés, Sugarbush invites leisurely lunches. Spilling out from the lovely Lightfoot leather shop, its shady tables are set in lavender-lined gardens filled with white irises. Pull up a wicker chair on the pretty bougainvillea-shaded terrace and order from the regularly changing menu of homemade favourites: pancakes, quiche, hearty lasagne & pies. $–$$

Taste Tea Room & Brew Bar [157 D3] 6293 Kwacha Rd, Olympia; m 0975 000247; e thetastefam@gmail.com; ⌚ 09.00–18.00 Tue–Thu, 09.00–22.00 Fri & Sat. From an extensive array of global tea to weekend live music sets by local Zambian artists, Taste is a peaceful, laid-back spot serving lunch & cocktails alongside home décor & holistic lifestyle gifts. $–$$

The Zambean Coffee Co [167 F2] 6 Nyati Cl; ⌚ 09.00–16.00 Mon–Sat. Tables inside & out in a quiet garden offer a relaxed setting for this unassuming café. Enjoy a freshly ground coffee or a glass of South African wine, with tasting notes, backed up by 'gourmet' sandwiches (think smoked chicken with honey wholegrain mustard, rocket, pecan nuts & avocado). Delicious cakes – especially the carrot cake – add to the treats, & there's free Wi-Fi. $–$$

Vasilis [167 F1] Manda Hill Mall; ⌚ 08.00–20.00 daily. Take a break from shopping for coffee & cakes or pizza & baguettes at this modern café-cum-bakery. $

ENTERTAINMENT AND NIGHTLIFE

For delicious drinks in a stylish setting, the lobby bar at **Latitude 15** (page 170) is a great spot, as is 'The Other Side' where hotel guests are welcome to drink and enjoy the weekly live music performances. **Il Portico** (page 171) has a live band on Friday and Saturday nights. Lively **O'Hagans** Irish pub (Woodlands Mall; 0211 262156) hosts a band on Thursday nights, as does the Intercontinental Hotel (Haile Selassie Ave; 0211 250000). The Misty Jazz Restaurant (Levy Mall, Church Rd; 0211 234121; m 0972 460116; ⌚ noon–23.00 daily) is a long-standing live-music venue (from jazz to DJ sets) complete with cocktail bar and cosy dining.

For live, local music, like Zambian kalindula guitars, and African DJ sets, **Chef's Gallery** [159 F4] (Alick Nkhata Rd) is the current hotspot.

SHOPPING

While Lusaka's traditional, vibrant **markets** (page 177) continue to thrive, and are well worth a visit if you have the time, it is the ubiquitous shopping malls that now take centre stage in the retail sector.

The complex at **Manda Hill** [167 F1] (w shopmandahill.com), on the Great East Road, revolutionised shopping in Lusaka when it was first opened. Modern and clean, with plenty of parking and a conspicuous security presence, it became the preferred place to shop for both visitors and many local people. It now offers two-storey parking and feels exactly like any shopping mall in the West. Come on a Saturday afternoon and you'll see Lusaka's fashionistas seeking out the latest trends alongside families doing the week's grocery shopping.

A stone's throw to the east, on the other side of the road, the **Arcades** complex [159 E3] (f Arcades.Shopping.Centre) has more of an entertainment and restaurant bias, but it still offers a range of shops, including music and video stores and a SuperSpar supermarket. There's also a weekend curio market, popular for souvenir shopping (page 174), a petrol station and round-the-clock guarded parking.

The most central of the city malls is **Levy** [166 B3] (f levyshoppingmall), widely known as Levy Park, which – with its mix of shops, restaurants, cafés, cinema and hotel – is breathing new life into the western side of the city.

In the wealthier suburbs, smaller shopping complexes include **Crossroads** at Leopards Hill [159 H6], **Woodlands** [159 G7], and the more established Kabulonga [159 G5]. To the south, **Makeni Mall** [158 B7] and Cosmopolitan Mall [158 B7] offer fast-food chains, supermarkets and an array of banks, tech and clothing shops.

Shops at Lusaka's malls are usually open Monday to Friday, from around 09.00 to 18.00, but at weekends, most shops close earlier, especially on Sunday when midday or early afternoon is the norm. Shops elsewhere in the city are usually closed on a Sunday.

FOOD AND SUPPLIES Fresh fruit and vegetables can of course be picked up from local markets (page 177) and various street stalls. Most of Lusaka's visitors tend to stick to one of the large **supermarkets** though, which are similar to those found in Europe or America. Sizeable supermarkets – Shoprite, PicknPay, SuperSpar, Woolworths – can be found in all of the large shopping malls (see opposite). There are some smaller alternatives, including:

Food Lover's Market [166 B3] Levy Park. A good bet, with good quality, seasonal vegetables, meat, bread & hot food to take away.

Melisa Supermarket [166 D1] Great East Rd, Northmead; [159 G5] Chindo Road, near Kabulonga shopping centre. Small, well-established Lusaka chain, & one of the best. More expensive than its larger rivals, its high-quality produce & on-site bakery make it popular with expats & more affluent locals alike. A great place to stock up for a road trip.

BOOKS AND MUSIC

Bookworld [167 F1] Manda Hill; [166 A3] Cairo Rd; [159 G5] Arcades; [159 G6] Pinnacle; [158 B7] Cosmopolitan; ☎ 0211 225282, 268329, 274591, 255470. Zambia's largest book and stationery chain, Bookworld can be found in many of Lusaka's larger malls (Manda Hill has the flagship) and is *the* place for a wider range of literary interests, including Zambian literature & poetry, flora and fauna field guides, and road maps.

Sounds [159 E3] Arcades; [159 H6] Crossroads. A reasonable selection of music CDs and some headphones.

CAMPING AND OUTDOOR EQUIPMENT Most of the basic outdoor equipment can be found at **Game** [167 F1] (Manda Hill) or [158 B7] (Cosmopolitan Mall).

African Wild Track [159 E3] East Park Mall; m 0977 617416. For an extensive selection of fishing tackle & a range of branded outdoor essentials from walking boots to GPSs.

Mudpackers [159 H7] Leopards Hill Business Park; m 0975 869007; ⏲ 08.00–16.30 Mon–Fri. A specialist 4x4 & camping outfitter offering advice & quality equipment, including gas canisters & refilling.

CAR REPAIRS AND SPARES As spare parts have become more readily available, so vehicle repairs have become more straightforward to arrange here. Specialist dealers with service centres and parts include:

Alliance Motors Zambia (Land Rover) [159 G7] 38717 Great East Rd, Chainama; m 0971 245459

Ford Zambia Parts & Service (CFAO) [6a B3] Sheki-Sheki Rd; m 0972 190160; w ford.vehicle-centre-zambia.com

Southern Cross Motors (Mercedes & Mitsubishi) [158 B7] Kafue Rd; ☎ 0211 844780; w southerncross.co.zm

Toyota Zambia [166 A2] Cairo Rd; ☎ 0211 229109, 229113; m 0971 268000; w toytazambia.co.zm

Many fuel stations will be able to help with replacing tyres and more general spares. Alternatively, try:

Autoworld [158 B4] Downtown Mall, Kafue Rd; ☎ 0211 223207, 237716, 237719; e info@autoworld.zm; w autoworldzm.com; ⏲ check website – opening hours vary by branch & day. HQ at Downtown Mall with other outlets on Lumumba Rd, Cairo Rd, Freedom Way & at Woodlands Mall. Reliable operation handling servicing & basic repairs, & with Sun opening at Woodlands and Freedom Way.

TS Tyre Services [166 A3] Cairo Rd; ☎ 0211 235901; m 0979 833291; e sciarrino1973@gmail.com; [167 E3] Embassy Mall, Kafue Rd; & in [159 G5] Kabulonga, next to the Melisa Supermarket; ⏲ 07.30–21.00 Mon–Sat, 08.00–20.00 Sun; book appointment via f TS.TyreSevices (sic).

CRAFTS, CURIOS AND GIFTS For typical African carvings, basketware and curios, you probably won't get better value or a wider selection than at Kabwata Cultural Village (page 178). Every Sunday a regular outdoor curio market is held at the Arcades [159 E3], or you could try the small craft market at the back of the outdoor market at Northmead [166 D1], opposite Melisa Supermarket (park at the supermarket), which sells some good malachite bracelets, necklaces and a wide selection of carvings.

Specialist shops afford the opportunity to browse at leisure, without the hassle of bargaining. There are also some wonderful ethical collectives and individuals driving quality and empowerment through Zambian crafts.

37D Gallery [159 H6] 37d Middleway, Kabulonga; m 0973 006919; e curator@thestartfoundationtrust.org; ⌚ 09.00–17.00 Mon–Fri, 10.00–15.00 Sat. A smart, contemporary gallery showcasing fine art & sculpture from emerging & established artists with a Zambian connection. 25% of art sales go directly to the gallery's stART Foundation charity, dedicated to encouraging development & creativity in young, disadvantaged Zambians.

✷ **Collective** [167 6G] Los Angeles Bd (behind Longacres Market); m 0969 307286, 0968 975964; w lusakacollective.com; ⌚ 09.00–16.30 Mon–Fri, 10.00–14.00 Sat. Super, ethically minded souvenir shop in the heart of Lusaka, with smaller outlets at the Wildlife Discovery Centre (page 180) & Lusaka airport. From monochrome lino prints to delicious organic honey, shaggy woven lampshades to intricate basketry – & so much more! – the Lusaka Collective is a curated collection of artisan produced souvenirs from around Zambia. A wonderful treasure-trove of handmade design.

Jagoda Gems [159 H6] 37d Middleway, Kabulonga; ☎ 0211 220814; w jagodagems.com. Long-established specialists with experience in sourcing genuine Zambian gemstones and creating original pieces of jewellery.

Jewel of Africa [167 E5] 8 Nyerere Rd; ☎ 0967 750777; e rashmisharma@jewelofafrica.com; w jewelofafrica.com; ⌚ 09.00-18:00 Mon–Fri, 10.30–13.30 Sat. With 3 branches in Lusaka & outlets at Lusaka & Livingstone airports, Jewel are an established & accredited Zambian jewellery supplier.

Lightfoot Zambia [159 H7] Sugarbush Farm, Leopards Hill Rd; m 0978 047773; w lightfootzambia.com; ⌚ 08.00-17.00 daily. Hand-crafted Zambian leather handbags, made at the on-site workshop. Stylish & original, they can be made up to order. Jewellery, fabric toys, gorgeous textiles, bespoke furniture (can be shipped) & ethnic home accessories are a feast for the eyes & make excellent souvenirs.

OPTICIANS

Phil Opticians ☎ 0955 250430; w philopticians.com. 10 branches across Lusaka's largest shopping malls, inc Leopards Hill Mall [167 H7] m 0956 562774; Arcades [159 E3] ☎ 0211 250430; Crossroads [159 H6] & Woodlands [159 G7].

Vision Care Opticians ☎ 0970 200008; w visioncarezambia.com. 8 branches across Lusaka, inc Manda Hill Mall [167 F1]; East Park Mall [159 E3]; Levy Park [166 B3].

PHARMACIES

Bell Pharmacy [159 G5] Kabulonga Mall; ☎ 0779 600643

Jubilee Chemist ☎ 0211 255556/7, 265331, 238216. Branches at Cairo Rd [166 A4], Crossroads [159 H6].

Link ☎ 0211 231124, 324011; w linkpharmacy.co.zm. Well-established, efficient pharmacy with branches at Manda Hill [167 F1], Arcades [159 E3], Levy Park [166 B3], Woodlands [159 G7] & East Park [159 F3].

PHOTOGRAPHIC AND COMPUTER SUPPLIES

Computer Express Carousel Mall, Lumumba Rd; ☎ 0211 225035; e sales@compex.co.zm; w compex.co.zm; f ComPexLsk. Computer, laptop & business-tech hardware & accessories.

Phil Photo [166 B4] Cairo Rd; 0211 225572; branches at Manda Hill [167 F1]; Arcades [159 E3] & Crossroads [159 H6]. Phil's sells cameras, memory cards, etc, & offers a printing service.

BANKS AND CHANGING MONEY

BANKS For most visitors, the banks and ATMs at Manda Hill, Arcades, Levy Park and almost all other shopping complexes are the most convenient. There is a Barclays ATM at the Southern Sun Ridgeway and ATMs are installed in many supermarkets and fuel stations.

CHANGING MONEY Use any bank or a bureau de change to change money wherever possible; otherwise stick to a hotel – though these generally offer poor rates of exchange and charge steep commissions. Wherever you change money, don't forget to take passport ID with you.

COMMUNICATIONS

INTERNET Wi-Fi is readily available across Lusaka, and is free of charge in most of the better hotels and guesthouses, as well as restaurants and cafés. Some of the larger hotels also have dedicated business centres with internet facilities.

POST AND TELEPHONE Lusaka's busy main **post office** is in the centre of Cairo Road [166 B4]. If you're just looking for stamps, it's probably quicker to go to one of the smaller post offices around the city. There's parking behind the post office (K2), though you can expect a bit of hassle from touts here.

Both the main post office and the one at Ridgeway have a bureau de change where rates are on a par with those of the banks.

The major **mobile-phone** providers have countless branches throughout the city. Top-up cards are easily available from shops, garages and street vendors at major road junctions.

COURIERS If you need to send something valuable or ship large souvenirs, a courier is far more reliable than the postal service. Lusaka's main couriers are:

DHL (Zambia) 3039 Makishi Rd; 0211 376400; w dhl.co.zm
FedEx Enock Kavu Rd; 0216 221411; w fedex.com/zm
Mercury Express Logistics/TNT 6392 Dundudza Chididza Rd, Longacres; m 0971 269390-29; w mercury.co.zm

OTHER PRACTICALITIES

EMBASSIES AND HIGH COMMISSIONS IN LUSAKA The Zambian Department of Immigration carries a comprehensive list of the foreign embassies and consulates based in Lusaka (w zambiaimmigration.gov.zm). The following is a selection:

Angola (embassy) 6660 Mumana Rd; 0211 292277
Botswana (high commission) 5201 Pandit Nehru Rd; 0211 250555
Canada (high commission) 5210 Independence Av; 0211 250833
DRC (embassy) 1124 Parirenyatwa Rd; 0211 235679
European Union 4899 Los Angeles Bd; 0211 251140
Finland (embassy) Haile Selassie Av; 0211 251988

France (embassy) 31F Leopards Hill Cl; 0971 054128
Germany (embassy) 5219 Haile Selassie Av; 0211 250644
India (high commission) 1 Pandit Nehru Rd; 0211 253159–60
Ireland (embassy) 6663 Katima Mulilo Rd; 0211 426900
Italy (embassy) 5211 Embassy Pk; 0211 250781
Kenya (high commission) 5207 United Nations Av; 0211 250722
Malawi (embassy) 5202 Pandit Nehru Rd; 0211 265768
Mozambique (high commission) 9592 Kacha Rd; 0211 220333
Namibia (high commission) 30A Mutende Rd; 0211 211407/8
Nigeria (embassy) 5203 Haile Selassie Av; 0211 253177
Norway (honorary consulate) 5831 Mwange Cl; m 0956 839736
South Africa (embassy) 26D Cheetah Rd, Kabulonga; 0211 260497
Sweden (embassy) Haile Selassie Av; 0211 426100
Tanzania (embassy) 5200 United Nations Av; 0211 253323
UK (high commission) 5210 Independence Av; 0211 423200
USA (embassy) Kabulonga Rd, Ibex Hill; 0211 357000
Zimbabwe (embassy) 11058 Haile Selassie Av; 0211 254006/12/18

EMERGENCIES AND HEALTH CARE

Emergencies In the event of an accident, or for a serious medical condition, don't hesitate to use the emergency number given with your medical insurance. Note, too, that many adventure/safari companies, lodges and camps subscribe to an emergency medical evacuation service. Good travel insurances will also cover you for use of their service, although authorisation for this in an emergency can take time. Their regional offices are:

Specialty Emergency Services (SES) Emergency 0977 770302, 0962 740300; General 0211 273302; e sales@ses-zambia.com; w ses-zambia.com

The government-run **University Teaching Hospital** [167 G6] (Nationalist Rd; 0211 251451) has a department for emergencies, but it is sadly overstretched and best avoided if possible. More up to date is the Levy Mwanawasa General Hospital [167 G2] (Great East Rd; 0211 285464; m 0968 769140), also a public hospital, which was opened in 2011 with the aid of Chinese finance, and has its own casualty department.

General health care For less life-threatening conditions, either your embassy or hotel should be able to recommend a doctor or clinic. A sick foreign traveller will usually be accepted by one of the well-equipped clinics used by the city's more affluent residents without too many questions being asked at first, though proof of comprehensive medical insurance will make this all the more speedy. Some are affiliated to specific insurance companies, so it would be wise to check this first if you can. Among the most well known, offering 24-hour medical attention, are:

Care for Business (CFB) Medical Centre [167 F2] 4192 Addis Ababa Dr; 0211 252917, 254396/8; m 0979 700100; w cfbmedic.com.zm
Fairview Hospital [166 D4] Chilubi Rd; 0211 373000; w fairview.co.zm
Medcross Hospital [166 C3] Makishi Rd; m 0972 072922; w medcrosszam.com
Victoria Hospital [159 E3] 5498 Lunsenfwa Rd; 0211 290985; w victoriahospitals.org

TRAVEL AGENTS There is no shortage of travel agents in the capital, but attentive and efficient service isn't as common. In addition, many have their own favourite properties or trips, and will recommend those, regardless of what would suit you best.

Most safari arrangements are best made as far in advance as possible. Unless you are travelling totally independently (driving or hiking, and camping everywhere), you should ideally book with a good specialist tour operator before you leave home (page 92). This will also give you added consumer protection and recourse from home if things go wrong. By booking ahead, you also have the best chance of getting into the places you want to visit.

If you do choose to book locally, try one of Lusaka's better travel agents – or one for which you have a reliable personal recommendation, and always pay by credit card as it will give your money some degree of protection. The following companies are familiar with the requirements of international travellers:

Juls Africa [159 E2] 5507 Libala Rd, Kalundu; ☎ 0211 291712, 292942, 292979, 293972; e res@julstravel.co.zm; w julstravelzambia.com. Well-established, family business covering travel arrangements from car hire to international flights & safari bookings.

Shamba Travel and Tours [167 C2] Unit 5, Block A, East Park Mall; m 0962 458529; e shambatravel@travelport.co.zm, mfourie@shamba.co.zm; w shambatravel.com. Professional company offering everything from car hire to accommodation & flight bookings.

Voyagers [167 E4] Suez Rd; ☎ 0211 375700; m 0977 860648; e tours@voyagerszambia.com; w voyagerszambia.com. Lusaka office of this recommended travel agent, with its own car-hire division.

SPORT AND ACTIVITIES

The larger and more luxurious **hotels** have their own fitness suites and pools; some have spa facilities, too. Lusaka also has an outdoor, Olympic-size **municipal swimming pool** – the '90 Days Legacy Pool' at the Olympic Youth Development Centre [167 G2] (Great North Rd; w oydc.org.zm; 🕘 usually Oct–Apr)

There are myriad sports clubs, with four **rugby** teams playing at the Lusaka Showgrounds alone, and two **golf** clubs: Lusaka Golf Club at Longacres [159 F5] (Los Angeles Bd) and Chainama Hills [159 G3]. The National Sports Development Centre (NASDEC) at Lusaka Showgrounds [167 G1] has tennis courts and the city's best **squash** courts (glass-backed), plus equipment hire and friendly staff.

WHAT TO SEE AND DO

MARKETS Like most African cities, Lusaka has numerous markets: some focused on everyday essentials for the local population and a few craft and curios markets primarily aimed at international visitors. Both merit time. The hectic community markets are fascinating to wander around, but pay attention to your belongings and don't take anything valuable with you.

Most of the city's market stalls concentrate on fish and vegetables, plus new and secondhand clothes. There'll be plenty of others, though, selling everything from baskets to tobacco, bicycle parts to an assortment of hardware. Do look for the interesting traditional-healer stalls, tinsmiths and furniture makers.

The more relaxed of the two main markets for visitors is **Kamwala Market** on Independence Avenue [166 B5]. Stalls here are predominantly owned by the city's Chinese and Lebanese communities.

On the western side of Cairo Road, the **New City Market** – widely known as 'Soweto' Market – is on Lumumba Road [166 A4], which in itself is lined with street vendors peddling their wares. This is the city's biggest market, lively and interesting – it's even popular with adventurous expats on Saturday mornings. Here in particular it's important to dress down for a visit, and don't even think of taking any valuables with you.

There are two other large markets in the centre, both smaller than the New City Market. The **Central Market** is near the Kulima Tower on Chachacha Road [166 A4], and **Comesa Market** (or Luburma) is off Independence Avenue near the Kafue Road fly-over bridge [166 A5]. Comesa is the preserve of traders from across the region, importing goods from Botswana, Zimbabwe, Namibia, Mozambique and Angola. In all of these you'll find clothing donated by charities from the West, with shoes piled up in great heaps. This trade, known as *salaula*, has badly affected Zambia's indigenous clothes industry – which previously thrived on the production and sale of printed cotton fabrics, like the common *chitenjes*. This is why *salaula*'s long-term value as a form of aid is hotly debated.

Many visitors will find Pakati Market, the Sunday **street market** at the Arcades [159 E3] (🕘 10.00–17.00), less daunting, though bargaining here is as important as in the bigger markets.

Somewhat different in character is the genteel bazaar held on the last Saturday of each month at the **Dutch Reformed Church** [159 G5] (Kabulonga Rd; 🕘 08.00–18.00). With a US$1 entrance fee, it's a good place for gifts and crafts, from jewellery to paintings and handmade clothing and carvings from all over central Africa. It's a friendly and relaxed place to have coffee and cakes, to savour Chinese and Indian snacks, or to find good biltong.

MUSEUMS AND CULTURE

Kabwata Cultural Village [167 E7] (Burma Rd; 🕘 08.00–17.00) The rondavels of the Kabwata Cultural Village are all that remain of 300 similar huts, which were built in the 1930s and '40s by the colonial government to house Lusaka's black labour force. They were designed with just one room, to house single men whose families were expected to remain in the rural areas rather than become permanent urban settlers.

Between 1971 and '73 the government demolished most of the huts to construct the flats now seen nearby. Fortunately, in 1974, 43 rondavels were saved and turned into a 'cultural centre' with the aim of preserving the country's cultural heritage. Today, many of the rondavels house artists from all over Zambia, who live and work here. In addition to wood- and stone-carvers, you'll find jewellery and other crafts, much of it the work of a women's co-operative based at the centre, as well as some interesting textiles. Sadly, the centre isn't in a great state of repair, and plans to upgrade and revitalise it have so far come to nothing. Nevertheless, it is probably the city's best spot for buying hand-carved crafts and curios. Large wooden hippos are generally cheaper than equivalent carvings at the craft centre near Victoria Falls in Livingstone. Haggling is key.

Lusaka National Museum [166 C5] (Independence Av; 🕘 09.00–16.30 daily, exc Christmas & New Year's Day; entry US$5/$3 adult/child; no photography) The Lusaka National Museum is an interesting diversion in the city: not least for the impressive art and photographic exhibition on the ground floor that features changing exhibitions by contemporary Zambian painters and sculptors.

The rest of the museum has sections devoted to archaeology and ethnography, political and social history, as well as a life-size rural village, complete with rondavels and model people, depicting traditional village life. The ethnography section is one of the most interesting, with exhibits of the material culture of various Zambian ethnic groups, including musical instruments, pottery and basketwork, and a popular display of artefacts relating to witchcraft and initiation ceremonies. Don't miss the display of masks, particularly the Makishi masks of the Northwestern Province.

The political-history displays feature colonial, independence-era and present-day leaders, with a clear emphasis on Kenneth Kaunda's liberation struggle. There's a well-stocked shop selling a good range of baskets and other crafts, and a few relevant books.

School groups tend to visit the museum between Wednesday and Saturday, so aim for the beginning of the week if you want to visit at a quiet time.

Freedom Statue [167 C5] (Independence Av) This memorial to fallen freedom fighters is just west of the National Museum. The statue, of a man breaking his chains, symbolises Zambia's liberation from the colonial yoke.

Presidential Burial Site [167 F5] (Embassy Park, Independence Av; ⌚ 08.30–16.30 daily; US$15/8 adult/child) Opened to the public in 2012, this mausoleum complex honours the memory of Zambia's recent presidents: Levy Patrick Mwanawasa (1948–2008), his predecessor in office, Frederick Chiluba (1943–2011), and the most recent incumbent, Michael Sata (1937–2014).

Each of the presidents buried here has an individual memorial designed to reflect his character, policies and time in office. For Mwanawasa, the architect incorporated a traditional stool to represent that he was a sitting president, with four boot-shaped legs to denote his four keynote policies and desire to 'stamp out' corruption, and eight steps, one for each of his years in office. For Chiluba's memorial, the ten pillars, for his ten years in office, are beneath a roof topped with a cross, indicating his Christian beliefs, and a small village house to remember his commitment to empowering Zambians with housing. The memorial for President Sata, completed in 2018, is designed in the style of King Soloman's Temple, Jerusalem in testament to Sata's inauguration pronouncement that he would 'rule Zambia using the 10 Commandments'.

The rather steep entrance fee includes a guide.

Henry Tayali Visual Arts Centre [167 G1] (Lion Ln, Lusaka Showgrounds; ☎ 0211 254440; m 0955 254440; ⌚ 08.00–17.00 Mon–Fri, 10.00–16.30 Sat–Sun) In the middle of the Lusaka Showgrounds, opposite Manda Hill, this interesting art gallery has permanent as well as changing exhibitions of contemporary Zambian art. Items on display are for sale, at prices negotiated with the artist. The centre is probably the best place in Lusaka from which to buy Zambian paintings, and sometimes carvings and sculptures.

OUTSIDE THE CITY

Kalimba Reptile Park [159 H2] (☎ 0211 213272/847190; ⌚ 09.00–17.00; entry K70–100/35–50 adult/child under 14) This well-established, well-run park has good displays of crocodiles, indigenous snakes, chameleons and tortoises. Knowledgeable guides share information about all of the reptiles, many of whom have been rescued by the on-call snake team, and brave and curious visitors can touch and hold the pythons.

There are also fishing ponds for anglers – or young enthusiasts who can borrow basic bamboo rods and bait – as well as crazy golf, a children's playground, volleyball court and two swimming pools. Drinks and snacks are available, with popular croc-burgers – from their own farmed animals – a major attraction or barbecue grills and charcoal available for DIY picnic lunches.

If you're self-driving with a fridge, check out the farm shop for supplies: delicious sausages and boerewors, free-range Pekin duck, bream and crocodile all on offer.

Lusaka National Park [159 H7] (🕘 06.00–18.00 daily; entry K30/15 adult/child; K10/vehicle) Some 16km southeast of the city from Crossroads shopping mall, along Leopards Hill Road, Zambia's newest national park was unveiled by President Lungu on 4 June 2015 with the aim of introducing city dwellers to some of Zambia's natural wildlife. Incongruously close to a zone earmarked for commercial development, it covers an area of just $46km^2$, making it also the smallest of the national parks, bar the tiny Ngonye Falls.

The land enclosed for the park has suffered over the years from deforestation, and is now largely scrub with rocky outcrops, few mature trees and no natural water. Tree shade is limited too, and poaching has been a problem since the first animals arrived. Despite that, the park has been stocked with a range of herbivores, including wildebeest, eland, hartebeest, sable antelope, zebra and kudu – though whether or not they can be spotted from a vehicle is largely a matter of luck. Pride of place in their own heavily protected enclosure is given to two (dehorned) white rhino.

Visitors are not permitted to enter the park on foot, so you'll need a vehicle to explore the game loops. On the main roads a standard saloon car should be fine, but elsewhere you'll need a high-clearance vehicle to negotiate the rocks – and potentially a 4x4 in the rainy season. There are toilets at the entrance gate, and at the large picnic site some 8km from the gates, where there are also a couple of viewing platforms, but signage is poor, so ask at the gate to see a map before you set off.

If you're an international visitor heading on to the country's more established safari areas, there will likely be more urban activities that absorb your time in Lusaka, however, it is worth noting that in 2021, Game Rangers International opened an informative **Wildlife Discovery Centre** (**m** 0971 609777; **e** WDC@gamerangersinternational.org; 🕘 09.00–15.00 daily; US$15/5 adult/child) within Lusaka National Park, raising its international appeal considerably. Beautiful murals adorn rondavels focusing on Zambia's different habitats, and there's the opportunity to view orphaned elephants from a raised observation deck at feeding time (🕘 11.30–13.00 daily) and learn about the work of conservation organisations operating across the country's national parks. With an on-site café for homemade treats and an ethical souvenir shop selling lovely handcrafted products from Collective (page 174), it's a worthy stop, especially for those new to safari or travelling with youngsters.

9

Livingstone and the Victoria Falls

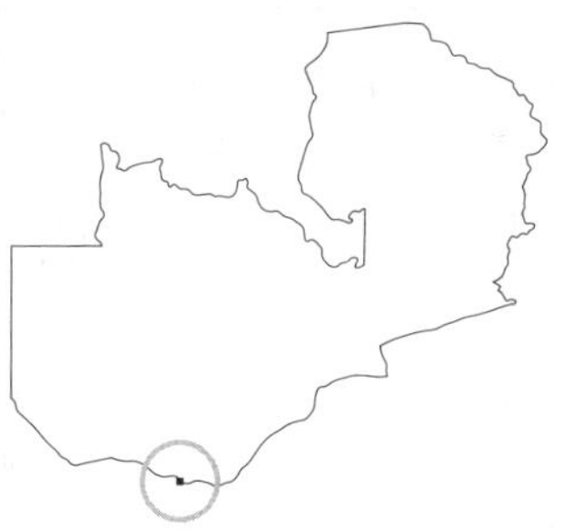

Livingstone is probably better oriented towards visitors than any other corner of Zambia. In spite of this, visitors travelling north from Zimbabwe are attracted simply by the Victoria Falls. The town of Livingstone itself often remained unseen, being less well known than the small Zimbabwean border town that shares the name of the waterfall. However, as a result of Zimbabwean political instability, Livingstone has developed rapidly since the early 2000s and now plays host to a number of tour operators and lodge owners who cut their teeth across the border – Zimbabwe's loss has very much been Livingstone's gain. Additionally, there has been an impressive push to develop local infrastructure and improve the cleanliness of the city, which continues today.

The Zambian and Zimbabwean sides offer different views of the Falls themselves, and if you have time it is worth seeing both sides to appreciate the whole waterfall. It's worth noting, though, that at present Livingstone is the preferred destination for most people visiting the Victoria Falls. Historians might note that most adventure activities like rafting, bungee jumping and microlighting originally started on the Zambian side of the Falls, before being taken over by more commercial Zimbabwean companies.

HISTORY

We can be sure that the Falls were well known to the native peoples of southern Africa well before any European 'discovered' them. After the San/Bushmen hunter-gatherers, the Toka Leya people inhabited the area, and it was probably they who christened the Falls Shongwe. Later, the Ndebele knew the Falls as the aManza Thunqayo, and after that the Makololo referred to them as Mosi-oa-Tunya.

However, their first written description comes to us from Dr David Livingstone, who approached them in November 1855 from the west – from Linyanti, along the Chobe and Zambezi rivers. Livingstone already knew of their existence from the locals, and wrote:

> I resolved on the following day to visit the Falls of Victoria, called by the natives Mosioatunya, or more anciently Shongwe. Of these we had often heard since we came into the country: indeed one of the questions asked by Sebituane [the chief of the Makololo tribe] travelling was, 'Have you the smoke that sounds in your country?' They did not go near enough to examine them, but, viewing them with awe at a distance, said, in reference to the vapour and noise, 'Mosi oa tunya' (smoke does sound there). It was previously called Shongwe, the meaning of which I could not ascertain. The word for a 'pot' resembles this, and it may mean a seething cauldron; but I am not certain of it.

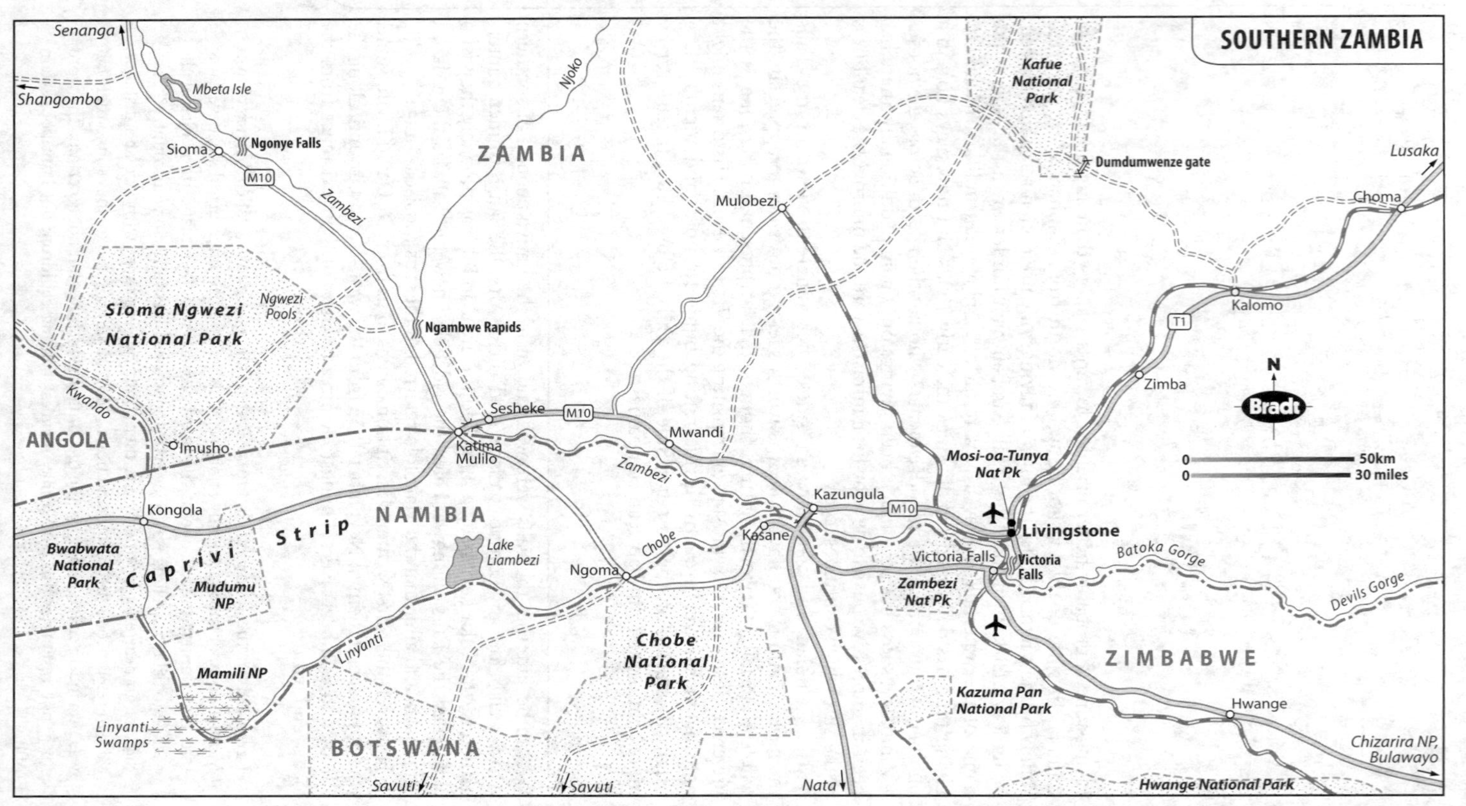
SOUTHERN ZAMBIA
Senanga
Shangombo
Mbeta Isle
Sioma
Ngonye Falls
M10
Zambezi
ZAMBIA
Njoko
Kafue National Park
Dumdumwenze gate
Mulobezi
Lusaka
Choma
Kalomo
T1
Zimba
N
Bradt
0 50km
0 30 miles
Sioma Ngwezi National Park
Ngwezi Pools
Ngambwe Rapids
Kwando
ANGOLA
Imusho
Sesheke
Katima Mulilo
Mwandi
Zambezi
Mosi-oa-Tunya Nat Pk
Kazungula
Livingstone
Kongola
NAMIBIA
Caprivi Strip
Lake Liambezi
Kasane
Victoria Falls
Batoka Gorge
Devils Gorge
Bwabwata National Park
Mudumu NP
Ngoma
Chobe
Zambezi Nat Pk
Chobe National Park
ZIMBABWE
Mamili NP
Linyanti
Linyanti Swamps
Kazuma Pan National Park
Hwange
BOTSWANA
Chizarira NP, Bulawayo
Savuti
Savuti
Nata
Hwange National Park

Livingstone continues to describe the river above the Falls, its islands and their lush vegetation, before making his most famous comment about sightseeing angels, now abused and misquoted by those who write tourist brochures to the area:

> Some trees resemble the great spreading oak, others assume the character of our own elms and chestnuts; but no one can imagine the beauty of the view from anything witnessed in England. It had never been seen before by European eyes; but scenes so lovely must have been gazed upon by angels in their flight. The only want felt is that of mountains in the background. The Falls are bounded on three sides by ridges 300 or 400 feet in height, which are covered in forest, with the red soil appearing among the trees. When about half a mile from the Falls, I left the canoe by which we had come down this far, and embarked in a lighter one, with men well acquainted with the rapids, who, by passing down the centre of the stream in the eddies and still places caused by many jutting rocks, brought me to an island situated in the middle of the river, on the edge of the lip over which the water rolls.
>
> From the autobiographical *Journeys in South Africa.*

Those who bemoan the area's emphasis on tourism should note that there must have been sightseeing boat trips ever since David Livingstone came this way.

Being the most eastern point reachable by boat from the Chobe or Upper Zambezi rivers, the area of the Falls was a natural place for European settlement. Soon more traders, hunters and missionaries came into the area, and by the late 1800s a small European settlement had formed around a ferry crossing called the Old Drift, about 10km upstream from the Falls. However, this was built on low-lying marshy ground near the river, buzzing with mosquitoes, so malaria took many lives.

By 1905 the spectacular Victoria Falls Bridge had been completed, linking the copper deposits of the Copperbelt and the coal deposits at Wankie (now Hwange) with a railway line. This, and malaria, encouraged the settlers to transfer to a site on higher ground, next to the railway line at a place called Constitution Hill. It became the centre of present-day Livingstone, and many of its original buildings are still standing. A small cemetery, the poignant remains of Old Drift, can still be made out on the northern bank of the Zambezi within the Mosi-oa-Tunya National Park.

In 1911 Livingstone became the capital of Northern Rhodesia (now Zambia), which it remained until 1935, when the administration was transferred to Lusaka.

GEOLOGY

The Falls are, geologically speaking, probably a very recent formation. About a million years ago, the Zambezi's course is thought to have been down a wide valley over a plateau dating from the Karoo period, until it met the Middle Zambezi rift – where the Matetsi River mouth is now.

Here it fell about 250m over an escarpment. However, that fast-falling water would have eroded the lip of the waterfall and gouged out a deeper channel within the basalt rock of the escarpment plateau – and so the original Falls steadily retreated upstream. These channels tended to follow some existing fissure – a crack or weakness, formed when the lava first cooled at the end of the Karoo period. At around the Batoka Gorge these fissures naturally run east–west in the rock, parallel to the course of the valley.

By around the Middle Pleistocene period, between 35,000 and 40,000 years ago, this process had formed the Batoka Gorge, carving it out to within about 90km of the present Falls.

However, as water eroded away the lip of the Falls, its valley gradually turned north, until it was almost at right angles to the basalt fault lines which run east–west. Then the water began to erode the fissures and turn them into walls of rock stretching across the valley, perpendicular to it, over which gushed broad curtains of water.

Once such a wall had formed, the water would wear down the rock until it found a fault line behind the wall, along which the water would erode and cause the rock subsequently to collapse. Thus the new fault line would become the wall of the new Falls, behind the old one. This process resulted in the eight gorges that now form the river's slalom course after it has passed over the present Falls. Each gorge was once a great waterfall.

Today, on the eastern side of the Devil's Cataract, you can see this pattern starting again. The water is eroding away the rock of another fault line, behind the line of the present Falls, which geologists expect will form a new waterfall a few thousand years from now.

LIVINGSTONE

GETTING THERE AND AWAY

By air Harry Mwaanga Nkumbula International Airport (code LVI) in Livingstone is just 5km northwest of the town centre on Airport Road.

The glass entrance foyer has pleasant waiting rooms, airline offices, a bank (🕘 08.00–16.00 Mon–Fri, 08.15–14.30 Sat) with an ATM, a post office and several car-hire kiosks. You can also buy sundries such as sweets and postcards, and there are curio shops for last-minute purchases. If you're after extra security for your luggage, there's a bag-wrapping service for US$10 per bag, located in the same cavernous hall as the check-in desks.

A simple snack bar (🕘 08.00–18.00 daily) serves substantial local dishes, but once you've passed through passport control, neither the bar nor the shops offer anything more substantial than snacks. As if in recompense, though, there's now a duty-free shop and a couple more curio outlets, including Kubu Crafts and Jewel of Africa. Free Wi-Fi is available throughout.

Airlines The airport is served by a number of scheduled airlines and charter companies.

International airlines In June 2023, the national airline, Zambia Airways, launched a direct, daily flight to Johannesburg (1hr 30mins). South African carrier Airlink also flies this route daily, as well as operating a daily flight to Kruger Mpumalanga Airport (1hr 40mins). Kenyan Airways flies twice weekly to both Cape Town (3hrs 10mins) and Nairobi (3hrs 15mins).

LIVINGSTONE & VICTORIA FALLS

For listings, see from page 190

Where to stay

1 David Livingstone Safari Lodge & Spa......B4
2 Limbo Lodge......C1
3 Maramba River Lodge......C4
4 Protea Hotel Livingstone......C3
5 Royal Sichango Lodge......B4
6 Stanley Safari Lodge......D5
7 Victoria Falls Waterfront......B4

Off map

Taita Falcon Lodge......D7

Where to eat and drink

8 Golden Leaf......C3
Victoria Falls Waterfront......(see 7)

Off map

Elephant Café......A2

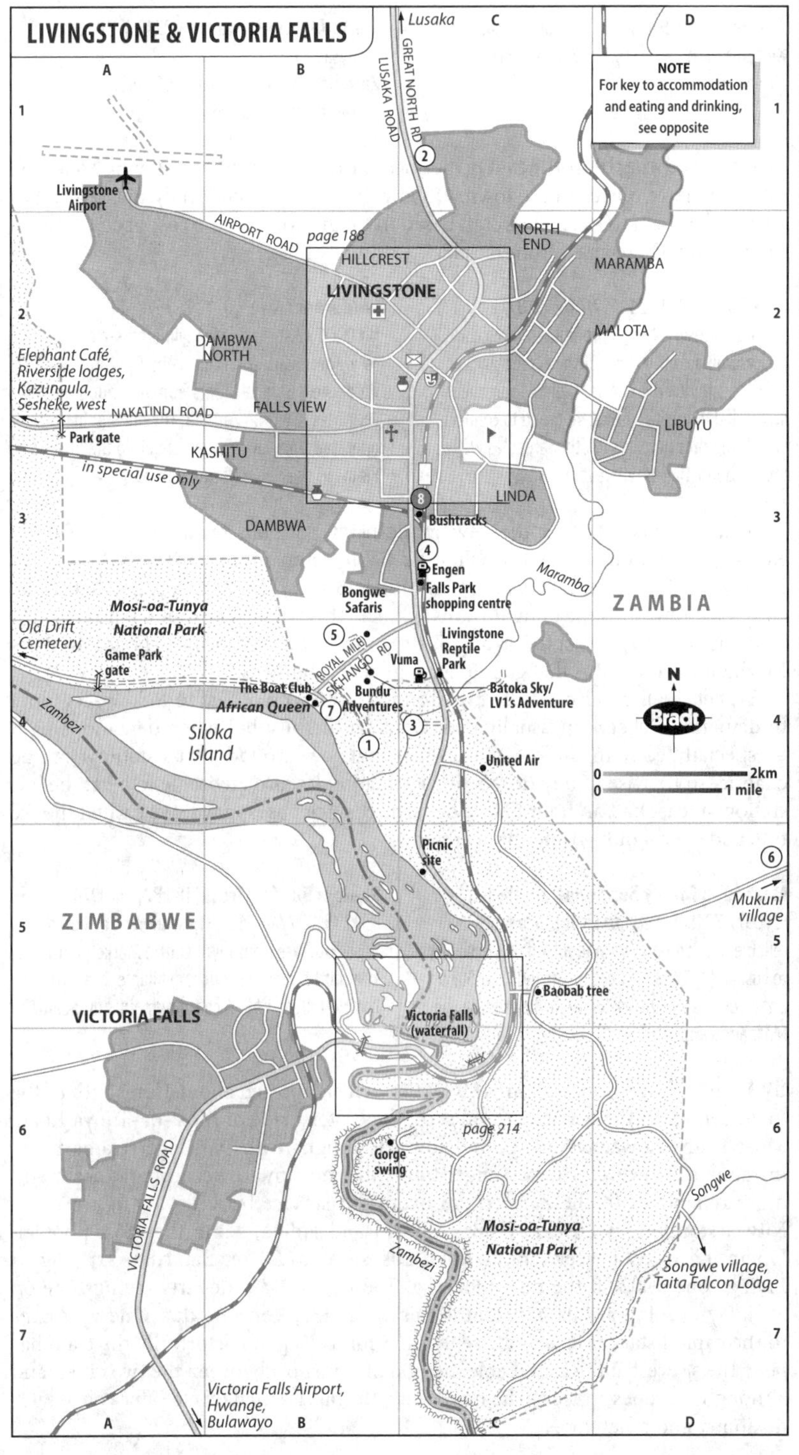

LIVINGSTONE & VICTORIA FALLS
NOTE
For key to accommodation and eating and drinking, see opposite
Lusaka
GREAT NORTH RD
LUSAKA ROAD
Livingstone Airport
AIRPORT ROAD
page 188
HILLCREST
LIVINGSTONE
NORTH END
MARAMBA
MALOTA
LIBUYU
DAMBWA NORTH
Elephant Café, Riverside lodges, Kazungula, Sesheke, west
NAKATINDI ROAD
FALLS VIEW
Park gate
KASHITU
in special use only
LINDA
DAMBWA
Bushtracks
Engen
Falls Park shopping centre
Bongwe Safaris
Maramba
ZAMBIA
Mosi-oa-Tunya National Park
Old Drift Cemetery
Game Park gate
ROYAL MILE
SICHANGO RD
Livingstone Reptile Park
Vuma
Batoka Sky/ LV1's Adventure
The Boat Club
African Queen
Bundu Adventures
Zambezi
Siloka Island
United Air
0 2km
0 1 mile
Picnic site
Mukuni village
ZIMBABWE
Baobab tree
VICTORIA FALLS
Victoria Falls (waterfall)
page 214
Gorge swing
Songwe
VICTORIA FALLS ROAD
Mosi-oa-Tunya National Park
Zambezi
Songwe village, Taita Falcon Lodge
Victoria Falls Airport, Hwange, Bulawayo

Airlink m 0979 481903; w flyairlink.com

Kenyan Airways ☎ 0211 271042; w kenya-airways.com

South African Airways ☎ 0213 323031/3; w flysaa.com

Zambia Airways m 0771 012345; w zambia-airways.com

Internal and charter airlines Of the local airlines that fly into Livingstone, the following have offices in the town. Other charter companies do fly to the city, but it's rare for them to have an aircraft based in Livingstone, so the cost of chartering a flight to anywhere apart from Lusaka is extremely high.

Proflight ☎ 0211 252452/476; m 0977 335563; e reservations@proflight-zambia.com; w flyzambia.com. An established company offering scheduled & charter flights. Their direct, scheduled flights to Lusaka are timed to connect with Proflight's transfers to other areas, as well as international flights wherever possible.

Wilderness Air ☎ 0213 321578–80; m 0966 770485; e info@wilderness-air.com; w wildernessdestinations.com. Operates all of Wilderness Safaris' flights from neighbouring countries & within Zambia. The only flights operated from Livingstone are up to the Busanga Plains in the Kafue National Park.

By bus Opened in 2023, the new, modern intercity bus terminus is on Kafubu Road, although one of the town's most reliable companies is currently Mazhandu Family Bus Service which is based on Mutelo Street [188 B2]. Buses gather in the early morning, most heading towards Lusaka. This trip takes around 6 hours.

If you want to go west to Kazungula or Sesheke your best bet is to board the daily Mazhandu Family Bus that goes to Mongu via both towns.

Expect the first buses to leave at around 06.00, with others to follow according to demand. Tickets can usually be bought on the bus, but when demand is high – especially early in the morning, when touts are around – bus stations can be chaotic, so it's wise to buy tickets the day before. It's also advisable to be at the bus station at least half an hour before departure, since buses may leave early if they're full, and overbooking is not unheard of.

Mazhandu Family Bus Services [188 B2] m 0977 794889. Perhaps Livingstone's most reliable bus company, with regular daily departures to Lusaka (K350) & services to Kazungula (K50) & on to Sesheke (K70).Tickets can be booked via the Mazhandu app.

Shalom Bus Services [188 B2] m 0970 833235, 0977 668621. These vibrant coloured buses operate from Town Centre Market, with standard & luxury services available, the latter having toilets, WiFi & charging points on board.

By train The railway station [189 D7] is well signposted about 1km south of the town centre on the way to the Falls, on the eastern side of Mosi-oa-Tunya Road. Most trains nowadays are geared towards freight with passenger trains being infrequent. However, the passenger trains that do run are becoming quicker and more reliable, with the *Zambezi*, an overnight service between Livingstone and Kitwe, stopping at Lusaka, Kapiri Mposhi and Ndola, being the most popular. Operating once a week, trains leave Lusaka at 07.30 on Saturday, arriving in Livingstone at 02.00 the next morning. The return train departs Livingstone on Monday evening at 20.00, reaching Lusaka at 13.20 on Tuesday. One-way fares to the capital start at K70 and rise to K135 for a sleeper. Historically the train has been the slowest and least reliable method of transport between the two cities, and although this does appear to be improving, the bus is still likely to offer you greater flexibility and reliability.

Driving For details of driving between Livingstone and Lusaka, see page 233.

Those heading **west**, into Namibia's Caprivi Strip, Botswana or western Zambia, should take the Nakatindi Road – signposted as the M10 – past the lodges by the river. After about 70km this comes to the Zambezi River at Kazungula – where Namibia, Botswana, Zimbabwe and Zambia all meet at a notional point. Here you can continue northwest within Zambia to Sesheke, or take the ferry across the Zambezi into Botswana, near Kasane. The drive from Livingstone to Sesheke takes about 2½ hours. Note that the last 40km section from Kazungula to Sesheke has more pot-holes than tarmac.

GETTING AROUND

Orientation Livingstone town itself is fairly compact and surrounded by several small township suburbs, sprawling out from its centre. Much bigger than the Zimbabwean town of Victoria Falls, on the other side of the river, the town has two main business areas concentrated along the all-important Mosi-oa-Tunya Road. Sections of this are lined with classic colonial buildings with corrugated-iron roofs and wide wooden verandas, some restored and others in a state of disrepair.

The larger and busier central business district begins atop a small hill just past the museum, while in the lower part of town is a smaller but growing retail area known as '217'. Developments further south have introduced a new shopping area between Livingstone and the Falls. Navigation is easy, even without a map, though signposts are often missing or may point to establishments no longer in existence.

Drive north out of the city, and the main street leading to the capital becomes Lusaka Road. Head south for about 10km and you reach the Zambezi River and the Victoria Falls themselves, and the border post to cross into Zimbabwe via Victoria Falls Bridge. Many visitors choose to stay close to the Falls at one of Sun International's two hotels, but there are now several options on this side of town.

Travel west from town on the M10 Nakatindi Road and you'll find yourself driving parallel to the north bank of the Zambezi upstream towards Kazungula and the ferry to Botswana. Signposts to the left point to small, exclusive lodges perched at picturesque spots on the river's bank.

By taxi or with a tour operator Livingstone town is small enough to walk around, as is the Falls area. However, if you are travelling between the two, going to the airport, or in a hurry, then use one of the plentiful – if battered – light-blue taxis that congregate near the old Shoprite at the main taxi stand [188 B2] or on Mosi-oa-Tunya Road opposite the curio market in the park [188 E3]. All taxis are supposed to carry a fare chart, though you will be lucky to see one. A taxi between town and either the Falls or the airport will cost around US$10 for up to four passengers. A taxi out to the riverside lodges will cost from around US$15, depending on the location; some are a considerable distance from town. Competition among taxi drivers can be fierce, so be sure to negotiate for the best deal and agree on the price in advance.

While you can negotiate to hire a taxi for the day to take you around town, to the Falls and to outlying areas, you'll have a more informative trip with one of the licensed and more knowledgeable tour operators. For details, see page 211.

By bus Local minibuses run to the Falls from the Town Centre Market in the centre of Livingstone throughout the day. The buses only depart when they are full, so expect the 10-minute journey to be cramped. Expect to pay around K5 for the journey.

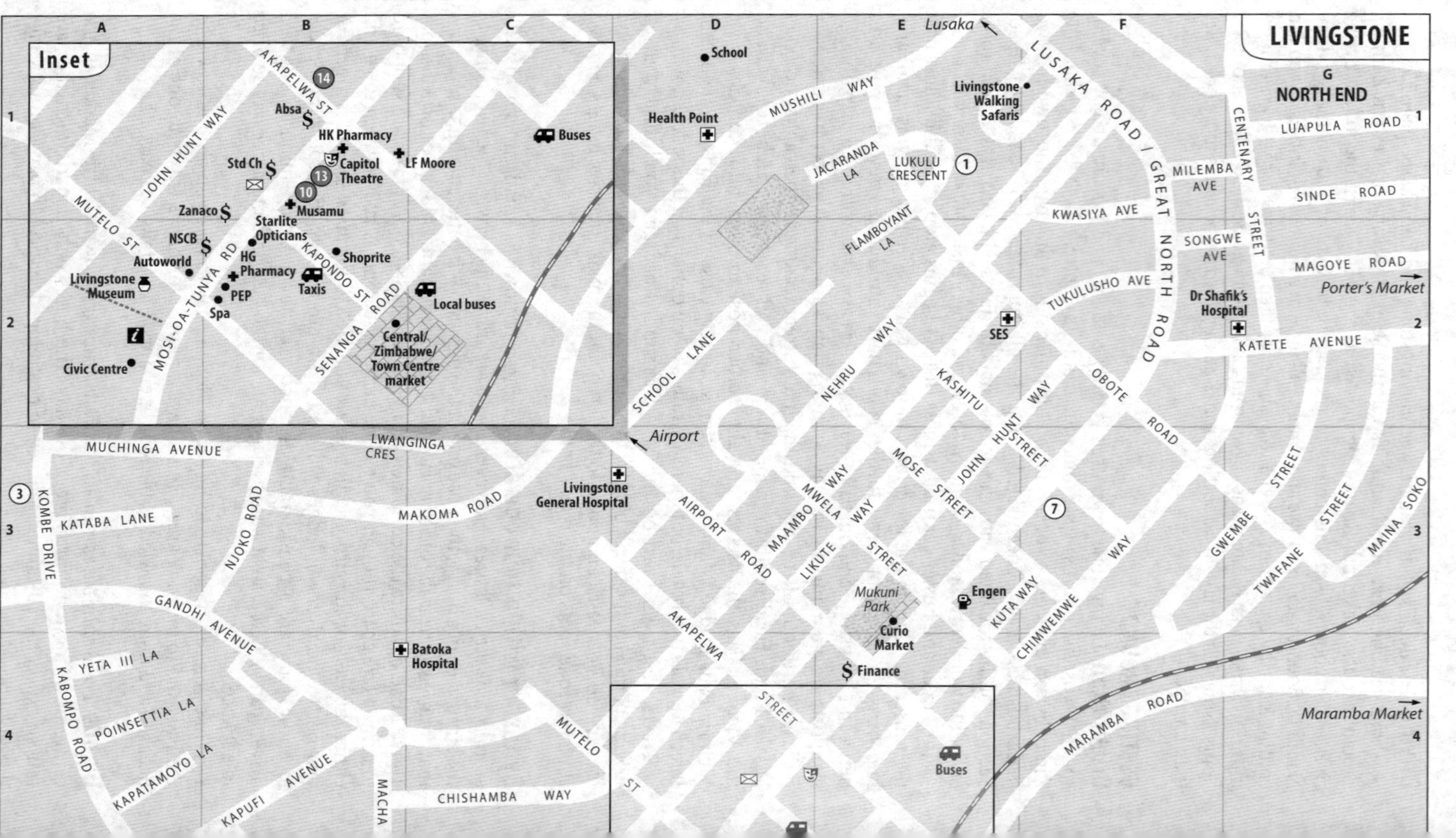
LIVINGSTONE
NORTH END
Inset
Lusaka
Airport
Porter's Market
Maramba Market
LUAPULA ROAD
SINDE ROAD
MAGOYE ROAD
CENTENARY STREET
KATETE AVENUE
MILEMBA AVE
SONGWE AVE
Dr Shafik's Hospital
LUSAKA ROAD / GREAT NORTH ROAD
KWASIYA AVE
TUKULUSHO AVE
OBOTE ROAD
MAINA SOKO
STREET
TWAFANE STREET
GWEMBE STREET
CHIMWEMWE WAY
KUTA WAY
MARAMBA ROAD
Livingstone Walking Safaris
LUKULU CRESCENT
JACARANDA LA
FLAMBOYANT LA
MUSHILI WAY
SES
KASHITU WAY
JOHN HUNT STREET
MOSE STREET
NEHRU WAY
MWELA WAY
MAAMBO WAY
LIKUTE STREET
Engen
Mukuni Park
Curio Market
Finance
Buses
School
Health Point
SCHOOL LANE
AIRPORT ROAD
AKAPELWA STREET
MUTELO ST
Livingstone General Hospital
LWANGINGA CRES
MAKOMA ROAD
Batoka Hospital
CHISHAMBA WAY
MACHA
KAPUFI AVENUE
NJOKO ROAD
GANDHI AVENUE
MUCHINGA AVENUE
KATABA LANE
YETA III LA
POINSETTIA LA
KAPATAMOYO LA
KABOMPO ROAD
KOMBE DRIVE
AKAPELWA ST
JOHN HUNT WAY
MUTELO ST
MOSI-OA-TUNYA RD
KAPONDO ST
SENANGA ROAD
Absa
Std Ch
Zanaco
NSCB
Autoworld
Livingstone Museum
Civic Centre
Starlite Opticians
HG Pharmacy
PEP
Spa
Musamu
HK Pharmacy
Capitol Theatre
LF Moore
Shoprite
Taxis
Local buses
Central/ Zimbabwe/ Town Centre market
A
B
C
D
E
F
G
1
2
3
4

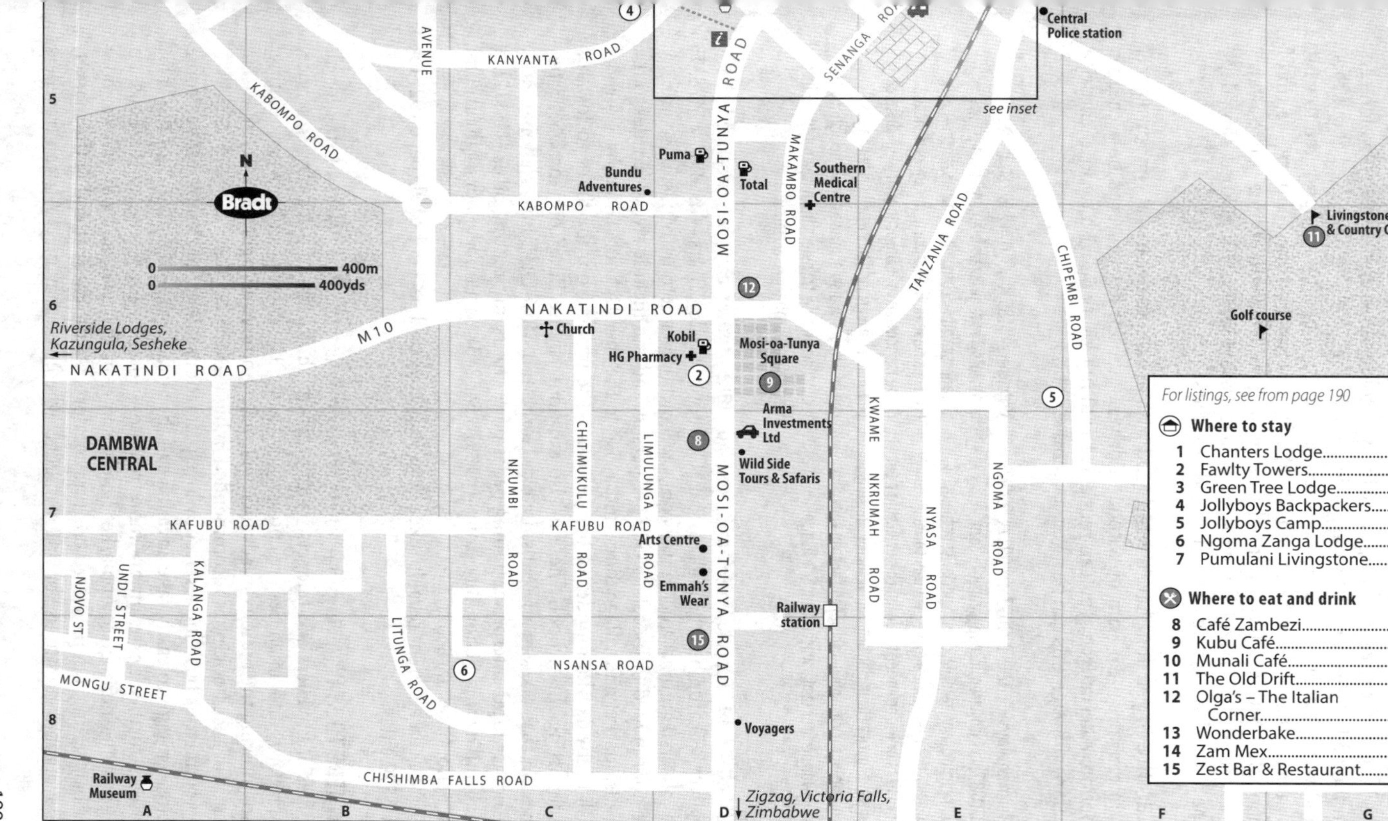
For listings, see from page 190
Where to stay
1 Chanters Lodge.....E1
2 Fawlty Towers.....D6
3 Green Tree Lodge.....A3
4 Jollyboys Backpackers.....C5
5 Jollyboys Camp.....E6
6 Ngoma Zanga Lodge.....C8
7 Pumulani Livingstone.....F3
Where to eat and drink
8 Café Zambezi.....D7
9 Kubu Café.....D6
10 Munali Café.....B1
11 The Old Drift.....G6
12 Olga's – The Italian Corner.....D6
13 Wonderbake.....B1
14 Zam Mex.....B1
15 Zest Bar & Restaurant.....D8
Central Police station
see inset
KANYANTA ROAD
AVENUE
KABOMPO ROAD
SENANGA ROAD
Puma
Bundu Adventures
Total
MAKAMBO ROAD
Southern Medical Centre
TANZANIA ROAD
CHIPEMBI ROAD
Livingstone Royal Golf & Country Club
Golf course
Bradt
400m
400yds
NAKATINDI ROAD
M10
Riverside Lodges, Kazungula, Sesheke
Church
Kobil
HG Pharmacy
Mosi-oa-Tunya Square
Arma Investments Ltd
Wild Side Tours & Safaris
MOSI-OA-TUNYA ROAD
KWAME NKRUMAH ROAD
NYASA ROAD
NGOMA ROAD
DAMBWA CENTRAL
NKUMBI ROAD
CHITIMUKULU ROAD
LIMULUNGA ROAD
KAFUBU ROAD
Arts Centre
Emmah's Wear
Railway station
NJOVO ST
UNDI STREET
KALANGA ROAD
LITUNGA ROAD
NSANSA ROAD
MONGU STREET
Voyagers
CHISHIMBA FALLS ROAD
Railway Museum
Zigzag, Victoria Falls, Zimbabwe

Driving yourself Driving in Livingstone is pretty straightforward, though watch out for the none-too-subtle speed humps along Mosi-oa-Tunya Road.

Most lodges and hotels have secure parking, as do many restaurants. If you're parking on the street in town, you're likely to come across any number of volunteers to look after your car or to wash it for you. There's nothing organised about this, and you're under no obligation to accept their help, but if you're prepared to trust someone then – in spite of considerable protestations to the contrary – a tip of about K2–3/US$0.50 is about right, depending on the length of time you're away.

There are several 24-hour fuel stations on the main Mosi-oa-Tunya Road. Nowadays, the price of fuel, both diesel and unleaded, is the same nationwide (page 113).

Car hire If you don't have a vehicle and wish to explore the area at your own pace, you can hire a car with or without a driver – the former can even be a cheaper option. Alternatively, you can rent a 4x4 with full kit if you wish to do a self-drive safari, although this can be a very expensive option.

Hemingways ☎ 0213 323097; m 0977 866492, 870232; e info@hemingwayszambia.com; w hemingwayszambia.com. Specialist vehicle hire, with or without a driver, for day tours, transfers or independent safaris. Their reliable fleet of new Toyota Hilux double-cab vehicles are fully equipped for camping, including rooftop tents, long-range fuel tank, water tank & a fridge.

Voyagers [185 A4] ☎ 0212 627800; e rentals@voyagerszambia.com, livingstone@voyagerszambia.com; w voyagerszambia.com. From its base at the airport, Voyagers Rentals is the franchisee for Europcar, with self-drive & chauffeur-driven vehicles in all price ranges & styles. They can also arrange trips throughout the region, including transfers from Kazungula & into Botswana, Zimbabwe & Namibia.

By bicycle Bicycle hire and guided bike tours can be arranged with Oliver Sikatumba through Local Cowboy's Cycle Tours (m 0977 747837; e oliversikatumba@rocketmail.com; w cowboybicycletourslivingstone.com). A 4-hour guided tour costs US$30 per person, and can include riverside rides to the Falls, market and village tours, and a visit to the small school started by 'Cowboy' Cliff Sitwala, the founder of the company. The profits from the tours go towards supporting this school. There is also a 6-hour Nature Bike Tour for US$35 per person that takes in the Falls, Batoka Gorge and Mosi-Oa-Tunya National Park. Another local enterprise running pedal-power tours and renting bikes (US$12/24 half/full day) is Action Bike Tours (m 0978 545283; e actionbiketours@gmail.com; w actionbikesafari.com).

You can also rent reliable bikes from **Jollyboys** backpacker hostel (page 192) for US$20 a day.

WHERE TO STAY Livingstone offers an enormous variety of places to stay for all types of travellers and budgets. With excellent choices in all price ranges, service, standards and amenities are consistently rising. The choice can be overwhelming, so knowing the options in advance will make finding the right place much easier, and advance booking is recommended in high season.

Numerous bush lodges occupy lovely situations along the Zambezi River, some close enough to easily take advantage of the attractions and activities of the Falls; others further upstream are more remote. Closer to town, and to the Falls, an increasing number of upmarket hotels, some on the river, and others in a more urban setting, offer Western creature comforts. At the cheaper end of the market, staying in a guesthouse or in-town lodge, where you may meet African travellers or volunteers from overseas, can add a multi-cultural dimension to your visit, while backpacker accommodation tends to cater strictly to the international budget traveller.

In town Hotels in Livingstone itself are still relatively spread out, with some in town, and others on the road south towards the Falls. Establishments listed here are roughly in order of price.

Even the most unobservant visitor in Livingstone can't help but notice the multitude of signs pointing to **guesthouses** all over town, but standards vary immensely. Many are new to tourism and others cater to the local market rather than to overseas visitors. One thing is for certain: the Western image of a guesthouse – a charming and personal B&B – is not to be found here...yet. Rather, a 'guesthouse' can be anything from a basic hostel to a quasi mini-hotel. Some are old, converted homes with smallish rooms, limited facilities and lower prices; others are newly constructed with restaurant, bar, pool, air conditioning and other mod cons, and priced accordingly. Interior decoration leans either towards the basic and functional, perhaps with the odd ethnic touch, or tends to be overblown, with an abundance of velvet, chrome and multi-patterned fabrics. Inevitably new places crop up all the time so it's worth looking around to see what catches your eye and which location suits you best; there are numerous options around the water tower to the north of town, and several along the road to the airport, too. Always ask to see the room and facilities before booking in, as there's no shortage of choice. Options here are listed by price bracket and then alphabetically.

For the budget-minded, nothing beats Livingstone's popular **backpackers'** hostels. Generally clean, convenient and cheap, they are ideal for independent travellers – but can be crowded at times. As a one-stop shop, they offer shared and private rooms, camping, booking agency, restaurant, bar, kitchen, laundry, pool and even a built-in social life.

Hotels

Protea Hotel Livingstone [185 C3] (80 rooms) Mosi-oa-Tunya Rd; ☎ 0213 324630; **e** reservations@phlivingstone.co.zm; **w** protea.marriott.com. Adjacent to Falls Park shopping centre, this surprisingly elegant hotel opened in 2008. From the entrance, flanked by giant pots overflowing with water, a wide tiled lobby, with a formal restaurant to one side, leads in turn through to a courtyard. Here, there's a rectangular swimming pool with its own bar & plenty of loungers. Dark-wood furniture & classic styling define the rooms, some of which face the courtyard. The hotel has its own activity centre, while for the more work orientated, there are conference facilities, free Wi-Fi access & a business centre. There's also a secure car park. **$$$$**

Ngoma Zanga Lodge [189 C8] (10 rooms) 963 Kariba Cres Livingstone; ☎ 0213 325006; **m** 0976 325554; **e** ngomazangalodge@yahoo.com; **w** ngomazangalodge.com. An easy 1km walk from the centre of Livingstone, Ngoma Zanga is a friendly lodge with thoughtfully decorated hotel rooms & a self-catering double. There's a lovely swimming pool, an eclectic, curio-filled lounge & a thatched restaurant. The team will happily arrange activities in & around the Falls area. **$$$–$$$$**

Guesthouses

Chanters Lodge [188 E1] (11 rooms) Lukulu Cres; ☎ 0213 323412; **e** richardchanter@gmail.com; **w** chanters-livingstone.com. Chanters was one of the first guesthouses in Livingstone & stands in a leafy residential area off Obote Av, about 1km north of town.

En-suite rooms – some with bath & shower, others just a shower – vary in size from 'singles' (with a dbl bed) to family accommodation, but all have AC, sat TV & fridge. The public rooms are pleasant, with tables & chairs extending on to a patio & garden at the back, around a small pool. There's also secure parking & Wi-Fi. The restaurant is open all day until 21.30. **$$**

Limbo Lodge [185 C1] (12 chalets) 7671/7673 Lusaka Rd; ☎ 0213 322096; **m** 0955 780330; **e** limbolodge@gmail.com; **w** limbolodge.com. A tranquil option in a lovely garden, Limbo offers warm hospitality & good value about 100m on the road heading north out of town. Grass-thatched chalets are spread across green lawns & each has 2 rooms, which can interconnect to form a family room & its own en suite. There's a restaurant & bar, a swimming pool, & a large conference room & secure parking. **$$**

Pumulani Livingstone [188 F3] (6 rooms) Mosi-oa-Tunya Rd; ☎ 0213 320981; **m** 0964 017019, 0954 516518; **e** pumulanizambia@yahoo.com. Conveniently located on the main road with secure parking, this peaceful guesthouse works well for self-drivers. A converted house, each room is decorated with a mixture of traditional & modern African décor, although they are close together & can lack privacy. Each room has tea-/coffee-making facilities, fridge, DSTV & Wi-Fi. **$$**

Green Tree Lodge [188 A3] (5 chalets, camping) 2015 Kombe Dr; ☎ 0213 322631; **e** info@greentreelodgezambia.com; **w** greentreelodgezambia.com. Individual en-suite chalets with secure parking alongside make this an attractive proposition for the self-driver. The clean, dbl chalets are set among fruit trees with their own veranda & good facilities. It's also possible to camp on the grass, close to the pool & Mambo restaurant where meals are available. **$–$$**

Backpackers

Fawlty Towers [188 D6] (34 dorm beds, 33 rooms) 216 Mosi-oa-Tunya Rd; ☎ 0213 323432; **m** 0972 250154; **e** info@adventure-africa.com; **w** adventure-africa.com. Just south of the turn-off to Nakatindi/Kazungula Rd, you can't miss Fawlty Towers. This large, popular international backpackers' place – look for the blue, mural-covered building – feels spacious & a bit more upmarket than the other backpacker options in Livingstone. Light & clean dorm rooms sleeping 3–8, neat en-suite room & new garden twin rooms are all reasonably priced & have access to a self-catering kitchen, BBQ, lively bar, comfortable lounge, pool table & even a spa.

There's a tropical garden shaded by mango trees & coloured with bougainvillea around an inviting pool. Tea & coffee are on hand all day, & free pancakes are offered poolside each afternoon. There's even a laundry service at US$10 per bag.

Fawlty Towers is quiet, secure, well run & tremendously convenient for the centre of Livingstone. The atmosphere is informal & lively, & it's a great place to meet other travellers, but the bar closes early so you can still get a reasonable night's sleep. There is free Wi-Fi available throughout the hostel & they offer free transport & transfers to Victoria Falls (5 days/wk) for K20 pp. *Dorm bed US$12; en-suite room US$55; garden twin US$65.* **$–$$** *exc b/fast.*

Jollyboys Backpackers [189 C5] (14 en-suite rooms, 11 with shared ablutions, 50 dorm beds, camping) 34 Kanyanta Rd; ☎ 0213 324229/322086; **e** enquiries@backpackzambia.com; **w** backpackzambia.com. The ever-popular Jollyboys occupies a tree-shaded site just behind the museum, a 2-min walk from the town centre. Owner-operated & managed by the helpful & friendly Kim, Sue & John, its reputation as the quintessential backpackers' lodge remains undimmed.

The main facilities are set within a large, central thatched courtyard, with the dorms, reception area & ablutions around the perimeter. There are also 14 en-suite twin & dbl rooms with AC & mosi nets. Mixed dorms come with 4 beds, 8 beds with AC, or – the cheapest – 16 beds, all with bedding included, fans & sharing a good-sized toilet & shower block with endless hot water. In the back garden are 2-bed A-frame thatched chalets & some lawned camping space, both sharing ablution facilities.

In the middle of the 'quad' is a wonderful sunken lounge – 'The Pillow Pit' with a firepit & colourful kitenge cushions – a perfect spot to chill out, read & meet fellow travellers. Above is a wooden deck from which you can see the spray from the Falls. A covered sitting area has comfy seating & table tennis, & looks out to an enticing rock swimming pool, lawns & gardens. Adjacent are the open-plan bar with sat TV, & a restaurant, where you can enjoy a home-cooked meal at reasonable prices – the burgers & smoothies are particularly good. There's also a separate self-catering kitchen. Bikes can be hired (US$20/day), & there's a laundry service, book exchange (K2 per book, with proceeds to charity), Mon-night movie, free weekly town walk, secure parking & short- & long-term baggage storage.

There's also a free pick-up service from the airport, by arrangement & free lifts to the Falls at 10.00 daily.

The atmosphere is relaxed & unpretentious, & even when it's busy, the bar shuts by 23.00 so noise isn't a major issue. *En-suite room US$68/80/90 sgl/dbl/tpl; shared ablutions room US$48–63 sgl/dbl; dorm bed US$20; camping US$12 pp.* **$–$$** *exc b/fast.*

Jollyboys Camp [189 E6] (24 dorm beds, 9 en-suite rooms, 6 twin chalets, camping) 80 Chipembi Rd; ☎ 0213 324756; e enquiries@backpackzambia.com; w backpackzambia.com. This offshoot of Jollyboys, owned & run by the same people, is close to the golf course, less than 10mins' walk to the centre of town. It has all the hallmark offerings of its well-known parent, but with a greater focus on family accommodation. This comes in the form of twin & dbl en-suite rooms, including a family room, 6 twin chalets, & 4- & 6-bed dorms with shared ablutions. For campers, there are spaces both for tents & – with power points, water & lights – for 4x4 vehicles with rooftop tents. All guests can use the bar where sports are typically shown on sat TV, self-catering kitchen, braai facilities, Wi-Fi, short- & long-term baggage storage, secure off-street parking, swimming pool, & free pick up from the airport. Evenings around the firepit offer the chance to mull over the day's activities, kids are catered for with their own jungle gym. *En-suite room US$68–80 sgl/dbl; shared ablutions room US$48–63 sgl/dbl; dorm bed US$20; camping US$12 pp.* **$–$$** *exc b/fast.*

Jungle Junction [map, page 194] (4 chalets, 5 huts, camping) Bovu Island; m 0978 725282; e stay@junglejunction.info; w junglejunction.info. About 1hr's drive from Livingstone, this popular backpackers' hang-out is based on its own island in the Zambezi. Just a 10 min mokoro ride from the shore, its launch site is suitable only for 4x4s & can be difficult to find; it isn't signposted. It's therefore essential to book in advance via email, & transfers can be easily arranged to the lodge from Livingstone, or from the Victoria Falls or Kazungula border posts.

Facilities are still rustic, but the setting is splendid: indigenous shade trees, sandy beaches & sweeping river views. Large, reed-walled chalets are built on stilts with wood floors, mesh windows, mosi nets & a veranda with river views. 5 smaller 'fisherman's huts' are simple A-frame structures with raised wooden floors, & are constructed from local reed & thatch. They are very simple, & without walls, windows or doors they are very open to the environment. The huts come furnished with beds, all bedding & mosquito nets. Both of these room types share a basic ablution block, with flush loos & hot showers, which is also used by the campsite. Here, there's plenty of space to pitch a tent on the sandy shore, & there's a kitchen with utensils, charcoal & essentials provided. Hot water is provided in the showers from a wood boiler, & there are also propane-powered fridges & a solar-power system is available for recharging batteries.

The barefoot bar with its river views is undoubtedly the most popular place to hang out in camp, & in the adjacent dining room & library, books line shelves made of mekoro. The restaurant serves fairly standard fare such as chicken curry, spaghetti Bolognese & beef stew, served with fresh vegetables & salads (🕘 all day; full b/fast or lunch US$7; dinner to US$12). A small shop sells curios & clothing made from colourful African chitenje material, which can be made to fit by the resident tailor.

A one-off charge of US$25 pp covers activities for the duration of your stay. These include fishing, nature walks, village visits & trips taking you hippo watching or to a secluded swimming spot. Think twice before venturing into crocodile-infested waters, though, no matter how safe it is deemed; crocs quickly become habituated to people & may lurk in the shadows. Fashioning your own fishing rod out of a reed pole is quite novel, or you can hire tackle & a guide (*US$12/day for 2 pax*). The lodge has built, & is still heavily involved with, a community school opposite the island on the mainland, & guests are welcome to visit. Transfers & all boat activities are by mokoro, which are fun but potentially perilous. *Hut US$25 pp; chalet US$35. Camping US$10 per tent per night.* **$–$$**

Beside the Zambezi: upriver *Map, page 194*

Livingstone's riverside lodges are for the most part spread along the shores of the Zambezi leading west from the town off Nakatindi Road. As well as the more

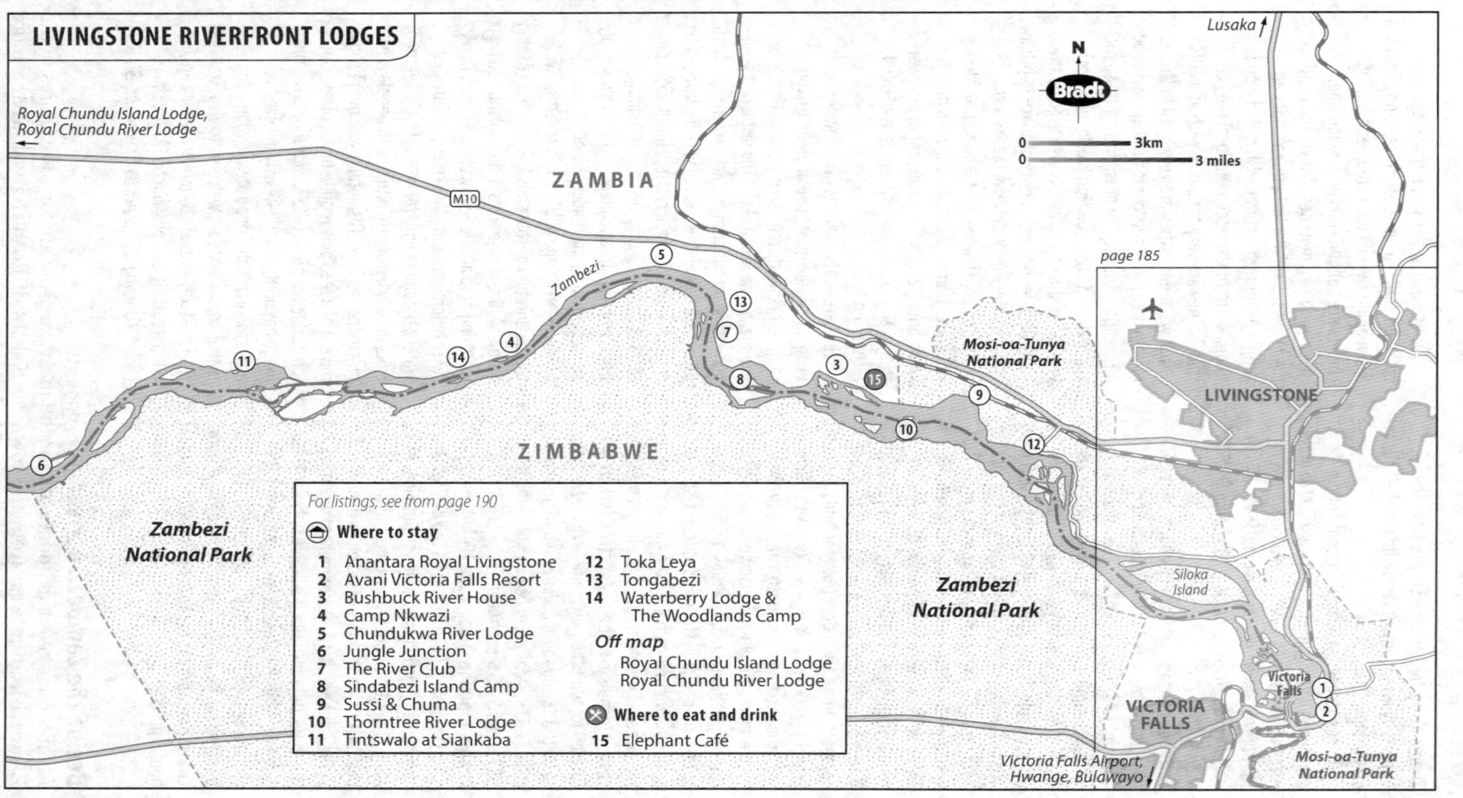
LIVINGSTONE RIVERFRONT LODGES
Royal Chundu Island Lodge, Royal Chundu River Lodge
ZAMBIA
M10
Zambezi
ZIMBABWE
Zambezi National Park
Mosi-oa-Tunya National Park
LIVINGSTONE
page 185
Siloka Island
Victoria Falls
VICTORIA FALLS
Lusaka
Victoria Falls Airport, Hwange, Bulawayo
0 3km
0 3 miles
For listings, see from page 190
Where to stay
1 Anantara Royal Livingstone
2 Avani Victoria Falls Resort
3 Bushbuck River House
4 Camp Nkwazi
5 Chundukwa River Lodge
6 Jungle Junction
7 The River Club
8 Sindabezi Island Camp
9 Sussi & Chuma
10 Thorntree River Lodge
11 Tintswalo at Siankaba
12 Toka Leya
13 Tongabezi
14 Waterberry Lodge & The Woodlands Camp
Off map
Royal Chundu Island Lodge
Royal Chundu River Lodge
Where to eat and drink
15 Elephant Café

exclusive lodges, there are now a few more accessible offerings further upstream, including a couple of campsites. The following are listed from east to west.

Toka Leya (12 tented chalets) Contact Wilderness Safaris, page 419. Set within the national park, some 5km from Livingstone, Toka Leya's green canvas tents & timber decking blend into the riverine environment. Although each tented chalet faces the river, some lie well back, glimpsing the water through the trees rather than affording a panoramic view. Raised on wide wooden verandas, the rooms are airy & spacious with 4-poster beds (3 family rooms have a separate twin room at the back), Persian-style rugs & high-backed, leather armchairs.

The understated style runs through to the main lounge & restaurant area, segmented into 'rooms' by squashy sofas, with linking walkways to a bar, tree-shaded deck where steps lead down to a small sandy section of beach – a wonderful place to have dinner when the water is low. Nearby, sunloungers surround a small infinity pool, & by the river there's a simple spa for massages & manicures; for the more energetic, there's a riverside gym with AC. Dinner is often taken at a group table, though it can be served privately on your own deck, & there are individual tables during the day. Particularly popular at lunchtime is pizza, freshly prepared out of a wood-fired oven. There's also free Wi-Fi throughout the camp.

Boat trips from the lodge's jetty, 2hr game drives & 1½hr birding/nature walks are all possible, as are trips to the Falls, museum & market; most other activities can be booked. Environmental issues are high on the agenda, with a filtration system for drinking water, solar geysers for hot water, & a worm farm for kitchen waste; guests can even plant a tree as part of a project to replace lost specimens along the river. *US$750–950 pp sharing FB, inc local drinks, laundry, 2 activities/day, exc spa treatments.* ⏲ *All year.* ♛♛♛♛

Sussi & Chuma (12 chalets, 2 houses) Contact Sanctuary Retreats: **w** sanctuaryretreats.com. Named after the Zambian bearers who carried David Livingstone's body from Zambia to Dar es Salaam after his death, Sussi & Chuma lies within the national park, just 15mins' drive from Livingstone. Set among riverine ebony forest & constructed high up on wooden platforms, from the outside Sussi & Chuma's chalets are reminiscent of rustic treehouses. Inside though, the rooms have a smart, modern feel to them. Polished wooden floors, high thatched ceilings with whitewashed rafters & natural fabrics make the rooms calm & airy. There's a powerful shower & a large bathtub (complete with candles & bath salts) in the corner of the open-plan room. Wooden doors with large glass windows at the front of the chalet open out onto an elevated wooden deck, where a couple of wicker armchairs allow you to admire the views of the Zambezi. Alternatively, if privacy is preferred, the 2 separate Chuma houses each have 2 en-suite bedrooms, a private plunge pool, & a chef & butler.

Raised walkways connect the chalets to a large 2-storey thatched central area, which mirrors the circular design of the rooms. Upstairs, a sitting room with comfortable sofas & a bar have views over the river. Below, the dining area extends onto a circular deck where meals may be taken with other guests, or individually, as you prefer. The lodge has its own wine cellar, but can order specific wines on request. A short walkway leads to a sheltered bend of the river, the location of a large infinity pool & a sundowner deck with firepits. Spa treatments are available using Africology products, also sold in the gift shop. Reliable Wi-Fi is available in all of the rooms, but not in the main areas.

Activities include game drives or walking safaris, which can easily be combined with a rhino walk allowing a close up experience with Mosi-oa-Tunya's small population of white rhino. Also on offer are boat cruises at sunrise & sunset, fishing, a village tour, & visits to the Falls. *US$755–1,150 pp/sharing (1–3 nights) FBA, inc local drinks, laundry, 2 guided activities/day, park fees. Children under 6 in houses only.* ⏲ *All year.* ♛♛♛♛

Thorntree River Lodge (8 suites; 2 family) ☎ +27 21 701 0270; **e** info@africanbushcamps.com; **w** africanbushcamps.com. The most luxurious lodge within the broader confines of Mosi-oa-Tunya National Park, Thorntree sits on private land 12km from the Falls (10 mins from town) & is clearly signposted. The camp was purchased in 2015 by African Bush Camps, an established owner-run safari company with a number of camps in Botswana & Zimbabwe. Under their guidance, the lodge has undergone a complete transformation. Seriously sophisticated &

stylish, this beautiful lodge is a glamorous tented camp with every modern comfort & high levels of service.

The main area is a duo of stone walled, peaked tents where a central fireplace makes for cosy evenings & glazed folding wall leads on to an expansive deck overlooking the Zambezi. There are 4 seating areas filled with an array of beanbags, sofas & benches, all thoughtfully arranged under an eclectic arrangement of lights. The dining room, complete with a temperature-controlled wine cellar & open kitchen serves delicious à la carte lunches & 3-course dinners, though meals can be enjoyed almost anywhere you wish. There's also a circular, sandy boma where cushion-covered benches surround a sculpted firepit – perfect for drinks & camp chatter before or after dinner.

Although all of the usual Livingstone activities can be arranged here, the lodge itself is lovely enough to simply stay & relax, especially after the early starts of safari. There's a lovely, 2-tier infinity pool overlooking the river, a small library, TV room &, in 2 traditional-style Lozi mud huts, a spa & gym.

The suites themselves are characteristically elegant. Raised off the ground, you enter through a heavy door fashioned from reclaimed teak railway sleepers into an elegant space filled with light & contemporary African art. The glazed front wall opens on to the riverfront deck, complete with plunge pool, & the beautiful bedroom is restful in blue & neutral shades, with copper accents & a well-appointed en-suite bathroom. The family suites offer the same style but combine 2 en-suite tents, linked by a connected walkway, and two plunge pools. These rooms are immediately adjacent to the main area.

Tented suites US$603–974 pp sharing, FB, inc airport transfers & community levy. Children all ages welcome. ⌚ *All year.* ♛♛♛–♛♛♛♛

Bushbuck River House (8 rooms, camping) e bushbuckriverhouse@gmail.com; w bushbuckriverhousezambia.com. Situated 16km from town, Bushbuck lies just outside the national park. Take the first left after leaving the main road, cross the railway, turn sharp left following the railway line back, then turn towards the river for about 1km. A traditional thatched farmhouse & a smaller thatched cottage, added in 2013, are both in a quiet spot with good river views & reportedly excellent home-cooked meals. The main house has 4 en-suite rooms, while the 'Waterbuck Cottage' contains 2 suites, each with 2 bedrooms & a shared bathroom. One of the suites also has a self-catering kitchen downstairs. The accommodation here is comfortable & affordable, & is very much in the style of a shared house rather than the other lodge-style properties on the river, which may afford you slightly more privacy. Both camping & self catering are further options. Relax in the attractive poolside boma, watch the river from a high viewing platform, or chill in the lounge with DSTV, including Sky Sports. ♛♛

The River Club (11 chalets) ☎ 021 1391051; reservations: ☎ +27 72 517 4880; e reservations@theriverclubzambia.com; w theriverclub.africa. Perched on a rise beside the Zambezi, The River Club is an expansive restored 1940s homestead with a distinctly colonial-era décor & formal service to match. It's an intimate lodge, set in securely fenced grounds with green lawns, organic vegetable gardens & even its own helipad. Most guests are transferred from Livingstone by boat, a scenic 10-min ride, but for those who wish to drive the turning off Nakatindi Rd is clearly signposted.

Well spaced along neat pathways, 7 large, thatched chalets are built on stilts amid indigenous riverside trees, with stunning views over the Zambezi below. Free-standing teak furniture, quality fabrics & beautiful (if slippery) polished floors feature in these split-level rooms, along with 2 bathrooms, one featuring a claw-foot bath. Additionally, 2 River Suites (1 wheelchair accessible) carry the same amenities, but also have their own decks & plunge pools set in small private gardens, while the Family Suite features 2 bedrooms with its own pool. Secluded at the far end of the lodge, the Princess Mary Suite is a double storey unit accommodating 4 adults in 2 en-suite bedrooms. With its own garden, lounge area, bar & dining area it can act autonomously from the main lodge.

The main building enjoys magnificent river views from wide verandas where afternoon tea & sundown cocktails are served. Inside, there's the reception, a small gift shop, cloakrooms, a formal dining room with a magnificent teak table, a comfortable lounge, a massive double-sided fireplace & a well-stocked library. Antiques & colonial-era pictures add to the Edwardian ambience, while Wi-Fi access throughout brings a touch of the 21st century. Beautifully presented meals prepared in the strict kosher kitchen are elegant affairs featuring pre-set dinner menus that change daily. Typically guests dine together, but individual tables can be arranged, & for absolute privacy there's a riverside 'gazebo'. Opposite the main building, & built in the same style, is a 'summerhouse', ideal for small groups with its own lounge & dining table, snooker room & small library.

Overlooking the river is a lovely pool surrounded by sunloungers & shaded by over-sized umbrellas. Walkways, illuminated at night, cross the sweeping lawns, dotted with palms & brightly coloured bougainvillaea. Croquet, boules & bush golf are gentle diversions, & for the more active, there's an all-weather tennis court & a 2½km nature-walk/running track around the 20ha property. A wellness centre provides massages & other treatments, while below is a small gym, with a sauna & jacuzzi. All other Falls' area activities can be booked direct from the lodge.

Suite US$656/688, luxury suite US$740/782, Princess Mary suite US$809/861 all pp sharing, low/high season, FBA, inc local drinks, laundry, exc spa, tourism levy (US$12 pp/day), transfers & off-site activities. Children over 6.

♛♛♛♛–♛♛♛♛♛

Tongabezi (5 cottages, 7 houses) m 0979 312766; e reservations@greensafaris.com; w greensafaris.com. Set on a sweeping bend of the Zambezi, 15km west of the town centre, Tongabezi remains one of the most exclusive & individual lodges on the north side of the Zambezi. Its lovely setting is matched by excellent service from a team of first-class local staff. In 2020, it became part of Green Safaris, whose ethos in sustainability, community development & originality match perfectly with Tongabezi's own.

Overlooking the river are 5 beautiful thatched cottages, full of character & furnished with contemporary Zambian fabrics & furniture. Deep cushioned sofas, large beds, linen curtains, large en-suite bathrooms with river-view claw-foot bathtubs, & wide river-view decks. There are also 7 creatively designed, & some amusingly named, houses. Each is original in style & structure, & 3 have one side completely open to the river: the secluded Bird House, the open-fronted Tree House, wound around 3 large ebonies, & the boho-chic Honeymoon House – once cited as 'worth getting married for'. Each has a king-size bed & impressive en-suite bathroom with inviting tub. In an elevated spot, the split-level Nut House has a cool Zanzibari vibe, with pretty lanterns, baraza benches and moulded arches. Completely enclosed, the large folding French doors open onto a lovely deck with its own infinity plunge pool overlooking the Zambezi. Closer to the river, the substantial Dog House has 2 elegant, open-plan bedrooms, surrounded by concertina glass doors, & 3 interconnected wooden decks, including an infinity plunge pool, lounger area & bar. Then, tucked away from the river in its own lush, private patch, is the Garden Cottage. Ideal for families or 2 couples sharing, it comprises 3 separate buildings – 2 spacious, en-suite dbl rooms & an open-sided lounge with fireplace– set in a rough horseshoe around a private pool. Each of Tongabezi's houses is carefully secluded from its neighbours, & has the services of a dedicated private valet. For the ultimate in exclusive-use, consider Tangala, the luxurious, 4-bedroom family home – complete with 2 resident dogs – with 250m of private riverfront, a large pool & oodles of homely, relaxing corners.

All Tongabezi's guests are welcome at the thatched, riverside boma, shaded by creeper-clad ebony trees & incorporating the bar, dining room & 2 intimate lounge areas, one with a fireplace. Right on the river are 2 thatched lounge areas with comfy chairs. One, aptly named Look Out, has stunning views from its upper storey, & also has a small library, desks & even a private dining area (which must be pre-booked); it's an attractive place to relax. Further relaxation comes in the form of in-room massages, manicures & pedicures. There's a large swimming pool, with sunloungers & a laid-back pool bar.

Towards sunset, everyone gathers outside around a roaring campfire for sundowners & hors d'oeuvres. Meals are sumptuous affairs, cooked to a high standard & served on the riverside deck, in the dining room, or even in your own cottage. By special arrangement & when the water isn't too high, couples can dine under the stars on Tongabezi's floating 'sampan', with each course hand delivered by canoe – a romantic & memorable occasion.

The lodge's ethos is confirmed by its school, Tujatane, which is run to provide free education for the over 300 children of Tongabezi staff & all local villages within walking distance. School visits are popular with guests, & many contribute to the school & the children's future education.

Guided sunrise & sunset boat trips from the lodge's jetty, canoeing, birdwatching trips, fishing, game drives (to Mosi-oa-Tunya National Park), island picnics, village visits, shopping excursions, museum tours & gorge walks are all included (exc park fees & museum entrance). Mountain bikes are available to visit Simonga village & explore the surrounding area. With advance notice, & at extra cost, guests may also sleep on Sindabezi Island (see below), or have a meal on Livingstone Island (page 215), beside the Falls. *River Cottage from US$815, House from US$1,023, both pp sharing FBA, inc local drinks, laundry, levies, exc transfers, park fees.* ♛♛♛♛

✷ **Sindabezi Island Camp** (5 chalets) Contact via Tongabezi (page 197). A short, 2km boat (or canoe) trip downstream from Tongabezi, Sindabezi Island offers barefoot luxury on an island retreat, just a stone's throw across the water from Zimbabwe's Zambezi National Park. Sindabezi was built with a strong focus on the environment, with all waste water recycled & hot water from solar geysers; it's widely regarded to be one of the most environmentally friendly properties on the river. Its individually designed en-suite chalets are carefully spaced around the shore of the sandy island for maximum privacy. With solid wood furniture, beautifully crafted, natural chandeliers & shiny copper basins, these are tastefully appointed; 2 have outdoor baths, & one even has its own 'beach'. All are raised on decks & are open on 3 sides, with canvas roll-down walls for protection from the elements. There's a campfire for evening star-gazing, a deck high in the ebony trees with commanding views of the river & a river-view plunge pool. A relaxed open-sided dining area with teak decking is just one of the settings for meals prepared by the island's own chef, & the pop-up Sindabezi Sand Bar is a full bar set up on an ever-changing, powder-white sandbar in the middle of the Zambezi – perhaps the most idyllic of river sundowner spots.

Game is often sighted on the riverbanks, & there's often a hippo sleeping behind the camp's kitchen. With your own guide, you can explore the river & surrounding islands by boat or canoe, or go walking, fishing & birdwatching, as well as take part in all activities run at Tongabezi itself. *Chalet from US$650; honeymoon chalet from US$715, both pp sharing FBA, inc drinks, laundry, transfers to/from island.* ♛♛♛–♛♛♛♛

Chundukwa River Lodge (5 chalets, 1 cottage) **m** 0969 641797; **e** reservations@chundukwa.com; **w** chundukwariverlodge.com. Situated 25km from Livingstone, Chundukwa is owner-run by the Zambian-born Doug & Gail, who are both incredibly friendly & passionate hosts. Its en-suite thatched chalets are raised on stilts along the riverbank. The chalets, each named after a local bird, are open fronted allowing views of the river, which can flow under the chalets during high water. Each room has a full-sized mosi net, fan & electric blankets for the winter. At the edge of the lodge is a self-contained cottage, Chundu, that sleeps 4 adults & 2 children & has its own swimming pool: perfect for families. In the thatched main area is the lounge & dining room, the lodge prides itself on the quality of its home-cooked food, & nearby there's a rock plunge pool. In keeping with the theme this area is open plan with views across the river to Chundu Island & Zimbabwe's Zambezi National Park beyond. Chundukwa is also the home of the Livingstone Polocrosse Club (page 220), evidenced by the pitches & horses & large stable yard next to the entrance road. Horseriding can be arranged (*1½ hr horse trail around US$55*) for both novices & more experienced riders, although other activities can also be organised through the lodge. *Chalets US$500–546 pp FB inc airport transfers, Victoria Falls trip, laundry & bed levy. No children under 10. Chundu Cottage US$300-450 pp/night, self-catering, min 4 guests, inc laundry & housekeeping & Wi-Fi.* ♛♛♛♛

Waterberry Lodge & The Woodlands Camp (7 chalets; 3 tents) ☎ 0213 327455; enquiries +44 (0)1379 873474; **e** reservations@waterberrylodge.com; **w** waterberrylodge.com. Waterberry Lodge is set in a secluded position on the banks of the Zambezi, about 35mins' drive from Livingstone. It's a friendly, understated place, offering style, comfort and service at a modest price tag. Constructed of neat brick & thatch, Waterberry's rooms are dotted around lovely landscaped gardens, which include a lagoon & nature trail, making this a wonderful spot for birdlife.

The rooms themselves, all named after local birds, are light, comfortable & clean. Polished concrete floors, splashes of vibrant colour, wrought-iron details & traditional thatched buildings all add to their character. Rooms all have en-suite bathrooms, AC, fans & mosi nets. Most are grouped around the main building & swimming pool, but 2 larger rooms are set further back, with a private deck over the lagoon, & a secluded honeymoon suite sits at the river's edge. The 2-storey family room next to the main area is spacious & can sleep up to 6 people, but parents should keep in mind that the site is open, & frequented by hippos, so a degree of caution is needed with children. Families may also be interested in Waterberry's River Farmhouse, a 5min walk from the main lodge & sleeping up to 10, with its own pool, shady veranda, comfortable bedrooms & the option of its own chef.

For keen birders & those seeking a secluded, peaceful hideaway, Waterberry has now also opened 3 large, well-appointed tents – The Woodlands – in their own wilderness spot, dotted with waterholes popular with birds & bushbuck. Tucked away at the back of the gardens, this quiet little camp has its own butler & guard, with a shared open-sided lounge & campfire. Meals can be taken on your private terrace or guests are welcome to use all the facilities at Waterberry Lodge.

The 2-storey central building at Waterberry has a dining area & ground-floor terrace, while upstairs the main bar & lounge are open under deep thatch, with magnificent views over the lawns, river & Zambezi National Park beyond. There are plenty of seating areas, a few reference books, & a well-stocked bar. Meals – tailored to fit around individual activities – are served in the dining area, on the sundeck, or on the terrace overlooking the pool, & there are island picnics & traditional bush dinners, too.

Activities offered are very flexible ranging from sunset & daytime cruises to birding, fishing, a tour of the Falls, & village & market visits. *Lodge US$546, Farmhouse US$614, Woodlands US$441, all pp FBA, inc drinks, laundry, airport transfers & bed levy.* ♛♛♛

Camp Nkwazi (10 chalets, 13 camp pitches), m 0973 048830; e info@campnkwazi.com; w campnkwazi.com. Situated on the banks of the Zambezi, shaded by riverine forest, Camp Nkwazi celebrated its 10th anniversary in 2023. Its en-suite, tented chalets are well spaced out, some with a river view, & others overlooking a lagoon at the rear of camp. Each stands slightly elevated off the ground & is constructed from canvas walls on a wooden frame, with a brick bathroom at the back & a private wooden deck at the front. Inside the rooms are neat & modern, with polished wooden floors & dbl or twin beds covered by walk-in mosi nets. Each chalet has a private parking spot, an outside braai, & a small kitchen with an electric hob, kettle, microwave & fridge, so they serve the independent traveller well. However, if guests prefer they can eat in the camp's restaurant, located in the main area, a redbrick structure with a canvas roof that also incorporates a fully stocked bar, comfortable lounge, & a wooden deck projecting over the river.

This main area is accessible via ramps, & 2 of the chalets are also set up for wheelchairs, with ramps, larger bathrooms & handrails in the shower & next to the toilet, meaning this is one of the few lodges in the area that caters well for travellers with mobility problems.

Across from the lagoon several camping areas have been cut out of the thick bush, but retain plenty of privacy. This is certainly one of the better-designed campsites in the area. Smaller pitches for 3 or 4 vehicles & larger areas for overlanders each have their own ablution blocks, with free electricity provided, large BBQ area & hot-water supply. Boat trips (US$40 pp) are offered on site, & the camp can book activities in town or at the Falls. *US$160/245 pp self-catering/FB; exc laundry, airport transfers. Camping US$25 pp.* ♛♛

Tintswalo at Siankaba (7 chalets) reservations +27 217 730900, lodge 0964 443189; e reservations@tintswalo.com; w tintswalo.com. Now part of the South African Tintswalo group, Siankaba is a classically styled lodge 35km from Livingstone, followed by a 7km track through open bush & a 5min boat ride. The lodge lies on 2 separate islands linked by suspension bridges. On one, spacious chalets, all named after African waterfalls, are reached along raised wooden walkways & nestle like bird hides among the trees that overhang the banks, their decks an ideal place to watch the river in complete privacy. In contrast to the half-canvas walls & roof, the heavy furniture & chintzy furnishings are very classic, with colourful velvet headboards, matching armchairs & floral accent cushions. Polished teak furniture sits on polished teak floors, offset by thick oriental rugs. Stately beds with an integral ceiling fan are hung like 4-posters with pristine white mosquito nets, & good reading lights complement the otherwise subdued lighting. Set on a platform to the rear are a claw-footed bathtub & twin pedestal basins with views towards the river, as well as a shower & separate toilet. Tucked discreetly away is a safe & fridge.

The adjacent island serves as the epicentre of the camp. Here you'll find the spacious restaurant & comfortable bar/lounge area, with natural décor & tables out on the stone terrace for alfresco dining. Among the trees is a secluded pool with stylish sunloungers, & nearby there's a small spa offering a range of treatments from hot-stone treatments to full-body massages. In addition to the treatment rooms in the spa, massages are available outside by the pool, or on the privacy of your room's deck. A 1½km nature trail also runs around the island, providing ample opportunities for birdwatching.

Activities include a sundowner cruise, birding & fishing excursions, & a mokoro trip among the islands. Mountain bikes are supplied for guests' use, & village walks – taking in a visit to the local school & returning by mokoro – are popular, too. The school, Mandia, is a government-run establishment that – along with other community projects like the nursery school – is supported by a trust fund operated by the lodge. *River tent US$660–740 pp sharing/sgl FB, inc local drinks, transfers to/from Livingstone airport, & lodge activities. No children under 12.* ♛♛♛

Royal Chundu River Lodge (10 chalets) lodge: ☎ 0213 327060; reservations: ☎ +27 21 3002439; **e** reservations@royalchundu.com; **w** royalchundu.com. Zambia's only Relais & Châteaux property, Royal Chundu is a firmly upmarket lodge on a peaceful, wooded stretch of the river. About 63km from Livingstone, & just over 1hr's drive from the Falls, two sets of rapids ensure that the lodge sits on a practically private section of the Zambezi, visited by just the occasional canoeist from the nearby village, & a haven for birds.

Solid thatched chalets are stretched along the riverbank, secluded by waterberry & water-pear trees. Concertina doors at the front of the chalets provide views of the river, & open up onto a smart wooden deck. Inside, mosi nets envelop the king-size bed & side tables, fronted by comfortable chairs. Bathrooms have twin showers, twin basins, a separate toilet & bidet. The rooms are light & airy, with colourful artwork & terrific African fabrics adding character and style. With a dressing area, safe, Wi-Fi, mini bar & tea & coffee making station it feels like a very smart hotel room with distinctly African roots.

At the heart of the lodge, linked to the chalets by wide wooden walkways, a large, sparkling infinity pool overlooks the river, bordered by neat lawns & with shaded day beds for R&R. B/fast is usually served out on the expansive deck, while dinner may be either in the firelit boma – perhaps with entertainment from the local villagers – or in the formal dining room. Ingredients for the meals are impressively all sourced from a 3km radius of the lodge, with traditional Zambian ingredients incorporated into the meals; there's even a very interesting Zambian cultural tasting menu available. Meals can be accompanied by a good selection of (rather pricey) fine wines available from the cellar, & cigars are also available.

There's a large, open-sided lounge, with a lovely mosaic bar & plenty of books (including railway memorabilia belonging to owner Hugh O'Mahoney's father), squashy sofas & coffee tables, while above – carefully shielded for noise – are a TV lounge, small library & computer room, with more comfy chairs. (There's also Wi-Fi throughout – but no mobile phone coverage.) A new floating riverside spa has added a further level of luxury to this already swanky lodge.

The lodge has good links with the local village, which guests can visit, & where many of the items in the curio shop are made. Other activities include boat cruises, fishing, canoeing & bush walks. While it's too far from the Falls for easy access, the lodge operates full-day trips combining the Falls with lunch on Livingstone Island & an evening on the *Royal Livingstone Express*. *US$1,095 pp FBA, inc airport transfers, drinks, 2 activities/day.* ♛♛♛–♛♛♛♛

Royal Chundu Island Lodge (4 suites) Contact via Royal Chundu, see left. Just a short boat trip upstream of Royal Chundu River Lodge, its exclusive sister-lodge is set on its own 1km² private wooded island, overlooking the Katombora Rapids. It is staffed with its own chef & guide, & equipped with a boat, ensuring that activities, too, are exclusive. Standards are on a par with those at the main lodge, but the suites here are larger, even closer to the river & boast a wider frontage, with an outdoor, lamplit bath on the deck, a shower that's open on 2 sides, & a more spacious sitting area to one side of the room. The main building incorporates 2 lovely lounges with contemporary comforts & a dramatic blue, painted fireplace wall & a dining area for full silver-service dinners. Boma dinners are an alternative option, with b/fast usually taken on the deck, where a small infinity pool looks across to Zimbabwe. A 3–4km nature trail takes in the huge jackalberries, baobab trees & python creepers that characterise the island, or you can participate in any activities offered by the main lodge. *US$1,340 pp FBA, inc airport transfers, drinks, 2 activities/day.* ⌚ *All year.* ♛♛♛♛

Game park, Falls and Gorge environs The development by Sun International of a prime spot close to the Falls has introduced a whole new style of accommodation to Livingstone. Other accommodation to the south of town has in recent years been augmented by lodges built away from the river, affording the advantages of open bush but without the high prices associated with a riverside location. Many of the following are actually much closer to the Falls than those situated on the upper river to the west of Livingstone, and are listed as if heading south from Livingstone towards the Falls, then out towards the gorges.

Royal Sichango Lodge [185 B4] (7 chalets, camping) Sichango Rd; m 0974 189914; e info@bushfront.com. Bordering the national park, Royal Sichango is a few km upriver from the Falls, & about 5km from town. Formerly Bushfront Lodge, but under new management in 2023, the simple, en-suite thatched chalets are set among indigenous vegetation with abundant birdlife. For campers there are 3 individual pitches with ablutions & a braai area. The main lodge area has sat TV, free Wi-Fi, a large bar/lounge & a restaurant. All meals are served here, & snacks are always available, & there's a small pool for cooling off. *Chalet US$150/room; Camping US$20.* **$$$**

Victoria Falls Waterfront [185 B4] (23 rooms, 20 tents, camping) off Sichango Rd; ☎ 0213 320606–08; m 0968 320606; e waterfront@safpar.com; w safpar.com. This large, secure & affordable riverside complex, within the unfenced area of Mosi-oa-Tunya National Park is only 4km upstream from the Falls, is well equipped & positioned to take advantage of all Livingstone's activities. Its large teak deck, from which you can often see the spray from the Falls, is one of the best places to watch the sunset over the Zambezi. Outside, among palm trees, is a sunken pool overlooking the river. 8 large A-frame thatched chalets house individual rooms that are comfortable, light & airy with ethnic touches.

Beyond the main building is the Adventure Village with a large natural-style rock pool, another bar & a thatched auditorium where daily activity briefings are given & rafting videos are shown in the evening, accompanied by a BBQ. In the gardens here, 20 permanent tents are perched on wooden platforms, each with 2 beds with bedding & linen (or bring your own). Nearby ablutions are clean & spacious, with flush toilets & hot & cold showers. Further along, a separate grassed camping area has its own ablutions, BBQ & washing-up area; taking about 75 campers, it gets pretty noisy when it's busy with overland trucks. SafPar's activity centre is located upstairs in the main area, offering a full range of activities & excursions, many that they operate themselves (page 212); you will often begin & end your activities at the Waterfront, even if staying elsewhere in Livingstone. Among these are 2 boats offering b/fast, lunch or sunset **cruises** (*US$60–75 pp inc canapés, drinks & park fees*) from the Waterfront's own jetty. The larger Mukambi takes up to 100 people & tends to draw a more lively crowd, while the more upmarket Mabushi takes up to 25 passengers, & is perfect for families or those wanting a quieter cruise. Every Oct, the Zambezi Whitewater Challenge is organised by the lodge owners, SafPar – a testament to their adventure sports' origins. *Chalet room* **$$$$**; *tent US$30 pp, B&B; camping US$15 pp.*

David Livingstone Safari Lodge & Spa [185 B4] (77 rooms) ☎ +27 104 425888; e cro@aha.co.za; w thedavidlivingstone.com. This efficient 5-star hotel under steep thatch occupies an impressive spot on the Zambezi, and makes the most of its wide river frontage. The entrance lobby, restaurants, rooms & even a good-sized infinity pool command excellent views of the river, where the 3-deck *Lady Livingstone* (page 216) awaits passengers to cruise along the Zambezi every sunset. Huge basketwork lampshades & wooden sculptures dominate the décor, conveying a strong sense of Africa. Concrete walkways with rustic pole railings lead across the sprawling site to tastefully appointed rooms, each furnished in dark wood with AC, large, flat-screen TV, safe & walk-in mosi nets (helpfully encompassing bedside lights & a phone). Glazed folding doors lead to a small balcony with a couple of chairs, while behind lies a modern bathroom with separate toilet & shower. 2 rooms are specifically designed for travellers with mobility problems, while 5 suites each have a lounge/bar area & an indoor jacuzzi. There's an Afro-Arabian fusion restaurant – Kalai, a cocktail bar, & waterside terrace serving drinks, snacks & light lunches. Other facilities include a spa, gym & gift shop. **$$$$$** *inc 1 activity/day (sunset cruise or Vic Falls tour).*

Maramba River Lodge [185 C4] (10 chalets, 26 tents, camping) ☎ 0213 324189; **m** 0976 587511; **e** reservations@marambariverlodge.com; **w** maramba-zambia.com. This well-established lodge & campsite, founded in 1991, lies 4km from the Falls, down a short, bumpy track just south of Livingstone Reptile Park. Situated within the national park on the banks of the Maramba River, it is a real oasis in the bush, with green lawns & mature trees, hippos, elephants & birds aplenty. The lodge has a relaxed atmosphere, & with a shaded pool, children's play area & several family rooms it works well for families. It's important to note though that wildlife does walk through the grounds, so children still need to be supervised at all times. The lodge is well appointed with an activity booking office, craft shop, fully licensed riverside bar, simple restaurant, & free Wi-Fi is available in the communal areas.

There are 4 types of accommodation. The thatched en-suite chalets (with 2 or 4 beds, mosquito nets & fans) are bright & airy, in a pretty location under mopane & mahogany trees. 9 spacious luxury tents combine lodge comfort with the pleasures of camping. They are en suite (with tiled bathroom & open-air shower) & have handcrafted furniture, including a dbl & a sgl bed under walk-in mosi nets & a small veranda. Simpler accommodation comes in the form of 10 twin-bedded safari tents under thatch, with chairs, clothes storage, electricity & en-suite facilities. Simpler still, there are 7 small dome tents, fitted with twin beds & a lockable drawer. They have a dedicated ablution block, & a covered main area overlooking the river. The small campsite is very popular, so it's wise to book in advance; campers share an ablution block with hot showers & laundry facilities. *Camping US$25/15 adult/child; chalets US$145–169 pp; tents US$125–280; family chalets US$335/444 4/6 people; all B&B inc morning & afternoon tea.* **$$$**

Anantara Royal Livingstone [map, page 214] (173 rooms) Mosi-oa-Tunya Rd; ☎ 0768 850446, 0213 321122; **e** royallivingstone@anantara.com; **w** anantara.com. This opulent 5-star hotel is situated in extensive grounds. Spacious, elegant interiors, with an old-world attention to detail & service are de rigueur. Outside, broad, shady verandas overlook sweeping lawns leading to an unparalleled frontage along the Zambezi, with the 'smoke' from the Falls rising tantalisingly close. A 15-min walk along the river brings you to the Falls themselves via the direct access point that is the preserve of the two Sun International hotels, or guests can be escorted by porters in pith helmets on one of the hotel's 'club cars' (golf-cart style). The hotel is in the national park; zebra, impala & giraffe are often seen grazing in the grounds.

All rooms have twin or king-size beds & are fitted with AC, sat TV, radio, blu-ray DVD player, minibar, safe & phone; 2 rooms are fully equipped for travellers with mobility problems. Tasteful & comfortable, if on the small side, each room has its own private balcony, & benefits from the services of a butler. Should all this not be sufficient, there are also 4 suites.

Meals are served either in the excellent à-la-carte restaurant where live piano music is often played in the evenings (page 205), or outside on the veranda, while for a special occasion private candlelit dinners on the lawns can be arranged at extra cost. The long, wood-panelled bar has a relaxed, colonial air. A sundeck built on stilts over the Zambezi makes a pleasant spot to enjoy a sundowner drink, & when the spray from the Falls is visible in high water the view is spectacular, although the deck can get incredibly busy in the evenings. There's also a smaller, private deck nearby that can be reserved for groups. A grand swimming pool overlooks the river, & makes a great place to relax in the afternoon. The Royal Livingstone has a well-equipped & air-conditioned gym, while those in search of pampering can visit the Royal Spa (page 221) with its white massage tents spread along the riverbank.

No activities are included in the cost of the hotel, but the concierge can help to organise any of the activities in the Livingstone area, & the hotel even has its own helipad should you wish to arrive & depart in style.

Considerably more expensive than the adjacent Avani, the Royal Livingstone caters for a very different market – those seeking traditional standards of décor & service in a truly gracious setting. If you'd like to indulge without the high price of accommodation, consider sundowners on their magnificent riverside deck, or a highly civilised afternoon high tea in the lounge (⌚ 15.00–17.00 daily; US$50 pp). **$$$$$**

Avani Victoria Falls Resort [map, page 214] (212 rooms) 393 Mosi-oa-Tunya Rd; ☎ 0213 321122; m 0978 777044–7; e victoriafalls@avanihotels.com; w avanihotels.com. Known as the Zambezi Sun until Minor International took over a controlling share in 2014, Avani is the lively 3-star sibling of the Royal Livingstone, & what a contrast. Crenellated walls are more reminiscent of a north African mosque than of southern Africa, their deep desert red contrasting with the Zambian sky. Vervet monkeys, the bane of the staff, cavort through the colourful grounds as if through a children's playground. Although the hotel is only 5 mins' walk from the Falls there are no views of the river. Instead balconies from each room overlook the extensive lawns where impala, zebra & giraffes freely wander among the ironwork animal statues dotted around the grounds. Well designed, if rather compact, the rooms are very comfortable – the standard of a good international business hotel – but with considerably more flashes of colour & individuality. Each has AC, sat TV, free Wi-Fi, safe & phone, with a bath & shower en suite. 2 rooms are adapted for travellers with mobility problems.

In addition to the extensive buffet **restaurant** (*US$40 pp*), there's a relaxed alfresco grill beside the pool that snakes through the grounds, often accompanied by a live band or dancers, or – adjacent to The Falls activity centre – a simple café. If you want something more formal it's possible to eat in the Royal Livingstone's restaurant, which is similarly priced, but you will need to book in advance, & its dress code requires trousers rather than shorts. You can use the Royal's spa, too – although on-site massages can be organised here. The complex also includes a children's club & playground, & business & conference centres. Ultimately, though, everything hinges on the location. Just a few hundred metres' walk from the lip of the Falls & the curio market, & with unrestricted access, the hotel's position is unbeatable. **$$$$$**

Stanley Safari Lodge [185 D5] (10 cottages) Contact Robin Pope Safaris, page 292. Set some distance back from the river & bordering the Mosi-oa-Tunya National Park, Stanley Safari Lodge was taken over by Robin Pope Safaris in 2011. Positioned at the top of a hill, the lodge enjoys sweeping views down towards the Zambezi, & spray from the Falls is often visible when the river is in full flow. It's best suited as a place to chill out, relax & unwind. Advance reservations are essential, with almost all clients arriving by air & collected at the airport. Should you be driving yourself, turn east off the main road to the Falls almost opposite the Royal Livingstone & continue past a large baobab on your right, bearing sharp right after 500m, then following the road towards Mukuni village for a further 2km. The turning (⊕ 17°54' 1.45 S, 25°53'39.32 E) is on the rise of a hill, on the left, just after the sign for Munali Farm.

The lodge is set behind a high electric fence, but once inside all is calm & spacious. Large, fairly formal gardens with a central infinity pool face west towards the Zambezi. The main building is a beautifully designed thatched affair with an open-aspect lounge, bar & dining area, & the 'map room' (with a laptop & free Wi-Fi) deserves to be popular with guests. Above is a further sitting area, while below, a wine cellar allows candlelit tastings of a range of South African, French & Italian wines. Permutations for serving dinner are many – including the option of a dining table *in* the infinity pool!

5 stylish open 'cottages', each slightly different but most with an open front & a view towards the Zambezi, are built in a half-moon shape, with king-size or twin beds, a 'loo with a view' & an outside shower & bath; a closed cottage has a similar layout but with a solid front. The Honeymoon Suite is an open suite with its own plunge pool & fireplace, while the family suite, which is also open fronted, is 2 bedroomed, & works well for children. It has a shallow paddling pool, & a bucket shower set outside around a tree, giving younger children

the opportunity to experience in safety the fun of living in the bush. There are also 2 closed suites, Livingstone & Stanley, decorated in a colonial style with a lounge, fireplace, covered terrace, & private plunge pool. The Stanley Suite has 2 en-suite bedrooms so it also works well for families.

Throughout, the décor is both stylish & comfortable, with good use of wood, stone & natural fabrics, & plenty of space. Activities offered by the lodge include mountain biking, rhino tracking in the national park, & village & museum tours. The lodge can easily arrange external activities around Livingstone. *Cottage US$415–520, open suite US$460–610, closed suite US$520–680, pp sharing, all FBA; inc local drinks, laundry, airport transfers.* **$$$$$**

Taita Falcon Lodge [185 D7] (7 chalets, camping) lodge 0213 327046, reservations 0213 321850; **e** info@taitafalcon.com; **w** taitafalcon.com. ⊕ 17°58.879'S, 25°54.654'E. Perched on the very edge of Batoka Gorge, with the raging waters below, Taita's view is breathtaking to say the least. It is a 45-min drive from Livingstone, for which you'll need a high-clearance vehicle, & a 4x4 during the rains. The lodge has its own helipad, but drivers should follow the main road from town towards the Falls, take the well-signposted left turn opposite the entrance to the Royal Livingstone, then go right at the baobab tree. From here, follow the signs for about ½hr along 11km of long, winding track, passing through Songwe village.

The lodge is named after the rare Taita falcon that frequents cliffs & gorges, especially in the Zambezi Valley – & this area is one of the best in Africa for spotting them. They are small (less than 30cm long) with cream to brown underparts – no bars or markings – & a strong, fast style of flight. Look for them especially in the evenings, perhaps trying to catch swallows or bats on the wing. Verreaux's (black) eagles, peregrine falcons & many other raptors & small birds are also resident, numbering among the 234 bird species recorded here.

The lodge is pleasant & informal surrounded by indigenous gardens & with personable service. Its rustic en-suite chalets are constructed of stone, timber & reeds under thatch, with pull-down rush 'windows', a simple sliding door, & locally made beds, tables & chairs. With a shower, basin & toilet at the back, & a separate outside shower in a garden area at the front, they're open in design, but entirely private. 2 can be made up as family rooms, sleeping up to 5; the rest are dbls or trpls. Electricity is from a generator.

Narrow pathways, accessible by wheelchair, weave through the bush parallel to the cliff, linking the chalets to the bar & restaurant. In front of the bar, overlooking the gorge & Rapids 16 & 17, downstream of the Falls, is a great place both to spot birds & to watch the rafters down below. That said, & although the chalets are set back from the precipice, I'd be wary of letting children run wild here. There's a nice small pool for a dip, encompassed by a tiled patio with adjacent small lawn.

A couple of kilometres from the lodge is a small campsite – Peregrine's Nest Bush Camp - with 3 pitches, set well apart with their own ablution blocks & a generator for power 18.30–21.30, but with no river view. Campers can use the lodge's bar & restaurant if they book in advance, but not the pool.

Included in some of the lodge rates are a tour of Songwe village & one of 4 activities: a game drive, a sunset cruise, a town tour, or a visit to the Falls. Other activities include guided bush & bird walks, hiking trails in & around the gorge (equipped hikers can do 2–3-day hikes) & fishing (for the fit – it's a steep walk!). Taita Falcon Lodge is a relaxing place in a remote spot – albeit only 12km from the Falls. Adrenalin junkies, though, could feel cut off from the epicentre of things. *US$205–240 pp FB; inc airport transfers, village tour & a bush & bird walk. Camping US$20 pp.*

WHERE TO EAT AND DRINK Meals are usually included in the rates of the upmarket, riverside lodges, and the food will be of a very high standard indeed. Many of the larger hotels' restaurants also serve international cuisine of a good quality, although the better of these can be expensive places to eat.

In recent years, several independent restaurants have opened up in Livingstone, offering a wide variety of world cuisines, at prices often cheaper than the hotel restaurants. Although generally good quality, few of the town's restaurants are fine dining; fresh, tasty meals will tend to be hearty rather than haute cuisine. We've listed the current pick of the bunch here but it's always worth asking locally about the latest openings. In addition, there are several small cafés & chain restaurants in town. For a few kwacha, these serve the usual fare of pre-packaged chips, burgers, samosas, sandwiches and soft drinks. All are in the centre of town, along Mosi-oa-Tunya Road. Falls Park shopping centre [185 C3] and Mosi-oa-Tunya Square [189 D6] are useful sources of fast food with an outside seating area. Most are open every day until around 21.00.

Cafés

For something homemade & tasty, the best café by far is Kubu Café.

✷ **Kubu Café** [189 D6] Kabompo Rd; m 0977 653345; e kubucafe@zamnet.zm; ⌚ 08.00–23.00 Tue–Sat, 08.00–17.00 Sun–Mon. Next to Livingstone Fire Station, this consistently good café is a super spot for a full English breakfast, fresh salad, shwarma or simply a great cup of coffee & a slice of delicious carrot cake. There is ample seating both inside & outside, a children's play area, community noticeboard, book exchange & some great locally produced crafts & farm produce to buy. The café serves milkshakes & coffees that go well with a slice of one of their homemade cakes. More substantial meals such as burgers, pizzas & steaks are also available, & there's a reasonably stocked bar. Wi-Fi is available to paying customers. $–$$$$

Munali Café [188 B1] Mosi-oa-Tunya Rd; ⌚ 08.00–21.00 Mon–Sat, 08.00–20.00 Sun. Another pleasant café in the centre of Livingstone, it serves pastries, samosas, sandwiches & basic hot food, & is a good place for a cheap & quick meal, & the coffee is as good as any that you'll find in Livingstone. $

Wonderbake [188 B1] Mosi-oa-Tunya Rd; ⌚ 08.00–21.00 Mon–Sat, 08.00–20.00 Sun. This Zambian chain is in a convenient location for a quick snack, though it's often crowded. Expect fresh bread, samosas, pies, & coffees should you need a jolt of caffeine. $

Zam Mex [188 B1] 4557 Kunawa Rd; ⌚ 08.00–23.00. Near the bus station, this no-frills snack stop is operated by Spanish NGO Kubuka, to help fund their local community projects. Cheap local & Mexican fare, predominantly to locals and backpackers. $

Restaurants

Avani Victoria Falls Restaurant & Poolside Grill [map, page 214] Mosi-oa-Tunya Rd; ☎ 0213 321122; w avanihotels.com; ⌚ restaurant 06-30–10.30 & 18.30–22.30 daily; poolside grill 10.30–22.00 daily. As you'd expect in a large resort, there's an extensive, international buffet dinner in 'The Theatre of Food', as well as a lively alfresco restaurant serving poolside Western fare, ideal for light lunches &, when there's live music, it's good value for an evening out. African boma dinners are a Sat night option. $$$$$

✷ **Elephant Café** [map, page 194] Nakatindi Rd, Mosi-oa-Tunya National Park; ☎ 0973 403270; w safpar.com. Upstream of the Falls, inside the national park, the award-winning Elephant Café is far from a café: it's a sophisticated set-menu restaurant serving delicious, locally produced organic food, beautifully presented on a wooden deck over the Zambezi. Its name comes from the hand-reared rescue elephants who live here & with whom guests can interact. Road transfers are possible but it's pretty special to take the 30min Jetboat trip through the park. Reservations essential. No children under 4; only children over 10 can interact with elephants. *US$140–230pp (price varies by time of day & road/boat access).* $$$$$

The Old Drift Restaurant [189 G6] Anantara Royal Livingstone, Mosi-oa-Tunya Rd; ☎ 0213 321122. For old-world elegance & comfort, good service & fine dining, try the Royal Livingstone's à la carte restaurant: The Old Drift. It's formal & reasonably expensive – a good opportunity to get out of khaki safari kit. Enjoy a pre-dinner cocktail on the riverside Kubu deck, complete with views of rising mist from the Falls & resident grazing zebra. There is also a genteel afternoon tea option – though be warned: vervet monkeys might try to steal your food – & a cosy piano bar complete with its own gin menu. Be sure to book any dining in advance; if the hotel is full they don't take outside reservations. $$$$$

Victoria Falls Waterfront [185 B4] Sichango Rd; ☎ 0213 320606–08. The magnificent setting of SafPar's riverside watersports complex makes this a good place to dine after a day on the river (you can stay here too). Enjoy snacks, meals & sundowners on the banks of the Zambezi at affordable prices. The food is good & plentiful with the usual variety of crowd-pleasing steaks, wraps, burgers & wood-fired pizzas served by friendly staff. There is also a full bar. While it is out of town, it's the kind of place you might go for a meal & stay for hours to savour the chilled riverside ambience. **$$$–$$$$**

Golden Leaf Indian Restaurant [185 C3] 1174 Mosi-oa-Tunya Rd; ☎ 0213 321266, **m** 0974 321266; **w** ngolide-lodge.com; ⏲ 12.30–22.00 Tue–Sun. Serving homemade Indian delicacies here for over 20 years, this small, authentic restaurant has a good reputation, convivial atmosphere & loyal following. Consistently one of the better places to eat in town, the extensive menu includes fish masala, kadai chicken, spicy chilli naan & an extensive range of vegetarian dishes. You can order a take-away or eat in, although due to its popularity it's advisable to book in advance. **$$–$$$**

✷ **Olga's – The Italian Corner** [189 D6] 20 Mokambo Rd; ☎ 0977 229083; **e** olgasproject2022@gmail.com; **w** olgasproject.com; ⏲ 07.00–22.00 daily. Close to the Catholic church, this is *the* place for traditional stone-baked pizzas, as well as pasta dishes & salads. A thatched eating area incorporates crafts & furniture made by members of the Local Youth Community Training Centre & a school for disadvantaged & vulnerable youngsters, with profits from the restaurant fed directly back into the education centre. The restaurant has free Wi-Fi, & take-away is available. 9 rooms are also available in a guesthouse overlooking the lush garden. **$$–$$$**

Zest Bar & Restaurant [189 D8] 2616 Mosi-oa-Tunya Rd; **m** 0978 109392; **f** zestbarandrestaurant; ⏲ 08.00-midnight daily. Opposite Zambian Railways, this casual spot is a local favourite serving popular espetadas (Brazilian hanging kebabs), pizzas, traditional Zambian fare – *vinkubala* (caterpillars) & *kapenta* (small fish) – as well as sharing platters. **$$–$$$**

Café Zambezi [189 D7] Shop 214, 217 Area, Mosi-oa-Tunya Rd; **m** 0213 323189; **e** michelle.cafezambezi@gmail.com; **f** CafeZambezi; ⏲ 08.00–21.00 Mon–Sat, 08.00–20.00 Sun. A popular local spot serving a well-regarded Jamaican goat curry, barbecue fare, burgers & Zambian beef stew. The best place to sit is under the mango tree in the outside courtyard. **$**

ENTERTAINMENT AND NIGHTLIFE Livingstone's **nightlife** centres largely around dancing and drinking, although the bars at various restaurants offer a pleasant atmosphere if you simply want to relax and chat. For relaxed sundowners, join the crowd at the Victoria Falls Waterfront [185 B4], overlooking the river, or for lively DJ nights try The B' Hive Cafe [185 C3] most nights.

For live music, there's a band at Avani (page 203) most evenings and at weekends. Traditional dancing can be seen at The Victoria Falls Waterfront, though you'll need to check times and dates with them.

The New Fairmount Hotel [188 E3] has the neon-lit Club Fairmount (☎ 0213 320723; ⏲ normally 20.00–04.00 Thu–Sat, but phone to confirm) that's generally jam-packed at weekends.

SHOPPING With both the Falls Park shopping centre [185 C3] and Mosi-oa-Tunya Square [189 D6] (commonly referred to as the 'Shoprite Centre'), options for shopping in Livingstone have improved considerably in recent years. There are also a couple of markets, and several shops along the main Mosi-oa-Tunya Road. Opening hours are usually around 09.00–17.00 Monday to Friday, and Saturday mornings, unless otherwise stated.

Food and drink Although you can find most things in Livingstone, you may still have to visit several shops, and imported gourmet items are harder to come by and expensive.

Of the **supermarkets**, the newer Shoprite [189 D6] (Mosi-oa-Tunya Sq; ⌚ 08.00–20.00 daily) is the largest and has the best selection (The original Shoprite on Kapondo Street [188 B2] is an entirely different affair, so don't get them confused!), although the new branch of Spar Super Store on the corner of Mutelo St [188 B2] (Mosi-oa-Tunya Rd; ⌚ 07.00–20.00 daily) is also useful and well stocked.

For somewhere less corporate, for fruit and vegetables, try the Zambian open-air **markets**. Positioned around town, these have fresh tomatoes, onions and other basic fruits and vegetables, and are generally cheaper than the supermarkets, although some haggling may be required. If it's just **meat** you're after, cross Mosi-oa-Tunya Road to Pama Meats for a selection of beef, poultry and pork, or try Shopper's Butchery [188 B1] (John Hunt Way, behind post office). Wonderbake and Munali Café [188 B1] sell good fresh-baked **bread** and pastries.

Books and magazines Several of the curio shops stock wildlife reference books and regional travel guides. Kubu Café has a small secondhand bookshop selling books (K5) and slightly out-of-date magazines (K2). Jollyboys (page 192) has a book-exchange system, as do many other places to stay in town. Current magazines may be harder to come by. Your best bet is the Spar in the centre [188 B2] or Shoprite at Mosi-oa-Tunya Square [189 D6] – though be warned, magazines are expensive and tend to be several months old, so be sure to check the issue date. Oddly, the street vendors in front of the Capitol Theatre [188 B1] often have more recent ones at much lower prices, but this is very hit or miss.

Clothes You can pick up clothing essentials at the PEP store [188 B2] (Mosi-oa-Tunya Rd, opposite Zanaco), or at Power Sales, a few doors down from the same bank, though you'll need to be selective. There are also plenty of shops selling a hotchpotch of stuff that includes assorted clothing, mostly from China – so it can become rather a mission (or adventure) to find what you seek. For more fashionable wear try the clothing stores at Falls Park shopping centre [185 C3] or at the Avani Victoria Falls Resort [map, page 214], though these will be pricier. For shoes, there's Bata [188 B1], though both the selection and sizes are rather limited.

Despite its shortcomings on fashion, Livingstone is a great place to find African wear – brightly coloured shirts, skirts and dresses, some complete with matching caps or headscarves – and garments can often be made to order with a few days' notice. *Chitenje*, the colourful lengths of traditional African cloth, can be found at most of the small Indian shops on the main road and on Kuta Way, parallel to the main road, or at any of the local markets (page 218). Clothes can be made up at Emmah's Wear (see below) from your own fabrics or theirs.

Crafts, curios and gifts If you like bargaining and have lots of patience, then try one of the craft markets (page 218), either in town or next to the Falls. Alternatively, look out for the informal craft market in the car park at Falls Park shopping centre [185 C3], where curio vendors lay out their goods on a more ad hoc basis.

If time isn't on your side, or you don't fancy the hassle of bargaining, one of the following might suit you much better.

Emmah's Wear [189 D7] 121 Mosi-oa-Tunya Rd; **m** 0977 432957; **e** emmahwear@gmail.com; ⌚ 08.00–17.00 Mon–Fri, 08.00–12.30 Sat. Just north of the railway station, opposite the police post, Emmah's can tailor-make anything from clothing to tablecloths, quickly & affordably. Bring your own fabric (bought at a local market or an Indian shop in town) or choose one at their shop, & expect to pay from K180 for a simple skirt & K280 for a dress. There's also a small craft shop here.

Mosi-oa-Tunya Arts Centre [189 D7] 123 Mosi-oa-Tunya Rd. Just next to Emmah's Wear on the main road, the Arts Centre is an open-sided shop that looks like a small market. It sells a range of art from life-size iron sculptures of bulls, to more practical items like paintings & locally made jewellery. You can expect to engage in some haggling to get a reasonable price, but it's less pushy than some of the larger craft markets.

Museum Curio Shop & Art Gallery [189 A2] Livingstone Museum. The museum's curio shop showcases Zambian handicrafts & basketware. A wide selection of Zambian paintings & other art by local artists is for sale – everything from wildlife to people to abstract.

Women in Mining Jewellery Project [map, page 214] The Falls, Mosi-oa-Tunya Rd; ⏲ 08.00–18.00 daily. If it's gemstones or jewellery you're after, this shop linked to the Association of Zambian Women in Mining (AZWIM) could be the place to find it.

Zambezi Jewels [map, page 214] 147 Mosi-oa-Tunya Rd; ☎ 0213 324567; ⏲ 09.00–18.00. Located just next to Avani's activity centre, Zambezi Jewels has an interesting collection of handcrafted jewellery from across Zambia. The staff are helpful & it's a non-pressured environment for souvenir shopping.

Pharmacies For cosmetics, toiletries or medicines there are several good pharmacies stocking a selection of items including insect repellents, beauty products, suncreams, medical supplies, baby supplies, batteries and more. Each has a trained pharmacist, who can also offer advice on medications and fill prescriptions. Otherwise, the Spar Super Store in the centre [188 B2] and Shoprite in Mosi-oa-Tunya Square [189 D6] sell a variety of beauty products and basics.

Health & Glow Pharmacy [188 B2 & 189 D6] Mosi-oa-Tunya Rd; ☎ 0967 319251, 0961 457104; w healthandglowpharmacy.com; ⏲ 08.00–19.00 Mon–Sat, 09.00–13.00 Sun. With branches opposite Mosi-oa Tunya mall & next to Munali Cafe, these well-stocked shops have helpful, knowledgeable staff.

HK Pharmacy & Photo Studio [188 B1] Mosi-oa-Tunya Rd, next to Capitol Theatre; ☎ 0213 324296; ⏲ 08.30–19.00 Mon–Fri, 08.00–14.00 Sat. Get your prescriptions filled & photos digitally printed at the same time. They also have a wide selection of beauty products.

L F Moore Chemists [188 C1] 133 Akapelwa St; ☎ 0213 321640; ⏲ 08.00–17.00 Mon–Fri, 08.00–13.00 Sat. Established in 1936, L F Moore is a Livingstone institution. It remains one of the best-stocked chemists in town, with friendly staff who will go out of their way to help.

Link Pharmacy [189 D6] Mosi-oa-Tunya Sq; ☎ 0213 324222; ⏲ 09.00–18.00 Mon–Fri, 09.00–17.00 Sat, 10.00–14.00 Sun. If this well-stocked chemist doesn't have what you want, they can usually get it from their Lusaka store.

BANKS AND CHANGING MONEY Livingstone has several major banks and various bureaux de change dotted throughout town. Most of the banks have ATMs, for which you'll generally need a Visa card rather than MasterCard. More convenient, but with the least favourable exchange rate, is to change money at a hotel or lodge.

Avoid the freelance 'money-changers' who tend to congregate around the Capitol Theatre and at the border. No matter how carefully you watch, they always take advantage of unsuspecting (and even suspicious) tourists by short-changing them somehow.

The major **banks** are situated around the post office area, parallel to the main Mosi-oa-Tunya Road [188 D4]. Typically they open Monday to Friday 08.00–16.00, and sometimes on Saturday mornings, but get there early if you want to avoid long queues. The spacious air-conditioned interior and more private exchange facilities of Zanaco make it the preferred choice in town.

Many of these banks operate a **bureau de change** service and you can also exchange money at the post office, though rates are likely to be lower at the private **bureaux de change.**

Banks

Absa Bank Cnr Akapelwa St & Mosi-oa-Tunya; 0211 430014
Atlas Mara John Hunt Way; 0213 320122
First National Bank (FNB) 360 Mosi-oa-Tunya Rd; 0211 366 800. Inc ATM & Forex.
NSBC Maina Soko; 0213 322649. Also at airport, inc ATM.
Stanbic Mosi-oa-Tunya Sq; 0213 324353
Standard Chartered 0213 220489. Also at Falls Park, inc ATM [185 C3].
Zanaco Cnr Mutelo St & Mosi-oa-Tunya Rd; 0213 321901

Bureaux de change

Zampost [188 B1] Mosi-oa-Tunya Rd, in post office complex; 0213 322472; 08.00–16.30 Mon–Fri, 08.00–12.30 Sat
Zampost [185 C3] Falls Park; 0213 324797; 09.00–12.30, 12.45–17.00 Mon–Fri, 08.00–12.30 Sat

COMMUNICATIONS

Internet Driven by increasing expectations from international travellers the majority of accommodation, and many restaurants, now offer free Wi-Fi access and/or computers with internet access. As such the number of internet cafés in Livingstone has declined in recent years, although there is still a reliable one at PostNet near the Capitol Theatre [188 B1] (08.00–18.00 Mon–Fri, 08.00–13.00 Sat). While rates are low and comparable, at around K1–2/hour, the standard of computers, speed and service varies; high-speed service in Livingstone is pretty rare, and the service often goes down during the common power outages. For those with a laptop, Kubu Café (page 205) offers Wi-Fi to customers, so is a good place for a great cappuccino while you check your emails.

Post and courier You can't miss Livingstone's post office [188 B2] (912 Mosi-Oa-Tunya; 0213 322002; 08.00–18.00 Mon–Fri, 08.00–14.00 Sat) in the centre of town in a sprawling complex of banks and shops, adjacent to the main road. If you splurge on a giant wooden giraffe or a heavy sculpture at the curio market, there are reliable international couriers who can assist.

DHL Mosi-oa-Tunya Hse; 0213 320044
FedEx 912 Mosi-Oa-Tunya; 0213 321133

Telephone The prevalence of Wi-Fi and use of WhatsApp makes phone calls a great deal easier and cheaper than they once were. Any visitors spending any amount of time in Zambia, and especially those on long-stays or self-drive trips, are advised to purchase a local SIM card. Those for Airtel, MTN and the state-owned Zamtel are easily obtainable from numerous outlets across town; look out for their signs at shopping malls and on Mosi-oa-Tunya Road. Expect to pay around US$4 for a week's unlimited data on a prepaid SIM card; for around US$10, you can purchase a 30-day, 25GB data bundle. After purchasing your SIM card (less than US$1), it must be registered at the main office of the supplier before it can be used. Airtel, MTN and Zamtel all have offices on Mosi-oa-Tunya Road and you will need to present your passport to complete the registration process.

OTHER PRACTICALITIES

Car repairs and spares The two biggest workshops in town are Foley's Africa (639 Industrial Rd; 0213 320888; **e** info@foleysafrica.com; **w** foleysafrica.com;

⌚ 08.00–17.00 Mon–Fri, 08.00–13.00 Sat), which caters for Land Rovers; and Bennet Quality Engineering, also known as Harry's workshop [185 C3] (☎ 0213 322380; m 0978 308936; e hbennett@iconnect.zm), opposite Falls Park. Bennett services most of the tour operators' vehicles in town and is your best bet for more serious problems.

For more basic repairs, punctures and tyre repairs, the main fuel stations will usually have someone who can assist. If it's parts or vehicle accessories that you need, the most central place is the large, well-signed Autoworld [188 A2] (Mosi-oa-Tunya Rd; ☎ 0213 320264; e autoworld@zamtel.zm).

Emergencies Medical facilities are limited in Livingstone, and the local hospitals are not up to the standard of those in the West, but in the event of an emergency you can contact the facilities listed below.

Should you need an **optician**, head for Falls Park shopping centre [185 C3] or try Sunbird Opticians [188 B1] (3 Nongo Kalimba House, Mosi-oa-Tunya Rd) or Starlite Opticians [188 B2] (357 Mosi-oa-Tunya Rd). For pharmacies, see page 208.

Dr Shafik's Hospital [188 G2] 1115 Katete Av; ☎ 0213 321130 (24hrs); m 0955/0966/0977 863000; e shafikhosp@rocketmail.com. Dr Shafik is a surgeon & the hospital can also provide doctor consultations, nursing care & medication.

SES [189 E2] Speciality Emergency Services Emergency control centre ☎ 0977 770302, 0962 740300; m 0977 740306/8; e livingstoneparamedics@ses-zambia.com; w ses-zambia.com. Rapid emergency response teams with air ambulances can be deployed 24/7 from Lusaka & Kitwe, plus helicopters stationed in Livingstone.

Tourist information The Zambia Tourism Board [188 A2] (Mosi-oa-Tunya Rd; ☎ 0213 321404/87; e ztb@zambiatourism.org.zm; w zambiatourism.com; ⌚ 08.00–17.00 Mon–Fri, 09.00–noon Sat) has an office at the tourist centre next to the Livingstone Museum, easily spotted for the two-seater plane outside. Here you can expect pleasant, friendly staff working with limited resources. You can pick up brochures and get referrals, but agents and tour operators (see opposite) are usually better geared to assist you with actual bookings.

Travel agents For international airline tickets and fares, your best choice is:

Southend Travel [188 E4] Liso House, 106 Mosi-oa-Tunya Rd; m 0978 544666; e southendlvi@yahoo.com; ⌚ 08.00–17.30 Mon–Fri, 08.00–13.00 Sat. Experienced, long-established agents for SAA, British Airways, Kenya Airways, Lufthansa & Ethiopian Airways, among others. Able to advise on special air fares, & also for the Intercape Mainliner bus service (page 100).

WHAT TO SEE AND DO

The area around Victoria Falls has been a major crossroads for travellers for over a hundred years. From the early missionaries and traders, to the backpackers, overland trucks, package tourists and safari-goers of the last few decades – virtually everyone passing through the region from overseas chooses to stop here. This has created a thriving tourism industry and, apart from simply marvelling at one of the world's greatest waterfalls, there are now myriad ways to occupy yourself for a few days. Some of these are easily booked after you arrive; one or two are better pre-arranged.

The past few decades have witnessed a huge shift in the area's atmosphere. Visitors used to be from southern Africa, with perhaps the odd intrepid backpacker and the fortunate few who could afford an upmarket safari. Now the sheer volume of visitors to the Falls has increased massively. This increase, especially noticeable in the proportion of younger visitors, has fuelled the rise of more active, adventurous pursuits like white-water rafting, bungee jumping, river boarding and other thrill-based pastimes.

A genteel cocktail at a luxury hotel is no longer the only high point of a Livingstone visit for most people. You are more likely to return home with vivid memories of the adrenalin rush of shooting rapids in a raft, or the buzz of accelerating head-first towards the Zambezi with only a piece of elastic to save you.

TOUR OPERATORS In a town where tourism is such big business, almost everyone – from hoteliers to car-hire companies to taxi firms – can handle bookings for individual activities. Those listed here are the specialists. For flight operators, see page 186.

Many companies offer **guided sightseeing tours** around Livingstone, including visits to traditional villages, local markets, museums, the Falls, game park and historical sites. While some activities can be organised without notice, others need to be pre-booked, so it's as well to be organised if you don't want to be disappointed. Rates almost always include transfers from your accommodation, within a reasonable radius.

If you are staying in one of the smart riverfront lodges, sightseeing tours for guests using their own guides and vehicles are generally included. Bushtracks Africa, Wild Side Tours & Safaris and Safari Par Excellence are popular operators, although there are many others (see below). Of these, Wild Side is run by people who have lived in Livingstone for years, and who understand the place well; it can personalise tours to suit individual requirements, while the larger Bushtracks runs set trips aimed largely at guests at many of the top hotels and lodges. Several other specialist operators have combined under the marketing umbrella of the Livingstone's Adventure Group, making a convenient one-stop shop for their activities. In all cases, trips are professionally run with competent guides. Most tours can be either standalone or in combination with others.

Abseil Zambia [189 D6] Mosi-oa-Tunya Rd; ☎ 0974 327877; e res@zambeziecoadventures.com. Gorge swinging, abseiling, highwiring & 'flying-fox' activities at their site atop the 5th gorge on the Zambian side, some 5km from the Falls.

African Queen/African Princess [185 B4] Contact Livingstone's Adventure (page 216). Two luxury catamarans operating b/fast, lunch & dinner trips.

Angle Zambia ☎ 0213 327489; m 0977 707829/780670; e info@anglezam.co.zm; w zambezifishing.com. Half-day, full-day & multi-day sport fishing trips with experienced guides. Also owns Barotse Tiger Camp on the Barotse Floodplain (page 486).

Batoka Sky Adventures [185 B4] Maramba Aerodrome, off Sichango Rd; contact Livingstone's Adventure. Microlights & helicopters for scenic flights over the Falls, game park & upper river.

Bongwe Safaris [185 B3] ☎ 0972 112181, 0976 012590; e enquiries@bongwesafaris.com; w bongwesafaris.com. Good, ethical operation running game drives, walking safaris & river cruises, with links to excellent projects tackling conservation & Livingstone's human-wildlife conflicts.

Bundu Adventures [185 B4] Sichango Rd; m 0978 770175; e info@bunduadventures.com; w bunduadventures.com. Bundu offers rafting, riverboarding, kayaking, canoeing, hydrospeed surfing & low-water swimming in the rock pools beneath the Falls.

Bushtracks Africa [185 C3] Mosi-oa-Tunya Rd; ☎ 0213 323232; e operations@bushtracksafrica.

com; w bushtracksafrica.com. One of the best & most reliable tour operators in Livingstone, Bushtracks is located just south of the railway station, where the railway line crosses the road. It's an effective one-stop shop for everything from game drives & river cruises to day trips to Botswana, as well as operating the *Royal Livingstone Express*.

Gwembe Safaris [185 C4] Livingstone Reptile Park, Mosi-oa-Tunya Rd; 0213 321733; m 0967 777719; e gwemsaf@gmail.com; f livingstonecrocpark. Booking agents, tour operators, & owners of the reptile park.

Jet Extreme Zambia 0213 321375; m 0977 388465; e info@jetextremezambia.com; w jetextremezambia.com. Runs 90km/h jet boat trips in the Batoka Gorge, & operates the cable car out of the gorge at rapid 25.

Kayak the Zambezi m 0971 565044; e kayak@thezambezi.com; w thezambezi.com. The kayaking specialists for novice & experienced paddlers alike. Will help you plan day trips & longer expeditions as well as offering river surfing in the tubing wave at Rapid 11 in Jul (for experienced riders only!).

Livingstone's Adventure [185 B4] 4023 Sichango Rd; 0213 323589; m 0978 770175; e reservations@livingstonesadventure.com; w livingstonesadventure.com. This umbrella organisation with good insurance coverage groups together a variety of activities: the *African Queen*, Batoka Sky (helicopter & microlights), Livingstone Quad Company, Makora Quest (canoeing), Victoria Carriage Company (horseriding) & Victoria Falls River Safaris. Booking several trips attracts a discount. To experience the Zambezi from 2 angles, they offer 'combo' trips featuring aerial sightseeing (helicopter or microlight) & a river-canoe safari or sedate river cruise.

Livingstone Quad Company [185 B4] Maramba Aerodrome, off Sichango Rd; contact Livingstone's Adventure (above). Quadbike excursions either from the aerodrome on an 'eco-trail' or on a local 'village trail'.

Livingstone Rhino Walking Safaris [188 F1] 4 Nakambala La; 0213 322267; m 0977 450716; e gecko@zamnet.zm; w livingstonerhinosafaris.com. Guided walks in Mosi-oa-Tunya NP with ½-day activities taking in the usual walking safari or tracking the national park's star attraction – the resident white rhino. Min age 12.

Makora Quest Contact Livingstone's Adventure (see left). Livingstone's most established canoe operator, with extensive local knowledge & friendly service.

Ride Zambezi Chundukwa River Lodge; m 0979 549558; e chundukwahorse@microlink.zm; w chundukwariverlodge.com. Organises various guided rides depending on preference & experience, using horses from the stables at Chundukwa River Lodge. All abilities & ages.

Safari Par Excellence [185 B4] Zambezi Waterfront & Activity Centre, Sichango Rd; 0213 320606; m 0968 320606; e zaminfo@safpar.com; w safpar.com. One of Livingstone's larger tourism enterprises, 'SafPar' is a one-stop shop for everything you need. The company also operates the *Lady Livingstone* & The Elephant café (page 205).

Shearwater Adventures +263 134 4471; m +263 773 461716; e reservations@shearwatervf.com; w shearwatervictoriafalls.com. Bungee jumping, gorge swing, safari drives, elephant encounters & more.

Taonga Safaris [185 B4] Sichango Rd, next to the Boat Club; 0213 322508; m 0977 878065; e info@taonga-safaris.com; w taonga-safaris.com. Lively booze & barbecue cruises catering mainly to backpackers.

Thorn Tree Safaris 0974 436267; e thorntreesafaris@yahoo.com; f ThornTreeHouseLivingstone. Super range of cycle tours (sedate to challenging) & bespoke safari options stretching far and wide.

United Air Charters 0213 323095; e info@uaczam.com; w uaczam.com. Operates a fleet of helicopters for scenic & charter flights from its spectacular base on Baobab Ridge, to the east of Mosi-oa-Tunya Rd.

Victoria Carriage Co Contact Livingstone's Adventure (see left). Horse-drawn carriage trips on Sun International property & horseriding in the bush near the Falls.

Victoria Falls River Safaris Contact Livingstone's Adventure (see left). Aluminium 'safari' boats with shade, akin to the 4x4 of the river, can go far beyond the reach of conventional craft.

Wild Side Tours & Safaris [189 D7] 131 Mosi-oa-Tunya Rd; 0213 323726; m 0978 323726; e karien.kermer@outlook.com. Located in a restored railway house in the 217 area; look for the big 'i' sign indicating tourist information. Owner operated, & one of Livingstone's long-time tour companies, Wild Side offers a full service including village & town tours, game drives, cultural tours, activities & transfers, as well as online accommodation booking.

VICTORIA FALLS The Falls are 1,688m wide and average just over 100m in height. Around 550 million litres (750 million during peak months) cascade over the lip every minute, making this one of the world's greatest waterfalls. Closer inspection shows that this immense curtain of water is interrupted by gaps, where small islands stand on the lip of the Falls. These effectively split the Falls into smaller waterfalls, which are known as (from west to east) the Devil's Cataract, the Main Falls, the Horseshoe Falls, the Rainbow Falls and the Eastern Cataract.

Around the Falls is a genuinely important and interesting rainforest, with plant species (especially ferns) rarely found elsewhere in Zimbabwe or Zambia. These are sustained by the clouds of spray, which blanket the immediate vicinity of the Falls. You'll also find various monkeys and baboons here, while the lush canopy shelters Livingstone's lourie among other birds.

The flow, and hence the spray, is greatest just after the end of the rainy season – around March or April, depending upon the rains. It then decreases gradually until about December, when the rains in western Zambia will start to replenish the river. During low water, a light raincoat (available for rent on site) is very useful for wandering between the viewpoints on the Zimbabwean side, though it's not necessary in Zambia. However, in high water a raincoat is largely ineffective as the spray blows all around and soaks you in seconds. Anything that you want to keep dry must be wrapped in several layers of plastic or, even better, zip-lock plastic bags.

The Falls never seem the same twice, so try to visit several times, under different light conditions. At sunrise, both Danger Point and Knife-edge Point are fascinating – position yourself carefully to see your shadow in the mists, with three concentric rainbows appearing as halos. (Photographers will find polarising filters invaluable in capturing the rainbows on film, as the light from the rainbows at any time of day is polarised.) Moonlight is another fascinating time, when the Falls take on an ethereal glow and the waters blend into one smooth mass which seems frozen over the rocks.

On the Zambian side (entry international visitors US$10/20 child/adult; free under 6 year; vehicle US$5; gate ⌚ 06.00–18.00 daily) Viewing the Falls here could not be easier, and every season brings a reason to visit. For photographers, the area is best explored in the early morning, when the sun is still behind you and illuminates the Falls, or in the late afternoon when you may catch a stunning sunset. If you visit when the river is at its lowest, towards the end of the dry season, then the channels on the Zambian side may have dried up. Yet, while the Falls will be less spectacular then, their fascinating geology, normally obscured by spray, is revealed. In recent years, the diversion of water to generate power has been curtailed so the flow of water is more constant, and there is generally some water flowing over the edge on the Zambian side.

The main path leads along the cliff opposite the Falls, then across the swaying knife-edge bridge, via scenic points, photo stops and a good vantage point from which to watch bungee jumpers. This finishes at the farthest west of the Zambian viewpoints.

A third path descends right down to the water's edge at the Boiling Pot, which is used as a raft launch site during the main rafting season. It is a beautiful (but steep) hike down, first navigating big cement steps, then through palm-fringed forest and

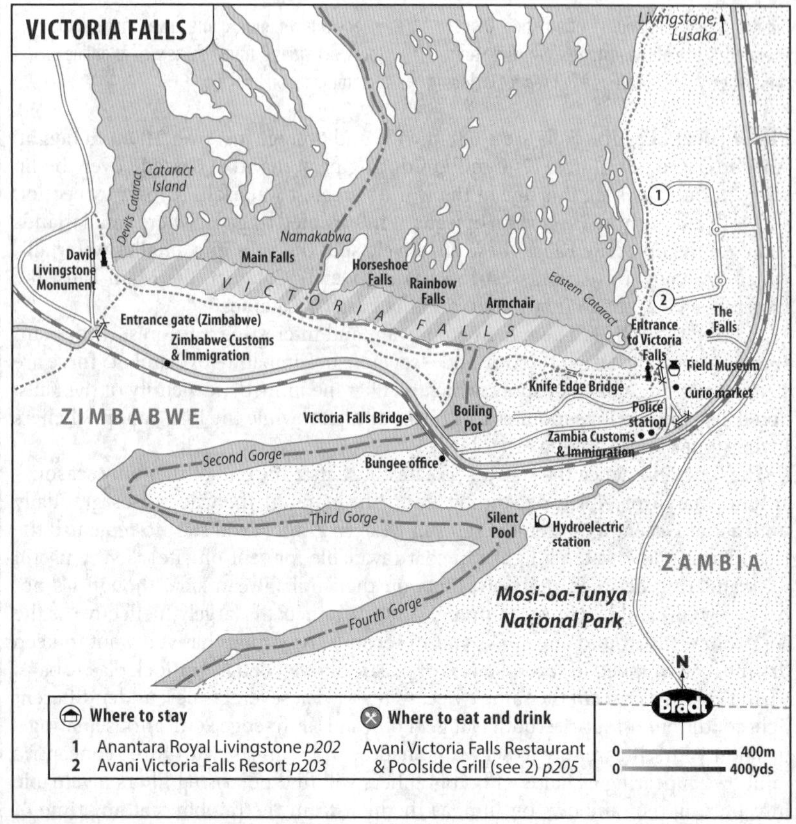

finally scrambling over boulders, but well worth the long, hot climb back as long as you have good footwear. Take a picnic and relax by the river if you've time (and if you notice a smell of urine, it's probably from the monkeys!).

Viewing the Falls by moonlight (US$100 pp) is possible for four days at full moon, including two days before and one day after. Watch for a lunar rainbow at this time, too; it's an amazing sight. It's best not to go alone, as elephants occasionally wander about.

If you are touring on your own a helpful starting point is the small information centre or **field museum**, directly across from the Falls entrance, which provides a good overview of the origins of Victoria Falls. The museum is packed full of informative exhibits and interesting photos covering the area's fascinating geology, archaeology and history, complete with an excavation right in the middle. Knowledgeable guides are on hand to answer questions, or you can explore at your leisure. Snacks and cold drinks are available in the shop next door.

While you can easily explore on your own, most tour operators offer excellent guided tours of the Falls (both Zimbabwe and Zambia sides) and the surrounding area, either standalone or in combination with historical, cultural, game-viewing and other sightseeing tours. These are highly informative with professional guides offering detailed explanations of the formation of the Falls and gorges, the river, local history and flora and fauna. Tours cost around US$25–35 per person, including entrance fees.

From the Zimbabwean side (entry international US$25/50 child/adult; free under 6 years; lunar tour US$100; ⌚ Sep–Apr 06.00–18.00; May–Aug 06.30–18.00), Viewing the Falls is more regulated here. The entrance to the Falls can be reached via paths from the Victoria Falls Hotel, the Kingdom Hotel and just opposite Ilala Lodge. There is a small ticket booth and display at the entrance gate, which is a few hundred metres from the Zimbabwean border post. Tickets are valid for the whole day, so you can return for no extra cost during the same day. There's also a car park for self-drivers too. Be prepared, however, for the mandatory hassle of generally pleasant but very persistent vendors and 'guides' along the way. Perhaps the easiest way to organise to see the Falls is through a tour operator, who will arrange visas and transfers as well as entry fees. Alternatively, make an afternoon of it and have tea at the Victoria Falls Hotel. Visiting in the afternoon, when the angle of the sun offers the best views, is ideal.

If you're planning to visit independently, it'll cost around US$10 to get a taxi to the border from Livingstone, though several properties offer shuttle bus services. You will need to clear customs and immigration at the border (⌚ 06.00–22.00) in order to explore the Zimbabwe side of the Falls, as well as the town of Victoria Falls itself. Although Zambia removed the need for a visa for many nationalities, this is not the same for Zimbabwe. Visitors to the Zimbabwean side of the Falls need to purchase a visa at the border. The cost is currently US$55/70 sgl/dbl entry for UK, Irish & Canadian citizens; US$30/45 sgl/dbl entry for citizens of USA, Australasia and much of Europe.

Technically this area is within the Victoria Falls National Park – and you will find a map of the paths at the entrance. Start at the western end, by Livingstone's statue – inscribed with 'Explorer, Missionary and Liberator', and overlooking the Devil's Cataract.

Visiting the viewpoints in order, next is the Cataract View. If water levels are low, and the spray not too strong, after clambering down quite a steep stairway you will be greeted by views along the canyon of the Falls. Climbing back up, wander from one viewpoint to the next, eastwards, and you will eventually reach the slippery-smooth rocks at Danger Point.

Few of these viewpoints have anything more than brushwood fences and low railings to guard the edges – so going close to the edge is not for those who suffer from vertigo. Viewing the Falls by moonlight is possible by special arrangement.

If you are keen to visit the town of Victoria Falls it's easily walkable or just a short taxi ride away. Taxis are readily available from the border post and car park opposite the Falls, and the one-way trip into the town centre should cost you US$5–10, depending on your willingness to haggle.

LIVINGSTONE ISLAND (US$110 inc transfers, park fees, guide & gourmet meal; ☎ 0213 327450; m 0978 291886; e livingstoneisland@greensafaris.com; w livingstoneisland.com) Livingstone Island (also known as Namakabwa Island) lies in the middle of the great waterfall, and is the island from which Dr Livingstone first viewed the Falls. Trips are run exclusively by Green Safaris at Tongabezi (page 197) between July and March (subject to water levels), with guests transferred to the island from the Royal Livingstone launch site by boat. There you'll have the opportunity to take in the scene – gazing over the edge, perhaps chancing a thrilling dip in the Devil's Pool right on the Falls edge, and having a gourmet meal in an exclusive setting. Five trips are offered daily; choose either morning (called 'breezer'), with a full English breakfast, gourmet lunch, or afternoon high tea with a full bar and hors d'oeuvres.

When the water's at its lowest, around October and November, you can sometimes walk across the top of the Falls, climbing over rocks, exploring pot-holes and crossing small streams along the way – it's even possible to swim at the very edge of the Falls at the right time of year. These activities are now permitted only if booked through Tongabezi. (Aside from the fact that the island is private, there is a risk of being stuck on top of the Falls should water levels unexpectedly rise. If you were to attempt the walk alone, you would almost certainly be turned back by national park scouts.)

RIVER CRUISES Floating on the Upper Zambezi with a glass in one hand, and a pair of binoculars in the other, is still a pleasant way to watch the sun go down, even if nowadays booze-cruise boats operate round the clock (you can choose from breakfast, lunch, sunset or dinner cruises), and sometimes all congregate close together. Whatever type of boat you choose, taking a gentle look around the Zambezi's islands, surrounded by national parks on both sides of the river, is one of the region's highlights.

African Queen [185 B4] (Livingstone Adventures; US$65 pp b/fast, mid morning or lunch cruise, US$75 pp sunset cruise; all inc open bar & a meal or canapés) On the Zambian side, surely the most elegant and leisurely way to experience the river is aboard the *African Queen* or its sister boat, the *African Princess*. These old-style double-decker riverboats complete with gleaming brass cruise regally upriver from their dock on the aptly named but sadly dilapidated Royal Mile. (The name is derived directly from royalty, for it was from here that George VI and his entourage took a launch onto the river during their visit in 1947. Today it is known more prosaically as Sichonga Road.) In the rarified atmosphere on board, guests sip cocktails or soft drinks to the rhythmic accompaniment of xylophones, or marimba, that sound the vessel's imminent departure. As the boat makes its stately way upstream, you may spot the odd hippo, crocodile or elephant – or even, if you're very lucky, a white rhino – not to mention numerous birds. Such luxury doesn't come cheap, but the price includes an open bar (with a charge for premium and imported brands) and a substantial finger buffet. Breakfast, lunch and dinner cruises are also available.

Lady Livingstone [185 B4] (SafPar Sunset US$75 pp, inc drinks & snacks, exc park fees US$10; b/fast cruise US$75; lunch cruise US$80 pp) Based at David Livingstone Safari Lodge, the *Lady Livingstone* takes up to 144 passengers on three decks. While it is similar in design to the *African Queen*, it's clearly more modern. The bar is at one end, giving the passengers more room to circulate, and the choice of drinks is generally wider than on its rival. Snacks are served as three courses during the course of the cruise, ending with 'delicious chocolate truffles' and brownies. The most popular excursion is the 2–2½-hour sunset cruise, departing between 16.00 and 16.30, but there are also lunch and breakfast cruises.

Other boats On the Zambian side, smaller craft plying the same route are organised by Victoria Falls River Safaris, Safari Par Excellence and Taonga Safaris. All have an open bar and are generally popular with backpackers. Typically cruises last around 2½ hours and cost around US$60–75 per person. Most of the lodges along the upper stretches of the Zambezi offer boat cruises away from the crowded waters near the Falls, usually as one of their inclusive activities. Here you can cruise in solitude, taking in the scenery, prolific birdlife and wildlife along the banks of the Zambezi National Park. Hippos, elephants and crocodiles are commonly seen as well as waterbuck, bushbuck and even buffalo.

Victoria Falls River Safaris uses specialised propeller-free aluminium boats, which can get within 200m of the Falls, and to stretches of the Zambezi unreachable by other boats (US$100 pp, min 2 passengers).

FISHING EXCURSIONS (Angle Zambia: US$125/255 ½/full day inc lunch; multi-day trips on request) Among the angling fraternity, the Zambezi River is synonymous with great fishing for prized tiger fish and Zambezi bream. If you dream of hooking a 'tiger' then a memorable day on the river with a knowledgeable guide can help make it come true. Angle Zambia, with their excellent local knowledge and friendly, personalised service, has been in operation since 2000 and is highly recommended. Owner-operated by Vivienne Simpson, it runs half- and full-day fishing trips on the Upper Zambezi, about 30km from Livingstone. Catering to both novice and experienced anglers as well as fly-fishermen, the company has three 6m aluminium boats complete with fish finders, sunshades and radio communications to their base. Trips include fishing tackle, boat hire, fuel, transfers, a qualified guide and refreshments.

ROYAL LIVINGSTONE EXPRESS (Bushtracks; dinner train dep 16.00, summer 17.00 Sat; Sun lunch safari if demand is high enough; US$170 pp, inc transfers, dinner & drinks; children welcome, recommended age 12+ in evening) The whistle of a steam loco rarely fails to stir a frisson of excitement, and Livingstone's foray into steam has proved a considerable success since its inaugural journey in late 2007. A joint venture between Bushtracks and Sun International, the train brings Zambia's railway history to life. It is pulled by one of two locomotives, the first of which – the 10th class *Princess of Mulobezi*, built in Glasgow in 1924 for Rhodesian Railways – until recently took pride of place in Livingstone's Railway Museum. The second, Loco 204, is a 12th-class locomotive originally built in 1924. Both have been restored with meticulous attention to detail by Ben Costa, a Zimbabwean railway engineer with a passion for the iron horse; the locos and attendant wooden carriages are polished until they gleam. Many of the train's staff have the railways in their blood, some tracing their railway ancestry back three or more generations.

The train starts its 15km journey in a purpose-built station next to the Bushtracks office, getting up steam as it passes excited children and families gathering for the evening meal, heading to the Victoria Falls Bridge in time to witness the sun set behind the Falls. Wine, beer and soft drinks are served in air-conditioned comfort, with a cash bar on board for those who prefer spirits. Large windows, as well as an observation car, ensure good visibility for all, with game such as elephants and antelope often spotted en route to the bridge. For a photo opportunity of the train itself the best time is at the Palm Grove Run Around, where passengers are able to disembark and watch as the locomotive detaches itself from the front of the train and attaches itself to the opposite end. After a 20-minute sundowner on the bridge itself, an unhurried five-course dinner is served as the train makes its way back towards Livingstone, prepared and served by staff from the Royal Livingstone Hotel, in an atmosphere enhanced by soft lighting and classical music.

CULTURAL ATTRACTIONS AND TOURS

Museums Given its fascinating history, it is no surprise that Livingstone has several good museums. The main Livingstone Museum is the most important of these, and certainly one of the best in the country.

Tours (1½hrs, inc entry fees & transfers, US$54/27 adult/child, Bushtracks) can be organised to visit the Livingstone Museum or the Railway Museum, or both. Although you can readily visit on your own, an organised tour is an easy alternative, especially as part of a full day's sightseeing trip, with transfer included.

Livingstone Museum [188 B2] (567 Mosi-oa-Tunya Rd; **w** livingstonemuseum.org; US$5/3 adult/child; ⌚ 09.00–16.30 daily) In a prime position in the centre of town, Livingstone's main museum more than justifies a visit. To start with, there's an excellent three-dimensional map showing how the Zambezi River flows over Victoria Falls and downstream into the gorges, which puts everything into good perspective. There are several galleries focusing on the origins of humans in Zambia, the history of man in the country up to the modern age, the natural history of the area and an impressive gallery on traditional village life including a life-size village household. Watch out, too, for the David Livingstone gallery, with a unique collection of the famous explorer's personal possessions, including many of his letters: it's a must.

The museum often has special exhibitions, including an interesting comparison of traditional villages to modern towns. Sculpture and paintings by Zambian artists are also displayed and available for sale, as are local handicrafts and curios. The staff are friendly and knowledgeable and guided tours are included.

Railway Museum [189 A8] (National Heritage Conservation Commission; Chishimba Falls Rd; US$15/7 adult child; ⌚ 08.30–16.30 daily) Located on the site of the Zambezi Saw Mills, this collection of beautifully preserved old steam locomotives and memorabilia, and displays on railway history, originally belonged to the artist David Shepherd. It celebrates the iron horse's history in Livingstone since the 3ft 6in narrow-gauge railway was built by the British in 1905. Sadly a serious fire took its toll on the collections, and the museum building itself is looking a bit run-down, but the engines themselves are in good condition, and will be of interest to railway buffs. Fortunately, the 1924 10th Class 156 out of Glasgow that used to take pride of place has now been put to work hauling the *Royal Livingstone Express* (page 217). There is also a small but informative Jewish museum on the site, a research centre & one of the oldest libraries in Zambia (⌚ 09.00–17.00 Mon–Fri).

Field Museum [map, page 214] Directly across from the entrance gate to Victoria Falls, next to the curio market, this is signed as an information centre, but is more of a small interpretation centre. It's well worth a visit for an understanding of the geology, archaeology and history of the Falls.

Markets Livingstone has many colourful local markets. In addition to the large and fascinating Maramba Market [188 G4], there is also Porters' Market, further north [188 G2]. For something smaller and closer to town, try Zimbabwe, Central or Town Centre Market (take your pick of the names!), down the road from Shoprite and next to the minibus station [188 B2].

At the heart of Livingstone's community, these markets offer everything from fresh produce to secondhand clothes (called *salaula*), from hand-fashioned metal pots to live chickens, from *chitenjes* (the traditional African cloth) to handcrafted wood furniture and more. A company called Bushtracks runs 1½-hour **market tours** (US$54 pp).

Craft markets Just inside the Zambian border, by the entrance to the Falls, is an outstanding curio market [map, page 214]. The carvers and traders come mostly from Mukuni village, though the goods come from as far as the Democratic Republic of Congo and Malawi. In town itself there's **Mukuni Park Curio Market** [188 E3] (🕘 06.00–20.00 daily), where local artisans, craftsmen and traders sell their wares from newly constructed permanent stalls along the edge of the park. Both of these are excellent places to buy wood and stone carvings, handicrafts, chessboards, masks, drums, baskets and the like, and are open during daylight hours throughout the week. There are usually about 20 or 30 individual traders, laying out their wares separately, and competing with one another for your business. The best buys are *makenge* baskets (these come exclusively from Zambia's Western Province), malachite and heavy wood carvings: hippos, elephants, rhinos, giraffes and smaller statues, often made out of excellent-quality, heavy wood. However, do consider the ethics of encouraging any further exploitation of hardwoods. Note, too, that some wooden items, especially wooden salad bowls and tall giraffes, are prone to cracking once you get them home due to changes in climate, and that very rarely are 'antiques' sold at craft markets anything other than fakes. Unless you have the expertise to tell the difference, it's better to buy such artefacts from a reputable shop in town.

Vendors will vie hard for your attention, and you can expect to bargain hard, hearing all sorts of prefabricated stories as to why you should pay more. When you start to pay, you will realise how sophisticated the traders are about their currency conversions, reminding you to double-check any exchange rates. Traders will accept most currencies and sometimes credit cards.

For something rather less demanding, there's an ad-hoc craft and curio market in the car park at the Falls Park shopping centre [185 C3]. Buying items from street traders, however, is illegal, so stick to the designated markets.

Village visits (Mukuni Village: Bushtracks US$40, SafPar US$55) While some of the lodges organise independent visits to local villages for their guests, there are also several organised trips to different locations. Most popular among these is **Mukuni village,** a settlement of about 7,000 Leya people to the east of the Falls. An organised tour here, lasting around 2½ hours, will give you a glimpse of how local people live and work in a traditional setting along with informative explanations. You can visit local huts, view villagers at work, watch curio making and even sample traditional beer and food. However, Mukuni village, with its proximity to the Falls and popularity with tour operators, relies heavily on the tourist trade, so tends towards a commercial, rather than authentic, feel, with often relentless though friendly pressure to buy curios made there.

Some operators organise less commercial tours which involve clients going to smaller villages, perhaps visiting local markets to buy food which they then prepare in the village and eat with the locals while having some language lessons (and of course a walk around the village).

Further afield is **Songwe village**, about a 40-minute drive through the bush, and less commercial as it receives fewer tourists. The Livingstone Quad Company also offers guided quadbike excursions to villages and the bush (US$140 pp; 🕘 07.00–14.00). Alternatively, if your heart is set on a more remote village off the beaten path and you have the time, Bwaato Adventures offer a day trip some 45km upriver to one of the rural villages along the Zambezi.

Historical tour of Livingstone (Bushtracks 1½hrs US$54 pp; Wild Side 2½ hrs US$60 pp) Livingstone, the capital of Northern Rhodesia from 1907 to 1935, has a fascinating history marked by many old historical buildings and accented by colourful characters, intriguing tales and a once-vibrant social life. A guided historical tour through town – on foot and by vehicle – will trace the town's history from frontier town to modern-day tourist capital, including the first hospital, school, library, churches, sports clubs, shopping districts, the old North Western Hotel and other historical sites.

African heritage tour (Bushtracks ½ day; US$137 pp, inc park fees & bottled water, min 4 people) Dubbed the 'Mists of Time' tour, this trip takes in the Victoria Falls and one of the local villages. In the hands of Russell Gammon, whose family history in Africa dates back to the 19th century, the aim is to bring these sites to life through the stories of those who have left their mark on Livingstone over the years.

Music and dance The opportunity to see local dance theatre is offered by the Livingstone Performing Arts Foundation (0977 371700; e lipafzm@yahoo.com). The group's *Dancing Around Zambia* (*US$20*) is performed regularly at Avani resort (page 203) and features traditional dancing and drumming in a celebration of Zambia's diverse culture, although they are always coming up with new shows. For details of performances and venues, contact them direct.

SPORTS AND SPAS Many of Livingstone's hotels and lodges have small gyms, trained massage therapists and even tennis courts for their guests to use. Some facilities are open to all and are worthy of specific mention.

The Livingstone Sports Festival (w lsf.co.zm) hosts the annual Zambezi International Regatta in September. With alumni from Oxford and Cambridge rowing teams taking part alongside prestigious universities from Zimbabwe, South Africa and the USA, school rowers, corporate teams and the truly Zambian 'mokoro sprint', it's a fun water festival, whether you're racing crocodiles or cheering from the banks.

Polocrosse Not surprisingly in a town with such a strong colonial history, horseriding is popular locally. Polocrosse (f ZambiaPolocrosse) is a fast-paced mix of polo and lacrosse at which Zambia excels. Currently ranked second in the world, their 2024 World Cup squad have high hopes for success.

The home of the Livingstone Polocrosse Club is a little way out of town at Chundukwa River Lodge (page 198), whose stables house many of the club's horses. Lodge owner Doug Evans is also a Zambian National Polocrosse coach, and has coached for the world cup. During the season, which runs from April to September, the sport attracts a good following locally and invariably ends in a great party.

Golf Established in 1908, the Livingstone Royal Golf and Country Club was once a popular social and sports club, complete with tennis and lawn bowling. Sadly, it has once again fallen into disrepair.

Across the border in Zimbabwe, the Elephant Hills Golf Course (US$30/45 9/18 holes; US$20 club hire; US$40 golf cart hire; $12 caddy fee) is an 18-hole course designed by Gary Player where golfers share the fairways with warthogs, impala and monkeys.

Massages and pampering Indulgent massage treatments and calming spa facilities make for blissful pampering after the exhaustion of international travel, sightseeing, adventure activities and bumpy 4x4 safaris. You'll find treatments available in Livingstone for a range of budgets, be it at Jollyboys backpackers' hostel or one of the luxury riverfront lodges. Some of the better spas that welcome walk-in guests are detailed below.

David Livingstone Safari Lodge & Spa [185 B4] ☎ 0213 324601; e spamanager@dlslandspa.com; ⌚ 08.00–19.00 daily. A more classic spa set up with professional therapists & an array of body & beauty treatments.

Royal Livingstone Spa [map, page 214] Royal Livingstone Hotel; m 0978 7770447; e spa.aroy@anantara.com; w anatara.com; ⌚ 08.30–19.00 daily. With 4 billowing white tented gazebos on the banks of the Zambezi & the spray from the Falls as backdrop, this is an idyllic outdoor spa. A number of packages, from Auyervedic to aromatherapy massage, body wraps & an extensive range of beauty treatments, are on offer. Divine pampering using natural Terre d'Afrique products & must be booked in advance.

Ruby Spa & Salon 9732 Mukambo Rd; m 0977 386998. This affordable salon offers hair & beauty care including massages, manicures, pedicures & facials.

THRILLS AND SPILLS The Falls area is indisputably *the* adventure capital of southern Africa. There is an amazing and seemingly endless variety of ways to get your shot of adrenalin: white-water rafting, canoeing, bungee jumping, kayaking, abseiling, gorge swinging, riverboarding or simply a flight over the Falls.

None comes cheaply. Most are upwards of US$100 per activity, which adds up quickly. If you wish to do multiple activities, check out the many combination packages on offer. These can be slightly cheaper than booking individually. There are also choices of operator for most of these, so if you book locally, shop around to find something that suits you before you decide. Prices won't vary much, but you will find the true range of what's available. Whatever you plan, expect to sign an indemnity form before your activity starts.

On the Zambian side there is a single cable car at Rapid 25 to bring clients out of the gorge after rafting trips, with the cost included in the activity price.

Flight of Angels Named after Livingstone's famous comment, 'Flight of Angels' describes any sightseeing trip over the Falls by microlight or helicopter. This is a good way to get a feel for the geography of the area, and is surprisingly worthwhile if you really want to appreciate the Falls. If you're arriving from Kasane, or leaving for there, consider combining a sightseeing flight and an air transfer. Otherwise any of these trips can be readily booked by agents in the area.

Microlight [185 B4] (Batoka Sky Adventures; ☎ 0213 323589; w livingstonesadventure.com; US$185 pp/15mins, US$366 pp/½hr, inc transfers from Livingstone & Victoria Falls town & aviation fee; weight limit 100kg unless notified in advance) This is a totally different experience from a light aircraft: essentially sightseeing from a propeller-powered armchair 500m above the ground; it's the closest you can come to soaring like a bird over the Falls.

Microlights take only one passenger plus the pilot. Because the passenger sits next to the propeller, cameras cannot be carried for safety reasons. However, for US$20 you can arrange to be photographed above the Falls from a camera fixed to the wing. Flights are operated out of Batoka Sky's Maramba Aerodrome and within 5 minutes are over the Zambezi. A 15-minute flight takes in a circle over the Falls and the islands in the river. The longer flight then continues upstream before crossing over the national park. Microlights are affected by the slightest turbulence, so if you book in advance, it's best to specify early morning or late afternoon, when conditions are ideal.

Helicopter (Typically US$189/250/360 pp for 15/22/30 mins, inc transfers from either Livingstone or Victoria Falls) This is the most expensive way to see the Falls, but it is tremendous fun. A 15-minute trip takes in the Falls and the national park. Longer trips, lasting between 22 and 30 minutes, will also include a sweep down into the Batoka Gorge, flying down the river just above the rapids. The 30-minute trip also passes over local villages and the town of Victoria Falls on the Zimbabwe side, or provides some aerial game viewing over Mosi-oa-Tunya National Park. At extra cost, you can stop in the gorge at Rapid 22, 'Bobo Camp', for a 1- or 2-hour picnic (min six people). Alternatively, if you plan to raft, riverboard or ride a jet boat, you can get an exhilarating lift out of the gorge by helicopter – at extra cost of course, but including a scenic flight over the Falls and Zambezi gorges. Flights are operated by United Air Charters, in four- and six-seater helicopters from the aptly named Baobab Ridge just south of town, and Batoka Sky, based at the Maramba Aerodrome, in three-, four- or six-seater craft. All are designed to give each passenger a good view, though it's difficult to guarantee the best view at the window seats as passengers are placed in the helicopter according to weight and balance safety requirements. You can purchase scenic helicopter footage for US$20 after your flight. Note that Batoka Sky will fly with just two people.

Bungee jumping (US$168 per solo jump; no refund if you change your mind. Min age 14, but under-18s require attendance of parent or guardian & their signature on the indemnity form. Min/max client weight 40/120kg (88/265lb). ⌚ 09.30–17.00, or from 10.00 at high water due to spray from Falls) There's only one company organising bungee jumping: African Extreme, part of Shearwater Adventures and an offshoot of the original New Zealand pioneers, Kiwi Extreme. Solo or tandem, you jump from the middle of the main bridge between Zambia and Zimbabwe, where the Zambezi is 111m below you. It is among the highest commercial bungee jumps in the world, and not for the nervous.

You can book in advance, either direct or through a tour operator, or simply turn up at the bridge and pay there. There's a bar on site, and digital photos and videos of your jump are available.

Bridge walks (US$68 pp 1½ hour tour, min 2 people) There's no-one better positioned to show you the ins and outs – no, make that ups and downs – of the Victoria Falls Bridge than the bungee folks, whose intimate bridge knowledge will not only fascinate you but have you clambering around and underneath the bridge like a monkey. With safety harness on and accompanied by guide, you have the opportunity to explore the bridge's superstructure while hearing all about its construction and riveting history. While not as adrenalin-charged as bungee jumping, it's still bound to get your heart beating faster as you navigate your way high above the Zambezi. Remember to take your passport (no visa necessary).

Abseiling, high-wiring, gorge swing and slide (Trio of activities US$230 pp inc insurance, transfers, drinks & snacks; gorge swing only US$158/105 dbl/sgl; flying fox or cable slide only US$53) A very popular addition to the adventure menu is the Zambezi swing, a cable swing set across the gorge which, together with a 90m-high cable slide (flying fox), abseiling (rappelling) and 'rap' jumps (rappelling forwards) down the side of the gorge, offers daring fun for all ages. These are currently offered by both Abseil Zambia at the top of the fifth gorge on the Zambian side, and Shearwater Adventures from their site on the bridge (see page 212).

At Abseil Zambia, the swing is a fixed 135m cable spanning the gorge. Participants are harnessed to ropes attached to the cable's sliding pulley and, after stepping off the cliff face, experience a heart-stopping 53m, three-second free-fall, followed by an exhilarating pendulum-like swing across the gorge, accelerating up to 140km/h (with a pull of roughly 2½ times gravity) for some 2 minutes before being lowered to the ground. Described by participants as 'even more thrilling than bungee jumping', it's definitely not for the faint-hearted, though participants as young as eight and as old as 76 have braved it. It's even possible to try it out in tandem.

A slightly tamer alternative is the high wire or flying fox, set on another static cable stretched across the gorge. With harness and pulley, you leap off a platform and 'fly' (slide) across the gorge some 90m above the ground. It can be done in either a sitting or a flying position, and is suitable for children.

Except for the flying fox, be prepared to hike some 30 minutes out of the gorge after each go.

A full day's activity allows you to go up, down and over the gorge to your heart's content. Lunch, beer and cool drinks are included and sundowners are offered. Videos or disks of your activities are available at extra cost. It's also possible to spend just a half day, or to do any activities on their own.

The site is 5km from the Falls. If you're driving yourself, turn off the main road to the Falls just before the Avani Victoria Falls Resort, and follow the signposts.

Canoeing on the Upper Zambezi (Canoeing US$170 ½/full day inc b/fast or lunch & park fees; overnight US$280) Canoeing down the Upper Zambezi is a cool occupation on hot days, and the best way to explore the upper river, its islands and channels. Zimbabwe's Zambezi National Park stretches all along the western shore providing ample opportunity for game viewing, while lodges, farms, villages and bush dot the Zambian side as you head downstream to the upper reaches of the Mosi-oa-Tunya National Park. The silence of canoes makes them ideal for floating up to antelope drinking, elephants feeding or crocodiles basking. Birdlife is prolific – you may hear the cry of the African fish eagle or see pied kingfishers hover and dive. The large number of hippos that call this stretch of the river home can provide excitement, but the river is wide and you need to show them respect by giving them plenty of space. If you follow the instructions of your guide they shouldn't cause you any problems.

A variety of options is available, from half- to full-day excursions, combo canoeing and game drives, and even overnight camping trips with the evening spent under the stars. You'll find any of them generally relaxing, although paddling becomes a bit more strenuous if it's windy. All canoe trips are accompanied by a licensed river guide, and sometimes also a motorboat for additional safety. Canoes range from two-seater open-decked kayaks to inflatable 'crocodiles'.

There are some sections of choppy water if you'd like a little more excitement, though it's possible to avoid most of these easily if you wish. Trips concentrating on these shouldn't be confused with the white-water rafting beneath the Falls (see page 224).

For those who'd like the experience but don't want to paddle, canoe operators also run guided 'float' trips known as the Livingstone Drift on the Upper Zambezi. Participants can paddle when they feel like it or simply float downstream on a raft.

No prior canoeing experience is necessary, and once you are used to the water, the better guides will encourage you to concentrate on the wildlife. Lunch is typically served on an island. Trips are run by Makora Quest, Bundu Adventures and Safari Par Excellence, with the latter two also running float trips using rafts. At Tongabezi, canoeing for guests is included in the rates.

White-water rafting The Zambezi below the Falls is one of the world's most renowned stretches of white water. It was the venue for the 1995 World Rafting Championships, and rafting is now very big business here, with keen competition for tourist dollars. (About 50,000 people now go down the river every year, paying about US$160–180 each. You can do the sums.)

Experienced rafters grade rivers from I to VI, according to difficulty. Elsewhere in the world, a normal view of this scale would be:

Class I	No rapids, flat water.
Class II	Easy rapids, a float trip. No rafting experience required.
Class III	Intermediate to advanced rapids. No rafting experience required.
Class IV	Very difficult rapids. Prior rafting experience highly recommended. No children.
Class V	For experts only. High chance of flips or swims. No children or beginners.
Class VI	Impossible to run.

The rapids below the Falls are mostly graded IV and V. This isn't surprising when you realise that all the water coming slowly down the Zambezi's 1.7km width is being squeezed through rocky gorges that are often just 50–60m wide.

Fortunately for the rafting companies, most of the rapids here may be very large, but the vast majority of them are not 'technical' to run. This means that they don't need skill to manoeuvre the boat while it is within the rapids, they just require the rafts to be positioned properly before entering each rapid. Hence, despite the grading of these rapids, they allow absolute beginners into virtually all of the rafts. That said, you should think very carefully about committing yourself if you have no experience. Boats do flip over, and the consequences can be severe. It's also important to ensure that your chosen operator will give a thorough safety briefing before departure, explaining what to do in the event of a capsize.

High or low water, and which side of the river? Rafting is offered from both Zambia and Zimbabwe by a wide range of companies.

From July to January, when the water is low, full- or half-day trips leave from the Boiling Pot just below the Falls: a spectacular start to the day. This period, when the river's waves and troughs (or 'drops') are more pronounced, is probably the best time to experience the Zambezi's full glory.

In high-water months (February to July), only half-day trips are offered, starting below Rapid 9 on both sides of the river. Note that when the river is highest its rapids may seem less dramatic, but it is more dangerous, due to the strong whirlpools and undercurrents. If the water is too high, rafting is suspended until it recedes to a safer level.

The trips A typical rafting trip will start with a briefing, covering safety/health issues, giving the plan for the day and answering any questions. Once you reach the 'put-in' at the river, you will be given a short safety/practice session to familiarise yourself with the raft, techniques and commands that will be used to run the rapids. Half-day trips typically run from rapid 1 to 10 in the morning (the more extreme of the rapids), and 11 to 25 in the afternoon, which are of a lower grade (II-IV) and therefore slightly less challenging. A full day's rafting is needed to get all the way from rapid 1 to 25. Lunch and cool drinks are included. It's also possible to organise a multi-day trip of between one and five days with SafPar.

The climb up and out of the gorge at the end of the trip can be steep and tiring, especially in hot weather, but on the Zambian side, a cable car at Rapid 25 has made this a thing of the past – albeit at a price (though the cost of the lift is included in SafPar's rates). Alternatively, most companies offer a heli–raft combo, whereby you can opt to fly out instead at additional cost. Beyond the obvious advantage of 'taking the easy way out', the heli flight is an exhilarating end to an exciting day, zipping you out of the gorge with a bird's-eye view of the rapids you've just run and the Falls as well.

A trained river guide pilots every raft, but you need to decide whether you want to go in an oar boat or in a paddle boat. In an oar boat expect to cling on for dear life, and throw your weight around the raft on demand – but nothing more. Oar boats are generally easier and safer because you rely on the skills of the oarsmen to negotiate the rapids, and you can hang onto the raft at all times. Only occasionally will you have to 'highside' (throw your weight forward) when punching through a big wave.

In a paddle boat the participants provide the power by paddling, while a trained rafting guide positions the boat and yells out commands instructing you what to do. You'll have to listen, and also paddle like crazy through the rapids, remembering when and if you are supposed to be paddling. You can't just hang on! In paddle boats you are an active participant and thus are largely responsible for how successfully you run the rapids. The rafting guide calls commands and positions the boat, but then it's up to you. If your fellow paddlers are not up to it, then expect a difficult ride. Paddle boats have a higher tendency to flip and/or have 'swimmers' (someone thrown out of the boat).

Originally, only oar boats were run on the Zambezi. However, nowadays paddle boats have become more popular as rafting companies compete to outdo each other in offering the most exciting rides. There is, of course, a very fine line between striving to be more exciting, and actually becoming more dangerous.

With either option, remember that people often fall out and rafts do capsize. Trips are always accompanied by a number of safety kayaks though, and safety records are usually cited as excellent. Serious injuries are said to be uncommon and fatalities rare.

Rafting operators (US$100/150 pp ½/full day inc transfers & gorge lift or cable car at Rapid 25 if appropriate; min age 15) All rafting companies offer broadly similar experiences. To gain a competitive edge, some now offer freebies like dinner and sundowners in their prices, so it's well worth asking around and comparing what's included, as this changes from time to time. The rapids are numbered from 1 to 25, starting from the Boiling Pot, so it's easy to make a rough comparison of the trips on offer.

Zambian operators include Bundu Adventures and Safari Par Excellence. All offer videos and photos of your trip at a rather extortionate additional cost. A shorter, 3-hour trip from rapids 1 to 7 is also available through Bundu Adventures, at US$150 per person, including swimming under the Falls, a video of your trip and river fee.

In addition to day trips, there are four-day expeditions as far as the proposed Batoka Gorge Dam site, while seven-day expeditions reach the mouth of the Matetsi River. These offer more than the adrenalin of white water, and are the best way to see the remote Batoka Gorge, though trips are few and far between.

Riverboarding (Riverboard US$130; riverboard & raft combo US$200 pp full day inc transfers, light b/fast, lunch & sundowner; min age 15) For a more up-close and personal encounter with the Zambezi rapids, adrenalin junkies can try their hand at riverboarding (also known as boogie-boarding) or combo riverboarding and rafting. After donning your fins, lifejacket and helmet, you and your foam board (the size of a small surfboard) will have an opportunity to 'surf' the big waves of the Zambezi, after being taught basic skills in a calmer section of the river. A raft accompanies each trip and takes you downstream to the best spots of the day. Here you can try finding the best 'standing waves' where you can stay still and surf as the water rushes beneath you. Experts can stand, but most will surf on their stomachs. It's thrilling for the fit who swim strongly, but not for the faint of heart. Trips are offered by both Bundu Adventures and Safari Par Excellence.

White-water kayaking (Kayak the Zambezi: experienced kayakers US$125/190/450 pp; ½/full day/3 day, inc lunch & transfers; tandem US$220 pp Aug–Jan; kayak hire US$30) Yet another option for white-water enthusiasts is kayaking in the gorge. Those without experience can try tandem kayaking in Topolino Duo kayaks; a qualified guide sits in the back, piloting and manoeuvring the kayak through rapids, while you sit in front and assist with paddle power. In all cases you must be a confident swimmer; kayaks, smaller and lighter than rafts, may capsize in bigger rapids, and although your guide will attempt to right it by executing an 'Eskimo roll', you (and your guide) may have to swim the rest of the rapid.

There are also multi-day courses for experienced kayakers and fully outfitted multi-day expeditions by special arrangement.

Jet boating (Jet Extreme US$116 pp, inc transfers, drinks & cable car) Another adrenaline activity on the river, but on the flatter sections of water between rapids 23 and 27. Undertaken in a 22-seater, 700-horsepower jet boat, the trip up and down the river reaches speeds of up to 90km/h, with 30 minutes of sharp turns and swift navigation of the small rapids ensuring that all occupants of the boat get suitably wet. The trip also includes a tour of Mukuni village on the way to the activity, as well as the 8-minute, 220m trip down into the gorge, and back out again at the end.

WILDLIFE ENCOUNTERS

Mosi-oa-Tunya National Park (Park entry US$10 (self drive US$15) pp/day; vehicle US$15/day; guided game drive US$50 pp; game walk US$85 pp) Much of the Zambian area around the Falls is protected within the Mosi-oa-Tunya National Park, until 2009 the smallest national park in Zambia, which now has a fenced off area of 66km². The original area, about half this size and known as 'the game park', lies in the middle, and this is where walks and game drives take place. The newer area stretches along the river in both directions. Visitors can also see the cemetery at Old Drift, the site of Livingstone's first settlement.

Getting there and around You can drive yourself around easily, or go with one of the many operators (page 211) who run 4x4 trips into the park. The three lodges inside the park – Toka Leya, Sussi & Chuma and Thorntree River Lodge – also offer their guests guided drives or walks from the lodge. For the more adventurous there are 3-hour walking safaris, led by licensed safari guides from Livingstone Rhino Walking Safaris (US$85 plus US$25 transfer & park fees). Beyond the excitement of tracking game on foot, these are an excellent way to learn about the flora and fauna. The best time to go for birds is early in the morning, but walks also take place in the afternoon.

Flora and fauna The park boasts tracts of riverine vegetation, dry mixed woodland and mopane trees. A few hours' driving could yield sightings of most of the common antelope and some fine giraffe, as well as buffalo, elephant and zebra. Although outside of the historical range of the white rhino, several attempts have been made to establish a population in the park. Sadly, the first attempts failed due to poaching and, in 2020, a mother and calf were tragically killed by a speeding driver at night in the national park. Today, only one white rhino remains. Always protected by armed rangers, it can sometimes be spotted from game drives, but a rhino walk with Livingstone Rhino Walking Safaris (US$85) will give you a much better chance of a sighting, and a much closer experience. Wild dog are also present: a pack recently crossed the river from Zimbabwe. There are, however, no lion, leopard or other cats present.

Birdwatching Birdwatching isn't normally regarded as an adrenalin sport, but with the outstanding avifauna to be found in and around the Falls, serious 'twitchers' might disagree.

Even the casual visitor with little interest will often see fish eagles, Egyptian geese, numerous kingfishers, bee-eaters, Hadeda and sacred ibis, and various other storks, egrets and herons. Meanwhile, avid birders will be seeking the more elusive birds like the rare Taita falcon, as Batoka Gorge is one of the best sites to look for them. Rock pratincoles have almost as restricted a distribution (just following the Zambezi), but can often be seen here balancing on boulders by the water's edge and hawking for insects, while African skimmers can be found nesting upon sandy shores of islands. Look in the riverine forest around the Falls and you may spot a collared palm thrush rummaging around; again, these are really quite rare birds recorded in only a few areas. In contrast, African finfoot occur throughout sub-Saharan Africa, but are always shy. They prefer slow water, overhung with leafy branches, and they find the upper sections of the Zambezi perfect, so are often seen there if you look when it's quiet. Back on land, keep an eye out for birds of prey; on a recent visit, a martial eagle was spotted surveying our early-morning walk from on high.

Birdwatching excursions are an offered activity at many of the lodges along the river, often included in the nightly rate. Experienced guides can take you out either on foot or on the river. Alternatively, you can arrange to go out with a knowledgeable member of BirdWatch Zambia (w birdwatchzambia.org), formerly known as the Zambian Ornithological Society, who will be able to guide you to some great viewing spots and help with identification and general birding knowledge. The group has an active forum on Facebook for up to the moment information and assistance.

Horseriding and horse-drawn carriages Riding along the Zambezi and through the bush is a wonderful way to experience nature up close. Trips for all levels are offered from the fantastic stables at Chundukwa River Lodge (page 198). The extremely experienced team here are skilled at pairing riders with suitable horses. There are a mixture of Quarter Horses, Quarter Horse cross Boerperds, Basotho ponies and thoroughbred crosses. Many of the thoroughbred horses are used either for local polo and successful polocrosse teams (the Livingstone Polo Club is based here) and all of the horses are well cared for and well behaved.

Trips can last from as little as an hour up to half a day and there are also champagne breakfast trips, and pony trails led by a guide on foot for younger children.

Livingstone Reptile Park [185 C4] (Gwembe Safaris: entry US$15/7.50 adult/child; f livingstonecrocpark; ⌚ Thu–Tue) Just to the south of Livingstone, the Reptile Park (still signposted 'Livingstone Crocodile Park') offers the opportunity to see some huge crocs at close quarters – from behind the safety of a chain-link fence or from covered walkways – and to get some great photographs. Well-informed and friendly guides offer explanations about the behaviour and history of the animals, and feeding times (usually early afternoon) are posted at the entrance. The park plays a valuable role in the local community, capturing and housing snakes and crocodiles that could pose a danger to the public, and also running education trips with visiting groups from local schools and the wider community learning about these dangerous creatures, and in many cases developing a new-found respect for them. Picnic tables are set in the landscaped grounds and there's a café serving the park's signature 'Croc Bite'.

The park also features some of Zambia's snakes, housed in glass cages. It, hopefully, will be your only chance to see Africa's most dangerous snakes – black mamba, cobra, puff adder – up close and personal; you can even hold the 'safe' snakes to get a feel for them. There is also an activity centre here where visitors can book any of a wide range of activities or to go on one of Gwembe's game drives in the Mosi-oa-Tunya National Park (in which case, you get free entrance to the reptile park).

Walking with lions and cheetah The opportunity to walk with lion cubs and cheetah is well advertised in Livingstone. The animals are bred specially for these programmes and for some visitors the activity is clearly very appealing and unusual. The authors' personal views are that this venture is unethical, and we would urge anyone considering taking part to read the box opposite for information on the controversy surrounding this activity.

OTHER ACTIVITIES

Quadbikes (Eco Trail US$80, 1hr; village trail US$140, 2½hrs, inc transfers; other destinations & tailormade trips also available) Guided quadbike (four-wheel motorbike) excursions are operated by the Livingstone Quad Company. Choose from a 1-hour 'eco-trail' at Batoka Land (starting at Maramba Aerodrome), consisting of 17ha in and around the unfenced portion of the national park, or a 2-hour trip venturing out into the bush to explore African villages and the landscape by the Zambezi gorges. Participants are given an introduction and a chance to practise before heading out on the trail of their choice.

Segway tours (e touroperations@bushtracksafrica.com; US$39 pp; min age 7 & with good balance) If your idea of fun is to glide along laid-out trails to observe wildlife such as giraffe, baboons, zebra, impala and monkeys, this is for you. No experience is necessary, since coaches are on hand to teach the basics of riding the two-wheeled, stand-on segway. Operated by Bushtracks on Avani Victoria Falls Resort property.

SAFARIS AROUND THE FALLS AREA

Livingstone is well placed for day-trip safaris, both in Zambia's Mosi-oa-Tunya National Park (page 226) and in Victoria Falls and Zambezi national parks across the river in Zimbabwe.

If you are seeking a four- or five-day excursion from the Falls area, there are several superb game parks within easy reach. Some of the local operators (page

THE ETHICS OF WALKING WITH LIONS

There are now several operations in Africa which offer visitors the opportunity to pay to touch, stroke and walk with baby lions. All cite their 'projects' as part of larger conservation initiatives to 'save lions', some with the backing of charities (often small charities, very closely linked with the projects in question). The problem with this for conservationists is two-fold: first, what happens to the cubs when they grow older; and second, are these projects really doing any valuable conservation work?

WHAT HAPPENS TO ALL THE BABY LIONS? When lion cubs reach about 18 months old, they become too large and dangerous to be mixed with people. Lions typically live for about 16 years in the wild and up to 25 in captivity. If they have spent time as cubs mixing with people, then they cannot be released into an unfenced area, because sooner or later they'd probably come across local villagers – and with no fear of humans they'd be likely to kill.

Most of Africa's national parks and really wild areas are unfenced. It doesn't take much to do the maths and estimate the number of adult lions that each of these projects will produce every year. These will all need to be housed in fenced areas stocked with game for them to eat. Many conservationists claim that there just aren't enough such areas, and they point out that 'lions breed like rabbits' when given the right conditions.

Considerable controversy was stirred up by a *Sunday Times* article by Chris Haslam in February 2008 entitled 'African lion encounters: a bloody con'. This looked at one such operation and alleged that, once adult, the original lion cubs were likely to be used for 'canned hunting' on farms in South Africa. The paper was unable to prove that farms in South Africa which had received lions from the project in question had definitely used the lions for canned hunting, and hence issued a retraction. However, you only have to search the internet to realise that there's great debate over the ethics of such operations.

VALUABLE CONSERVATION? Many leading lion conservationists question if there is any conservation value at all in most of these projects.

They argue that habitat destruction and human encroachment are the real conservation issues that need to be addressed for conserving Africa's lions, and observe that there is little evidence of these commercial operations doing any meaningful work of this type. They also question the wisdom of randomly mixing lion populations, which risks introducing deleterious genes or diseases into established lion populations.

So we'd urge you to think carefully about the ethics of your actions and to try to look beyond the fine words of the commercial concerns involved. Your few hours of fun may come at a hefty price.

211) run trips from Livingstone, and for backpackers there are usually a few operators running buses or trucks to Windhoek, Maun or even Harare. Like cut-down overland trips, these often stop at parks on the way.

VICTORIA FALLS NATIONAL PARK, ZIMBABWE Like the northern side of the river, a good section of Zimbabwe's land around the Falls is protected – though only the rainforest area, criss-crossed by footpaths to viewing points, is actually fenced off. If you are feeling adventurous, then follow the riverbank upstream from Livingstone's statue. (If the gate is closed beyond the statue, then retrace your steps out of the entrance to the rainforest; and turn right, then right again, down Zambezi Drive, to reach the outside of that gate.)

This path runs next to Zambezi Drive for a while. After almost 2km, Zambezi Drive leaves the river and turns back towards town, passing a famous baobab tree called the Big Tree. From there the path continues for about 8km upstream until it reaches A'Zambezi River Lodge, just outside the gate to the Zambezi National Park. This is a very beautiful, wild walk but, despite its innocent air, you are as likely to meet hippo, elephant or buffalo here as in any other national park. So take great care as you admire the view across the river. You may also want to plan ahead and arrange a pick-up from A'Zambezi back into town, or alternatively just ask the hotel on arrival.

ZAMBEZI NATIONAL PARK, ZIMBABWE This park borders the Zambezi River, starting about 6km from Victoria Falls and extending about 40km upstream. You cannot walk here (without a professional guide), so you need a vehicle, but there are several Zimbabwean operators running morning and afternoon drives through the park who will collect you from any of the main hotels.

The park is actually bisected by the main road from Victoria Falls to Kazungula/Kasane (which has long been an unlikely, but favourite, spot for sightings of wild dogs). Better game viewing is to be had from the roads designed for it: the Zambezi River Drive, or the Chamabondo Drive.

The former is easily reached by driving out of town along Park Way, past the Elephant Hills Hotel and the Victoria Falls Safari Lodge. This road follows the river's course almost to the end of the park, and there are plenty of loop roads to explore away from the river.

The Chamabondo Drive has a separate entrance on the road to Bulawayo. Take a right turn just before the road crosses the Massive River, about 7km out of town. This leads past several pans and hides until it terminates at Nook Pan, from where you must retrace your steps as there are no loop roads.

The park has good populations of elephant, buffalo and antelope – especially notable are the graceful sable which thrive here. The riverfront is beautiful, lined with classic stands of tall winterthorn trees, *Acacia albida*. Note that when wet this park is often impossible to drive through in a 2WD, and when dry some of the roads remain in poor condition.

KAFUE NATIONAL PARK, ZAMBIA Geographically speaking, the southern side of Kafue is quite close to Livingstone, but the practicalities of getting to the park are trickier than they look. The area is remote and relatively underdeveloped, and it can take 4½ hours just to reach the park gate, and another 2 hours along weather-dependent roads to reach the first lodge. To get here you will need a fully kitted 4x4, a GPS and some off-road driving experience, or the help of a local tour operator. This is not a day trip from Livingstone. For details, see page 414.

CHOBE NATIONAL PARK, BOTSWANA This is often suggested as a day trip from the Falls, but is really too far to be worthwhile. (You end up arriving after the best of the morning's game viewing is finished, and leaving before the afternoon cools down sufficiently for the game to re-appear!) However, the Chobe riverfront, around Serondela, probably has higher wildlife densities than any of the other parks mentioned here. So if you can cope with the sheer number of vehicles there, it may be worth a trip for a few days. Its luxurious lodges (and high park fees) mean that northern Chobe is always expensive. In spite of that, day trips with some of the major operators are extremely popular. A typical trip with Wild Side (US$180 pp) will incorporate a game drive, boat cruise and lunch at one of the hotels. Bushtracks includes a morning riverboat on the Chobe River, with an afternoon game drive (US$195 pp). Longer trips are also available. Jollyboys offers a full-day excursion (US$160 pp) which includes all transfers, a light breakfast, lunch and a game drive and boat cruise along the river.

There are regular transfers between Victoria Falls and Kasane (in Botswana, beside the park) which take around 2 hours. Then stay at Chobe Game Lodge, Chobe Chilwero or Elephant Valley Lodge – the three lodges in that section of the park. Either can easily be arranged by a good tour operator before you arrive, or by a travel agent in Livingstone. The lodges in Kasane, outside the park, don't compare (though Impalila Island Lodge or Ichingo Chobe River Lodge on the opposite bank of the river are little-known options that are both excellent value, and cheaper).

Alternatively, if you have a good 4x4 then you can drive yourself around and (advance reservations essential) camp at the basic, unfenced site at Ihaha. Take all your food and equipment with you, and watch for the baboons.

HWANGE NATIONAL PARK, ZIMBABWE Zimbabwe's flagship national park has three established public camps that provide excellent value, basic accommodation and camping. It also has several more basic camping spots at picnic sites.

Alternatively there are a few more expensive private lodges in the park, most of them towards the south side of the park's road network in an area of Kalahari sandveld.

CHIZARIRA NATIONAL PARK, ZIMBABWE One of Zimbabwe's wildest and least visited parks, Chizarira requires patience, lots of driving skill, and a 4x4 – and that's just to get there. Unfortunately this isolated and cash-starved park was hit heavily by poaching, and the wildlife is now scarce and skittish, but the wilderness experience is excellent.

There are no lodges operating in the area, but there are a number of campsites that can be used as self-driving bases, although you will need to bring all your own supplies, including water. Alternatively, Leon Varley and his team run walking safaris here and have been doing so for years. They're a first-class operation.

KAZUMA PAN NATIONAL PARK, ZIMBABWE This small, little-visited national park borders Botswana between the Zambezi and Hwange national parks. It is used for walking safaris more than for driving, though the environment is very different. It consists of a huge, almost flat depression – a grass-covered pan surrounded by forests that are dominated by the familiar mopane and teak trees.

Only a few groups are allowed into the park at any time, each requiring a fully licensed walking guide – which effectively limits access to organised operators.

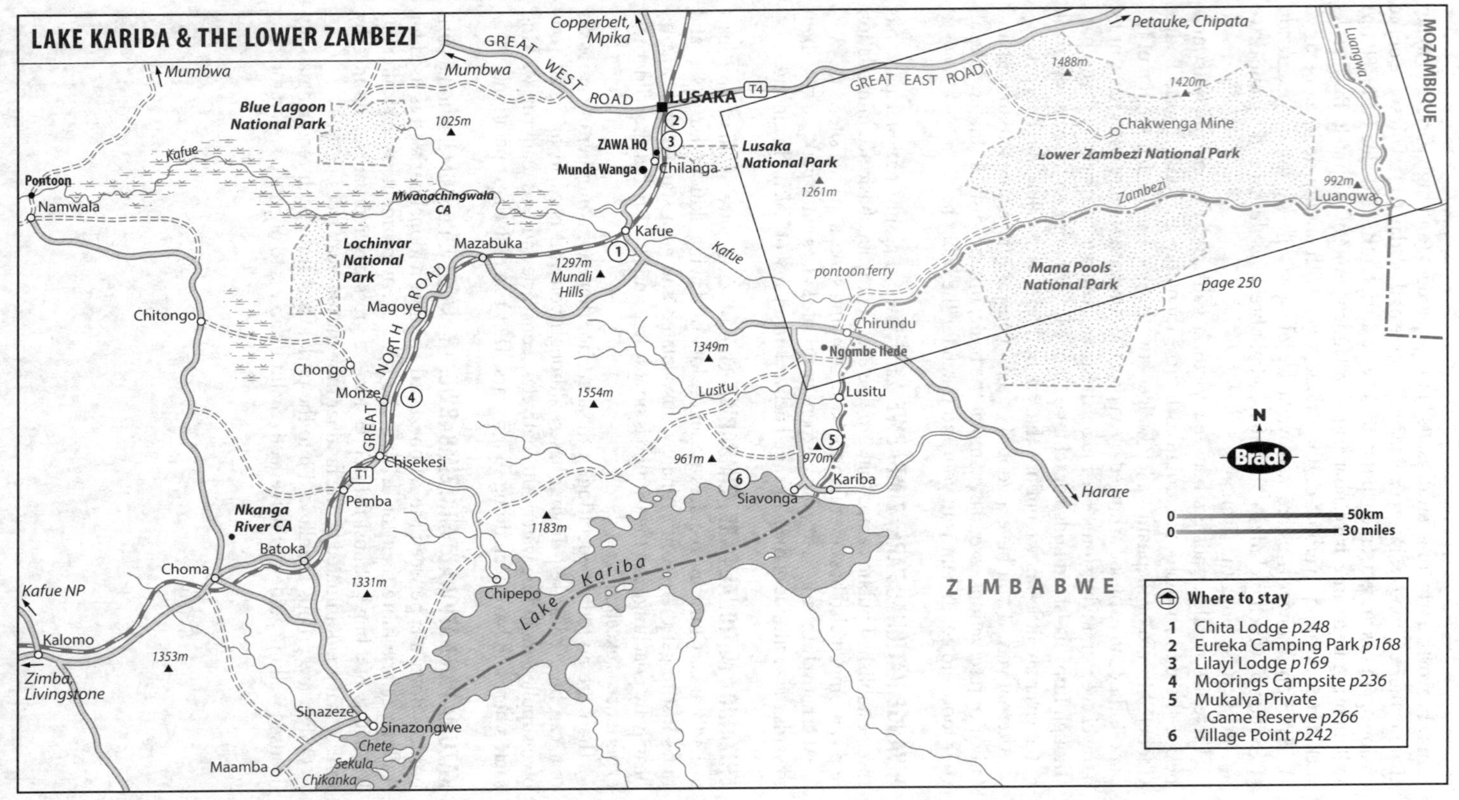

LAKE KARIBA & THE LOWER ZAMBEZI
Copperbelt, Mpika
Petauke, Chipata
MOZAMBIQUE
Mumbwa
Mumbwa
GREAT WEST ROAD
LUSAKA
T4
GREAT EAST ROAD
1488m
1420m
Luangwa
Blue Lagoon National Park
1025m
ZAWA HQ
Munda Wanga
Chilanga
Lusaka National Park
1261m
Chakwenga Mine
Lower Zambezi National Park
Zambezi
992m
Luangwa
Kafue
Pontoon
Namwala
Mwanachingwala CA
Lochinvar National Park
Mazabuka
Kafue
Kafue
1297m
Munali Hills
pontoon ferry
Mana Pools National Park
page 250
Chitongo
Magoye
GREAT NORTH ROAD
Chirundu
Ngombe Ilede
1349m
Chongo
Monze
1554m
Lusitu
Lusitu
N
Bradt
961m
970m
Chisekesi
T1
Kariba
Siavonga
Harare
Pemba
1183m
Nkanga River CA
0 50km
0 30 miles
Batoka
Choma
Lake Kariba
ZIMBABWE
Kafue NP
1331m
Chipepo
Where to stay
1 Chita Lodge p248
2 Eureka Camping Park p168
3 Lilayi Lodge p169
4 Moorings Campsite p236
5 Mukalya Private Game Reserve p266
6 Village Point p242
Kalomo
1353m
Zimba, Livingstone
Sinazeze
Sinazongwe
Chete
Sekula
Maamba
Chikanka

Lake Kariba and the Lower Zambezi

Zambia's border with Zimbabwe is defined by the course of the Zambezi as it slowly meanders towards the Indian Ocean. Below the Victoria Falls, the Zambezi flows east, sometimes northeast, with the greatest features of this section of river being artificial: Lake Kariba, between Zambia and Zimbabwe, and Lake Cabora Bassa, in Mozambique.

The photogenic skeletons of submerged trees, spectacular sunsets and days spent messing about on boats have drawn visitors, both local and international, to Lake Kariba since its creation in 1959. The laid-back lakeshore towns of Sinazongwe and Siavonga are pleasant spots to relax, take a boat trip, fish and visit the islands of Chete – large enough to be a credible wilderness destination with good wildlife – and Chikanka, with the possibility to stay overnight.

Below Kariba Dam, the Zambezi continues through the hot, low-lying Lower Zambezi Valley. National parks and fantastic safari camps flank both sides of the river, offering some of the best game viewing in the country and the winning combination of safari on land and water. For a magical day, combine tracking wild dogs and lions with sundowner boat trips to spot kingfishers alongside herds of elephants quenching their thirst. This is also the place to canoe down one of the world's great rivers – albeit avoiding hippos.

LIVINGSTONE TO LUSAKA *See also map, page 182*

This main tar road is only 485km, but it seems longer. There are three toll stations along the way, at Zimba, Choma and Kafue, each charging K20 per vehicle (US$1.10) and it's best to have the correct change to hand. The tarmac is largely faultlessly smooth, particularly as far as Mazabuka, though there are a few rough patches to negotiate, and speed humps in the towns, so allow about 7 hours for the journey if you're planning on a straight run, and stick to a safe 80km/h or so.

Better still, stop along the way and explore, including Choma's small museum and craft shop, and Coffeeberry Café outside Mazabuka. If you've more time, detour to Sinazongwe and on to one of Kariba's islands (page 246).

If you're planning to stop overnight, try Masuku Lodge at Nkanga River Conservation Area (page 235) or the super Moorings Campsite (page 236) at Monze (even if you don't have your own camping gear).

KALOMO This small town, about 126km from Livingstone and 347km from Lusaka, marks the turn-off from the main road towards Dumdumwenze gate, the access point for the southern section of Kafue National Park. The turning is clearly signposted. See page 434 for details of this route, and note that a 4x4 is essential to drive in the park.

There's a Kobil **fuel** station (⊕ KAFUEL 17°01.673'S, 26°29.259'E) on the main road, just south of the Kafue turn-off, but don't bank on it; while generally reliable, fuel availability cannot be guaranteed. There is a small snack shop and an Absa ATM here, and a Barclays Bank (inc ATM), district hospital, chemist, post office, several churches and a long-running Christian mission around town. There are a few basic accommodation options here if you really need somewhere to stay. Two sites nearby merit a passing mention:

Administrator's House (US$5/3 adult/child) Some 6km from the tar road, between the centre of Kalomo and its main suburb/township, this national monument dates to around 1903–04. It was built for the Administrator of Northwestern Rhodesia, as appointed by the British South Africa Company. Then Kalomo was the 'capital' of the territory, and the house is said to be the first non-traditional brick house built in Northern Rhodesia.

Kalundu Mound About 3km north of Kalomo, on the main road, is a slightly raised mound of earth (a matter of just a few metres) through which the road passes. This marks the site of an Iron-Age village, and the mound is the accumulated debris of many centuries of occupation.

It was excavated in the late 1950s and early 1960s when the road was being built, and the archaeologists estimated that it might have been occupied as early as the 4th century AD, although it was certainly full of people from about AD800–1300. The occupants during this latter period are sometimes referred to by Zambian archaeologists as following the 'Kalomo Tradition'.

CHOMA Choma (⊕ 16°48.547'S, 26°59.302'E) is a bustling, friendly market town, about 285km from Lusaka and 188km from Livingstone. The main road between the two, here called Livingstone Road, runs through the centre of the town, and on (or just off) it you'll find all the amenities of small-town life: shops, market, cafés, post office, internet facilities, five reliable fuel stations, branches of several major banks with ATMs, a good Spar supermarket, and a general hospital and pharmacy. Perhaps more surprisingly, there's a super little museum (see below). North of the town, roadside craft stalls mingle with those of the charcoal sellers, and you may also see local fishermen touting their catch by waving it in the face of passing cars.

Where to stay With your own transport, we'd recommend staying in the lodge or campsite within Nkanga River Conservation Area (page 235). In town, there are numerous smaller guesthouses, all with similarly simple facilities: **Leon's Lodge** (12 rooms; ☎0971 624852; **$$**), **Richland Lodge** (19 rooms; ☎0971 044730; **$$**), **Golden Pillow Lodge** (16 rooms; ☎0979 563563; **$$**) and **Kozo Lodge** (40 rooms; Livingstone Rd; ☎0977 619665; **$$**).

Where to eat and drink Most of the guesthouses can arrange meals and snacks. Food is also served at the museum and freshly baked treats are available at Wonderbake, behind Spar, and the supermarket itself sells take-away dishes.

What to see and do The popular **Choma Museum and Crafts Centre** (m 0979 323929; e chomamuseum@gmail.com; w chomamuseumartgallery.weebly.com; ⏲ 08.00–17.00 daily; admission US$2/1 adult/child) is on the main road through town. In addition to a collection of regional artefacts related to the Tonga people, the centre focuses on contemporary crafts and – to a lesser extent – art, showcasing the work of rural craftspeople throughout the area. There's a café, craft shop and children's playground.

NKANGA RIVER CONSERVATION AREA (Entry US$15 pp) About 5km north of Choma there's a signpost to Nkanga, 20km away on a good dirt road; it is also easily reached on the tarred road from Namwala. Here you'll find a conservation area that incorporates three local farms, and protects antelope including sable, eland, puku, hartebeest, wildebeest, kudu, tsessebe and many other species. The area is also one of Zambia's 'Important Bird Areas' (IBA), with a total of 439 species noted. These include Zambia's only endemic bird, the Zambian (Chaplin's) barbet.

As it's a conservation area that sustainably manages its populations of native game, some hunting is also conducted, though this does not interfere with the photographic visitors. Visitors may not walk around the farm without first obtaining permission.

Where to stay

Masuku Lodge (6 rondavels) 0213 225225; m 0966 763172; e masukulodge@gmail.com; f Masukulodge. Overlooking a dam within the Nkanga conservation area, Masuku Lodge is managed by Rory McDougall, a specialist safari birding guide, & Dori Glasspool. There are 6 thatched, en-suite rondavels with comfortable twin/dbl beds, sitting in neat lawned gardens. Guests dine together at one table in a central lounge/dining area & there's a friendly, home-from-home vibe. The lodge is particularly suited to birding, though much of the farm's game can also be spotted, including sable, kudu, zebra, eland & bushbuck. There's a swimming pool, wrought iron chairs round the campfire & some good walks & game drives (*US$20 pp*) on offer. A great overnight stop if you're self-driving between Lusaka & Livingstone. *US$360/dbl dinner B&B, exc conservancy fee.* ⏲ *All year; advance booking essential.* **$$$**

Nkanga River Conservation Area Camp Site 0213 225592; m 0977 863873/766260; e nansaibm@gmail.com. Basic campsite on the riverbank. Largely the domain of bushbuck, Cape clawless otter & countless birds, there's a communal shelter for campers, with firewood & the facility for BBQs, plus cold showers, toilets & electric lights. It can be cold by the river, especially May–Jul, & mosquito protection is essential. Guide game & birding walks can be arranged, as well as fishing for bream & barbel. Nkanga also runs valuable educational bushcamps Apr–Oct for groups (min 14) of children aged 7–16, covering bush knowledge, skills & outdoor activities. *Camping US$15 pp, exc conservancy fee.* ⏲ *All year; advance booking essential.* **$**

BATOKA Little more than a market-lined road with a small post office, Batoka is significant for visitors as the turn-off for Sinazongwe and Lake Kariba, which is signposted to the east of the road. It's almost the midway point between Livingstone (222km) and Lusaka (251km).

CHISEKESI The linear community of Chisekesi, 270km from Livingstone, boasts a useful fuel station. Just to the north is the **Mayfair Guesthouse** (m 0965 872476) offering rooms and camping.

Chisekesi is the turn-off to Chipepo Harbour and some of the non-commercial Kariba islands, at a distance of 92km. This is one of the settlement areas of the Tonga people who were displaced when the dam was constructed (Siavonga/Lusitu is another).

After the dam was built, ZESCO was committed to restoring the road that connects Siavonga with Sinazongwe and southwest to Sianzovo with its amethyst mines and market, but this remains inconsistent and rough going in parts. (As an aside, stones have in the past been sold illegally here by Senegalese traders known as the Masenesene.) Beyond Sianzovo a rough road continues to Syagulula, and on a further 15km to Devil's Gorge. You'll need some large-scale maps of the area, but the scenery is rewarding. A similarly poor road connects Sianzovo market back to Kalomo.

MONZE Monze's large grain silos are testament to the fertile land surrounding the small town. Vital grain-growing aside, Monze (MONZE ⊕ 16°15.436'S, 27°28.588'E) has a useful fuel station, some immaculate, fee-paying toilets at The Roadside and Moorings Campsite to the north of town, which is an excellent spot to spend the night.

Where to stay *See map, page 232*

Moorings Campsite (3 chalets, camping) **m** 0956 619491, 0954 945452; **e** mooringscamp.enquiries@gmail.com; **w** mooringscampsite.com. Much more than just a campsite, Moorings offers shady camping pitches with access to hot showers, a self-catering kitchen, restaurant & bar, as well as en-suite chalets, a craft centre & even a doctor at the weekends. Clearly signposted to the east of the main road, about 11km north of Monze and 50km south of Mazabuka, this is probably the best place to camp between Livingstone & Lusaka. The campsite is set in a grassy field, dotted with huge trees, on a mixed 2,600ha farm, supplementing the income from cattle, maize & soya. The site is also well placed for Lochinvar National Park, about 2hrs' drive away. Do ask managers James & Kim about the birding; keen birders may spot the Zambian (Chaplin's) barbet here.

Campers pull up alongside one of a number of open-sided thatched rondavels that are dotted about the field, each with electric light & space for a large open fire, with wood available. You can hire a tent if you don't have your own, & for non-campers there are small, en-suite brick-built chalets, 1 suitable for a family. The ablution block is spotlessly clean & visitors may use the small kitchen – with a limited menu available if you don't fancy cooking; there's also a large, airy bar area with plenty of chairs.

Visitors to the campsite are welcome to look around. Owner Thea Savory originally came to Monze from the Netherlands to work in the local hospital. Now she runs a medical clinic which is free for the farm's permanent workers & their families; other patients pay a small fee. The farm effectively has its own primary school, too, & partially funds secondary education.

Finally, there is the Malambo Women's Centre & Craft Shop, where local women come together for adult education & to make & sell brightly coloured quilts, cushion covers & Tonga basketry. Moorings is much more than just a campsite & it is well worth breaking your journey here. Booking not required. *Camping US$8 pp; chalet US$40/60 dbl/family. Firewood US$2/bundle* ⏲ *All year.* **$$** *exc b/fast.*

Excursions from Monze

Fort Monze (Entry US$5/2 adult/child; vehicle US$5/day) About 16km to the west of the town is the site of Fort Monze, which was one of the first police posts established in Zambia by the colonial powers. Founded in 1898 by the British South Africa police, led by Major Harding, the post was demolished in 1903 when the colonial authorities had a much firmer grip on the country. All that remains is a small, neglected graveyard and a monument in the shape of a cross to the soldiers who died here from blackwater fever. Although signposted from town, access to Fort Monze is only possible by 4x4 in the dry season, and the track is in very poor condition.

Lochinvar National Park Lochinvar National Park, northeast of Monze, has been designated as a wetland of international importance for its very special environment. It's about 48km from Monze, and if you have an equipped 4x4 and some time to explore, then it could be worth a visit. See page 447 for details.

MAZABUKA This large, bustling, tree-lined town, 349km from Livingstone and 124km from Lusaka (⊕ 15°51.489'S, 27°45.747'E), is at the centre of a very prosperous commercial-farming community. The huge Zambia Sugar company (locally referred to as the Nakambala Estate) dominates the area, and you'll see their fields of mono-culture sugarcane lining the main road either side of town.

Aside from a number of **fuel** stations, there is a major branch of Shoprite and a Choppies **supermarket** in the centre of town, branches of several major **banks** with ATMs, a couple of internet cafés, a pharmacy and a 24-hour private **hospital**, Victoria Hospital, on the eastern edge of town. For vehicle spares, try **Autoworld** (17–19 Nyerere Road; t 0213 230134; e mazabukasales@autoworld.co.zm).

Where to stay Although Mazabuka has a wide range of simple guesthouses there is little to choose between them. The listings here are among the better-quality options, with en-suite rooms and secure parking. Camping is possible on the lawn at Namasheke Gardens B&B on Chachacha Road.

Golden Pillow Lodge (10 rooms) Livingstone Rd; t 0213 231026; m 0968 838383; e goldenpillow.mazabuka@gmail.com. One of a trio of Golden Pillows along this route, offering simple, motel-style rooms & meals. $–$$

Nak Guest House (10 rooms) Nakambala Sugar Estate; m 0955 230484. On the Nakambala Sugar Estate, these neat, thatched chalets are clean & comfortable, overlook lush lawns & benefit from the reasonable, if slow, on-site restaurant, Plantations. $

Where to eat and drink Mazabuka boasts perhaps the best spot for a homemade meal or peaceful refreshment stop on **the entire Livingstone** to **Lusaka** route: Coffeeberry Café. In addition, most guesthouses can arrange a simple meal; or for take-away options, Mazabuka's supermarkets sell ready-made food and there are several fast-food joints – of varying quality – in town, among them a branch of the pasta/pizza chain Panarottis, next to the Oryx Fuel Station on the main road.

✱ **Coffeeberry Café** Tanderra Estates entrance, Livingstone Rd; m 0966 646836; e coffeeberrymaz@gmail.com; f coffeeberrymaz; ⏱ 07.00–17.00. With a shady veranda & relaxing gardens, Coffeeberry serves super coffee & scrumptious cakes, alongside a garden-fresh menu featuring breakfast burritos, wood-fired pizza, sandwiches & burgers. All dairy is homemade – from mozzarella to ice cream – and everything from the coffee beans to the strawberries & meat are sourced locally. Service can be slow but you can WhatsApp or call in a take-away order in advance if you don't want to delay your journey, though part of the joy here is in the serenity of the stop. Look out for wine tastings & music nights here (booking required), & check out the gift shop for locally made souvenirs. $–$$$

Plantations Nakambala Sugar Estate; t 0955 230484. Serves simple meals of chicken schnitzel, fish & steak with chips in its open, thatched dining area & at quiet garden tables on the lawn. $–$$$

Around Mazabuka

Mwanachingwala Conservation Area This conservation area on the Kafue Flats, some 25km north of Mazabuka, covers about 470km² beside the Kafue River. It combines land contributed by the local community of Chief Mwanachingwala with some of the private commercial farms in the area, and is rich in birdlife as well as being home to the Kafue lechwe and the shy sitatunga.

Those who make the journey are welcome to walk, fish, visit the large, semi-permanent fishing village or hire a mokoro to explore the area's hidden lagoons. Any income generated from activities in the conservation area is ploughed back into the local community.

For access, in the dry season only, you'll need a 4x4. Head south of Mazabuka towards Livingstone for around 5km, then turn right on Ghana Road, cross the Kaleya Stream, then after 3km or so take another right to Etebe School. A further 3–4km brings you to a turn-off to Mamba Fishing Camp; you're then on the Kafue Flats.

In theory, information about the area is available at the municipal offices in Mazabuka, near Shoprite, and this is where arrangements to visit should be made. However, there's no guarantee that the office will be staffed, so be prepared to ask around and allow plenty of time.

MAZABUKA TO LUSAKA This final stretch of the journey between Livingstone and Lusaka covers a distance of 131km. Pot-holes come and go, so as always, it's best not to exceed 80km/h.

The road passes through the Munali Hills, where – 56km north of Mazabuka – there's a sign to **Munali Hills historic site**, a stone cairn 1km along the Munali Pass road commemorating Livingstone's passage through the hill pass that separates the Lusaka high plateau from the Kafue Flats. (Munali, meaning 'you have been' or 'you have passed through', was the nickname given to Livingstone.)

Further north, you come to the small town of **Kafue**, which is the turn-off to Chirundu and the Lower Zambezi, and to Siavonga on Lake Kariba. Look out at the junction for roadside stalls selling baskets, from small decorative items to large linen numbers. For details of this road and the town itself, see page 247.

The final 50km of the route, from Kafue to Lusaka, is fairly plain sailing as far as Chilonga, but from here the steadily increasing level of traffic spreading out from the capital has the potential to cause delays.

LAKE KARIBA

Lake Kariba was created by the construction of a huge dam, started in November 1956 and completed in June 1959. It was the largest dam of its time – 579m wide at its crest, 128m high, 13–26m thick – and designed to provide copious hydro-electric power for both Zimbabwe and Zambia. It was a huge undertaking that turned some 280km of the river into around 5,200km² of lake. It has six 100,000kW generators on the Zimbabwean side, and five on the Zambian side – although the electricity generated here is promptly sold to Zimbabwe. The total construction cost was £78 million.

In human terms, construction of the dam immediately displaced thousands of BaTonga villagers, on both sides of the border, and took the lives of 86 workers in the process – around 18 of whom are entombed within the dam's million cubic metres of cement. It has opened up new industries relying on the lake, just as it closed off many possibilities for exploiting the existing rich game areas in that section of the Zambezi Valley.

It inevitably drowned much wildlife, despite the efforts of Operation Noah to save and relocate some of the animals as the floodwaters rose. However, the lake is now home to rich fish and aquatic life, and several game reserves and lodges are thriving on its southern shores.

For the visitor, Zambia's side of the lake is less well developed than Zimbabwe's and lacks a national park, but it's got a laid-back vibe, great fishing opportunities, and the small resorts of Siavonga and Sinazongwe make pleasant places to relax and base yourself for outings on to the lake. Only on its islands, Chete and Chikanka, will you find much game.

A commercial ferry, Kariba Ferries (☎ +263 261 2146176; e reservations@karibaferries.co.zw; w karibaferries.com; $145/75 adult/child inc meals), runs the length of the lake on the Zimbabwean side between Kariba and Mlibizi carrying both passengers and vehicles on the 22-hour journey; otherwise the only way to go on the lake is to rent a boat or houseboat, or to visit one of the islands (pages 241 and 246).

HEALTH AND SAFETY AROUND THE LAKE

Bilharzia Bilharzia is found in Lake Kariba, but only in certain parts. Unfortunately, it isn't possible to pinpoint its whereabouts exactly, but shallow, weedy areas that suit the host snail are likely to harbour the parasites; you're unlikely to contract bilharzia while in deep water in the middle of the lake.

See page 129 for more detailed comments on this disease. Local people who engage in fishing, bathing and water activities consider it an occupational hazard, and are regularly treated to expel the parasites from their bodies (those who can afford the treatment, that is).

Animal dangers The lake contains good populations of crocodiles, and a few hippos. Both conspire to make bathing and swimming near the shore unsafe. However, it is generally considered safe to take quick dips in the middle of the lake – often tempting, given Lake Kariba's high temperatures and humidity. The crocodiles have apparently not yet learned how to catch water-skiers.

SIAVONGA

Approaching Siavonga The road to Siavonga (⊕ 16°32.371'S, 28°42.545'E) leaves the main Lusaka–Chirundu road (page 247) a few kilometres west of the Chirundu Bridge over the Zambezi. It's marked by a police checkpoint, and a motley selection of corrugated metal craft stalls. From that turn-off, it is some 71km of rolling tarred road to the roundabout in Siavonga, mostly through areas of subsistence farming. From Lusaka to Siavonga takes around 3½ hours. The area is relatively densely populated, largely the result of 'forced migration' when the dam was built and entire villages, such as Lusitu (⊕ 16°08.050'S, 28°44.329'E), which now lies along this road, were relocated. You can expect animals wandering over the road, so drive slowly. While straight after the rains this makes an attractive drive, enhanced by some marvellous ancient baobabs, the problems of erosion and overgrazing make it a more challenging route at the end of the dry season, with numerous gullies cut into the powdery red soil. It is, however, a good route for roadside stalls – selling baskets in a range of sizes and numerous pieces of quartz, for which you'll need to be prepared to bargain very hard. (Be aware, too, that some of these 'gemstones' are broken pieces of insulation glass.)

About 15km after the turning off the main road, there's a track to the left (⊕ 16°07.948'S, 28°44.290'E) leading to the archaeological site of **Ngombe Ilede** (US$15/7 adult/child; vehicle US$5/day), some 13km away in a stark landscape devoid of all but baobabs. The site is now considered to be a 16th-century burial ground; 1960s archaeologists found 'richly adorned human skeletons' here, with exceptional gold, glass beads and bronze bangles that likely link them to Portuguese and East African traders of the time. Designated a national monument, the name translates 'the cow that is lying down' after a partially horizontal local baobab.

Nearing Siavonga, the road winds its way around the hills in steep spirals, affording some superb views, before finally dropping down into the town, on the edge of Lake Kariba.

Like the town of Kariba, its Zimbabwean neighbour over the dam, Siavonga has a strange layout as the result of being built on the upper sections of three or four hills – the lake's artificially created shore. What started out as a camp for the builders working on the dam in the 1950s eventually developed into a quiet holiday resort focusing on lake activities.

Getting there and away The easiest way to get to Siavonga is to drive yourself. Minibuses do ply the route between here and Lusaka each day, leaving only when they are full and costing about K80 one way. It's also possible to take a scheduled bus to Chirundu and then a taxi for the second leg of the journey; alternatively, for a more direct and possibly more comfortable journey, contact a travel agent in Lusaka or Livingstone, who could arrange a private transfer.

Getting around The small town is quite spread out, and the roads curve incessantly, sticking to the sides of the hills on which the town is built. Each of the hotels is tucked away in a different little cove or inlet, and to get from one to another usually involves several kilometres of up-and-down, winding roads. So while you could walk everywhere, you'll find it much easier with your own transport.

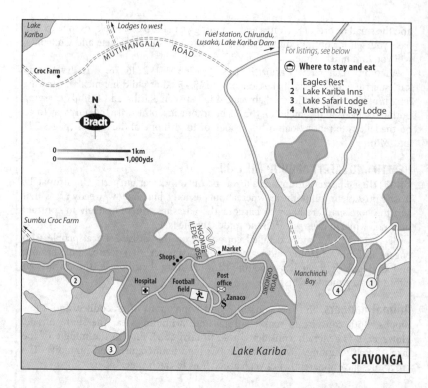

Where to stay and eat *Map, above, unless otherwise stated*
Siavonga has a surprising amount of accommodation considering its size and relatively few attractions (though the lake itself is a powerful draw). Being just a

3-hour drive from Lusaka makes it a convenient conference getaway destination – the stock trade for almost all Siavonga's hotels – or for a weekend break for city folk. Full board, rather than just B&B, can be good value, especially as there are no sparkling local restaurants. On a quiet night, you can find a good bed at a reasonable price. Campers have less choice, but are well catered for at Eagles Rest and Sandy Beach.

West of Siavonga, there are various simple lodges along the shoreline, reached by taking the turning to the west about 2km north of town (⊕ 16°24.290'S, 28°43.763'E). It's a very rough track, for which a high-clearance vehicle is essential, and a 4x4 in the rainy season. For the more westerly lodges, it's more sensible to arrange a boat transfer with the lodge concerned than to drive yourself.

On the lake itself, there are boats for hire by the day or for memorable overnight excursions (see below). To rent a houseboat on Lake Kariba, try Lake Kariba Inns or Eagles Rest (see below), or try the specialist Lake Kariba Houseboats (+263 4291 2027; e maureen@karibahouseboats.com; w karibahouseboats.com) based just across the border in Zimbabwe, who have an extensive range of boats and extremely helpful staff.

Lakeside

Lake Safari Lodge (70 rooms) Simamba Rd; 0211 511148; m 0978 659584; e bookings@lakesafari.com; w lakesafari.com. This attractive, if slightly dated, hotel is perched on a rocky headland slightly above the lake, about 1km from Siavonga harbour. En-suite rooms, the best with a lake view, spread out between the main building & a private slipway into the water. There's a restaurant, a late-night bar (busy at weekends) & 2 great swimming pools. Several boats can be hired by the hour. **$$$$**

Lake Kariba Inns (50 rooms) 0211 511249; m 0977 770480; e info@karibainns.com; w karibainns.com. With its pleasant gardens, complete with resident zebra & impala, good views, & wide range of facilities, the efficient Lake Kariba Inns is the best of Siavonga's options. Fresh, bright rooms, some with verandas overlooking the lake, & 7 villas with their own private pools, are popular with conference groups & families alike. A large bar & restaurant, 4 swimming pools complete with multiple waterslides, pedalos, a gym & spa keep everyone happy. Boat trips, fishing & kapenta rig tours can be arranged, with steep stairs leading down to the water where the Inn's 30-person pontoon boat, *Chipembere*, & its houseboat, *Takamaka* (see right), are moored. **$$$**

Manchinchi Bay Lodge (30 rooms); m 0976 849814; e info@manchinbaylodge.com. Dated rooms, albeit clean, with lakeview verandas, tropical gardens, a large swimming pool & sunset cruises on the *Manchinchi MV*. **$$$**

Eagles Rest (12 chalets, camping) m 0967 688617, 0978 869126; e bookingeaglesrest@gmail.com (hotel/camping), steveeaglesrest@gmail.com (boats); f eagles.rest.siavonga. Less than 10km from the Kariba Dam wall, Eagles Rest's compact, air-conditioned chalets are geared to self-catering with fridges, basic kitchen equipment & a BBQ overlooking the bay. The adjacent tree-shaded campsite is beautifully located, with an ablutions block & points for electricity & water. There's a modest restaurant/bar (**$$–$$$**) & lively, thatched beach bar. With its pool & beach volleyball, the place is popular with families, who can canoe on the lake (K20 pp/hr) or take part in dam wall cruises (K550 up to 12 people) & sunset cruises (K750/12 people). Boats can also be hired for fishing trips (from K500/hr up to 4 people), with fishing tackle available to rent. For houseboat cruises on the *Bateleur*, see page 242. River canoe safaris & hikes can be organised with notice. *Chalet US$75 dbl B&B; camping K100 pp.* **$$**

Houseboats

Takamaka [not mapped] (8 berth) Contact Lake Kariba Inns (see left). Refurbished in 2022, this 2-storey pontoon-style houseboat has 4 cabins sharing 2 bathrooms, a plunge pool, bar & the option of self-catering or full board. You'll be accompanied by a small crew & a tender boat for fishing expeditions & forays to the shore. *US$950/night for up to 12 guests; US$60 pp/day for Kariba Feast. All FB inc fishing, exc drinks.*

THE TRAP *Heather Chalcraft*

According to legend, the name of Kariba should be *kariwa*, 'the trap', for long ago a lake behind the hills broke through and the violent torrent tore out the gorge; when the water subsided it left behind a massive stone slab, the *kariwa*, until it collapsed.

The real trapping of the river took place on 2 December 1958, when the peaceful course that the Zambezi had run for centuries was stopped in its stride. This was the day on which the gap in the wall was closed. Less than 100 years ago, the Kariba Gorge was considered an obstacle to river navigation, for in its 26km the river ran fast. In 1912, a district commissioner visiting from Southern Rhodesia (now Zimbabwe) reported on the potential dam site with a view to irrigation of the Zambezi Valley. Ten years later, it was suggested as a source of hydro-electric power but, as in 1912, there was no money available for this. By 1937 it was recognised that the potential of Zambia's copper mines could not be realised without cheap electrical power but it was only in 1951 that Kariba was recommended as a suitable site for the construction of a dam.

The project was dogged by controversy. A similar scheme had already been suggested on the Kafue River, but the experts backed Kariba as it was the bigger of the schemes. When the announcement was made in March 1955 that the dam was to be built at Kariba there was outrage north of the Zambezi where politicians called it the 'Great Betrayal'.

Finance for the dam, a total of £80 million, came from a variety of sources, including the World Bank, the Colonial Development Corporation, the British South Africa Company and the Rhodesian Federal Government. The closing date for tenders was 17 April 1956 and one tender arrived in Salisbury (now Harare) with only 10 minutes to spare – the aircraft with the courier from Italy had been delayed due to a technical fault. Three months later, the main contract for the construction of the dam and south-bank power station was awarded to an Italian firm – Impresit South Africa – at a value of over £25 million. Another Italian-controlled firm, Rhodesia Power Lines, was awarded the contract for the transmission lines at a value of nearly £10 million. The British companies that had tendered for the job were outraged.

Bateleur [not mapped] (10 berth) Contact Eagles Rest (page 241). A relatively large boat offering overnight trips sleeping up to 12 passengers – 3 cabins sleep 6, plus 6 on the upper deck, with a jacuzzi for relaxing, & waterskiing & fishing options. *US$100 pp/day based on 10 passengers.*

West of Siavonga

Village Point [map, page 232] (4 chalets, 3 huts, camping) **m** 0966 289005; **e** nessylewis@yahoo.co.uk. **f** Village-Point-Lodge. On a peninsula in Lotri Bay, 40km west of Siavonga (30min boat transfer), Village Point is laid-back with strong community links. Tall, open-fronted chalets are comfortable & make the most of the lakeview & breeze; the Mango Grove huts & campsite are good budget options. *US$60 pp FB, exc drinks. Camping US$15, or US$30 with hired tent.* **$$**

Other practicalities Siavonga is quite a sleepy, relaxed place. Groceries can be bought at the simple **supermarket**, bakery and two local markets, and there's a **post office** and two **banks** with ATMs: Zanaco and **ZNC.** The latter, together with the civic centre (where you'll find the police station and a courtroom), form the 'town centre' which is perched on one of the hills. There is **no fuel station**: fill up at the Puma or SGC garages on the M15, just before the turn-off to Siavonga from Lusaka.

One of the earliest contracts awarded, to Costain, was for the construction of Kariba township, where those involved in the building of the dam would live for the duration. Original estimates were that the township would take two years to complete, but this was cut down by a third. Work went on for 18 hours a day, seven days a week, with temperatures sitting at 43°C at 22.00 and 32°C at 05.00. Fitters took to carrying tools in buckets of water to prevent them becoming too hot. Houses, from foundations to door locks, were being completed at the rate of three every two days. A bank was built from start to finish in nine days.

The building of the dam was an outstanding engineering feat. A great river which could in the space of a few hours become a raging torrent had to be tamed; the site was remote with no roads leading to or from it; the gorge in which they had to work was narrow; and the temperatures and humidity were high. In November 1956, the first skip of concrete, two tons of it, was poured. This was only the first of nearly three million tons used in the wall – enough to pave a road from Zambia to Russia. On 22 June 1959 the last skip of concrete was released on the curve of the wall by the federal Prime Minister, Sir Roy Welensky – ten months ahead of schedule despite the floods of 1957 and 1958 when the Zambezi did its best to fight man's intentions.

Meanwhile virgin bush was being cleared to the north for the transmission lines – a job which was started in 1955 and was to take four years. The trees, which would be covered with water, were being pulled down and work was commencing on the south-bank power station. For those who worked at Kariba, they needed no references or testimonials – they only had to say 'I worked at Kariba' and the job was theirs. But there were human tragedies too – a number of people lost their lives during the construction of the dam; some are still buried within the wall. Eight of Chief Chipepo's people who were forcibly being moved to higher ground were killed during violent clashes with the police. And the human tragedies continue for those displaced people…

First published in The Lowdown, *January 2004*

What to see and do

On the lake Most of the activities in Siavonga revolve around the lake: boating, fishing and watersports such as windsurfing, tubing and waterskiing (though note the comments on safety on page 239). Canoeing trips are available through Eagles Rest (page 241).

Lake cruises and sunset trips are offered by all the hotels and lodges, from around K60 per person, depending on the type of boat and the numbers on board. They are also able to organise longer boat trips, perhaps to do a spot of fishing, or to visit the dam wall.

Visiting the dam Lake cruises to visit the dam wall can be organised through various hotels, including Eagles Rest. It's also possible for visitors to take a walk over the dam wall. If you have your own transport, simply present your passport to the customs office at the Zambian border post, then drive down the border road to the car park. From here, you can walk along the wall, enjoying an east–west view of lake and gorges, huge spillgates, and Zambia and Zimbabwe's power stations.

Note that both Zimbabwe and Zambia are acutely aware of the vulnerability of the dam to damage or terrorist attack. So don't appear 'suspicious' and always ask before taking photographs – it may be just a wall to you, but it's of vital importance to them.

Kapenta rig tour Kapenta are small, sardine-like fish, similar to whitebait, that were introduced on commercial grounds into Kariba in the 1960s (see below). Since then, fishing for them has become an important new industry around the lake, in both Zimbabwe and Zambia. When dried, kapenta are tasty, high in protein, and very easy to transport: an ideal food in a country where poorer people often suffer from protein deficiency.

Look out over the lake at night and watch the fishing rigs use powerful lights to attract the fish into their deep nets. These are then brought back to shore in the early morning, sun-dried on open racks (easily smelled and seen), and packaged for sale. Short tours lasting a couple of hours in the early evening can be arranged to one of these rigs through the hotels in Siavonga, and you'll bring back fresh kapenta to eat.

THE FOOD OF THE PAINTED WOMEN *Heather Chalcraft*

Fishing for kapenta (*Limnothrissa miodon*) is an important commercial enterprise on Lake Kariba, giving a living to a significant number of people around the lake. It first came to the towns and cities of Zambia from Lake Tanganyika, although as early as 1860 the explorer Richard Burton had described the use of circular nets lowered from a canoe to catch fish attracted by the light of an *mbaula* (a wood-fired brazier). Today, kapenta rigs have enormous lights on the surface and are fitted with the same circular nets, although they are much larger, and the lights are lowered into the water. The lights attract the fish and, when there are sufficient numbers, the net is lifted to the surface with the catch.

The possibility of introducing kapenta into Lake Kariba was considered as early as 1956, although the first experimental attempts began in 1952. Under the supervision of Dr George Coulter, Senior Fisheries Officer in the then Northern Rhodesia, a brood of sardine fry of the genus *Limnothrissa* was netted near Mpulungu and placed into two galvanised-iron transport tanks. They all died within 5 hours. A second method, whereby the fry were caught in a large polythene net and placed in polythene bags, resulted in a greater survival rate, although mortality was still high. However, some individual fry survived and were growing beyond the maximum transportation size, so a trial run to Kariba of 350 fry was attempted. These were transported by road to Abercorn (now Mbala) Airport, by air to Kariba Airport and by road to the lakeshore.

At Kariba, 7½ hours after capture, 45% of the fry had survived. Half of these were introduced immediately to a lakeside storage dam where they all died within a few minutes, possibly because of a difference in water temperatures. The next day only 14 of the original 350 were still alive. These were placed in a keep-net in the lake where they lived and grew for more than three months until a storm wrecked the net and the fry escaped into the lake. Albeit accidentally, the first introduction of sardines to Lake Kariba had taken place.

But it was still not known whether they would find conditions suitable for breeding, nor which of the two species involved would be the better. Investigations were carried out and by September 1966 it was decided that

Crocodile farms Siavonga has a couple of private crocodile farms, both open to the public: Kaliolio, located on the Mutinangala Road, and Kandilo, which is visited by Manchinchi Bay Lodge.

SINAZONGWE Zambia's second small town on Lake Kariba is roughly equidistant between Livingstone and Siavonga. It is a typical small Zambian town, originally built as the fishing and administrative centre for the southern lakeshore area, and is used mainly as an outpost for kapenta fishing. Despite the town's location, its centre is actually up the hill away from the lake, with a couple of simple restaurants and a small hospital. When the lake was first flooded Sinazongwe was a much busier harbour and even had the lake's only lighthouse. Although its prosperity has somewhat faded, it is well placed to become the hub of operations for Zambian tourism to Lake Kariba, and its first campsite has been developed into attractive self-catering chalets.

Getting there and away There's a good tar road from Batoka, signposted to Maamba Mines, on the main Lusaka–Livingstone road (30km northeast of Choma),

Limnothrissa miodon, the larger, less specialised species, would be the one. *Limnothrissa miodon* was known to grow to 17cm in Lake Tanganyika and did not require such deep water for laying its eggs as the other species. Further experiments on the catching, handling, keeping and transportation of the sardines were undertaken until, in 1969, fish of varying sizes were caught in Lake Kariba and identified as kapenta, suggesting that they had not only survived but also bred in their new environment. The Kariba kapenta grew much smaller than the Tanganyika ones, reaching sexual maturity before a length of 5cm and rarely growing beyond 6cm.

The first attempts to catch the kapenta were made using banana boats, lights and scoop, and lift nets. The catches were not spectacular but large numbers of fish could be seen under the lights, and by the end of the first year some had been caught 64km east of Sinazongwe. It was not until 1976 that commercial fishing of kapenta started on the Rhodesian (Zimbabwean) side of the lake, followed by the Zambian side in the early 1980s, after Zimbabwe's independence. At night one can see the flickering lights across the dark waters of Lake Kariba. These are the fishing rigs at work. Catches are seasonal as during the summer months the kapenta move inshore to breed in protected bays. Commercial catches rise again after March when the adults return to open waters. However, if the rain has been poor, there is less food for them, which means poor harvests for fisherfolk (and for the fish and birds which feed on them).

But it is not only on Lake Kariba that man, fish and birds benefit from this 'silver gold'. These hardy little fish are sucked into the turbines and spewed into the stilling pool below the dam. They survive, only to fall prey to the hundreds of tern and kingfishers that are waiting for their dazed emergence at the dam's tailrace. Survivors have even made the 220km journey through a river devoid of plankton and infested with predators, to establish new shoals in Lake Cahora Bassa in Mozambique.

From an article first published in The Lowdown, *January 2004*

which stretches to within 17km of Sinazongwe, before becoming a reasonable, all-weather gravel road. Driving time to/from Lusaka is approximately 4–5 hours, or from Livingstone 3–4 hours.

Sinazongwe lies almost directly beneath the flight-path between Livingstone and the Lower Zambezi National Park – between which there are occasional direct charter fights. Organising a seat on these would be tricky, but may be possible; check with a knowledgeable tour operator.

Where to stay

Lakeview Lodge (3 chalets) m 0962 667752, 0974 052922; e reservations@lakeview-zambia.com, lakeviewzambia@gmail.com; f lakeviewkariba. Under the same ownership as Mukalya (page 266), this tranquil lodge is an ideal place to unwind, with just lizards & kingfishers for company. Overlooking the lake from their secluded terraces are thatched chalets, simply but attractively furnished with en-suite showers & ceiling fans to aid the breeze from the lake. Lawns lead down to the reed-fringed lakeshore, backed by large boulders that shelter a small sandy beach. There's an attractive dining room with tables on the veranda, a waterfront swimming pool & an entertainment area. Activities feature day trips to Chikanka Island (*K1,400/up to 6 people, exc lunch*); sunset cruises (*K135 pp*); & guided walks on Chete Island (*K300 pp*). For details of Chikanka & Chete islands, see below. **$$$**

ISLANDS ON LAKE KARIBA Of the numerous islands on Lake Kariba, only two are currently inhabited, Chikanka and Maaze; Chete's lodge has been closed for some years.

Chete Island Chete is the largest island on the lake, and after a quick glance at the map you'll realise that it's much nearer to the Zimbabwean mainland (150m) than it is to Zambia (15km). This is because the border is defined as the deepest part of the Zambezi's old river course, not a line through the middle of the lake. In fact, the island lies just offshore from Zimbabwe's Chete Safari Area – so it's no surprise that it's become recognised under Zambia's national parks system as a private wildlife reserve and bird sanctuary.

Chete is in a remote southern part of the lake, isolated except for the distant nocturnal lights of the kapenta rigs. The island's game isn't tame, nor as dense as you'll find in the Luangwa or the better areas of the Kafue, but there is a sense of solitude and wilderness such as only a wild island like this can give. Its closest point of contact is really Sinazongwe, 17km away across Lake Kariba.

Much of the bigger game migrates between Zimbabwe and the island. This is especially true of the elephant bulls, but there's also a resident breeding herd of around 50 elephants on the island. A small pride of lion frequents the island, too. Then there are perhaps half-a-dozen leopard, a herd of eland, and plenty of waterbuck, bushbuck, impala and some magnificent kudu. Not forgetting the many crocodile and hippo that surround the shores, and a wide variety of birds – some 161 species have been counted on Chete and the neighbouring Sikula Island. Vultures circle in the thermals over the high ground, and a solitary martial eagle may be spotted over the centre of the island, while lower down, numerous smaller birds come to the fore, including little bee-eaters and colourful blue waxbills.

Typically, a guided walk across the centre of the island takes around 2 hours. The landscape is very varied, similar in parts to Zimbabwe's Chizarira and Matusadonna national parks. Areas of dense cover, rugged interior woodlands and gorges contrast with lightly wooded clearings criss-crossed with game tracks; nearer the shore, the terrain opens up into expansive floodplains. There are no roads here, and now that the lodge is closed, the island is totally deserted.

Chikanka Island Chikanka Island is now strictly an archipelago of three islands due to a rise in the level of the lake since it was formed, although at the end of the dry season, you can sometimes walk between the three. It lies about 8km from the Zambian mainland, 10km west–southwest of Chete and 18km southwest of Sinazongwe. Covering 240ha (2.4km^2), it is smaller than Chete, and is also privately owned.

The islands are mostly wooded, with mopane trees, marulas and the occasional baobab contrasting with the stark skeletons of drowned trees in the surrounding lake. Rock figs display their intricate root system; wild purple morning glory entwines its way through the waterplants along the shoreline, and dwarf plated lizards flash their brilliant blue tails as they dart among the rocks.

Chikanka has some plains game, including kudu, impala and bushbuck, and elephants occasionally visit too. Not surprisingly, there are also hippos and crocodiles around the shores, so it's not sensible to swim, but guided game walks are offered. The channels between the islands boast a good variety of fish, including bream, tiger fish, Cornish jack and bottlenose.

Where to stay

Chikanka Island Fishing & Game Lodge (8 chalets) Contact via Lakeview Lodge (see opposite). Closed at the time of writing, it's worth checking with Lakeview Lodge if these lovely stone-clad, en-suite chalets have reopened when you're in the area. The dawn view over the lake to Zimbabwe is stunning.

LUSAKA TO CHIRUNDU

It takes at least 20 minutes to slough off the increasing urban sprawl of Lusaka before you're on an open road, beyond Chilanga. Some 50km south of the city, you'll come to the town of Kafue and, shortly before the busy turning to Livingstone (marked by a police checkpoint), cross over the wide and slow Kafue River that is also heading to join the Zambezi. From here the road gradually, consistently and occasionally spectacularly, descends. It leaves the higher, cooler escarpment for the hot floor of the Zambezi Valley, before passing the turn-off to Siavonga and crossing the busy bridge at Chirundu into Zimbabwe.

This tar road is an important commercial artery, so is kept in reasonably good repair, though you can expect some outbreaks of pot-holes on the lower sections of the escarpment. Between Kafue and Chirundu, lumbering trucks struggle to negotiate the steep, sharp bends, with breakdowns common and accidents all too frequent.

Occasional stalls set up on the side of the road sell seasonal fruit and vegetables, but the best spot for carved wooden animals, drums, baskets and other crafts is at the turn-off to Livingstone, just south of Kafue town. If you decide to buy, and you're flying home, remember that large carvings such as giraffes have to be put in the plane's hold, so make sure that they are very carefully packed.

KAFUE Geographically sandwiched, Kafue town sits on slightly raised ground between the meandering Kafue River and the rising granite hills of the central Zambian plateau. A rapidly growing, straggling industrial town, it's home to a large-scale fishery, quarry, commercial farming, a steel plant, and the nearby hydro-electric dam at Kafue Gorge.

For refreshments and supplies, **Kafue River Mall** is the best stop, with a PicknPay supermarket, selection of fast food outlets, a pharmacy, optician, Barclays bank and a mobile-phone shop. There is also a post office, bus station and several **fuel** stations in town.

Where to stay and eat Options in town are limited to a clutch of small, simple guesthouses that predominantly serve the town's industries.

Chita Lodge [map, page 232] (61 rooms; camping) Great North Rd; **m** 0979 562176; **e** reservations@chita.co.zm; **w** chita.co.zm; ⊕ CHITAK 15°48.382'S, 28°12.632'E. About 5km south of Kafue, Chita is a riverfront lodge with a restaurant, swimming pool & an eye on the local conference market. Camping is permitted (US$8.50/tent) & BBQ facilities are available (US$6). **$$$**

House of Excellence Guesthouse (14 rooms) 1723 Kaseba, off main rd; **m** 0975 269671. One of the better options, with en-suite rooms, a restaurant & secure parking. **$$**

CHIRUNDU BORDER AREA A few kilometres before Chirundu, just 500m after the turn-off to Siavonga and Kariba and another police checkpoint, is the **Chirundu Fossil Forest** (entry US$15/7 adult/child), a small area around the road where the remnants of petrified trees from the Jurassic Period can be seen strewn on the ground. Note that it's illegal to remove any fossils from the site.

The approach to Chirundu is lined with truck parks harbouring lorries waiting to get across the border to Zimbabwe. It's a place where people come and go, with few staying around. In 2018, the town got its first shopping mall, close to the border post, and with it the welcome arrival of a Shoprite **supermarket**. There are several **banks**, a **post office,** a good mission **hospital** and a couple of **fuel** stations.

Getting to the Lower Zambezi

By car The unsignposted dirt road to Gwabi River Lodge and the Lower Zambezi branches east from the main road about 200–300m from the border. To find it, turn left at the entrance to the town itself, opposite the sign to the Zanaco Bank, and continue past the bus station. After about 2km you'll pass the sign for Machembere on your right, then a further 10km on is the Gwabi turn-off, to the left. From here, after another 2km, the road heads towards the Kafue River where a 2km stretch of tar heralds a modern bridge. Much as the old pontoon across the river could be time consuming, there's no denying that it had considerably more character than the stark new construction, complete with incongruous urban streetlights, that has recently replaced it.

By public transport The Juldan Motors **bus** between Lusaka and Harare passes through Chirundu and will stop on request. If you'd like to get a taste of the Zambezi River, ask the driver to let you off in Chirundu, then you can take a taxi to one of the riverside lodges (see below). Alternatively, you can get a minibus to Chirundu, costing about US$5 per person from Lusaka, or consider a taxi from Lusaka, which at US$80–100 might be worth it for a group.

Where to stay Despite a handful of cheap lodgings in Chirundu itself, the town is no place to linger. You'd do far better to continue out of town to one of the riverside options before crossing the Kafue River to the north.

Gwabi River Lodge [250 B4] (11 chalets, 8 tents, camping) ☎ 0950 089068; **m** 0966 345962; **e** admin@gwabiriverlodge.com; **w** gwabiriverlodge.com (⊕ GWABI 15°55.889'S,

28°52.266′E). On an undulating site on the Kafue River, 3km from its confluence with the Zambezi, Gwabi offers various overnight options, the best being the river-view chalets & the tree-shaded camping area along the river. There's a pool, games room, dining area & full-day excursions can be arranged, inc game drives – albeit a 2hr drive to the national park from here – tiger fishing, river safaris & village walks. *Chalet US$46–83/52–95 pp sharing/sgl B&B; tent US$35/44 exc b/fast; stone tent US$20 pp exc b/fast; camping US$14 pp.* ⏲ *All year.* **$–$$$**

Machembere Lodge [250 A4] (5 chalets, camping) m 0977 758691, 0968 642102; e machembere123@gmail.com; f machemberelodge. Down a bumpy 1½km track about 2km from Chirundu, Machembere is notable for its wide river frontage & lush gardens, the pride of owner Hilary Vlahakis. A waterfront main area, lovely pool, comfortable, low-key cottages & a tree-shaded campsite (US$6). ⏲ *All year.* **$$**

LOWER ZAMBEZI VALLEY

The Lower Zambezi Valley, from the Kariba Dam to the Mozambique border, has a formidable reputation for wildlife and striking beautiful wilderness, leading UNESCO to designate part of the Zimbabwean side as a World Heritage Site. Two national parks protect the environment and wildlife on either side of the Zambezi – Mana Pools National Park in Zimbabwe to the south and, to the north, Lower Zambezi National Park in Zambia. Given the propensity of some of the bigger animals to regularly cross the river, especially elephant and buffalo, this makes for a very large area of the valley devoted to wildlife conservation.

However, take a look at a map of the Zambian bank and you'll realise that the land up to 55km east from the Kafue River (from Gwabi River Lodge) is not in the national park at all; the river defines the border with the Chiawa Game Management Area (GMA), which is owned by the operators within the area, obtained with permission from the chieftainess. Only to the east of the Chongwe River are you in the national park.

As you might expect, the game densities increase as you travel east, with the best game in the national park itself, and fewer animals on the privately owned land nearer to Chirundu. The situation is similar on the opposite bank of the river, in Zimbabwe, so if you want optimum game viewing then do get into the park if you can, or at least near to it.

Time in the Lower Zambezi is magic. The ability to combine land- and water-based activities makes for an extra special safari. Here you can mix action-packed game drives tracking wild dogs with the tranquillity of a lunchtime boat cruise, or canoeing at eye-level with antelope and thirsty elephants with trying your hand at world-class tiger fishing. There are myriad ways to explore the park and its wildlife, but it's hard to beat simply sitting back to watch the sun dip over the escarpment, G&T in hand, from the middle of the Zambezi.

GEOGRAPHY From Chirundu to the Mozambique border, the Zambezi descends 42m, from 371m to 329m above sea level, over a distance of over 150km. That very gentle gradient (about 1:3,500) explains why the Zambezi flows so slowly and spreads out across the wide valley, making such a gentle course for canoeing.

From the river, look either side of you into Zambia and Zimbabwe. In the distance you will spot the escarpment, if the heat haze doesn't obscure it. At around 1,200m high, it marks the confines of the Lower Zambezi Valley and the start of the higher, cooler territory beyond which is known as the 'highveld' in Zimbabwe.

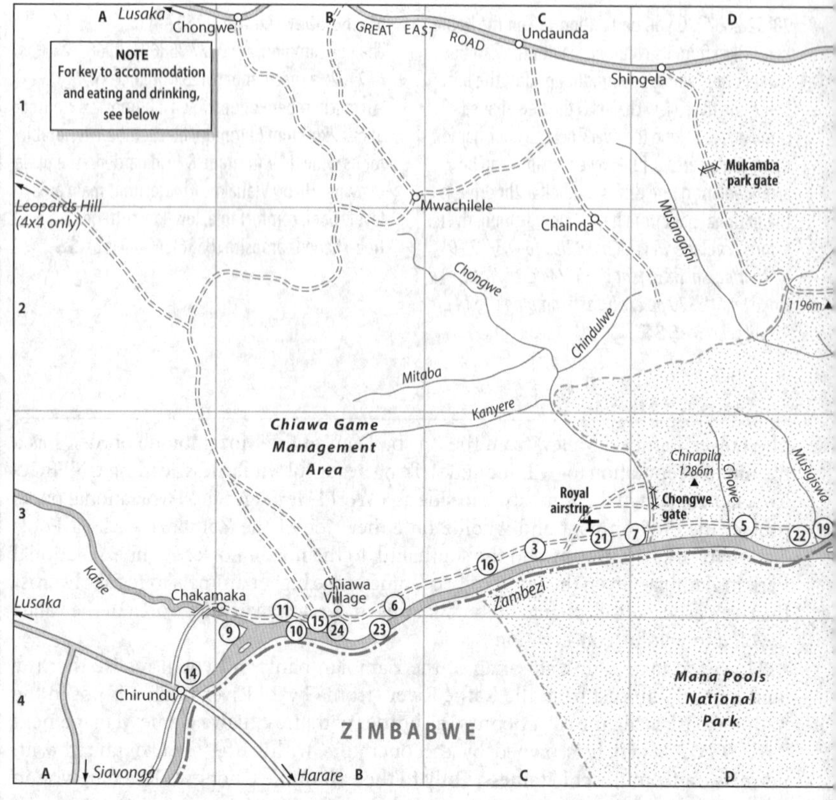

The valley is a rift valley, similar to the Great Rift Valley of East Africa (though probably older), and it shares its genesis with the adjoining Luangwa Valley. The original sedimentary strata covering the whole area are part of the karoo system, sedimentary rocks laid down from about 300 to 175 million years ago. During this time, faulting occurred and volcanic material was injected into rifts in the existing sediments. One of these faults, the wide Zambezi Valley, can still be seen. In geologically recent times, the Zambezi has meandered across the wide valley floor, eroding the mineral-rich rocks into volcanic soils and depositing silts which have helped to make the valley so rich in vegetation and wildlife. These meanders have also left old watercourses and oxbow pools, which add to the area's attraction for game.

So look again from one side of the valley to the other. What you see is not a huge river valley: it is a rift in the earth's crust through which a huge river happens to be flowing.

FLORA AND FAUNA

Flora Most of the park, made up of higher ground on the sides and top of the escarpment, is thick bush – where game viewing is difficult. This is broadleafed miombo woodland, dominated by brachystegia, *julbernardia*, *combretum* and *terminalia* species. Fortunately, there's little permanent water here, so during the dry season the game concentrates on the flat alluvial plain by the river.

Acacia species and mopane dominate the vegetation on the richer soils of the valley floor, complemented by typical riverine trees like leadwood (*Combretum imberbe*),

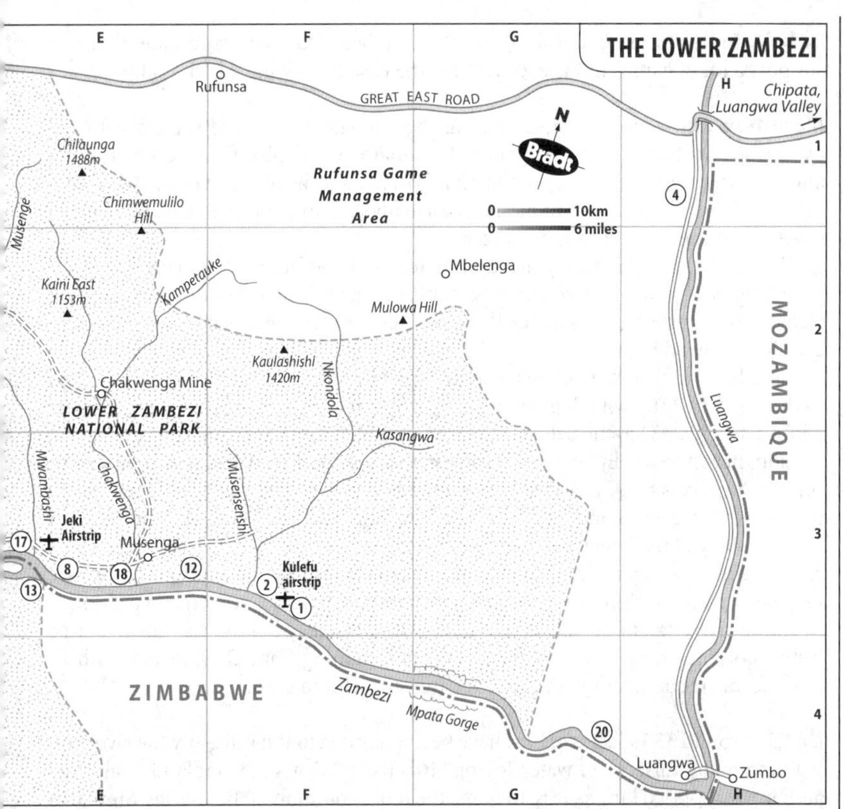

ebony (*Diospyros mespiliformis*) and various figs (*Ficus* species). Here the riverine landscape and vegetation are very distinctive: similar to the Luangwa Valley, but quite different from other parks in the subcontinent.

Perhaps it is the richness of the soils which allows the trees to grow so tall and strong, forming woodlands with carpets of grasses, and only limited thickets of shrubs to obscure the viewing of game. The acacia species include some superb specimens of the winterthorn (*Faidherbia albida*, which used to be known as *Acacia albida*), and the flat-topped umbrella thorn (*Acacia tortilis*). Both of these produce seedpods which the game love, the former looking like apple-rings, the latter being tightly spiralled seedpods which are very nutritious (19% protein, 26%

THE LOWER ZAMBEZI

For listings, see from page 257, unless otherwise stated

Where to stay

1 Amanzi........F3
2 Anabezi........F3
3 Baines' River Camp........C3
4 Bridge Camp Luangwa *p271*........H1
5 Chiawa Camp........D3
6 Chiawa Cultural Village........B3
7 Chongwe Camp........D3
Chongwe House........(see 7)
8 Chula Island Camp........E3
9 Gwabi River Lodge *p248*........B4
Kanyemba Island Bushcamp......(see 10)
10 Kanyemba Lodge........B4
11 Kiambi Lower Zambezi........B3
12 Kutali........E3
13 Lolebezi........E3
14 Machembere Lodge *p249*........A4
15 Mukuyu........B4
16 Mvuu Lodge........C3
17 Mwambashi River Lodge........E3
18 Old Mondoro........E3
19 Potato Bush Camp........D3
20 Redcliff Zambezi Lodge........G4
21 Royal Zambezi Lodge........C3
22 Sausage Tree Camp........D3
23 Tsika Island Camp........B4
24 Wildtracks Lodge........B4

carbohydrate, 5% minerals). It all results in a beautiful, lush landscape that can support a lot of game, and is excellent for the ease of viewing which it allows.

Mammals The Lower Zambezi has all the big game that you'd expect, with the exceptions of rhino, giraffe and cheetah. Buffalo and elephant are very common, and can often be seen grazing on the islands in the middle of the river, or swimming between Zimbabwe and Zambia. It is normally safe to get quite close by drifting quietly past these giants as they graze.

The antelope in the valley are dominated by large herds of impala, but good populations of kudu, waterbuck, bushbuck, zebra and the odd duiker or grysbok also occur. Giraffe are notable for their absence – in fact, there's no record of them ever having lived here.

Lion, leopard and spotted hyena are the major predators, and having re-appeared in the valley in 2015, wild dogs are thriving, with an ever-growing pack denning near Jeki Airstrip in 2022 to the delight of visitors and BBC film-makers.

Lions have historically been very visible in the park. Back in 1995, I saw a marvellous pride of in excess of 30 animals. Though the lion prides have since split, perhaps in part due to a predominance of males, watching big cats hunt is still a Lower Zambezi special. Many of the larger trees have branches made-to-measure for leopards, which are sometimes seen on night drives, and increasingly during the day, too. There have long been plans to reintroduce cheetah here but these have not yet come to fruition.

In the river, crocodile and hippo are always present, but look also for the large water monitor lizard, or *leguvaan*, and the entertaining Cape clawless otter, which both occur frequently though the latter are very seldom seen.

Birds Around 350 species of bird have been recorded in the valley. By the river you will find many varieties of water-loving birds like pied, giant, woodland, malachite and brown-hooded kingfishers, to name the more common of the species. Similarly, darters, cormorants, egrets and storks are common, and fish eagles are always to be found perching on high branches that overlook the river. Less common residents include ospreys, spoonbills, Pels' fishing owl and African skimmers, and the river is rich in waders, both resident and migrant, including squacco heron.

CONSERVATION

Poaching In the 1940s, due to numerous severe outbreaks of sleeping sickness, several villages were evacuated from this area, which became a hunting concession from the 1960s. Although the valley was classified as a national park in 1983, in the mid-1980s, commercial poaching for ivory and rhino horn completely wiped out the park's black rhino population, and threatened to do the same to the elephants. Fortunately, the CITES ban on the world ivory trade did much to stop this; the elephant population in the park is now good, and the Lower Zambezi's game is generally in good shape. That said, as in most national parks, three types of poaching still occur in the Lower Zambezi: commercial ivory, commercial bushmeat and subsistence (mostly snaring). However, ZAWA teams stationed around the park, with the assistance of Conservation Lower Zambezi, are active in ensuring daily law-enforcement patrols minimise the impact on wildlife.

Conservation Lower Zambezi Committed to the conservation and sustainable use of the valley's wildlife and natural resources, Conservation Lower Zambezi (CLZ; w conservationlowerzambezi.org) focuses on wildlife protection, education and supporting local community development.

Funded by the camps in the Lower Zambezi and concerned individuals and companies, CLZ provides logistical support – food, fuel and communications – to the ZAWA patrol teams, mounts aerial patrols and facilitates research projects. It is also responsible for the park's guide training scheme. On the community front, schoolchildren from the surrounding communities are able to learn about their local wildlife through visits to the activity centre, and CLZ is also addressing the concerns of human–wildlife conflict in the surrounding GMA.

Supporting CLZ helps to protect the wildlife and environment in this area from illegal killing and degradation, both through short-term law enforcement and long-term community involvement.

More recent is the establishment of the Lower Zambezi Conservation Trust (**e** info@lzct.org), a partnership between the local community and tour operators to conserve wildlife and the environment within the eastern GMA.

GETTING THERE There are three means of getting into this area: by road, by air and by boat – or any combination of these. Most visitors stay at one of the private camps as a base, and go for game-viewing drives, walks and trips on the river from there. Arriving by air is certainly the fastest means of transport. Planes land at one of several airstrips in the valley, including Royal Zambezi, Jeki and Kulefu, with the drive to and from the lodges being an activity in itself. A few lodges can arrange for transfers by road and river from Lusaka, though this tends to be very expensive.

More economical, for those with their own vehicle, is to drive to Gwabi River Lodge (page 248) and arrange to be collected from there by boat; again, this is an experience that is an intrinsic part of a trip. Alternatively, the well equipped can drive themselves all the way (see below), but this is neither an easy nor a fast option.

Finally, there are popular canoe safaris (page 255) that run along the river, using simple temporary fly-camps at night.

Visiting independently The adventurous and well equipped can drive in with their own vehicles, either staying at lodges or camping – which usually involves bringing all supplies as well as camping gear. Note that the only fuel available within the whole area is to be found at Gwabi River Lodge (page 248), which also offers minor repairs, including tyres.

The roads into the park need a 4x4 vehicle (ideally two, for safety's sake) but are not difficult driving in the dry season, though the going can be very slow. Get detailed maps of the whole valley before you leave Lusaka, and pack a compass and GPS. Getting lost among the labyrinth of game-drive loops is all too easily done.

From Chirundu As you enter Chirundu from the north, turn left onto a dirt road signposted to Zambezi Breezers and Gwabi River Lodge, and follow this road for about 8km to the smart new bridge across the Kafue River (⊕ CHIAWP 15°56.667'S, 28°52.500'E). Once across the bridge you'll be in the Chiawa GMA. The tarmac runs out almost immediately and at this point the road splits; take the right fork (the left one leads to a Zambeef installation) then it's largely a case of sticking close to the river, and following the main track. As far as Chiawa village, this runs alongside fertile fields, where maize, paprika, bananas, mangoes and beans are the staple crops, and passes numerous small homesteads. About 16km from the bridge, a sign for Chiawa Cultural Village (⊕ CHIACV 15°50.230'S, 29°07.061'E) marks a fork; for the national park, bear right here, towards Chiawa village.

The western entrance to the national park, Chongwe gate, lies about 46km from here, or 62km from the bridge. The route is pretty clear as far as Royal airstrip, which you'll pass on your right. However, about 3km beyond the airstrip you come to a fork (⊕ FKAIR 15°43.046'S, 29°19.308'E). Bear left here, and another 4km or so will bring you to the Chongwe River. Depending on the crossing point, which can vary, you'll come to the Chongwe gate into the national park (⊕ CHONGG 15°42.093'S, 29°20.045'E) after 2km or 4km.

Once inside the national park itself, the terrain is dominated by broad plains, dotted with baobab trees and inhabited only by plains animals and birds, before eventually dropping down into *albida* forest where shallow lagoons among the trees attract brightly coloured saddle-billed storks.

From the Great East Road For those heading for the eastern side of the park, there's a little-known access road that starts from the Great East Road, some 100km east of Lusaka. It's rough, slow going, and easy to get lost; travelling in convoy is a must and a GPS essential. To find the start of the road, go past Chongwe village, then turn right shortly after the village of Shingela (⊕ TUSHIN 15°14.188'S, 29°10.032'E). From here, follow the road to the Mukanga gate (⊕ MUKANG 15°21.015'S, 29°17.135'E). Shortly after the gate there's another checkpoint marking the entrance to the Chakwenga Mine. The road then drops over the escarpment, a steep descent culminating in a series of sandy riverbeds, and the main game-viewing area on the valley's floor in the Kulefu area, eventually coming out at ⊕ TUCHMN 15°36.577'S, 29°40.167'E, between Jeki airstrip and Old Mondoro. You'll need to allow at least 5 hours from the Great East Road to Kulefu.

From Lusaka Another equally poor 4x4 track starts from Leopards Hill Road in Lusaka, and gradually deteriorates as it winds its way steeply down the escarpment. Back-up is essential as very little passes this way, and there's a real danger of rolling your vehicle. The track finally emerges at ⊕ EXLEOP 15°55.880'S, 28°57.205'E, opposite cultivated fields and close to Chiawa village.

ACTIVITIES Most of the lodges along the river offer similar activities, concentrating primarily on drives, boat trips, walking safaris, canoeing and fishing, but each has its own individual atmosphere and areas of expertise, and some specialise. Outside the park, some of the lodges also offer village visits or trips to Chiawa Cultural Village.

Game drives Day and night drives, both in the Chiawa GMA and into the Lower Zambezi National Park (🕘 Jun–Oct), are high on the list of priorities for most visitors. They are offered by almost all camps, whether they're located inside or outside the park – though it's worth remembering that the further you are from the national park, the less game you're likely to see; game drives on the west of the GMA can be uneventful.

If you're self-driving into the park, the Lower Zambezi park fee will be US$30 per person per day for international visitors, with an additional US$15 per day for overseas registered vehicles and K25.50 per day for local vehicles. This day rate is valid from sunrise to sunset (06.00–18.00) – no night driving is allowed for self-drive vehicles. For those staying in safari lodges or camps, the relevant fees are often, but not always, included in their rates so do pay attention to what's included when booking.

Walking safaris Walking safaris with a professional guide are widely available in Lower Zambezi's safari camps, affording visitors the opportunity to get closer to the wildlife on its terms. There are strict exams for guides in Zambia, walking requiring the highest qualification. It is also mandatory to be accompanied by an armed scout. We would strongly recommend that you never go walking with an unqualified guide, or even a guide in whom you don't have the utmost trust. With an experienced guide, walking is invigorating, engaging and physically active – something that can otherwise be lacking on 4x4 safaris. Most walks last between 2 and 4 hours, and are done as a morning activity from a lodge or camp. They are usually arranged a day in advance to ensure that an armed guard is available from the park's department.

Birdwatching Some gentle birdwatching is usually built into most walks, drives or boating trips. With a range of habitats, the region is a great place to spot avian wildlife at any time, but especially from September to March, when migrants from central Africa can be spotted in the area. Serious birdwatchers might want to arrange private vehicles to ensure that they can stay as long as desired in certain areas and to ensure silence at sightings.

Fishing Fishing on the Zambezi – primarily for tiger fish – is offered by most outfits. It is at its best when the waters are clear, from around May to June until towards the end of the year, with the prime season for tiger fishing around September and October. Catch and release is obligatory in the national park and some lodges also operate a no-live bait policy. Fishing permits are normally obtained by the lodge on behalf of their guests. There's a ban on fishing between December and February.

Canoeing Canoeing on the Zambezi is a firm favourite for the more adventurous. It's a terrific way to relax in the open air and see the river, while doing some gentle exercise and game viewing at the same time.

Most operators use stable Canadian-style fibreglass canoes which are 5.7m long, and large enough for two people plus their camping equipment and personal belongings. Trips are usually limited to a maximum of five canoes led by a fully qualified canoe guide; while this means that the guide has control over the group, you could still occasionally find yourself closer to a pod of hippos than to your trusty guide.

Broadly there are two different ways to go canoeing. You can opt for this as an activity from a lodge or camp, or you can paddle from A to B, sleeping on islands or at points on the bank along the way.

Canoeing guides and safety In the 1990s the question asked about these trips was always 'Which section should we canoe?'. Now it is more usually 'How qualified is the guide?'. This is important both for safety reasons and to help you make the most of your trip.

Canoe safaris were started on the Zimbabwean side of the river in the early 1980s, led by qualified canoe guides who had to pass national parks' examinations. In the early 1990s, with the emergence of the Lower Zambezi National Parks Wildlife Protection Programme, Zambia also started canoe safaris. Today's canoeing guides on the Lower Zambezi are fully qualified wildlife guides with further stringent training in canoeing and water safety.

You should understand from the outset though that canoeing on this river, including the channels, has a risk attached to it that no guide can ever take away. Even with the very best of guides, it's possible to get into dangerous, even life-threatening, situations with both hippos and crocodiles. Although the safety record among the best canoe operators is exceptional, situations when these animals injure or even kill visitors are not unknown. That said, the vast majority of such encounters are with local Zambian fishermen, making theirs a particularly hard and dangerous life. For the visitor, canoeing with, and listening to, a good guide who knows the river will give you the best chance of avoiding dangerous situations, and of escaping those that prove unavoidable.

Short trips from a camp or lodge Most of the lodges and camps along the Lower Zambezi offer canoeing as a morning or afternoon activity, typically taking about 3 to 4 hours, and occasionally extended to a whole day with a game-drive finish.

Depending on the location of the lodge, you'll either be driven upstream with the canoes, and will then paddle back to the lodge, or you will paddle downstream, and be returned to your lodge by boat or on a game-drive vehicle. Increasingly, rather than use the main river, lodges are focusing on a couple of narrower side channels that are more sheltered and tend to offer more in the way of game. These include the Nkalangi Channel and, further east, the beautiful Chifungulu Channel, deep inside the national park.

Canoeing from a lodge has several advantages. First, there's no hurry, so your guide can build in time to pause and observe the game along the river; second, if you're at a good lodge then you're probably spending all your canoeing time in a prime game area, within or close to the park; third, you're not committing yourself to more than 3 or 4 hours paddling; and finally, you've got a comfortable bed lined up for the night back at camp.

Longer overnight trips: from point to point On these trips you put all your kit in the canoe, and paddle downstream for a number of days. Typically, you'll carry tents and food, and camp along the way.

Physically, you will feel tired at the end of a day, but canoeing downriver is not excessively strenuous (unless you meet a strong headwind), and no previous experience is demanded. To some extent that feeling of exertion often leads to a feeling of achievement at the end of the trip, which increases with the length of the trip and the distance covered.

Costs normally include basic camping kit, food (and wine with the evening meal), guide, canoes, paddles, etc. Transfers are extra.

Which section to canoe? Broadly, canoe safaris vary according to the length of time available. Typically the shortest, taking two nights/three days, covers the section of the river from Chirundu to around Mvuu Lodge. The second, from Chirundu to the mid-Mana Pools region, features larger numbers of game and birdlife due to the proximity of national parks on both sides of the river, and takes three nights/four days. Slightly longer, at four nights/five days, is to paddle as far as the Chongwe River on the borders of the Lower Zambezi National Park. Undoubtedly the wildest option runs the whole length of the two national parks, from the Chongwe River, passing through floodplains and the spectacular Mpata Gorge, and ending at the confluence of the Luangwa River some 163km downstream; for this, allow at least five nights/six days.

Canoeing operators Although most lodges offer canoeing as an activity from camp, there isn't the choice of trips, or operators, doing longer canoe trips here that there was in the early 1990s. There is one dedicated specialist for longer trips:

River Horse Expeditions m 0967 862626; e info@riverhorsesafaris.com; w riverhorsesafaris.com. River Horse is a dedicated canoe safari operator in the Lower Zambezi that has been paddling this stretch of water for 20 years. Individuals, families (over 15 only) & groups paddle & fly-camp their way downstream with licensed guides. 4 trips are on offer; the shortest route starts at Breezes River Lodge at Chirundu & involves canoeing 56km in 2 nights/3 days & is known as the Zambezi Short (from US$510 pp). More energetic is the 5–6-night/6–7-day Great Zambezi Canoe Safari (from US$1,450 pp, min 4) heading 163km east from Chirundu to Mupata Gorge. Trips can also be tailormade & combined with local community projects. There's normally a maximum of 5 18ft 2-man Canadian-style canoes per safari. No children under 15 unless by prior arrangement.

Chongwe Falls (⊕ CHONGF 15°41.173'S, 29°18.581'E) These accessible falls on the Chongwe River, which forms the western boundary of the Lower Zambezi National Park, make a beautiful picnic spot with some good birding. You can clamber up the rocks to see the falls from above, or try your hand at fishing, but don't be beguiled by the still waters; there are large crocodiles lurking in there so a cooling dip is out of the question.

Cultural tourism Several of the lodges at the western end of the valley offer village trips. Some arrange these on an informal basis, but others take in **Chiawa Cultural Village** [250 B3] (⊕ CHIACV 15°50.230'S, 29°07.061'E; admission K50 pp), which is about 25km east of the bridge and clearly signposted. Access is either by boat, or by road. If you're driving, ask for directions shortly after the signpost, and you'll probably find a gaggle of children vying with each other to show you the way.

The village was established with funds from the African Wildlife Foundation to showcase the cultural traditions of the local Goba people, and at the same time to raise funds for orphans and other vulnerable people within the community. In this way, people from the villages around the national park get the chance to benefit from the conservation of wildlife and the not-inconsiderable wealth that tourists bring to the area.

Visitors who come by appointment are usually greeted by a group of dancers, an interactive display that can be considerable fun. A guide is on hand to explain the history of the Goba people and to look at many aspects of traditional village life: from cooking and medicinal herbs to clothes, toys and weapons. There are full-size village huts, an interesting museum/interpretive centre, a curio shop, and even a look-out post for elephants (with a great view of the river). If you just turn up, it's very much more low key, and although you can camp here, facilities are rudimentary in the extreme.

WHERE TO STAY There are several lodges in the valley and a few campsites as well. Almost all are good, but their styles vary widely, from traditional thatched and/or tented lodges to more permanent structures with something of a hotel feel. For the most part, power is either solar generated or supplied by battery, so needs to be used sparingly. With advance booking and a 4x4, you can drive yourself into any of these, but most people arrange for a transfer by road or charter flight. All bar one of the establishments listed to the west of the national park are in the Chiawa GMA.

Within the Lower Zambezi National Park Staying within the national park itself offers the optimum wildlife experience, with access to the park's finest areas quite literally on the doorstep. All overnight visitors within the national park are required to pay park fees (US$25), tourism concession fees and a conservation levy (the last two vary by camp, with the concession fee set by DNPW), and together this will total between US$85 and US$120 per person per night. Some lodges include one or all of these charges in their rates, others do not. The conservation levy goes towards excellent organisations like Conservation Lower Zambezi (page 252), an organisation committed to the protection of the wildlife and habitat of the national park and the Chiawa GMA, but each camp chooses who they will support independently. In addition, water activities within the national park incur separate park charges. The rates are subject to change with little notice, but at the time of writing they included boating/canoeing at US$20 per person per day and an angling permit at US$40 per person per day. Children aged 5–13 years pay 50% of these activity fees. The charges can add up quickly and significantly, so be sure to check with your camp in advance which, if any, of these additional fees will apply to your stay.

The camps and lodges are listed in alphabetical order.

Amanzi [251 F3] (4 suites) **e** res@amanzizambezi.com; **w** amanzizambezi.com; ⊕ 15°36.516'S, 29°47.163'E. Ranged along a low rise above a tranquil channel of the Zambezi, just a 5min drive from Kulefu airstrip, Amanzi is the smaller, more intimate sibling of Anabezi, used by small groups seeking an exclusive-use lodge with a stylish but rustic touch. In the open-sided central area, raised up on stilts, wicker & canvas chairs sit on wooden decking that snakes around trees overlooking the water. Down below, sunloungers sit alongside a small pool & there's a riverside firepit.

The suites – each of them long & narrow – are designed to make the best of the location, with a wall of gauzed picture windows facing the Zambezi. Amanzi might be simpler than its sibling, but creature comforts are plentiful: poster beds have a fan inside the mosquito net; there's a comfortable lounge area, dressing room with a big shower, a separate 'loo with a view' & a timber deck with swinging chairs. 2 of the chalets are built closer together with a linking walkway, so would work well for families. Activities are as at Anabezi, with the same degree of flexibility. *US$570–854 pp Apr–Jun & Nov, US$835–1,380 pp Jul–Oct, all FBA inc most drinks, exc park fees.* ⏲ *Apr–Nov.* 👑👑👑–👑👑👑👑

Anabezi [251 F3] (12 chalets) **m** 0967 786398; **e** res@anabezi.com; **w** anabezi.com; ⊕ 15°36.630'S, 29°46.192'E. Along almost 500m of high, raised wooden walkways, the simply huge, canvas suites here (just 4km from Kulefu airstrip) overlook the Zambezi or Mushika floodplain, both of which are frequented by a variety of wildlife.

The chalets here are simply huge: canvas-roofed structures with reed walls, fronted by a series of sliding glass doors. These open onto a long shaded deck with day beds & a plunge pool. At one end there's an open-air shower, toilet & basin; in the centre, a second indoor bathroom complete with bathtub. Twin or king-size beds with bedside tables are enveloped in mosquito nets, & there's a substantial sitting area with solid-wood furniture & a proper sofa. Extra beds can be added for children.

Activities take in the range of game drives (day & night), walking, fishing, canoeing & boat trips, led by a very good guiding team which aims for flexibility. While private guiding isn't always possible, all guests have a 'window' seat in very comfortable game-drive vehicles. *US$950 pp Apr–Jun & Nov, US$1,350 pp Jul–Oct, all FBA inc most drinks, exc park fees.* ⏲ *Apr–mid Nov.* 👑👑👑👑

✷ **Chiawa Camp** [250 D3] (9 tented chalets) ☎ 0211 261588; **m** 0977 767433; **e** res@chiawa.com; **w** chiawa.com; ⊕ CHIAWA 15°41.058'S, 29°24.829'E. Set beneath a grove of mahogany trees, about 8km (30mins' drive) inside the national park, Chiawa is the oldest camp in the valley (opened in 1991) & continues to set the bar high. Carving out a well-earned reputation as one of Zambia's top safari lodges, Chiawa has consistently improved & evolved over the years, while driving myriad good-practice & conservation initiatives in the park. Headed by the dynamic Cumings family, it's run by professional staff & good guides determined to maintain its friendly & highly efficient standards.

Being within the park, Chiawa is only open during the dry season, so is largely built of timber, canvas & reeds. Though the setting remains wild – the simple sand pathways make popular elephant highways – the camp itself has become considerably more stylish over the years. Rebuilt afresh in 2020, its waterfront tents are light & spacious with comfortable beds, superb picture 'windows', stylish, locally produced furniture & pole-shaded verandas. Soak in the claw-foot bath, laze in the hammock, dip your toes in the sunken lounge plunge pool – & keep your binoculars to hand for the frequent passing wildlife. There's also a wonderful Safari Suite, which is ideal for families (min age 8 unless the whole camp is booked for exclusive use).

Central to the camp is an open riverside structure with a proper bar & well-designed lounge area filled with plenty of beautiful books, a cabinet of safari curiosities & plush sofas; stairs lead up to a laid-back seating & viewing area in the rafters. Most meals are taken in the central dining area, overlooking the campfire & river, but other venues feature too: the floating champagne lunch on the pontoon boat is particularly special, as are the BBQ bush dinners under the stars.

From walking safaris & 4x4 trips (inc night drives), to motorboat excursions & canoe trips along the river or the Nkalangi Channel: activities are exceptionally flexible here. Game-drive vehicles have bean bags for camera kit & window seats for all. Few visitors just want to fish, but Chiawa maintains a top reputation for serious fishing trips for tiger fish (all catch & release; no live bait). Right in camp, a solid hide towers above an area where elephants come to drink, while a reed hide downstream is accessed by boat, & a third, behind the camp, by vehicle. For those after a cooling dip, there's a large, secluded pool backed by decking & sunloungers, & some gym equipment for working off the teatime treats. There's even a small gift shop for a touch of souvenir shopping.

As part of its commitment to the development of conservation education, Chiawa & its guests fund the education of 140 children in local village schools, & it is a top contributor to the funding of anti-poaching, environmental education programmes & conservation in the area. All appropriate for a camp whose very name means 'the one who shares'.

Most guests fly to Royal airstrip, followed by a short drive & boat ride to the lodge. Private flights from elsewhere, including the Luangwa, can be organised.

Safari tnts US$1,325 adult/sharing, US$495–695 child/sharing May–Jun & mid-Oct–mid-Nov, US$1,755 adult/sharing, US$495–695 child/sharing Jul–mid-Oct; Safari suite (min 2 adults) US$1,620–2,065 adult/sharing, US$495–695 child/sharing; all FBA, inc local drinks, laundry & all park, conservation, tourism & carbon offset fees, exc fishing permits. Children age 8+ in tents & 5+ in suite. ⌚ *May–mid Nov.* ♛♛♛♛–♛♛♛♛♛

Chula Island Camp [251 E3] (5 tents) **m** 0974 173403; **e** info@classiczambiasafaris.com; **w** classiczambiasafaris.com. Chula Island Camp is, as its name suggests, on an island in the Discovery Channel. However, being set back from the Zambezi, there are no real river views here, it's a wild location of reed-fringed lagoons & open dambos, & the camp here definitely feels more rustic & little rough around the edges compared to the likes of sister camp Kutali (see below). Sand pathways lead to 5 separate tents, a couple under the deep shade of Natal mahoganies, with simple furnishings & separate open-air bathrooms with warm water bucket-showers & flush toilets. The main mess tent is a simple shade with a wooden dining table, trestle table bar & campfire circle of directors' chairs. Dining is communal & hearty fare is enjoyed alfresco. All activities, excluding canoeing, start with a short boat ride to the mainland where daily game drives and walks take place.

Kutali and Chula are often used in combination, with guests spending a few nights in both locations.

US$580 pp/sharing May–Jun, US$780 pp/sharing Jul–Oct, all FBA, exc transfers, Medivac, park & conservation fees. Private guiding (4x4 or boat) US$350-500/day; transfers US$280/vehicle (2-4pax) from camp to Lower Zambezi airstrips; US$500/vehicle from camp to Chirundu/Zim border. Children 14+. ⌚ *May–Nov.* ♛♛–♛♛♛

Kutali [251 E3] (5 tents) **m** 0974 173403; **e** info@classiczambiasafaris.com; **w** classiczambiasafaris.com. Opened in 2018, Kutali is the only true fly camp in Lower Zambezi National Park – neat tents with simple facilities, & all in lightweight, temporary structures. The focus here is on back-to-basics safaris concentrating on the environment & wildlife, & less on the modern conveniences & increasingly plush surroundings found in other safari camps. The 5 sand-coloured tents are well spread out along a beautiful stretch of riverbank, under a shady canopy of old winterthorn trees. Simple but inviting, each has excellent full-mesh panels (with roll-down blinds), affording great views from inside, comfortable metal-frame beds on rugs, practical furnishings, solar hurricane lights & an en-suite open-air bathroom, complete with a hot water-bucket shower, flush toilet & fluffy towels.

The central area is an open-sided mess tent with wide views through the albida grove to the river. There's a simple bar, cushioned area on woven palm mats, directors' chairs & a communal dining table, where all meals are shared. There's a charging station at the small bar but no Wi-Fi.

A river crossing to the mainland national park means game drives operate in a great area at the heart of the park, but this camp's raison d'etre is non-motorised activities. Walking (6–7km linear trips) on their private islands is a popular option, with good guides and barefoot crossings on shallow water channels. If you're keen to do a lot of walking here it's important to mention this when booking to ensure that the camp can secure enough walking scouts (a legal requirement), which has proved an issue in the park in recent years. Canoeing on varied channels – Inkalange, Chifungulu or Discovery – & the main river is equally popular, with groups of up to 8 heading out on the water under the guidance of camp staff. *US$580 pp/sharing May–Jun, US$780 pp/sharing Jul–Oct; all FBA, exc transfers, Medivac, park & conservation fees. Private guiding (4x4 or boat) US$350–500/day. Transfers US$280/vehicle (2–4 people) from camp to Lower Zambezi airstrips; US$500/vehicle from camp to Chirundu/Zim border. Children 14+.* ◷ *Jun–Nov.* ♛♛–♛♛♛

Lolebezi [251 E3] ☎ +27 21 701 0270; **e** contact@africanbushcamps.com; **w** africanbushcamps.com. Part of the African Bush Camps collection, Lolebezi is the newest lodge in the Lower Zambezi (opened in June 2022) & makes for a striking addition. Designed to be an enticing, swanky safari destination, it's aimed at image-conscious, luxury travellers & is quite different from anything else in Zambia. It's youthful & edgy in décor with boutique city hotel vibes alongside locally crafted furniture & impressive grass weavings, with a striking fusion of African craftsmanship & modern design throughout.

The 2-storey, open-sided main area, overlooking the main pool deck & the confluence of the Zambezi and Discovery Channel, is the hub of social activity at Lolebezi. The curved, cushioned riverfront lounge & dining area sit either side of a circular walkway, a spot frequented most nights by a resident honey badger. The Italian green-marble bar is perfect for sipping cocktails on a jade velvet bar-stool, while the waterfront firepit lends itself to laid-back star-gazing. The halal kitchen is open all day, with meal times & dining locations completely flexible. From build-your-own pizza & tapas lunches to boma BBQ nights, or simply a midday scoop of ice cream, the catering team here are keen to please & good company.

Accommodation is in 4 signature suites & 2 vast family suites. The signature suites are wonderful, glass-fronted contemporary spaces. Clad in old railway sleepers & filled with beautiful Zambian basketry weaving, a sumptuous bed & comfortable furniture, they are extremely stylish. There's a huge bathroom complete with a glorious green bath, & an indoor & outdoor shower. Quirky decorations from industrial black shower heads to swinging leather chairs & designer light fittings are all around, but the real draw remains the panoramic river view. An opening glass wall runs along the entire front of each suite, affording a stunning waterfront vista & easy access on to the wide, private deck. Spanning the length of the suite, & complete with loungers, a thatched 'sala' seating area, & an infinity plunge pool, the decks are super places to watch the water & its wildlife visitors.

Activities at Lolebezi are varied & flexible. There are opportunities for game drives, guided river excursions by boat or canoe, walking safaris & fishing. For guests keen to exercise, there's a separate gym, while those keen to be pampered can enjoy spa treatments in a beautiful treatment room. Children of all ages are warmly welcomed (though only over 16s can go canoeing & on walking safaris). There's a games room on the upper level, complete with a pool table, table tennis, large TV & even a PlayStation for those so inclined.

Unlike all of the other camps in the Lower Zambezi National Park, Lolebezi plans to remain open year-round, but driving is unlikely to be possible during sections of the Green Season (Nov–Apr), when activities will be limited to boating safaris. During this time, when the river is high and fast, we would not advise travellers to go canoeing because of the speed of the current. *US$479 pp Jan–Mar & Dec, US$1,154 pp/sharing Apr–Nov, all FBA, inc transfers, park & conservation fees & laundry, exc spa.* ⏲ *All year.* ♛♛–♛♛♛♛♛

Mwambashi River Lodge [250 E3] (9 tents, 1 chalet) **e** mwambashi@gmail.com; **w** mwambashiriverlodge.com. ⊕ MWAMRL 15°38.392′S, 29°34.681′E. This exclusive-use, private camp hosts groups of up to 22 people & cannot be booked by individual travellers. Mwambashi is centred around an open-sided, thatched boma, home to wicker furniture, adorned with kubu-cloth cushions, a dining room & bar, all of which overlook the Zambezi across the lawn. There are 9 forest green, classic safari tents, tastefully decorated, & with open-air, en-suite bathrooms to the rear. 2 suites – the Reed & Zambezi – offer more solid structures, the latter also featuring its own small pool. Activities from bush picnics to game drives, canoeing to sunset boat trips are on offer; fishing is possible but limited equipment means that anglers are advised to bring their own kit. There is separate gym building with large openings to catch any breeze & equipment comprises weights, running, crossfit & rowing machines. While researching this edition, we encountered Mwambashi guests widely spread out on a morning jog along the Jeki airstrip; a highly questionable activity in a park where lions and significant numbers of elephants roam everywhere & where walking requires an armed scout to be present. ⏲ *Apr–Nov.* ♛♛–♛♛♛

✷ **Old Mondoro** [251 E3] (5 chalets, 1 family suite) **w** chiawa.com; contact via Chiawa (page 258). ⊕ OLDMON 15°37.839′S, 29°41.423′E. Owned & run by the experienced team at Chiawa Safaris, Old Mondoro is a class act. Surrounded by open woodland alongside the Zambezi, it's an intimate bushcamp focused on superlative wildlife experiences & quality guiding.

A smart, immaculately furnished, open-sided central area is the focus of camp life. Sumptuous sofas in soft grey, an inviting dining table and perfectly curated details invite guests to hang out, socialise & relax here. It's beautiful & comfortable, with a focus on looking outward to the wildlife wandering through camp & the river. Fantastically attentive & engaging staff are always around to help.

Named after birds, there are only 5 well-spaced chalets & a family suite here. Unassuming from the outside, each chalet sits under khaki canvas like a perfect little house. There is great beauty in the simplicity & care that has created these safari boltholes. Pale, moulded concrete interiors, dark, varnished pole walls & wide picture windows in the canvas are all stylish & well considered. Inside, beds & linens are pristine, while the huge outdoor bath & shaded deck both overlook the lush, hyacinth-filled lagoon, a favourite spot for kingfishers & wallowing elephants. And while some of the natural materials may be rustic, there's everything you could want, from banks of sockets for charging batteries & running computers to gas geysers for hot water, fans & good bedside lights. Away from the chalets, close to the main area, is a family chalet, its 2 en-suite rooms (1 dbl, 1 twin) with an interlinking door.

The camp focuses on walking, day & night game drives, game viewing by boat, canoe trips & fishing. There's great leopard sightings & elephant numbers around camp & even a resident aardvark in camp (best sightings of this illusive creature are the week after full moon). Despite a considerable upgrade & superb standard of food & service, the remote & open location means that this is still very much a bushcamp experience – albeit a luxury one – for those seeking an emphasis on guiding & wildlife. Certainly one of the best bushcamps in Zambia. Max 8 guests in camp unless exclusive use.

Bush chalet US$1,325 adult/sharing, US$495–695 child/sharing May–Jun & mid-Oct–mid-Nov; family tent US$1,755 adult/sharing, US$495–695 child/sharing May–Jun & mid-Oct–mid-Nov; all FBA, inc local drinks, laundry & all park, conservation, tourism & carbon offset fees, exc fishing permits. Children age 12+. ⏲ *May–mid-Nov.* ♛♛♛♛–♛♛♛♛♛

Potato Bush Camp [250 D3] (4 tented chalets) **w** potatobushcamp.com; contact via Sausage Tree, page 262. A short walk from Sausage Tree, Potato Bush has a simpler, more contemporary feel than its sibling, the broad canvas roofs of its central area & chalets lending a hint of the east. Low, open-sided wooden walkways and chalets set on plinths mean that the camp can enjoy a longer season than Sausage Tree, as rises in water levels are less crucial.

Cream canvas stretched over rosewood frames creates the walls & roofs of the chalets & the main area, instilling a sense of light & space. The chalets are entered from the back, but bifold wooden doors open to a river view, with a 2-person hammock swinging by each private plunge pool. Inside are twin or king-size beds draped in walk-in mosquito nets, cream-coloured couches, & an open-fronted bathroom with twin basins, shower & bath. A 2-bedroom family chalet is set further back than the others at the end of camp, with a dbl-sized plunge pool. All have fans & 24hr electricity. In the central area, solid-wood furniture runs to a beautiful rosewood dining table, balanced by a couple of intimate seating areas looking out towards the firepit by the river.

Under the new ownership of Green Safaris, with a strong professional team linked to that of Sausage Tree, & the same range of activities, this is a small, relaxed camp that benefits from high standards. Min stay 3 nights.

US$3,710 pp/sharing Apr–May & Nov, US$4,685 pp/sharing Jun–Oct, all FBA for 3 nights inc domestic flights, drinks, park & conservation fees. Children 4+.

Apr–Nov.

Sausage Tree Camp [250 D3] (8 chalets) Green Safaris (page 292); **w** greensafaris.com; ⊕ SAUSTR 15°40.675'S, 29°28.692'E. In a beautiful riverside position, Sausage Tree is usually accessed by a short flight to either Jeki or (closer) Royal airstrip on the lodge's own plane (domestic flights included in rates). The sausage tree for which the camp was named has long since washed away, but mature Natal mahoganies give plenty of shade, & sandy paths add a very natural, bush feel.

The large, canvas suites all have broad panoramic terraces overlooking the Zambezi & comfortable interiors. Accessed from raked sand paths running along the back of the suites, each has an elegant, circus-like roof, polished floors, big beds, deep leather armchairs & a private plunge pools. Each chalet is the responsibility of an individual *muchinda* or butler, though the camp is much less formal than this might suggest. The cream canvas roofs extend to the living & dining areas, & matching umbrellas that shade tables & chairs on the wooden deck. Most meals are taken here or by the firepit, but they may turn up in some surprising venues. Almost out of sight is a 25m infinity pool, with a river view that definitely justifies swimming a length or two. Out of camp you'll typically do 2 activities a day, to include game drives (day & night), canoeing, walking, boating or fishing, but it's very flexible; midday activities can be organised, as can full-day drives with a picnic. One of the camp's main assets is the proximity of a lovely backwater, the Chifungulu Channel, which runs parallel to the main river for about 14km & makes a great area for a gentle paddle. It's popular with the local hippo population, too, not to mention elephants & buffalo & some wonderful birdlife. As an aside, *chifungulu* is the local name for *Combretum microphyllum*, the 'flame creeper' that grows up winterthorn trees here & colours the trees blood red in July.

In mid-2023, Green Safaris bought this long-established lodge to complete their trio of Zambia's best known national parks. Having created fine, trail-blazing, all-electric camps in South Luangwa & Kafue over recent years (pages 309 & 425), it'll be exciting to see the changes they have planned for Sausage Tree! Min stay 3 nights.

US$4,685 pp/sharing Apr–May & Nov, US$6,080 pp/sharing Jun–Oct, all FBA for 3 nights inc domestic flights, drinks, park & conservation fees. Children 8+.

Apr–Nov.

Outside the national park in the Chiawa GMA These properties are listed alphabetically.

Baines' River Camp [250 C3] (8 chalets, 1 family cottage) +27 33 342 7498; **m** +27 82 806 4074; **e** reservations@bainesrivercamp.com; **w** bainesrivercamp.com. ⊕ BAINES 15°45.743'S, 29°13.913'E. On a wide riverfront site just 16km west of the national park, most of Baines' guests arrive by plane at the nearby Royal airstrip. With its soft-grey metal roofs, cream-painted walls & glazed windows, it looks solid & cool, akin to a smart club, with professional yet friendly service to match.

As you step down into the main area, the first impression is of space, oodles of it: in the lounge with its large fireplace & leather sofas, in the rather masculine bar, even in the 'boardroom' that doubles as a library & study centre. There's

Wi-Fi in the main area, & computer stations with laptops in the lounge. Step outside & you'll find a firepit tantalisingly close to the river, & a narrow 11m pool.

Sharing the river views are colonial-style chalets with comfortable dark-wood furniture & private verandas. Expect AC (until 22.00), glazed windows, carpeted floors, king-size or twin beds beneath ceiling fans, & a smart bathroom with separate toilet; each chalet (2 of them smaller than the others) boasts a minibar, hairdryer & safe, & 2 feature outdoor showers. Baines' Cottage has 2 en-suite bedrooms with a dining/lounge/kitchen area.

Activities are flexible with recommendations of the best times to fish, canoe along a channel of the Zambezi, laze on the river or do a game drive (in the GMA or national park) happily forthcoming. With 72hrs notice, walking is an option. *Chalet US$675/895 pp sharing low/high season, all FBA, inc most drinks, laundry, airstrip transfers & park fees. Min stay 2 nights. No children under 6. ⌚ Mar–Dec.* ♛♛♛–♛♛♛♛

Chiawa Cultural Village (camping) [250 B3] ⊕ CHIACV 15°50.230'S, 29°07.061'E. The valley's cultural village (page 257) will accommodate campers on a dusty site by the river beneath a couple of sausage trees. You'll need to bring all your own supplies (even the water here is sporadic), & ablutions are basic in the extreme. There are without doubt better options. *US$15 pp.* **$**

Chongwe Camp [250 D3] (8 tents, 2 suites) ☎ +27 60 6424004; **e** travel@timeandtideafrica.com; **w** timeandtideafrica.com. ⊕ CHONRC 15°42.911'S, 29°20.287'E. Chongwe has an enviable location, on the banks of the Chongwe River, which marks the boundary between the GMA & the national park, at its confluence with the Zambezi. The concentration of game here is good (albeit not quite as good as within the park itself) but without the high daily charges levied by the park's authorities. Most visitors arrive on scheduled flights at Royal airstrip, or occasionally by boat from another camp.

Neat, Meru-style tents are set up on platforms along the river, each with dbl or twin beds, a small, shaded riverbank porch & a semi-open, rustic bathroom with ochre-cement & rush walls offset with stylish furnishings. At the south end of camp, right at the confluence of the Chongwe and the Zambezi Rivers, are Chongwe's 2 original suites, enclosed by funky, free-form walls. The Albida is the larger, with 2 en-suite octagonal tents linked by a stylish canvas-canopied lounge/dining area. The Cassia Suite has just 1 large tent, with a private lounge & dining area, perfect for honeymooners. Both have private plunge pools, riverfront campfires & the option of private dining.

The hub of camp life is the central sandy dining & firepit area, shaded by an old winterthorn (*Faidherbia albida*), its pods beloved of the local elephant population. Overlooking the river, there's also an informal lounge & bar, decked out with cushion-covered curving benches under canvas canopies, with board games & books. To cool off, there's a large pool & lovely earthen hide. The atmosphere is informal & friendly, with knowledgeable & informative staff on hand.

Chongwe offers all the standard safari activities & good guiding. There's also the option of walking upstream along the Chongwe & returning by canoe. Birdwatching is good here, explained in part by the proximity of the Lower Zambezi escarpment, & children of all ages are welcome in camp (not on all activities though). *Standard tent US$870 pp, sharing Apr–May & Nov, US$1,040 pp sharing Jun–Oct; suites US$1,000pp Apr–May & Nov, US$1,370 pp sharing Jun–Oct, all FBA, inc most drinks, laundry, park fees & conservation levies. ⌚ Apr–mid-Nov.* ♛♛♛–♛♛♛♛

✷ **Chongwe House** [250 D3] ☎ +27 60 6424004; **e** travel@timeandtideafrica.com; **w** timeandtideafrica.com. ⊕ CHONRH 15°42.488'S, 29°20.259'E. At the end of a wonderful winterthorn grove, this utterly unique, 4-bedroom private retreat lies on the banks of the peaceful Chongwe River, with a spectacular view of the mountainous escarpment. Organic in form, the entire house is built around a wild-wood frame so its structure & adobe walls follow the natural lines of the branches used. There is not a straight line to be seen! The main room looks out over the deck & a large pool to the river & mountains beyond. Furniture in the living area has been carved from a single huge fallen winterthorn tree, as if it had come to rest across the room, while embedded in the ceilings are pastel-coloured pebbles from the river. Each of the ground-floor bedrooms is entered through a tunnel, rather like walking through a cave; the curved entrance gives privacy without the need for doors. Their bathrooms have water pouring out of the stone ceiling instead of the normal shower rose, & upstairs the showers are waterfalls. There are wooden 'taps', & the basins have been carved out of wood & white marble by the Zambian artist, Eddie Mumba. From the bedrooms, the sitting room & the deck you will have game in view, feeding & watering; even the unusual baths in the upstairs bedrooms afford a view across the bush, including the huge elephants attracted by the house's winterthorn trees. The house is completely autonomous, with its own chef, safari guide & vehicle, giving groups complete flexibility over their activities. *US$1,000 pp Apr–May & Nov, US$1,370 pp Jun–Oct; FBA, inc most drinks, laundry, park fees & conservation levies. Min 6 adults. ⌚ Apr–mid Nov.* ♛♛♛♛

Kanyemba Island Bushcamp [250 B4] (4 chalets) Contact Kanyemba, see below. The largest island on the Zambezi, some 7km long & 2km wide, is privately owned by Kanyemba Lodge, & home to their exclusive bushcamp. It's a rather romantic affair, this, its secluded reed-walled chalets raised high on stilts with canvas flaps opening on to tree-shaded decks over the river & private bathrooms on a platform in the trees. Even the LED 'fairy lights' have a slightly romantic quality! More prosaically, there's a radio on hand in case of emergency. Meals – to the same standard as those at the lodge – are served in an open thatched dining area above the river. There's a firepit here, too, as well as a simple bar & a small plunge pool.

With a resident elephant population & good birding, the island is the base for Kanyemba's bush walks; these & all other activities are as at the lodge. *US$440/590 pp sharing/sgl, all FBA, inc most drinks, park fees. No children under 12. ⌚ mid-Apr–Nov.* ♛♛♛

Kanyemba Lodge [250 B4] (6 rondavels, 1 family unit) **m** 0977 755720; **e** info@kanyemba.com; **w** kanyemba.com. ⊕ KANYEM 15°56.265'S, 28°55.919'E. Just 1km from Kiambi, Kanyemba was opened in 2002 by Zambian-born Italian Riccardo Garbaccio. From its bougainvillea-adorned entrance to the expanses of green lawns along the river, it's an attractive, well-run place with Italian-influenced cuisine – including a pizza oven.

Cool, spacious stone-&-thatch rondavels (1 of them a honeymoon suite with plunge pool & garden) are tasteful & stylish, with locally made solid wood furniture, a walk-in wardrobe area, en-suite shower & a wooden veranda facing the river. For families, the rondavels can take an extra 2 beds, or there's a larger house with 3 en-suite rooms. The understated décor runs through the thatched & partially open-sided central restaurant/bar, with an upper lounge area from which there's a superb view of the river through the rafters. To the front, a stone terrace is shaded by a wild mango tree, & chaise longues are set by a lovely infinity pool near the river. There's a good gift shop & the lodge is connected to mains electricity.

Activities include game walks on the private Kanyemba Island, where the birding is good & you might encounter wildlife such as elephant, waterbuck, bushbuck & even buffalo. There are also boat trips, canoeing, fishing (tackle included), village walks, sunset cruises & even a trip to the neighbouring Chakalaka banana farm. Full-day trips to the national park can be organised (& are included for those staying 3 nights or more); these take a boat to the gate, then driving from there. Unusually for this area, Kanyemba is open almost all year. *US$440/590 pp sharing/sgl, all FBA, inc most drinks, park fees. ⌚ Mar–5 Jan.* ♛♛♛

Kiambi Lower Zambezi [250 B3] (6 chalets, 8 Meru tents, 2 cottages, camping) reservations **m** 0966 655878, 0977 876003; **e** info@kiambi.com; **w** kiambi.com. ⊕ KIAMBI 15°55.849'S, 28°55.440'E. The first lodge that you come to in the GMA, Kiambi lies at the confluence of the Zambezi & Kafue rivers, with views across to Kanyemba Island. It is clearly signposted 12km from the Kafue bridge, with relatively easy 4x4 access & reasonable rates, the camp is popular with w/enders & can get very busy. Power is supplied by mains electricity, & fuel, firewood, charcoal & ice are available.

There are stone chalets, Meru tents, 2 self-catering cottages & a flat, grassy campsite. High over the river, Kiambi's lounge/bar has great views from its stone terrace, which features a small pool & makes a good spot for fireside dinners which are open to all.

Kiambi offers guided canoe trips, from 3hr to 4-day expeditions, tiger fishing (equipment hire available) & boat trips. *Chalet with AC US$178 pp sharing; self-catering cottage US$235 pp (up to 8); camping US$16 pp; 2-man tent/bedding US$20 pp.* **$$**

Mukuyu [250 B4] (1 tent, 1 rondavel, camping) **m** 0977 851361, 0977 246564; **e** mkuyucampingsite@gmail.com;

f MukuyuCamp; ⊕ 15°49.937'S, 29°07.680'E. Mukuyu has an open site down a 1½km track with hippo-cropped lawns sloping down to the river. A traditional thatched shelter & simple bar is matched by a similarly styled shower/toilet for campers, & a small en-suite chalet built of heavy poles & thatch. The friendly owner, Kennedy, will serve meals by arrangement, drive you into the national park in his safari Land Cruiser (US$120 pp, min 4 people), arrange laundry or organise a canoe or boat trip. The camp is all very rustic & low key but the service impeccable & the boat & vehicle well maintained. Boat trip US$200/150/80 full/half day/2hrs. *Chalet US$100 dbl, B&B; camping US$15pp.* ⌚ *All year.* **$**

Mvuu Lodge [250 C3] (11 tents, camping) lodge m 0966 363762; res m +27 79 524 8709; e info@mvuulodge.com; w mvuulodge.com. ⊕ MVUU 15°45.913'S, 29°13.122'E. This laid-back & flexible lodge is particularly popular with the angling fraternity. It's 18km west of the national park, & visitors either drive themselves here or arrive by boat from Gwabi River Lodge. There's a generator for power, but lighting is largely provided by paraffin or battery lamps. Wooden hippos roam the deck above the river, in front of a 3-sided central area with a proper bar & bar stools, & Wi-Fi access. Squashy leather sofas & cane chairs complement wooden tables set up for individual dining. There's a firepit by the river & a pool bubbling on the lawns. Paths through the grass link to the en-suite twin-bedded walk-in tents (1 for families) & the campsite. 8 of the tents have partially open, stone bathrooms & wooden terraces, some looking across to the river. The remaining 3 tents are set up for self-catering, each with its own firepit, braai & cooking equipment; you just bring the food. For self-drivers, camping is available too. The pitches are pricey but all come with an element of luxury: each of the 7 sites (4 beside the river) has its own braai area, firepit, private shower & flush toilet, with an attendant to provide firewood & clean pots & pans. Bliss! With advance notice, campers may also dine in the restaurant (dinner US$35 pp + VAT), & you can hire a dome tent, too (US$10). Activities include sundowner cruises *(US$44 pp)*, fishing *(US$75–80/130–140 half/full day, exc fuel)*, ½-day canoe trips *(US$95–102 pp)* & game drives *(US$60 pp in GMA; US$80–125 pp in national park; min 3 people). US$280–325 pp sharing FB & sunset cruise, exc drinks, activities, transfers, scouts, park & conservation levy; US$385 family, self-catering; camping US$30–35 pp; 25% sgl supplement. Children all ages, 50% discount for ages 4–10. Airstrip transfer US$12 pp each way.* ⌚ *Mar–Dec.* **$**

Royal Zambezi Lodge [250 C3] (15 tented chalets) m 0966 748249/0970 010124; e res@royalzambezilodge.com; w royalzambezilodge.com. ⊕ ROYAL 15°43.641'S, 29°18.876'E. Just 4km west of the national park, with a full 3km of river frontage, Royal Zambezi is linked to Royal Air Charters, allowing the lodge to operate their own daily schedule into the Lower Zambezi, which is open to everyone at any lodge. Many guests fly into Royal airstrip; alternatively, leave your vehicle at Gwabi River Lodge & transfer by boat, taking about 1½hrs.

Imposing gates set the scene for the main building, where lounge & dining areas, each with outside fireplaces, lead off from a huge lobby. The welcome here is warm & friendly, & the service is good. Meals, at individual tables, are served from an à-la-carte menu, with many 'surprise' out-of-camp dining experiences on offer. Outside, a wide terrace offers more relaxed seating & dining options, & a walkway leads to the bar, built around the trunk of a large sausage tree. En-suite tented chalets under thatch are accessed along a concrete path at the back of the lawned site, separated by rough pole screens for privacy. Inside, crisp bed linen, feather pillows & fluffy blankets offer contemporary comfort, while picture windows & a porch facing the river draw your eye to the lovely views. There are 2 categories of room: deluxe & presidential, both of which have a private plunge pool & several are suitable for families. Children are warmly welcomed & well catered for here, not least because the managers' own children are growing up here.

This is very much a holiday place, with free-flowing activity options & times, allowing you to do as much or as little as you like. Chill out in camp by the infinity pool or at the award-winning spa, browse in the gift shop, or take part in activities both in the GMA & the park: day & night game drives, walks, gourmet picnics, bush dinners, fishing, canoeing along a channel of the Zambezi & 3hr hikes into the mountains are all on the agenda. With a large team of guides, they aim for private guiding, but this isn't guaranteed. *Deluxe* *rooms US$675 pp/sharing Jan–May & Dec, US$970 pp/sharing Jun–Nov; suites US$819 pp/sharing Jan–May & Dec, US$1,113 pp/sharing Jun–Nov; family unit (2 adults, 2 children) US$2,208 Jan–May & Dec, US$3,172 Jun–Nov; all FBA, inc most drinks; exc park fees (US$85 pp/day), spa, shop, fly fishing, fishing tackle (US$25/day). No sgl suppt. Min stay 2 nights. ⏱ All year.* 👑👑–👑👑👑👑

Tsika Island Camp [250 B4] (3 chalets) **m** 0976 175476; **e** tsika@hudzam.com; **f** Tsika-Island; ⊕ TSIKA 15°51.205'S, 29°06.583'E. A rustic, self-catering (with a chef available to assist) bushcamp on a small island (2½km x 1½km) about 35km upstream from Chongwe River Camp. It's an unspoiled spot, shaded by winterthorn trees with sandy paths leading to the rather quirky riverfront chalets, with ochre ferro walls under shaggy thatch, pole-framed windows & reed blinds. 3 lovely but simply furnished dbls with solar lighting & a pole walkway leading to a toilet, basin & bucket shower. (1 chalet can take 2 extra beds.) It's a low-key camp, with an open-sided, thatched lounge-dining area & riverside firepit; a small plunge pool with a nearby pizza oven are the only modern luxuries present. The island offers good birding & is a permanent home to a couple of porcupines. Elephant & hippo sometimes wander onto the island, & dangerous game is present here as all over the national park, so a scout is needed to walk the perimeter. Boat trips & fishing are on offer, as are visits to the cultural village that's almost opposite. Boat transfers to the national park can be arranged for game drives. *US$35/50 child/adult (min 6 people over w/ends & holidays), exc boat hire & transfers.* **$$$**

Wildtracks Lodge [250 B4] (4 tents, 3 chalets, camping) **m** 0961 084576; **e** info@wildtracks-zambia.com; **w** wildtracks-zambia.com. ⊕ WILDT 15°56.463'S, 29°00.288'E. Well maintained & very family friendly, Wildtracks is clearly signposted 15km east of the bridge, down a 3.3km track. It's a family-run place with the emphasis on environmental education & reservations are essential. Safari tents & chalets come in various sizes & configurations (2–6 beds), most sharing ablutions, though the secluded 'honeymoon' chalet by the river has its own bathroom. You need to bring all your own food & drink, but staff are on hand to prepare your meals, & there's a dining area & attractive 2-storey boma. There are 3 separate camping pitches (max 8 people each), each with private ablutions & a braai area. Bring everything you need except firewood & ice (available for sale).

Wildtracks is popular with school groups, which explains a large swimming pool, child-focused walks, an obstacle course, geocaching & superb climbing on an old baobab tree (US$12 pp). River cruises (US$68 boat/2hrs) & fishing (US$108/180 half/full day per boat; tackle & bait US$10–15/day) round off the options, both including 20 litres of fuel, with rods available for hire. *En-suite chalet US$336 dbl; tent US$84 dbl; camping US$9/18 child/adult.* $$$

West of the national park

Mukalya Private Game Reserve [map, page 232] (9 rooms) **m** 0974 052922; **e** reservations@mukalya.co.zm; **w** mukalya.com. On the banks of the Zambezi River, just 40km north of Lake Kariba, Mukalya is a stylish lodge set in immaculate, manicured gardens within its own 300ha private game reserve. Entering into the welcoming main area, deep-cushioned leather sofas, cow-hide rugs, oversized footstools & lovely, textured blue cushions invite relaxation, as do the efficient staff. It's an open-fronted, thatched space, immediately overlooking the river, & care & thoughtful design are evident in every detail: sculptural aloes sit in brass pots on a carved elephant console table, dugout canoes have been turned into shelving & a large fireplace sits in a neat pebble-stone wall beside games of bao for evening entertainment. There's an adjacent oval pool, campfire & terrace dining, where delicious meals come with a waterfront vista.

The 9 lovely rooms are constructed from a mix of khaki canvas, stone walling, reed poles & polished concrete, & are all quite beautiful. Individually decorated, all spacious with tastefully pared-down interiors, they are relaxing spaces with comfortable beds, lovely linens & thoughtful furniture. From a crimson, riverview bath to a shaded daybed or pretty mosaic patterning, each room has original features, & a few can be booked on a self-catering basis with access to a separate, shared kitchen & even a culinary assistant (US$15/day).

This is not a place to rival the wildlife experiences within the national park or Chiawa

GMA, so don't come expecting herds of elephants & hunting lions – albeit, you may spot big game in neighbouring Zimbabwe on a boat trip. Activities here range from gentle reserve walks & game drives to see antelope, giraffe & resident birdlife, swimming in hot springs, valley quadbiking, boat trips & fishing (best Mar–Dec if you're after tiger fish). There's also a massage treatment room & an open-air, rooftop gym. *US$458–524 pp/sharing; family rooms US$420 pp/4 people; FBA inc 2 daily activities, bicycles, sauna, local drinks, exc fishing, spa & transfers. Self-catering US$75–105pp/sharing. Children all ages welcome: 50% discount when sharing with adult.* ⌚ *All year.* ♛♛

East of the national park There are normally a few small camps operating east of the national park and the Mpata Gorge. These are usually accessed from the village of Luangwa, or Luangwa boma, which is some 85km from the Great East Road (page 254), or can be reached by charter flight from Lusaka. A long-running, reliable option is:

Redcliff Zambezi Lodge [251 G4] (7 chalets) ☎ 0957 920026; e reservations@redcliff-lodge.com; w redcliff-lodge.com. Redcliff Zambezi is tucked away in a GMA between the dramatic Mpata Gorge & the village of Luangwa on the Mozambique border. Accessed by 10min boat transfer from the village of Kavalamanja (parking available), the focus is very much on tiger fishing, though safari activities are also available. *US$135 pp/sharing FBA; exc bar, transfers.* ♛♛

11

The Luangwa Valley

This lush rift valley, enclosed by steep escarpment walls, is one of the continent's finest areas for wildlife. Four national parks protect parts of the area: South Luangwa, North Luangwa, Luambe and Lukusuzi. Separating these are game management areas (GMAs), which also contain good populations of game. This entire valley is remote but, for the enthusiast, the wildlife is well worth the effort made to get here.

For most visitors, South Luangwa National Park (known locally as just 'the South Park') is by far the most practical park to visit in the valley. This is the largest of the parks, with superb wildlife and many excellent camps. Organising a trip to South Luangwa is not difficult, and its infrastructure is easily the best. However, it is still a very remote park, and so most visitors arrive on trips organised outside Zambia. A few arrive independently and, though this is possible, it does limit their accommodation and activity choices.

The more intrepid may also organise a safari from the South Park into North Luangwa, which is even more remote and exclusive. Its wildlife is now flourishing, thanks to some intensive conservation efforts over the past decade, and the few safaris that do run concentrate on taking small groups for purely walking trips.

Luambe National Park is much smaller than either the South or the North parks, and there's one camp there that makes a good stopover if you're heading that way. The birdwatching is good, as with the other parks, though there is less game.

Finally, Lukusuzi National Park is something of an unknown quantity. Few people have even visited this park and there are currently no facilities or camps there.

THE GREAT EAST ROAD

The Great East Road leads from Lusaka to Chipata, the Luangwa's 'gateway', and onwards over the border into Malawi. It's a long drive: about 570km of tar, which is good in places, and pot-holed in others. There are regular buses – though you'll need to take a coach from Lusaka early in the morning (04.00–07.00) to be sure of getting to Chipata by evening. There's relatively little en route. At Chongwe village you'll find a couple of fuel stations, banks and a good local produce market. From here, the road begins to climb the escarpment, affording lovely, far-reaching views but also an increasing number of pot-holes, so do be careful. The turning to Luangwa village itself is marked by a cluster of large signboards (the smallest of which is the actual road sign), otherwise continue onwards past the small police post and over Luangwa Bridge, after which you'll enjoy considerably better road conditions. Passing through the linear villages of Nyimba, Petauke amd Katete, you'll be able to pick up simple, local snacks, drinks, fuel (each village has multiple stations but some may require cash payment) and find a bank, before arriving at

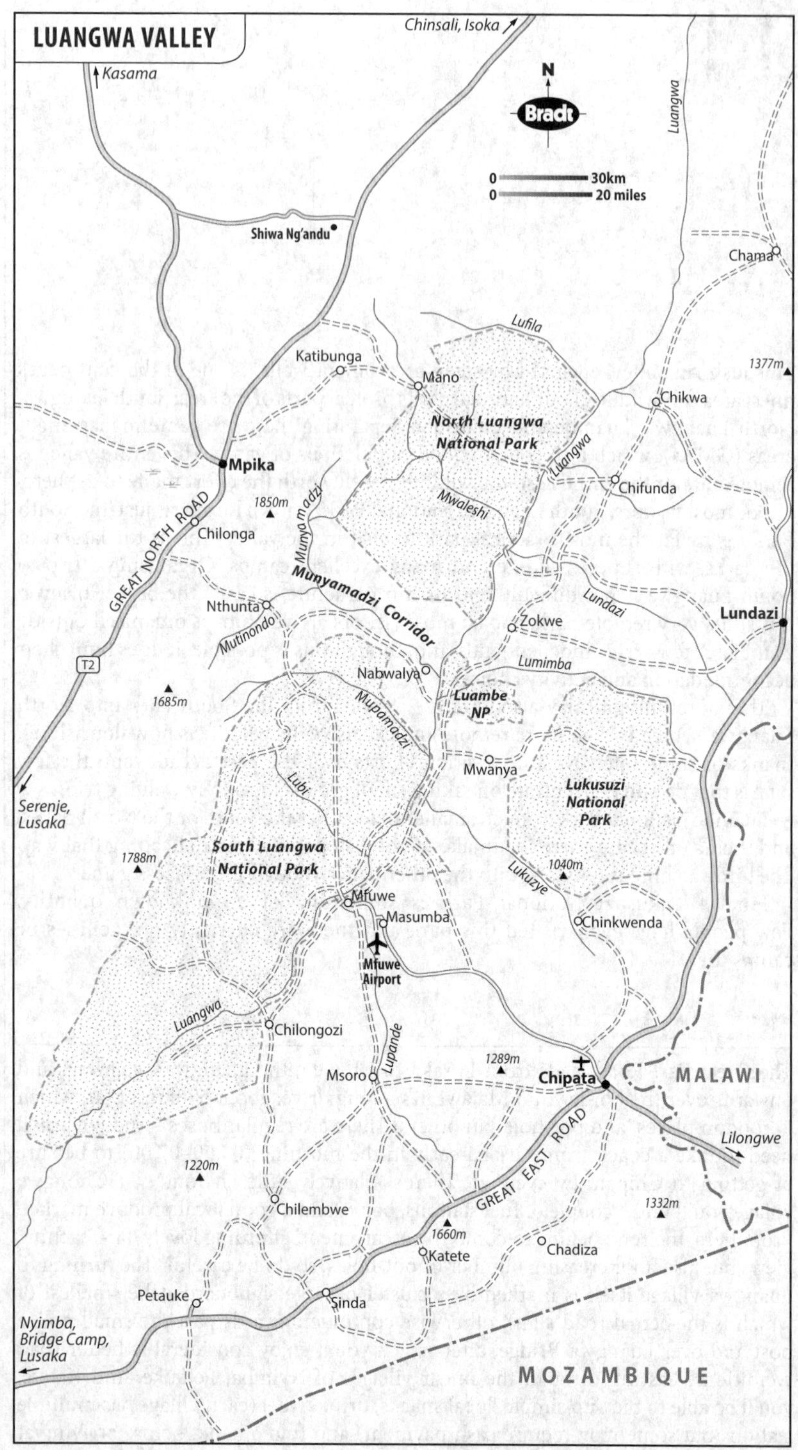

LUANGWA VALLEY
Chinsali, Isoka
Kasama
N
Bradt
0 30km
0 20 miles
Luangwa
Shiwa Ng'andu
Chama
Lufila
Katibunga
Mano
1377m
Chikwa
North Luangwa National Park
Luangwa
Mpika
Chifunda
Mwaleshi
1850m
Munyamadzi
Chilonga
GREAT NORTH ROAD
Munyamadzi Corridor
Lundazi
Nthunta
Lundazi
Mutinondo
Zokwe
T2
Nabwalya
Lumimba
Luambe NP
1685m
Mupamadzi
Mwanya
Serenje, Lusaka
Lubi
Lukusuzi National Park
South Luangwa National Park
1788m
1040m
Lukuzye
Mfuwe
Masumba
Chinkwenda
Mfuwe Airport
Luangwa
Chilongozi
Lupande
1289m
Msoro
Chipata
MALAWI
GREAT EAST ROAD
Lilongwe
1220m
Chilembwe
1332m
1660m
Chadiza
Katete
Petauke
Sinda
Nyimba, Bridge Camp, Lusaka
MOZAMBIQUE

Chipata. The road does in fact continue on to the little-visited town of Lundazi, notable for its anachronistic castle.

As with all driving in Zambia, observe the speed limit, be aware of other road users who may take unnecessary risks and avoid driving at night.

LUANGWA RIVER AREA The impressive suspension bridge over the Luangwa is some 225km east of Lusaka, or 329km west of Chipata. Just 1.9km west of this is a turning to the village of Luangwa (or Luangwa boma), which lies at the confluence of the Luangwa and the Zambezi rivers, close to the border with both Mozambique and Zimbabwe. Near the turning is a small market where there are baskets for sale.

Where to stay and eat

Bridge Camp Luangwa [251 H1] (10 chalets, camping) Feira Rd; m 0973 682286, 0953 745376; e isengeluangwasafaris@gmail.com, @ bridgecampluangwa; ⊕ 15°00.191'S, 30°12.547'E. The obvious place to stay in the area, especially on the Lusaka–Malawi route, this budget camp offers simple, thatched chalets & level camping on a hill overlooking the Luangwa River towards Mozambique. Clearly signposted, just 3km from the Luangwa Bridge market on the Great East Rd, there's a refreshing pool, bar & restaurant – open to passing visitors as well as stopovers. **$**

NYIMBA Some 98km east of the Luangwa Bridge, huge speed humps announce the presence of this small town, which has a fuel station, bank with an ATM, central bus station, post office and a small market.

Where to stay and eat

Taitana Lodge (6 rooms) Great East Rd; m 0979 710390. A number of lime-green A-frame chalets with basic interiors. **$–$$**

Thula Lodge (4 rooms, camping) Great East Rd; 2km east of Nyimba. Very basic rooms & simple meals of nshima, chicken & steak. Camping allowed, making this a handy option on a long drive. **$–$$**

PETAUKE Surrounded by fields of cotton, sunflower and soya, Petauke is a small town with a **fuel** station, **bank**, district hospital, local shops and a handful of guesthouses.

Where to stay and eat

Chimwemwe Executive Lodge (40 rooms) 2260m Boma Road; m 0968 807900; e info@chimwemwelodge.com, f chimwemwelodge.Petauke.Zambia. Established as one of the better stops along this route, Chimwemwe has 40 rooms in thatched chalets, a tree-shaded campsite, restaurant & communal firepit. **$$**

Petauke Plateau Guesthouse (12 rooms) Off Ukwimi Rd; m 0763 556222; e petaukeplateau@gmail.com; f Petauke-Plateau. Opened in 2021, this guesthouse has a modern look, swimming pool & a residents-only restaurant serving salads & grilled meats. **$$**

KATETE Another fairly nondescript town some 79km west of Chipata, Katete is home to a large mosque, a useful **filling station**, a **Finance Bank**, **post office**, and half-a-dozen grocery **shops**. There's also a Catholic church on the southern side of the road at the western end of town and the St Francis Mission Hospital. If you're interested in volunteering, or in cultural tourism, check out Tikondane Lodge (page 272). If you are catching the bus from Lusaka, the journey to Katete is about 7 hours long and you can ask the bus to drop you at Tiko Lodge or take a taxi there (about 5 minutes) from Katete bus station.

Where to stay

Tikondane Lodge (17 rooms, 14 dorm beds, 1 rondavel) Great East Rd; m 0777 501737; e tikoeducation@gmail.com; w tikondane.org. Next to the hospital, about 2km west of Katete, this lodge was set up to raise funds for the Tikondane Community Centre, which brings together skills training, early childhood & adult education programmes (in particular the '22 steps out of poverty' programme for subsistence farmers). Guests are welcome to get involved at several levels: teaching their own subject, perhaps joining classes for drumming or dancing, learning the local language or helping make peanut butter or soap. A structured programme of longer voluntary work means that even those with just a few weeks can contribute to the project. Computer skills, fundraising, basic teaching & reading are much valued, but the list is seemingly endless! Volunteering packages cost US$225/week including meals & accommodation & run from 8 days to 12 weeks. In order to help foster local traditions, the lodge works with 3 villages, & organises a number of 'cultural safaris'. One option features a visit by oxcart to watch the Chewa initiation rites: Chinamwali for women & Gule Wamkulu, the 'ghost dance', for men. You are invited into homes in the village & a vegetarian meal is included. Accommodation in the lodge varies from en-suite family or dbl rooms to simple dormitories, & there is also campground & a restaurant with a licence. *Dbl room US$25; dorm bed US$8; camping US$5 pp*. **$**

CHIPATA Chipata (⊕ CHIPAT 13°38.557'S, 32°38.796'E) is a small bustling town that is more than just a junction en route to South Luangwa; it is also a border town just 30km from Malawi. Known in colonial days as Fort Jameson, and now the capital of Eastern Province, Chipata stands in a valley, surrounded by quite a fertile area of subsistence farms with low bush-covered hills around. To the east of town is an attractive mosque; in the centre are banks, fuel stations and a few large supermarkets (Spar, Choppies & Shoprite), which are recommended for stocking up if you're self-driving into South Luangwa.

Getting there and away Note that there is an ongoing programme of reconstruction work on the roads into and out of Chipata.

By bus There are regular coach services between Chipata and Lusaka – reliable operators include Power Tools Logistics (3 daily services), Johabie and Kobs. The fare is around K350 one way and buses depart in the morning, taking around 7 to 8 hours to reach Lusaka. In the other direction, there are twice-weekly buses to Lilongwe in Malawi for around K180 one way. For travel to and from Mfuwe, Green Bus and Jonda Bus operate a daily service. The town's bus station is a little way off the main road, near the main township and market, and is not a place to hang around after dark. Alternatively, there are taxis available.

Where to stay and eat *Map, opposite*

Most visitors continue to the Mfuwe area, down in the Luangwa Valley, if they can. However, if you arrive late then staying in Chipata is a wise move, and hitchhikers could easily end up here for a night or two due to lack of lifts. There are several good places to lay your head or get a meal, of which Mama Rula's is probably the most geared to travellers rather than the business market.

Protea Hotel Chipata (40 rooms) Great East Rd; ☎ 0216 222905; e reservations@phchipata.co.zm; w proteahotels.com/chipata. Just 2km west of town, 300m from the turn-off to Mfuwe, the Protea has all the accoutrements of a good modern mid-range hotel for corporate as well as leisure travellers. The clean, functional dbl rooms have standard in-room facilities. There's a lounge area & outside, against a backdrop of the Kanjala Hills, the restaurant spills out on to a terrace

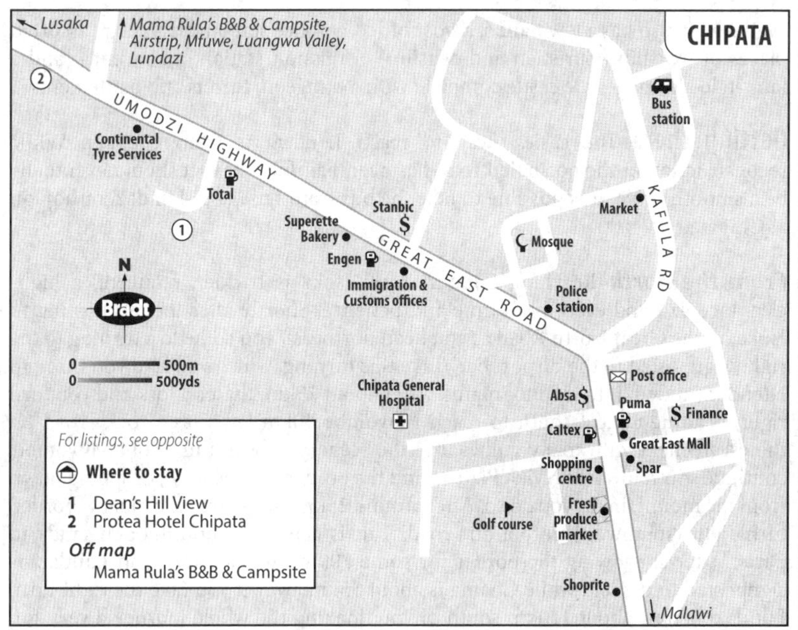

where there's a good-sized pool, with a bar & umbrella shade. **$$$**

Mama Rula's B&B & Campsite (13 rooms, camping) Old Lundazi Rd; **m** 0960 341236; **e** richardsbnjm@gmail.com. In a quiet location, Mama Rula's is well signposted north of town, about 6km down the main Mfuwe road. A level shady campsite spreads across a large lawn under a canopy of marvellous red mahogany (*Khaya anthotheca*) trees & the odd banana or papaya. There are very basic, shared ablutions & a tree-shaded pool. It's a little run down these days but a secure, leafy spot for overnight spots. **$–$$**

Dean's Hill View (6 rooms, camping) **m** 0979 392721. Overlooking Chipata, this tropical, tree-shaded site offers camping pitches – not all level – & very simple rooms away from the noise of town. Basic ablution facilities (some visitors report the need for renovation), garden hammocks, rustic picnic tables & friendly, accommodating staff always on hand. *Room US$25; camping US$8.* **$**

Other practicalities As you arrive by road from Lusaka, the first of several **fuel** stations is on your right, well placed for those continuing north to Mfuwe. The heart of the town, however, is a couple of kilometres beyond this, past the police station and around a sharp bend. There are various **banks** with ATMs. If you're continuing on to Malawi and need to exchange cash for Malawian kwacha, watch out for money sharks, especially around the fuel stations.

For supplies, start at the large, very well-stocked Spar in the Great East Mall (🕘 07.30–20.00 daily). Further southeast there's also a branch of Shoprite, set back from the right side of the road. The main market is out towards the bus station, but for fresh produce check out the small market close to Shoprite.

LUNDAZI About 180km north of Chipata, well off any obvious route for travellers, lies the small, friendly town of Lundazi. It's perched high above the eastern side of the Luangwa Valley, and close to a quiet border crossing to Malawi.

Lundazi has no large supermarkets, but plenty of small, local **shops** where you can buy most essentials. There are a lot of farming areas around, so fresh produce is available. It also has a few **banks**, a **post office**, a police station, an airstrip, assorted places of worship (Christian and Muslim), a mission station, a convent – and a fairy-tale Norman-style castle complete with a dungeon, turrets and battlements.

Getting there The easiest way to reach Lundazi is from Chipata. While reconstruction of the pot-holed road has been painfully slow, it should eventually be a smooth drive. It is possible to take the bus from Lusaka to Lundazi or hop on at Chipata.

From the north Reaching Lundazi from Isoka is trickier, requiring a high-clearance 4x4 and even more time and patience. Shortly after the left turning to Isoka on the Great North Road as you head northeast, you come to a turning to the right, signposted to the 'airport bar'. Take this turning, which will lead you through Ntendere and up into the mountains. After about 75km, there's a fork and you turn right, heading almost south to reach Muyombe 50km later. It's a rocky road on the escarpment with many gullies, but the scenery is beautiful. From Muyombe, continue south towards Nyika Plateau and the border with Malawi, dropping down from the mountains as you do so. After around 25km, just before the Malawi border, turn right (southwest) onto a dirt road. This is generally good, though sandy in parts. After shadowing the border for some 70km, there's a fork and Lundazi is signposted to the left, while Chama is about 35km away if you take the right turn. Lundazi is now about 110km south of you; making the whole journey a very full day's drive from Isoka.

From the Luangwa Valley Both of the two roads from the Luangwa Valley are impassable during the rains, and even in the dry season require hours of hard 4x4 travel. The better of them leaves the main road on the east side of the valley about 20–25km north of Luambe National Park. It then climbs up the escarpment directly to Lundazi, about 130km away. It's a 4- to 5-hour drive.

The second turns eastwards around the northern boundary of South Luangwa National Park and then cuts up the escarpment through Lukusuzi National Park. It then joins the Chipata–Lundazi road some 60km south of Lundazi (120km north of Chipata).

 **Where to stay** If the lure of staying in a castle appeals, it's an option here – that said, manage your expectations of anything plush and regal. Otherwise the town has several other basic resthouses and motels, the best of which is listed below.

Country 24 Lodge (7 rooms) Old Air Strip; m 0955 455943; e lundazicountry24@gmail.com. Opened in 2018, this is best place in town. Neat, clean & modern rooms, with en-suite bathrooms & AC, plus there's a decent restaurant (grilled chicken with rice & vegetables for less than K100). They will allow you to camp with roof tents in the car park for around K300, but given rooms are only K500, it's probably worth staying in the hotel. *Rooftent camping US$16; rooms US$28.* **$–$$**

Lundazi Castle Hotel (17 rooms) Great East Rd; m 0977 348532. Dick Hobson's excellent *Tales of Zambia* (page 511) tells of how the district commissioner in the late 1940s, Errol Button, needed to build a resthouse here. Tourism was then taking off & visitors needed to stop between Nyika Plateau & the Luangwa Valley (the same could be said today!). Button designed & oversaw the construction of a small castle in Norman style, with thick walls & narrow slits for archers, overlooking a lake. It has a dungeon, high turrets at each corner & battlements all around. It was christened 'Rumpelstiltskin' after the fairy-tale character favoured by his daughter, & cost a mere £500 to build at the time. The castle quickly became very popular & was extended in 1952 to accommodate more visitors.

Today, the castle is a very basic hotel & very cold in winter. All but 4 of the poorly maintained rooms share bathrooms, though running water is not always available – & only the more expensive rooms have hot showers. There is a lounge & a restaurant where simple dishes are served. **$**

MFUWE If you are heading to South Luangwa National Park on safari, whether by air or road, then you're likely to be aiming for a dot on the map marked 'Mfuwe': 'the gateway to South Luangwa'.

For a long time, most visitors' only experience of Mfuwe was the small single-storey, international airport 25km southeast of town, where most of the valley's visitors still arrive and depart today. It's an organised hub for vehicles from the valley's many safari camps, where welcoming, khaki-clad guides stand ready to whisk new arrivals straight through Mfuwe village and onwards to all corners of the national park.

In recent years, however, Mfuwe itself has blossomed, and now merits a stop on your way in or out of the park. Its population has grown and Mfuwe's points of interest have recentred on the village itself. No longer simply a necessary airport destination, an increasing number of high-quality, eclectic handicraft shops and hands-on activities now sit alongside local shops, bars, homes and small farm stalls of neat vegetable pyramids.

Driving along the D104 from the airport towards the Luangwa River bridge and park entrance, you'll pass bike-repair workshops under trees, craftsmen carving furniture, neat village houses with washing hung to dry and groups of

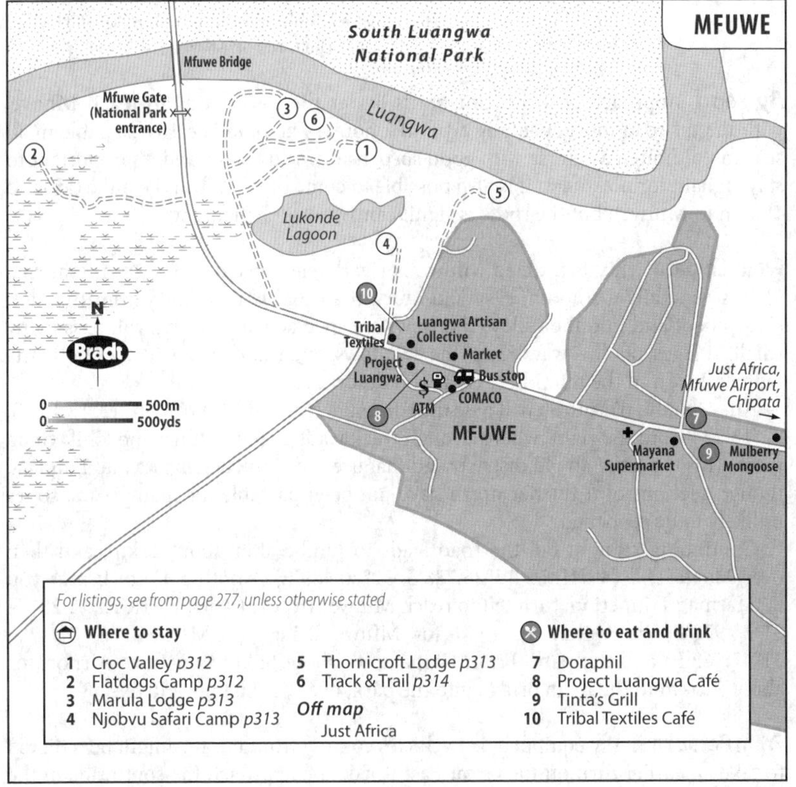

waving schoolchildren. This is very much a small, working, rural African town. The economy here is good, thanks largely to tourism and associated development initiatives, and there's an air of positive activity and pride.

Getting there and away

By air The vast majority of international visitors arrive by air into Mufwe International Airport (⊕ MFUAIR 13°15.281'S, 31°55.933'E). The small airport, housed in a single terminal building, has a bank with an ATM – useful if you arrive after closing – and currency exchange, a café, toilet facilities and a couple of curio shops.

Charter flights (page 108) are commonplace here, but Mfuwe also enjoys a regular, scheduled flight service. Proflight operates flights from Lusaka throughout the year; the number of weekly flights depends on the time of year, but during peak safari season (May–Oct) there are up to three flights a day. They also operate direct, daily flights between Mfuwe and the Lower Zambezi (Royal & Jeki airstrips) during safari season.

With a customs and immigration facility at the airport, international routes are also available to Johannesburg (Proflight via Lusaka) and to Malawi's capital, Lilongwe, and some of its national parks (Proflight & Ulendo Airlink).

Proflight Mfuwe airport ☎ 0971 246950; **m** 0777 034742; **e** reservations@proflight-zambia.com; **w** proflight-zambia.com; ⌚ 08.00–17.00 daily. The main scheduled, domestic carrier in Zambia.

Ulendo Airlink ☎ +265 (0)179 4638; **m** +265 (0)992 961201; **e** reservations@flyulendo.com; **w** book.flyulendo.com. Small, reliable airline offering scheduled & charter international flights between Mfuwe & Lilongwe, as well as internal connections within Malawi.

By road Approaching from Chipata is by far the easiest way to reach Mfuwe, with the tar road journey taking around 2 hours. The road is easily passable in all seasons, although a vehicle with good suspension is advisable and it's important to stay vigilant for pot-holes. It is also possible to come by road from Petauke (around 190km to Mfuwe), but the route is significantly more challenging.

From Chipata The turn-off to Mfuwe is clearly signposted just west of Chipata. This is generally a smooth, easy and quick road that winds down from the high escarpment and into the valley. The views are spectacular, and you will pass many small villages on the way. Keep the windows open and you will feel both the temperature and the humidity rise as you descend.

After around 65km you will pass the Chisengu turn-off (⊕ TUSLNP 13°18.131'S, 32°13.234'E) to the right, where a rough track leads to the Kauluzi and Chikwinda gates. This is part of an old district road that used to connect Chipata and Lundazi, though sections of it further north have not been passable for many years, so it's unlikely to be reopened.

Continuing straight on, the road leads to Jumbe after about 16km, and then over Mpata Hill (⊕ HILL2 13°26.728'S, 32°20.489'E). Another 15km brings you to a tarmac T-junction: turn left to reach Mfuwe Airport (⊕ MFUAIR 13°15.281'S, 31°55.933'E) in 3–4km, or right for Mfuwe Bridge (⊕ MFUBRI 13°5.917'S, 31°47.162'E) and the park. From Chipata, it's about 95km to Mfuwe Airport, or about 115km to the main bridge into the park, over the Luangwa River.

From Petauke Fully equipped 4x4 vehicles coming from Lusaka might be tempted to take an earlier turn off the Great East Road, and approach the south side of the park via a turn-off from Petauke. We haven't driven this road; it's very rarely used and is much slower and more difficult than the Chipata road (see opposite), though also more scenic and interesting. It's about 150km to the park's southern gate at Chilongozi from Petauke, then a further 40km to Mfuwe, during which time you're unlikely to see any other vehicles. We do not advise attempting this route at all during the wet season.

In the dry season, for those who have the back-up and want to try this, here are some old directions and GPS waypoints. Turn off the Great East Road at Chabisa, next to the Puma fuel station (fill up here), and head towards Petauke (⊕ PETAUK 14°17.730'S, 31°20.253'E). It's 4km until you pass the police station, on the right. Then turn left and continue up the hill, taking a left fork after about 200m (⊕ PETS01 14°14.982'S, 31°20.280'E). There are some reports of a veterinary checkpoint with a shoe/tyre disinfectant point and a K100 council levy from driving though the village of Lusangazi. Continue to head for Ukwimi, which is about 50km of ungraded, often extremely narrow track, following this route:

⊕ PETS02 13°56.842'S, 31°36.867'E
⊕ PETS03 13°50.448'S, 31°35.188'E
⊕ PETS04 13°48.282'S, 31°34.699'E
⊕ PETS05 13°47.971'S, 31°34.555'E
⊕ PETS06 13°46.096'S, 31°35.789'E
⊕ PETS07 13°38.386'S, 31°34.774'E
⊕ PETS08 13°37.398'S, 31°34.609'E
⊕ PETS09 13°34.183'S, 31°34.183'E
⊕ PETS10 13°31.152'S, 31°34.360'E
⊕ PETS11 13°25.981'S, 31°33.354'E
⊕ PETS12 13°26.011'S, 31°33.593'E
⊕ PETS13 13°22.746'S, 31°36.775'E

This brings you to the Chilongozi area and the now-defunct Nyamaluma pontoon (⊕ NYALUM 13°22.630'S, 31°36.974'E). From here you have to continue roughly northeast, shadowing the east bank of the Luangwa, and will eventually emerge into Mfuwe, just east of the bridge.

By bus/taxi Both Jonda and Juldan operate a daily bus service from Lusaka, via Chipata, departing around 04.00–05.00 and arriving in Mfuwe 12 hours later. It should cost around US$12. Small groups of travellers may consider hiring a vehicle and driver for a reasonable rate, but make sure you agree on a precise drop-off location and remember that Mfuwe Airport and the centre of Mfuwe village (the fuel station is a good point) are 25km apart.

Where to stay *Map, page 275*

Nearly all international visitors arriving in Mfuwe head straight to safari camps and lodges. Most, but not all, are within the national park boundaries, and those that are not are extremely close to it. Given this universal safari focus, we have included all accommodation options, bar one, within the South Luangwa *Where to stay* listings to aid comparison (page 298). The option listed here is close to the airport and may be useful if you arrive late by road or are on a tight budget.

Just Africa (3 rooms, 4 chalets) Mfuwe Rd; **m** 0979 696503; **e** kadewele@just-africa.com; ⊕ 13°12.123'S, 31°54.949'E. Some 3km from the airport, Just Africa is owned by an engaging, entrepreneurial local woman, Misozi Kadewele, & is recommended for those on a tight budget. Most rooms & chalets have an en-suite shower (water heated by wood-fired boilers) & toilet. These are basic but clean, the beds have mosi nets & there's electricity for charging – including an unexpected solar-&-battery inverter system in the chalets. Game drives & village visits can be organised. Self-catering is possible, although dinner – typically nshima & relish (*US$6–10 pp*) with drinks – is available for guests. **$**

Where to eat and drink *Map, page 275*

There are a couple of spots on the main Mfuwe Road for a cold drink and a bite to eat, ideal if you decide to spend an afternoon away from camp, doing some shopping and taking in 'town life'. In addition, Project Luangwa and Tribal Textiles (page 279) have good, small cafés on their premises.

Doraphil Restaurant Mfuwe Rd; m 0966 860859, 0975 868663; e doricakamanga38@gmail.com. Opposite Mayana supermarket, local female entrepreneur Dorica offers good food & a friendly atmosphere. It's best to book in advance to sample the thali-style Zambian meal (vegetarian options) or the highly regarded chicken schnitzel, and you're welcome to bring your own drinks. $$

Tinta's Grill Mfuwe Rd. Next to Mayana supermarket, Tinta Mweetwa's café serves a selection of Western & Zambian fare at simple tables inside & out. There's a Zanaco ATM being installed in the adjoining building & long-term plans to add some accommodation here too. $$

Other practicalities Along Mfuwe Road in the heart of town, you'll find all of the key shops and services. There's a **fuel** station with a Zanaco **ATM** (if it's not working, there's one outside Tinta's Grill & at the airport), several **pharmacies** and hardware stores, , a **Comaco** store selling fair-trade peanut butter, honey and grain, and a well-stocked shop: **Mayana**, selling good cuts of meat (the excellent Chipata butcher also supplies several lodges), as well as milk, eggs, snacks and dry goods. Tucked in the streets behind are a local clinic, church, mosque and several schools.

What to see and do If you're staying in or near Mfuwe, it's worth spending a few hours here having a look at what's on offer and gathering some good-quality souvenirs. There are a number of hands-on craft activities on offer, from designing and printing cushion covers to making beaded jewellery. In addition, there's a couple of seriously impressive conservation and development organisations that'll gladly tell you about their work protecting the environment, wildlife and improving the lives of the local community, and plenty of opportunities to chat to the friendly people who live and work here. A few places that should definitely be on your itinerary are:

The Bush-Spa at Mfuwe Lodge Mfuwe Lodge; m 0979 306826; e info@bush-spa.com; w bush-spa.com; ⌚ 08.00–17.00 daily. This must be the most unlikely location for a full-scale spa. Overlooking a lagoon are 3 treatment rooms – 2 singles & a dbl – set within a large, thatched structure that also features a wet deck area & a jacuzzi. Watching elephants while having a massage must be for some the ultimate in game-viewing!

The brainchild of Nathalie Zanoli, the award-winning spa was opened in 2007, & offers a chance for local women to work within the tourist industry, which is otherwise largely dominated by men. Nathalie trains them in a range of techniques using indigenous products, such as those extracted from the sausage tree (*Kigelia africana*) or the baobab (*Adansonia digitata*), taking on board African holistic practices. Massages or wraps, facials or pedicures, hydrotherapy or reflexology: there are numerous options, all priced by the hour rather than according to the treatment.

The spa is open to all visitors to South Luangwa. The team visits lodges in the Mfuwe area to offer in-room treatments, but they can also arrange free transfers to the spa itself from camps in the vicinity.

Luangwa Artisan Collective Mfuwe Rd. Alongside Tribal Textiles, the Luangwa Artisan Collective is an open-air market space showcasing the works of several entrepreneurial Mfuwe artisans. From skilled weavers to carpenters, metalworkers & painters, their handcrafted products are all fairly priced & carefully made. Beautiful woven floor mats, cleverly collapsible

above (TT) On the Munde River in Western Province, the Lozi people fish together with traditional fishtraps on agreed days to ensure fairness of the catch PAGE 471

below (SLF) Home to the fantastical shoebill, thousands of black lechwe and now cheetah, the Bangweulu Wetlands are an idyllic, lily-strewn lattice of channels and floodplains PAGE 365

Water is a lifeline for wildlife, who crowd ever closer to the rivers, waterholes and lakes as the dry season advances. Sit and watch for some magical moments. Pictured: Black lechwe, Bangweulu Wetlands PAGE 365

above (MM)

The Ngonye Falls were formed by a similar process to Victoria Falls, with erosion taking advantage of cracks in the area's basalt rock PAGE 465

below (TH)

above (CEM) Africa's most distinctive tree, the seemingly upside-down baobab, makes for an iconic sunset backdrop

left (TH) Blood lily (*Scadoxus multiflorus*)

below left (TH) Leopard orchid (*Ansellia africana*)

below right (TH) Protea

Liuwa Plain hosts Africa's second largest wildebeest migration of around 30,000 animals which traverse these vast grasslands, pursued by predators, from November PAGE 473

above (TT)

Forming the northern boundary of the lush South Luangwa National Park, the steep, tree-covered Muchinga Escarpment lies at the end of the Great Rift Valley PAGE 280

below (SS)

above (JWL/AWL) Zambia's pioneering walking safaris are perhaps the best in Africa: superb guiding, first-class bushcamps and relaxed wildlife

left (RAS) All are accompanied by a guide and an armed national parks' scout, and are available in all the main national parks PAGE 149

below (FdE)

right (CS)

Large parks, few vehicles and good guiding mean you'll often enjoy incredible wildlife sightings alone PAGE 39

below (CS)

The mighty Zambezi: seek its source, wonder at Victoria Falls and take a gentle canoe safari through Lower Zambezi National Park PAGE 152

bottom (SHS)

Safaris are special: from morning coffee alongside giraffes to barbecue feasts under the Milky Way PAGE 91

Millions of fruit bats descend on Kasanka National Park between October and December PAGE 351 (I/D)

lampshades, carved animal sculptures & silhouette metalwork trees are all excellent souvenirs, with 100% of the sale price benefitting these talented people.

Mulberry Mongoose Mfuwe Rd; 0978 051814; m 0767 383012; e info@mulberrymongoose.com; w mulberrymongoose.com. In a new building, clearly signposted on the main Mfuwe road, this wonderful, ethically minded jewellery company, owned by Kate Wilson & run by a team of 8 determined local ladies, make jewellery from locally sourced materials: scarlet-coloured lucky beans, guinea-fowl feathers, old Zambian coins &, most famously, repurposed steel wire from poachers' snares. This celebrated 'snare-ware' range is fashioned by hammering long coils of thick steel wire, shaping & cutting it into earrings, bracelets & necklaces, often interspersed with semi-precious stones, copper, freshwater pearls, wooden beads & vegetable ivory (a hard, white palm nut). It is labour intensive, physical work, undertaken by local women developing and perfecting a new craft. The snare wire used to create Mulberry Mongoose jewellery is provided by park rangers clearing these lethal traps from South Luangwa; for each piece purchased, a US$5 donation is made to fund these vital anti-poaching missions. Worth visiting for a special souvenir. You can also book a 2hr jewellery making workshop. Not only will you bead your own piece to take away, but you can try your hand at bending & flattening the steel snare wire – after which, you'll definitely have even greater respect for the strength of the ladies working here!

Project Luangwa Mfuwe Rd; m 0974 250152; e info@projectluangwa.org; w projectluangwa.org. Many of the lodges in South Luangwa have brought their various community projects under one umbrella: Project Luangwa. The project aims to improve the long-term economic prospects of the community while avoiding negative impacts on the natural environment, in part by developing & improving education in the area. This includes raising the standards of more than 20 schools that have previously had little or no support & – more ambitiously – increasing the number of children who attend school in the first place. A specific focus is education for girls, aiming to address why so few attend, & why those who do so often fall behind the boys.

And the project isn't just focused on children. They also work with young adults to develop vocational training both in order to improve their employment prospects & to enable some to start their own small businesses; they run a fantastic eco-stove project; help with provision of clean water sources; & help address conservation issues such as deforestation through exploring alternatives to firewood.

There are numerous ways to support their work, from purchasing handcrafted bags, cuddly toys & fabrics in their lovely Mfuwe shop to taking time out to sip coffee or snack on samosas in their on-site café. And when you're done shopping & eating, it's well worth taking some time to wander around their wonderfully muralled shop to learn about their many projects from the clear infographics. The staff will be delighted to talk to you about their outreach work in the community, too. If you do wish to donate the money goes directly to great causes: for US$10 you can gift a family a stove & for US$15 you can provide a girl with sanitary products to enable her to stay in school. There are also opportunities to sponsor a child for a year in education, pay for the football team to reach their away games or fund a teacher. Every one of their projects is carefully considered and managed to ensure the most effective and beneficial use of the money raised.

Tribal Textiles Mfuwe Rd; 0976 815114; e hello@tribaltextiles.co.zm; w tribaltextiles.co.zm. In a new location in the centre of town, this beautifully laid-out home décor shop is Mfuwe's original craft retailer. Started in 1991 to create sustainable, well-paid local employment, Tribal Textiles has gone from strength to strength & now sells perhaps Zambia's best hand-painted textiles. Contemporary, African-infused designs, environmentally conscious processes & quality products are on display. In the pretty garden, under shade-cloths, you can see a few of the friendly team working on new pieces & learn about their low-tech manufacturing process. Prices are reasonable for handcrafted pieces (credit cards accepted), with 5% being donated to a range of great organisations – from the primary school & orphanage to local wildlife conservation groups. It also offers half-day 'Art Safari' workshops where you can design & make your own cushion cover or shopping bag – a lovely opportunity to produce a memorable souvenir and chat to the local team.

(Park fees US$25 pp/day; self-drivers US$30 pp/day plus US$15 per vehicle/day or K17 if Zambian registered; bed levy US$20/night) There are many contenders for the title of Africa's best game park. The Serengeti, Amboseli, Ngorongoro Crater, Etosha, Kruger, Moremi and Mana Pools would certainly be high on the list. South Luangwa has a better claim than most. Some of these other areas will match its phenomenally high game densities. Many others – the lesser known of Africa's parks – will have equally few visitors. One or two also allow night drives, which open up a different, nocturnal world to view, allowing leopards to be commonly seen and even watched while hunting.

However, few have South Luangwa's high quality of guiding together with its remarkable wildlife spectacles, day and night, in the isolation of a true wilderness. These elements, perhaps, are how the contenders ought to be judged, and on these the South Luangwa Park comes out as one of the highest on the list.

HISTORY

Note on prehistory Some of the earliest evidence of humans in south-central Africa is currently emerging from excavations in and around the South Luangwa National Park. Stone tools dating to at least 2 million years ago have been found, and all other periods of the Stone Age are represented in the park. There is also evidence emerging of early farmers in the valley, appearing by AD400. As yet there are no sites accessible to the public, but plans have been afoot for some years to build a museum at Mfuwe, on the site of the old cultural centre at Nsendamila, to showcase the valley's rich prehistory.

From the 8th century *With thanks to John Hudson OBE for his help in preparing this text*

With the Zambezi established as a trade route by the 8th century, it seems reasonable to assume that small settlements were also appearing on the neighbouring Luangwa River, though it is harder to navigate and was, at that time, probably used mainly to reach the abundant game of the valley, rather than for any trading purposes. Records tell us that Zumbo, on the eastern banks of the Luangwa, was founded in 1546 by the Portuguese – their first settlement in what is now Zambia – and one can only surmise that Luangwa township itself, situated at the strategically important confluence of the Luangwa and Zambezi rivers, must have been founded at around that time too. Both these settlements were subsequently abandoned and resettled, until about 1763 when Zumbo was recorded as having 200 Portuguese families living within its boundaries.

In the 19th century the area was crossed by many European explorers who came to hunt, trade, bring the Gospel or simply to satisfy their curiosity. Around 1810–20, a trading post was opened at Malambo, some 100km north of Mfuwe. This was on the main trade route from Tete to Lake Mweru, which had first been established by Lacerda as early as 1798.

In his last book, *Kakuli*, Norman Carr quotes a Portuguese captain, Antonio Gamitto, as writing of the Luangwa in around 1832:

> Game of all kinds is very abundant at this season of drought; great numbers of wild animals collect here, leaving dry areas in search of water…we can only say that this district appears to be the richest in animal life of any we have seen.

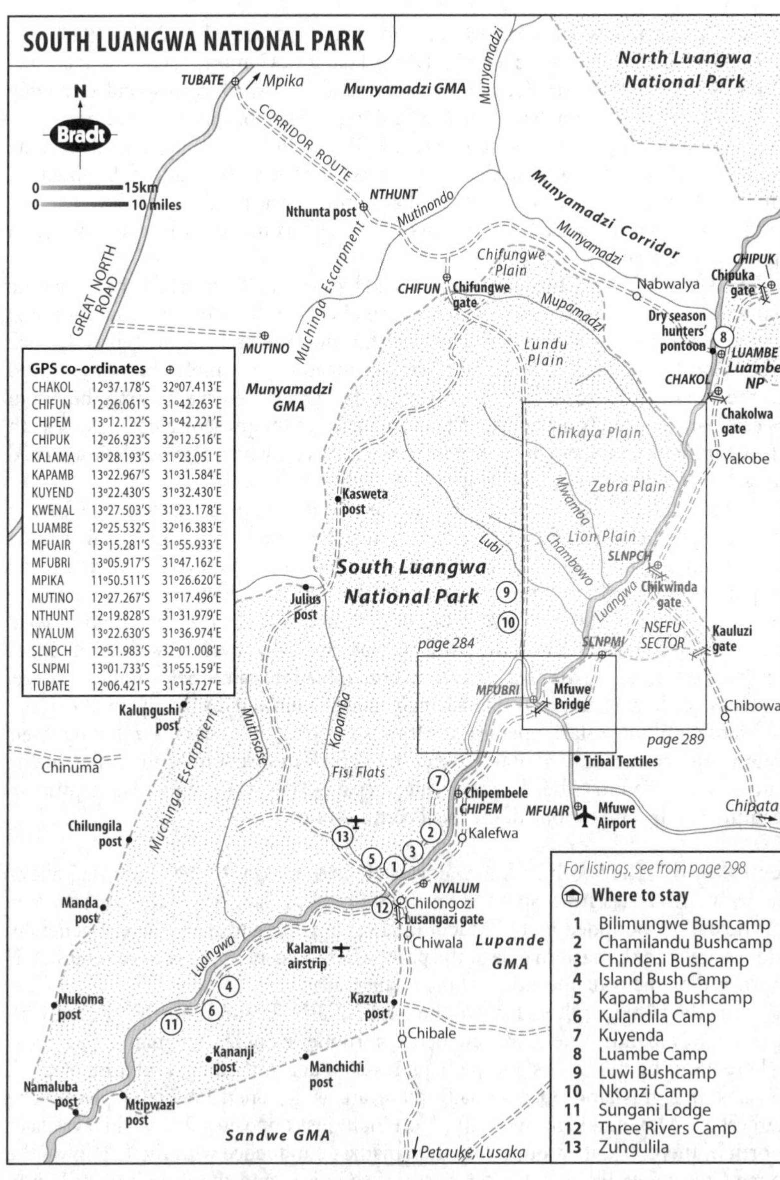

Later, in December 1866, when Livingstone crossed the Luangwa at Perekani (a place north of Tafika and south of Chibembe), he was just one of many Europeans exploring the continent. He commented:

> I will make this land better known to men that it may become one of their haunts. It is impossible to describe its luxuriance.

In 1904 a Luangwa Game Park was declared on the eastern bank of the river. However, this was not maintained, hunting licences were given out to control allegedly marauding elephants, and the park came to mean little. Then on 27 May 1938 three parks were defined in the valley: the North Luangwa Game Reserve, the Lukusuzi Game Reserve and the South Luangwa Game Reserve – which corresponded roughly to the present park, though without the Chifungwe Plain or the Nsefu Sector.

In the following year, Norman Carr and Bert Schultz were appointed as game rangers and villages within the reserves were moved outside its boundaries. Initially Norman Carr recommended that hunting safaris be started, but over the coming decade he realised that visitors would also come for what are now called 'photographic safaris'.

In 1949 the Senior Chief Nsefu, prompted by Norman Carr, established a private game reserve on the Luangwa's eastern bank, between the Mwasauke and Kauluzi rivers. A safari camp was started here which sent some of its income directly back to the local community. (Norman Carr was ahead of his time!) This soon moved to the site of the present-day Nsefu Camp. The chief's reserve became the Nsefu Sector, which was absorbed into the boundaries of the present park – along with the Chifungwe Plain, north of the Mupamadzi River – when new legislation turned all game reserves into national parks on 15 February 1972.

In the later years of his life, Norman Carr lived at Kapani Safari Lodge, having played a pivotal role in the history of the valley by pioneering commercial walking safaris, upon which South Luangwa has founded its reputation. He remained an important and highly outspoken figure to the end, and devoted much energy in his latter years to development projects designed to help the surrounding local communities to benefit from the park. He was especially involved with local school projects, encouraging the next generation of Zambians to value their wildlife heritage.

His excellent example is increasingly being followed by many of the more forward-thinking safari operators. More and more operators are taking their role in the community seriously, often by sponsoring schools and clinics in the surrounding countryside. Kawaza Village (page 313) is a highly visible tourism venture run by and for one of the local communities.

GEOGRAPHY The South Park now covers about 9,050km² of the Luangwa Valley's floor, which varies from about 500m to 800m above sea level. The western side of the park is bounded by the Muchinga Escarpment, and from there it generally slopes down to the eastern side of the park, where, except in the extreme south, it is bordered by the wide meanders of the Luangwa River.

Near the banks of the Luangwa the land is fairly flat, and mostly covered with mature woodlands. There are few dense shrubberies here, but many open areas where beautiful tall trees stand perhaps 10–20m apart, shading a mixture of small bushes and grassland. Occasionally there are wide, open grassland plains. The largest are Mutanda Plain in Nsefu, Lion Plain just opposite Nsefu, Chikaya Plain north of there, Ntanta around the Mupamadzi's confluence with the Luangwa, the huge Chifungwe Plain in the far north of the park, and the little-known Lundu Plain, south of the Mupamadzi River. These are not Serengeti-type plains with short grass; instead they usually boast tall species of grasses and often bushes. It is their lack of trees that makes them open.

Understandably, the highest density of animals (and hence camps) is around the Luangwa River. However, increasingly camps are being set up elsewhere in the park. The trio of bushcamps run by Norman Carr Safaris is located along the Lubi (or Luwi) River, one of the Luangwa's smaller tributaries, while temporary walking camps run by Robin Pope Safaris are sited beside the Mupamadzi River rather than the Luangwa.

The Luangwa River For the visitor, perhaps the most notable feature of the Luangwa Valley is the pristine river that runs through it. Take a close look at it: very few rivers of this size in Africa (or anywhere else!) have been so unaffected by man. There are no dams on it, no commercial agriculture along its banks, and incredibly little pollution. Hence here you can still see the seasonal fluctuations of water levels and flooding which lead to the dynamic nature of a river in a really natural state. It's not only beautiful but also textbook geography.

Note how the river's twisting curves cut easily through the valley's fertile soil, leaving a sprinkling of crescent-shaped oxbow lakes, or *wafwas*, in their wake. Every year new sandbanks arise as its original banks are cut back and the river's course changes with the floods. Just look at the number of riverside camps and lodges that, over the years, have either moved or gradually been swallowed up by river erosion.

GEOLOGY The Luangwa Valley is a rift valley, similar to the Great Rift Valley of East Africa, though probably older, and it shares its genesis with the adjoining Lower Zambezi Valley. The original sedimentary strata covering the whole area is part of the karoo system, sedimentary rocks laid down from 175 to 300 million years ago.

During this time, faulting occurred and volcanic material was injected into rifts in the existing sediments. One of these faults is the wide valley that the Luangwa now occupies. In geologically recent times, the Luangwa meandered extensively across the wide valley floor, eroding the volcanic rocks and depositing mineral-rich silts. These meanders also left behind them old watercourses and oxbow pools. The most recent of these can still be seen, and they are an important feature of the landscape near the present river.

FLORA AND FAUNA

Vegetation To understand the Luangwa Valley's vegetation, the base of its productive ecosystem, consider the elements that combine to nurture its plants: the water, light, heat and nutrients. Rainfall in the valley is typically 800–1,100mm per annum – which is moderate, but easily sufficient for strong vegetation growth. Occupying a position between 12° and 14° south of the Equator, the valley lacks neither light nor heat. (Visit in October and you may feel that it has too much of both.)

However, the key to its vegetation lies in the nutrients. The Luangwa's soils, being volcanic in origin, are rich in minerals, and the sediments laid down by the river are fine, making excellent soils. Thus with abundant water, light, heat and nutrient-rich soils, the valley's vegetation has thrived: it is both lush and diverse.

Unlike many parks, the 'bush' in the Luangwa is very variable, and as you drive or walk you'll pass through a patchwork of different vegetation zones. See page 30, for more detail, but the more obvious include some beautiful mature forests of 'cathedral mopane'. South of Mfuwe, just outside the national park on the way to the salt pans south of Nkwali, is one area where the mopane are particularly tall.

Along the Luangwa's tributaries, which are just rivers of sand for most of the year, you'll find lush riverine vegetation dominated by giant red mahogany trees (*Khaya anthotheca*, formerly known as *Khaya nyasica*) and *Adina microsephala*. Sometimes you'll also find Natal mahoganies (*Trichilia emetica*), and African ebony trees (*Diospyros mespiliformis*). There are several locations in the park where the latter form dense groves, casting a heavy shade on the sparse undergrowth. Look for such groves where the tributaries meet the Luangwa; there's one beside Mchenja Camp, and another near Kaingo.

Elsewhere are large, open grassland plains. Chief among these are probably the plains in the Nsefu Sector. These surround some natural salt springs, which attract crowned cranes in their thousands.

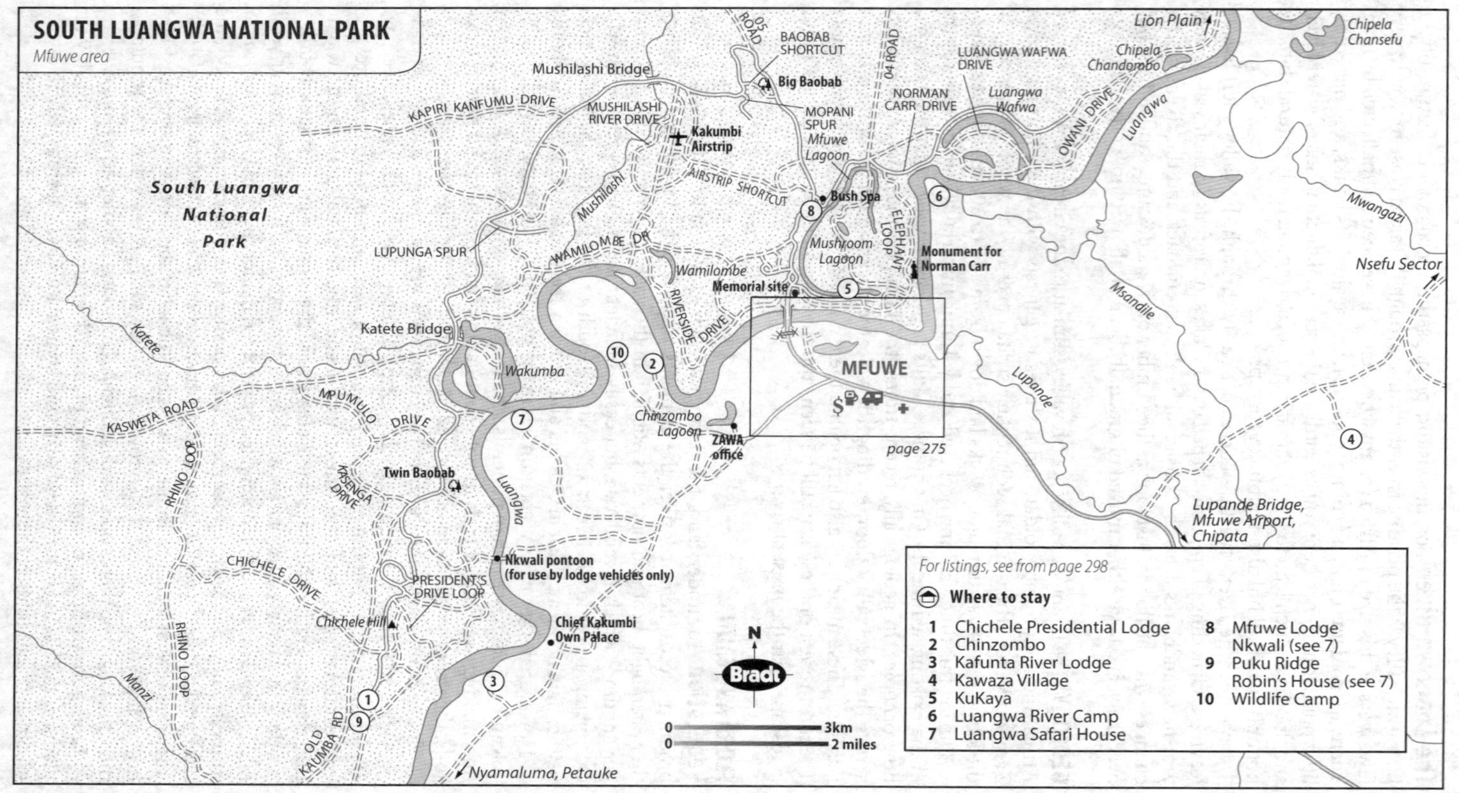

SOUTH LUANGWA NATIONAL PARK
Mfuwe area
South Luangwa National Park
Mushilashi Bridge
KAPIRI KANFUMU DRIVE
MUSHILASHI RIVER DRIVE
Kakumbi Airstrip
05 ROAD
BAOBAB SHORTCUT
Big Baobab
MOPANI SPUR
Mfuwe Lagoon
04 ROAD
NORMAN CARR DRIVE
LUANGWA WAFWA DRIVE
Luangwa Wafwa
Chipela Chandombo
Lion Plain
Chipela Chansefu
OWANI DRIVE
Luangwa
AIRSTRIP SHORTCUT
Bush Spa
Mushilashi
LUPUNGA SPUR
WAMILOMBE DR
Wamilombe
Mushroom Lagoon
ELEPHANT LOOP
Monument for Norman Carr
Memorial site
Mwangazi
Nsefu Sector
Msandile
Katete
Katete Bridge
RIVERSIDE DRIVE
Wakumba
MFUWE
Lupande
MPUMULO DRIVE
KASWETA ROAD
Chinzombo Lagoon
ZAWA office
page 275
Twin Baobab
KASENGA DRIVE
RHINO LOOP
Luangwa
Lupande Bridge, Mfuwe Airport, Chipata
CHICHELE DRIVE
Nkwali pontoon (for use by lodge vehicles only)
PRESIDENT'S DRIVE LOOP
Chichele Hill
Chief Kakumbi Own Palace
Manzi
OLD KAUMBA RD
Nyamaluma, Petauke
N
Bradt
0 3km
0 2 miles
For listings, see from page 298
Where to stay
1 Chichele Presidential Lodge
2 Chinzombo
3 Kafunta River Lodge
4 Kawaza Village
5 KuKaya
6 Luangwa River Camp
7 Luangwa Safari House
8 Mfuwe Lodge
Nkwali (see 7)
9 Puku Ridge
Robin's House (see 7)
10 Wildlife Camp

Antelope and other herbivores With its rich vegetation, the Luangwa supports large numbers of a wide variety of animals. Each species has its own niche in the food chain, which avoids direct competition with any other species. Each herbivore has its favourite food plants, and even species that utilise the same food plants will feed on different parts of those plants. This efficient use of the available vegetation – refined over the last few millennia – makes the wildlife far more productive than any domestic stock would be if given the same land. It also leads to the high densities of game that the valley supports.

The game includes huge herds of buffalo, commonly hundreds of animals strong, and seemingly endless family groups of elephants; both are particularly spectacular if encountered while you are on foot. Despite Zambia's past poaching problems, South Luangwa's elephants are generally neither scarce nor excessively skittish in the presence of people. Just north of Mfuwe Lodge, you'll find an open plain with few trees, just the skeletal trunks of an old cathedral mopane forest. This has always been attributed to elephant damage from the 1970s, before ivory poaching became a problem, when there were around 56,000 elephants in the park (100,000 in the whole Luangwa Valley) – though recent research suggests that soil changes and even heart rot disease may have contributed to the trees' demise.

The park's dominant antelope species are puku and impala. While impala are dominant in much of southern Africa, including the Zambezi Valley and throughout Zimbabwe, puku are rare south of the Zambezi. They form small breeding groups which are exceedingly common in their favourite habitat – well-watered riverine areas. Groups are dominated by a territorial male adorned with the characteristic lyre-shaped horns.

Luangwa has a number of 'specialities' including the beautiful Thornicroft's giraffe (*Giraffa camelopardalis thornicroftii*). This rare subspecies differs from the much more common southern giraffe, found in Mosi-oa-Tunya National Park, south of the Zambezi, and throughout southern Africa, in having a different (and more striking) coloration. Thornicroft's have dark body patches and lighter neck patches; their colour patches don't normally extend below the knees, leaving their lower legs almost white; and their faces are light or white. Fortunately, around the Mfuwe area there is a widespread traditional belief that people who eat giraffe meat will get spots like those of a giraffe. Hence giraffe are rarely hunted by the local people, and are even very common in the GMA to the east of the river, outside the national park.

Cookson's wildebeest (*Connochaetes taurinus cooksoni*), a subspecies of the blue wildebeest found throughout sub-Saharan Africa, are endemic to the valley. They are more common in more northerly areas of the valley, such as the North Luangwa, and Norman Carr's wildlife guide (page 512) maintains that they also seem to favour the east side of the river, rather than the west. That said, in South Luangwa you've also a fair chance of seeing them in the Nsefu Sector, and on Lion Plain, and particularly around Mwamba Bushcamp area. They differ from the blue wildebeest in having cleaner colours, including slightly reddish bands, and being a little smaller and more compact.

Another special of the Luangwa Valley is Crawshay's zebra (*Equus quagga crawshaii*), a subspecies of the more common plains zebra, which is found in much of the subcontinent. Crawshay's zebra occur east of the Muchinga Escarpment – in the Luangwa Valley and on Nyika Plateau – and lack the brown shadow-stripe that plains zebra usually have between their black stripes.

In contrast to these examples, it is the common waterbuck (*Kobus ellipsiprymnus*) that is found in the valley, rather than its rarer subspecies, the defassa waterbuck

(*K. e. crawshayi*), which is found over most of the rest of Zambia. The common waterbuck has the characteristic white 'toilet seat' ring on its rump, whereas the defassa has a white circular patch.

Other antelope in the park include bushbuck, eland and kudu. The delicate oribi occur occasionally in the grassland areas (especially Chifungwe Plain), while grysbok are often encountered on night drives. Reedbuck and Lichtenstein's hartebeest also occur, but not usually near the river, while sable are occasionally seen in the hills near the escarpment. Like sable, roan antelope seem to be most frequently seen in the hills – often on the roads south of Chichele, although in the late dry season there are frequent sightings in the Chikoko area, on the fringes of Chifungwe Plain, and in the 'corridor' area between the North and South parks.

A special mention must go to the hippopotami (and crocodiles) found in the rivers, and especially in the Luangwa: their numbers are remarkable. Look over the main bridge crossing the Luangwa at Mfuwe – sometimes there are hundreds of hippo there. Towards the end of the dry season, when the rivers are at their lowest, is the best time to observe such dense congregations of hippo. Then these semi-aquatic mammals are forced into smaller and smaller pools, and you'll appreciate their sheer numbers. These congregations reach their peak in October and November when, for example, you'll find a concentration of 1,000 hippo in just 2km of river, in the Changwa Channel, north of Chibembe.

Predators The main predators in the Luangwa Valley are typical of sub-Saharan Africa: lion, leopard, spotted hyena and wild dog. During the day, the visitor is most likely to see lion (*Panthera leo*), the park's most common large predator. Their prides are relatively easily spotted, at least in the dry season when the grass is low, and to witness one of their hunting trips makes a gripping spectacle.

CARNIVORES IN ZAMBIA'S NATIONAL PARKS

Because large carnivores such as African wild dog, lion and cheetah are naturally wide-ranging and low density, they require immense areas to survive and are therefore very susceptible to human impacts such as habitat loss, disease and persecution. Consequently, the presence of these species is synonymous with large, relatively intact ecosystems, and Zambia's national parks are a case in point.

With nearly one third of the country managed for wildlife through national parks and adjacent game management areas (GMAs), Zambia is home to a number of threatened large carnivore species (many of whose populations extend into neighbouring countries such as Malawi). Of these, the African wild dog, or painted dog – once found throughout most of sub-Saharan Africa – is now one of the continent's most endangered carnivores, with Zambia one of only six countries to have a viable population. The immense Kafue National Park is thought to have the country's largest number of wild dogs, followed by the Luangwa Valley.

Intensive conservation work on these dogs was initiated in 1998 in the Lower Zambezi National Park with the formation by Dr Kellie Leigh of African Wild Dog Conservation. This has since broadened into the Zambian Carnivore Programme (ZCP; 0216 246199; **e** zambiacarnivores@gmail.com; **w** zambiacarnivores.org), which, working in collaboration with DNPW, is focused on conserving Zambia's large carnivores and the ecosystems on which they depend. Fully field-based and operating across seven national parks and seven GMAs, the ZCP uses an

South Luangwa has made a name for itself among the safari community as an excellent park for leopard (*Panthera pardus*). This is largely because leopard hunt nocturnally, and Zambia is one of the few African countries to allow operators to go on spotlit game drives at night. Estimates made while filming a BBC documentary about leopards in the park suggest an average leopard density of one animal per 2.5km² – roughly twice the density recorded in South Africa's Kruger National Park. So perhaps the reputation is justified. In our experience, night drives in Luangwa with experienced guides do consistently yield excellent sightings of these cats – at a frequency that is difficult to match elsewhere on the continent. In contrast to this, there have been no reports of cheetah in the park for a number of decades, and are highly likely to be extinct in the park.

The populations of wild dogs seem to oscillate over a period of years. A study of wild dogs in Zambia by Kenneth Buk in 1994 (page 512) suggested that the Luangwa holds Zambia's second-largest wild dog population, even though this was badly depleted by an outbreak of anthrax in 1987. Since the late 1990s, wild dog have gradually been making more appearances. They're now regularly seen, with a particularly high incidence of sightings south of Mfuwe, near the Nkwali pontoon, from around February to May. Recent research suggests that their numbers are building up (see opposite).

Birds The Luangwa boasts the rich tropical birdlife that you would expect of such a fertile valley. This includes species that prefer a dry habitat of plains and forests, and those that live close to water. It is difficult to mention more than a few of the Luangwa's 400 species, but several books listed on page 512 cover the region's birds. As the Luangwa is situated between southern and east Africa, keen birdwatchers may want to arrive with two field guides, each describing birds

interdisciplinary approach of research, conservation and education to ensure the best chances of survival for Zambia's large carnivores.

With over 4,000 person days in the field in 2021 alone, they conducted over 7,500 patrols to check large carnivores for snare damage, vaccinated close to 3,000 domestic dogs against rabies, mapped the human encroachment patterns for all of Zambia and portions of seven neighbouring countries, conducted 335 educational safari drives for 2,500 community members, supported seven Zambian students through Wildlife Conservation degrees at university, and welcomed 31 Zambian women as conservation biology and vet trainees. From publishing scientific studies to engaging the community through radio programmes and collaborating with local partners, their work has been tremendously successful. In 2021, for the first time in over 15 years, no snared wild dogs were detected in the Luangwa, a record number of young conservation trainees joined the organisation and ZCP joined the African Conservation Leadership Network,

As a visitor to Zambia's national parks, you can join the effort. Of course, fundraising to support their conservation projects is always needed but, in addition, because cheetah and wild dog can be individually identified by their coat patterns, any photographs you take of these sightings in Zambia can be invaluable to research and conservation efforts. You can submit yours direct to ZCP through the email submission form on their website.

from one region, so that between them they will cover the full range of species encountered in the valley. Better still, bring a good guide to southern Africa's birds, like Newman's guide, and buy Aspinwall and Beel's Zambian guide locally (page 512). Alternatively, get hold of a single guide to the birds of sub-Saharan Africa or the more concise Collins Illustrated Checklist to the *Birds of Southern Africa*. Many bird guides, such as Newman's and Sasol's come with apps for smartphones and tablets, which can aid with easy identification and include bird calls.

Species of note include flocks of crowned cranes occurring on the marshes of the Nsefu Sector; the colonies of iridescent carmine bee-eaters that nest in sandy riverbanks in September and October; the African skimmers found along the river; and the giant eagle owls which are sometimes picked out by the spotlight on night drives.

The best time for birds is the summer: the rainy season. The birds' food supply is then at its most abundant, and the summer migrants are around. Just drive into the park during the rains and it becomes immediately apparent that both the vegetation and the birdlife are running riot. Dry plains have sprouted thick, green vegetation mirrored all around in shallow water. Flocks of egrets, herons and storks wade through this, around feeding geese and ducks.

Many species breed here, including storks that often form impressive colonies. There are several sites of tall trees in the Nsefu Sector which, when surrounded by shallow water, regularly become breeding colonies. The most amazing of these has half-a-dozen huge trees filled with nests of yellow-billed storks in their spectacular pink breeding plumage. This is one of the Luangwa's most remarkable sights.

CONSERVATION IN SOUTH LUANGWA

Hunting and poaching South Luangwa has always been Zambia's 'most favoured park'. Over the years it has been given a disproportionately large share of the resources allotted to all of the country's national parks. Many would argue that this has been to the detriment of the other parks, though it did enable it to fight the plague of commercial poaching, which hit the country in the 1980s, with some success. The poachers came for rhino horn – which is sold to make dagger-handles in the Middle East and Chinese medicines for the Far East – and, of course, for ivory.

Sadly the valley's thriving black rhino population was wiped out, with the last confirmed sightings in the Luangwa in 1987, and offically declared extinct in Zambia in 1998. (One or two sources suggest that a couple of individual animals may have been left in the wild, but this was probably just wishful thinking.) However, the good news is that a project to reintroduce black rhino into a specially protected area within the North Luangwa National Park is progressing well, with a small population having been established. This is a long-term project though, and it's likely to be decades before the South Luangwa sees its own rhino population again.

Fortunately, the valley's elephant populations didn't fare as badly as the rhino; they were only reduced. In recent years, thanks in part to the CITES ban on the ivory trade, they have bounced back – and South Luangwa, especially, has very healthy, large herds of relaxed elephants.

Today there is minimal poaching in the park, as demonstrated by the size of the animal populations, and certainly no lack of game. Only in the nervous elephant populations of North Luangwa does one get any echo of the poaching problems of the past.

Conservation South Luangwa (**e** rachel@slcszambia.org; **w** slcszambia.org) Formed in 2003 in order to support the Zambia Wildlife Authority and Community Resource Boards, Conservation South Luangwa (CSL) pulled together the work of

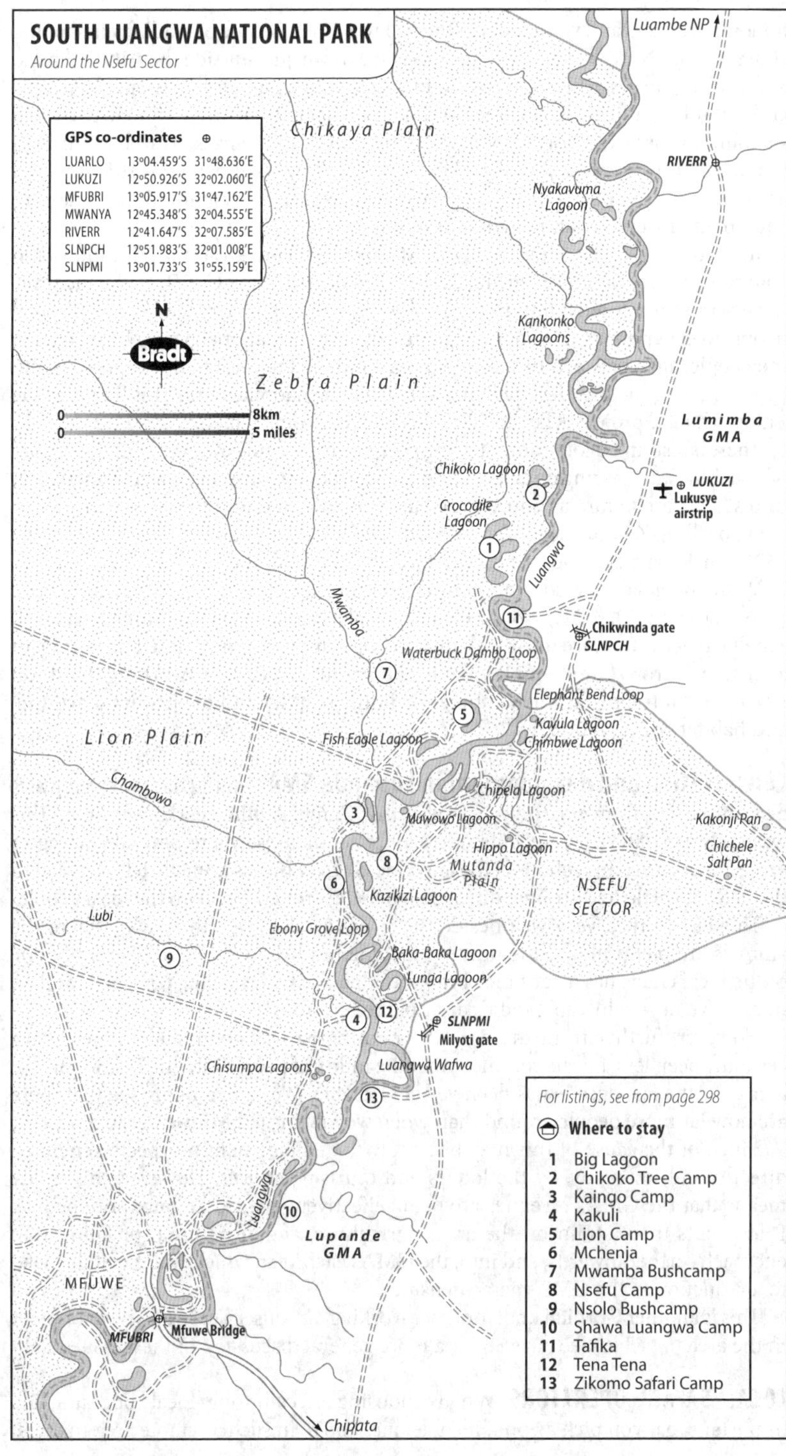
SOUTH LUANGWA NATIONAL PARK
Around the Nsefu Sector
GPS co-ordinates
LUARLO 13°04.459'S 31°48.636'E
LUKUZI 12°50.926'S 32°02.060'E
MFUBRI 13°05.917'S 31°47.162'E
MWANYA 12°45.348'S 32°04.555'E
RIVERR 12°41.647'S 32°07.585'E
SLNPCH 12°51.983'S 32°01.008'E
SLNPMI 13°01.733'S 31°55.159'E
N
Bradt
0 8km
0 5 miles
Luambe NP
Chikaya Plain
RIVERR
Nyakavuma Lagoon
Kankonko Lagoons
Zebra Plain
Lumimba GMA
Chikoko Lagoon
LUKUZI
Lukusye airstrip
Crocodile Lagoon
Luangwa
Mwamba
Chikwinda gate
SLNPCH
Waterbuck Dambo Loop
Elephant Bend Loop
Kavula Lagoon
Chimbwe Lagoon
Lion Plain
Fish Eagle Lagoon
Chambowo
Chipela Lagoon
Muwowo Lagoon
Kakonji Pan
Hippo Lagoon
Chichele Salt Pan
Mutanda Plain
NSEFU SECTOR
Kazikizi Lagoon
Lubi
Ebony Grove Loop
Baka-Baka Lagoon
Lunga Lagoon
SLNPMI
Milyoti gate
Chisumpa Lagoons
Luangwa Wafwa
Luangwa
Lupande GMA
MFUWE
MFUBRI
Mfuwe Bridge
Chipata
For listings, see from page 298
Where to stay
1 Big Lagoon
2 Chikoko Tree Camp
3 Kaingo Camp
4 Kakuli
5 Lion Camp
6 Mchenja
7 Mwamba Bushcamp
8 Nsefu Camp
9 Nsolo Bushcamp
10 Shawa Luangwa Camp
11 Tafika
12 Tena Tena
13 Zikomo Safari Camp

honorary rangers and volunteers in the valley at the frontline of wildlife and habitat conservation. Now with its own premises in Mfuwe, just outside the national park, and 120 employees, CSL continues to focus on managing the coexistence of people and wildlife, and protecting the wildlife and habitats of the national park and surrounding area. Supported by many of the camps in the park, as well as through membership fees and donations, CSL employs many local people – 105 of whom are community scouts – providing them with salaries, accommodation, rations, equipment, incentives and ongoing training.

In addition, it is actively involved in local conservation education and engagement programmes. During the tourism dearth of the COVID-19 pandemic, the organisation hired a hundred out-of-work guides and arranged for 3,300 local people to experience the wonder of game drives in the national park. Nearly 60% of the people, aged between three and 90 years old, had never had the opportunity to experience this before, despite living alongside the national park. This 'Experience. Enjoy. Protect.' project is key to CSL's engagement commitment.

There is also an ongoing anti-snaring programme to build awareness of the impact of poaching and snaring on the wildlife and the local environment; a veterinary unit to rescue snared animals and treat village animals, and an impressive five-strong anti-poaching K9 unit. They also introduced chilli fences and chilli patrollers (page 352) to help farmers whose crops are threatened by wildlife.

With financial rewards for joining community clean-ups, collecting snares (636 snares in 2020/21!), the provision of elephant-safe grain stores and chilli 'smelly fences' to ward off elephants, co-operative planting and harvesting of alternative crops, and employment opportunities, CSL is working hard on practical solutions to mitigate human–wildlife conflict and to encourage wildlife and habitat conservation.

Conservation and development in Lupande GMA South Luangwa has always been protected from poaching in a way that Zambia's other parks were not. This wasn't always 100% effective, but it was a lot better than elsewhere. Several years ago a project was started in sections of the Lupande GMA, which is immediately adjacent to the national park, to distribute direct cash benefits from the park to the local people.

This has worked very well beside the river (ie: alongside the park), where the animals are plentiful and the hunting income has been very good. Certainly one of the local chiefs has a very nice brick-built palace with satellite television and an impressive new twin-cab Land Cruiser parked in front.

However, further from the park the hunting isn't as good, and the fees have certainly been less. Locals comment that the influx of people into the Mfuwe Bridge area over the last decade has been very noticeable. We can certainly see that there are now far more people around than when we first visited Mfuwe decades ago.

Much of the cause of this may be simply the employment prospects generated directly, and indirectly, by the lodges and tourism services. However, this influx means that the GMA's revenues are being effectively divided among more people. It also puts more strain on the area's agriculture, and areas used for cultivation encroach further towards, and into, the GMAs each year, which will inevitably lead to a reduction in the GMA's game densities.

This is another Gordian knot for those working on conservation and development in the area to tackle. See page 33 for a more general discussion of these issues.

LOCAL SAFARI OPERATORS When choosing a camp or local operator, it's important that you pick a good, reliable one. You're in such a remote area that you

CHIPEMBELE WILDLIFE EDUCATION CENTRE

Chipembele (☏ 0216 246108; e info@chipembele.org; w chipembele.org; ⊕ CHIPEM 13°12.122's, 31°42.221'E) came about through the determination of Steve and Anna Tolan, who retired from the British police force in 1998 to invest in their dream of educating children in conservation matters. With a passion for African wildlife born of years of travelling and reading, they set about building an education centre, which was finally opened on the eastern bank of the Luangwa River, about 16km southwest of Mfuwe, in 2001. The centre has a large interpretive room complete with displays and exhibits, and visitors are welcome by prior arrangement.

Chipembele's work focuses on teaching through active involvement and fun. Children come for the day from schools all over the area, spending time en route spotting game that many of them may never have seen before.

From this central project, Anna has branched out into an extensive conservation outreach programme in the local schools, school improvement projects and a pupil sponsorship scheme, while Steve has taken on anti-poaching work and forestry protection. Rehabilitation of orphaned and injured animals is a further aspect of their work, together with an active involvement from other conservation organisations in the area.

can't afford to have problems. One safeguard is to seek advice from a reputable, independent overseas tour operator. For all except the budget camps, you should find that booking your trip through them will be cheaper than booking directly with the camps.

Perhaps also check out Expert Africa's website, w expertafrica.com (even if you're not arranging a trip with them), as we will be posting updates there for all to see. Many of the smaller one- or two-camp operations are excellent. Meanwhile, here are the contact details and selected snippets of background information on a few of the higher-profile safari operators, in alphabetical order:

The Bushcamp Company ☏ 0216 246041; m 0978 770055; e info@bushcampcompany.com; w bushcampcompany.com. Formed in 2000, The Bushcamp Company is still run by its main founding director, Andy Hogg, despite having been bought by a US-based billionaire philanthropist, Paul Allen, in 2010.

Originally an amalgamation of 2 very old bushcamps (Chamilandu & Kuyenda), 2 new ones (Bilimungwe & Chindeni) & the larger Mfuwe Lodge, which remains the hub of their operations, The Bushcamp Company has continued to expand its operations. 2 further bushcamps were created in the south of the park – Kapamba in 2005 & Zungulila in 2008 – &, more recently, an exclusive-use property (The Director's House) & small lodge (KuKaya) which opened in 2022.

Bushcamp Company has carved out a niche by offering small, remote, high-quality bushcamps in the southern section of the park, with a solid base in Mfuwe. Each camp is different & each offers day & night drives in the park, although walking is the main focus at several of the camps. Note that it's possible to walk from Chamilandu to Chindeni to Bilimungwe to Kapamba to Zungulila.

Chiawa Safaris ☏ 0211 261588; m 0977 767433; e res@chiawa.com; w chiawa.com. Chiawa Safaris are renowned for their excellent Lower Zambezi camps, Chiawa & Old Mondoro (page 258 & 261), having pioneered tourism in the region back in 1989. In 2020, they brought their skills & vision into South Luangwa in partnership with Chichele Safaris to open Puku Ridge & more recently Chichele Presidential Lodge. Both of these Luangwa camps have been stunningly reimagined & now operate with the slick, high standards of accommodation, guiding & service evident in all the Chiawa camps.

Green Safaris m 0979 312 766; e reservations@greensafaris.com; w greensafaris.com. Following the success of their eco-camps in Kafue National Park (page 414), Green Safaris opened their first camp in South Luangwa in 2021: Shawa Luangwa Camp. Unlike the personal ownership common in the valley, Green Safaris is owned by a small group of genuinely ethical, Dutch investors, headed by Vincent Kouwenhoven & Daniel Allcock. Determined to bring true sustainability to safari camps, the entire camps run on 100% solar energy & vehicles are all electric, making for wonderfully quiet game drives. With great staff & community empowerment schemes, they're a new-style force for good.

Kafunta Safaris 0977 182993; e bookings@kafuntasafaris.com; w kafuntasafaris.com. Kafunta Safaris own a trio of camps in South Luangwa: Kafunta River Lodge, Island Bush Camp & Three Rivers. Owned & run by Ron & Anke Cowan, an Australian-German couple who've been resident in the valley since 1990, they offer driving & walking safaris from their base on the edge of the national park. Kafunta has been instrumental in promoting local boys' education through the Mfuwe junior football league: no school, no football!

Remote Africa Safaris 0216 246185; e reservations@remoteafrica.com; w remoteafrica.com. Founded by John & Carol Coppinger, Remote Africa Safaris is a small, high-quality operator with truly innovative ideas, & a keen focus on sustainability, guiding & classic safari experiences. They run excellent camps across 3 parks: Tafika & the Chikoko Trails walking camps (Chikoko, Crocodile & Big Lagoon) in South Luangwa, & Mwaleshi & Takwela in the North Park, & Shoebill Island Camp in the Bangweulu Wetlands. John used to run Wilderness Trails in the valley, & is regarded as one of the most experienced guides in the region. His camp guides include Bryan Jackson & Isaac Zulu, who are experts in their own right. John is one of the very few people to have canoed the length of the Mwaleshi & Luangwa rivers & was the first to run river safaris in the park. With the longest serving team in the Valley – from kitchen hands to guides – Remote Africa is a formidable group. This is unquestionably one of the Valley's very best operators, & with the addition of John & Carol's daughter Jennifer & her husband Nick to the management team, the future of Remote Africa looks great.

Robin Pope Safaris 0957 090441; e info@robinpopesafaris.net; w robinpopesafaris.net. This excellent & highly reliable company was founded by Robin Pope, who was raised in Zambia, trained by Norman Carr, & is one of the country's top wildlife guides. His English wife, Jo, was the first woman to qualify as a walking guide in the valley – but it is her efficiency with the marketing & business side of the operation that make her legendary. Together with a very good team they built up what is probably the valley's most complex set of camps & trips, including Tena Tena, Nkwali & Nsefu, river safaris, & a range of different walking safaris (including some true mobiles & various 'special-interest' safaris in & beyond the valley). In 2010 Robin & Jo handed over the helm of RPS to a Malawi-based Dutch couple, Ton & Margeaux do Rooy – although Robin continues to lead a few interesting safaris, & Jo's marketing skills are in demand, not least by the Zambia Tourism Board.

Shenton Safaris 0216 246064; e info@kaingo.com; w shentonsafaris.com. Established by third-generation conservationist Derek Shenton & jointly run with his Australian wife, Jules, a zoologist & keen photographer, Shenton Safaris runs Kaingo Camp & Mwamba, both lovely safari camps in a great game area with a strong focus on good guiding & wildlife photography. Although Derek & Jules are now raising their family in Lusaka, they frequently visit both the camps & their boho-chic style & grounded conservation vision is very much in evidence. Notable is the value they place on using game hides to view & photograph wildlife unobtrusively, & a keenness to organise 3 activities a day for those who wish to maximise their safari time. The Shenton family also owns Forest Inn, near Mkushi (page 333).

Time+Tide (formerly Norman Carr Safaris) South Africa +27 60 642 4004; e info@timeandtide.com; w timeandtideafrica.com. In 2018, Norman Carr Safaris joined the Time+Tide collection, along with Chongwe in the Lower Zambezi, King Lewanika in Liuwa Plains & Chinzombo in South Luangwa. Known for exceptional bush knowledge, Norman Carr's was a pioneer of walking safaris, & 4 bushcamps – Nsolo, Luwi, Kakuli & Mchenja – have remained true to these roots. If you want to walk between different bushcamps, going from one to the next every few days, then the walk down the dry Luwi River is difficult to beat. A more recent addition to the

Time+Tide portfolio is the stylish Chinzombo, which brought levels of luxury not previously seen in the park when it opened & continues to set a very high bar for high-end safaris. All are excellent camps & Time+Tide rightly retains one of the best reputations of any company in the valley. It is currently one of only 2 companies to organise regular river safaris in the Green Season & the only camp to accept children of all ages in all of its camps (though naturally not on all activities, such as walking).

GETTING THERE

By air The majority of visitors to South Luangwa fly in to Mfuwe (page 275). During the main safari season, from June to the end of October, it is one of the easiest places in Zambia to reach by air.

By road Whether you're staying inside the national park or in a camp on its periphery, the route to South Luangwa will take you straight through Mfuwe village. Everything is very clearly signposted. After the fuel station, there's a tar road to the left towards Kafunta, Nkwali, Chinzombo and the lodges and camps on the southern side of Mfuwe. The turning to various lodges outside the park, including Marula Lodge and Track and Trail, is a little further on the right, and after that there's a turning to the left to Flatdogs Camp. At the Mfuwe Bridge (⊕ MFUBRI 13°5.917'S, 31°47.162'E) over the Luangwa River, you'll need to stop to pay park fees at the DNPW office on the left – watch out for the baboons that congregate around the office here!

Approaching from the south Most self-drivers will approach South Luangwa on the all-weather, tar road from Chipata, while the more adventurous may prefer to tackle the scenic route from Petauke. Both of these routes are essentially heading for Mfuwe and driving directions are detailed on page 276.

Approaching from the north Driving to South Luangwa from the north, Luambe or Mpika is a totally different story: it requires a small expedition of at least two well-equipped 4x4 vehicles, driven by experienced bush drivers with a high degree of self-reliance. Ensure you are travelling with a reliable GPS, like Tracks4Africa (page 103) and perhaps monitor online forums such as iOverlander (**w** ioverlander.com) for the most recent road conditions experienced by 4x4 drivers.

From Mpika via the Corridor Road and '05' Driving south from Mpika, down into the Luangwa Valley between the North and South parks, and then crossing the Mupamadzi into South Luangwa, is possible only in the dry season – but it's probably the trickiest of the ways to get here. See the section on getting to Luambe National Park, entitled *From Mpika via the Corridor Road,* on page 328, for the start of the route. After turning east from the Great North Road (⊕ TUBATE 12°6.421'S, 31°15.727'E) about 40km south of Mpika, you will need to follow the road in a southeasterly direction for 37km before you pass Nthunta scout camp (⊕ NTHUNT 12°19.447'S, 31°32.232'E) and then drop over the escarpment and eventually reach the Mutinondo River. About 8.8km after crossing this, there's a left turning which leads to Nabwalya village and the Luangwa River (though the pontoon across the river is no longer operational).

To reach the national park, don't turn left to Nabwalya but continue straight on, then after a further 7.3km you will reach the Chifungwe gate (⊕ CHIFUNG 12°26.061'S, 31°42.263'E), just before the Mupamadzi River. This is the boundary

NORMAN CARR AND THE ORIGINS OF LUANGWA'S SAFARIS

The success of safaris in the Luangwa Valley is due in no small measure to one man: Norman Carr. Originally a ranger within the newly formed game reserves in the valley, Carr was quick to spot the potential of tourism as a lucrative source of income for the park. Although originally an advocate of hunting safaris, Carr soon recognised that there was an alternative – and one that didn't involve hunting down and killing the local fauna.

By 1950, Carr had persuaded Senior Chief Nsefu, paramount Chief of the Kunda people in the Luangwa Valley, to set aside some of their land to establish a private reserve on the eastern bank of the Luangwa River. (Interestingly, a reliable local historian maintains that the colonial provincial commissioner was nervous about this. He feared that ultimately the local people would lose both their land and their access to collect salt at the pans in the centre of the Nsefu Sector. His concerns proved valid when, 20 years later, the Nsefu Sector was combined into the national park.) In partnership with the chief, Carr founded Nsefu Camp in 1952. The camp was close to the present-day Nsefu Camp (it's still visible on the Nsefu Luangwa Wafwa), though it was subsequently moved when the river changed its course.

In 1961, Carr set up his own wilderness safaris, based out of another camp, Kapani. This had been established in 1960, when he was warden of the Luangwa Valley, and it was here that he stayed with Big Boy and Little Boy, the two lions that he famously kept as companions. Kapani Camp lay just north of the Nsefu Sector, close to today's Tafika. In 1961, Carr leased what later became known as Old Lion Camp, close to Kapani Camp but on the opposite (western) bank of the Luangwa River.

In those days the whole operation was basic, with Carr wading across the Luangwa every morning to fetch his clients from Old Lion Camp to take them on a walking safari. Further camps were tried by the lower Kapamba River in 1963, and the Mwaleshi in the north of the reserve, but neither was commercially viable. The venture to Mwaleshi ended with the unfortunate death of one of the guides, Peter Hankin, who was killed by a lioness.

Carr was more successful with his next venture. In 1965, he started walking safaris out of Chibembe Camp, just north of the Chibembe/Luangwa confluence (close to the now-closed Zebra Plains Camp). With this as a hub, he established a circuit of several small pole-and-grass bushcamps, with his clients walking from camp to camp. Nine years later, he built Chibembe Lodge on the east bank; as this was larger and built of permanent materials, it had to be sited outside the park. With this as his main base, he continued to use the old Chibembe Camp as a walking bushcamp. This modus operandi of a number of small, temporary walking bushcamps working like satellites for one more permanent lodge is still used by several of the valley's more traditional operations today.

Carr's clientele in those early days came mainly from the UK, with a few from Southern Rhodesia (now Zimbabwe), South Africa and America. The expense of travelling to and from Zambia ensured that such safaris were a very expensive, elite activity.

Two years after Chibembe Lodge, Mwamba Bushcamp was constructed on the East Mwamba River, close to present-day Crocodile Bushcamp. This was the first exclusive bushcamp, a place where clients could hire the whole six-bed camp and have their own vehicle and guide. Other camps and lodges followed, including Chikoko and Kasansanya (1974). In 1977, Carr founded Chinzombo, on the same site as the present day Chinzombo, which could be reached all year (Chibembe had always been inaccessible during the rains); Kakuli was built in 1984, and, finally, Kapani Safari Lodge in 1986.

NORMAN CARR'S LEGACY Nsefu Camp was the Valley's first camp for photographic safaris: safaris that focus on wildlife viewing as opposed to wildlife hunting. From the outset, one of its founding principles was that the indigenous people, the traditional owners of the wildlife, should benefit from the visitors. This mirrors the approach to conservation and development that has been recently adopted by most of those working in this sector. (In the jargon, it is now called 'community-based natural-resource management'.) Norman Carr was a conservationist far ahead of his time.

Not only did Carr start a number of these camps in the Valley, he also implemented education projects, and worked alongside and helped to train many of those who are now the valley's most experienced guides. These include:

- **Robin Pope** came into the valley in 1976, working with Carr at Chibembe and then Nsefu Camp. In 1986, Pope took over Tena Tena, which was established around 1983 as one of Nsefu's walking bushcamps, and branched off to start what grew into perhaps the Valley's most successful safari operation, Robin Pope Safaris. Pope stepped back from the day-to-day running of the safari company and camps in 2010, although he still guides some specialist safaris to Liuwa Plains, where he is a director of African Parks Liuwa.
- **John Coppinger** started as a guide at Nsefu in 1984, while Pope was manager. He managed Nsefu for a few years, and then became general manager of Wilderness Trails, which ran Chibembe, Nsefu, Big Lagoon and a travel agency in Lusaka at the time. He left in 1994 to start his own operation, Remote Africa Safaris, based out of Tafika and specialising in walking safaris. His daughter Jennifer has now joined him at the helm, alongside her husband Nick, to continue their guiding excellence.
- **Isaac Zulu** originally studied as an agriculturalist but was trained by Carr from 1974. He guided in the valley for many years, including at Chibembe in the late 1980s. Eventually he left the valley in 1989 and worked with Tongabezi in Livingstone, returning to the valley in 2001 with Chilongozi Safaris (now defunct). He's currently guiding again with Coppinger at Remote Africa Safaris.
- **Abraham Banda** was trained by Carr in 1989, having come straight from Kapani School (set up by Norman to offer local children the chance of a good education). Banda is now one of the leaders of the new generation of Luangwa guides, managing safari operations at Norman Carr Safaris from its new flagship camp Chinzombo. In addition, he runs a very successful charity to support Yoseffe School, and a number of other community projects.

The way that the Luangwa Valley's safari business has created opportunities for an increasing number of locally born people like Banda, both in education and tourism, is part and parcel of why Norman Carr started safaris in the Luangwa over 60 years ago. Perhaps his greatest legacy is not the wealth of high-quality walking safaris here, but the impressively strong conservation and development ethics that now underpin virtually all of the better, long-standing safari operations in the valley.

to South Luangwa National Park, reached about 69km from the Great North Road. The community campsite here (⊕ MUNYAM 12°22.410'S, 31°35.779'E) has unfortunately closed, but you can still free camp here, and it's a beautiful spot. Crossing the Mupamadzi (which should only be attempted when low) is tricky, but then it's a simple, if long, journey to head due south.

About 3km after the Mupamadzi crossing you reach a junction (⊕ MUNYAM 12°26.778'S, 31°43.791'E): to the right is a seldom-used road that skirts round the western boundary of the park before ending up near Bilimungwe Bushcamp 140km later, the road quality is poor and there's nowhere to stop off along the way; to the left is the '05' road (see below) which is also little used but will take you right across the heart of the park, skirting the western side of Zebra Pans. About 55km after the Mupamadzi, you will reach the deep sand of the Luwi River (⊕ 05LUWI 12°56.381'S, 31°45.468'E) near Nsolo Bushcamp, and then some 10km after that you join the network of all-weather roads in the Mfuwe area, just north of the 'Big Baobab' and Mfuwe Lodge (see map, page 284).

From Luambe See page 327 for details of this route in reverse, and backtrack.

LESSONS IN BUSH TRAVEL

In early November 2002, two German visitors borrowed a brand-new 4x4 to explore the South Luangwa. The car was a small, low-slung saloon, one of the latest models and very much state-of-the-art. It had on-board computers to control much of the vehicle, from the engine to the suspension.

Coming from Mpika, they entered the Luangwa Valley by the tricky 'corridor' road, successfully reaching the remote Chifungwe game scouts' camp. They planned to take the road known locally as the '05', which passes near the old site of Zebra Pans Bushcamp, before eventually reaching a crossroads near Nsolo Bushcamp, and then the heart of the Mfuwe area. It's a dead straight road (with a bearing of about 5°), mostly through thick bush. It's used very little, and was sure to be very quiet then as all the valley's bushcamps close at the end of October.

All went smoothly until they were crossing the Mupamadzi River, about 3km after the scouts' camp. Halfway across, they got stuck. Then the driver realised that he hadn't locked his hubs (some 4x4 vehicles require one to physically turn a switch on the wheels), so he got out in the river and turned the hubs. Surprisingly, they managed to drive to the other side.

All seemed well and the pair continued south, but 25km further along the road, the car died. Water had got into the wiring; the car's computer had shut down and with it the engine. If the car had broken down in the river, the two men would have been only 3km from the scouts' camp. Now they were 28km away. As is normally wise, they decided to wait with their car for a passing vehicle to summon help. Unfortunately, 24 hours later, not one vehicle had passed by. The '05' is one of many bush roads in Africa which may see only a handful of vehicles per year; just because it's marked on the maps, it is a mistake to assume that it's used frequently!

The men were starting to feel desperate. They had told nobody local what their plans were; nobody was expecting them anywhere. Nobody would raise an alarm. All they had with them was some fruit juice, water, butter and cheese, and the water was running out fast. They decided to walk to find help – southwards towards Mfuwe. After 25km, the elder of the two men, sore and tired, could walk

GETTING AROUND

In your own vehicle South Luangwa's network of roads is not as extensive as you might expect. A few all-weather roads (mostly graded gravel) have been built in the park around the Mfuwe area – accessible over the main bridge into the park. There's also an isolated network around the camps owned by the Bushcamp Company, in the south of the park. These are the only roads that can be relied upon during the wet season.

Elsewhere, the park has seasonally passable roads that are (optimistically) marked on some of the maps. Such tracks follow both banks of the Luangwa, north and south of Mfuwe, and a few penetrate westwards into the park. In the areas near camps, there are numerous 'loop' roads, which leave these main tracks and return to them. These are just side roads for game viewing, and trying to be precise about their position is pointless – they are usually made simply by the passage of a few vehicles, and will disappear again very swiftly once the vehicles stop and the rains come.

Note that if you are driving your own vehicle around the park then you are limited to being in the park from dawn to dusk. You are not allowed to stay in and

no further. They agreed that he should stop there, while the younger, fitter man would continue.

Then their fortunes turned: it rained. The older man, who had been sitting in temperatures of 43°C during the day, took off his clothes and lay on the ground to soak up the water. At 16.00 the next day, he was discovered at the side of the road by a scout patrol. He was naked and approaching delirium; the scouts estimated that he was about 3 to 4 hours from death.

Meanwhile, the younger man had continued walking through the night, but lost the main road while avoiding a small herd of elephants. Miraculously, in the morning he stumbled across Nsolo Bushcamp. Being November, everything had just closed down for the rains, but a rummage through the bins uncovered tin cans, while the dry river nearby yielded water where the elephants had dug up the bed with their tusks. Boiling the water in the cans on an open fire, the man felt better. The next morning, the scout patrol who had found his friend followed his tracks to Nsolo, and found him there. He was relatively well, although concerned by the two lionesses who had been watching him closely.

Both men were very lucky and now safe – but what of the car? It took 9 hours to tow it northwards and back across the river. Then it rained for two days, and the river flooded – making the road impassable. Anyone who knows the area would have told them that November was a crazy time to drive across that river.

Meanwhile, a mechanic flew up to attempt repairs. Plugging his laptop into the car, he restarted its computer and had it working in minutes. Apparently it just needed resetting! Later the men learnt that it would have been possible to shut down the computer entirely.

There are many lessons to draw from this, but the big picture is clear. Unless you're an experienced old Africa hand with a good network of local contacts, unless you take good advice, and drive a vehicle that you know, then driving yourself around the more remote corners of Zambia is asking for trouble. Just because this book indicates GPS positions and bush tracks, it does not mean that these routes are suitable for drivers who aren't experienced in remote African travel.

drive around after dark; only local safari companies have licences to conduct night drives. (Note also that the Nkwali pontoon marked on many maps is not for use by private vehicles.)

Without a vehicle If you have organised your camps and lodges in advance then you can relax. A vehicle will be waiting to take you to camp, and there's no need to think ahead. If you haven't organised this before you arrive, then you may be limited to a handful of budget options based in the Mfuwe area. If your budget is higher, then you might consider taking advantage of the cell reception at the airport to phone a few of the more upmarket camps (or ask one of the safari vehicles usually waiting outside the airport to radio for you) to see if they have any space left. This is unusual, and don't expect bargains (you won't find any), but it is a real waste to get all the way here and then not make the most of the park. So if you can, splash out on the best place that you can afford. If you'd like to rent a vehicle or discuss a responsible, budget-friendly game drive (guided or not), contact Personal Touch:

The Personal Touch m 0978 459965; e info@personaltouchsafaris.com; w personaltouchsafaris.com. Owner Ben Koobs rents out 4x4 Toyotas (no mileage restrictions) for self-driving in the park, with the option of adding a 2-person roof tent & camping kit. They also offer game drives within or around the park, with an accompanying guide & spotter. Airport/lodge transfers within the South Luangwa NP & trips to Kawaza & other community projects are also possible. *US$150/day 4x4 Toyota rental; US$100/1 game drive; US$225/all-day drive inc guide, spotter & fuel, exc park fees.*

Maps Accurate, up-to-date maps of the South Luangwa are difficult to come by but a couple may be available in Lusaka. One showing South Luangwa and Luambe national parks was compiled for the national tourist board, and is useful in giving the general scheme of the area's roads. Otherwise the information on its reverse side is fairly dated, and so not very valuable.

A second, very different map concentrates on just the South Luangwa National Park. This was produced in 1989 using aid donations and shows the landscape and vegetation in considerable scientific detail; it's a scholarly work. Its reverse side details the various land systems in the area: the different combinations of land form, rock, soil and vegetation in the park. This is a fascinating map, but the camps and roads are long out of date, and will be of very little use for navigation.

In the unlikely event that you need to navigate yourself around the park, the *Hupe Zambia Road Map* includes a detailed map of the South Luangwa National Park and is best used as a physical back-up for a GPS loaded with the Tracks4Africa (w tracks4africa.co.za) GPS maps of the area or, better still, with the excellent Tracks4Africa app, which would also be essential for visitors to Luambe or Lukusuzi.

WHERE TO STAY We've seen the park several ways over the years – from hitchhiking in and camping, self-driving around the park, and flying in with advanced bookings at lodges and small bushcamps. Without question, much of the Luangwa's magic is in being guided by some of Africa's best guides – in an open vehicle or, especially, on foot. They know this area, and its flora and fauna, like the back of their hands and it's an absolute privilege to share in their knowledge and experience.

Upmarket camps and lodges Most of South Luangwa's camps aim at upmarket visitors from overseas. Given the park's remote location, this is not surprising. They incur great difficulties and costs in communicating, organising supplies and actually getting their clients into and around the valley. Add to this the fact that the climate and environment mean that most camps can only operate for five or six months of the year, after which they pack up, returning to rebuild their camps after every rainy season. Thus, they have some very good reasons to be costly.

The rates at these camps, generally including all meals and activities, and often your bar bill and park fees too, are around US$500–1,200 per person per day. Most offer a special 'safari rate', typically about 5–10% cheaper than the normal rate, if you stay in camps run by just one operator for seven nights or more. This can be very convenient and is certainly recommended. It will provide a welcome continuity while you visit totally different camps. Such combinations include Chinzombo and Time+Tide's bushcamps; Robin Pope Safaris' Nkwali, Tena Tena and Nsefu; Tafika and Remote Africa's walking bushcamps, not to mention their camps in North Luangwa and Bangweulu Swamps; and Mfuwe Lodge and the camps of the Bushcamp Company. Equally, Puku Ridge can be combined with Chiawa Safaris' camps in Lower Zambezi with a similar discount, and Green Safaris offer combinations with their Kafue and Livingstone camps.

A few camps offer discounts in the quieter parts of the season if you are a resident of Zambia, but overall the best safari deals are usually available from overseas operators (page 92) who specialise in Zambia; their volumes of business give the most experienced of these operators access to significant discounts.

Note that although many of the camps cost around a similar level, their atmospheres and styles differ significantly – so take time to understand their differences and choose carefully. We have included detailed descriptions specifically to help you decide on what is best for your particular needs. The valley's camps, in alphabetical order, include:

Bilimungwe Bushcamp [map, page 281] (4 chalets) Contact Bushcamp Company, page 291. ⊕ BILIMU 13°23.295'S, 31°34.198'E. Some 46km (as the eagle flies) southeast of Mfuwe (3hrs drive), Bilimungwe stands about 100m from the Luangwa, slightly upstream of its confluence with the Kapamba River. Meaning 'chameleon' in the local Kamanga tongue, the camp dates back to 1996, though was completely rebuilt in 2011 with modern interiors, while keeping enough rustic reed-and thatch design choices for it to still suit the environment & retain its bushcamp vibe. The central area has been beautifully designed as a raised wooden deck & a tall thatch roof intertwined around the trunks & branches of natal mahogany & winterthorn trees. Nest-like, cushion-covered wicker chairs, a bar & candlelit dining table occupy the main space, while on a lower deck colourful scatter cushions enliven the bench seating & just a stone's throw away there's a sandy firepit in the open. Overlooking a trio of permanent waterholes, it's a wonderful spot to relax & watch wildlife.

Very comfortable thatched chalets have walls of cane & reeds topped with mosquito gauze. Concertina doors open on to an extensive deck, allowing waterhole views from the beds, & giving the huge rooms a light & airy feel. With plentiful wood incorporated into the design, plus an ingenious stone-enclosed outdoor shower in addition to the indoor bathroom, the rooms manage to feel both modern & natural in design. The camp mixes walking safaris & game drives, with some flexibility built into guests' choice of activities, & many choose to combine a stay at Bilimungwe with other Bushcamp Company camps, some of them within walking distance. Specially adapted photographic vehicles are also available. *US$740–935 pp FBA, inc bar, laundry, airport & inter-camp transfers, park & conservation fees. Children over 12 years.* ⌚ *mid-May–Dec.* 👑👑👑

Chamilandu Bushcamp [map, page 281] (3 chalets) Contact Bushcamp Company, page 291. ⊕ CHAMIL 13°19.023'S, 31°38.526'E. About 2hrs' drive southwest of Mfuwe, Chamilandu is set up as a bushcamp for walking safaris, & is one of the more rustic properties in this area of the park. The camp is set on the banks of the Luangwa facing the N'Chindeni Hills, which look beautiful in the late afternoon sun & the rooms, set on high wooden decks, take full advantage of the views. The reed & thatch chalets are smartly furnished with king-size or twin ¾ beds under mosquito nets, and are completely open to the front. En-suite bathrooms have open-air showers, dbl washbasins & flush toilets. At night, there's solar-powered lanterns but little else to detract from the moon & stars.

The camp's central area is close to the river, while a short walk brings you to a smart, thatched hide overlooking 1 of the 7 oxbow lagoons that surround the camp; a great spot for lunch or to watch game. Game drives are offered as an alternative to the usual walks. There is only one resident guide, but several floating guides who work for Bushcamp Company bring some flexibility to the activities. Walking between Chamilandu, Chindeni, Bilimungwe & Zungulila – with your luggage taken ahead for you – can usually be arranged as there's only about 10km between each camp. *US$740–935 pp FBA, inc bar, laundry, airport & inter-camp transfers, park & conservation fees. Children over 12 years.* ⌚ *Jun–Nov.* ♛♛♛

Chichele Presidential Lodge [map, page 284] (10 suites) Contact Chiawa Safaris, page 291; ⊕ CHICHE 13°10.008'S, 31°42.605'E. Chichele was built in 1972 as President Kaunda's private lodge in the Luangwa. High up atop President Hill, it's in an area where the Luangwa River starts to come much closer to the escarpment, & it's got an incredible view! Having passed from the government through several private safari operators, it's now in the very experienced hands of Chiawa Safaris, who were diligently renovating the lodge into something spectacular at the time of writing. Given their outstanding success at neighbouring Puku Ridge, we are excited to see this luxurious reimagining. Prices will doubtless be high; but service & décor will match. ♛♛♛♛♛

Chikoko Trails (2 camps) Contact Remote Africa Safaris, page 292. True walking camps, accessed on foot, Chikoko Trails comprises 2 delightfully bijou bushcamps: Chikoko Tree Camp & Big Lagoon. Slightly upstream of their parent camp, Tafika, & on the opposite bank of the Luangwa, this is around the spot where David Livingstone crossed the Luangwa in 1866 & where Norman Carr first set up a walking camp in the park. Little seems to have changed since either men were here: it remains a beautiful corner of the valley with excellent game densities.

Being in a wilderness area, all your luggage & supplies are carried into & between camps by porters. From Tafika, this means a brief drive along the river, followed by a quick canoe crossing & then a gentle wilderness walk with your guide & scout.

The camps themselves are very simple, reed-built structures, thoughtfully constructed & with comfortable beds & hot showers. Food, cooked by the chef in a ground oven (do check this out), is impressive & delicious. But to focus on the camps themselves is to somewhat miss the point; Remote Africa's guides are among the valley's most experienced – so though simple, these are among the valley's very best bushcamps in wonderful wilderness areas. *US$535–610 Jun–Oct; all FBA, inc bar, laundry, current park fees, airport & inter-camp transfers. Sgl suppt US$300.* ♛♛♛♛

Big Lagoon [map, page 289] (3 chalets) Further from the river, about a 40min walk, Big Lagoon opened in 2022 in a wonderful location. Tucked on the edge of an ebony forest, overlooking a large lagoon, the neat, en-suite reed chalets have open-front, picture 'windows' to make the most of the vista. There's a simple lounge/dining room & a great deck cantilevered over the lagoon – a perfect spot to sit, binoculars in hand, & watch the birds and wildlife coming to the water. ⌚ *Jun–Oct.*

Chikoko Tree Camp [map, page 289] (3 chalets) Only about 10mins' walk from the Luangwa, beside the small, seasonal Chikoko Channel, Chikoko's simple, grass-walled chalets are more like tree houses. Reached by wooden stairs, & raised about 3m off the ground, their bedrooms have low sides & are open to the front, providing a good vantage point for spotting wildlife but with the height giving the nervous an added sense of security. There's a canvas shade above the beds to keep off the sun & any rain, & downstairs is a private flush toilet & shower (hot on request). ⌚ *25 May–31 Oct.*

Chindeni Bushcamp [map, page 281] (4 tents) Contact Bushcamp Company, page 291. ⊕ CHINDE 13°22.056'S, 31°36.426'E. About 7km further upstream than Bilimungwe, Chindeni is also about 3hrs' drive south of Mfuwe. It stands on the banks of a large, semi-permanent lagoon, which stretches away from it on both sides. The main river is about 1km away, & in the near distance rise the N'Chindeni Hills, overlooking the park's eastern boundary.

Chindeni's large, well-spaced tents are raised up on hardwood decks, hidden in the vegetation. They're lined with soft-brown canvas, rising to 3 pinnacles, like a trio of miniature big tops. Beneath the centre are twin or dbl beds, flanked by an en-suite shower, toilet & twin basins; & open basketwork chairs with cushioned footstools. Outside, twin hammocks on a private shaded veranda invite you to laze away the afternoon. It's all very light: lots of polished, light wood & neutral fabrics give the rooms a modern, minimalist feeling. At the heart of the camp a sturdy split-level deck overlooks the lagoon, furnished with low wicker armchairs & a stylish fire circle. Ebony & tamarind trees provide shade, while shelter for the separate dining & lounge areas comes from 2 large canvas-topped 'gazebos' held up by heavy poles & featuring lovely, natural chandeliers.

It's usual to combine time here with stays at Bilimungwe, or the company's other camps. Here, too, day & night game drives & walks are available, with some flexibility over activities. *US$740–935 pp FBA, inc bar, laundry, airport & inter-camp transfers, park & conservation fees. Children over 12 years.* ⌚ *May–Dec.* ♛♛♛

Chinzombo [map, page 284] (6 villas) Contact Time+Tide, page 292. ⊕ 13°6.334'S, 31°45.733'E. Situated just outside of the park, overlooking a wide bend in the Luangwa River, Chinzombo is a contemporary camp with a long history. Opened in its current form in 2013, it's built on the site of one of the valley's first safari camps, from which Chinzombo gets its name.

This latest incarnation of Chinzombo was designed by top safari camp architects Silvio Reach & Lesley Corstens, who designed some of Botswana's top camps as well as the iconic North Island in the Seychelles. The design is decadent & luxurious, aligning it more closely with the boutique styling of Botswana's safari camps rather than the more understated style of many in Zambia.

The minimalist structure of the main area is comprised of a metal frame & white-washed wooden decking, cleverly built around existing trees, leaving the sides completely open. Lots of leather, canvas & wooden fittings in the lounge & bar give the camp a very colonial atmosphere, but there are also plenty of modern amenities such as a Nespresso coffee machine & a swimming pool towards the river. A firepit perched on the river bank provides a great spot to eat breakfast & watch the sun rise.

Chinzombo has 6 spacious villas, one of which has 2 bedrooms for families, which closely match the design & décor of the main area. They have king-size or twin beds complete with full-size mosi nets & 'evening breeze' AC units, which quietly & effectively cool the air around the beds. Through a curtain is an open-plan en suite with a shower (hot & cold), twin basins, & a large bath. Mains electricity allows amenities in the rooms such as a mini-bar, tea- & coffee-making station & Wi-Fi. The gauze panels at the front of the villas can be rolled up, leading to a private deck with a plunge pool & ample comfortable seating.

Private guiding is included as standard for each booking, giving complete freedom over your choice of activities; these include drives & walks in the park, privately accessed by a short boat trip across the river from camp.

Chinzombo has overseen the training of several local women & offers a range of spa treatments in the privacy of your own villa. This adds to the comfort & luxury of the lodge, making it a good place to end your safari, usually after spending time at Time+Tide's bushcamps. Do be aware that the area around Chinzombo is much busier with other vehicles compared to the more remote areas of the park. *US$1,270–1,750 pp sharing FBA inc standard bar, laundry, airport & inter-camp transfers, exc spa. Children all ages welcome.* ⌚ *All year.* ♛♛♛♛–♛♛♛♛♛

Island Bush Camp [map, page 281] (5 chalets) Contact Kafunta River Safaris (page 292). About 2hrs' drive south of Kafunta, Island Bush Camp stands on the banks of the Luangwa River, in the remote south of the park, where the river no longer forms the border of the national park but rather runs through it. Guests are normally driven from Kafunta, along a dirt track, a journey that can take 2–3 hrs. With its twin chalets raised up on platforms, reed walls open to the river & en suites with bucket showers, it offers a truly rustic add-on to Kafunta, in an area primarily reserved for walking. The 'kitchen safari' is part of the bushcamp experience here, & it's always impressive to see how 'bush chefs' manage so wonderfully with minimal equipment & only a basic wood-burning stove. *US$615 pp sharing, FBA, inc drinks, park fees.* ⌚ *25 May–Oct.* ♛♛♛

Kafunta River Lodge [map, page 284] (10 chalets) 📞 0977 182993; **e** bookings@kafuntasafaris.com; **w** kafuntasafaris.com. ⊕ KAFUNT 13°9.785'S, 31°44.360'E.

On a spacious site beside the river, Kafunta was built from scratch in 1998 by a team including Ron & Anke Cowan, who now own & run the camp. Its central dining/bar area under a huge thatched roof is very impressive – built around a wild mango tree. Dinner is often served by candlelight on an open-air deck to the front, with great views over the floodplains. There's a small wildlife hide cleverly built into the underneath of this deck, a lovely sunken campfire circle &, beside the bar, an infinity pool & hot tub supplied by a natural geothermal hot spring, discovered when the camp was drilling for their borehole. Set behind the main area, under a giant fig tree, there's a small bush spa offering massage & beauty treatments, & a gym hut.

Kafunta has 10 thatched chalets, each elevated off the ground. Paned windows are set into cool grey stone walls, & a set of doors at the front lead onto a private veranda. Each of the 8 'standard' chalets are spacious & pleasantly furnished for comfort; 2 'luxury suites' have more space, including an upper deck which can act as a viewing platform or an extra bedroom for 1–2 children. All chalets have a minibar, kettle & ceiling fan, as well as a shower, twin basins & flush toilet. The suites also have large bathtubs.

Walking safaris are possible, but activities generally centre on 4x4 game drives (day & night). Kafunta is 9km from the Mfuwe Bridge, but its drives normally access the park across the Nkwali pontoon, only 1.5km from the lodge.

Kafunta also operates Island Bush Camp & Three Rivers Camp (pages 301 & 311). *US$505–650 pp sharing, FBA, inc bar, laundry, park fees, airport & inter-camp transfers. Sgl suppt US$150 FBA*. ⌚ *Apr–5 Jan.* ♛♛♛

Kaingo Camp [map, page 284] (6 chalets) Contact Shenton Safaris, page 292. ⊕ KAINGO 12°55.370'S, 31°55.441'E. Where the seasonal Mwamba River meets the main Luangwa River, this small, independent camp looks over the water towards the Nsefu Sector from beneath a picturesque grove of mahogany & ebony trees. Kaingo is owned & run by Derek Shenton, a quiet, unassuming conservationist, & his dynamic wife, Jules. Their complementary talents & long-term dedication to wildlife, environment & local community lend the lodge a calm, established air, while innovation & contemporary styling keep Kaingo feeling fresh & inviting.

Operating since 1993, & with its excellent head guide, Patrick Njobvu, guiding in the area for over 30 years, the safari experience here is as reliable as it is special. The thatched, open-sided *chitenge* lounge & dining area is large & cool, with an incredible bar made from an old leadwood tree trunk. Outside, a lower deck is cantilevered over the river – perfect for game viewing & delicious afternoon teas hosted by Catherine, the wonderful executive chef.

Spread out along the riverfront, each of Kaingo's neat, thatched chalets are tastefully decorated with polished concrete floors, handcrafted timber beds, tumbled glass light fittings, natural indigo-dyed rugs & beautiful black & white photography. They are elegant & uncluttered. Sliding doors have mesh panels ensuring both a bedtime view & cooling breeze. All chalets have en-suite bathrooms with beautiful rain-shower mosaics, a decadent outdoor bath, international charging stations, solar lighting, a veranda & small private deck, complete with huge beanbag, over the river. For families or a couple seeking exclusivity, The First House is a wonderful retreat, furthest from the main area, with a circular, en-suite master bedroom, a lounge (can be a large second bedroom), sweeping veranda, complete with alfresco dining under a lovely looped chandelier & a deck for watching frolicking hippos & basking crocodiles below.

Close to the camp are several hides – the 'elephant' & 'hippo' hides, & the seasonal 'carmine bee-eater' & 'Wild dog lagoon' hides – as well as several mobile hides. These are fairly unusual in the Luangwa, & have been widely used by film-crews from both the BBC & *National Geographic*. If you're too active for a noon siesta, or are keen on photography, these are worth a visit. In fact, photographers are particularly well catered for at Shenton Safaris' camps, with camera dust covers & bean bags provided in vehicles, a media room available for editing images & a guaranteed outside seat on game drives with only 4 people per vehicle.

As well as the usual walking safaris & game drives (day & night), there are picnics in the bush & trips to the hides; many Kaingo guests opt for 3 activities a day. With advance notice, it's possible to arrange camping trips from Kaingo geared towards fit people looking for a minimalist set-up (*extra US$600/1–2 people*), as well as nights in the elephant hide next to the river, & on the Numbu Platform in a vast open savannah (*both extra US$200/2 people*). *Standard US$819–1,023; Family House (aka the First House) US$1,324–1,579 all pp (adult) sharing FBA, inc drinks, current park fees.* ⌚ *20 May–Oct.* ♛♛♛♛

Kakuli [map, page 289] (5 chalets) Contact Time+Tide, page 292. Overlooking a wide bend in the Luangwa, a camp was first started here in 1984 by Norman Carr. *Kakuli* is the local word for an old buffalo bull which has left the main herd, & by association was also Norman Carr's nickname among the local people before he died.

Kakuli is linked to Nsolo & Luwi camps, respectively 15km & 20km away, by the seasonal Luwi River, which makes 3-day walks between these 3 sister camps a very interesting option.

Its neat reed chalets are lovingly rebuilt every year, when their design is often tweaked & refined a little, but never strays far from its rustic bushcamp roots. On a polished concrete base, each room has a large thatched roof & completely open front, affording a terrific panorama from the feather-topped beds. Leather chairs, matt black furniture, a hanging chair on the terrace & quality wool blankets are all stylishly understated. A curtain separates the en-suite bathrooms & there are indoor & outdoor hot showers hidden from view.

The dining-room/bar area is simple & comfortable: a thatched, reed-walled structure with 2 open sides, a sprinkling of leather, canvas & cushioned chairs & a good bookshelf. A suspended deck with built in fireplace overlooks the floodplain.

The camp offers both walking & driving, day & night, & it's possible to sleep out under the stars in simple 'fly camp' mosquito net cubes. Seasonal boat trips are on offer & children of all ages are welcome in camp (though not on all activities). A stay here is usually combined with some of its sister bushcamps, Luwi, Nsolo & Mchenja, & also Chinzombo for those looking to add some luxury into their trip. *From US$840 pp sharing FBA inc drinks, exc park fees.* ⌚ *Jan–15 Nov.* ♛♛♛♛

Kapamba Bushcamp [map, page 281] (4 chalets) Contact Bushcamp Company, page 291. ⊕ KAPAMB 13°22.967'S, 31°31.584'E. This one of the Bushcamp Company's camps, a 3½hr drive from Mfuwe, is quite different from the rest. Unencumbered by a 4th wall, each of Kapamba's stone-walled chalets is open fronted, with sweeping views of a floodplain around the Kapamba River – which is shallow enough to paddle through barefoot or even to sit in during the dry season for a delightful sundowner or intimate dinner. Wrought-iron gates span the front of each chalet, offering protection from unwanted visitors & creating a spider-web effect against the African sky. Inside, each chalet is warm & stylish, with a clear north African influence in its design. En-suite bathrooms are twin showers above a bath the size of a small plunge pool (a happy accident, resulting from a specification given in centimetres, which the builders assumed was in inches!). The rooms are more stylish & contemporary than a traditional bushcamp, but nestle comfortably in with the surrounding environment.

Activities include walking, driving & night drives in the area around camp, which has plentiful wildlife but few other vehicles. Similarly to Bushcamp's other properties, if the camp is full then there will be 2 resident guides; if not there will be 1 while the company's floating guides provide guests with some flexibility over their choice of activities. *US$740–935 pp FBA, inc bar, laundry, airport & inter-camp transfers, park & conservation fees.* ⌚ *Apr–Jan.* ♛♛♛♛

KuKaya [map, page 284] (6 chalets) Contact Bushcamp Company, page 291. 2.5km from the main gate, KuKaya is a new lodge in the heart of the Mfuwe area. Overlooking a deep oxbow lagoon, its 6 substantial thatched chalets are contemporary & comfortable, with modern furnishings, handcrafted basketry, natural fabrics & muted colours. Chalets have a relaxed lounge/dining area, en-suite bathroom with an outdoor shower & inviting bedroom, though the waterfront decks, complete with private plunge pool, firepit & cushioned loungers, are the highlight. There are 2 hides in camp, which are great for photographers & birders, & all the usual safari activities (walking & game drives). With proximity to Mfuwe, community visits are possible & spa treatments can be booked at the nearby Bush Spa. This is a good game area, so simply sitting back with your binoculars or ice-cold drink, watching the wildlife pass by is equally lovely. In the main area, The Deli serves fresh, seasonal food & the bar offers drinks all day. *US$670–720 pp FBA, laundry, airport & inter-camp transfers, park & conservation fees; exc bar. Children all ages. Open all year.* ♛♛♛♛

Kulandila Camp [map, page 281] (4 tents) ☎ +44 7760 966011; e reservations@sungani.

com; **w** sungani.com; ⊕ KULAND 13°27.342'S, 31°25.558'E. Under a canopy of lala palms & towering riverine trees, Kulandila sits between the Luangwa River & a large lagoon that shares its name. Overlooking the meandering river, this lovely, bijoux camp offers a bygone safari feel with a contemporary twist. Opened in 2022, alongside its larger, sister camp Sungani (page 309), the canvas & pole construction of the central area takes in the incredible panorama of the river in the foreground, affording game-viewing from the lounge & super sunsets from the friendly bar. There's a lovely linked pool deck, shaded terrace for alfresco meals & neat sand paths leading to the 4 tents. Inside them, warm wooden headboards, super-size walk-in mosquito nets, leather ottomans, brass details & campaign-style folding furniture all lend the interiors a classic camp aesthetic. There's a small, raised seating area at the front & en-suite bathrooms to the rear, while the open-air bath-with-a-view is a lovely addition. Activities, as at Sungani, can be on foot or by vehicle, & photographers are well catered for. *US$1,065 pp sharing mid-May–mid-Jun & mid–end Oct, US$1,365 mid-Jun–mid-Oct. All rates FBA, inc flight/road transfer from Mfuwe, laundry, park & conservation levies.* ⌚ *mid-May–Oct.* ♛♛♛♛

Kuyenda [map, page 281] (4 rondavels) Contact Bushcamp Company, page 291. ⊕ KUYEND 13°22.430'S, 31°32.430'E. About 75 mins' drive south of Mfuwe, this small, very traditional bushcamp concentrates on walking safaris with the occasional drive. It overlooks the Manzi River, a sand-river tributary of the main Luangwa.

The simplest & most rustic of Bushcamp Company's camps, Kuyenda is a true back-to-nature experience where walking safaris are at the heart of camp life. Until his death in 2022, the camp was run by Phil Berry – the Valley's most experienced guide with a legendary reputation for his knowledge of the area's wildlife – and his vivacious partner, Babette. While they are no longer here, Kuyenda remains a camp for old Africa hands & classic safari connoisseurs. The simple round chalets, made of thatch & reeds, have en-suite toilets & showers open to the sky (hot water is brought on request), beds veiled by mosquito netting, atmospheric paraffin lanterns & wide mesh-covered panoramic windows. It's unfussy & very peaceful.

Though walking is the main focus here, drives are also possible, including night drives that are always a feature of time here. Returning to the camp when it's dark is a great pleasure as the whole camp is lit by glowing hurricane lamps which look magical as you approach across a wide sand river. *US$600–775 pp FBA, inc bar, laundry, airport & inter-camp transfers, park & conservation fees.* ⌚ *Jun–Nov.* ♛♛♛♛

Lion Camp [map, page 289] (10 chalets) ☎ 0216 246024, **m** 0965 156181; **e** info@lioncamp.com; **w** lioncamp.com. ⊕ LIONCA 12°53.089'S, 31°58.032'E. Situated inside the park around 3hrs' drive from Mfuwe, stylish Lion Camp stands on the edge of an oxbow lagoon, or wafwa, overlooking an open plain.

At the heart of the camp, seating areas under thatch form a horseshoe around a central fireplace. Parallel to the lagoon, a narrow ribbon of deck edges a similarly narrow infinity pool. At the back, the walls lined with black-&-white wildlife photos, are a large bar & a full-size billiard table; a separate lounge with TV for wildlife DVDs & Wi-Fi, & a well-stocked curio shop. Dining is flexible – with locations moved from one meal to the next.

High wooden walkways lead to the chalets, themselves on wooden platforms with French windows leading onto decks overlooking the lagoon. They're solid, spacious structures under thatch with timber-clad canvas walls, gauze windows & stylish interiors: polished wood floors, contemporary, industrial style furniture & soft furnishings in calm, neutral tones. The en-suite tents have chairs on the deck for relaxed game-viewing & a decanter of port to accompany evening star-gazing. The Deluxe Suite has a bath on the deck for indulgent relaxation, & the Honeymoon Suite a 'star-bed' platform. There's 220V inverter power in each chalet, & locks on the doors – a rarity in the Luangwa!

Activities revolve around game drives & walking safaris, & there are photographic safari weeks with local wildlife photographers throughout the year, as well as great workspace – complete with charging points – for those keen to look at their digital imagery.

It's a professionally run lodge in a wildlife rich, yet remote, area of the park. The facilities are impressive & it has a much more solid structure than some of the more traditional properties in the area, so it may not suit people looking for a simple bushcamp.

Luxury Suite US$856–1,055 pp sharing; Deluxe Suite US$995–1,325 pp sharing; all FBA, inc bar, laundry, airport & inter-camp transfers, exc park fees. No children under 10. ⌚ 21 May–Oct. ♛♛♛

Luangwa River Camp [map, page 284] (5 chalets) Contact Robin Pope Safaris, page 292. ⊕ LUARLO 13°04.459'S, 31°48.636'E. In a riverside setting 10km northeast of Mfuwe, overlooking the South Park, Luangwa River Camp is a well-established property that was taken over by Robin Pope Safaris. Featuring a small, double-level infinity pool sunk into the tiered wooden deck along the front of the lodge, surrounded by vibrant green banana trees & overlooking a manicured lawn & the river beyond, it has a spacious, tropical feel. There's a large L-shaped, open-plan lounge & dining area with wide, cushioned seats that have a beautiful wide outlook, a curved corner bar & neatly laid tables.

Deep sand pathways lead to the 5 cream-rendered brick & thatch chalets, which are spacious & classically furnished, with bifold doors opening on to a small semi-circular terrace overlooking the riverbed. En-suite bathrooms are huge, with showers concealed behind curved walls & claw-foot or sunken baths, & mains electricity enables the use of spotlights, hairdryers, fans & other 'luxuries', making the lodge a good introduction to a safari holiday or suitable for anyone who prefers more solid accommodation.

Aside from walking safaris & game drives, usually in the national park, there are boat trips when the river is sufficiently high, & cultural trips are easily within range, too, including visits to Chipembele Wildlife Education Centre (page 291), Kawaza Village (page 317), & various other craft & village projects. It's all very flexible – right down to the option of a holistic massage! *US$480–635 all pp FBA, inc drinks, laundry, airport & inter-camp transfers, exc park & community fees. Children over 12 years.* ⌚ *Apr–Nov.* ♛♛♛

Luangwa Safari House [map, page 284] (4 bedrooms) Contact Robin Pope Safaris, page 292. Built in 2005 near to Nkwali (page 307), this large & traditional-looking house has a carefully crafted structure based around the trunks of 25 ancient leadwood trees. From the front entrance, a huge pivoted door opens into the spacious main room, some 12m high, with comfy sofas, large marble dining table & full-height views of the bush through 1 open wall.

There are 4 grand bedrooms, each individually styled & reflecting a different material from copper to glass. Open-tread wooden staircases made from massive reclaimed slabs of wooden banana tree lead to 2 of these rooms; both with balconies supported like drawbridges. All are highly original & styled on a grand scale, with king-size or twin beds & very large en-suite bathrooms.

Despite that, the focus is on the outdoors. Terraces lead to an infinity pool, & a wooden jetty extends away from the house to an open-sided lounge deck constructed around a group of huge ebony trees in the middle of an often-dry lagoon. Nearby a waterhole attracts families of elephants, which can be easily observed from a sunken hide. During the day, a double-storey wall of the lounge, & a section of each bedroom wall, are opened up completely, turning the outside into a continuation of the living space inside. At night a clever system of insect-proof mesh, wrought-iron grills &, if necessary, waterproof panels slot into place to close up the house & keep it cosy.

The house can only be booked in its entirety by a single group, & comes with a private chef, house manager, safari guide & game-viewing vehicle, giving guests complete flexibility over their schedule. Although often referred to as a 'family house', Luangwa Safari House really best suits small groups of adults, or at least adults & older children, who will appreciate the openness of its design & the complete flexibility of its high-quality activities. *US$4,050–4,980 (sleeps 8) rate for house per day FBA, inc drinks, laundry, airport transfers, exc park & community fees. Children over 7.* ⌚ *15 Mar–15 Jan.* ♛♛♛♛

Luwi Bushcamp [map, page 281] (4 tents) Contact Time+Tide Safaris, page 292. A further 10km up the Luwi River from its sister camp, Nsolo, Luwi is as beautiful as it is rustic. Standing on polished timber deck under a stand of tall shady trees (*Vitex, Breonadia & Khaya anthotheca*), looking out over a small plain, its small, elegant mess tent manages to achieve an intimate feel in spite of being entirely open-sided. Watch the sunset from the leather Chesterfield sofa, G&T in hand, enjoy communal lantern-lit dinners & watch the wildlife cross in front of camp. The pale tents are equally stylish, with an en-suite shower & a small veranda, complete with the obligatory directors chairs.

A very short walk from camp leads to a large, permanent oxbow lagoon at a bend in the river (usually frequented by a pod of about 60 hippos, & a range of water birds). The joy of a remote camp like Luwi is the opportunities for great walking safaris: either for day walks based here, or for walks linking with Nsolo, Kakuli & Mchenja bushcamps. Games drives are possible – although there's always a vehicle in camp to investigate interesting noises at dusk – & the camp seldom takes more than 7 guests. Luwi is often combined with its sister bushcamps, allowing a mixture of walks & drives in different areas of the park, & there's a 'sleepout' option available at a supplement. *From US$800 pp sharing, all FBA inc drinks, transfers, laundry, exc premium drinks, spa. Children of all ages (not walking safaris).* ⌚ *20 May–15 Nov.* ♛♛♛♛

Mchenja [map, page 289] (5 chalets) Contact Time+Tide, page 292. Mchenja stands in one of the very best locations of any camp in the Valley, beside the Luangwa River at the end of a serenely beautiful grove of African ebony trees (*Diospyros mespiliformis*, which are known as *muchenja* in the local ChiNyanja dialect).

The golden reed chalets all have thatched roofs supported on dark wooden poles, with roll-down canvas panels to the otherwise open font. Polished concrete floors, minimal but thoughtful furnishings, lovely beds with crisp white linen, a cane drinks trolley & a veranda overlooking the water are all terrific. The en-suite bathrooms are open-air & there's a decadent free-standing bath with river views. There's solar lighting & charging available but no Wi-Fi or phone signal. For families, there's a 2-bed, 2-bath chalet available.

The airy dining area & small lounge are under thatch, & there is a small freshwater pool overlooking the river. Food & activities are reliably good & the camp usually offers activities on foot & by vehicle. About 30km from Mfuwe (2½hr game drive), Mchenja stands opposite the Nsefu Sector, between Nsefu Camp & Tena Tena. It makes a good last stop at the end of a walking safari, being an easy 10km walk (3–4hrs) from either Nsolo or Kakuli. *US$840–1,140 pp sharing all FBA inc drinks & transfers, exc premium drinks. Children all ages.* ⌚ *20 May–15 Nov.* ♛♛♛

Mfuwe Lodge [map, page 284] (18 chalets) Contact Bushcamp Company, page 291. ⊕ MFUWEL 13°4.725'S, 31°47.441'E. This smart, long-established lodge is the hub of the Bushcamp Company operations & it stands in a prime location overlooking the picturesque Mfuwe Lagoon in the centre of the park's all-weather road network. The wildlife here is prolific & relaxed, though it is the park's busiest area. The lodge's history dates back many years, having been rebuilt from scratch in the 1990s by the Bizzaro family, owners of the successful Club Makokola in Malawi; it was, & remains, relatively big in the context of the Luangwa's tiny camps.

Each of Mfuwe's painted brick-&-thatch chalets overlooks a lagoon from a broad veranda, complete with directors' chairs. Inside, beds are encased in walk-in mosquito nets & cooled by AC, there's a writing desk, safe, drinks & a seating area. The contemporary bathroom has dual washbasins, a separate toilet, & a shower with a view. Larger family rooms & suites are split level, some with a bath.

Mfuwe has a vast lobby & at the end of the dry season it's the scene of an extraordinary sight: a whole family of elephants who come through to feast on the wild mango trees beyond. For most guests, a large pool, squashy sofas, huge fireplaces & an open-air dining area with pizza oven are the greater draw! The food is good & the bar well stocked. Added bonuses are the Phil Berry Centre, housing a proper library & photographic studio, as well as a good curio shop, internet access & its own lagoon-side spa (page 278). Morning & afternoon/night drives are in Land Rovers with 3 rows of individual seats, & walks are also possible, though keen walkers would be best to combine a stay here with time at one or more of the company's bushcamps. *Lodge US$560 pp FBA inc park fees & conservation levy, exc drinks. Suites US$620 pp FBA inc park fees & conservation levy, exc drinks. Children all ages.* ⌚ *All year.* ♛♛♛

✷ **Mwamba Bushcamp** [map, page 289] (4 chalets) Contact Shenton Safaris, page 292. ⊕ MWAMBA 12°52.973'S, 31°55.940'E. About 6km north of Kaingo, only a morning's walk away, lies Mwamba, Kaingo's delightful satellite bushcamp. Located at the confluence of the East Mwamba & main Mwamba rivers, the approach to the camp is lovely, following the dry, sandy riverbeds through mopane forest, ebony groves & grasslands. The camp itself is shaded within a grove of particularly beautiful ebonies (*Diospyros mespiliformis*). A neatly swept, open-air circle is at the heart of camp life. There's a banqueting table for social dinners, a fabulous bar lit by beaded chandeliers amid python vines on a huge ebony, and a little lounge area where comfortable sofas & carved Malawi chairs cluster beside a reference bookshelf, under a triangular shade cloth. There are deep cushioned chairs around an adjacent metal firepit & a large birdbath to attract passing avian visitors.

Nearby, the 4 small, traditional bamboo reed-&-thatch chalets have rustic-chic interiors with delicate beaded linens, comfortable beds, charging facilities & gauze skylights, enabling guests to enjoy the stars from their beds. Large, open-air, en-suite bathrooms (with hot bucket shower & flush toilet) sit to the side of the bedrooms, which also have a small private seating area overlooking the riverbed.

Walking & driving safaris are on offer & the camp has its own hide, focused on a waterhole that regularly attracts birds & passing wildlife. It's a very personal camp & activities are very flexible. The wildlife in the area is excellent & it's one of South Luangwa's best spots for Cookson's wildebeest, & eland are sometimes spotted in the area. *US$886.50–1,088 pp sharing, FBA, inc drinks, transfers, laundry, current park fees.* ⌚ *Jun–1 Nov.* ♛♛♛♛

Nkwali [map, page 284] (6 rooms, Robin's House, Luangwa Safari House) Contact Robin Pope Safaris, page 292. ⊕ NKWALI 13°6.989'S, 31°44.414'E. Nkwali is the main base for Robin Pope Safaris. It overlooks the Luangwa & the park beyond from the Lupande GMA which encompasses some beautiful tall acacia & ebony woodlands, a favourite haunt for giraffe & elephant. As you turn left just before the main bridge at Mfuwe, Nkwali is well signposted. Take the road for about 5km, then turn left just before the end of the tarmac. Take this for about 2km, then turn right for a further 4km.

Each of Nkwali's comfortable rooms has a high thatched roof resting on 3 creamy-white walls, leaving the front completely open with views of the river, plus grill-like doors for the evening. The chalets are furnished with dbl or twin beds surrounded by a walk-in mosi net & hanging shelves. In the en suite at the back the shower is open to the sky while the toilet & two basins are under cover. 5 of the chalets are the same size, while the 6th is larger & can act as a family room with the extra beds. All are on mains power with a back-up generator.

The camp feels rustic but comfortable & the main area is a guest focal point. The bar is spectacularly built around an ebony tree, & there's a small swimming pool behind the dining room. The proximity to the river & a nearby waterhole often attracts game close to camp.

Most activities from Nkwali are drives into the park, which is accessed either by boat across the river, or over the conveniently close Nkwali pontoon. Walks are led into both the park & in the surrounding GMA; often you'll just cross the river by boat & walk from there. The camp has permission to run walking safaris throughout the year.

It's usual to combine time here with time at Tena Tena &/or Nsefu camps, further north – when Nkwali often works best as the first camp on the itinerary. Nearby there are also 2 safari houses: the child-friendly 2-bedroom Robin's House (page 308) & the rather more quirky & stylish 4-bedroom Luangwa Safari House (page 305). Both are close to Nkwali, but they run with their own chefs & guides, so don't impact upon the character of Nkwali at all.

US$495–710 pp FBA, inc drinks, laundry, airport & inter-camp transfers, exc park & community fees. ⌚ *All year.* ♛♛♛

Nsefu Camp [map, page 289] (6 rondavels) Contact Robin Pope Safaris, page 292. ⊕ NSEFU 12°56.236'S, 31°55.289'E. Nsefu is superbly situated on the Luangwa River, in the middle of the Nsefu Sector. It was first opened in 1951 by Norman Carr – making it Zambia's oldest safari camp – & moved to its present location in 1953. In late 1998, the camp was bought by Robin Pope Safaris, who completely rebuilt & refurbished it, but it remains an old-school safari camp in a good wildlife area.

Nsefu's original row of small, round rondavels remain, each with a shady wooden veranda overlooking the lawn towards the river. Inside, they are simply furnished, with AC & fairly small rooms by modern safari standards. At the back, each room steps down to a partly open, en-suite bathroom.

The camp is simply furnished, with a square, thatched main area housing a bar & lounge. Deep-cushioned sofas overlook the Luangwa to the front & a pumped waterhole, complete with a small reed hide from where thirsty bushbuck, impala & busy gold weavers can be observed undisturbed.

Dining is often beside the riverbank, or elsewhere under the skies, & the atmosphere is relaxed. A stay here is often combined with Nkwali, Tena Tena, or one of RPS's walking safaris. *US$695–995 pp FBA, inc drinks, laundry, airport & inter-camp transfers, exc park & community fees. US$495 pp Green Season.* ⌚ *22 Jan–Mar; 22 May–20 Nov*. ♛♛♛♛

Nsolo Bushcamp [map, page 289] (5 chalets) Contact Time+Tide, page 292. Set on a sweeping bend of the seasonal Luwi River, with a permanent waterhole to the front, Nsolo focuses on a central *chitenje* in the shade of mahogany & sausage trees. This is an airy thatched room with low reed walls & low-key furnishings: a simple bar, soft sofas & view to the alfresco dining table and campfire. Meals are sometimes also held in the sand river, lit by the soft glow of hurricane lamps.

The large chalets are built on wooden decks with reed walls & high thatched roofs, each has either twin beds or a dbl under a walk-in mosquito net. En-suite bathrooms are open to the stars with a flush toilet & shower with a view. A dbl door opens onto a tree- or thatch-shaded private deck, with comfortable chairs & a great view over the river. Solar lights are used in the evenings & no Wi-Fi or mobile signal is available.

The camp was named for the *nsolo* or honeyguide bird (*Indicator indicator*). It lies 9–10km inside the park from the main Luangwa River, directly west of the Nsefu Sector in a sandy area dominated by mopane trees, with veins of shady riparian forest. Game drives are on offer but walking is the major attraction. On my first visit to Nsolo in 1995 the ranger for our walks was Rice Time, a sprightly Zambian hunter who strode through the bush with speed & confidence – despite being over 70 years of age. Sadly he died in 2006, but there is a memorial for him in camp, & his stories are still told & re-told. A stay here is usually combined with visits to Nsolo's sister camps, & with Luwi 10km to the east & 15km west to Kakuli & Mchenja, a few days spent walking down the sand river between the camps makes a great trip. Nsolo is also a great base if you're keen to do a sleepout under the stars.

From US$800 pp sharing, all FBA inc drinks, park fees, exc premium drinks. Children all ages. ⌚ *20 May–15 Nov*. ♛♛♛♛

✷ **Puku Ridge** [map, page 284] (8 suites) Contact Chiawa Safaris, page 291. Puku Ridge is simply stunning. Reopened in 2019, it has brought a new level of contemporary style & sophistication to South Luangwa. Developed in its current form by the experienced team at Chiawa Safaris, Puku Ridge stands on the side of a rocky outcrop, overlooking the lovely Kakumbi Dambo floodplain, on the south side of the park. Mushroom-coloured walls, fan-like pole shading, tiered timber decking & natural, Scandi-African styling set the tone throughout.

The linear main area is completely open to the panoramic view of the floodplain. Festooned with myriad woven lanterns & thoughtfully laid out to give space for diners, with relaxed lounging beside the excellent reference library, & swinging chairs arranged to take in the impressive view. On the meandering decking below, you can scan the horizon with spotting scopes to discover which wildlife is approaching the permanent waterhole immediately in front of camp or take to what is perhaps Zambia's most decadent photographic hide below the main deck to catch eye-level shots of the animals. There's a campfire circle off the main deck, where buffet breakfasts & after-dinner drinks are served, & the friendly, quietly efficient team are always on hand. Food is fine-dining – fresh, original & lovingly presented – & a highlight of a stay here.

The 8 suites are tranquil havens spread out along the rocky hillside. Walls are a mix of safari canvas & sliding glass; there's a rooftop star bed & organically shaped outside deck, complete with curved seating, plunge pool & shaded dining area. The interiors are refined: pale timber furnishings, crisp cotton & linen fabrics, leather-strapped mosquito nets & copper accents. There's a pillow menu, lights in the wardrobes, efficient AC & an indulgent slate-grey bath, if you aren't tempted with the outdoor shower. This is very much a luxury retreat.

But it's not just the beautiful interior design, exceptional details & panoramic vista that give Puku Ridge its edge, the team here are superlative. Every staff member, from the waiters to the guides, chefs to housekeepers, & the fantastic management, have this lodge running on wheels, making it a super slick operation.

The guides here are highly skilled & game drives (day and night) are productive & varied, with daily walking safaris available. *US$1,325–1,755 pp sharing FBA inc park fees & airport transfers.* ⌚ *Apr–Nov*. ♛♛♛♛

Robin's House [map, page 284] (2 bedrooms) Contact Robin Pope Safaris, page 292. The exclusive-use 5-bed Robin's House stands on the riverbank near Nkwali, under a grove of large ebony trees. Originally the home of Robin & Jo Pope themselves, it's homely & functional, but it's still comfortable & tastefully decorated. It has a central sitting room & 2 large bedrooms (a dbl & a trpl), each with its own bathroom. Large windows give great views across the river, & there's a grassy garden complete with a swimming pool overlooking the river. The house has a private guide, hostess & chef, so it's ideal for families &/or those seeking more privacy. Those with older children, & larger groups, might consider Luangwa Safari House (page 305) as a more appropriate alternative. *US$650–825 pp FBA, inc drinks, laundry, airport transfers, exc park & community fees. Min 2 adults, 1 child.* ⏲ *All year.* ♛♛♛♛

✷ **Shawa Luangwa Camp** [map, page 289] (5 tents) **m** 0979 312766; **e** reservations@greensafaris.com; **w** greensafaris.com. Opened in June 2021, Shawa is Green Safaris' first camp in the Luangwa Valley, named after the camp's well-known head guide, Jacob Shawa, a protégé of Robin Pope. This contemporary eco-camp sits in a prime location on the banks of the Luangwa River, overlooking the national park. Original in architectural design, the main area is entirely open, with an exposed steel superstructure & a magnificent Natal mahogany shading its alfresco dining area. Soaring ceilings, khaki metalwork & linear riverview decks give the place a relaxed, modern vibe somewhere between a New York loft & a boat club. It's edgy but familiar & has its sights set firmly on the water ahead & the wildlife in the park beyond.

From the main area, neatly brushed paths lead to the lush lower lawn & loungers around the lovely, deep swimming pool; the rooms stretch along the riverbank. Each of the 5 canvas suites (2 of which are interconnected by a private walkway for families) are tucked deep into the riverine forest. Accessed up a flight of timber stairs, the distinctive, teepee-like en-suite tents are a first in safari camp design. Inspired by chimneys & built to funnel the hot air away on steamy days, they are both fun & functional. High ceilings, tent sides that open horizontally to create shade & offer lovely panoramic views of tree canopy & open timber decks, lend an immersive, treehouse feel to the experience. There's a small toilet cubicle inside each tent, a sunken bath & a wonderful, hidden power shower on the deck (in fact, it's perhaps the best bush shower in the Luangwa!). Deep mattresses, fine linen, a good breeze & sounds of the bush will lull you to sleep, & in the morning there's a lovely deck to listen to the birds, watch the grey tree frogs & scan for lions & hippos on the riverbank opposite.

The entire camp runs on solar energy – with an impressive solar farm on site & Green Safaris are committed to environmentally responsible travel. As such, they were the first company to pioneer electric vehicles & boats in their Kafue camps, and they now operate an all-electric fleet at Shawa. The experience is magic – silent journeys in the wilderness allowing you to hear the guide at all times, to slow or stop to observe & photograph birds & animals without any disruption, & to listen to the sounds of the bush as you travel. After decades of game driving all over Africa, we were utterly captivated by 'silent safari' – it's a game changer. Game drives are available day & night, as well as walking safaris with experienced guides. The team at Shawa can arrange visits to community development projects run by Project Luangwa (page 279) & are happy to invite wildlife researchers from Conservation South Luangwa (page 288) to talk about the conservation initiatives taking place in the national park. *US$625 pp sharing Jun & Nov, US$905 pp sharing Jul–Oct, all FBA inc park fees, conservation levy & laundry. Children 9+.* ⏲ *May–2 Jan.* ♛♛♛–♛♛♛♛

Sungani Lodge [map, page 281] (7 tents) **m** +44 7760 966011; **e** reservations@sungani.com; **w** sungani.com; ⊕ SUNGAN 13°27.556"S, 31°24.148"E. Opened in 2022, Sungani Lodge is the most southerly camp in South Luangwa National Park, located in its furthest reaches. An elegant, high quality camp with owners experienced in running luxury camps & having a keen eye on community & conservation, it's a great addition to Luangwa. Not least because the arrival of Sungani, & its sister camp Kulandila (page 303) a little downstream, will have significant benefits to the anti-poachng efforts of this region of the park. To have an area, previously little visited & inaccessible, open up to game-drive vehicles & scouts offers the wildlife here far greater protection, which in turn benefits the park-wide conservation of all wildlife.

The lodge itself is raised on decking overlooking a beautiful lagoon. Very much a family-owned &

run establishment, there's a relaxed, homely feel here but with a raft of low-key luxuries in all its details. Natural materials, open panoramic vistas & classic safari colours abound, with a spotting scope, antique chess board & thoughtful library leading guests to laid-back leisure pursuits in a host of different spaces. There's also a sparkling pool, complete with loungers under the trees, for middle of the day siestas, small gift shop & a well-equipped, air-conditioned gym for the energetic. Delicious meals are served under the trees on the deck or at the communal table, & the attentive staff are always on hand to chat and help.

The 7 spacious tents – one of which can accommodate a family with 2 children & the Directors' tent which boasts a host of mod-cons – are all equally beautiful. Polished concrete floors keep them cool, tasteful furniture, muted colours & lovely linens make them restful, while the lagoon-view claw-foot bath, shaded private deck & plunge pool all add to the sense of wild indulgence. Activities naturally focus on wildlife and wilderness experiences: game drives in vehicles complete with camera rests for photographers, bush picnics on the banks of the Luangwa River, photographic hides perfect for watching the lagoon wildlife, & walking safaris.

Access to the lodge is by 20–30min light-aircraft hop from Mfuwe airport on the camp's own plane (4 passengers), which is included in the rates, or a 3hr road transfer. Thought has also been given to guests with limited mobility & the lodge is wheelchair friendly (NB door width 80cm), though it's always best to discuss specific needs with them in advance. *US$1,465–1,915pp sharing mid-May–mid-Jun & mid-Oct–mid-Nov, US$1,915–2,065 mid-Jun–mid-Oct, all FBA, inc flight/road transfer from Mfuwe, laundry, park & conservation levies.* ◷ *All year – green season on request.* ♛♛♛♛♛

✷ **Tafika** [map, page 289] (6 chalets) Contact Remote Africa Safaris, page 292. ⊕ TAFIKA 15°51.250'S, 31°59.811'E. Founded by John & Carol Coppinger in 1995, Tafika stands on the bank of the Luangwa, overlooking the national park. John's years of experience in the Valley are augmented by the experience of several other top guides working here, including Bryan Jackson, who has been part of the Remote Africa team from the beginning. In fact Tafika's guiding is among the best in the valley. In recent years, John & Carol's daughter Jennifer & her husband Nick – both qualified guides – have joined them at the helm. Bringing new energy & refining of camp's fine details, Tafika's fundamental DNA is unchanged & safaris here are consistently excellent.

The blonde reed-&-thatch chalets are immaculately constructed around the lawned gardens above the river. The interiors are natural & rustic in material but carefully & thoughtfully decorated to ensure maximum comfort & practicality. Linen is contemporary African themed, large lockboxes will fit even the largest camera bags, the fans & in-room charging points are useful, & the laundry service is efficient. The large family chalet, built around the trunk of a stunning sausage tree (*Kigelia africana*), has 2 bedrooms, while the new honeymoon suite is very similar to the standard rooms, but has a king-size bed, dbl showers & a private hammock. All the rooms have spacious en-suite facilities to the rear, including a flush toilet & excellent shower open to the skies. Lighting is by solar-powered storm lanterns.

The main bar/dining area has comfortable chairs & large, circular dining tables, though dinner is a relaxed affair, often eaten together outside. Tafika is not ostentatious but it is very high quality: the food is superb (do check out their incredible vegetable garden, from where much of the food comes), the atmosphere friendly & unpretentious & the guiding truly expert.

Game activities include day & night drives, as well as walking safaris. It's also possible to do a mountain-bike safari, cycling through the local village & then into the park itself. Alternatively, you could cycle to the school & clinic supported by Tafika (as you might expect, the camp is closely connected to the local community, which it supports extensively). With such a large guiding team at Tafika there are almost never more than 4 guests per vehicle, & they are extremely accommodating in arranging your activity choices. There's a productive hide at the back of the camp, which makes an excellent spot to hang out between activities, as well as hides further afield to view the carmine bee-eaters & lagoon.

During the dry season, Tafika acts as the hub for Remote Africa's Chikoko Trails (page 300) walking safaris, as well as Mwaleshi & Takwela, their camps in North Luangwa National Park (page 318), & Shoebill Island Camp in Bangweulu Wetlands (page 374). In the Green Season, Tafika offers a great 'Stork Special' rate, when it has near exclusive access to the incredible yellow-billed stork colony in the Nsefu Sector. *US$900–1,100 pp (Jun–mid Nov) FBA, inc bar, laundry, current park fees, airport & inter-camp transfers. Stork Special (May) US$495 pp, FBA, inc bar, laundry, current park fees, airport & inter-camp transfers. Children from 8.* ◷ *May–15 Nov.* ♛♛♛♛♛

Tena Tena [map, page 289] (6 tents) Contact Robin Pope Safaris, page 292. ⊕ 12°59,089'S, 31°53,655'E. Tena Tena is a widely recognised name in safari circles. Having moved 1km upstream from its original site in 2012 (due to river erosion threatening the camp), it now overlooks a stretch of the Luangwa River at the southern end of the Nsefu Sector of the park, about 20km northeast of the bridge at Mfuwe.

The main area at Tena Tena is a large, circus-like tented roof supported by rustic poles & shaded by twin vine-covered Natal mahoganies. The upper level has a sweeping & well-stocked bar, a comfortable lounge, & a large dining table with director's chairs. From here, the ground is tiered organically over several levels, creating a series of intimate seating areas. Tree trunks are carved into rough, throne-like chairs, & cushioned baraza benches make for perfect siesta or game viewing spots. All overlook the distant Luangwa River & there's a spotting scope for scanning for approaching animals.

The large, square safari tents sit on a solid base & are comfortably furnished with 3 sides of mesh walls for ventilation & views, & cream curtains for privacy & a sense of security if preferred. Each tent has an open en-suite shower & toilet with low walls overlooking the river from the edge of the riverine trees, & a sandy semi-circular terrace at the front. They are spaced well apart in the trees & make for peaceful retreats in the middle of the day.

Activities concentrate on morning & afternoon walks, & game drives (including night drives). A stay here is often combined with Nkwali, Nsefu (camp or bush camping), or one of Robin Pope's walking safaris. *US$830–995 pp FBA, inc drinks, laundry, airport & inter-camp transfers, exc park & community fees.* ◷ *22 May–Oct.* ♛♛♛♛

Three Rivers Camp [map, page 281] (5 tents) Contact Kafunta River Safaris (page 292). In 2017, Kafunta Safaris opened a bushcamp at the confluence of the Luangwa, Lusangazi & Kapamba rivers at the southern end of the park. Its 5 tents are comfortably furnished with open-sided en-suite bathrooms & circular private decks. Each tent also has a platform 'star bed' that can be set up outside your room for an immersive 'sleep out' in the bush. Activities focus on safari drives & walks, with it being possible to walk the 7km south to Island Bush Camp. *US$680 pp sharing, FBA, inc drinks, park fees.* ◷ *25 May–Nov.* ♛♛♛

Zungulila [map, page 281] (4 tents) Contact Bushcamp Company, page 291. ⊕ ZUNGUL 13°21.117'S, 31°30.928'E. Situated in an untouched part of the park, Zungulila focuses on exploring some of the most untamed sections of bush on foot (though drives are possible). Routes include the Hippo Pools trail along the Kapamba River, or guests can walk to or from its sister camp, Bilimungwe. With its dark wood furniture & kilim-style floor rugs, the camp itself is redolent of the days of the early explorers. Its 4 large tents, with views of the river from their shaded decks, have many comforts, from classic dressing tables & solar lighting to partially open-air bathrooms with a separate toilet & alfresco copper bath, relaxing sunloungers & a small plunge pool. There's a central campfire boma, communal dining table, & an eclectic array of chairs in the small lounge area. At the end of the day, you can even cool off with a feet-in-the-river sundowner! Access is usually by 3½hr transfer from Mfuwe Lodge, but there's also an airstrip close by. *US$605 pp sharing, FBA, inc bar, laundry, airport & inter-camp transfers, exc park fees.* ◷ *Apr–Jan.* ♛♛♛♛

Budget and mid-range camps South Luangwa National Park is not an ideal safari destination for the impecunious backpacker. Hitchhiking into the park from Chipata is difficult (flying is the best way to arrive 'independently'), and there are no touts selling cheap safaris. There are a few budget camps as well as a lot of smaller, more exclusive ones (with all-inclusive rates). The latter don't cater well for unexpected visitors; they're best booked in advance.

If you want to be independent, then come in your own fully equipped 4x4 – as then you can see the park for yourself. That said, although driving yourself around is fun, it's a pale shadow of the experience that you get at one of the better small lodges. Note, too, that self-drive vehicles may not be driven in the national park when it's dark; only registered guides can conduct night drives. Make sure that you bring supplies of food (fresh vegetables and other limited provisions can be bought locally), and the best maps that you can buy in Lusaka.

Most budget travellers who come to the Luangwa arrive in overland trucks. These travel between Malawi and Zimbabwe, stopping here and in Lusaka. They usually stay, together with a few backpackers and independent travellers, at one of Luangwa's less expensive camps, most clustered around the Mfuwe Bridge area.

Croc Valley [map, page 275] (6 chalets, 16 tents, 10 backpacker beds, camping) ☎ 0216 246074; m 0977 175172; e reservations@crocvalley.com; w crocvalley.com. Upstream of the main Mfuwe Bridge, this large, leafy camp has a range of simple accommodation options & camping pitches available but is feeling somewhat tired & run-down these days. Shaded by Natal mahogany, ebony & sausage trees, & with extensive river frontage, it has a large, open-fronted bar & lounge area overlooking the Luangwa & basking crocodiles on the sandbanks below. There's a sizeable swimming pool, some gym equipment, a volleyball net, table tennis & a small kitchen for self-caterers. Accommodation options range from green Meru safari tents to rustic riverfront chalets, terraced family & backpacker rooms, & small twin bed 'eco tents'. The interiors are all very basic. Camping pitches for 4x4 roof tents & standard tents are available with braai facilities. All safari activities can be arranged at the reception desk. *River tent US$216/264; Chalet US$192–240; Rooms & Eco-tent US$150, all pp sharing, FBA exc 10% service charge & government levies. Camping US$15 pp.* ⌚ *All year.* ♛–♛♛

✷ **Flatdogs Camp** [map, page 275] (10 tents, 6 chalets, 2 exclusive use) ☎ 0216 246038; e info@flatdogscamp.com; w flatdogscamp.com. ⊕ FLATDO 13°6.298'S, 31°46.546'E. The local nickname for the crocodile, 'flatdog' was an apt choice when the original campsite was opened in 1992 at the old crocodile camp near the Mfuwe Bridge. In 2000, Flatdogs moved to its present site on about 100ha of land beside the river, where a great deal of wildlife wanders by to drink, including a good population of giraffe, attracted by the acacia trees. It's a really lovely spot, with plenty of shade from winterthorn (*Faidherbia albida*) & mahogany (*Trichelia emetica*), & a terrifically friendly & knowledgeable team.

Flatdogs today is an extensive & imaginatively designed camp. It includes an open-plan bar, 2 lovely swimming pools, a shop for bush kit & an à-la-carte restaurant serving delicious meals (including vegetarian food) all day. The bar & restaurants are open to non-residents, & it's a cheerful, sociable spot in the evenings.

There's a wide range of accommodation available here, from classic safari tents to chalets & exclusive-use safari pads, but all are well spread around the grounds & share the same main facilities.

The 6 chalets are housed in 3 double-storey, thatched buildings with each divided into 2 light, bright en-suite rooms, which work perfectly for families or travelling couples. Each building has a communal kitchenette with self-catering equipment, complimentary hot drinks & a wraparound veranda. A larger family chalet has a lovely mezzanine floor with river viewing deck, & comfortably sleeps up to 7 in its spacious, airy rooms. For greater privacy, there are 2 exclusive-use safari houses. A 2min drive from the main area, the innovative Jackalberry Treehouse has 2 en-suite bedrooms & a completely open sitting room on a decked platform overlooking a small dambo, while the Crocs Nest is a large tented riverfront house. It has 2 en-suite rooms (a dbl & a twin) joined by a large living & dining area, & a large deck outside has a private pool overlooking the river.

Across the lawn from the main area, there are also 10 comfortable, en-suite safari tents; the luxury are larger & have views across the river; while the smaller standard tents have a bush view.

Activities include day & night drives in the park (max 6 people per 4x4 vehicle), walking safaris, & all-day drive/walks (if you're staying on a room-only rate, activities are charged at US$89/100 pp low/high season, inc park fees). The camp is smart, relaxed, professionally run & has done a consistently excellent job of empowering & training up local people. It's also well suited to those on a tighter budget, especially as accommodation & activities can be booked separately. *Chalet US$350–455; Standard/luxury tents US$268–370/US$320–430 pp FBA inc park fees, laundry airport transfer; Treehouse US$1,554–1,955 (4 people) FBA inc park fees, laundry & transfers; Croc Nest US$1,830–2,385 (4 people) FBA inc park fees, laundry & transfers. Room only rates available. Children all ages.*

Kawaza Village [map, page 284] (6 huts) For details of this cultural village, see page 317.

Marula Lodge [map, page 275] (11 chalets, 6 tents, 9 backpacker beds) m 0763 455789; e marulalodge22@gmail.com; w marulasouthluangwa.com. In a beautiful position, just upstream from the main Mfuwe Bridge, Marula is just before Croc Valley & Track & Trail Rivercamp.

Used mainly by local groups, Marula's spacious, en-suite chalets, are dotted over well-kept lawns. All chalets have high ceilings, concrete floors, mosquito nets & a ceiling fan. 7 of the chalets (5 dbl, 2 twin) are smaller with louvered windows, which may add a sense of security for a more nervous traveller, but may feel rather restrictive to others. Close by 2 newer rooms are more spacious & have an airy feel to them. Lined along the riverbank are 6 dome tents with a communal bathroom, & another 2-storey building has a dormitory with 9 beds upstairs, & an office below. The camp has mains electricity, with both Wi-Fi & mobile reception available.

The camp's focal point is a large central dining area with open sides & a bar. Wholesome, halal food is served in the à-la-carte restaurant, although guests are also welcome to self-cater. Fridges & freezers are available on site, & the camps chefs are more than happy to help you cook. Game drives & walks are offered & there's a pool near the river. *Chalets US$235–255; Tent US$205–220; Dorm US$200–205. All pp sharing FBA, exc park fees & walking safaris (US$25 pp).* ⌚ *All year.*

Njobvu Safari Camp [map, page 275] (9 chalets) m 0976 942984, 0964 410521; e info@njobvusafari.com; w njobvusafari.com. Cousins Thomas & Nicholas Njobvu opened this small lodge in their hometown in Nov 2019. Having both worked at a couple of the valley's top camps, it's excellent to see these 2 local guides start their own place. Overlooking the Lukonde Lagoon, their camp has a lovely spot with sweeping views from its main deck & en-suite chalets. The high-thatched, ochre chalets are simply furnished with dbl beds & jaunty African fabric, & each have timber shutters opening on to a small deck, with waterfront locations where you can watch fishing parties of water birds. *Chalet US$325 pp, FBA inc park fees, exc alcohol.*

Nkonzi Camp [map, page 281] (4 tents) m 0978 733265; e info@jackalberry.net; w gavinopiesafaris.com; ⊕ 12°58.615'S 31°44.988'E. Located along the banks of the seasonal Mushilashi River, deep inside the park, Nkonzi is an intimate tented camp, owned & run by experienced guide Gavin Opie & his wife Rosie. Even by South Luangwa standards, this camp is off the beaten track.

Opened in 2015, the camp has a strong focus on sustainability, with a borehole being the only permanent fixture of the camp. Every aspect of this low-key bushcamp is removed at the end of each season & restored in time for the next. The 4 small, green, walk-in tents have comfortable beds, gauze windows & canvas flaps at the entrance allow light & a breeze into the tents, but also make them largely mosquito proof. At the back of each tent open-air bathrooms are surrounded by reed walls & contain a bucket shower & flush toilet.

The communal area is delightfully simple – a taut canvas shade over a communal dining table & small lounge area. Reed walls conceal the simple bush-kitchen & an array of solar panels that power the camp. The focus at Nkhonzi is very much on a simple, back-to-nature wilderness experience.

Walking safaris are the main focus of the camp, which are often led by Gavin, who with over 25 years of experience guiding & running safari camps in Zambia is a patient and knowledgeable man to spend time with in the bush. Day & night game drives are also possible. While there is plentiful wildlife in the area, its true draw is the isolation from other camps & the wilderness experience. *US$650–750 pp FBA, inc airport transfers, laundry, local drinks & park fees.* ⌚ *Jun–Oct.*

Thornicroft Lodge [map, page 275] (10 chalets) 0961 672538; e info@thornicroft-lodge.com; w thornicroft-lodge.com. 1km downstream of the confluence of the Luangwa & the Lupande rivers, Thornicroft aims at both the local market & international visitors – & is more mid-range than budget. Each solid chalet here has stones & wood inset into its walls, with large mesh windows to allow the breeze in & keep the chalets cool during the summer, & a large thatch roof providing insulation during the colder winter nights. Inside is en suite, with comfortable beds & white linen inside a walk-in mosquito net, plus a desk & hanging space. Outside a veranda overlooks the Luangwa, which is eating away at the bank to get closer every year. At the heart of the lodge is a quirky swimming pool in the shape of Zambia, & nearby a huge thatched building incorporates the restaurant, bar & lounge area, where tea & coffee is available all day. Morning & afternoon/night game drives are offered as standard, & walking safari (*US$120*) & village excursions (*US$15*) are chargeable extras available on request. *US$242/285, exc drinks, airport transfers, laundry & park fees.* 🕘 *All year.* 👑👑

Track & Trail River Camp [map, page 275] (10 chalets, camping) ☎ 0216 246020; **m** 0977 600556; **e** info@trackandtrailrivercamp.com; **w** trackandtrailrivercamp.com. ⊕ 13°09.979'S, 31°79.261'E. Track & Trail is a lovely, efficient Dutch-owned, mid-range camp just 5 mins' drive from the park entrance. Right next to Croc Valley, it overlooks the river & is reached along the same track. Thatched en-suite chalets of a split-level design each have a private veranda & a narrow balcony allowing guests to take advantage of the river views. The rooms are tastefully decorated with African artwork, & dbl beds downstairs are supplemented by 2 sgl beds on the upper level, all of which are surrounded by large mosi nets. Towards the back of the property, the shady campsite offers individual pitches with water, electricity, BBQ facilities & 2.4m-high raised platforms for pitching tents with a view. All campers share a central ablution block. Campers can store food in the main bar area fridge or eat in the restaurant, where the food is very good, & there's an excellent coffee machine behind the very funky bar. Hammock chairs & quirky seedpod lampshades speak to the owner's artistic streak. Overlooking the river & a popular hippo sandbank, there's an unusual above-ground pool to keep cool, an open-sided gym rondavel to provide an opportunity for some exercise, & a spa offering a range of aromatherapy & massage treatments.

In addition to guided safaris on foot & in an open game vehicle, this is a good place to pick up photography tips from owner-photographer Peter Geraerdts, who also runs photographic workshops from the camp. *Chalet US$385–475; Tent US$299–349. All pp sharing, FBA inc park fees, airport transfers & laundry. Camping US$15–17 pp.* 🕘 *All year.* 👑👑

Wildlife Camp [map, page 284] (9 chalets, 7 safari tents, camping, bushcamp) ☎ 0216 246026; **e** info@wildlifezambia.com; **w** wildlifezambia.com. ⊕ WILDLI 13°6.320'S, 31°45.133'E. This popular, buzzing camp, still large by Luangwa standards, has been leased & run from the WECSZ (page 98) by the helpful Herman Miles since 1992. As the lease fee goes towards conservation/development projects, by staying here you are contributing to a good cause. By its own admission, 'Wildlife Camp does not offer luxury – we offer the bush!' – & indeed the camp makes a good exploration base if you have your own vehicle. If you're driving, pass the airport & turn left just before the main Mfuwe Bridge, following the signs to Nkwali, the Wildlife Camp & others. Routes differ slightly in the dry season, but in the wet season you pass the entrance to Kapani, now closed to guests, then carry on through mopane woodland for about 3km until you see the Wildlife Camp signs; the camp is shortly after that.

Each of the chalets (with 2–4 beds) & twin-bedded safari tents is en suite; all are clean & pleasant, but not luxurious. For those with their own kit, there's a huge campsite within a large grove of mopane trees, with plenty of shaded spots along the river to set up camp. As with any big-game location, don't even think about sleeping outside without a closed tent. In addition to an ablution block, the campsite has thatched shelters, & its own pool & bar. Basic kitchen equipment is available both for the chalets & at the campsite, or with 24hrs notice you can arrange for staff to cook for you. Either way, you'll need to bring your own food; there are a few shops in Mfuwe where you can pick up supplies. Note that there are monkeys in camp, so don't leave food lying around.

The bar/restaurant is often busy & always relaxed. It overlooks a floodplain & the main Luangwa River beyond, & serves both à-la-carte meals & snacks. There are exceedingly popular day & night game drives (*US$50 pp/min 3*) &, between Jun & Nov, walking safaris (*US$50–60 pp/min 3*) on WECSZ land & in the park; the 4-tent bushcamp (about 2–3km from the main camp) makes a great overnight walking safari option. If you have your own vehicle you can drive yourself into the park during the day, though only licensed guides are allowed to conduct night drives. Village tours are also possible (*US$3 pp*). *Chalet US$156–244 pp sharing; Bushcamp US$290 pp sharing, both FBA inc airport transfers & laundry, exc park fees & bar. Chalet US$48–70 self-catering (cook hire US$30/ day); Tent US$32–52 pp SC; Camping US$10 pp. Discounts for WECSZ members. Main camp children all ages.* ⌚ *All year.* ♛–♛♛

Zikomo Safari Camp [map, page 289] (9 chalets, camping) ☎ 0955 798752; **m** 0975 684643; **e** inquiryzikomosafari@gmail.com; **w** zikomosafari.com. ⊕ ZIKOMO 13°01.400′S, 31°53.646′E. Zikomo, meaning 'thank you' in the Chichewa language, is a new camp that opened in 2012 on the border of the Nsefu Sector of the park. The camp is owned & run by David & Victoria Wallace, a couple from the USA. To get to the camp, head north on the road from Mfuwe to Luambe & the turning to Zikomo is well signposted approximately 14km from the turning in Mfuwe.

Zikomo is spread out under a section of riverine forest along the eastern bank of the Luangwa. Although it's situated in the GMA, its proximity to the Nsefu Sector means it has easy access to some excellent areas of the park for walks & game drives. Also, there's often plenty of wildlife around camp. The main area in the centre of the camp is raised slightly from the ground, with completely open sides & a high thatch roof covering a dining area, modest bar & lounge area with plenty of wicker furniture. Close by is a small, irregular swimming pool, with several sunloungers overlooking the river.

The chalets at Zikomo come in 2 styles, with 4 being raised chalets with timber frames, reed walls & high thatch roofs, & 5 chalets with walls constructed from local sand & soil. Both of these rooms are comfortably furnished with both dbl & sgl beds, & are decorated with plentiful African fabrics from Tribal Textiles. Being constructed entirely from natural materials, these rooms feel quite rustic, but they come with modern amenities such as flushing toilets & hot showers in the en-suite bathrooms, & power sockets in the rooms. There is also Wi-Fi available in the main area. The shady campground is also on the riverbank, with 5 separate pitches & shared ablution blocks. Campers are welcome to make use of the facilities at the main lodge. *US$580 May–Nov pp sharing FBA; inc park fees, bar, airport transfers, laundry. Camping US$15.* ⌚ *May–Nov.* ♛♛♛

Other types of trips/accommodation

Mobile safaris There's a lot of hype about mobile walking safaris. Perhaps images of Livingstone or Stanley striding through deepest Africa with an entourage of trusty porters and guides are to blame. I don't know. But these days, let's be honest, it is somewhat different. The term 'mobile safari' is overused.

It used to mean that you set off with all your kit on the backs of porters and camped where you stopped. Think, for a moment, of the consequences of this. You'll realise that it resulted in either very basic camping stops with few facilities, or more comfortable camps requiring a safari of enormous cost. It also required total freedom to camp where you liked, which is now limited and controlled by ZAWA for very good reasons.

Although the term 'mobile safari' is often abused, there is one operation in South Luangwa National Park that comes close to running a proper mobile operation:

Robin Pope's Mobile Safaris Contact Robin Pope Safaris, page 292. Between mid-Jun & Sep, RPS organises about 22 mobile walking safaris along the Mupamadzi River, in the far north of the park. The trip itself lasts 6 days & 5 nights; participants also spend at least 1 night prior to the trip at Nkwali, & 1 at the end at Nsefu or Tena Tena – though a few more days either side would be ideal.

The walks are about 10km per day & a truly mobile camp is used, moved by the back-up vehicle to meet you. The camp has comfortable walk-in tents (each with twin beds), shared hot & cold showers, shared long-drop toilets, & a staff of 8 or 9. Typically they'll use 3 different sites for the 5 nights, & the choice depends on the game & the walkers' interests.

Trips are organised on fixed dates each year, & take a max of 6 people. They are always oversubscribed, & sometimes booked up a year or 2 in advance. The real attraction of these trips is, firstly, that they are just walking in a wilderness area. There's no driving, & you are away from everything but the bush. Secondly, you're in a small group that stays together with just 1 guide. You get to know each other & have a lot of time with one of the valley's best guides. They're very relaxing. (As there is no sgl supplement while walking, these trips are popular among sgl people.) *US$5,197–6,285 for 7 nights, inc costs of Nkwali & Nsefu, exc park fees.* 🕘 *mid-Jun–Sep.*

Fly-camping In Africa, the term 'fly-camp' usually means a simple campsite with a campfire and a small, very simple tent – or possibly just a mosquito net. This is obviously a far cry from the luxurious en-suite tents of most modern safari camps – but camping like this out in the bush, with nothing around you apart from the darkness, does have a real appeal for many cosseted travellers. They're ideal for the thrill of no-frills camping in the bush – expect a bucket shower under a tree and a long-drop toilet – but there's certainly no better way to feel close to the wildlife at night.

Lodges have operated fly-camps in some areas of Africa for years – most notably the Selous Game Reserve in southern Tanzania – but they're still new to the Luangwa. The main companies offering them are listed here. Robin Pope Safaris uses small, walk-in tents for these nights, while Time+Tide and Shentons usually use mosquito net cubes.

- **Robin Pope Safaris** (page 292), which terms them 'Bush Camping', and offers them as individual nights, or for two to three days as you walk between Tena Tena and Nsefu.
- **Time+Tide** (page 292), which offers what it terms 'Luwi River sleepouts' – usually for just one night, for a maximum of four people, and as part of a walk between their bushcamps.
- **Shenton Safaris** (page 292) have a less well-known option called 'camp-outs' available for guests residing at Mwamba – they go north of the camp for one night with a maximum of four guests.

River safaris River safaris are only possible around February to April, depending on the water level in the Luangwa River; then, this is the only way to get around most of the park. See page 87 for more comment on the wet season – but from that you'll realise that the rain is usually in short, sharp, late-afternoon bursts. The rest of the day is often sunny – for photographers the clarity and quality of the light is extraordinary. So if you've been on safari quite a bit, but only seen the Luangwa (or southern Africa) in the dry season, you should aim to make a trip during the rains. You won't see the density of animals that you'll find in October, but the place comes alive with animals and plants you just don't see in the dry season, and the birdlife is phenomenal.

For ten months of the year most of the river's tributaries are sand rivers, but for just a few months they fill with water. Often they are lined by tall old hardwood trees. In a few areas the trees open out onto wide, shallow floodplains, usually dotted with egrets, waders or geese, while in the middle are several nesting colonies for storks and herons, of which the most well known are those in the Nsefu Sector of the park. These rely on a high water level, and the birds won't nest unless the area is flooded. (This is probably a protection mechanism against nest raiders who would be deterred by the water at the foot of the trees.) The main one of these is a huge colony for yellow-billed storks, which take on a beautiful, delicate pink hue when breeding and collectively make for an amazing sight.

Two operations, Time+Tide (page 292) and Robin Pope Safaris (page 292) currently run river trips during the rainy season.

CULTURAL TOURISM Though wildlife is often the main draw of the Luangwa Valley, increasing numbers of visitors are enjoying meeting the local people and learning more of their traditional lifestyles. Cultural tourism is gradually taking off. Currently this has two main points of focus:

Kawaza Village [map, page 284] (m 0976 373126; e nkhomasams464@gmail.com; f KawazaVillageTourismProject). Jointly developed between Robin Pope Safaris and local villagers, and now part of the wider Project Luangwa, Kawaza is an efficient and viable small business for the village which involves visitors staying either for an afternoon, or (much better) overnight. Here they can spend time with people from this Kunda community and learn more of their daily ways of living, traditions and culture.

It started as an effort to end the villagers' feeling of exclusion. Some of the communities around Mfuwe felt that many overseas visitors arrive and leave without any meaningful form of social contact with them. They also wished to get involved in tourism, to raise funds for their school and to support vulnerable members of their community (orphans and the elderly). The scheme is run by a committee of villagers, with Felix John Kalubu, headmaster of the adjacent school, as secretary. His predecessor, David Mwewa, explained to me that the objectives were 'to provide an authentic Zambian experience and raise money for the community'.

Kawaza is a real village and visitors are encouraged to participate in its normal everyday life – to help the women cook nshima and relish, to visit the local traditional healer, to tend the crops, to try fishing, or to visit the local school, church or clinic. Villagers will tailormake an agenda to suit your interests and time – with an overnight stay (see below) the best option.

The effects of the project on the community are gradually showing. Some of the villagers are learning more English in order to communicate better with visitors. David commented, 'When the visitors first came the villagers could not imagine dancing together with a white person or eating together. But when guests come to the village they join in all the activities…when they see the villagers putting up a roof they join them…The visitors like it that way.' Further, the community is benefitting directly, as a proportion of the income goes towards financially supporting orphans and elderly people in the community, as well as providing the local school with textbooks, computers, and transport for pupils and staff.

The village is a 30–45-minute drive from the Mfuwe Bridge, depending on the time of year and the route taken. Transfer costs vary between operators, but the village tour is US$40 pp.

Where to stay

Kawaza Rondavels (6 huts) A handful of rondavels have been built just for visitors: small, clean huts of traditional design with thatched roofs. These have mattresses on simple wooden bedsteads, with spotlessly clean sheets & mosquito nets. Visitors also have their own separate long-drop toilets & rondavels for bathing (using a large tin bowl & a scoop for the water). The food is grown locally & prepared in the village – including tasty cassava for breakfast, with coffee, tea & milk.

Activities are really just taking part in whatever is going on when you are there, & whatever you are interested in. That might mean going into the bush to the village's plots of arable land, collecting local plants & herbs, preparing the food, or even going to help teach a class at the school. Depending on the time of year, you may be allowed to see some (though not all) of the initiation ceremonies for the young people. (As you'd expect, men attend only the men's ceremonies & women only the women's.)

Of special interest, usually arranged on request, would be a visit to a traditional healer, or a local clinic, or a meeting with the area's senior chief Nsefu – the paramount chief of the 6 local chiefs. In the evening, the community's elders tell traditional stories or sing songs around the campfire.

If you've never really tried to put yourself in a totally different culture, then spend a night here. It'll make you think about your own culture as much as Kawaza's, & you'll remember it long after you've forgotten the animals.

Guests staying at most camps in the Luangwa can add a night at Kawaza to their itinerary, with rates depending on the individual camp & the cost of transfers. *Rondavel US$80 pp FBA.*

Nsendamila Cultural Village Very close to the hub of the Mfuwe area, Nsendamila village has been closed for several years, but now offers a small selection of curios for sale. It is easily found by turning left towards Nkwali just before the Mfuwe Bridge, followed shortly by another turning to the left. The village was originally built by the local communities, with funding from various charities and NGOs, its traditional rondavels laid out to demonstrate a local village's way of life. Further plans – for a cultural and heritage centre with drama productions, and for a small museum to house prehistoric artefacts from the Luangwa Valley – have yet to come to fruition. The village is also the site of Uyoba Community School, built and sponsored by the CSL, at which visitors are welcome.

NORTH LUANGWA NATIONAL PARK

(Park fees US$20 pp/day; self drive US$25 pp/day & vehicle US$15/day; bed levy US$20 pp per night) North Luangwa National Park, known simply as 'North Park' in Zambia, is a region veined with the tributaries of the Luangwa River that hug its eastern fringe and, like South Luangwa, remains inaccessible for six months of the year. But when it is open, the privileged few who venture here can stay in its clutch of simple, intimate camps, and explore enormous tracts of untamed land, largely on foot, in the company of seasoned guides. For adventures and wilderness enthusiasts, it's absolutely magic.

Covering about 4,636km² of the Luangwa Valley, it's half the size of the South Luangwa National Park (aka 'The South Park'). It shares the same origin as the South Park, being part of the same rift valley, and its eastern boundary is also the Luangwa River. It has the same geology, soil types and vegetation as South Luangwa, and so its landscapes are very similar.

However, unlike the South Park, which is basically bounded by the steep Muchinga Escarpment to the west, the North Park takes in a lot of this within its protection. About 24% of North Luangwa lies within the escarpment, compared with about 5% of South Luangwa. This means that North Luangwa has a more diverse range of habitats, which is especially interesting for birdwatchers, although there are also mammals found on the hill which aren't normally seen on the valley floor.

From a conservation point of view, it also means that much of the catchment area of North Luangwa's main rivers falls within the boundaries of the park – giving the park authorities more control of its rivers and habitats.

For visitors to the wilderness camps, perhaps the park's most important natural feature is the Mwaleshi River – which is unlike the Luangwa or any of its tributaries in the South Park (except, possibly, stretches of the Mupamadzi). It's a permanent river that flows even in the heat of the dry season, when it's generally very clear and shallow.

THE PARK'S ZONES For the visitor, it's important to understand that North Luangwa is now 'zoned'. Most of the southern side of the park is strictly reserved as a wilderness area. It has very few roads and is currently used only by two small camps, which concentrate on walking safaris. The only way to visit this is to arrange your trip with one of these operators, and stay in one of these tiny camps. If you're not staying at a camp, then you cannot even pass through this area; you'll find clear signs and even booms across the tracks.

However, north of this is a 'zone' that was opened to wider access in 2002. Now it's possible for experienced travellers to bring fully equipped vehicles into the park, and drive through from east to west, or vice versa. Access is strictly restricted to the

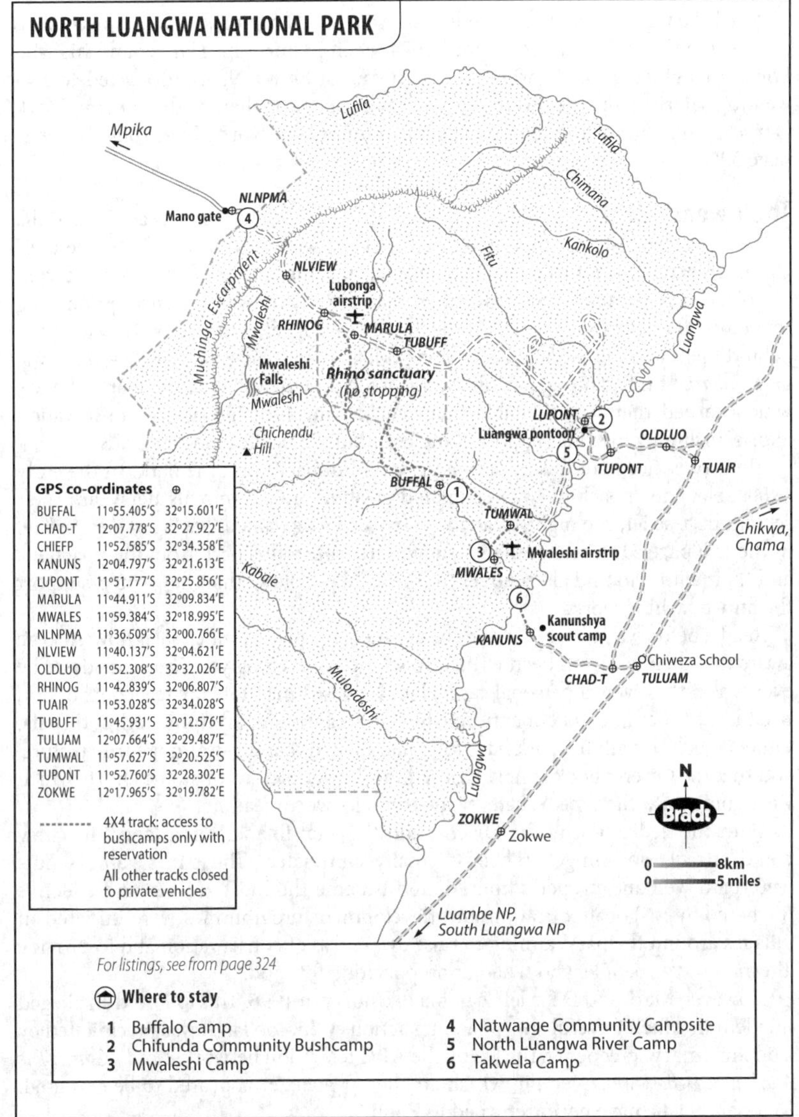

GPS co-ordinates ⊕

BUFFAL	11°55.405'S	32°15.601'E
CHAD-T	12°07.778'S	32°27.922'E
CHIEFP	11°52.585'S	32°34.358'E
KANUNS	12°04.797'S	32°21.613'E
LUPONT	11°51.777'S	32°25.856'E
MARULA	11°44.911'S	32°09.834'E
MWALES	11°59.384'S	32°18.995'E
NLNPMA	11°36.509'S	32°00.766'E
NLVIEW	11°40.137'S	32°04.621'E
OLDLUO	11°52.308'S	32°32.026'E
RHINOG	11°42.839'S	32°06.807'S
TUAIR	11°53.028'S	32°34.028'S
TUBUFF	11°45.931'S	32°12.576'E
TULUAM	12°07.664'S	32°29.487'E
TUMWAL	11°57.627'S	32°20.525'S
TUPONT	11°52.760'S	32°28.302'E
ZOKWE	12°17.965'S	32°19.782'E

---------- 4X4 track: access to bushcamps only with reservation

All other tracks closed to private vehicles

For listings, see from page 324

Where to stay

1 Buffalo Camp
2 Chifunda Community Bushcamp
3 Mwaleshi Camp
4 Natwange Community Campsite
5 North Luangwa River Camp
6 Takwela Camp

more northerly zone, which has one main track across it and several side-tracks. This is a new way to see parts of this remote park, while getting between Luambe National Park and the Great North Road. It also opens up the possibility of an interesting (if challenging) circular drive around eastern Zambia.

HISTORY

Before the mid 1980s Without the conservation efforts and funds that were devoted to South Luangwa, the country's premier game park, the North Luangwa National Park has until recently been a 'poor relation'. Poachers hunting rhino and elephant met less resistance there, and local people crossed its boundaries freely in search of food. The impact on the game was inevitable.

North Luangwa remained a wilderness area for many years, officially accessible only to the Game Department, until 1984 when Major John Harvey and his wife Lorna (daughter of Sir Stewart Gore-Browne, of Shiwa Ng'andu) started to run walking safaris here. They were the first safari operators here and their son, Mark Harvey, runs one of the four camps currently in the North Park (*Buffalo Camp*, page 325).

The Owens' ideal In 1986 a couple of American zoologists – Mark and Delia Owens – visited the park in search of an African wilderness in which to base their animal research, and returned in October '87 to base themselves here. They came from a project in Botswana's Central Kalahari Game Reserve, with an uncompromising reputation for defending the wildlife against powerful vested interests. They also had behind them an international best-selling book about their experiences – *The Cry of the Kalahari*. This had brought conservation issues in Botswana to a popular audience, which earned them considerable financial backing for high-profile conservation efforts, including the vital support of the Frankfurt Zoological Society (FZS).

Their presence here was to have a profound impact upon the park. In the early 1980s, elephant poaching was estimated at about 1,000 animals per year. Their second best-seller, the highly readable *Survivor's Song* (called *The Eye of the Elephant* in the US; page 513), relates their struggles to protect this park from the poachers, and their efforts to find alternatives for the local people so that they would support the anti-poaching work.

Read it before you arrive, but don't be alarmed: the place is much safer now. Also be aware that their book has been written to sell. It's an exciting yarn, but does describe events as if they were a personal campaign. It doesn't mention any real contribution to education, development or anti-poaching from anyone apart from Mark and Delia. Others involved with the park have long maintained that this was not a true picture, and that the Owens' book simply ignored the 'bigger picture' of all the efforts which were going on at the time. Whatever the truth, it's worth reading.

With the dedication of the Owens, and the vital financial assistance that they could attract, poaching has been virtually eliminated. The park's game scouts were paid well and properly housed, and became the most zealous and effective in the country. Local education and development programmes were initiated in villages around the park, aiming to raise awareness of conservation and to provide alternatives for people who relied upon poaching for food.

However, Mark and Delia left Zambia in a hurry in 1996. This followed an alleged incident in which forceful anti-poaching actions went too far. It was precipitated by a documentary screened in the US by the ABC television network, *Deadly Game: The Mark and Delia Owens Story*, in which an alleged poacher appeared to be executed. Mark and Delia have never returned to Zambia.

NORTH LUANGWA CONSERVATION PROJECT Perhaps the real, lasting legacy of Mark and Delia is that they introduced the Frankfurt Zoological Society (FZS) to North Luangwa. The FZS's constant financial support over more than 30 years has done an amazing amount to safeguard this terrific park. Thanks to them, and other important donors, the privately financed North Luangwa Conservation Project continues to support the park and its authorities.

The NLCP's input has concentrated on support for the law enforcement effort, through training and the supply of essential field equipment, rations, vehicles and the building of houses for the field staff. Thus the park's scouts continue to be keen, well trained and well motivated. They also help to conduct regular aerial surveys of large mammals, records of which stretch all the way back to the late 1980s, and to maintain and gradually expand the road network – as well as other aspects of the park's management and conservation.

Various programmes continue to support the communities around the park. These vary from a conservation education programme, with material that is specific to this area, to work on land-use plans – to get the nearby communities to think critically about their future and how they can generate income, while safeguarding some of their natural resources for the future. In late 2022, the formidable community-backed conservation efforts of the team here were globally recognised (see below).

The rhino Meanwhile, wildlife goes from strength to strength here. In 2003 five black rhino were reintroduced, and I was lucky enough to be there to watch as these first animals were fitted with a radio transmitter prior to their release into a large, fenced off, intensive protection zone at the heart of the park. A further ten were added in 2006, five more in 2008, and a final five in 2010. There have been several setbacks, such as the unfortunate deaths of six rhinos from disease and intraspecific

NORTH LUANGWA'S GLOBAL GOLD FOR CONSERVATION

At the end of 2022, the United Nations held a global Biodiversity Conference (COP15). Its aim was to halt and reverse worldwide nature loss. The conference addressed unsustainable practices from pollution to over-exploitation of resources, agreed global targets, and sought to ensure that finance was available to back environmentally sustainable initiatives through the newly created Global Biodiversity Fund. It also commended and shared best practice.

The IUCN Green List is the global gold standard for nature conservation that meets 21st-century environmental challenges in a way that is fair, effective and respectful of local communities. It's a demanding set of assessment criteria, but at COP15, North Luangwa National Park was awarded Green-List status for conservation excellence – one of only 61 protected areas meeting the mark globally. Chosen as a beacon to showcase long-term, successful conservation results for both people and nature, it's a huge accolade for the dedicated conservation team in this wild and beautiful park.

From supporting the creation of a micro-finance system for eco-friendly community businesses to ensuring the ongoing protection of Zambia's only black rhino population and the country's largest elephant population, the North Luangwa Conservation Project has a proven track record in successful conservation outcomes and positive community development.

fighting in 2011, but also huge successes such as the birth of a number of calves, and never losing an individual to poaching. The total population of rhino stood at 34 by 2015, a real achievement for conservation in the valley, and though the number of rhino are now kept secret, the population here is currently known to have one of the fastest growth rates in Africa.

These are the only black rhino in the country; their presence is a strong sign of how secure the North Luangwa is, and that the park expects to enjoy the long-term support of the FZS. It's worth noting that while there are 4x4 tracks through the protection zone, no-one is currently allowed to stop within the fenced area. Other animals, however, can get under or over the fencing; it is only the rhino that are kept within the zone.

The future for North Luangwa seems bright – and Zambia's positive experience of having a national park run with the strong support of a donor-funded private organisation has helped it to look to the future in places like Liuwa Plain, where an analogous project is progressing well, and in the Bangweulu Wetlands.

FLORA AND FAUNA In general, the flora and fauna of the North Park are the same as those found in South Luangwa (page 283). However, the inclusion of the escarpment in the park certainly brings a new dimension to the flora here. An excellent example is the road from Mano down from the escarpment, which is about 12km long. This brings you from the two-storey woodlands of the upper and plateau escarpment, with a lightly closed canopy of semi-evergreen trees 15–20m high, and down through the miombo woodlands on the hills to vegetation more typical of the valley as most people know it.

Often there are bird species here that aren't usually found on the valley floor, and sometimes sable antelope, bushpig or blue monkeys. In the dry season, look also for signs of elephant, which often move into the mountains.

On the valley floor, the ecosystems of the two parks, and the native game species found therein, often seem virtually identical. The North Park has some east African bird species that don't occur further south – like the chestnut-mantled sparrow weaver, the white-winged starling and especially the yellow-throated longclaw – but the differences in species are minor.

However, several differences are apparent. You're more likely to see Cookson's wildebeest (*Connochaetes taurinus cooksoni*), one of the valley's endemic subspecies. The population seems much larger in the north of the valley than in the south. However, you won't find any giraffes here, as they don't seem to occur much north of the Mupamadzi River. (Phil Berry kept reliable records of a few sightings here until about the mid '80s. John Coppinger comments that in his years operating to the North Park since 1990, he's only ever received a report of one giraffe…and that was probably lost!)

Eland, the largest of the antelope, are more common here, and hartebeest are also seen more often than in the South Park. Given their long lifespan, and slow regeneration after poaching, elephant are skittish in the North Park and still relatively scarce. The population is growing, but it'll take a long time before they are as numerous, or as relaxed, as they are around Mfuwe. Buffalo herds seem to be even larger than those in the South Park, and there are some very strong prides of lion. Hyena are also common; those in the North Park seem to hunt more than those in the South, and have developed a tactic of chasing puku into the Mwaleshi River in order to catch them. Those in the South Park tend perhaps to do a little more scavenging, and less hunting. Then, of course, there are the reintroduced black rhino – see page 321.

GETTING THERE The vast majority of visitors to North Luangwa come to one of the few safari camps specifically for walking safaris within the park, and that's certainly the way to get the most out of the area. Typically a three- to five-night stay at one of the walking camps is perfect. Most safari visitors (and there are only a few hundred in the average year) combine a walking trip here with time in the South Park, and fly between the two. For the cognoscenti, it's one of Africa's top safari destinations.

By air Transfers to and from North Luangwa are normally organised as part of your safari package, on small four- to six-seater light aircraft. A short hop here by light aircraft from Lukuzi or Mfuwe (both in South Luangwa) takes about 20–45 minutes and costs in the region of US$350 per person.

Driving The adventurous and experienced may now drive themselves through the north side of the park. Although the access roads from the Mpika area are graded, and even those within the park are reasonably well maintained, it's a very remote and wild area, so you'll need two fully equipped 4x4 vehicles, the expertise to use them, and a high degree of self-sufficiency. See page 296 before you even consider this! Then directions are as follows:

From Mpika via Mano gate There are now two roads to North Luangwa National Park from the Mpika area, the new route being considerably closer to Mpika. The established route, a turning off the Great North Road (⊕ TUNLNP 11°26.378'S, 31°44.307'E), is well signposted just over 60km northeast of Mpika, and 28km south of the turning to Shiwa Ng'andu. There are a few buildings at the junction, a place called Luanya, and the altitude here is 1,556m. Follow this well-maintained track for about 32km, and carry straight on when another sign points left (⊕ TUNLN2 11°35.698'S, 31°55.229'E). It's then a further 11km to the Mano gate (⊕ NLNPMA 11°36.509'S, 32°00.766'E), by which time you've descended about 390m from the Great North Road.

The road glories in the name of the Kalenga Mashitu Range Road. It starts just over 5km north of Mpika, where you turn east towards the North Luangwa (⊕ TU2NLP 11°47.056'S, 31°27.663'E). The only signpost is to Katibunga High School. This, too, is a graded road, initially running parallel to the mountains through woodland, enlivened here and there by the pink and cream blooms of protea flowers. After 38km, you'll go through the village of Katibunga, a prosperous-looking mission station dominated by the Church of Christ the King and now run by Tanzanian monks. A further 21km will bring you to a signpost, where you turn right to the national park. From here the road narrows, and after another 9.4km brings you to the Mano gate.

Mano itself is outside of the park, but this is where you sign in, pay your park fees and find out about the latest park news. The staff are generally very helpful, and usually have reasonably accurate maps charting the route that you are allowed to take across the park. (Self-drivers are only allowed into the south of the park if staying at one of the bushcamps, and must stick to the road, driving directly to camp with no deviations. Breaking these rules can result in removal from the park and a hefty fine!) Note that if you're driving to one of the lodges, you must get to the park gate no later than 16.00. If you're camping, the obvious first stop is the Natwange Community Campsite (page 326), not more than 1km further down the road; a second campsite, Chifunda, lies just beyond the pontoon that marks the eastern access point to the park.

From Luambe National Park Approaching North Luangwa from Luambe, you'll be travelling on the east side of the Luangwa River – very much a continuation of the road from South Luangwa to Luambe. (See page 327 for directions.)

Starting at Chipuka gate (⊕ CHIPUK 12°26.923'S, 32°12.516'E), which marks the northern edge of Luambe National Park, you'll be driving north through some very rural country with a scattering of remote villages. About 9km after the scout camp you need to take a very sharp left turn (⊕ TULUA1 12°25.313'S, 32°16.547'E).

Some 17km or so after that turn, you'll reach the very basic Zokwe scout camp (⊕ ZOKWE 12°17.965'S, 32°19.782'E), which is followed by a lovely stretch of fairly undisturbed cathedral mopane woodland. Around 30km after Zokwe, there's a junction in the track (⊕ TULUAM 12°7.664'S, 32°29.487'E) at Chiweza village school. Turn left here, and continue for another 2.9km until there's a right turn onto another track at ⊕ 12°07.778'S, 32°27.922'E.

(Continuing straight on would lead to a crossing of the Luangwa near the old Kanunshya gate, but this entry to the park is exclusive to the operators who work there, and there is no public right of access.)

Hence take a right turn at ⊕ CHAD-T ⊕ 12°07.778'S, 32°27.922'E and continue north and slightly east for about 28km until you cross an airfield. Just beyond this, turn left (west) at ⊕ TUAIR 11°53.028'S, 32°34.028'E. After another 5km you pass a place called Old Luelo Camp (⊕ OLDLUO 11°52.308'S, 32°32.026'E), and then about 8.5km later, take a right turn (⊕ TUPONT 11°52.760'S, 32°28.302'E). The road ahead is a game track. After almost 7km you'll pass the entrance to Chifunda Bushcamp (⊕ CHIFBC 11°51.645'S, 32°26.066'E), then another 0.4km brings you to a T-junction. Turn right for 200m or so to reach the manual pontoon across the Luangwa (⊕ LUPONT 11°51.777'S, 32°25.856'E; *no charge*) into the North Park. Note that the pontoon takes one vehicle only and is normally operated from 1 June until the end of October, but it's always wise to check in advance. The pontoon is usually monitored by the park's very sharp scouts. In case of vehicle problems they can arrange for help, but a substantial vehicle recovery fee will be payable.

WHERE TO STAY *Map, page 319*

Northern zone The only permanent camp currently in the northern zone is Luangwa North Camp. However, for those who are self-sufficient and driving themselves through the northern zone of the park, there are three simple community camps, two to the west, by the Mano gate, the second close to the Luangwa pontoon in the east of the park. Alternatively, you can camp at Luambe Camp (page 329) in Luambe National Park.

Southern wilderness area Being very remote, and only accessible for part of the year, the park's southern zone – the walking wilderness area – is a difficult place for a safari company to operate. Hence for many years there have been only two or three camps here, all of which concentrate on walking rather than driving. North Luangwa offers an experience that is even more remote and isolated than the rest of the valley, and you can guarantee that you won't be disturbed by anyone else while walking here.

Both of the park's bushcamps stand on the banks of the Mwaleshi, one of the few sources of water for the game, which consequently gravitates to it. It is shallow enough to be easily crossed on foot, allowing you to follow game back and forth across the river. This isn't usually an option beside the main Luangwa, but is easy here. Certainly in the heat of October I relished the cool of paddling across it and even the chance to just sit down in the middle with a drink at sundown. Having such a convenient, cool stream next to camp does make a big difference to both your comfort in the heat and your game viewing.

If you're driving yourself, you will have to leave the park by either the Mano gate or the Chifunda gate. If the latter, do be aware that the road that runs north, parallel to the Luangwa River, is very rarely used, so be prepared for fallen trees, and give yourself plenty of time.

The North Luangwa camps are listed in alphabetical order.

Buffalo Camp (7 chalets) m 0976 970444; e kapishya@shiwasafaris.com; w shiwasafaris.com. ⊕ BUFFAL 11°55.405'S, 32°15.601'E. Situated close to the Mwaleshi River, surrounded by plains, this small, no-frills, walking camp is owned & run by Mark Harvey, who was born & brought up at Shiwa Ng'andu. At the time of writing, the camp was temporarily closed, but will likely reopen again for adventurous travellers. ♛–♛♛

✱ **Mwaleshi Camp** (4 chalets) Contact Remote Africa Safaris, page 292. ⊕ MWALES 11°59.384'S, 32°18.995'E. John Coppinger set up Mwaleshi Camp for Wilderness Trails in 1989, then retained control of it when he set up his own operation, Remote Africa Safaris. Almost all visitors fly between South & North Luangwa national parks; it's a 35min hop from Lukuzi Airstrip, near Tafika, or 45mins from Mfuwe. Remote Africa has its own plane & charming pilot, making this an easy hop. A minimum stay of 3 nights is sensible.

About as remote as bushcamps get, Mwaleshi is a delightfully simple yet well-equipped camp whose reed-&-grass chalets are set on the southern bank of a scenic stretch of the Mwaleshi River. It's within the rhino sanctuary area & guests here have been lucky enough to enjoy sightings. Each has a flush toilet & hot shower en suite, under the stars. There's an attractive thatched dining & bar area, also overlooking the river, & a small riverside shelter so you can cool off in the heat of the day. The permanent manager/guide is one of the experienced team from Remote Africa Safaris – so it's a top-class operation & one of our favourite bushcamps in Africa. Walking really is the activity here (very convenient, given the amount you'll be tempted to eat of their excellent food), & the first time you get on a vehicle from camp may well be when you're leaving. That said, the presence of a vehicle enables walks further afield, a day trip to Mwaleshi Falls, or even the occasional night drive. Mwaleshi offers beach fly-camping 'sleep outs' at no extra charge if everyone in camp is keen on immersive adventure. If you do, your afternoon activity will end riverside for a flame-cooked dinner, before you snuggle into your riverbank bed – a cosy camp mattress on the beach, under a cube of netting, giving magical views of the Milky Way overhead. *US$700 pp sharing mid-Jun–Jul, US$750 pp sharing Aug–Oct, all FBA inc bar, current park fees, exc premium wines.* ⏲ *15 Jun–Oct.* ♛♛♛♛

North Luangwa River Camp (4 chalets) m 0750 288083; e northluangwariverlodge@gmail.com; w luangwaexplorers.com. North Luangwa River Camp sits on the riverbank under the shade of leadwood trees. Linked by raised walkways, the 4 thatched, woven-reed rooms are relatively close together but all enjoy river views of the Luangwa & Lutaba confluence. Interiors are simple but comfortable, each with an en-suite bathroom & small deck. Self-drivers are welcome, with camping & self-catering options available. A 45min drive from the Chifunda Pontoon, it's worth asking the rangers at the pontoon to radio ahead to advise of your arrival time. *US$330 pp FB inc walking safaris & all meals, exc bar & park fees; US$150 pp SC (chef available for US$25/night); Camping US$35 pp.* **$$–$$$$**

Takwela Camp (4 chalets) Contact Remote Africa Safaris, page 292. At the confluence of the Luangwa and Mwaleshi rivers, Takwela is Remote Africa's newest camp. Opened in 2019, this wilderness bushcamp has all the traits of a fine safari spot: simple reed & thatch cottages with open-air en-suite bathrooms, & inviting beds overlooking the sweep of blue river, often teeming with hippos. There's a small social bar & lounge, & a large open floodplain in front of the camp that provides great wildlife-viewing opportunities. It's an intimate, back-to-basics camp offering super walking as well as game drives in a lovely part of the park. Takwela benefits from the excellent guiding associated with Remote Africa, making this a great spot for experienced Africa travellers & real wildlife enthusiasts. A beautiful 10km walk from Mwaleshi (see left), it works particularly well in a walking safari combination. *US$700–750 pp FBA inc park fees. Children min age 12.* ⏲ *15 Jun–Oct.* ♛♛♛

Campsites around the North Luangwa

Chifunda Community Bushcamp (3 chalets, camping) 0216 246127; m 0978 014706; e bushcamp@itswild.org; w itswild.org. ⊕ CHIFBC 11°51.645'S, 32°26.066'E. This thriving community bushcamp on the Luangwa River, just 0.6km from the Luangwa pontoon, is the only survivor of 3 set up under an initiative sponsored by Community Markets for Conservation (COMACO), each employing local people – some of them ex-poachers – & with profits shared between local villages. It's a friendly site with great views.

Surrounded by tall, shady trees, Chifunda is an attractive, well-maintained site overlooking the national park. As well as camping, there are simple but spacious thatched chalets, each with large twin beds, solar lighting, open-air toilet & a big shower area. There's a central dining shelter where meals can be provided (*b/fast US$10, lunch/dinner US$15 pp*) or, if you bring your own food, they'll help with preparation. Guided walks (*US$15 pp*) can be organised, as can game drives in your own vehicle (*US$10 pp*), both exc park fees. Village visits (*US$10 pp*) are a further option. *Camping US$12 pp; chalet US$42 pp.* ⏲ *12 Jun–Oct.*

Natwange Community Campsite (Camping) m 0972 607672, 0967 834910; e info@natwange.org; w natwange.org. ⊕ NLNPMA 11°36.509'S, 32°00.766'E. Opened in 2002 with the help of the North Luangwa Conservation Project, Natwange is run by the local Mukungule community, & all the proceeds go into a fund that benefits the community. It's an ideal place to camp on the western boundary of the park. The campsite is set in beautiful thick *mushitu* forest on the banks of the Mwaleshi River, just 1km or so inside the Mano gate. Individual pitches have flush toilets, hot-water showers & fireplaces for BBQs, & there's a central shelter. Dome tents can be hired (*US$5/night*), with water & firewood provided, but otherwise you'll need all your own supplies.

You can walk along the river from here, arrange a visit to one of the local villages, or perhaps do a little birding or fishing (*guided birding US$10 pp/hr*). Look out for Ross's turaco & the uncommon green twinspot. *US$20/10 adult/child inc showers & firewood.* ⏲ *May–mid Dec.*

LUAMBE NATIONAL PARK

(Park fees US$15 pp/day; vehicle US$15/day; full fees payable in transit between North & South parks) This small park, just 254km^2, is situated between North and South Luangwa national parks and can be reached only between about May and October. The first serious rains turn the area's powdery black-cotton soil into an impassable quagmire – impossible even in the best 4x4. Even in the dry season the roads are not great, as the black-cotton soil sets into a series of hard bumps. The good news, though, is that these – including some self-drive game loops – are re-graded each year.

The park is administered by ZAWA, but the concession for the park was won by Luambe Conservation Ltd, a German-owned Zambia-based company with a mixture of German & Zambian management who run the only lodge within the park.

FLORA AND FAUNA Luambe is mostly riverine forest, and stretches of mopane woodland; some of this is beautiful, tall cathedral mopane with lots of space between the trees and very little undergrowth. There are also areas of miombo woodland and grasslands – including the open Chipuka Plains that are crisscrossed by streams and lagoons, and regularly visited on game drives.

Although the ecosystem is virtually identical to that of the North and South Luangwa parks, Luambe is a small park in the middle of a large GMA, where controlled hunting is allowed. Thus game densities are lower, and the game tends to be a bit more skittish than in the larger parks. That being said, game densities have recovered significantly under the auspices of the German NGO Communities for Conservation Society Cologne (although they no longer operate in the park). On

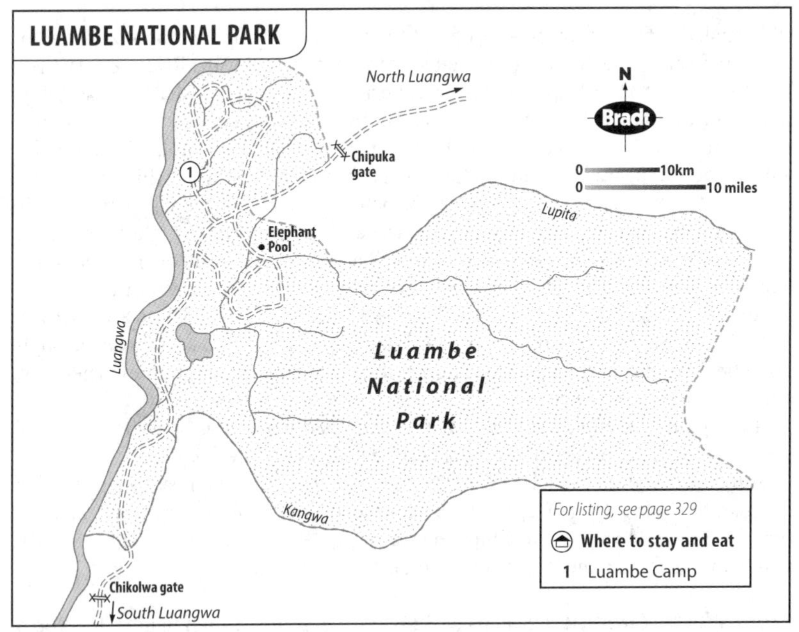

my last trip through here in June, I saw a sprinkling of small antelope – especially around the lodge and near the river: puku, impala, bushbuck, kudu, and waterbuck are common, and both the shy oribi and the endemic Cookson's wildebeest are occasionally seen. In addition to the huge numbers of resident hippo, the elephant population is rising, and there are also reports of increased sightings of predators such as lions, leopards and wild dog. With a bird count of around 400 species, it would be well worth investigating further.

GETTING THERE Many of the park's visitors are adventurous 4x4ers passing through, heading to or from the North Park.

If you are not driving, you'll probably need to charter a five-seater **plane** (pilot plus four passengers) from Mfuwe, which will cost around US$1,000 for a one-way trip to either airstrip. Alternatively, Luambe Camp can arrange road transfers from Mfuwe, which will take around 3–5 hours and cost US$120 per person, one-way (max 4 people). Luambe Camp can also arrange transfers to other locations on request. There are a couple of airstrips (Waka Waka and Luawata) approximately 45 minutes' drive from Luambe Camp, the transfer from Luawata including a short river crossing.

Driving Do read *Lessons in bush travel*, page 296, before you attempt to get to this remote corner by yourself! When you've taken heed of this, the directions are as follows.

From South Luangwa Approaching Luambe or North Luangwa from the South Park, you'll be travelling on the east side of the river. From Mfuwe, head north through the Nsefu Sector, and finally exit the park from Chikwinda gate (⊕ SLNPCH 12°51.983'S, 32°1.008'E). It is then about 3 hours' drive to Luambe, and perhaps seven to the edge of North Luangwa.

On this road, especially near the start, there are a number of small tributaries of the Luangwa to cross. Between about mid-June and the end of October these will usually be fairly easy; outside of that they can be very tricky. About 26km after Chikwinda gate, one of the more notable of these is the Lukusuzi River (⊕ RIVERR 12°41.647'S, 32°7.585'E). I know from experience that this is easier to cross going south–north than north–south, as the southern bank stopped me for about 5 hours on one muddy night in early June. Fortunately, virtually the whole of the nearby village soon appeared – many helped to push and manoeuvre, while some just came for the entertainment. I hope it was better than TV for the villagers, as their unstinting help certainly saved us from a wet and uncomfortable night in the river.

The turning east to the Lukusuzi National Park is (at least in theory) on the south bank of this river, although in practice very, very few people ever venture that way.

About 10km after the river you'll come to the Chakolwa gate (⊕ CHAKOL 12°37.178'S, 32°7.413'E), the entry into Luambe National Park. The road through Luambe is primarily thick black-cotton soil so is often hard and bumpy when dry, and impassable when wet.

It's re-graded each year, but was particularly bad when I last travelled this way shortly after the rainy season; leaving second gear was a novelty.

Some 18km later (⊕ TULUA2 12°28.869'S, 32°9.486'E) you'll pass a left turning to Luambe Camp (page 329), which is almost 3km away. Continuing north, a further 7km will bring you to Chipuka gate (⊕ CHIPUK 12°26.923'S, 32°12.516'E), which marks the northern edge of Luambe National Park.

From North Luangwa See page 324 for the route from Luambe to North Luangwa, and backtrack along that.

From Lundazi There's a 4x4 route from Lundazi to Luambe that is passable in the dry season only. It's a scenic drive of 140km or so, but not to be rushed, particularly when going down the escarpment.

From Mpika via the Corridor Road There is in theory a very difficult route into the Luangwa Valley which leaves the Great North Road south of Mpika, and involves the 'Corridor pontoon' across the Luangwa River, but it's a serious undertaking. Even in a good year it's viable only in the dry season – and unless the pontoon is operating, then only in September or October when the river is very low.

The 'Corridor' is the area between the North and South parks, usually used by professional trophy hunters (hunting on a sustainable basis). They have a few simple camps there, they make the roads, and they usually ensure that the pontoon across the Luangwa is working. But if there's no hunting in any given year, then many of the tracks through here will be impassable.

That said, in a normal year you can turn east from the Great North Road about 40km south of Mpika, at ⊕ TUBATE 12°6.421'S, 31°15.727'E – on the track that passes the old Bateleur Farm after 26km. The next landmark is Nthunta Scout Camp (⊕ NTHUNT 12°19.828'S, 31°31.979'E). About 46km from the main road you reach the Nthunta Escarpment, with its breathtaking view over the whole Luangwa Valley.

The road is very rough as it descends down the escarpment, but after about 11km (it feels longer) you will reach the Mutinondo River. Cross this, and after 8km there's a turning to the left which takes you to Nabwalya village, in the middle of the Munyamadzi GMA. In the dry season, the hunters usually keep a pontoon across the Luangwa, just south of here (near Nyampala Hunting Camp), which links up with the track between Luambe and the South Park. Unless the river is very low, it's absolutely essential to check that this is operating before you even consider embarking upon this route – since otherwise you cannot get through.

THE GOUGH MEMORIAL

High on the Nthunta Escarpment, near the Nthunta scout post, stands a small memorial to Mary Gough. Memories of the origins of this are hazy, but it's said that she was a woman who went (against all advice) to camp alone and unprotected for a long time on the Chifungwe Plain in the 1970s. Some remains of her body and clothing were found, from which it was deduced that she had been eaten by lions – and hence she was buried here.

I'm told that a few years later, during the height of Zimbabwe's war for independence, her son from Rhodesia (now Zimbabwe) came here to revisit the memorial. Local sources allege that he was a spy, who fed back information to the Rhodesian armed forces – resulting in the bombing of several bridges along the Great North Road. However, it seems he was never caught or charged with this – so the truth is uncertain.

Perhaps a reader could confirm or refute this rough history, so that I can expand on the facts and stories around this memorial in another edition!

If you were to carry straight on, instead of turning towards Nabwalya, you would be heading directly over the Mupamadzi River into the South Park. For those directions, see the section on getting to South Luangwa on page 293.

WHERE TO STAY *Map, page 327*

Luambe Camp (4 tents, camping) 0978 823331; e res@luambe.com; w luambe.com. ⊕ LUAMBE 12°25.532'S, 32°16.383'E. Just 3km from the road that links North & South Luangwa, Luambe Camp is currently the only lodge in the park, & is an ideal stopover for those driving between the 2 parks. While few overseas visitors will fly over the camps in the South Park to get here, there is a nearby airstrip, & the area can be seen as a destination in its own right.

Luambe sits in the cool & dense shade of the thick riverine vegetation, overlooking a deep section of the Luangwa River where hippos congregate in their hundreds as the water levels drop. The campsite has space for approximately 10 vehicles & tents, sharing a bathroom & cooking area, while the main camp has 4 safari tents along the riverbank, each with a private veranda, allowing guests to take advantage of the river views, & an open-air, en-suite bathroom allowing guests to shower under the stars. Power for the lodge will come from solar panels, while a mixture of solar geysers & wood boilers will supply hot water for the rooms.

Activities at Luambe include day & night game drives, usually in the Chipuku plains area of the park. Walks are also possible, as are guided bird tours where you can try & spot some of the park's more notable avian species such as Grimwood's Longclaw, or colonies of Bocage's weaver.

Luambe has a strong relationship with the local village of Chitungulu, located approximately 15km to the north, & the lodge purchases much of its poultry, eggs, vegetables & building materials from the village. In partnership with the Chitungulu Foundation, a local sustainable development charity, Luambe runs tours to the village where you can learn about daily life, & the conservation issues facing this isolated community. There is a significant conservation focus & Luambe works closely with the Zambian Carnivore Programme (page 286). *US$440/530 pp sharing/sgl FBA, inc laundry, drinks, exc park fees; US$340/430 pp sharing/sgl FB. Camping US$15 pp, inc hot showers & firewood, exc park fees. Children age 7.* ⊕ *May–Oct.* ♛♛♛

LUKUSUZI NATIONAL PARK

This remote park is on the eastern side of the Luangwa Valley, slightly higher in altitude than the other parks in the valley. There are no facilities here at all, and despite rumours of its privatisation it has seen no development. There's a manned scouts' post near the gate, and an exceedingly poor track leading through the park. It's uncertain how much wildlife has survived the poaching, though it is thought that the dominant predator here is the spotted hyena, rather than the lion. The vegetation is mostly miombo woodland, dotted with grassland.

GETTING THERE Visiting the park requires a major expedition. There is a track that turns east from the South Luangwa–Luambe track, and then continues through Lukusuzi National Park until it reaches the Great East Road. This track east to the Lukusuzi National Park starts (at least in theory) on the south bank of the Lukusuzi River (⊕ RIVERR 12°41.647'S, 32°7.585'E). See page 327 for more directions, but don't expect this turning to be very clear or well marked.

This track is bound to be impassable during the rains. The easiest approach to the park would be to take the Great East Road to Chipata, then turn north towards Lundazi. About 110km beyond Chipata there is a track on the left to Lukusuzi. It's strongly advisable to stop at the game scouts' camp at the park's entrance, and ask them about the condition of the roads. I haven't driven on either of these routes myself.

12

Bangweulu Wetlands Area

The spectacular Bangweulu Wetlands are, after the rains, a fascinating water wilderness similar in size to Botswana's Okavango Delta. This huge wetland area has its own endemic species of antelope, the black lechwe, who roam in herds of thousands on the floodplains, alongside a great variety of other antelope species, elephant and buffalo. The birdlife, enticed by the water, is fantastic and the papyrus reeds are a key breeding ground for one of Africa's strangest and rarest birds: the shoebill.

Nearby, Kasanka National Park is a jewel of a reserve, proving beyond doubt that small can be beautiful, while the grand manor house and estate at Shiwa Ng'andu are a must for anyone seeking an insight into Zambia's colonial history. Mutinondo Wilderness Area is ripe for modern adventurers, while hardcore safari enthusiasts can venture into the stunning and remote North Luangwa National Park (page 318), which can be accessed by road from these areas. Main attractions aside, there are numerous fascinating stops in this region – waterfalls, caves and old colonial monuments – the area where David Livingstone, literally, left his heart.

If you want to explore Zambia beyond the obvious trio of great game parks (Luangwa, Lower Zambezi and Kafue) then this is perhaps the first area that you should visit. The region is perfect for adventurous self-driving visitors with fully equipped 4x4s, but most of the main highlights here can also be visited on fly-in trips using light aircraft for transport.

THE GREAT NORTH ROAD

Access to much of the region is via the Great North Road out of Lusaka. For the most part this is a good tar road, almost pot-hole-free as far as Serenje, though beyond here watch out for some significant lapses in maintenance. From the turn-off at Kapiri Mposhi, the road passes Mkushi and Serenje, then on to Mpika further north. None of these towns is a really attractive destination for most visitors, but all can be useful bases for the area's real draws: Kasanka, Bangweulu, Mutinondo and Shiwa Ng'andu.

MKUSHI Some 92km from Kapiri Mposhi, Mkushi (⊕ MKUSHI 13°38.633'S, 29°23.976'E) is 1km north of the Great North Road, across the railway. Far from being just another stop on the TAZARA line, it's a thriving little town, the centre of a prosperous farming area, with a number of large commercial farms in the vicinity keeping cattle and cultivating cash crops. **Fuel** and provisions are easy to come by, with plenty of **shops**, a **post office**, **banks** (and ATMs) and a police post.

Getting there Several of the **buses** heading north stop in Mkushi. Mkushi is also a stop for **trains** on the TAZARA line between Kapiri Mposhi and Dar es Salaam (page 162).

BANGWEULU WETLANDS AREA

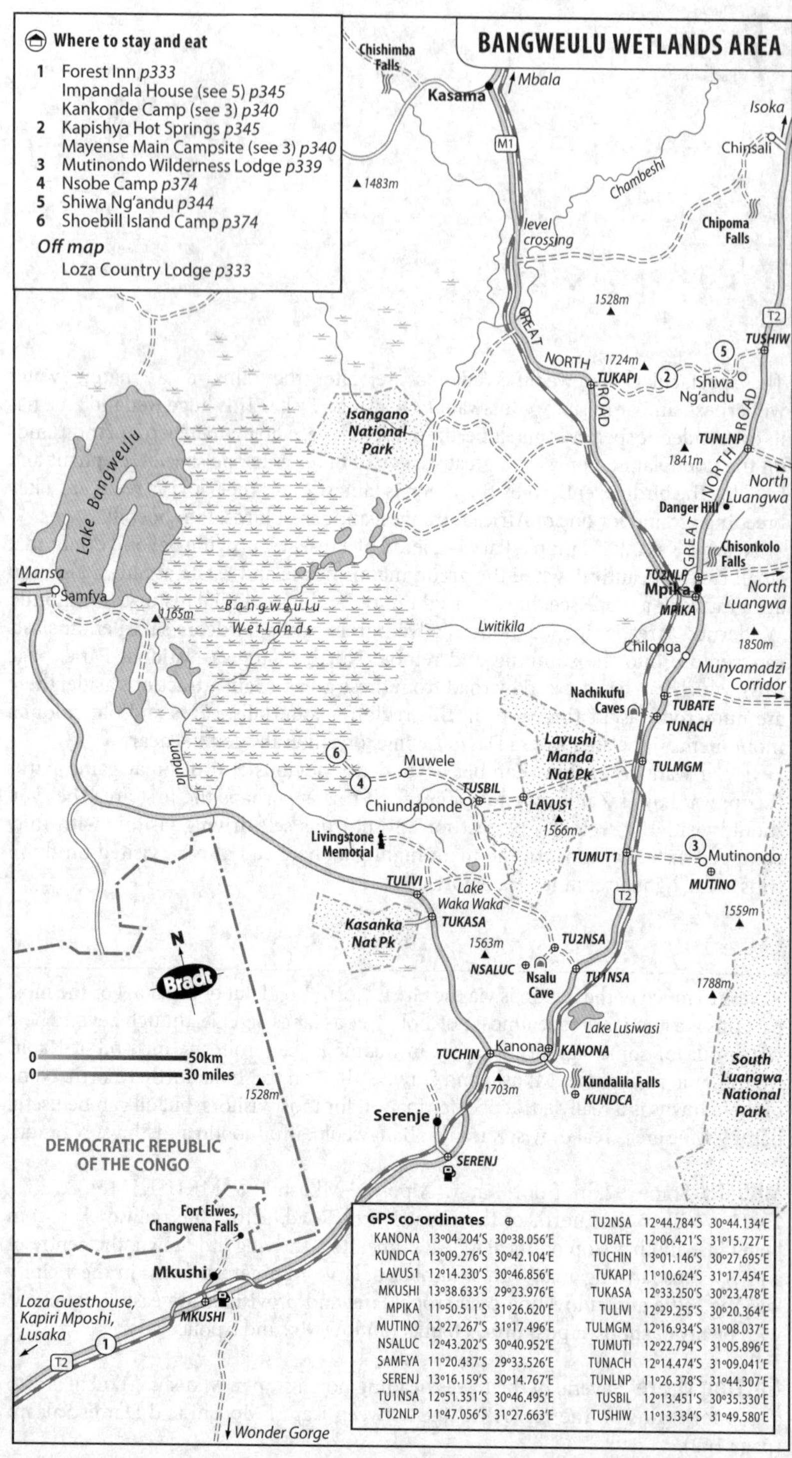

GPS co-ordinates ⊕

KANONA	13º04.204'S	30º38.056'E	TU2NSA	12º44.784'S	30º44.134'E
KUNDCA	13º09.276'S	30º42.104'E	TUBATE	12º06.421'S	31º15.727'E
LAVUS1	12º14.230'S	30º46.856'E	TUCHIN	13º01.146'S	30º27.695'E
MKUSHI	13º38.633'S	29º23.976'E	TUKAPI	11º10.624'S	31º17.454'E
MPIKA	11º50.511'S	31º26.620'E	TUKASA	12º33.250'S	30º23.478'E
MUTINO	12º27.267'S	31º17.496'E	TULIVI	12º29.255'S	30º20.364'E
NSALUC	12º43.202'S	30º40.952'E	TULMGM	12º16.934'S	31º08.037'E
SAMFYA	11º20.437'S	29º33.526'E	TUMUTI	12º22.794'S	31º05.896'E
SERENJ	13º16.159'S	30º14.767'E	TUNACH	12º14.474'S	31º09.041'E
TU1NSA	12º51.351'S	30º46.495'E	TUNLNP	11º26.378'S	31º44.307'E
TU2NLP	11º47.056'S	31º27.663'E	TUSBIL	12º13.451'S	30º35.330'E
			TUSHIW	11º13.334'S	31º49.580'E

Where to stay and eat Alongside a handful of basic places in Mkushi itself, there are two far more interesting and comfortable options within easy reach, with Forest Inn, 30km to the west, particularly geared to the needs of passing travellers.

In Mkushi

Motel Mariana (4 rooms, 10 chalets) Independence Av; m 0975 855455. On the left as you enter Mkushi along Independence Av, the thatched, ochre chalets in well-tended lawns are secure, if not especially stylish, & there is a pleasant pool. Twin rooms have TVs & en-suite showers; dbl-bedded chalets also have small fridges but neither have mosi nets. There's a simple bar & separate restaurant, where fish, steak, chicken & sharing platters ($) are served every evening.

Mirriam's Eco Café Great North Rd; m 0975 823424; ⌚ 07.00–17.30 daily. On the main road, 3km west of Mkushi, Mirriam's is a pleasant stop for coffee & cake, wraps (US$5) & burgers (US$4). Genuine commitment to recycling & mitigating waste, hence the name, with homemade food, a shady veranda & children's play area in the garden. **$$**

Beyond Mkushi *Map, opposite*

Forest Inn (11 chalets, camping) Great North Rd; m 0966 423388; e forestinnzambia@gmail.com; w forestinn-zambia.com. About 30km west of Mkushi, Forest Inn is clearly signposted to the south of the main road. The 4hr drive from Lusaka makes it a convenient & peaceful place to stop for lunch or overnight for those heading towards Kasanka, Mutinondo or Shiwa Ng'andu. Operating for over 2 decades, Forest Inn is owned & run by the Shenton family – the brother of Derek Shenton from Shenton Safaris in Luangwa (page 292) – who offer warm hospitality & a great deal of local knowledge.

The inn's thatched, en-suite chalets are bright & comfortable, each with outdoor seating, & set in well-tended grounds, filled with myriad cultivated plants, trees & even an old steam engine. The grassy campsite has its own well-lit shelter with BBQ facilities & a sizeable ablution block. The gate is kept closed, but there's a gatekeeper & guard on 24hr duty.

The restaurant (⌚ *06.00–20.30*), a good place to stop if you're driving through, serves good, farm-fresh produce, including excellent steaks ($$–$$$). Entertainment in the form of a pool table & darts is in the bar, while the lounge comes complete with a TV & a log fire on winter evenings. Signposted trails lead along short woodland walks – look out for the family of flying squirrels – & birding highlights include Boehm's flycatcher & chestnut-backed sparrow-weaver. Wi-Fi available. *Camping US$15 pp*. **$$**

Loza Country Lodge (10 rooms) m 0960 654306; e loza.lodge@gmail.com; w loza-guesthouse.business.site; ⊕ 13 43.515'S, 29 13.455'E. On the T2 road, 26km southwest of Mkushi, is a signpost to Loza. The 10km gravel track leads to the slightly Italianate farmhouse at the heart of this working farm, which makes for a peaceful overnight stop. Surrounded by lush lawns & neat flowering borders, the lodge's social terrace overlooks the swimming pool, pizza oven & fields beyond. Inside, the rooms are simply but personally decorated & most have an en-suite bath or shower. There are 2 interconnecting family rooms. Wi-Fi is available & home-cooked meals in the restaurant ($$–$$$$) feature fresh vegetables from the garden, which can be washed down with chilled beers & grappa from the farm's vineyard. **$$** *exc b/fast*.

Excursions from Mkushi There are a few interesting sites to the north of Mkushi, and one to the south, though you'll need a self-sufficient 4x4 to reach any of them. If heading north, note the proximity of the sites to the border with the DRC and check the security situation locally before you go. Make sure that you don't inadvertently drive too far, which would be surprisingly easy to do. Explaining an illegal entry into the DRC might not be fun.

Finally, if you are staying here, you're also within reach of Nsalu Cave and the Kundalila Falls (page 359).

Changwena Falls About 2 hours north of Mkushi, this is a very pretty waterfall, near to Fort Elwes and Mount Mumpu. Accessible along highly seasonal, rough forest tracks, it's important to be prepared and ask for local advice and directions from Mkushi before you set off. Camping is allowed just a few minutes' walk from the top of the falls.

The falls themselves are where a small stream leaves its dambo and cascades through a series of three rock pools. The rocks around are an attractive copper colour, helping to make this remote spot particularly beautiful, and a cooling dip after hiking is delightful.

Mount Mumpu Two hours northeast of Mkushi, along some extremely rough tracks in the North Swaka Forest Reserve, lies Mount Mumpu. With a summit elevation of 1,896m, a climb here rewards hikers with far-reaching, panoramic views but a good level of fitness is required to tackle some steep, rocky ascents and narrow crevasses. If you're interested in hiking here, perhaps in combination with Fort Elwes and Changwena Falls, guided (and catered) hikes are offered by experienced Mwamba Mwila (**m** 0977 713901; **e** mwilammwaba@gmail.com; **w** mwilaadventure.com) and allow for greater relaxation on lesser-trodden trails.

Fort Elwes Almost on the border with the DRC, Fort Elwes lies about 40km northeast of Mkushi at an altitude of 1,600m. The tracks to get there are in poor condition and it's not easy to find; ask locally for directions before you embark upon this trip.

The fort was built around 1896–97 by Europeans who came to seek gold in the area west of the Luangwa Valley. They feared reprisals from the local Ngoni people, if (as planned) the British attacked them near Chipata and the Ngoni were forced west.

It's an impressive place, with superb views of the hills in the surrounding area. Four huge drystone walls, some 2m thick and 3m high, form a rectangular building, which originally had a single entrance under one of them. Today it's disintegrating, but a few remnants of the original wooden structures still survive. The *National Monuments of Zambia* booklet (page 513) attributes the building to Frank Smitheman.

Lunsemfwa Wonder Gorge This steep, spectacular 300m-deep gorge marks the point where the Mkushi River meets the Lunsemfwa, and both cut into the sedimentary rocks of the Muchinga Escarpment. This is a very rural, remote area so you'll need a reliable and sturdy 4x4, good maps of the area, and someone to come and look for you if you get stuck.

The gorge – which is quite awesome – is 80km east of Kabwe and about 130km south of Mkushi, further south than what is known as Old Mkushi. The best vantage point is Bell Point, apparently named after a Miss Grace Bell, a friend of the first European to see the gorge, who visited in 1913.

Bell Point is designated as a national monument but there are places you can camp. From Bell Point, you can either scramble down to the bottom to keep exploring the gorge or simply sit and enjoy the elevated vantage point. The latter is recommended.

Getting there From Mkushi, at a signposted turn just northeast of Mkushi, head south for 100km towards Old Mkushi, before turning to Lunsemfwa. The turning for Bell Point viewpoint lies around 20km from Lunsemfwa, in a village confusingly also called Bell Point. Bell Point vantage point itself (⊕ 14°38.500'S, 29°08.600'E) is 35km away from this turning. After 1km there's a fork: take the right track. Ignore all turn-offs for 21km then, following an area of farmland, take a left on to a less-used track. The last village on the route lies 1km after this turning, after which the scenery grows ever more beautiful, despite the presence of a car wreck at 32km (a casualty, so it is said, of the Rhodesian war).

It's perhaps worth noting that the gorge is actually more easily accessed from Kabwe to the south (140km north of Lusaka), via Mulungushi, so could be incorporated into a route north from Lusaka if you're planning a self-drive adventure.

SERENJE Set in a valley in undulating countryside about 3km north of the main Great North Road, Serenje is 110km northeast of the turn-off to Mkushi. There are a couple of **fuel** stations, a **bank**, Catholic mission, teacher training college, **post office**, police station and a small hospital.

Getting there If you're **driving** yourself, turn off the main road at the Puma fuel station (⊕ SERENJ 13°16.159'S, 30°14.767'E). At the noisy and busy **bus** station, several buses a day stop between Lusaka (from K220 one way) and Kashikishi on Lake Mweru, while the Lusaka–Kasama **postbus** stops at the post office three times a week in both directions. Serenje is also a station on the **TAZARA** line (page 162).

Where to stay and eat Of Serenje's selection of guesthouses, one – the Mapontela – has long shone out above the others; it's also the best restaurant in town. Alternatively, **Villa Mbanandi** (m 0955 814657), further down the same road, is an adequate stop.

Mapontela Village Inn (8 rooms) 515 Ng'answa Rd; m 0979 587262. Serenje's established favourite is on the right as you enter the town, beyond the police station. It's a small warren of a place, run by a charming Zambian matriarch, Anna Mulenga, & her husband Steve Luker, a retired builder who came to Zambia with the Peace Corps. It has a smart exterior, shaded restaurant veranda, clean rooms & secure parking. It's a good spot to overnight or for lunch; the menu ranges from sandwiches to omelette & chips to nshima & steak ($–$$). **$–$$** exc b/fast.

Excursions from Serenje There are various waterfalls in the area, including the narrow but pretty cascades of Mulembo Falls, also known as Chipota Falls (⊕ MULEMB 13°13.067'S, 30°25.809'E). This is reached by turning off the main road 12km northeast of the Serenje turn-off, towards Kalwa Farm – a sadly rundown, self-catering guesthouse gifted to the Zambian Baptist Mission. After 4km, turn left just before the guesthouse, and immediately right. Just over 5km brings you to a rounded, domed rock, and a further 6.2km to the falls themselves. The right track leads to the falls, while straight on will take you to the river.

A little further afield are the beautiful **Kundalila Falls** (page 359).

MPIKA Though no bigger than Mkushi or Serenje, Mpika (⊕ MPIKA 11°50.511'S, 31°26.620'E) is a busy crossroads of a place which has an increasing air of affluence. Here the Great North Road forks: one branch goes to Kasama, Mbala, and Mpulungu on Lake Tanganyika; the other heads directly for the Tanzanian border at Nakonde. It is about a day's travel from Lusaka (8hrs), Mpulungu or the Tanzanian border, which perhaps explains why travellers often end up stopping here overnight, in spite of anything of particular interest locally.

Getting there Getting to Mpika is easy, with a choice of public transport if you are not driving.

By bus Daily local bus services link Mpika with Lusaka, Mbala and (to a lesser extent) northeast to Isoka and Nakonde. Depending on the operator, buses stop either next to the fuel station on the main road through town, or on the opposite side of the road. Sometimes, they will pick you up if you wave them down on the side of the road, but don't bank on it. The town is also serviced by the thrice-weekly postbus between Lusaka and Kasama.

By train Mpika is one of the stops between Kapiri Mposhi and Dar es Salaam, in Tanzania, on the TAZARA railway. Tickets on the express train between Mpika and Kapiri Mposhi cost K235 in first class, K181 in second and K154 in third.

The TAZARA station is about 5km out of town, and private pick-up trucks operate shuttle runs between the station and central Mpika, fitting as many people onto the vehicles as they can carry. The train rarely arrives on time so be prepared. If you arrive in the early hours of the morning then your options are to get one of these shuttles quickly, or to sleep rough on the station until daybreak and then try to get one. At times like this, the station is crowded but fairly clean and safe.

Tourist information Based at Bayama's Lodge (see below) the Mpika Tourism Association (MTA), a non-profit organisation founded with the help of Open Africa, offers local maps, a reservation service and information on local sights and tours.

Where to stay and eat

Mazingo Motel (34 rooms, camping) Great North Rd; t 0214 370314; m 0966 803919. ⊕ 11°48.570'S, 31°27.091'E. West of the road, 3km northeast of Mpika, this secure motel lies in pleasant gardens within a quiet compound. It offers basic en-suite rooms & a campsite with separate showers. Lunch & dinner available. **$–$$** exc b/fast.

Northern Rock Hotel (35 rooms) Great North Rd; m 0950 331640; e northernrockhotel@gmail.com; w northernrockhotel.com; f NorthernRockHotelMpikaZambia. Large, clean, en-suite rooms with a basic restaurant on the Great North Rd. **$–$$**

Bayama's Lodge, Pub & Grill (5 cottages, 3 rooms, camping) Casanova 5434; m 0977 410839, 0977 316143; e bayamakumpika@gmail.com; w bayama.de; ⊕ 11°50.733'S, 31°26.780'E. Behind zebra-striped walls, just east of the Great North Rd at the Kasama turn-off, Bayama (Bemba for 'uncle') has 5 cottages, 3 dbl rooms & camping is allowed. There's a bar, restaurant (traditional & international fare; $) & BBQ facilities, secure parking & tourist information. **$** exc b/fast.

Chintu Mukulu Community Campsite (3 chalets, camping) Great North Rd, Salamo Village; m 0978 064516; or contact Mutinondo (page 339). ⊕ CHINTU 12°16.601'S, 31°2.515'E. This community-run site lies close to the road about 83km south of Mpika. It has both simple chalets with bedding, & conventional tent pitches, sharing ablutions. Walks & cultural tours to the local Mpumba community to sample the traditional Bisa lifestyle are on offer, plus farming demonstrations (Nov–Jul). **$**

Fresh Air Lodge (12 rooms) Kasama Rd; m 0976 513500; e freshairlodge@gmail.com. Hidden behind vibrant walls, Fresh Air Lodge is unmissable. Simple, en-suite rooms, some with fridges & DSTV, & secure parking. **$**

Landmark Lodge (8 rooms) m 0966 400487. On the main road, perfect for easy stopovers, these large cottages are clean & functional with shaded parking outside. **$**

CIMS Restaurant Great North Rd. This clean place, opposite Melodies Lodge, claims to serve 'the best chicken & chips in Mpika', alongside more adventurous offerings such as ifishimu – caterpillar. There's a selection of bread, cakes, pies & dairy produce too, making it a possible place to put together a packed lunch. $

Other practicalities There are three **fuel** stations near each other on the Great North Road, close to the turn-off to Kasama. The most conspicuous of these has an **ATM** – and there's another ATM at Zanaco near the turning into the town; there's also a branch of the Finance Bank in town. For non-perishable **supplies**, GM Trading is worth a look. There's also a busy little market and roadside stalls for fruit and vegetables, and a couple of bakeries.

For **communications**, there are a couple of post offices, one at the Mpika–Kasama junction and one in the southeast in Mpika Boma. Should you be in need of vehicle **repairs**, ask at Bayama's Lodge (see opposite).

Excursions from Mpika There are a few interesting caves and waterfalls around Mpika, while both Mutinondo (page 339) and Shiwa Ng'andu (page 341) merit large sections of this chapter. To go anywhere away from the main roads, you'll need a self-contained 4x4 and experience, even in the dry season.

Nachikufu Caves (⊕ NACAVE 12°13.939'S, 31°08.693'E; entry US$10/5 adult/child; vehicle US$5; camping US$15 pp inc entry) The striking setting of this cave complex with its geometric San/Bushman rock paintings may be worth a detour, though taking admission fees into account, that's debatable unless you're planning to camp. When excavated in the 1940s Nachikufu Cave was estimated to have been occupied intermittently for about the last 15,000 years. This is no surprise when you consider that all the essentials for survival are here: a regular supply of water from a nearby stream, shelter provided by the cave, firewood in abundance, grass for bedding and a good supply of game and vegetable food sources from the local environment. The cave is also the 'type' site of the Zambian Late Stone Age, which is known to archaeologists as the 'Nachikufan Industry' (25,000–2,000 years ago). A small display of artefacts is kept within the cave entrance and access is only with the official caretaker, who is usually stationed on site, or contactable by a mobile number left on a nearby sign.

Both the rock shelter and the cave look north over a wide plateau, and are formed from a ridge of quartzite rock – perfect for stone tools. There's also a perennial stream about 500m away from the cave. The paintings themselves are fairly simple: various figures silhouetted in black, including a couple of elephants, a beautifully drawn antelope, and human figures, some of whom are depicted with bows and arrows and one with a spear. It has to be said, however, that they are not brilliant, and will be decidedly underwhelming if you've explored impressive rock art in other areas.

The signposted turning (⊕ TUNACH 12°14.474'S, 31°9.041'E) to Nachikufu is about 55km southwest of Mpika. This turning leads you north and west from the main road, over the TAZARA railway, and reaches the cave within about 2km.

Chipoma Falls (Entry US$10/5 adult/child; vehicle US$5; camping US$15 pp inc entry) About 20km south of Chinsali, the Chimanabuwi River drops 40m over a distance of 500m at this large set of rapids and cascades (⊕ CHIPOM 10°44.998'S, 32°00.284'E). It's a lovely spot for rock hopping, exploring and for a dip in the water. Although not an official site, camping is permitted in the shady parking area, where there's an open-sided shelter and long-drop toilets.

To reach the falls from Mpika, head north for Chinsali and Isoka and then turn left about 24km before you reach the turn-off for Chinsali (that's about 57km past the turning to Shiwa Ng'andu). Follow this road for around 6km, taking left turns at all the forks and junctions encountered, until you reach the caretaker's house by the falls.

Chisonkolo Falls (**w** diompika.org/lwitikila-school/chisonkolo-falls; ⊕ 08.00–22.00 daily*)* Also known as the Lwitikila Falls, this is a good place for a dip and lunch, or simply to wander. The falls are pretty rather than spectacular, with scope for walking in the surrounding woodland and up to see the views. It lies in a community area, with local people responsible for the site who also sell drinks and snacks. It's a quiet spot, except in August when there are various youth camps here, with all money raised going to the school.

To get to the falls from Mpika, take the road to Chinsali and Isoka for about 20km, until you see a right turn clearly signed to Lwitikila Girls' Secondary School (⊗ TOLWIT 11°43.600'S, 31°28.572'E). Follow this track uphill, turning right just before the school on to a smaller track leading directly to the falls (⊗ LWITIK 11°43.810'S, 31°29.674'E).

AROUND MPIKA

MUTINONDO WILDERNESS AREA Mutinondo Wilderness is a private 100km² reserve, started in 1995 by Mike and Lari Merrett, and still under their dedicated, meticulous care. The area encompasses a pristine section of verdant miombo woodland near the edge of the Luangwa Escarpment, complete with huge granite whalebacks, crystal-clear rivers, stunning waterfalls, pristine woodlands and some small wetland areas. There are great plants and birds, which all make for a lovely ambience.

It's a lovely bit of Africa to explore on foot or on bike, as well as being terrific value. Ideally you should plan on spending at least three nights here. While Mutinondo is quite off the beaten track (if there is a beaten track in this part of Zambia?!), it does have its own airstrip.

History Although this area has been occupied for centuries, as witnessed by the Iron-Age workings about 6km from the lodge, Mutinondo was first really put on the visitors' map in 1994, when Mike and Lari started looking for a place suitable for both conservation and tourism. Even having obtained the permission of the local authorities and chief, it wasn't until 2001 that they were able to start development. Throughout the process, they seem to have made every effort to develop the area sensitively, with minimum impact and maximum use of renewable natural resources, such as solar and wind power.

Flora and fauna Mike and Lari have strong ties to the academic community, and offer generous 'research rates' at their lodge. As such, the area's smaller flora and fauna has been meticulously catalogued – including over 1,000 plants, confirmed with help from teams at the Royal Botanical Gardens at Kew, as well as dozens of butterflies and a good range of the varied birdlife.

Flora The main vegetation here is classic miombo woodland, which is in pristine condition with plenty of *Brachystegia* and *Julbernadia* species. This is interspersed with numerous lush, herby dambos, many of which drain into permanent rivers and streams on the reserve. This water, together with the shade of the established woodland, makes the atmosphere relatively moist – which helps to promote such lush plant growth, making this a wonderful spot for *Aloe* species. Beside the rivers, you'll also find thin strips of riverine forest, and occasional patches of moist evergreen forest (*mushitu*). Judging by the thick lichens on the rocks and 'old man's beard' (*Usnea*) hanging from the trees, the air is very clean, and looking into the night sky you'll be hard pressed to spot any light pollution at all.

There is an impressive array of flowering plants, especially during and at the end of the rains. Among these are several species of proteas and a great range of orchids; many of the latter have been carefully relocated around the chalets after they were rescued from the trees felled to build the lodge's access road. During one visit I found a huge cycad in the woodland. At the end of winter, in mid-September, it's a magical place to witness the 'miombo flush', when the fresh new leaves bring a sea of colour across the woodland. If you're visiting during the rains, keep a look out for specimens of *Termitomyces titanicus*, which is the world's largest edible mushroom. The largest that Mike and Lari found had a diameter of about 85cm but they grow up to a metre in diameter. The local people have known about these for centuries; but it seems that they were first described to science as late as 1980.

Fauna Mutinondo is a good spot for birding and is one of Zambia's 'important bird areas', according to Birdlife International. The bird list available to visitors currently stands at 325 species, and is constantly growing. Obvious 'specials' include Anchieta's barbets, long-toed fluff tails, bar-winged weavers, half-collared kingfishers and Ross's turaco.

While Mutinondo is not primarily a game destination, if you spend enough time here you might find a variety of mammals, from duikers and klipspringer to sitatunga – though sightings are infrequent. As the area has remained protected, wildlife sightings are improving, with some of the larger antelope species like roan and sable sometimes seen grazing in the wetlands between September and November. Of much more interest really are the plants, flowers, trees, mushrooms and smaller wildlife, which also help to make walking here a real pleasure.

Getting there The Mutinondo turn-off on the Great North Road (⊕ TUMUTI 12°22.794'S, 31°5.896'E) is a few hundred metres south of Kalonje railway station on the TAZARA railway. It's about 12km southwest of the turning to Lavushi Manda, and 77km southwest of Mpika, or 364km northeast of Kapiri Mposhi. From the signboard to the lodge is a further 25km along a level track, which is accessible by 2WD year-round. There is a 5-ton weight limit on large camping vehicles.

Mutinondo's airstrip is just over 1km from the lodge (⊕ MUTAIR 12°26.998'S, 31°16.954'E), useful for those on a fly-in trip. Its 900m runway is suitable only for single-engine aircraft. Alternatively, with advance notice, it is possible to arrive at Kalonje by train, and arrange for the team at the lodge to collect you.

Where to stay and eat *Map, page 332*

For individual visitors there are three options: the lodge, nearby Mayense campsite and the self-catering camp, Kankonde. All are open year round, and share the same contact details. Activities available are detailed on page 340 and campers are welcome to make use of the honesty bar in the main lodge, or book in for wholesome, set menu meals (US$12 b/fast & lunch; US$18 3-course dinner). Note that special arrangements can be made for scientific, educational and school groups, which are warmly welcomed.

Mutinondo Wilderness Lodge (4 chalets) **m** 0978 198198, 0979 862545; **e** info@mutinondozambia.com; **w** mutinondozambia.com. ⊕ MUTINO 12°27.267'S, 31°17.496'E. The lodge is a lovely spot to stay – though quite idiosyncratic in its way, with both the chalets & the bar & dining areas carefully built around the rocks, each some distance from the other. Every effort has been made to source the building materials locally, & to use local skills & labour in the lodge's construction. The handmade bricks, stone & thatch used were all manufactured, quarried or harvested in the area,

& all the woodwork, including the furniture, was constructed by a father-&-son carpentry team from the village of Salamo. As you'd expect, most of the staff are from the surrounding villages.

Each of the chalets is large & individually designed: solid, but not luxurious. There are fireplaces (at an altitude of 1,400m, it can get very cold!), simple furnishings & great views over the wilderness; Mulombwa has a particularly spectacular balcony. Families & couples can be accommodated, with 3 of the chalets having an en-suite shower & separate toilet, while the last, arguably the most spectacular, has a separate bathroom with a home-built bath as well as a shower & a 'loo with a view'. Water is heated by individual solar heaters & wood-burning boilers. The cash bar operates on the honour system & the restaurant serves straightforward but substantial meals, including curries, casseroles & roasts. Limited Wi-Fi is available at the lodge, free of charge. *Standard US$125 pp/dbl, all FBA inc park fees & conservation levy; extra bed US$90 pp.* ♛♛♛

Mayense Main Campsite (8 pitches) This is a lovely campsite, with raven-proof storage cupboards, individual BBQ grills & picnic tables, good hot showers & clean long-drop toilets. As there are a limited number of pitches, some suitable for roof tents & some with shelters, you should consider booking in advance if possible. There's also a simple, thatched campsite room that is kitted out with 2 beds & all linen. There's plenty of help on hand for planning explorations, & hiking maps are available free of charge. The 1st bundle of firewood is free, then you'll pay K20/bundle. The campsite is adjacent to Mutinondo Wilderness Lodge; campers are welcome in the bar &, with advance notice, to dine here (3-course evening meal US$18). *US$20 own tent; campsite room US$36 pp; tent hire & bedding US$38.* **$$**

Kankonde Camp (1 s/c chalet, camping) ⊕ KANKON 12°24'S, 31°19'E. Some 11km from Mutinondo's main lodge & campsite, & a stone's throw from a swimming area on the Mutinondo River & the slopes of Mbuya Rock, Kankonde offers the independent traveller seclusion & greater freedom. Bar a caretaker to provide hot water, you'll need to be completely self-sufficient here. There's a single, open-sided grass chalet with a dbl bed (no bedding) & ample room for pitching tents (max 20 people). A long-drop toilet & 2 bucket showers, a BBQ grill & thatched nsaka *for dining and cooking, & a couple of large tables complete the* amenities. Firewood is supplied & water for bathing & drinking is sourced from the Mutinondo & is safe to drink or can be boiled if preferred, but otherwise you'll need to bring everything with you, including all bedding, food, crockery, cutlery, etc. Check in is at the main lodge to collect a map & other information before heading out to Kankonde. *Tent US$25 pp; grass chalet US$30.* **$**

What to see and do Mutinondo best suits those who feel comfortable exploring; it's a magical place for 'old Africa hands' who want to go off for hours on their own. It's less ideal for those who are new to the bush, although those with some degree of independence can hire one of the lodge's team to guide them around (US$25/day), and still have a great time. It's not the perfect place if you need your hand held all of the time, or if you're reluctant to abandon your vehicle, as there are relatively few motorable tracks (although there is one dry-season track which extends 25km to the escarpment). For lodge guests, activities are included in the rates; campers and those staying at Kankonde pay extra.

Walking and cycling There's a good network of trails, and the country is hilly without being particularly strenuous. The huge granite whalebacks are great for scrambling up, giving you access to superb views of the surrounding country and, in the east, to the Luangwa Escarpment and beyond. It would be very easy to spend three or four days exploring the tracks and whalebacks alone. Trail maps are available at the lodge, and several of the hiking trails are signposted with arrows and distances, but I'd also suggest that you take a GPS.

Dedicated and totally self-contained hikers who want something more challenging can arrange longer hikes here, including bush-camping stops. These might encompass the adjacent community-based conservation area, some of the magnificent escarpment waterfalls, or possibly even a long walk down into the Luangwa Valley. It's necessary to give advance warning to the lodge so they can make the appropriate arrangements with the local community. If you would prefer some support on the longer hikes you can arrange a guide and porters (US$70/guided trek) at the lodge. If you prefer cycling, you can also rent mountain bikes.

On the water There's a network of very clear rivers and waterfalls, with no crocodiles, hippos or bilharzia. (Though *always* double-check such a comment locally before you swim: the situation can change!) The rivers here have been re-stocked with indigenous fish: red-breasted, three-spot and green-headed bream – so fishing is possible, albeit on a strict catch-and-release policy.

There are two canoes stationed above one of the waterfalls, allowing you to float through the waterlilies along a tranquil, tree-lined section of the river. Alternatively, you can just enjoy swimming in the pools around the waterfalls.

SHIWA NG'ANDU

Background

The early days Shiwa Ng'andu was the inspiration of Stewart Gore-Browne. Born in England in 1883, Gore-Browne first came to Africa in 1902, at the tail end of the Boer War, and later returned in 1911 as a member of the Anglo-Belgian Congo Boundary Commission. On his way back to England, in 1914, one of his carriers guided him north towards Tanzania, passing beside Shiwa Ng'andu, the 'Lake of the Royal Crocodiles'. He intended to settle in Northern Rhodesia, so he negotiated with the local chief to buy the land around the lake – and then, after World War I, he returned to establish himself there. He borrowed money from his beloved Aunt Ethel, and began to build Shiwa.

Gore-Browne was uncomfortable with the colonial attitude towards the African people. He was determined to establish a utopian state, and in his hands Shiwa grew into a vast enterprise with schools and a hospital run with benevolent paternalism. By 1925, Shiwa Ng'andu was employing 1,800 local people.

Gore-Browne passed on skills to them, and together they built neat workers' cottages with tile roofs, as well as bridges and workshops and finally a magnificent manor house, set atop a hill overlooking the lake. Anything that could not be made locally was transported on the heads and backs of porters, along the arduous route from the nearest town, Ndola. At that time it took three weeks to reach Shiwa from Ndola: 70 miles on foot or horseback to the Luapula River, followed by a boat through the Bangweulu Wetlands, and a further ten-day walk from the Chambeshi River to Shiwa.

The heavy English-style furniture was made out of local wood; the large gilt-framed portraits and paintings, silver ornaments, and an entire library of books came from England. Everything came together to create an English country mansion in the heart of Africa – a testament to the determination with which Gore-Browne pursued his vision.

In 1927, when he was 44, Gore-Browne met and married Lorna Goldman, the 'ravishing' 18-year-old daughter of his first love, Lorna Bosworth-Smith. She came to Shiwa, threw herself into her husband's projects, and the estate and its inhabitants prospered. Gore-Browne built a distillery for the essential oils that he hoped to make into a profitable local industry. (Given Shiwa's remote location, the estate's produce had to be easily transportable: a non-perishable, valuable commodity of low bulk.) He had several failures, trying roses, geraniums, eucalyptus, peppermint and lemon grass with no success. Eventually, he succeeded with citrus fruit, which flourished and brought a good income into the estate…until a *tristezia* virus killed off the fruit trees. This hit the estate hard, forcing Gore-Browne to turn to more conventional, less profitable, agriculture.

Regrettably, the stresses of the estate and Gore-Browne's constant travelling took a toll on his marriage; it resulted in his separation from Lorna, who had found it difficult spending such a great deal of time alone at Shiwa with their two daughters, Lorna and Angela. Lady Lorna returned to live in London in 1945. She came back to Shiwa once, in 1958, and then never again. Even in England she would rarely speak of Shiwa; in December 2001 she died, aged 93.

In the meantime, Gore-Browne had become a rare political figure in Northern Rhodesia: an aristocratic Englishman, with excellent connections in London, who commanded respect both in the colonial administration and from the African people. He had been elected to Northern Rhodesia's Legislative Council as early as 1935, and was the first member of it to argue that real concessions were needed to African demands for more autonomy. He was impatient with the rule of the Colonial Office, and resented the loss of huge amounts of revenue through taxation paid to Britain, and 'royalties' paid to the British South Africa Company.

He was knighted by George VI and became mentor to Zambia's first president, Kenneth Kaunda, who, in 1966, appointed him the first ever Grand Officer of the Companion of the Order of Freedom, the highest honour ever bestowed on a white man in Zambia. He died, an octogenarian, in 1967, and today I believe that he remains the only white man in Africa to have been given a full state funeral. He is buried on a hill overlooking the lake at Shiwa – an honour only bestowed on the Bemba chiefs. In the words of Kaunda, 'He was born an Englishman and died a Zambian. Perhaps if Africa had more like him, the transition from colonial rule to independence would have been less traumatic.'

A highly readable and very successful historical account of the life and times of Stewart Gore-Browne and Shiwa Ng'andu, *The Africa House*, was first published in 1999 (page 511), although note that reservations have been expressed by the family about the historical accuracy of the book.

After Sir Stewart On Sir Stewart's death, the estate at Shiwa passed to his daughter Lorna and her husband, John Harvey, who lived in the house with their four children, Penny, Charlie, Mark and David. However, with the very poor agricultural soils, both the farm estate and the manor house proved difficult to run and maintain. In 1967 the Harveys bought a dairy farm near Lusaka, where both John and Lorna were murdered in 1992. On their deaths, the estate passed to three of Gore-Browne's grandchildren. Initially David took over its management, and by 1995 there were moves to turn the manor house into a museum. Finally, in 2000, Charlie Harvey bought the estate from his siblings and now runs it with his wife, Jo, and their two children, Tom and Emma.

Shiwa reinvented Until 2000, Shiwa typified an old English-style country estate that was gradually slipping back into the African bush. In 2001, Charlie and Jo sold their property and literally 'picked up' their entire farming business just north of Lusaka and translocated it 750km north to Shiwa. Together they brought endless farm equipment, 800 cattle, 600 sheep, 500 assorted wild game animals, eight horses, five cats and five dogs. It was a massive undertaking: for the cattle it was a three-day train ride, followed by a ten-day trek through the bush. With them came two large buses carrying the families – women and children – of the 34 men who had elected to follow the Harveys north.

Soon the house became a hum of activity, with builders and renovators raising much dust and gradually restoring Shiwa's past glory. When I visited Shiwa in 2003, some eight years after I'd first been there, the transformation was startling and impressive. The stranglehold of a slow, tropical decay had been arrested by sheer determination – and the whole feeling of the place had changed. Now it's a thriving family estate, combining a strong sense of history with a vibrant present and a solid future.

Before 2001, Shiwa's only real story – and the only reason to visit – was its history: Gore-Browne and the estate's past glories. Shiwa had been reduced to a curious anachronism in the African bush. By contrast, Shiwa's history is now just that: history. A visit here today will look at the past, but also explore the present: Shiwa's people, its animals and its environment – and how these are developing and changing. At one point during a stay here I saw a young carpenter making one of the internal windows over the courtyard. He was doing a good job, clearly deep in concentration. I asked him if he had also made some of the freshly painted windows on the outside of the house. 'No,' he replied, without pausing, 'my grandfather made those.'

So by all means come to Shiwa to wonder at its past, and the story of Sir Stewart; but expect to leave enthralled by the present – and intrigued by the apparently seamless continuity between the two.

Shiwa today

The manor house As you approach from the main road, the rectangular cottages built for farm workers come into view first, their whitewashed walls and tiled roofs saying more of England than of Africa. Then a red-brick gatehouse appears, its design of Italian influence. An old clock tower rises above its tiled roof, and through its main arch is a long straight avenue, bordered by eucalyptus, leading to the stately manor house.

Climbing up, the avenue leads through typically English gardens – designed on several levels with bougainvillea, frangipani, jacaranda and neatly arranged cypresses. These gardens have been restored with beautiful flowers and well-maintained lawns, though their maintenance represents a continuing battle with bushpigs and the increasing herds of antelope.

Above the front door is a small carving of a black rhino's head, a reminder that Gore-Browne had earned the local nickname of Chipembele, black rhino. At the centre of the manor is the square tiled Tuscan courtyard, surrounded by arches, overlooking windows and a red tiled roof. Climbing one of the cold, stone-slab staircases brings you into an English manor house, lined with old paintings and its wooden floors covered with old rugs.

Much of the old heavy wooden furniture remains here, including the sturdy chests; together with muskets and all manner of memorabilia, such as pictures of old relatives and regiments. Two frames with certificates face each other. One is from King George VI, granting 'our trusty and well-beloved Stewart Gore-Browne, esq' the degree, title, honour and dignity of Knight Bachelor. Opposite, President Kaunda appoints 'my trusted, well-beloved Sir Stewart Gore-Browne' as a Grand Officer of the Companion of the Order of Freedom, second division; it is dated 1966.

The library remains the manor's heart, with three huge walls of books, floor to ceiling, which tell of Gore-Browne's interests – Frouede's *History of England* in at least a dozen volumes, *Policy and Arms* by Colonel Repington and *The Genesis of War* by the Right Honourable H H Asquith. His wife was very keen on poetry: there is a classic collection of works by Byron, Shelley, Coleridge and Eliot among others. Gore-Browne left behind a wealth of diaries and personal papers, and much work is in progress cataloguing and archiving these. Central to the room is a grand fireplace, surmounted by the Latin inscription: *Ille terrarum mihi super omnes anculus ridet* – 'This corner of the earth, above all others, smiles on me'.

It's now possible to stay in the manor house (page 344).

Shiwa estate The working estate extends to include a farm, a well-stocked game-ranch, a lake, stables and all the support necessary for almost total self-sufficiency – directly employing a permanent staff of around 80, with another 120 or so working on a casual basis. It covers just over 100km² of land, and encompasses the domestic livestock, including thousands of hens, cattle, a productive dairy herd, sheep, pigs and Saanan goats, imported from the USA and whose milk is used to raise orphaned children. The game farm has expanded considerably over the years, with the assorted game continuously augmented to improve the existing herds' bloodlines, and increase the numbers. Shiwa boasts one of the largest breeding herds of pedigree Boran cattle in Zambia (originally imported from Kenya), its own abattoir in Mpika, as well as a butchery on the farm, where guests are welcome to buy their own meat. Pasture crops are grown largely to feed the livestock but the workers and their wives are encouraged to cultivate vegetable gardens and blocks of maize for their own consumption and for sale on and to the farm.

Gore-Brown's hospital has been brought back to life, thanks in part to grants from the British and German embassies – while smaller grants from diplomatic and private sources have enabled it to complete a very good maternity ward. The two government schools are now thriving once more, supplemented by tuition in IT from visiting international students.

Getting there

Shiwa Ng'andu is reasonably well signposted off the main road to Isoka and Nakonde; the turn-off (⊕ TUSHIW 11°13.334'S, 31°49.580'E) is about 87km northeast of Mpika. The manor house (⊕ SHIWAH 11°11.924'S, 31°44.289'E) is about 13km from this turn-off. The road then continues westwards to Kapishya Hot Springs and onto the Mpika–Kasama road.

Alternatively Shiwa can be reached directly from the Mpika–Kasama road; again turn off about 87km from Mpika (⊕ TUKAPI 11°10.624'S, 31°17.454'E). It's then a little over 30km to Kapishya, and about half of that again to the manor house.

Shiwa also has its own airstrip, so can easily be reached via charter flight from Lusaka or Mfuwe – a quick but expensive option.

Where to stay *Map, page 332*

There are three very different places to stay on the estate, listed here in order of proximity to the main house.

Shiwa Ng'andu Manor House (4 rooms) **m** 0973 311246; **e** shiwa@shiwangandu.com; **w** shiwangandu.com. ⊕ SHIWAH 11°11.924'S, 31°44.289'E. Charlie & Jo Harvey accept guests into their incredible home & make engaging & energetic hosts. Their guest rooms, hung with paintings from the Shiwa collection, are steeped in history & retain many original features, including fireplaces in which fires are lit on winter nights. Traditional hardwood furniture is complemented by new 4-poster bedsteads made on the estate, while en-suite bathrooms add a touch of modernity – but only a touch. Some have huge, old metal baths rather than modern showers & there's a prevailing aura of Edwardian style. Meals are very simple, home-cooked fare, much of it sourced on the farm, but served with style in the grandeur expected of the formal dining room. It's very much like staying in a quintessentially English stately home in Africa – which you'll realise isn't a contradiction in terms when you visit.

Jo & Charlie are very generous with the time that they give to their guests – but there is also a house manager on hand, & a professional guide to take you around the estate. Days are very full, with plenty of activities – you can choose what you'd like to do from a wide range of possibilities.

Most people come to Zambia on safari, then wonder about adding on Shiwa as an afterthought. That's sad, as I found my last stay here to be among the most interesting & engaging few days that I've spent anywhere in Zambia – a view backed up by the visitors that I've sent here over the years. If you do come, then allow at least 3 or 4 nights; any fewer would be far too frustrating for you! *US$480 pp Jan–Mar; US$500 pp Apr–Nov, FB inc estate activities & library/archive access.* ♛♛

Impandala House (4-bedroom house) Originally built by Gore-Browne in 1933, to house missionaries translating the Bible from English into Bemba, this quaint & simple farmhouse was renovated by the Harveys & opened to visitors in mid 2009. A 20-min drive from the main house, it, too, retains a sense of colonial times. Its bedrooms – 2 en-suite & 2 sharing a bathroom – are set over 2 levels. The comfortable lounge, dining room & wraparound veranda are furnished simply but appropriately, with some items brought from the main house. Though not as grand as the main house, it still has its fair share of history, & lays claim to being the site of the final signings of the Declaration of Independence of Zambia back in 1964. The house is ideal for families or friends travelling together, & makes a good, low-cost alternative to the main house. It's usually self-catering, but for international guests, with advance notice, the estate can supply groceries & cook. Fish, milk & bread can also be bought from local shops, & local farmers will often bring their home-grown vegetables around for sale. The house is fully staffed, including housekeepers & a local guide. *US$480 per night self-catering; US$220 pp FBA, exc horseriding & access to Shiwa House.* ⌚ *All year.* ♛♛

Kapishya Hot Springs (6 chalets, camping) m 0976 970444; e mark@shiwasafaris.com; w shiwasafaris.com. ⊕ KAPISH 11°10.263'S, 31°36.057'E. Kapishya is run by Mell & Mark Harvey, Sir Stewart's second grandson, a mine of local information & a top local guide. The camp lies on the Mansha River, set among picturesque gardens where individual plants are labelled with common & scientific names.

The thatched brick chalets are simple but comfortable, each sleeping 4, & with its own porch & brick floors covered with reed mats. Mosquito-netted windows & en-suite facilities that include large showers are standard. 2 of the chalets are dbl-storey, with a particularly good view of the river from the top & their own firepit. Mell's Restaurant serves a delicious fusion of international & Zambian dishes, with nearly all of the ingredients sourced from Kapishya's extensive vegetable garden & the estate farm. A rustic cash bar is well stocked, there's a small pool with a lounging deck next to a miniature set of rapids on the river, & relaxing massage treatments are available. There is also a large, grassy campsite on the riverbank, with good, hot showers, clean, flushing toilets & a dining shelter & BBQ (firewood provided). All visitors can use the lodge's communal facilities, with a 3-course dinner costing US$30, or opt to cater for themselves (chalet guests can use the camp's kitchen). To spice up the self-catering option, homemade jams & chutneys are for sale.

Kapishya Hot Springs themselves are a great attraction, as is the birding on the property (Ross's turaco is a relatively common visitor), but guests here can also take part in most of the activities on the Shiwa estate, be it a game drive or a lake trip. Alternatively, there are some lovely waterfalls nearby to explore yourself (page 348) & a number of mountain-bike trails in the area. In 2011, a horde of 60,000-year-old rock paintings was discovered, & it's possible to walk the 20mins from camp with Mark to see them. Additional cave paintings have been discovered since, although these are estimated to date back only 1,000 years. For those looking for a slower pace, Kapishya also has a spa, located at the edge of its gardens. Kapishya combines well with a visit to Buffalo Camp (page 325) in North Luangwa National Park, also run by Mark. With lots of advance notice, it's sometimes possible to pre-arrange vehicle transfers between the two areas. *US$70/125/160 pp sharing self-catering/dinner, B&B/FB; camping US$10/15 child/adult; US$20 b/fast & lunch; US$30 3-course dinner.* ♛

What to see and do Shiwa's a great place for a surprising variety of activities, so there's no question of being bored. For those staying at the manor house, these are generally included; for guests at Kapishya they're optional extras. Always bear in mind that numbers of visitors here are fairly small, so any reference to a 'tour' here generally means half-a-dozen visitors or fewer. Here are just a few of Shiwa's highlights.

Kapishya Hot Springs About 20km from Shiwa Ng'andu, the hot springs in the Manshya River at Kapishya were always a favourite spot of Gore-Browne's and a great place to unwind. Within a shallow part of the cool, rocky river, surrounded by *combretum* bushes and gently curving raffia palms (*Raphia farinifera*) is an inviting pool of hot spring water. It makes a great site for bathing. Those not staying overnight on the Shiwa estate can visit for the day (K75/150 child/adult).

Boating and rafting There are several activities possible on the water. It's lovely to take a slow boat trip around the edges of the lake, looking out for wildlife, from birds and otters to crocodiles, and it's also possible to do this by traditional *mokoro* (dugout canoe). During the fishing season, you can bring a rod and reel.

Alternatively, take a full-day trip around the lake, and then from there down the Manshya River to Kapishya, or from Kapishya to the Chusa Waterfall. These routes go over some small (Grade II) rapids, and are particularly good spots for birdlife (though do remember to protect any belongings in waterproof containers in case they should be thrown out).

Nature walks and drives Much of Shiwa estate is now a game area, so early morning walks or game drives can be very much a feature of staying here. Those not staying at the estate can self-drive around the area (US$20). It's a particularly good place to spot the elusive blue duiker, while the more common game includes puku, kudu, defassa waterbuck, Kafue lechwe, Lichtenstein hartebeest, common duiker, oribi, zebra, bushbuck, reedbuck, impala, yellow baboon, vervet monkey, grysbok and wildebeest.

The lechwe and the wildebeest are of a different subspecies than you'll find elsewhere in this part of northern Zambia; they're unlike those in the Luangwa and Bangweulu areas. With patience, sitatunga can usually be spotted from the hide, while bushpig, wild cat, civet, genet and clawless otters are around but often less visible. As in many of Zambia's isolated kopjes, there's a resident population of fairly elusive klipspringers.

One of the estate's natural highlights occurs in November, at the start of the rains, when thousands of straw-coloured fruit bats return to Shiwa to roost. For details of a similar spectacle at Kasanka, see page 351.

Guided walks The Shiwa estate, and the area around it, is a lovely place for scenic walks, with a number of stunning hills and sites of interest. It's as easy to have a good hour's walk alone as it is to stay out for the day with a local guide,

One notable spot is Nachipala Bareback Hill – a large granite whaleback which affords stunning panoramic vistas and a magnificent view of the lake. This is an energetic 3-hour walk from the manor house, and on the top a small cairn marks the spot where, on his last journey in 1867, Dr David Livingstone took compass bearings in his final attempt to find the source of the Nile.

Kapishya has developed a series of short, self-guided walking trails of 4–7km in length, some up and around the local hills, and one mostly along village paths by the river, through Bemba villages and fields, before finishing at the Chusa Falls. Maps with the routes are available at Kapishya, and guides, although not required, are available for a small fee.

Birdwatching Shiwa has been identified as a priority site for conservation and is listed as one of 42 'important bird areas' in Zambia (page 77). You can stroll around the estate and game ranch with or without a guide (there aren't usually any lion, buffalo or elephant here, so this is fairly safe), and some of the walks lead through beautiful raffia palm forests.

In total, over 380 species of birds have been seen on the estate. Birding highlights include palm-nut vultures, bat hawks, Ross's turacos, white-cheeked bee-eaters, white-tailed and blue flycatchers, Stanley's bustards, African finfoot, black-rumped buttonquail, long-toed flufftail, greater snipe, grass owls, black-chinned quail finch and a veritable kaleidoscope of different sunbirds. Down by the water, the swamps, rivers and lakes offer a haven for a variety of water birds, including pygmy geese; cormorants; yellow-billed, knob-nosed and white-faced teal; giant and lesser egrets; blue, grey, night and goliath herons; Fülleborn's and rosy-breasted longclaws; malachite, half-collared, giant and pied kingfishers; golden-rumped tinkerbird; splendid starlings; black-bellied seed cracker; Bocage's robin; bar-throated apalis; and white-headed saw-wing. Fish eagles and even ospreys may be spotted, as well as transient flocks of pelicans and flamingos.

Around the estate If you've time to spare then take a slow wander around the estate, and perhaps down to the lake, ideally with a guide. You will find an exceedingly positive atmosphere, with the local people very welcoming and friendly, and usually happy to talk about what they are doing.

The farm itself is run on commercial lines, but methods are far from the intensive farming beloved of the West. The environment is a key factor, and nothing is left to waste. This is no place for shiny new gadgets; spending an hour or so watching the sort of machinery usually confined to a museum being coaxed into life can be fascinating in itself. There are numerous community initiatives going on, too, from fish-farming to bee-keeping and bio-gas projects – as well as a variety of projects within the estate's hospital and school.

Tours of the manor house Guided tours of the manor house are by prior arrangement only. If you're staying at the manor house then this is merely a case of asking Jo and Charlie to show you around; it's delightfully informal and totally fascinating.

If you're staying at Kapishya, or just passing by, the only way to see some of the interior of the house is to contact Shiwa directly (page 344) and request a 'tour', which is usually possible for a small fee (around US$20 pp), which is donated to the local community fund. Within the house the tour is limited to the lower floors; the upper floors are strictly for the family and their guests. (Remember that this is a family home first, and a small exclusive guesthouse second, and you'll realise that neither the family, nor their guests, will want a steady stream of visitors looking throughout the house.) Also included are a game drive and a historical guided tour of the estate.

Shiwa's archives Putting Gore-Browne's extensive collection of diaries, letters and papers into an ordered archive has been a long-term project for Jo, and is still not complete. Guests interested in the manor house can have some access to this, on request; it's fascinating to read some of Gore-Browne's old diaries even if you're not an amateur historian. Then there's the enormous library, and Gore-Browne's collection of early records!

Historical tours on the estate Jo is a trained archaeologist, and has been in the forefront of excavating some of the older sites on the estate – already uncovering the kilns that were built to make the bricks and the tiles for the manor house, and the locations of an old summerhouse.

There are a number of other spots of historical interest, including the old hospital, the essential oils distillery, the traction engine and the graveyard – and any can easily be integrated into a historical tour of the estate.

Excursions from Shiwa Shiwa is really a destination in itself, and isn't often used as a base for excursions, although Kapishya makes quite a good base for visiting a few local waterfalls on the Mansha River, detailed below. If you ask the team at Shiwa or Kapishya, they will likely be able to arrange for a guide to go with you to make locating them easier.

Chusa Falls (⊕ CHUSAF 11°09.353'S, 31°33.093'E) Chusa Falls are the closest to Kapishya, making a good day trip. On foot, they're a distance of 7km away, or 10km by road. The falls are quite clearly a short series of three steps, each cascade being several metres high.

Senkele Falls (⊕ SENKEL 11°06.150'S, 31°21.922'E) These falls are a 15m drop on the Mansha River. The turn-off to them from the Mpika–Kasama Road is at ⊕ TUSENK 11°11.712'S, 31°18.903'E, about 3.5km north of the turning to Kapishya and Shiwa. From there the track turns north and continues for 10km. Continue north where the road forks, then after about 2km of high grass, stop at the deserted house; the falls are 100m from here. This would be an easy place to wild camp.

Namundela Falls (⊕ 11°06.760'S, 31°27.606'E) The stunning double Namundela Falls are about 2 hours' drive from Kapishya, followed by a 90-minute walk to the falls along the Mansha River. To get to them, head 28km west from Kapishya, turning north at Chilombo School (⊕ CHILOM 11°13.525'S, 31°24.624'E). Follow this track about 13km north and slightly east to the Anderson Farm (⊕ ANDERS 11°07.861'S, 31°26.542'E), and then further to the Kapololwe Homestead, marking the start of the walk along the river. There are plans to install a run-of-river hydro-electric power station at these falls, as exist on several of Zambia's waterfalls, which would increase reliable power supply to the area. Construction is yet to commence and, if other similar plants are anything to go by, shouldn't negatively impact the beauty of these waterfalls.

KASANKA NATIONAL PARK

(**w** kasanka.com; park fees US$10 pp/day; vehicle US$15/day; local registration K25.50/day; angling permit US$5) This small park is the first privately managed national park in Zambia. It is run by a charity, the Kasanka Trust, and the much-needed proceeds from tourism go directly into conservation and development of the park and its surrounding communities. Park fees are payable by all visitors, whether or not they are staying overnight, with the exception of those staying at the conservation centre, which is just outside the park boundary.

At just 390km² in area, Kasanka is one of Zambia's smallest national parks, but it encompasses a wide variety of vegetation zones: from dry evergreen forests, or *mateshe*, to various types of moist forest and permanent papyrus swamps. It's a delightful place to spend a relaxing few days at any time, when sitatunga are readily seen in the early morning and keen birdwatchers will find many pressing reasons to visit. In the later months of the year, Kasanka hosts a truly extraordinary wildlife spectacle: the annual bat migration.

HISTORY Kasanka was made a national park in 1972, but it was poorly maintained and poaching was rife until the late 1980s. Then an initiative was started by the late David Lloyd OBE, a former district officer, and Gary Williams, a local commercial farmer. With the approval of the National Parks and Wildlife Department and the local community, they started to put private money into revitalising the park.

In 1990, the National Parks Department signed a management contract with the Kasanka Trust, giving the latter the right to manage the park and develop it for tourism in partnership with the local community. In 2003, the Trust's management contract was extended by Zambia Wildlife Authority (ZAWA). The Trust, which is linked to a registered charity based in the UK and Netherlands, has trailblazed a model for the successful private management of a Zambian national park. It has been fortunate in gaining financial backing from various donors, including a substantial million euro donation from the French Facility for Global Environment (FFGM), but essentially it relies almost entirely on tourism income to fund its conservation activities.

The Kasanka Trust aims to manage the area's natural resources for the benefit of both the wildlife and the local people, and so it closely supports and consults with a locally elected community resource board.

In recent years, the Trust has been fighting hard to prevent the illegal deforestation of neighbouring Kafinda Game Management Area by Lake Agro Industries of Tanzania. Aside from the devastating effects on biodiversity of protected pristine forest being cleared for commercial agriculture and cattle ranching, Kafinda is an important buffer for Kasanka. The legal battle to stop encroachment into the forest was continuing at the time of research, with regular updates posted on the Trust's website.

GEOGRAPHY Kasanka is on the southern fringes of the Bangweulu Wetlands, and just 30km from the border with the DRC. It is almost completely flat and, lying at an altitude of about 1,200m, it gets a high rainfall during the wet season (about 1,200mm) which results in a lush cover of vegetation.

The park is dissected by two main rivers, the Kasanka and the Luwombwa, with a third, the Mulembo, on its northern boundary, but several smaller rivers and streams, and the evenness of the land, have resulted in an extensive marsh area known as the Kapabi Swamp. There are also numerous lakes, of which the biggest is the permanent Lake Wasa, though many of the others are really just small, seasonal dambos.

FLORA AND FAUNA

Flora The park's natural flora is dominated by miombo woodland, in which brachystegia species figure heavily. The local people use fire as part of their cultivation and hunting/gathering activities, which can spread into areas of the park, so some of this is less tall than it might be – perhaps reaching only 5m rather than its normal 20m. The park operates a programme of limited, controlled burning to reduce the damage caused by hotter fires later in the dry season.

There are also sections of much taller dry evergreen forest, where the tallest trees have an interlocking canopy, and the *mateshi* undergrowth is dense and woody. A good area for this is near the Mulembo River around the Katwa scout post.

Elsewhere you will find evergreen swamp forest, with some superb tall specimens of waterberry (*Syzygium cordatum*) and mululu, or red mahogany, trees (*Khaya

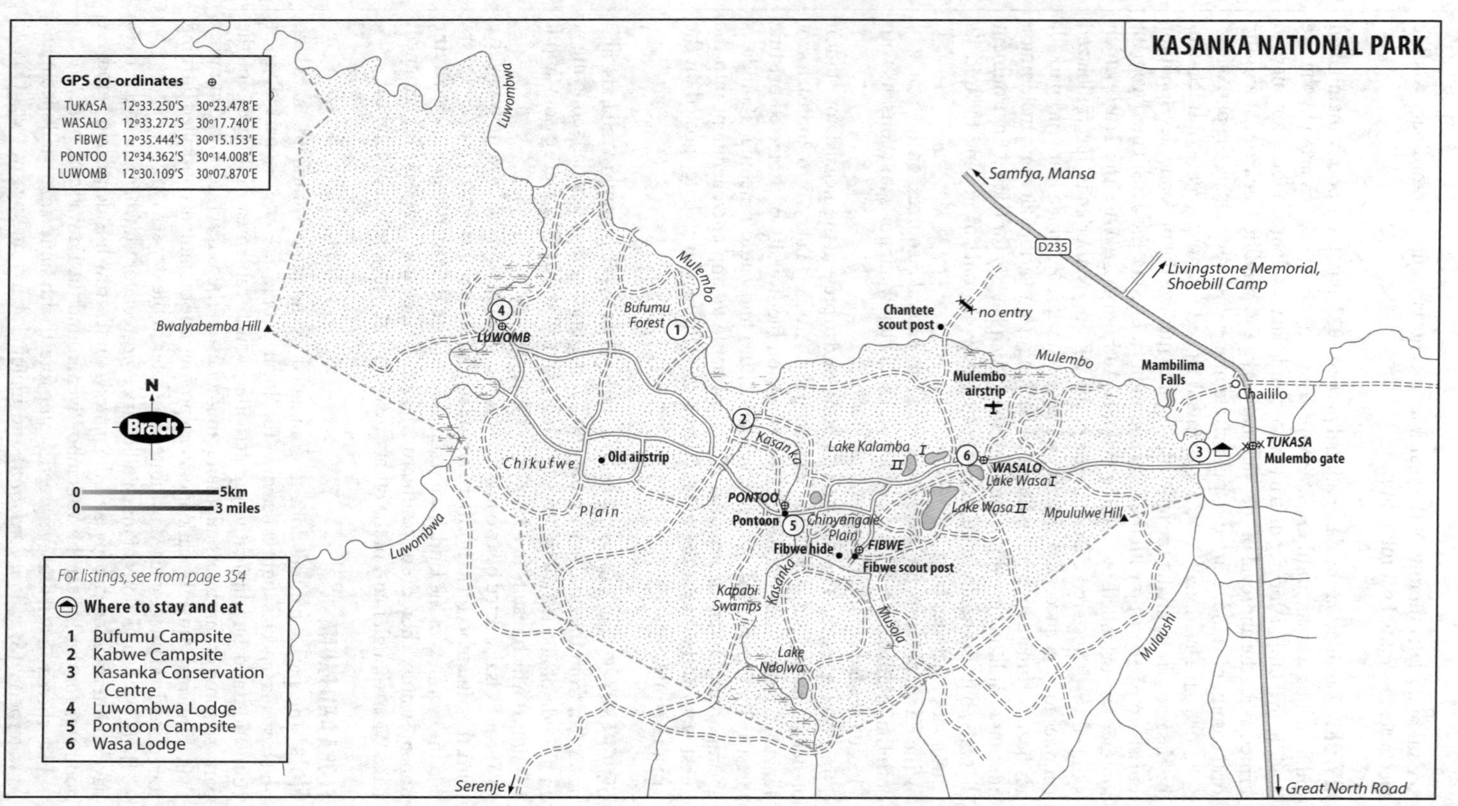
KASANKA NATIONAL PARK
GPS co-ordinates
TUKASA 12°33.250'S 30°23.478'E
WASALO 12°33.272'S 30°17.740'E
FIBWE 12°35.444'S 30°15.153'E
PONTOO 12°34.362'S 30°14.008'E
LUWOMB 12°30.109'S 30°07.870'E
Samfya, Mansa
D235
Livingstone Memorial, Shoebill Camp
Luwombwa
Mulembo
Bufumu Forest
Chantete scout post
no entry
Bwalyabemba Hill
LUWOMB
Mulembo
Mambilima Falls
Mulembo airstrip
Chaililo
N
Bradt
Kasanka
Lake Kalamba I
II
WASALO
Lake Wasa I
TUKASA
Mulembo gate
Chikufwe
Old airstrip
0 5km
0 3 miles
PONTOO
Plain
Pontoon
Chinyangale Plain
Lake Wasa II
Mpululwe Hill
Luwombwa
Fibwe hide
FIBWE
Fibwe scout post
For listings, see from page 354
Kapabi Swamps
Kasanka
Musola
Where to stay and eat
1 Bufumu Campsite
2 Kabwe Campsite
3 Kasanka Conservation Centre
4 Luwombwa Lodge
5 Pontoon Campsite
6 Wasa Lodge
Lake Ndolwa
Mulaushi
Serenje
Great North Road

nyasica). As an aside, one of the guides here told me a story of a biologist asking a local Chewa person the name of this tree, and getting the reply '*Khaya*', which means 'I don't know'!

Around the Fibwe scout post is one such area of forest, and the Fibwe hide (page 356) is perched in a huge mululu tree. Similar species also occur in the areas of riparian forest found by Kasanka's small rivers. One notable tree is the wild loquat (*Oxyanthus speciosus*), whose fruit is a major draw for bats.

Interspersed in these forested areas are seasonally flooded grasslands and swamps. The latter include large areas of permanent papyrus beds and *phragmites* reeds, often with very little open water to be seen. The wild date palm (*Phoenix reclinata*) is one of the most common species of tree found here. Keep a lookout, too, for the large tree-proteas that bloom spectacularly around May and June.

Mammals Poaching in the 1970s and '80s drastically reduced the numbers of animals in the park, but this seems to have had few long-term effects on the species now present. Many of these move into and out of the park quite freely and, as they gradually learn that the park is a safe haven, they are staying longer or becoming resident, and appear to be less shy.

Puku are the most common antelope here, and are found in a particularly high density along the Kasanka River. Other relatively common residents include bushbuck, reedbuck, Sharp's grysbok and the common duiker. Sable occur in good numbers, and a small herd of zebra was introduced in 2012, while Lichtenstein's hartebeest, roan antelope, blue duiker, buffalo and defassa waterbuck are more scarce. Elephants move through the park, but a recent count suggested that a population of about 35–50 was probably resident here.

Of particular interest are the shy sitatunga antelope, which can almost always be seen in the very early morning from the Fibwe hide (page 356). This hide offers one of the subcontinent's best opportunities for viewing these beautiful creatures in an undisturbed state – far superior to the fleeting glimpse of a startled sitatunga that you may get from a speedboat in places like the Okavango Delta. On occasion, 70 different animals have been spotted from here in the early morning. In addition, sitatunga are also regularly spotted along the Kasanka River near Pontoon campsite, where the park authorities are planning to set up a second hide.

The smaller carnivores are well represented in Kasanka, with caracal, side-striped jackal, civet, genet and Cape clawless otter all regularly recorded. Others, including leopard, serval, spotted hyena, honey badgers and the African wildcat, are more rarely seen. Lion are occasional visitors from the neighbouring Lavushi Manda National Park.

Mongooses are well represented: the water (or marsh), slender, white-tailed, banded, dwarf and large grey mongoose are all found here.

Given the park's proximity to the DRC, species that are typical of those equatorial rainforests (but rare for southern Africa), can also be spotted in Kasanka. For example, the blue monkey is often sighted in the *mushitu* forest, occurring together with the area's more common vervet monkeys. The baboons at Kasanka are unusual, too, a species known as the Kinda baboon that is smaller and more sociable than its better-known cousin in Zambia, the yellow baboon, and is the subject of a study by the Kasanka Baboon Project (**w** kasankababoonproject.com).

Bats Without doubt the most spectacular sight in Kasanka occurs around the start of the rains, in November and December, when 10 million straw-coloured fruit bats (*Eidolon helvum*) converge on the park to roost in the mushitu forest. It is

CHILLI FENCES

One of the greatest problems facing the successful operation of a national park is managing the conflict between conservation and community. Kasanka is no exception: with a small elephant population in an unfenced park, and a number of arable farms in the vicinity, problems are almost inevitable. Villagers understandably object to elephants trampling their valuable maize and cassava crops, but keeping the animals at bay is rarely straightforward.

In 2000, two researchers in Zimbabwe came up with a simple idea: chilli fences. The aim was to create a barrier that would repel the elephants without resorting to costly and often ineffective barricades or electric fencing. Based on the premise that elephants have a strong aversion to the smell of chillies, they had set up the Chilli Pepper Development Project (now the Elephant Pepper Development Trust, w elephantpepper.org). Using cheap, easily available materials, they created a fence made of wooden posts linked by sisal rope and hung with strips of cloth that had been doused in used engine oil and chillies. Their results were impressive.

Taking their research as a base, Victoria Paterson, a research student from Glasgow University, spent much of 2007 at Kasanka studying the potential of chilli fences for the villages around the national park. With a focus across five sites, she set up a series of fences, with control experiments to check the efficacy of the combination of materials, and worked with local farmers to explain the methods. Despite considerable resistance, some of the farmers have taken the suggestions on board, with very positive results for their crops.

One method of reinforcing the fences is to create a buffer zone between the precious maize crop and the elephant's forest habitat, by growing a secondary crop around it. The European potato, for example, doesn't find favour with elephants, so sowing this between the forest and the maize can help to persuade the elephant to look elsewhere rather than wading through a field of unappealing fare.

To mitigate the costs, villagers have been encouraged to use fibre for rope, and to grow chillies as one of their crops. Here, water is a huge factor, but if the chillies are grown alongside another, profitable crop that requires irrigation, such as rape, then a successful outcome is more likely.

Now, though, the elephants – thwarted of their free meal – have taken to heading for village grain stores, and so the cycle continues.

one of the largest mammal migrations on the planet. Sometimes known as flying foxes, each evening the bats pour out of their resting-place just after sunset, filling the sky as they fly in search of food. The bats have wingspans of up to 85cm, making a grand spectacle that is best observed from the area of the Fibwe hide (page 356).

Riverine animals In the lakes, rivers and swamps, hippo and crocodiles are common. It is also said that the slender-snouted crocodile, a typical resident of DRC's tropical rainforest rivers, occurs here – though it has not been spotted for many years and may no longer be present.

Birds Kasanka has lush vegetation with a wide range of habitats, including three large rivers, five natural lakes, a papyrus swamp (Kapabi) and real moist evergreen swamp forest. In this small area, some 477 bird species have been identified, including many 'specials', and the number continues to rise – so it's a very good place for quiet, undisturbed birdwatching.

The rivers, lakes and wetland areas have excellent populations of ibis, storks, herons, kingfishers and bee-eaters as well as many waterfowl. Water rails, greater and lesser jacanas, white-backed ducks and pygmy geese are common. Reed cormorants and African darters are easily spotted on the more open stretches of water, and larger birds include wattled cranes and saddle-billed storks. Around Lake Ndolwa and Wasa there have even been two sightings of the rare shoebill, which breeds in the Bangweulu Wetlands to the north, but this is exceptionally unusual.

Many species common in east or central Africa occur here, on the edge of their range (South African bird books just won't be enough!), like the grey apalis, olive sunbird, red and blue sunbird (Anchieta's), green lourie, Boehm's flycatcher, Boehm's bee-eater, Sousa's shrike, black-backed barbet, Anchieta's tchagra, and both Schalow's and Ross's turacos (the latter also known as Lady Ross's lourie). Meanwhile, a quiet drift in a canoe down the Luwombwa River should produce sightings of finfoot, giant and half-collared kingfishers, narina trogons and yellow-throated leaflove, to name but a few.

The more common raptors in the area are the bateleur, martial, crowned, Ayre's, African hawk and steppe eagles, plus the snake eagles (black-breasted, western-banded and brown) and the chanting goshawks (pale and dark). Kasanka's fish eagles are often seen and crowned eagles breed here. There are also several pairs of Pel's fishing owls.

GETTING THERE

By road It's around a 7-hour drive from Lusaka to Kasanka on reasonable tarred roads. From Kapiri Mposhi, head northeast for Serenje, where you should refuel as there's no fuel available in the park. Continue northeast for a further 36km, then take the main left turning along the D235, signposted to Samfya and Mansa. After another 55km, turn left for the park entrance, which is clearly signposted (⊕ TUKASA 12°33.250'S, 30°23.478'E).

If you're coming from Bangweulu, turn right 72km *after* the Luapula Bridge; do not follow the sign before the bridge to Kasanka Village and Mission. From Mpika, head 200km south on the Great North Road before turning right towards Mansa for 55km.

The entrance to the park, close to the eastern border, is clearly marked by the Mulembo gate and is always manned. Register and pay your entrance fees here before proceeding 12km to Wasa Lodge, bearing left at the fork after about 1km; or right if you're staying at the conservation centre, which is outside the park boundary.

By air Those flying in will come to the park's Mulembo airstrip, which is close to Wasa Lodge. By private charter with Sky Trails (page 110), it's an hour and a half from Lusaka or an hour from Mfuwe in the Luangwa Valley.

GETTING AROUND During the dry season Kasanka's roads are generally good, and accessible with a high-clearance 2WD. The manually operated pontoon (⊕ PONTOO 12°34.362'S, 30°14.008'E) across the Kasanka River has now been replaced by a narrow concrete bridge, thus improving access to the western side of the park.

Hardy 4x4 adventurers might consider the **Open Africa Nsobe Sitatunga Experience** (w openafrica.org), a route that takes in Kasanka, Lavushi Manda and Bangweulu to offer an interesting, if perhaps challenging drive.

GETTING ORGANISED Wherever you are going in the park, you should report first to Wasa Lodge. This is where you will book in for your accommodation, discuss meal requirements, arrange any activities and get directions to other parts of the park.

WHERE TO STAY *Map, page 350*

The Kasanka Trust (**m** 0960 753914, 0960 753977; **e** tourism@kasanka.com; **w** kasanka.com) runs all of the accommodation options in the park. Each operates slightly differently, particularly in terms of catering, and it's important to understand the implications before you decide where to stay. Although Kasanka can often accommodate 'drop-in' visitors who have their own food, booking in advance – for the campsites as well as the camps – is always a good idea.

Each of the **campsites** has flush toilets and bucket showers, with staff on hand to supply firewood, draw water, prepare hot showers, and give basic guidance to visitors. Campers need to bring all their own equipment and supplies, including drinking water.

Do remember that all visitors, irrespective of where they are staying, should report to Wasa Lodge before continuing further into the park.

Wasa Lodge (3 chalets, 5 rondavels) ⊕ WASALO 12°33.272'S, 30°17.740'E. The park's main camp is about 20 mins' drive from the main road, in a scenic spot on the shore of Lake Wasa. It's a fairly rustic set up, lit at night by small solar-powered lights, & all very low key. The 3 newer chalets are relatively spacious & comfortable, with en-suite facilities including hot water (shower only) & a sheltered veranda facing the lake. The older rondavels are smaller, their bucket showers filled on request, & the family chalet has 2 rooms sharing a bathroom. All beds have mosquito nets.

Most visitors to Wasa Lodge stay on a full-board basis, with well-prepared meals served inside or on a covered veranda in the central area, where there's also a good-sized bar. Occasionally, guests may arrange to bring their own food, which is then cooked & served by the camp's staff, but this must be agreed in advance.

Wasa has its own tree hide, close to the chalets & a superb vantage point over the lake, where sitatunga are often spotted in the early morning. Game drives & escorted walks can be organised from camp, while water-based activities start & finish at Luwombwa, 1hr's drive through the park. *All profits go to conservation initiatives. Rondavel US$175 Jan–Sep, US$230 Oct–Dec; chalet US$205–230 Jan–Sep; US$320–370 Oct–Dec; all FBA, inc drinks, activities (best pre-arranged) & laundry, exc park fees.* ⏲ *All year.* ♛–♛♛

Luwombwa Lodge (3 chalets) ⊕ LUWOMB 12°30.109'S, 30°07.870'E. Smaller & more rustic still than Wasa Lodge, the remote 'fishing lodge' sits on the bank of the Luwombwa River in the west of the park. It's a pleasant hour's drive from Wasa Lodge, so if you're arriving in the afternoon, allow plenty of time to get here before dark. If you're driving yourself, you'll need a high-clearance vehicle, with a 4x4 during or after the rains. The thatched, A-frame chalets are built of brick & are comfortable, if rather dark, with a small veranda over the river. Each has an en-suite toilet & shower (hot water on request), & a dbl & sgl bed beneath mosquito nets, while 2 of the chalets have an attic floor with twin beds.

Most visitors to Luwombwa bring their own supplies, which are prepared & served by the camp's very helpful staff. Alternatively, you could make arrangements in advance to stay on a full-board basis. The simple bar & dining area is made of reeds & thatch, & is dominated by a huge & quite magnificent mpundu (or mobola) plum (*Parinari curatellifolia*), which also shelters the camp's firepit, while a second dining shelter on the riverbank offers a superb birdwatching venue out of the sun.

River trips in 3-seater canoes with a guide (US$30 pp/min 2 people) can be organised all year, along with game drives (US$80/vehicle; US$50/guide for half day), Wasa Lake walks (US$15 pp plus scout escort) & cycle rides (US$25 pp/half day), & of course the bat experience for which many are drawn to Kasanka (page 357). *All profits go to conservation initiatives. Chalet US$60 Jan–Sep, US$80 Oct–Dec, self-catering, exc park fees. FB rates on request.* ⏲ *All year.* **$$$**

Kasanka Conservation Centre (4 rooms, 2 dormitories, camping) Accommodation at the conservation centre, about 2km from the park gate, is designed primarily for students or long-term researchers, but other visitors are welcome to stay here too. Rooms are small & basic, each with just enough space for twin beds with mosi nets; they are set up in pairs with a shared shower & toilet between them. A couple of 10-bed dormitories provides cost-effective accommodation for larger groups, and it's also possible to camp. Some meals can be provided from the on-site kitchen or visitors can cook for themselves, or join schoolchildren for a traditional lunch, & perhaps even some lessons. *Room US$32 pp; dormitory US$19 pp; camping US$10 pp. No park fees applicable.* ⌚ *All year.* **$**

Pontoon Campsite (3 pitches) PONTOC 12°34.385'S, 30°14.073'E. Set under a beautiful shady stand of red mahogany or mululu trees (*Khaya nyasica*) near the Kasanka River bridge, this gently sloping campsite has views towards the river & plains, offering some of the best sitatunga sightings in the park. Each of the 3 separate pitches has a simple bucket shower & flush toilet, but they share 2 cooking shelters with BBQ stands. *US$15 pp Jan–Sep; US$25 Oct–Dec.* ⌚ *All year.* **$$**

Kabwe Campsite (1 pitch) ⊕ KABWEC 12°32.457'S, 30°12.690'E. Overlooking the Kasanka River plain, this is a smaller, secluded site for up to 6 people, with a shower & flush toilet that were spotlessly clean when we visited. *US$15 pp Jan–Sep, US$25 Oct–Dec.* ⌚ *All year.* **$$**

Bufumu Campsite (1 pitch) ⊕ BUFUMC 12°29.783'S, 30°11.763'E. With a beautiful view of the open plain, a good shelter & BBQ, plus a toilet & bucket shower, Kasanka's newest campsite is pretty idyllic. A short walk from here takes you to the tallest tree in Zambia (page 357) in the Bufumu Forest. *US$15 pp Jan–Sep; US$25 Oct–Dec.* ⌚ *Mar–Dec.* **$$**

WHAT TO SEE AND DO

Activities

Activities Activities organised by the Kasanka Trust include escorted walks, cycling, day and night game drives, canoeing, motorboat trips and fishing. For those staying on an all-inclusive basis, these activities are included; for other guests, and for additional activities, see the rates below. All activities must be booked through Wasa Lodge and usually start from the lodge.

Baboon walks By arrangement with Wasa Lodge, it's possible to join researchers from the Kasanka Baboon Project (w kasankababoonproject.com) as they carry out their work monitoring the Kinda baboon. Walks (US$50 pp, inc tea & snack) take around 3 hours.

Bat safaris During late November and early December, bat safaris are run by two safari operators. Robin Pope Safaris (page 292) organises seven-night safaris which combine Luangwa River Camp in the South Luangwa (page 305) with three days at Wasa Lodge and a night in Lusaka. A similar trip is offered by Remote Africa Safaris (page 292) for their guests.

Bat viewing Between October and December, Kasanka's mushitu forest is the focus of an extraordinary bat migration that sees millions of straw-coloured fruit bats descend on the park (page 357). The bats are best seen near the Fibwe Hide, where public and exclusive viewing areas are opened especially for the season.

A guided bat experience (US$30 pp; US$200/group for exclusive use of the bat hide) affords the opportunity to view the bats emerging at sunset or returning from their nightly forage from an exclusive bat hide or platform on the edge of the Bat Forest. As well as the bats, there's the chance of spotting the variety of raptors that prey on them as they return to their roosts in the mornings, including the crowned eagle.

Boat trips Depending on the season, and thus the level of water, both motorboat (US$25 pp) and guided canoe trips (US$30 pp) can be organised on the Luwombwa

River. They also hire canoes for US$20, but I can highly recommend the excellent guided canoe trips: a magical way to spend a morning on the river.

Conservation and community projects With advance notice, visitors may arrange to see aspects of some of Kasanka's community-based conservation projects, and to meet their participants, or to visit a local school.

Fishing Anglers should head for Luwombwa Lodge, as the best waters for fishing are normally those of the Luwombwa River. The main species found here are vundu catfish and large-mouth, small-mouth and yellow-belly bream and occasionally tiger fish. The camp's cooks will prepare your catch for dinner, if you wish, but note that strict park rules allow only large fish to be removed for eating.

Fishing tackle cannot be hired from the lodges, so you'll need to bring your own. You must also obtain a permit from Wasa Lodge before heading out to Luwombwa, where you can hire a boat with a guide (US$30 pp, plus US$5 pp angling permit). No fishing is permitted between November and February.

Game drives and guided walks These can be organised with one of the park's own guides. Alternatively, you can drive yourself around the park, perhaps taking a guide with you if there is somebody free. A few places within the park are worth specific mention; see below for brief details. Specialist guides, such as expert birders, can also be organised with plenty of notice, a particular boon for the keen ornithologist. Game drive US$40 pp (max 6 people); guide US$25/up to 3hrs.

Scenic flights When there is a light aircraft stationed at Kasanka, usually between about May and November, it's possible to take a scenic flight over Kasanka and the Bangweulu Wetlands. The flight lasts about an hour, and costs US$600 for up to four passengers, or five with a child. Advance notice is normally required.

Walking trips With plenty of notice, it is possible for fully equipped and self-sufficient campers to organise a walking trip through the park with an armed game scout, staying at the different campsites as they go. This offers the chance to see the many different vegetation types, insects, birds and animals, and to discuss the bush, the project, and anything else at leisure, but note that your scout will not be a trained guide. US$25/3hrs.

Conservation centre A visitor centre close to the entrance to the park showcases Kasanka's conservation work and acts as an interpretation centre, with posters, displays, information and videos of the annual bat migration. The centre is just outside the park boundary in the surrounding GMA, so visitors here do not have to pay park fees.

Fibwe hide A magnificent mululu or red mahogany tree (*Khaya nyasica*), near to the Fibwe scout post (⊕ FIBWE 12°35.444'S, 30°15.153'E), can be climbed, using a basic ladder, to reach a platform some 18m above the ground. The views over a section of the Kapabi Swamp and the moist evergreen **Bat Forest** are excellent.

If you reach the hide in the early morning and climb quietly, your chances of seeing sitatunga are excellent. However, more leisurely risers should take heart: I have seen a number of sitatunga from here as late as midday. In short, this is probably the best place for seeing sitatunga in the wild anywhere in Africa – and so certainly one of the best tree-hides on the continent!

THE BATS

One of Kasanka's highlights is the magnificent tree-hide, perched high in a red mahogany tree overlooking the Kapabi Swamp. Most come here to spot sitatunga, but if you climb up on a late November afternoon, around the time the rains are beginning, then you'll also witness one of Africa's strangest wildlife spectacles. Between about 18.00 and 18.30, up to 10 million straw-coloured fruit bats will take to the air above you. These large, fruit-eating bats have wingspans up to about a metre. They start by circling overhead like a vast, slow whirlwind. Gradually, individuals and groups break off and spread out over the forest in search of wild fruits. For an amazing 20–30 minutes the sky is filled, as far as you can see, with squadron upon squadron of bats, heading off into the twilight.

'They come to roost in the evergreen swamp forest, near the Musola River,' Edmund said, gazing down through the canopy. 'It's very unusual vegetation for Zambia – only found near rivers. Tremendously fragile and easily destroyed,' he added. 'During the day the bats occupy just a small area. They hang off the mushitu trees in such numbers that they pull off the branches, leaving just the woody skeletons to hang on to. This lets light on to the forest floor which, together with the inordinate amount of fertiliser that they drop, promotes very rich undergrowth. Imagine, 8 million bats, weighing about 350g each... that's 2,800 tons of animals.' Edmund had clearly done his arithmetic before. 'The equivalent of a thousand elephants, hanging around in perhaps one hectare of forest, suspended from the trees,' he grinned.

Visiting this colony isn't for the faint-hearted, even during the day. Large crocodiles wander under the trees, far from the nearest water, scavenging for dead bats – along with vultures, gymnogenes and a host of other smaller predators. All of which provided further reasons why that high tree-hide was such a wonderful place to be.

Edited from an article by the author that first appeared in Travel Africa, *and reproduced by kind permission.*

It's also a particularly productive birding spot, with specials such as Ross's and Schalow's turaco, Boehm's bee-eater, black-backed barbet, Anchieta's tchagra, speckled mousebirds and various sunbirds often visible in the nearby forest. And during the bat migration, the hide offers a superb vantage point, especially at dusk when millions of bats leave their roosts en masse to search for food in the surrounding miombo woodland.

Bufumu Forest This pocket of dry evergreen forest, or *mateshe*, is home to the 'Big Tree', which is considered to be the tallest tree in Zambia. Towering 65m over the surrounding forest, it's a semi-deciduous *mofu* tree (*Entandrophragma delevoyi*) that's estimated to be 400 years old. Its existence owes much to the presence of royal graves at its foot, giving rise to the name 'sacred forest'. The tree is easily found from the Bufumu campsite, about a 5-minute walk to the north; ask the campsite attendant to show you the way.

Chinyangale Plain and Kasanka River Between the bridge over the Kasanka River and the Fibwe hide, a game-viewing road winds through the open plain with palm clumps and plentiful puku. Another road runs along the western side of the river, going downstream from the crossing. There are often large herds of puku here, and you'll frequently spot bushbuck and warthog.

Chikufwe Plain The Chikufwe Plain (⊕ CHIFUN 12°33.066'S, 30°09.645'E) is a large open area of seasonally flooded grassland on the western side of the park. The site of the old grass airstrip, it is a favourite place to spot sable, hartebeest and reedbuck. There is a loop road around the southern side of the plain.

Further afield By prior arrangement, usually between May and November, day trips to Shoebill Island in the Bangweulu Wetlands (page 365) can be organised for guests staying at Kasanka. Typically you'll leave the park by light aircraft at about 07.45, returning around 17.00. The charter flight doesn't come cheap; expect to pay about US$720 return for up to four passengers (or five including a child).

AROUND KASANKA AND BANGWEULU

There are several sites of interest in the area around Kasanka and Bangweulu, though you'll need a self-contained 4x4 to reach any of them, and local help for some.

LIVINGSTONE MEMORIAL A plain stone monument, under a simple cross, marks the place where David Livingstone's heart was buried in 1873, in the village of Chitambo. (The village has since moved, but Livingstone's heart – and the monument – remain.) After his death, from dysentery and malaria, his followers removed his heart and internal organs, and buried them under a *mpundu* tree that once stood where the monument is now.

In an amazing tribute, his two closest followers, Sussi and Chuma, then salted and dried his body before disguising it in a tree and carrying it over 1,000 miles to Bagamoyo (on Tanzania's coast). The journey took them about nine months. From there they took the body by ship to London, where Livingstone was finally buried with full honours in Westminster Abbey on 18 April 1874.

Twenty-five years later, in 1899, the Royal Geographical Society in London sent out a small expedition to cut down the *mpundu* tree and bring a section of its trunk, which had been engraved with the names of Livingstone and three of his party, to London, where it remains to this day.

The present Chief Chitambo, Freddy Chisenga, is the great grandson of the chief who received Livingstone. By appointment, the chief will receive visitors at his palace in Chaililo (sometimes spelled Cholilo or Chalilo) village, from where you can proceed to the memorial site.

Getting there The monument is clearly marked (if sometimes vaguely positioned) on most maps. The easiest route is to turn north off the Great North Road at ⊕ TUCHIN 13°1.146'S, 30°27.695'E towards Mansa and Samfya. After some 65km, or 10km beyond the sign for Kasanka National Park, turn right in Chaililo onto a dirt road. There is a signpost and a small market at this turning (⊕ TULIVI 12°29.255'S, 30°20.364'E). From here it's 27km from the memorial.

Follow the main track for 1km, turning left at Chaililo School (there's a sign to the chief's palace). After 500m, bear right to avoid the chief's palace, or left if you want to visit the chief. Then continue straight on, passing Mupopolo Health Centre, for about a further 25km, till you get to a clinic on the left. Here you should sign the visitors' book and will sometimes be asked to pay a small entry fee. The memorial (⊕ LIVMEM 12°17.970'S, 30°17.580'E) is signposted a little way beyond the clinic, to the left, just before Chipundu School. There are toilets on site.

On your return, it's best to avoid forking left along the old road which is marked on many maps, as this takes a very long time to get back to the tarmac road. It is, however, a useful short cut if you're heading towards Lake Waka Waka or the Bangweulu Wetlands.

KUNDALILA (NKUNDALILA) FALLS (⊕ KUNDAC 13°09.260'S, 30°42.119'E. Entry US$15/7 adult/child; camping US$1 pp) Kundalila, which means 'cooing dove', is one of Zambia's most beautiful waterfalls. Set in an area of scenic meadows and forests on the edge of the Muchinga Escarpment, the clear stream drops 67m into a crystal pool below; it makes a great place for a picnic among the granite boulders. Look out for blue monkeys that are said to inhabit the forests here, and some cheeky white-necked ravens.

At the bottom of the parking area, there is an old bridge across the Kaombe River. The path then splits and the right branch leads you to the top of the gorge. The left takes you on a longer walk to the bottom, where there's a beautiful pool for swimming, if you can bear the water's chill. Take a close look at a good topographical map and you'll realise that you're in one of Zambia's highest areas, at an altitude of around 1,500m, so it's frequently cool and windy but pleasantly devoid of mosquitoes.

Campers have the choice of three separate pitches in a simple, flat campsite, with a shared shelter and flush toilets (bucket refill system). There is no firewood or running water available here, so arrive fully prepared.

The daytime caretaker may also be able to take you to the nearby Kaudina Falls, and possibly also direct you to the Chilindi Chipususha Falls, on the Musumpu River.

Getting there About 65km beyond Serenje, turn southeast off the Great North Road at the small settlement of Kanona (⊕ KANONA 13°4.204'S, 30°38.056'E), where a good dirt track, albeit somewhat rocky in parts, is clearly signposted 'National Monument Kundalila Falls, 14km'. (If you were to take another right turn off this track almost immediately, you would reach the local ZAWA offices.)

Soon you'll cross the railway, then 6km further on there's a Kingdom Hall of Jehovah's Witnesses on the left, before finally reaching the falls. Generally you'll sign in with the caretaker, and pay your entry fee, either at the top of the track, or in the parking/camping area at the camping shelter.

NSALU CAVE (Entry US$10; camping US$15 pp, plus entry fees, although frequently unmanned) This huge semicircular cave, cut into Nsalu Hill, stands about 50m above the level of the surrounding plateau, and contains some excellent San/Bushmen rock paintings. Vandals have sprayed graffiti inside the caves in the past but thankfully the graffiti has faded much faster than the paintings, so once again most of the paintings can still be seen.

Archaeological investigations have demonstrated occupation for at least 20,000 years, firstly by Middle and Late Stone-Age people, and later by Iron-Age settlers. The oldest paintings are in yellow and include parallel lines, circles and loops. Later drawings were executed in rust-coloured paint, and even later ones in red and white paints used together. The last paints applied appear as grey-white pigments and have been applied rather clumsily. They contain animal fats and are thought to have been the work of Iron-Age settlers within the last 2,000 years.

Marked by clear, white painted arrows from the parking area, it's only a 10-minute walk to see the paintings and the view from the cave's mouth over the surrounding countryside is great. If you've lots of energy or plan on camping here, do scramble to the top of the hill for a fantastic panorama.

Getting there The cave is about a 45-minute drive from the main road. Head northeast on the Great North Road to the signpost for Nsalu Cave and turn left (⊗ TU1NSA 12°51.351'S, 30°46.495'E). This is between Serenje and Mpika, about 30km northeast of Kanona (where you turn to Kundalila Falls) and 15km north of Chitambo Mission Hospital.

Follow this road north for about 14km and then turn left at the rather marvellous sign to 'National Nonument' (⊗ TU2NSA 12°44.784'S, 30°44.134'E). After a further 8km this track ends and the cave (⊗ NSALUC 12°43.202'S, 30°40.952'E) is visible about halfway up the hill, on which a walking trail is marked. If you continue north past the 'National Nonument' sign, then you're heading to Lake Waka Waka, Chiundaponde and the Bangweulu Wetlands.

LAKE WAKA WAKA If you're looking for some relatively untouched bush and a quiet setting, where you're very unlikely to encounter anyone else, you'll find a lovely tranquil spot by this spring-fed lake. It's traditionally been good for walking and makes a convenient camping stop on the way to the Bangweulu Wetlands – albeit without facilities these days and with some rather off-putting reports of biting flies and mosquitoes. It's a pleasant lunch spot though and the views from the surrounding hilltops are panoramic. I'm reliably informed that the lake is safe to swim in, with no bilharzia, hippos or crocodiles – though I haven't done this myself. There are few settlements around here, and hence a scattering of game is present, including sitatunga and roan antelope, though both are skittish and scarce.

Getting there However you approach Lake Waka Waka, you'll need a high-clearance 4x4 vehicle in all seasons. Once you leave the main tarred roads, there's little traffic and of the most tracks are not well maintained.

From the west From the Great North Road, take the road north towards Mansa and Samfya for about 65km, turning right 10km after the sign to Kasanka National Park. (See the directions to the Livingstone Memorial, page 358.) About 1km from the tarmac, keep straight ahead at the Chaililo Basic School, rather than turning left to the Chief's Palace and Livingstone Memorial. Continue past Musangashi School for about 30km, before turning left (⊗ TUWAKA 12°31.524'S, 30°36.366'E) at a sign for Lake Waka Waka.

From the south There's a wonderful track from the Great North Road to Lake Waka Waka, but the more northerly sections of this are seldom used, so don't be lulled into taking half measures.

Start by turning north at the signpost for Nsalu Cave (⊗ TU1NSA 12°51.351'S, 30°46.495'E), 30km northeast of Kanona. After 14km you'll pass the left turning to Nsalu Cave (⊗ TU2NSA 12°44.784'S, 30°44.134'E), but you continue heading north-northwest. This track basically follows a watershed, with the Lukulu to the east, which drains into Bangweulu, and tributaries of the Kasanka to the west, which drain into the park. Thus with no rivers crossing it, it should be passable even during the rains. When I journeyed in late May, this road was particularly beautiful, though I don't think that more than half-a-dozen cars had been through since the previous December. The grass was high, the miombo woodlands apparently untouched, and there were very few villages.

About 22km north of the Nsalu turning, the track bumps over a very rocky hill (⊕ WAKHIL 12°36.573'S, 30°39.333'E), and becomes quite indistinct in places. Carry on, and aim for the junction of this track with the 'main' track from Kasanka to Chiundaponde, at ⊕ TUWAKA 12°31.524'S, 30°36.366'E. This is barely a kilometre from the lake.

CHIUNDAPONDE Chiundaponde is a typical small Zambian village that lies at the heart of the area covered by this chapter. The inhabitants are mainly small-scale farmers from the Bisa tribe. In the fields around the village they grow cassava, finger millet, sorghum, maize and groundnuts as their staple crops. Finger millet and sorghum are also used to make beer for selling; groundnuts are grown as a cash crop. Some also keep goats and chickens, either for subsistence or to sell, and you'll often have to avoid these as they wander across the road in front of your vehicle. Chiundaponde isn't really a destination for most visitors, but you will go through it if you're visiting the Bangweulu Wetlands, and so it's useful to be able to navigate to/from here.

For directions from Chiundaponde to the Bangweulu Wetlands, see page 358.

Getting there and away

From the south or west Follow the directions (page 358) from the Great North Road to the turning for Lake Waka Waka (⊕ TUWAKA 12°31.524'S, 30°36.366'E). From there, head on the track leading north – which bounces gently though miombo woodlands and, increasingly, small farming settlements. By 17km beyond the lake, you'll pass through a small village with a school where, like anywhere else here, you'll probably be the object of much curiosity and interest – if only from the local children. Although you'll be in third gear and the track is sandy in places, this isn't difficult driving.

After about 23km you'll cross a large dambo (⊕ DAMBO 12°21.947'S, 30°36.321'E), where the track follows a short causeway. A further 9km on and there's another large dambo to cross (⊕ DAMBO2 12°17.384'S, 30°35.407'E), and around 3km later there may be a sign to the new Nakapalayo village (see below) where you can stay. Some 6km after the second dambo, you reach Chiundaponde (⊕ CHSCHL 12°14.724'S, 30°34.741'E), where among other buildings you'll find a large school.

From the east Approaching from Mpika, leave the Great North Road about 65km from Mpika, and follow the directions (page 358) to get across Lavushi Manda National Park. In the dry season it takes about 3 hours to reach Chiundaponde from the turn-off. In the wet season, the Lavushi Manda road is so bad that you should consider an alternative route – perhaps even going all the way to Kasanka, and approaching from the west.

Where to stay and eat *Map, page 366*

Although many people will press on to reach Shoebill Camp, there's one option about 3–4km south of Chiundaponde that's worth considering:

Nakapalayo Homestay (9 local-style chalets, camping) m 0957 873480; ⊕ NAKAPA 12°16.542'S, 30°34.565'E. This community tourism project, started nearly a decade ago, is signposted from the main track between Chiundaponde & Waka Waka. The village has built extra chalets in traditional Bisa-style: neat, rectangular structures made out of traditional mud bricks with smooth, small, arrow-shaped open windows, & twin or dbl beds with mattresses & mosquito nets. They share very clean long-drop toilets, & bathrooms that are simply reed shelters with showers – buckets on a high shelf from which you scoop water over yourself.

Nakapalayo's people have been trained by members of the Kawaza Village community, in South Luangwa, and offer a variety of activities. Most visitors will take a wander around the village with one of the local guides to see, learn & try everyday activities like drawing water, pounding cassava or cultivating the fields. There are also opportunities to visit the village headman, or local chief, to learn about the culture & history of the Bisa people; to visit Chiundaponde School, the rural health centre or one of the local churches; to meet the village's traditional healer to learn about the medicinal uses of the area's flora; to take a bush walk to learn about traditional uses of the area's plants; & to enjoy dancing & storytelling around the fire. Locally made crafts are available to buy, & if you're staying, the villagers will also prepare tasty traditional meals for you. In return, you are asked to dress & behave modestly, with long trousers or skirts for women, & no public displays of affection, & not to give money or gifts to any individuals. Nakapalayo is worth supporting if you're passing through the area. Contact with Nakapalayo has improved with the arrival of WhatsApp, but if you have any trouble, the team at African Parks in Bangweulu (e bangweulu@africanparks.org) will do their best to assist. *Rondavels US$60 pp FBA, inc village tour & entertainment; Day visit US$15 pp.*

LAVUSHI MANDA NATIONAL PARK (Park fees US$10 pp/day; vehicle US$15/day) Bordering the Bangweulu GMA, this park is potentially interesting for its pleasant, undulating landscape and the Lavushi mountain range to the south. Sadly, it's lost a number of its animals to poachers over recent decades but there is little incentive to try and rejuvenate its fortunes by restocking it with game until tourism numbers here are substantially bigger.

For a period, the Kasanka Trust handled the management of the park as part of a donor-funded development project. They worked on anti-poaching and roadbuilding projects to create game-viewing loops. In 2017, however, the Kasanka Trust relinquished its management of the park to concentrate its efforts on Kasanka alone, requesting that the Department for National Parks & Wildlife (DNPW) seek an organisation with greater financial and management resources to manage Lavushi Manda. To date, the park remains solely under the control of DNPW and sadly some of the roads are increasingly neglected.

Geography Lavushi Manda is over three times the size of Kasanka, and covers 1,500km^2 including the Lavushi Hills. It is easily reached from the Great North Road, is almost equidistant from Serenje and Mpika, and the landscape is attractive and undulating. To the north the land slopes away, and the park's streams all drain into the Lulimala, Lukulu or Lumbatwa rivers and thence ultimately into the Bangweulu Basin.

Flora and fauna Miombo woodland covers most of the park, with some areas of riparian forest nearer the larger streams and many grassy dambos.

Mammals The park's history has left its mark on the wildlife, which remains relatively scarce and secretive. Nevertheless, remain it does, with antelope such as the common duiker, bushbuck, Sharpe's grysbok and southern reedbuck, although puku are thought to be extinct within the park. Unlike in Kasanka National Park, small groups of lion are resident in Lavushi Manda, as are leopard, side-striped jackal and spotted hyena. The Kinda baboon is widespread, especially near rock

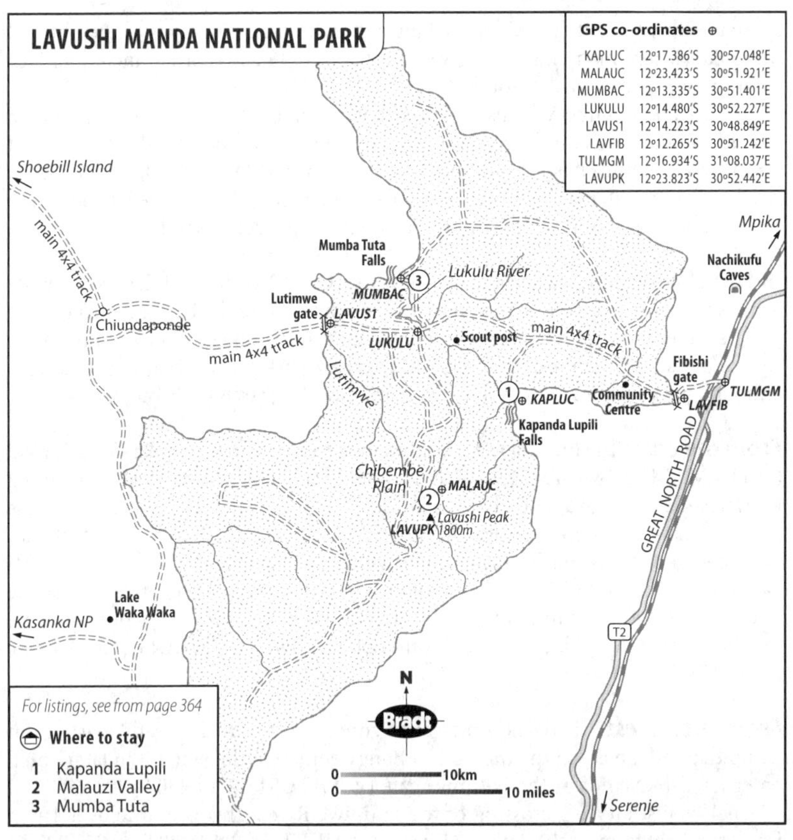

formations, and both vervet and blue monkeys are present. Hippo and crocodile are found in the rivers.

Birdlife Eminent ornithologist Frank Willems has catalogued a total of 366 birds in Lavushi Manda. Near the waterfalls, keep an eye out for African finfoot, long-tailed wagtail, black duck and other riverine species. Bohm's bee-eater, purple-throated cuckooshrike, olive-grey greenbul, Ross's turaco and black-backed barbet are among the many species that can be found in the evergreen forests along the rivers.

The Lavushi mountain range holds a range of rock-loving species. Verreaux's (black) eagle breeds near the peak and can be seen hunting the bush hyraxes and red rock rabbits that live here. Augur Buzzard, lazy cisticola, red-winged starling, mocking cliff chat, familiar chat and Reichard's seedeater are other typical species. The common sunbird on the bare parts of the mountains is eastern miombo double-collared sunbird, till very recently considered a subspecies but now thought to be a full species, while the western miombo double-collared sunbird is common in the surrounding woodlands. In the mountain gorges and elsewhere along streams, evergreen forests hold specials like black-bellied seedcracker and evergreen forest warbler.

The large dambos in the park hold many specials such as streaky-breasted and chestnut-headed flufftail, locustfinch, blue quail, black coucal, Fulleborn's longclaw and pale-crowned cisticola. Of special interest are the seasonal lakes Chibembe and Mikonko, where many interesting water birds have been recorded including jack snipe, a rare species this far south.

Almost all miombo woodland birds that occur in Zambia, can be found in Lavushi Manda. Relatively common are Anchieta's barbet (try the fig trees at Lutimwe Gate and Fibishi Community Centre), Anchieta's sunbird, Arnott's chat, Reichard's seedeater, miombo and rufous-bellied tit, yellow-bellied hyliota and black-necked eremomela. The ground hornbill is often seen as well.

Getting there Most easily accessed from the Great North Road, Lavushi Manda can also be reached from the western side at Chiundaponde. Driving through the park is a convenient route into the Bangweulu Game Management Area from the east, and makes an interesting diversion. There are park gates to both east and west, although park fees are not payable if you are travelling straight through.

From the east The turning to Lavushi Manda from the main Mpika–Serenje road (⊕ TULMGM 12°16.934'S, 31°8.037'E) is about 141km northeast of the D235 turning to Mansa and Kasanka, and about 60km from Mpika. A large signboard with the African Parks' logo points the way to Lavushi Manda and the Bangweulu Wetlands. This road goes across the TAZARA railway line, and enters the park via the Fibishi gate (⊕ LAVFIB 12°17.533'S, 31°04.400'E), which is a few kilometres east of the old gate (now the community centre). Continuing west, you'll eventually come to a new concrete bridge over the lovely Lukulu River (⊕ LUKULU 12°14.480'S, 30°52.227'E).

From the west There is only one good track which heads east from Chiundaponde, passing the turn-off to Bangweulu. A little over 20km later you'll enter Lavushi Manda at the Lutimwe gate (⊕ LAVUS1 12°14.230'S, 30°46.856'E) – which is just above a crossing of the Lutimwe River. This is a little over 10km from the bridge over the Lukulu River (⊕ LUKULU 12°14.480'S, 30°52.227'E) mentioned above.

Getting around For years, the main east–west road through the park has been dreadful. Driving is a challenge even in the dry season, with big muddy gullies and areas where the road has just been washed away. When I crossed the park in June some years back, I averaged about 15km/h. In the wet season, I'd expect this to be exceedingly time-consuming at best, and totally impassable at worst. A 4x4 is a must and do proceed with caution.

Where to stay *Map, page 363*

Three campsites were established in Lavushi Manda in 2011 but sadly, thanks to poor maintenance, basic facilities at all three locations are largely non-existent now: don't expect ablutions, firewood or running water. You'll need to be completely self-sufficient to stay here but you will be blessed with solitude in some lovely spots within easy reach of waterfalls and steams. If you want to camp, ask at the park gate; camping costs US$15 per person, per night, in addition to park fees.

Kapanda Lupili (⊕ KAPLUC 12°17.461'S, 30°57.902'E) Perched on a ridge close to the Lukulu River, Kapanda Lupili has views across open plains. It's a short walk from the falls of the same name, which flow strongly during the rainy season. At other times, you may with care be able to pick your way across the rocks to the other side. **$$**

Malauzi Valley (⊕ 12°23.423'S, 30°51.921'E) By a stream near the Lavushi Peak, this site looks over the palm-fringed plains of the valley, which support a fair amount of game. **$$**

Mumba Tuta (⊕ 12°12.335'S, 30°51.401'E) Right by the Lukulu River bridge, the campsite has a view of the Mumba Tuta Falls. It's fairly overgrown these days & facilities are largely limited to firepits alone. In theory it's possible to swim below the falls when the water's low, but there are crocodiles above – and hippos further downstream – so you'll need to be vigilant. **$$**

What to see and do A bit of forward thinking is essential if you want to make the most of your visit here. Lavushi Manda might make a good area for exploration if you are a very dedicated hiker, though you'll probably want to arrange for one of the scouts from the gate to accompany you. A more challenging trek is the climb up 1,800m Lavushi Peak (⊕ LAVUPK 12°23.823'S, 30°52.442'E), where you'll find klipspringer, bushy hyrax and white-necked ravens. Or consider a five-day hike across the eastern section of the park. Any of these options would require considerable time to plan and set up and a familiarity with wild camping and exploring in Africa.

THE BANGWEULU WETLANDS

In the local Bemba language, Bangweulu means 'where the water meets the sky'. Elsewhere, the Bangweulu Wetlands are often described, in clichéd terms, as one of Africa's last great wilderness areas. That might be overstating its case a little, but it is certainly sizeable and extraordinarily wild, and an area which very few people really know or understand.

Though most visitors' image of a wilderness area is an unpopulated, barren tract of land, the Bangweulu Wetlands encompasses numerous small villages. It remains home to some 50,000 local people, who still hunt and fish here, as their ancestors have done for centuries. They are as much a part of the landscape as the lily-strewn water channels and floodplains teeming with endemic black lechwe and hiding the rare, prehistoric-looking shoebill. Bangweulu is a place that grows on you the more you get to know it, and is well worth visiting to see a different side to Zambia.

PROTECTION OF THE WETLANDS Bangweulu is a conservation success story, but it took time and effort to achieve. Historically, conserving an area largely involved displacing the local people and proclaiming a national park. This clearly hasn't worked in much of Zambia: witness the minimal game left in many of the lesser-known parks. Then came a more enlightened approach of leaving the people on the land, and encouraging them to develop through sustainable management of their natural resources to preserve as much of the flora and fauna as possible. In Bangweulu, the area's population was growing, illegal hunting was rife, and there were fears for the future of the wildlife here.

The area was designated a Wetland of International Importance in 1991, and has also been defined as an Important Bird Area. When the WWF became involved in trying to help local communities to manage the area sustainably, the aim was to create a community partnership park (CPP) where illegal fishing would be stopped and the area intensively managed like a national park.

Then, in 2008, African Parks – already successful in turning round the management of Liuwa Plain National Park (page 473) in western Zambia – was invited by the local chiefs and community representatives to take over responsibility for the park and to protect the region's resources in partnership with the community and Zambia Wildlife Authority (ZAWA). The result was the 2010 declaration of the

Chikuni Community Partnership Park, an area of 2,900km² that is augmented by the 3,100km² of the surrounding Bangweulu GMA. Through education, training and law enforcement, they worked to restore and protect the environment, while monitoring fishing within the wetlands and implementing a seven-year programme of restocking the larger mammals. Over the years, African Parks faced many challenges, from complex issues concerning revenues with ZAWA, to an initial waning in support from local communities as seasonal fishing bans were

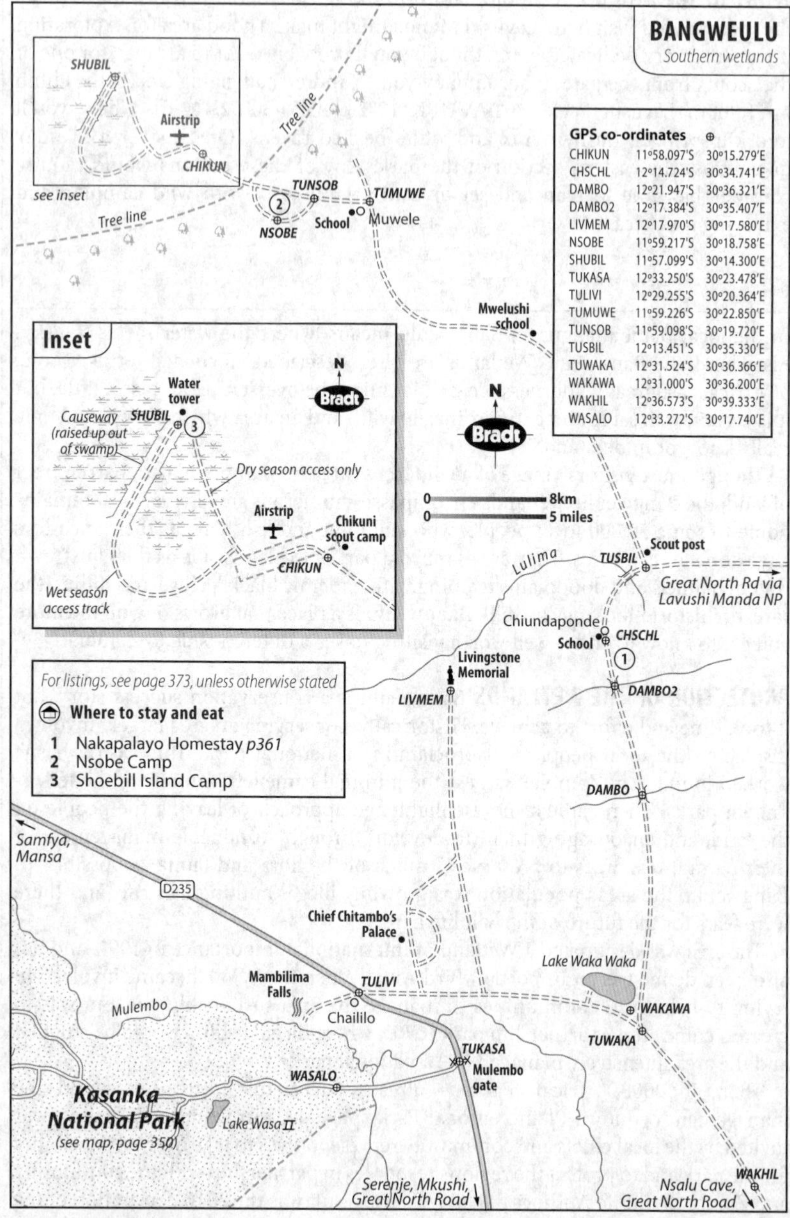

imposed in accordance with the national law. But the tide turned. Management issues with the national parks' authorities were resolved. The local communities began to reap the financial benefits of more sustainable fishing practices and other income-generating projects introduced by African Parks.

Bangweulu is now the largest employer in the region thanks to the significant numbers of village scouts employed in conservation and protection roles. In addition, an array of development projects have been created to help diversify the employment opportunities of the local communities. Seven hundred community members have been trained and are now directly involved in bee-keeping for honey production (1,895 hives to date), sustainable farming training has been provided to create community chicken- and goat-rearing programmes, and fisheries management education has helped enforce a seasonal fishing ban during breeding periods and improve fishing techniques. Everyone has benefitted from improved access to health care and investment in education, including the introduction of Zedupads (tablets featuring the Zambian school curriculum) to local schools and the creation of mini-libraries in 52 local primary schools.

Wildlife has naturally benefitted enormously from the conservation efforts of the last 15 years and a comprehensive management plan. Many of the antelope species found in the wetlands have shown great recovery, including black lechwe and sitatunga, while significant wildlife reintroductions have bolstered the area's animal populations: 95 buffalo from South Luangwa were moved to the area, along with a 250-strong group of waterbuck, zebra, impala and puku. Serval have been translocated into the park and, most recently, 2020–21 saw the historic return of cheetah to Bangweulu, with the successful translocation of ten cheetah to the area. The cheetah have certainly raised the park's profile and tourism interest in the area, with visitors reporting great sightings. This tourism revenue is key to the long-term sustainability of the wetlands and is a significant cause for celebration. And of course the shoebills, for which Bangweulu has such a strong reputation, are thriving. The new Shoebill Management Plan introduced in 2021 included the creation of a rehabilitation and breeding facility, which will undoubtedly make a tremendous difference to the outlook of this critically endangered species.

GEOGRAPHY The low-lying basin containing Lake Bangweulu and its wetlands receives one of the highest rainfalls in the country – over 1,400mm per annum. On the northwestern edge of the basin is Lake Bangweulu itself, about 50km long and up to 25km wide. This is probably the largest body of water within Zambia's borders, and an excellent spot for watching the local fishermen but, apart from the lake's remarkable white, sandy beaches, is of little interest to most visitors. It is easily reached at Samfya, a small town on the main road from Serenje to Mansa. See also page 399 for comments on Samfya and the surrounding area.

The more fascinating areas here are the vast wetlands to the southeast of the lake, which cover an area two to three times the size of the lake, and the seasonally flooded grasslands to the south of those wetlands.

The wetlands and grasslands are areas with few roads and lots of wildlife. It's one of the few regions of Zambia where the local communities are beginning to use the wildlife in their GMAs as a really sustainable source of income. There is little development here, just a small, tented lodge and a simple community-run camp for visitors who arrive on their own. The area still has many residents who continue to fish and eke out a living directly from the environment, but gradually the community development schemes are beginning to tap into tourism as a way to fund sustainable development.

FLORA AND FAUNA With access to the wetlands, the birdlife can be amazing and the animals impressive. However, choose the time of year for your visit very carefully: the type of fauna to be seen, and the activities required to see it, will vary hugely with the season.

Flora Fed by the Chambeshi, Luapula, Lukulu and Lulimala rivers, lush permanent swamps cover 6,000km^2 of the Bangweulu Wetlands. Filled with Cyperus papyrus, thick mats of floating grasses and Phragmites reeds, it's an enchanting watery ecosystem. Around the channels and swamps themselves, seasonally flooded grasslands, floodplains and miombo woodland provide surprising diversity.

Animals The positive effect on wildlife of African Parks' management cannot be understated: recovering populations and significant animal reintroductions have taken place here under their careful direction and supervision.

The speciality here is the black lechwe, an attractive dark race of the lechwe that is endemic to the Bangweulu area. The only other places where it has been recorded are the swamps beside Lake Mweru, where its status is now exceedingly questionable, and the Nashinga Swamps near Chinsali, where it has been re-introduced. It is much darker than the red lechwe found throughout southern Africa, or the race known as the Kafue lechwe which occur in the Lochinvar area. I think it's by far the most attractive of the three.

The current population in this area is estimated at 36,600 animals, and herds of thousands are common on the dry floodplains around the wetlands. As well as these huge herds of black lechwe, there are healthy populations of sitatunga, tsessebe, southern reedbuck, common duiker and oribi. In 2017, 250 zebra and impala were released to join the small breeding herds previously introduced to the park from a Lusaka game farm. These healthy herds are often visible on the plains. Elephant and buffalo are frequently seen, with 95 buffalo translocated from South Luangwa in 2019 to increase genetic diversity in the Bangweulu population.

Predators are less commonly sighted but spotted hyena and leopard are occasionally observed at dusk or dawn; on a night drive, side-striped jackal are very common. White-tailed mongooses, serval, civets and genets are also frequent nocturnal sightings.

In late 2020–21, seven cheetah were successfully translocated from South Africa to Bangweulu in a major species reintroduction effort and, thanks to being collared, are frequently seen by travellers on safari here. African Parks may even consider reintroducing rhino at a later stage.

Birds The Bangweulu area's big attraction is the unusual and rare shoebill (*Balaeniceps rex*; page 370): a giant, prehistoric-looking, grey bird, sometimes known as the whale-headed stork. The global population of shoebills in the wild is estimated at 8,000 birds, with a few hundred individuals estimated to live in the Bangweulu Wetlands, their southernmost habitat. These wetlands are a vital refuge for this very threatened species. Found only in tropical, central-eastern Africa, between South Sudan and Zambia, they do not migrate, and so are particularly sensitive to disturbance, be that from habitat loss or hunting. In Bangweulu, they breed in the papyrus between May and June, so it's essential that visitors are careful not to disturb them when the birds are sitting on their nests.

In 2008, when African Parks took over the management of Bangweulu's community-owned protection zone, the organisation implemented a successful 'Shoebill Guardian Programme', offering local people a financial incentive if they reported shoebill nests and helped to protect them until the birds fledged. In 2022, 26 community members were employed 24/7 between June and November to monitor 13 nests and their inhabitants. In tandem with researchers monitoring nests and chicks using camera traps, the scheme has been extremely successful, with a marked increase in fledglings over the years.

In recent years, it wasn't unusual to spot a shoebill near the staff house at Chikuni island, with rescued birds occasionally spending time here before being released to the wild. The scheme was taken to the next level in 2021 with the introduction of a long-term Shoebill Management Plan. Then in May 2022, in a first for shoebill conservation, the Shoebill Captive Rearing and Rehabilitation Facility opened in the Bangweulu Wetlands. Shoebills typically lay two eggs, though three have been documented, but it is only the first born that usually survives. The subsequent chicks to hatch usually die in the first week of life as a result of parental neglect or ruthless fratricide. The new breeding facility will incubate the second egg, collected by researchers and community guardians, as a means to increase overall bird numbers of this critically endangered species. It's a ground-breaking project – with only two known instances of shoebills having been reared in captivity previously recorded – and if successful could have an incredibly positive impact on global shoebill population numbers and scientific knowledge of the species.

Aside from the elusive shoebill, the birdlife in the wetlands is amazing throughout the year, making it well worth the effort required to get here. The commoner birds include the little, cattle, black and great white egrets; black-headed, purple, squacco and grey herons; sacred, glossy and hadeda ibis; knob-billed, yellow-billed, fulvous and white-faced whistling ducks; open-billed storks, pygmy geese, pratincoles and grey-headed gulls. Plovers are well represented, with blacksmith, wattled, three-banded, crowned, Caspian and long-toed varieties – and recently there's also been an influx of spurwing plovers.

Migrants that stop here while the floodwaters are high include flamingos, while pelicans and spoonbills are normally resident. Meanwhile Bangweulu is a very important reserve for wattled cranes, which occur in large flocks and are readily seen. (There are greater numbers here than almost anywhere else, with the possible exception of the Kafue Flats.) The wetlands' shallow waters are ideal for smaller waders, like sandpipers, godwits and avocets. Other smaller birds worthy of particular note include the swamp flycatcher, lesser jacana, white-cheeked bee-eater (aka blue-breasted in East African literature) and Fülleborn's and rosy-breasted longclaws (which is the local name for the birds known as pink-throated further south). There are plenty of raptors around, with fish eagles, marsh harriers and bateleur eagles particularly common. On the flat grass plains around the wetlands, Denham's bustards are frequently seen striding around.

WHEN TO GO There are many reasons to come to Bangweulu – only one of which is the birding. So choose your season carefully.

January and February are the heart of the rainy season, when the waters are rising. It's the worst time of year for the small, biting lechwe flies and other insects, so insect repellent is vital. Arriving with a head-net, covering your face and neck below your hat, would not be going too far.

This is a great time for birding, as many of the residents will be in breeding plumage, and there will be lots of migrants around – although shoebills usually arrive only at the end of February. The lechwe are in the swamps at this time, while other mammals have retreated to the woodlands on the margins of the water.

THE SHOEBILL'S TALE *Stephanie Debere*

The huge, rare and prehistoric-looking shoebill is found only in a few inaccessible spots between southern Sudan and northern Zambia – making it Africa's most sought-after species for birdwatchers.

Shoebills stand up to 1.4m tall, with a strong likeness to the dodo. They have always been named for their ungainly beaks, which resemble a wooden shoe, and older literature refers to them as whale-headed storks, while Arab traders knew them as *abu markub*, which means 'father of the shoe'. Their scientific name, *Balaeniceps rex*, means 'king whalehead'.

Shoebills can look rather sinister when viewed head-on, with their massive beaks and a frowning glare, but in profile they appear charmingly dolphin-like with a mouth that apparently smiles, and huge eyelashes. Despite this beguiling look, their mandibles are razor sharp; their upper bill ends in a curved hook that's used to pierce and hold their slippery prey. Their plumage is bluish slate-grey, with a slightly darker head which sports a small tuft of feathers that can be raised to form a crest. Their legs are long and dark, and their toes lack any webbing.

Shoebills inhabit a precise ecological niche: they specialise in feeding on large fish that live in poorly oxygenated waters of swamps and wetlands – particularly lungfish. They are usually seen standing motionless beside slow, deep-water channels, particularly in areas where fish concentrate – like the narrow channels where spreading waters spill out onto seasonally flooded areas. They remain still for hours, waiting for fish to surface for air, when they ambush with a swift and powerful strike. They will prey on species other than lungfish, and are also said to

Water levels peak in **March**, though the rains draw to a close only around April. From **May** the water levels start slowly to recede and travelling begins to get easier by the end of the month. This is the best time to go for shoebills, which are often seen within sight of Shoebill Camp, along with countless other wading and water-loving species. Like many of these birds, visitors to Bangweulu will often spend a lot of time wading if they're keen to see shoebills at close range!

Towards the end of this period and into **June and July**, the waters pull back from the flat, seasonally flooded plains around the wetlands, exposing large areas of fertile, open grasslands – like the Chimbwi Plain. These attract huge herds of black lechwe along with tsessebe and other herbivores from the woodland margins. It's a great time for game drives, with night drives often yielding genets, side-striped jackals, civets and various mongooses. In the wetlands, the water has receded further and the shoebills have moved closer to the lake – so seeing them involves longer mokoro (dugout canoe) journeys from Shoebill Camp. That said, in early June I managed half-a-dozen sightings in one long day – and even later in July you are still almost guaranteed to see a shoebill if you apply enough effort. Though days are warm, the nights are very cold – with temperatures dropping to almost freezing.

In **August and September** the floodplains and outer reaches of the wetlands become even drier; Shoebill Camp is no longer an island, and most wildlife viewing is done on foot or by 4x4. The shoebills have retreated into the permanent swamps, and it takes a bit of determination (and a mini-expedition) to get close to them, though in recent years it has been very possible to see them at this time of year. The take amphibians, water-snakes, monitor lizards, terrapins, rats, young waterfowl and, some sources report, even young crocodiles.

Although they prefer to hunt in fairly open areas, where it's easy for them to take off if disturbed, they nest in large, flat nests found in denser vegetation – often papyrus. Between one and three eggs are laid, though only one chick usually survives. It takes about four and a half months for this silvery-grey chick to fledge and become independent, then a further three or four years until it first breeds.

Taxonomists have long debated if the shoebill is a member of the stork, the heron or the pelican family, as various characteristics suggest one or another. However, DNA studies now conclude that shoebills are closely related to pelicans, but in a family of their own.

Given their restricted and remote habit, shoebills are incredibly difficult to study and consequently relatively little is known about them. Estimates of the total world population seem to be around the 5,000–10,000 mark. We know that their main stronghold is in the Sudd, in southern Sudan, and that they are also found in Murchison Falls National Park in Uganda, the Moyowosi-Kigosi Swamp in western Tanzania, Manovo-Gounda-Saint Floris National Park in the Central African Republic, and, allegedly, in Akagera National Park in Rwanda (though nobody on the ground in Rwanda seems to know about them!).

We also know that they are, sadly, occasionally sold for meat by local people and for profit by foreign collectors – as shoebills are one of the most expensive birds in the trade. So if you are fortunate enough to see them, try to keep your distance and minimise any disturbance.

Lukulu River is the focus of much wildlife, while concentrations of storks and other birds form 'fishing parties' in the remnants of drying pools where fish and snails are stranded.

By **October** the land is parched and dusty everywhere except deep in the heart of the wetlands, far from Shoebill Camp. In **November and December** the first rains bring some relief, as well as a flush of new grass on the plains, which attracts massive herds of black lechwe back from the wetlands, and tsessebe in more moderate numbers from the woodlands.

GETTING THERE Getting to Bangweulu isn't always easy. You'll need to do one of the following:

- Organise a special 'mobile' trip here with an experienced safari company. (I know of none that regularly runs trips here – although the Kasanka team will sometimes organise 4x4 transfers to/from Bangweulu.)
- Fly into here, and then continue by flying out. This is how most people visit; although not cheap it is the easiest way to organise, and the most relaxing way to visit.
- Drive in here with your own fully equipped 4x4. This isn't easy or quick, but it can be fun if you've an adventurous streak and can be self-sufficient.

Organised trips There's only one company working on the ground in this area at present: Remote Africa Safaris (page 292), who operate Shoebill Island Camp. You can book a trip with them directly or, more usually, arrange it through the tour operator (page 92) who is organising the rest of your trip in Zambia for about the same price as booking direct.

Cycling tours African Parks and the Kasanka Trust are keen to encourage cycling in the Bangweulu area. It is an authentic, adventurous way to see the plains, with good paths to cycle, friendly guides and wide open spaces. You'll be sharing the paths with local people, for whom bicycles are central to their way of life.

The cycling 'season' is during the traditionally dry months, between June and December and you can join a four-day guided mountain bike safari tour from Wasa Lodge to Kabwe Campsite for US$40 per person per day including bike, camping kit and all meals. In the past, groups have travelled from Kasanka, via Shoebill, all the way up to Shiwa Ng'andu and then into the Luangwa valley. Another good route would be Kasanka National Park–Shoebill/Chikuni–Lavushi Manda National Park. Interested cyclists should contact Kasanka or Shoebill Island Camp well in advance in order to arrange guides, park permits, river crossings and, if necessary, bush camping.

Fly-in trips These must be pre-arranged. You can fly in to Shoebill Camp, as there is an airstrip (called Chimbwe) at Chikuni, just 3km from the camp. You'll be transferred to the camp from there, and your activities will be arranged for you. There is currently no 'schedule' for these flight transfers, and so they are relatively costly for one person because you need to hire the whole plane. Consequently, the price becomes more economic for two or three passengers. Flying in will give you a fascinating view of the wetlands and surrounding plains that you just can't get from the ground.

Luangwa-Bangweulu Safaris These can be organised through Remote Africa Safaris (page 292) for guests staying more than four nights at camps in South Luangwa, using Tafika's own light aircraft to fly from Lukuzi airstrip to Chimbwe over the escarpment and Bangweulu's wetlands. Activities during the day include guided game drives, scenic canoeing excursions and cheetah tracking. This is an excellent way of combining Bangweulu with South Luangwa.

With advance notice, it is also possible to organise a day trip for guests at Kasanka; see page 348.

In early May, Robin Pope Safaris (page 292) operate a six-night 'Shoebill Safari' that combines a trip to Shoebill Camp with their Luangwa River Camp in the South Luangwa and Wasa Camp in Kasanka National Park.

Driving yourself From around November to early May, driving yourself on any of these routes can be very challenging – not to say wet, muddy and very slow. If you don't know what you're doing, you're likely to get stranded. By contrast, in the dry season it is fine, although note that there are very few vehicles on some of these tracks, and you always need a fully equipped 4x4 – with your own food and supplies. See also page 103 for details of the Open Africa route that covers this region.

From Chiundaponde to Chikuni If you're approaching from Waka Waka, then to reach Bangweulu just continue straight through Chiundaponde, heading roughly north. After leaving the village, you'll find the track bends slowly round to the right before crossing a small bridge. Barely 500m after this bridge is a left turn (⊗ TUSBIL 12°13.451'S, 30°35.330'E) onto a track which is small and easy to miss; this leads northwest to Bangweulu. This turning is about 4km east of Chiundaponde, and a fraction under 2 hours' drive from Waka Waka.

Barely 100m north of the turning is a scout post – and it's always worth checking with the scouts here for the latest news and directions. (There's a fairly reliable radio here that's in close touch with Chikuni and, in case of problems, could even reach Kasanka.) Follow the track northwest, and after about 19km you'll pass Mwelushi Middle Basic School. In another 20km you'll reach Muwele village (⊕ TUMUWE 11°59.226'S, 30°22.850'E) where the track splits; the left fork leads in a more westerly direction towards Chikuni. At times this track resembles more of a footpath than a road, but don't give up!

About 6km after the village, the road forks (⊕ TUNSOB 11°59.098'S, 30°19.720'E), with the left turn going to Nsobe Camp. If you continue straight on, without turning to Nsobe, you will soon emerge from low scrub into a plain of open grass, stretching for as far as you can see. (Look around you – that dark reddish colour on the horizon may just be thousands of black lechwe!) Here you'll see the start of a long causeway leading to Chikuni. In recent years it has been better, in the dry season, to follow the vehicle tracks which run parallel to the causeway. In the wet season you really need experienced, up-to-date local advice – which, when levels are low, will generally be to splash through the water on existing tracks. During periods when water levels are very high, Chikuni has been inaccessible by vehicle.

However you are proceeding across the plains, about 8km after the turning to Nsobe, you reach the Chikuni Research Post (⊕ CHIKUN 11°58.097'S, 30°15.279'E). Chikuni literally stands out as it's on top of a small rise in the plains, marked very clearly by a tall eucalyptus tree. This is one of the few trees within sight on the plains; there is another at Kaleha, about 8km east along the Lukulu River.

If you're going to Shoebill Camp then you need to have pre-arranged your stay, and Chikuni is often the rendezvous point where you leave your vehicle, and continue by mokoro; in any case, you should stop, check with the scouts, and sign the register. The scouts here have a radio to contact Shoebill Camp (as well as the ZAWA scout post on the road from Chiundaponde). Somewhere beyond Chikuni, depending on water levels, the wetlands begin.

From Chikuni to Shoebill You should pre-book your time at Shoebill Island Camp, so take advice from the Remote Africa team about how to get from Chikuni to Shoebill at the time of year when you are going. If the water's high (typically January to June) then you may need to leave your vehicle at Chikuni and reach the camp by mokoro.

Later in the year you should be able to drive, in which case you sign in with the scouts at Chikuni and then pass straight through. Follow the direction of the airstrip for part of its length, and then hit out at 30° to your right, where you should find the tracks of other vehicles to the Shoebill Island causeway. If in doubt, try scanning the flat horizon for Shoebill's distinctive rectangular water tower among a patch of small trees.

Facing the camp, you will need to bear slightly to the left in order to join the beginning of the causeway (or later on, depending on the water levels). However, the route varies a lot with the particular season, and so it's vital that you get directions from the team at Remote Africa, or the scouts at Chikuni, before you try to drive here. Regardless of season, extensive off-road 4x4 driving experience is necessary to embark on this route.

WHERE TO STAY *Map, page 366*

These days there are a few accommodation options in the Bangweulu area: Shoebill Island Camp, Nkondo Tented Camp, a couple of campsites and even a village homestay between Kasanka and Bangweulu, just outside Chiundaponde village (page 361). If you're on an organised trip, or flying in, then you'll likely be staying at Shoebill.

If you're driving yourself in a self-contained 4x4 with all your supplies (there is no other sensible way!) then you could possibly stop at Nakapalayo village on the way to Bangweulu. However, note that Shoebill Camp is further into the wetlands than the other camps – so most trips end up there at some stage!

Shoebill Island Camp (4 Meru-style tents, camping) Contact via Remote Africa Safaris (page 292); ⊕ SHUBIL 11°57.099'S, 30°14.300'E. Run as a collaboration between African Parks & Luangwa specialists Remote Africa Safaris, Shoebill Camp stands under trees on the western side of a small, permanent island, just 2.5km northwest of Chikuni as the stork flies. During the rains & for a few months afterwards, this is within the wetlands, surrounded by channels & lagoons. Later in the year, it's left high & dry & accessible by 4x4 from Chikuni (page 373).

Although recently rebuilt, Shoebill remains an old-style safari camp & facilities are simple. Each of the walk-in Meru-style tents has a private en-suite bathroom at the back, with a shower & a flush toilet. Solid timber furniture offers practical storage, there's a vibrant chitenge covered armchair & beds are comfortable. During the drier months when the campsite isn't flooded, it is also possible for adventurous self-drivers to camp here.

The camp's central area, with a fireside lounge, dining & bar make an excellent lookout point, & during your stay, do make the effort to climb the water tower for camp's best view over the swamps.

Shoebill Camp isn't luxurious by modern safari standards, but it is comfortable & remains by far the best option in this area, where the environment, flora & fauna are fascinating, & the activities (see below) can be excellent. This is a great destination for the adventurous who are keen on their wildlife, but it really needs to be booked in advance. *US$650 pp sharing, FBA inc park & conservation levies, cheetah tracking with the carnivore programme & visit to the shoebill rearing facility. Children 8+.* ⌚ *May–Oct.* 👑👑👑

Nsobe Camp (6 pitches) **e** bangweulu@african-parks.org; **w** africanparks.org. Nsobe was historically a hunting camp on the edge of the swamps, but now that that area has been afforded higher protection it has been taken over by African Parks. Run by the local community, Nsobe has sheltered sites with hot showers (on request), toilets, a rustic seating area & a small shelter for washing dishes. It's the location on the edge of the Chimbwe Plain that is the draw, with wide, far-reaching views. In time there may be reed-&-thatch chalets here, but at present it's purely for those with all their own camping kit & supplies, although firewood & water are available. *US$10 pp camping plus US$10 pp conservation levy, US$15 vehicle/night;* ⌚ *May–Oct depending on rains.* **$$**

WHAT TO SEE AND DO While the black lechwe are spectacular, the birdlife is Bangweulu's main attraction, and the ungainly shoebill (page 370) is a particular favourite among visitors.

Activities depend on the time of year; if there isn't enough water to travel through the swamps by canoe, the usual form of water transport, then the guides will take you walking over the floating reed bed in search of shoebills and other wildlife. Alternatively, drives will take you to the drier areas of the plains and into the surrounding woodlands.

Whatever you do – driving, walking (often wading!), boating and canoeing – all activities should be done with a guide.

For those staying at Shoebill Island Camp on a full-board basis, this includes activities. For campers, however, and those who are self-catering, activities are charged extra: US$30 per person for a half-day walk or canoe trip to visit the shoebill nests (note that only 5min is spent at the nest but it's a lovely scenic outing; up to 3 people); US$30 per person for a half-day game drive with a community guide (3–6 people); and US$40 per person for a pre-arranged cheetah monitoring encounter (children must be 12+).

As you might expect from an area which is seasonally flooded, and whose name translates as 'where the water meets the sky', Bangweulu is a largely trackless wilderness. It is easy to get lost if you simply head into it alone, and indiscriminate driving does a great deal of damage to both the soil structure and the ground-nesting birds. It is strongly recommended on safety and conservation grounds that 4x4 owners use one of the camps as a base for their explorations, and take local advice about where to go and how to minimise their environmental impact.

ISANGANO NATIONAL PARK

(Park fees US$5 pp/day; vehicle US$15/day) East of Lake Bangweulu, Isangano National Park covers 840km^2 of flat, well-watered grassland. The western side of the park forms part of the Bangweulu Wetlands, which are seasonally flooded.

While the park's ecosystem was originally the same as that of the Bangweulu GMAs, it is reliably reported that the game in Isangano has totally disappeared because of settlement, agriculture and the consequent subsistence hunting. There is no internal road network within the park at all, though there is quite a high density of subsistence farmers settled within its boundaries. With this in mind, it's very doubtful that Isangano will ever become a national park in anything but name. Visitors are advised to look toward the Bangweulu area if they want to visit this type of region. At least there is some infrastructure, and the local communities in the area will derive benefit from your visit.

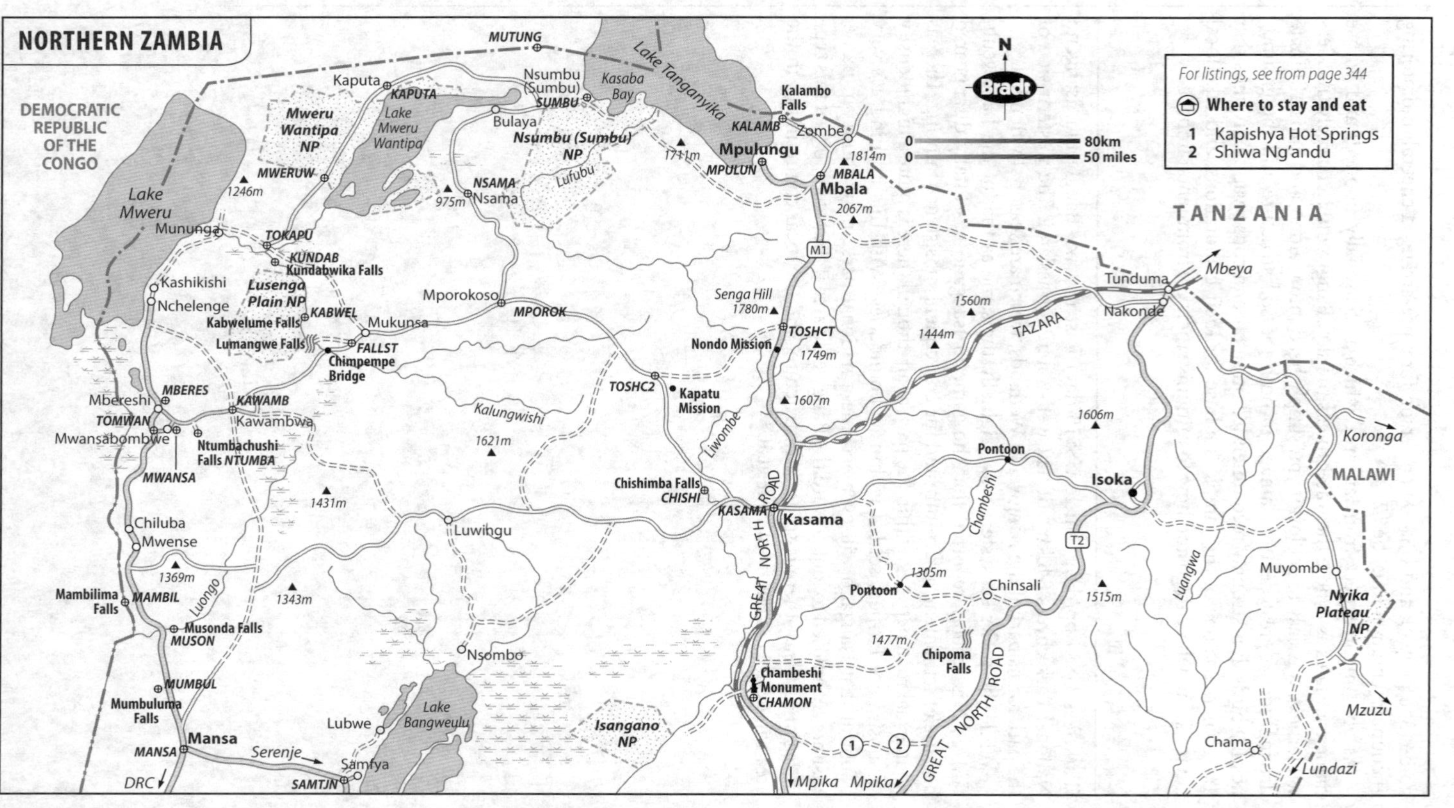

NORTHERN ZAMBIA
N
Bradt
0 80km
0 50 miles
For listings, see from page 344
Where to stay and eat
1 Kapishya Hot Springs
2 Shiwa Ng'andu
DEMOCRATIC REPUBLIC OF THE CONGO
TANZANIA
MALAWI
Lake Mweru
Lake Tanganyika
Lake Mweru Wantipa
Lake Bangweulu
Kasaba Bay
Mweru Wantipa NP
Nsumbu (Sumbu) NP
Lusenga Plain NP
Isangano NP
Nyika Plateau NP
GREAT NORTH ROAD
T2
M1
TAZARA
MUTUNG
Kaputa
KAPUTA
Nsumbu (Sumbu)
SUMBU
Bulaya
NSAMA
Nsama
MWERUW
Kalambo Falls
KALAMB
Zombe
Mpulungu
MPULUN
MBALA
Mbala
Mununga
TOKAPU
KUNDAB
Kundabwika Falls
Kashikishi
Nchelenge
Kabwelume Falls
KABWEL
Mukunsa
Mporokoso
MPOROK
Lumangwe Falls
FALLST
Chimpempe Bridge
Senga Hill
TOSHCT
Nondo Mission
TOSHC2
Kapatu Mission
Tunduma
Nakonde
Mbeya
MBERES
Mbereshi
TOMWAN
Mwansabombwe
KAWAMB
Kawambwa
Ntumbachushi Falls NTUMBA
MWANSA
Kalungwishi
Liwombe
Chishimba Falls
CHISHI
KASAMA
Kasama
Pontoon
Chambeshi
Isoka
Koronga
Luwingu
Chiluba
Mwense
Mambilima Falls
MAMBIL
Luongo
Musonda Falls
MUSON
Nsombo
Chinsali
Chipoma Falls
Luangwa
Muyombe
Chambeshi Monument
CHAMON
MUMBUL
Mumbuluma Falls
Mansa
MANSA
Lubwe
Serenje
Samfya
SAMTJN
DRC
Mpika
Mzuzu
Chama
Lundazi
Lufubu
1246m
975m
1711m
1814m
2067m
1780m
1749m
1560m
1444m
1607m
1606m
1621m
1431m
1369m
1343m
1305m
1515m
1477m

13

Northern Zambia

To explore northern Zambia properly, visiting its far-flung national parks and spectacular waterfalls, requires some determination and advance planning. Historically, all of the area's three main national parks have suffered from abuse and neglect over the years, but one, Nsumbu (also referred to as Sumbu), is leading the charge in revitalising and conserving these areas, which could lead to a promising future for the region. Bounded by Game Management Areas and Lake Tanganyika, one of the largest lakes in East Africa's Great Rift Valley, Nsumbu is home to a dedicated team of conservationists determined to restore its terrestrial wildlife to former glory and preserve the rich aquatic life of its waters. With traditional safari pursuits sitting alongside snorkelling, diving, fishing and beach barbecues, it's a special place to explore and recharge.

The north's other two large parks, Mweru Wantipa and Lusenga Plain, may take more time to get back on the safari map, as neither has organised facilities for visitors or good roads. Years of poaching have reduced the populations of game animals within them, and the wildlife that remains is shy and understandably wary of humankind.

Unlike some parts of the country though, many of northern Zambia's most beautiful scenes are outside of its national parks. It's an area rich in sweeping scenic views and spectacular waterfalls. Many a journey here – and some can be long given the conditions of the roads – can be broken with superb hikes and overnight stops at remote rapids or cascades.

Finally, a word about Nyika, a high plateau that straddles the Malawi border and provides the Luangwa with many of its tributaries. There are national parks on both sides of the border. Nyika Plateau National Park, on the Zambian side, is unlike anywhere else in the country: high mountains clothed in rolling heathlands and often draped with mist. It's a great walking destination, a cool respite after the heat of the Luangwa Valley and home to numerous endemic species. However, it's easiest to access from the east, from Malawi, and so we are just mentioning it here and you can read more about it in our Malawi guide (page 408).

GETTING ORGANISED

Most tour operators based in Zambia specialise in wildlife safaris, but one is especially well placed to handle northern Zambia (as well as further afield):

Thorn Tree Safaris m 0974 436267; e thorntreesafaris@yahoo.com; f ThornTreeSafaris. Run by Claire Powell & her husband, Sean Van Niekerk, from their Livingstone base (page 212), Thorn Tree Safaris is a mobile-safari operation organising bespoke adventures, safaris & cycling challenges countrywide, with a natural affinity to northern Zambia as Claire was born here & speaks the local language, Bemba, fluently.

GPS REFERENCES FOR NORTHERN ZAMBIA

CHAMON	10°54.634'S, 31°05.344'E	MPULUN	08°45.907'S, 31°06.368'E
CHIMBR	09°33.082'S, 29°26.937'E	MUMBUL	10°55.801'S, 28°44.178'E
CHISHI	10°06.465'S, 30°55.100'E	MUSON	10°42.856'S, 28°48.858'E
FALLST	09°32.239'S, 29°27.874'E	MUTUNG	08°33.839'S, 30°12.405'E
KABWEL	09°31.432'S, 29°21.267'E	MWANSA	09°49.250'S, 28°45.350'E
KALAMB	08°35.831'S, 31°14.397'E	MWERUP	08°53.572'S, 29°28.878'E
KAPUTA	08°28.503'S, 29°39.990'E	NSAMA	08°53.448'S, 29°56.896'E
KASAMA	10 °12.440'S, 31°11.290'E	NSUMBU	08°31.221'S, 30°28.629'E
KAWAMB	09°47.605'S, 29°04.675'E	NTUMBA	09°51.167'S, 28°56.652'E
KUNDAB	09°13.058'S, 29°18.258'E	SAMFYA	11°20.437'S, 29°33.526'E
MAMBIL	10°33.791'S, 28°48.858'E	SAMTJN	11°21.126'S, 29°29.453'E
MANSA	11°12.076'S, 28°53.451'E	TOKAPU	09°07.531'S, 29°12.996'E
MBALA	08°50.694'S, 31°22.325'E	TOMWAN	09°49.317'S, 28°45.474'E
MBERES	09°44.078'S, 28°47.350'E	TOSHCT	09°27.486'S, 31°13.136'E
MPOROK	09°21.831'S, 30°07.432'E	TOSHC2	09°40.270'S, 30°41.628'E

THE GREAT NORTH ROAD TO MPULUNGU

The Great North Road stretches from Lusaka through Kapiri Mposhi to Mpika. Here it divides, with the left-hand fork heading due north to Kasama then onward to Mbala and finally Mpulungu, on the shore of Lake Tanganyika – a mammoth 1,150km regional artery, tarred all the way and now largely free of the pot-holes that dogged it for many years.

KASAMA The bustling regional capital, Kasama is a centrally located little town, about 860km from Lusaka. It acts as a supply centre for much of the north of the country, so there are some well-stocked stores, and a relatively large amount of traffic coming into, and leaving, town. Visitors to northern Zambia will invariably end up spending some time here, even if only to refuel and buy a few soft drinks.

Getting there

By air There are no longer any regular flights to Kasama but the reliable, regional charter flight specialist Sky Trails (page 110) can arrange travel here.

By train The TAZARA station (page 110) is about 7km south of town, on the right as you enter from Mpika. This is your last chance to disembark at a major town before the railroad turns east, away from Lake Tanganyika, towards the border at Tunduma. The express train from Kapiri Mposhi to Dar es Salaam arrives in Kasama early on Wednesday at 03.19 and the slower 'Ordinary' train on Saturday at about 02.59. The trains pass through on their return journey 22.07 on Saturday and 00.11 on Wednesday respectively.

By bus Kasama is an important regional hub with buses connecting Lusaka with Lake Tanganyika in the far north stopping here, as well as those from the Copperbelt heading to Mpulungu. In 2021, a central bus station, Chikumanino, opened, allowing buses to and from all destinations to stop in the same place. Its metal structure is easily spotted from the M1 just northeast of Croc Roundabout in the heart of Kasama.

If you're heading east to Tanzania, it's usually fairly straightforward. The road to Nakonde, on the border, is pretty good, though it's worth checking the state of the roads at the end of the rainy season. If any of the pontoons are out of action, there's usually a sign on the way out of town. An alternative option is to take the TAZARA train.

Where to stay *Map, below*

There is no shortage of guesthouses in Kasama, though few stand out and price is no guide to quality. Quiet Kasembo is the best option, but for a central spot in town, try:

Kasama Lodge (11 rooms) Zambia Rd; ☎ 0214 221039; e enquiries@zambiahostels.com. **$–$$**

Kizya Executive Lodge (7 rooms) Mpika Rd; ☎ 0214 221797; m 0977 750147; e info@kizyalodge.com; w kizyalodge.com. **$–$$**

Out of town

Kasembo Guesthouse (14 rooms) Luwingu Rd; ☎ 0214 230065, 0214 221158; e kasemboguest@gmail.com, kasembofarms@gmail.com; ⊕ KASEMB 10°13.714'S, 31°07.506'E. Located 8km west of Kasama, Kasembo Guesthouse is on the farm of the same name. Founded more than 50 years ago & owned & run by the Missionaries of Marianhill, the 400ha organic farm offers accommodation for guests (of any creed) in large rooms (some en suite) grouped around a grassy central area, shaded by indigenous trees & near a good pool. It's a cool, tranquil spot, completely without hassle, & discussions with the missionaries can give you an interesting insight into the area. If you arrive in town & want to stay then ask at the Kasembo Supermarket opposite the central market. **$** *exc b/fast*.

Bushcamping Wild camping is safe pretty much anywhere in this region – just be sure to ask if you are near a village. The miombo woodlands and vast riverside

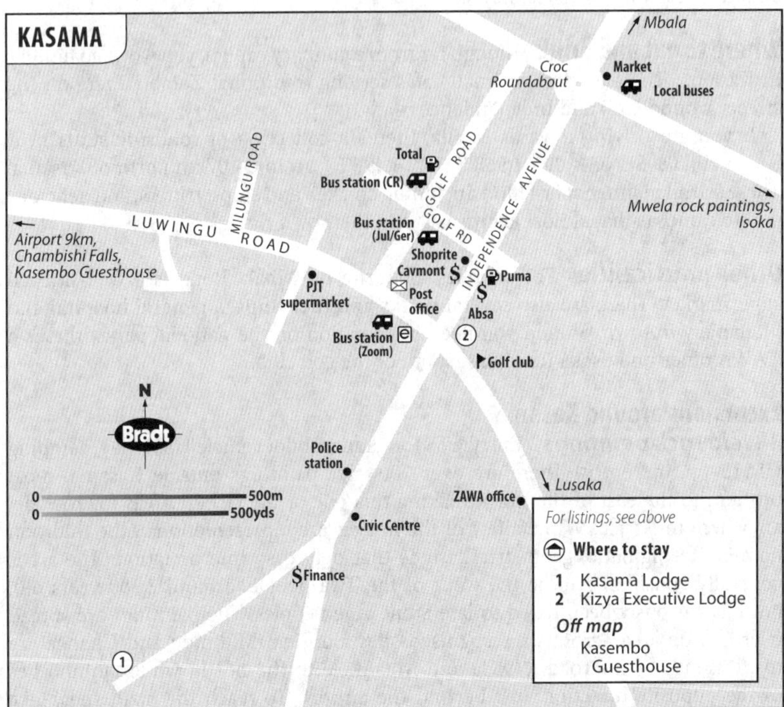

BORDER CROSSING INTO TANZANIA

Travellers on the TAZARA train will cross into Tanzania at Tunduma, some 245km northeast of Kasama. This is also a major crossing point for vehicles, with all the attendant queues and hassle that you might expect. The one-stop border (you exit one country and enter another in one place) is open from 08.00–20.00 Zambian time; be aware that Tanzania operates in a different time zone and is 1 hour behind Zambia (ie: the border is open 07.00–19.00 Tanzanian time). Be friendly, polite and respectful with all officials and have your paperwork and a pen at the ready. You will need:

A **Tanzanian visa**, currently US$50 for three months single-entry for most nationalities except Americans who are charged US$100 for a year-long, multi-entry visa. Both can be purchased online in advance of travel (w visa.immigration.go.tz) or at the border, but you'll need to pay in US dollars cash. There's a foreign exchange service at the bank near the immigration office.

To cross the border **with a vehicle**, you will require a **temporary import permit** (TIP) at a cost of US$25 for 30 days, in place of a 'carnet de passage'. This is supplied only on presentation of copies of your **passport**, an original or certified copy of the **vehicle's registration document**, **proof of insurance** and your **exit document from Zambia**. A month's Tanzanian **road tax** costs a further US$25, also payable in US dollars cash.

dambo at the defunct Kalungwishi State Ranch (2hrs drive from town) once made a fantastic, little-known stop, but the land was up for sale at the time of research, so enquire locally for the latest news.

Where to eat and drink Though far from a culinary capital, you won't go hungry in Kasama. There are lots of small cafés serving traditional Zambian fare on the streets around Golf and Independence roads.

If you are driving towards Mbala, there's a collection of **roadside stalls** near Senga Hill (⊕ SENGA 09°21.968'S, 31°14.496'E), around 107km north of Kasama. These sell all manner of fast food, including chicken and chips, fritters, and delicious potato samosas that almost justify a stop in their own right.

Other practicalities For supplies, Shoprite on Mbala Road is a well-stocked supermarket. There are also several **banks** and **fuel stops**, a **general hospital** and **pharmacy** in town. Should you need information on the national parks, there's a ZAWA office on Lusaka Road, just south of the golf club.

Excursions around Kasama

Mwela rock paintings (Entry US$15/7 adult/child; vehicle US$5/day; camping US$15 pp, inc entry) There are over 700 cave paintings outside Kasama, most of them to the east of the town, making this one of the richest areas for rock art anywhere in Africa. While a few of the images are representational, the tradition here is of enigmatic, geometric designs that defy easy interpretation. The art is generally considered to be the work of the Twa people, around 2,000 years old, but has variously been dated to late Stone-Age peoples. The paintings are spread over a wide area across six recognised sites: Sumina, Mulundu and Changa are to the south of the road; Mwela and Muankole to the north; while Luimbo lies in the opposite direction, just beyond the airport. To reach the main sites, take the road towards Isoka for about 6km until you see a sign indicating the national monument. Sign in at the kiosk with the caretaker, and he will lead you around the paintings (and would appreciate a tip at the end).

While it's possible to spend hours here, for most casual visitors just a few paintings will suffice to give an idea of the style and scale of the work. Highlights include the *Lion at Sumina*, and a series of three paintings on the Mwela site (⊕ MWELA 10°12.250'S, 31°13.958'E). An excellent book on the paintings, *Zambia's Ancient Rock Art: The Paintings of Kasama*, is available at the National Museum in Lusaka.

Chishimba Falls (Entry US$15/7 adult/child; vehicle US$5/day; camping US$15 pp inc falls visit) The Luombe River at Chishimba is partially harnessed to run a small, unobtrusive hydro-electric station, but the water that is left makes for a super series of waterfalls: one artificial and the other two natural. The uppermost 'main' waterfall, Mutumuna, has a drop of about 20m where it descends onto a rocky riverbed, and it's probably the prettiest of the three. In the centre, protected by a weir, is Kaela, more of a series of rapids than falls, with a large pool created by the weir. The third, Chishimba itself, is a short walk downstream. Here, water spouts over steep cliffs into a deep, rocky canyon that is, according to legend, inhabited by spirits. If you walk right down to the bottom you can stand behind the curtain of water with the rock face at your back and the water in front of you.

Close to the central weir, there's a shady picnic area and a waterside campsite with flush toilets, barbecue facilities and a visitor information centre. Walkways have been constructed between the falls, with thatched viewing shelters at strategic points, but note that at Chishimba Falls in particular there is a sheer drop that is not fenced, so it is important to take extra care. The helpful caretaker is usually happy to act as a guide.

To get to Chishimba (⊕ CHISHI 10°06.465'S, 30°55.100'E), head west out of Kasama on the tarred Luwingu Road towards the airport. Continue for 25km before turning right on to the wide gravel road to Mporokoso. After 11km, there's a clear signpost to the falls (⊕ TOCHIS 10°06.176'S, 30°55.694'E), and a parking area after 700m.

Chilambwe Falls (Entry US$5/3 adult/child; vehicle US$5/day; camping US$10 pp) About 72km from Kasama on the Mporokoso road, these lesser-known but nonetheless attractive falls are worth a stop. Tumbling 60m through moss-covered boulders and surrounded by indigenous trees, visitors can hike to the top of the falls, cool off in the spray or follow the river through open fields. Camping is permitted but there are no designated facilities.

Chambeshi Monument (Entry US$10/5 adult/child; vehicle US$5/day; camping US$15 pp, inc entry) At the north end of the bridge over the Chambeshi River, about 85km south of Kasama, this roadside monument (⊕ CHAMON 10°54.634'S, 31°05.344'E) marks the place where General von Lettow-Vorbeck, Commander of the German forces in East Africa during World War I, surrendered to Hector Croad, the British District Commissioner, on 14 November 1918.

Von Lettow-Vorbeck and his forces had marched south from German East Africa (now Tanzania). They didn't realise that the war in Europe had been over for three days until told by Croad. Upon hearing the news from the British, the Germans agreed to march back to Abercorn (now called Mbala) and there hand over their prisoners to the British. It seems as if it was all very civilised.

Part of the monument is a breech-loading field gun, made in 1890, which was the type that the German forces used during World War I.

Tiger fishing on the Chambeshi River One of Zambia's more remote fishing rivers, the Chambeshi offers tiger fishing in almost guaranteed isolation. With notice, mobile camping trips of two nights or longer can be organised between September and April by Thorn Tree Safaris in Livingstone (page 212).

MBALA The most northerly large town in Zambia, Mbala lies just off the Great North Road from Kasama, 25km from Lake Tanganyika and the Tanzanian border. Sitting on the edge of the plateau, 900m above lake level, the town enjoys relative cool before the merciless heat that accompanies the scenic descent into the rift valley and the end-of-the-road fishing port of Mpulungu.

Known as Abercorn when the country was under British rule, Mbala was a key strategic outpost for colonial administrators thanks to its location and pleasant climate. Today, it is a quiet backwater attracting few visitors thanks largely to its poor road connections and unrest in nearby DRC. It is however notable for the **Moto Moto Museum**, which is one of the country's best museums, and as the access point to Kalambo Falls (see opposite).

Mbala has a couple of **fuel stations**, **two banks**, a **post office** and even a small prison (the old prison building is now a historic monument). You can buy most things in the **shops**, including a decent selection of fresh fruit and vegetables.

Getting there and away Regular long-distance buses ply the route between Lusaka and Mpulungu, stopping at the bus station on Mbala's main street. Typically, southbound buses leave Mbala in the early hours of each morning. The one-way fare to Lusaka is around K300. There are also buses to Kitwe on most days.

Where to stay *Map, opposite*

Lake Chila Lodge (20 chalets, camping) m 0977 795241; e lakechilalodge@yahoo.com; ⊕ 08°50.389'S, 31°23.085'E. Just 1km northeast of town & right on the perennial Lake Chila, this lodge is set in pleasant gardens. En-suite chalets are spacious, & cheaper chalets & camping pitches are also available. There's a bar & restaurant – whose menu ranges from nshima to pasta & other Western-style dishes – & a vehicle & boat for excursions on the lake & in the surrounding area. In 2021, they opened a new property: Great Kalambo Falls Lodge (page 385) – not to be confused with Kalambo Falls Lodge on the lake – & can arrange transport between the two. **$$**

New Grasshopper Inn (22 rooms) Makanta Rd; 0214 450585. Within walking distance of the centre, this is a reasonably secure place with pretty basic rooms & a simple, local restaurant. **$** *exc b/fast.*

What to see and do

Moto Moto Museum (⊕ MOTOMO 08°49.265'S, 31°21.416'E; e motomoto.museum@yahoo.com; ⏲ 09.00–16.45 daily exc Christmas & New Year; entry US$5/3 adult/child) Opened in 1974, Moto Moto is an ethnographic museum and perhaps the best place in the country to see Bemba history and artefacts. At its heart is an extensive and well-presented collection of tools, craft instruments and exhibits connected to traditional ceremonies and witchcraft, originally assembled by Father Jean-Jaques Corbeil, a French Canadian missionary stationed at the nearby Kayambi Mission. The museum takes its name, though, from Bishop Joseph Dupont, nicknamed Bwana Moto as he smoked a pipe and was renowned for calling for *moto* (KiSwahili for 'fire'). A large-scale reconstruction of a local village serves to

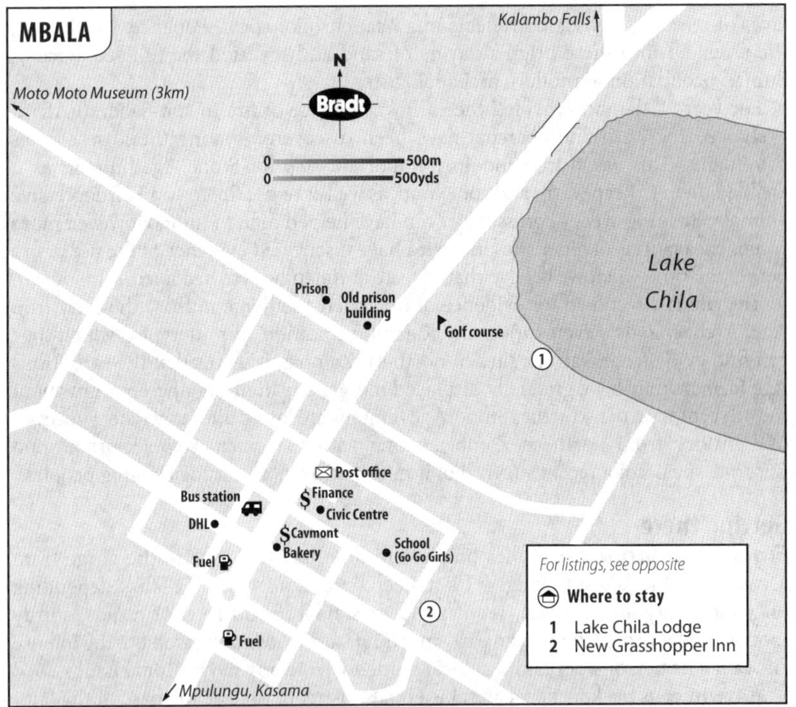

put the various artefacts into context, while explanations of the traditional roles of a husband and wife, for example, add fascinating depth. There is also a library popular with academic researchers and a reading shelter to encourage local youth literacy.

KALAMBO FALLS (⊕ KALAMB 08°35.831'S, 31°14.397'E; ⏱ 06.00–18.00 daily; entry US$15/7 adult/child, vehicle US$5/day, camping US$15 pp inc entry) For a short distance the Kalambo River marks the boundary between Zambia and Tanzania. At the Kalambo Falls, it plunges dramatically over the side of the Great Rift Valley in one, narrow vertical drop of about 221m. This is the second-highest waterfall in Africa (after South Africa's Tugela Falls), about double the height of the Victoria Falls, and about the 12th-highest in the world.

The falls certainly have the impressive statistics, but the real appeal lies in the drama of the setting. On either side of the falls, sheer rock walls frame the river valley far below: Zambia to the south, Tanzania to the north. A large colony of marabou storks breeds in the cliffs during the dry season. The falls themselves are at their most spectacular towards the end of the wet season, in February or March, though are worth visiting at any time.

Archaeology Though few visitors realise it, the Kalambo Falls are also one of the most important archaeological sites in southern Africa. Just above the falls, by the side of the river, is a site that appears to have been occupied throughout much of the Stone Age and early Iron Age. The earliest tools and other remains discovered there may be over 300,000 years old, including evidence for the use of fire.

It seems that the earlier sites of occupation were regularly flooded by the river. Each time this occurred, a fine layer of sand was deposited, thus preserving each layer of remains, tools and artefacts in a neat chronological sequence. Much later, the river cut into these original layers of sand and revealed the full sequence of human occupation to modern archaeologists.

For years Kalambo provided the earliest evidence of fire in sub-Saharan Africa – charred logs, ash and charcoal have been discovered among the lowest levels of remains. This was a tremendously important step for Stone-Age humans as it enabled them to keep warm and cook food, as well as to use fire to scare off aggressive animals. Burning areas of grass may even have helped man to hunt. However, more recent excavations of older sites in Africa have discovered evidence of the use of fire before the time when we believe that the site at Kalambo was occupied.

The site is also noted for evidence of much later settlement, from the early Iron Age. Archaeologists even speak of a 'Kalambo tradition' of pottery, for which they can find evidence in various sites in northern Zambia. It seems that the early Iron-Age farmers may have gradually displaced indigenous hunter-gatherers from about the 4th century AD: no further Stone-Age remains are found after that date. However, oral history from northern Zambia, along with the extensive rock art around Kasama, speaks of a recent survival of hunter-gatherers alongside farming peoples.

Getting there

From Lake Tanganyika It's possible to do a day-trip hike to the gorge from a couple of the lakeside lodges. It's a steep, strenuous climb (2–4hrs depending on your agility and energy), requiring a reasonably good level of fitness, sturdy footwear, plenty of water and an early morning start to avoid the worst of the intense rift valley heat. Consider taking a local guide to avoid any navigational issues.

Adventurous backpackers can take a boat upstream to near the base of the falls, hike up and stay overnight, either camping at the falls or staying at the relatively new Great Kalambo Falls Lodge, returning the following day. You will need to bring all your own food and equipment if you plan on camping.

There's a regular boat-taxi service between Chipwa and Mpulungu (page 388), three times a week, taking 2 hours in each direction. Boats leave the village of Chipwa very early in the morning, returning from Mpulungu the same day at around midday; as a *mzungu* (white person), you can expect to pay around K25. Since the times are very approximate, and you don't want to end up walking into the falls after dark, it may be better to negotiate a private trip with one of the fishermen at Mpulungu harbour.

A better option by far is to stay at one of the lodges nearer the falls – Mishembe Bay, Kalambo Falls Lodge or Isanga Bay. Then you can make a day hike to the falls.

From Mbala The falls are about 38km from Mbala, along a largely graded track. In the dry season it should be possible to get to within 1.5km in a 2WD vehicle, but certainly no further, and certainly not in the rains, but we would recommend a high clearance 4x4. The last stretch of road is an extremely steep and rocky descent, so you may prefer to park at Great Kalambo Falls Lodge (see opposite) and walk this last section.

Because of Kalambo's border position, policing it has been difficult in the past, and vehicles left unattended have been easy targets for theft. While this is still a potential hazard, there is a caretaker on site at the falls during the day and the arrival of the lodge has considerably reduced the risk.

Where to stay It's possible to **camp** at the falls themselves, with stunning views to the west across the rift valley. There's a caretaker on site all day, a shelter and some run-down ablution facilities. You will need to take all your provisions if you stay here, including water, as the pump is regularly out of order.

Great Kalambo Falls Lodge [map, page 386] (8 chalets, camping) m 0977 795241; e lakechilalodge@yahoo.com. Opened in late 2021 by the team from Lake Chila Lodge (page 382), this is the closest accommodation to the falls. (Do not confuse this lodge with the similarly named Kalambo Falls Lodge on the lakeshore.) Situated towards the end of the gravel road from Mbala, just before it becomes precipitous, it's a good option if you want to avoid the climb up from the lakeshore. About 1.5km from the waterfall itself, this low-key lodge has simple, red brick cottages, stone walkways, a basic restaurant & picnic tables dotted around the forest shade. It is also possible to camp here. **$** *exc b/fast*.

LAKE TANGANYIKA AND ENVIRONS

LAKE TANGANYIKA Lake Tanganyika is one of a series of geologically old lakes that have filled areas of the main East African Rift Valley. Look at a map of Africa and you will see many of these in a 'string' down the continent: lakes Malawi, Tanganyika, Kivu, Edward and Albert are some of the larger ones. Zambia just has a small tip of Tanganyika within its borders, but it is of importance to the country. Access to Lake Tanganyika grants Zambia a real port with transport links to a whole side of Tanzania and (during peaceable times) direct access to Burundi. It also makes this one corner of Zambia totally different from the rest of the country, with a mix of peoples and a 'tropical central Africa' feel.

There are some well-established lakeside lodges, those to the east within striking distance of Kalambo Falls, and two in the vicinity of the little-known Nsumbu National Park.

Geography Lake Tanganyika is the deepest of the Rift Valley lakes of central/east Africa, with a maximum depth of about 1,470m, and is the second-deepest lake in the world. It has an area of around 34,000km^2 and is estimated to be about 10–15 million years old. The surface layers of water are a tropical 24–28°C and support virtually all of the known life in the lake.

Well below these, where it is too deep for the sun's light to reach, are separate, colder waters. Below about 200m, these are deprived of oxygen and hardly mix with the upper layers. They are currently the subject of much scientific study.

The lake has a variety of habitats around its 3,000km or so of shoreline, ranging from flat sands to marshy areas and boulder-strewn shores.

Flora and fauna

Flora The geology of the rocks around the lake has led to the water being unusually hard (between 7° and 11° dH), alkaline (average 8.4 pH) and rich in minerals for a freshwater lake. It is not an ideal environment for normal aquatic plants, so these are generally found near the entry of rivers into the lake but not elsewhere. Various species of algae have adapted to fill this ecological niche, and extensive 'lawns' of grass-like algae cover many of the lake's submerged rocks.

Animals The water's excellent clarity, the lack of cover and the rocky shores do not encourage either hippo or crocodiles, though both are more common around the relatively undisturbed shores of Nsumbu National Park. They are also seen regularly near the mouths of rivers, and their presence must always be considered before you swim. The lake is a reliable source of water for game, which often comes

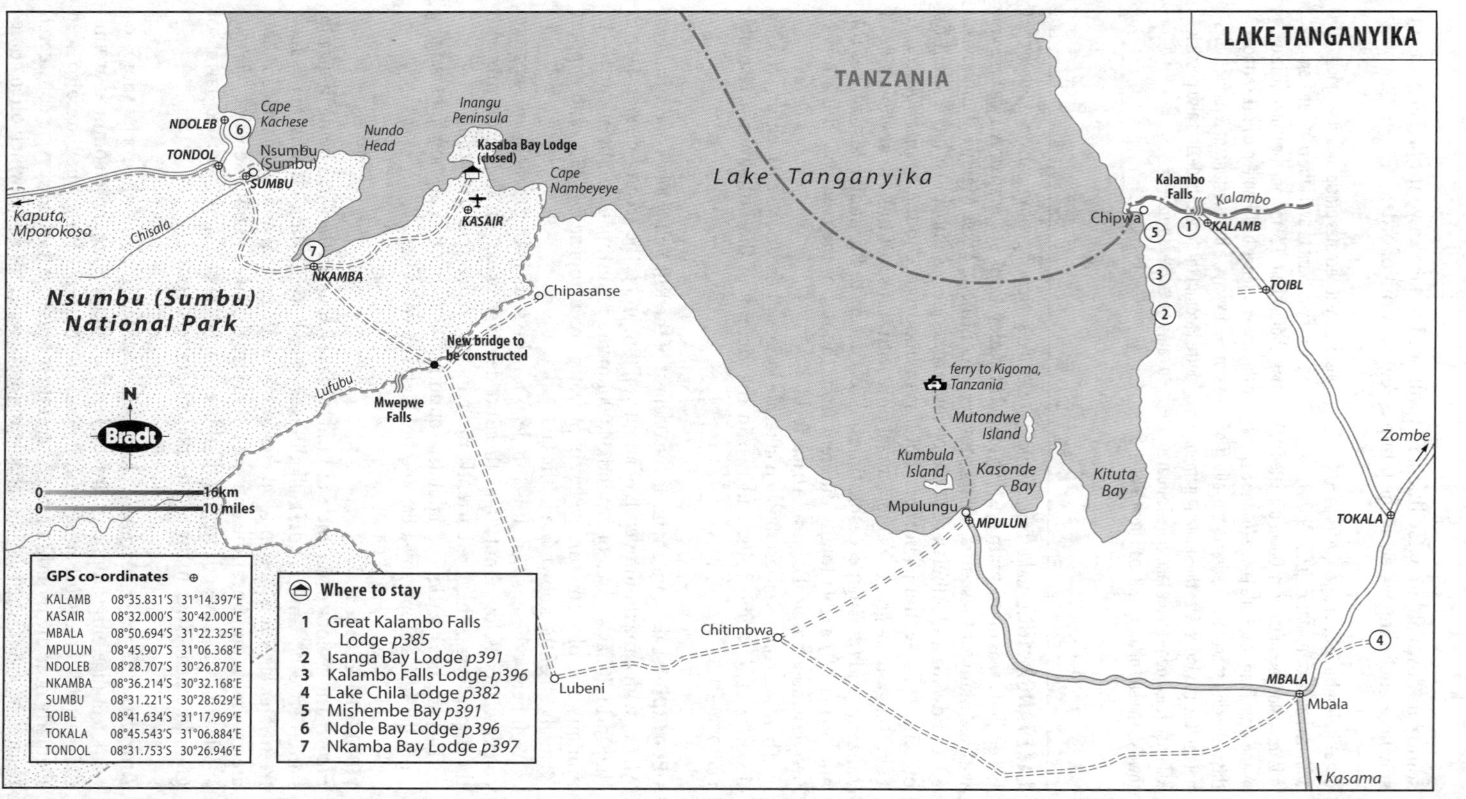
LAKE TANGANYIKA
TANZANIA
Lake Tanganyika
Cape Kachese
NDOLEB
TONDOL
Nsumbu (Sumbu)
SUMBU
Nundo Head
Inangu Peninsula
Kasaba Bay Lodge (closed)
KASAIR
Cape Nambeyeye
Kaputa, Mporokoso
Chisala
NKAMBA
Nsumbu (Sumbu) National Park
Chipasanse
New bridge to be constructed
Lufubu
Mwepwe Falls
Bradt
0 16km
0 10 miles
Kalambo Falls
Kalambo
Chipwa
KALAMB
TOIBL
ferry to Kigoma, Tanzania
Mutondwe Island
Kumbula Island
Kasonde Bay
Kituta Bay
Mpulungu
MPULUN
Zombe
TOKALA
Chitimbwa
Lubeni
MBALA
Mbala
Kasama
GPS co-ordinates
KALAMB 08°35.831'S 31°14.397'E
KASAIR 08°32.000'S 30°42.000'E
MBALA 08°50.694'S 31°22.325'E
MPULUN 08°45.907'S 31°06.368'E
NDOLEB 08°28.707'S 30°26.870'E
NKAMBA 08°36.214'S 30°32.168'E
SUMBU 08°31.221'S 30°28.629'E
TOIBL 08°41.634'S 31°17.969'E
TOKALA 08°45.543'S 31°06.884'E
TONDOL 08°31.753'S 30°26.946'E
Where to stay
1 Great Kalambo Falls Lodge p385
2 Isanga Bay Lodge p391
3 Kalambo Falls Lodge p396
4 Lake Chila Lodge p382
5 Mishembe Bay p391
6 Ndole Bay Lodge p396
7 Nkamba Bay Lodge p397

CICHLIDS

Cichlids are generally easy to keep in home aquaria, being small, colourful, and fairly undemanding. Several operations have sprung up around the lake in recent years to catch specimens for the pet trade, and fly them out to Europe and America. Indeed, one of the lake's lodges used to make most of its living from this, with tourism really just a sideline.

One of the characteristics of cichlids is the ability of individual species to adapt their colour at a very local level. Thus, one of the most popular cichlids for aquaria are the *Trophus sp*, which can be found in over 30 different colour morphs in different areas of the lake.

The largest of the cichlids found in Lake Tanganyika, indeed the largest in the world, is the nkupi (or emperor cichlid, to avoid confusion with the very different Zambezi fish, nkupi), *Boulengerochromis microlepis*, which grows up to 4kg in weight – in marked contrast to the tiny *Lamprologus multifaciatus*, which reaches a maximum length of just 1cm.

For a fascinating insight into the cichlids to be found in the lake, get hold of a copy of *Tanganyika Cichlids in their Natural Habitat* (page 512).

to drink during the dry season. Two reptiles are endemic to the lake: the fish-eating Tanganyika water-snake, *Lycodonomorphus bicolor*, and the venomous Tanganyika water cobra, *Boulengerina annulata*.

Birds The birdlife on the shoreline is generally good, and the species found here also tend to represent many more of the typical East African birds than can be found elsewhere in Zambia. The area's more unusual residents include purple-throated cuckoo-shrikes, white-headed saw-wings, stout cisticolas, and Oustalet's white-bellied sunbird.

Fish Lake Tanganyika and the other lakes in the rift valley continue to fascinate both zoologists and aquarists as they have evolved their own endemic species of fish. So far, well over 450 have been identified in Tanganyika, of which over 252 species are in the Zambian part of the lake (and of those, 82 have been identified as endemic in a report by the Ramsar Convention, under which much of Lake Tanganyika and the surrounding area is protected). Most of the lake's fish species are from the *Cichlidae* family – or cichlids (pronounced sick-lids; see above), as they are known. Many of these are small, colourful fish that live close to the surface and the shoreline. Here they inhabit crevices in the rocks and other natural cavities, avoiding the attention of larger, predatory fish that patrol the deeper, more open, waters.

The lake is the most southerly home of both the goliath tiger fish and an endemic species of perch from the *Lates* family, the silver or Tanganyika perch, *Lates angustifrons*. Three smaller species of perch are to be found in these waters, too, including the smallest, the buka, which along with kapenta is the target of commercial fishermen. There are also freshwater jellyfish which, interestingly, don't sting, and – very occasionally – a freshwater coelacanth is sighted.

What to see and do in and around the lake Most of the lodges around the lake can organise a range of watersports and fishing, though it's as well to be aware that if these involve a boat trip, costs will reflect the high cost of fuel. For additional activities around Nsumbu, see page 397.

Swimming, snorkelling and diving Tanganyika is a marvellous lake in which to go snorkelling, or even scuba-diving, as the numerous fish are beautifully coloured and there is seldom any need to dive deeply. Visibility depends on the state of the water, but can be as high as 10–20m in places. Halfway between Nsumbu and Mpulungu is a series of cliffs and drop-offs that are of particular interest to divers, while other popular diving spots include the area around Katete.

If you plan on any watersports, you must consider the safety issues. Both crocodiles and hippos are common in parts of the lake, though can be very localised. There is also the venomous if non-aggressive Tanganyika water cobra, which grows up to 2m. While it usually avoids swimmers, as terrestrial snakes avoid walkers, you should still watch out for it. There is some doubt about the existence of bilharzia in the lake but you should be aware of the possibility (and see page 129 for general guidelines). If you are considering taking a swim, ask advice from the locals about the precise place that you have in mind. They may not be infallible, but will give you a good idea of where is likely to be safe, and where is not.

Fishing Lake Tanganyika (and especially the Nsumbu area) has a first-class reputation in freshwater angling circles, because of the variety of fish that can be caught on rod and line. It is not unusual for visitors to catch a dozen different species in a single visit. The greatest appeal comes from the *nkupi*, the goliath tiger fish and the Nile perch, the last of which can reach an impressive 80kg in weight.

The best time for fishing is between November and March. Each February/March the annual six-day Tanganyika Angling Challenge (catch and release) takes place at Nsumbu, off the point near Nkamba Bay Lodge (page 397). A long-standing competition, increasingly focused on sustainability initiatives and donating funds to local conservation efforts of Frankfurt Zoological Society, it's a serious event that was once known as The Zambian National Fishing Competition. Fly-fishing is becoming increasingly popular, particularly for nkupi and the perch species. Some of the tropical cichlids will also rise to a smaller fly.

Commercial fishing is of significant importance, primarily for two species: the buka and the much smaller kapenta. There is considerable concern about the sustainability of commercial fishing on the lake, with the spotlight falling on both over-fishing, poor fishing methods and the impact of global warming on the breeding habits of the fish. Although fishing with nets is illegal within national park waters, the ban has traditionally been flouted. Law enforcement efforts and the creation of community-led fishery management areas have gone some way to reducing pressure in the park's waters in recent years.

MPULUNGU Sitting in the heat of the rift valley, about 38km from Mbala, Mpulungu is Zambia's largest port. It's a busy place and visited by many travellers, most of whom are Africans but with the odd backpacker and scientific researcher thrown in too. The atmosphere is very international, a mix of various southern, central and east African influences all stirred together by the ferries which circle the lake from port to port.

There is a strong local fishing community and a small but thriving business community, complete with a small contingent of expats and aid workers. So though Mpulungu might seem like the end of the earth when you get off a bus in the pitch-black evening, it isn't.

Getting there and away

By bus Mpulungu is at the most northerly end of the main bus route from Lusaka, via Kabwe, Kasama and every town in between. Buses from Mbala tend to arrive around 07.00, and return south in the small hours. There are several operators on the route, with Juldan Motors being well regarded. The 'terminus' is on the main road, beside the market – you cannot fail to go through it. There are also buses to Ndola every day, departing around midnight.

Driving Mpulungu is the final town on the Great North Road out of Lusaka. Long pitted with huge pot-holes, the descent from Mbala is now smooth tar and affords some great views of the lake. If you're transferring to one of the Nsumbu lodges, a taxi from Kasama airport to Mpulungu can be arranged for up to ten passengers, albeit at a hefty US$500 for the return trip.

By ferry Only one of the large international Tanganyika passenger ferries on Lake Tanganyika, the MV *Liemba*, remains operational – albeit in March 2023, it began

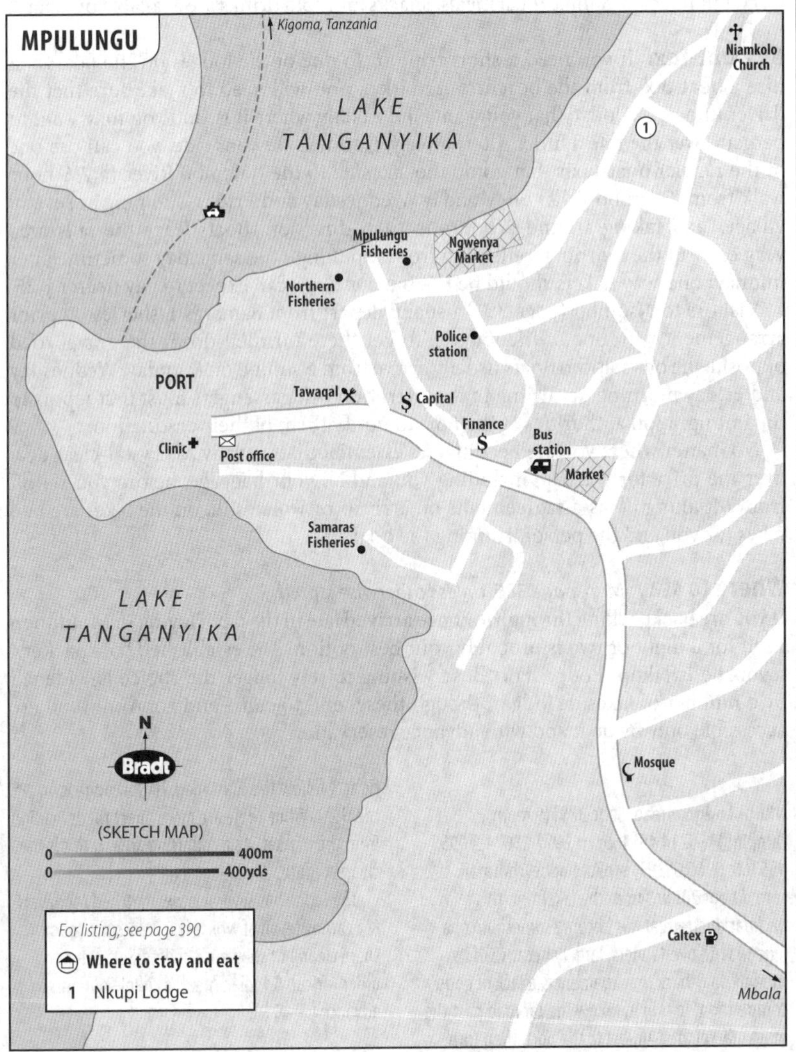

a temporary suspension of services for a full renovation as part of the Tanzanian government's commitment to improving marine transportation. It should resume service by 2024.

Once a World War I German warship and now the world's oldest passenger ferry, it plies the eastern side of Tanganyika between Kigoma in Tanzania and Mpulungu once a fortnight. Stopping at numerous villages en route, the journey to Kigoma takes around two and a half days, departing Mpulungu every other Friday morning – though actual times very much depend on the cargo. For precise dates, bookings and general information, contact: e info@mscl.go.tz.

Ferry tickets fall into three classes. There are ten en-suite, first-class cabins for two; at US$40 pp, they are well worth paying the extra for. The first-class cabins have a double bunk, while second-class cabins sleep four (US$35) and third-class passengers (US$30) take pot-luck seating around the ship. Bikes may be taken on the ferry, but not cars. Simple local meals, snacks and cold drinks are available on board.

By boat-taxi If you need a short trip out to one of the lodges on the lake then hire a boat-taxi from the beachfront market. You will need to make sure that the driver knows the lodge that you want, and exactly where it is, and you may want to bargain over the rate a little. Alternatively, if time is on your side, you can use one of the regular boat-taxis that go up the lakeside to the Kalambo River (a 2½-hour walk from Kalambo Falls) on Monday, Wednesday and Friday, stopping at several villages and taking around 2 hours in each direction. Boats leave the falls area very early in the morning, returning from Mpulungu the same day sometime after midday; one-way tickets should be K5, but a *mzungu* can expect to pay nearer K25.

Visitors to Nsumbu (page 391) usually depart from Samaras Fisheries by prior arrangement with one of the lodges. To get there turn left down the gravel road opposite the bus station. Boats usually arrive from Nsumbu on Monday, Wednesday and Friday morning, returning in the afternoon. All passengers must first report to the immigration authorities at the port to notify them of their destination.

No matter where you are heading, it's essential that you have a crystal-clear deal over the price for the trip, including you and all your baggage, before you set off from Mpulungu – as disagreements on arrival (or worse still, on the lake) are bad news for you and the person running the boat.

Where to stay *Map, page 386, unless otherwise stated*

If you are backpacking through, or have arrived late in the day, staying in Mpulungu itself for a night or two is probably your best option. The established backpackers' favourite is Nkupi Lodge. For those wishing to stay longer the choice is widened by a number of lakeside lodges, though these tend to come and go. Almost all are accessible only by boat and with advance reservation.

In town

Nkupi Lodge [map, page 389] (9 rooms, camping) 0214 455166; m 0977 456742, 0955 455166, 0966 69397; e nkupilodge@hotmail.com. About 20mins from the lakefront, this relaxed backpackers' retreat has become something of a legend with overlanders, largely because of its friendly, laid-back management & a lack of good competition. To find it, follow the tar road past the main market area almost to the port, then turn right & follow the coast road; Nkupi Lodge is on the right. While there are more direct roads leading from the market, it's a confusing area, & this is the clearest route.

The lodge has several large, thatched rondavels & a campsite, all of which (exc 1 en-suite room) share clean hot showers & toilets. Self-cater or order African & Indian meals a couple of hours in advance (**$–$$**).

Long-standing manager Charity & her son, Marino, are excellent & can arrange visits to Kalambo Falls, picnics, boat trips to the islands & swimming trips. *Camping K100 pp (own tent); K200–300pp chalet.* **$**

Lakeside lodges

Isanga Bay Lodge (6 chalets, camping) **m** 0973 472317; **e** bookings@isangabay.com; **w** isangabay.com. North of Mpulungu, about halfway to the Tanzanian border & within hiking distance of Kalambo Falls, Isanga Bay Lodge is reached by boat transfer from Mpulungu (US$150 return 6 people); there is safe parking in the town at Samaras Fisheries. Driving the poor 26km track from Mbala is not recommended, even in a 4x4.

3 thatched wooden chalets stand on stilts on 100m of beautiful white sandy beach, surrounded by coconut palms & indigenous vegetation. Overlooking the rocks are a further 3 stone chalets & a campsite with hot showers, braai stands, firewood & access to good meals & cold drinks in the central thatched *insaka*. Day visitors (US$6; 08.00–17.00) are welcome by appointment, with activities that include good snorkelling (US$35 pp) among the rocks, guided hikes to Kalambo Falls (US$40 pp), kayaking (US$5 pp) & even waterskiing. *Chalet US$65/105 dbl/family; camping US$15 pp.* **$$$–$$$$**

Mishembe Bay (Luke's Beach) (3 chalets, camping) **m** 0976 664999; **e** mishembebay@gmail.com; **f** mishembebayzambia. Also known as Luke's Beach, Mishembe is real Robinson Crusoe stuff – just a pure white sandy beach sheltered in its own bay – the last on the Zambian side of the shore. It is accessed in 30mins by private boat (US$150 return, up to 8 people) or by water-taxi from Mpulungu taking 1–3hrs (Mon, Wed & Fri). A self-catering hideaway hidden among the trees on wooden platforms overlooking the lake. There are 3 simple, open-sided en-suite chalets under thatch, space for camping, a well kitted-out kitchen & super snorkelling in the bay. It's a magical place, totally isolated, with great community links & very good value. *Chalets US$50 s/c; camping US$10 pp; exclusivity (whole bay) US$250/day.* ⌚ *All year.*

What to see Just a few kilometres east of Mpulungu, beside the lake, you may see a tall, rectangular turret rising above the shoreline as you head to Kalambo Falls or one of the lodges in a water-taxi. This isn't a fort, but the remains of one of Zambia's oldest churches, Niamkolo Church. It was originally built by the London Missionary Society around 1893–96, but abandoned in 1902 because of health problems suffered by the missionaries. The original buildings were burned, but in 1962 the walls were restored to their former height and cemented into place. Now they're all there is to see. At 80cm thick in places, they may last for another century yet.

NSUMBU (SUMBU) NATIONAL PARK

(Park fees US$10 pp/day; vehicle US$15/day; fishing US$30 pp/day) Nsumbu (also referred to as Sumbu) National Park covers about 2,020km^2, and borders on Lake Tanganyika. It also covers a small part of the lake, which means that those boating in these waters are subject to park entry fees, as well as those on land. To the north- and southwest, the park is adjoined by the 360,000ha Kaputa GMA, while between this and the park to the west is the smaller Tondwa GMA, which is leased out to a small professional hunting operator. These two act as a very effective buffer for the park, keeping the local subsistence hunters/poachers out and giving the game numbers a chance to increase. Combined with the presence of two (and potentially three) lodges in this area, this has made Nsumbu's future look very promising indeed.

On another promising note, Nsumbu is one of several parks in Zambia that have been designated as being 'viable game parks' under a study funded by the EU. In 2012, several prominent conservationists, led by Craig Zytkow from Ndole Bay, set up a non-profit organisation, Conservation Lake Tanganyika, to preserve and rejuvenate Nsumbu National Park and Lake Tanganyika. Now run as a partnership between Frankfurt Zoological Society and DNPW as the **Nsumbu Tanganyika Conservation Project (NTCP)**, it works to promote and protect the biodiversity in Nsumbu National Park and the surrounding area, conserving the elephant population, engaging the community in conservation, and supporting anti-poaching and infrastructure initiatives. It has great hopes for Nsumbu to return to its former glory as a haven for wildlife through its support for wildlife protection and management. It has created critical infrastructure for scout housing, provided an operations control centre and field equipment for patrols – on land and water – as well as critical scout training and recruitment. Combatting poaching on land is already quite a challenge but nothing like as difficult as trying to clamp down on illegal fishing in an area where virtually everyone depends on fishing for their livelihood and many regard it as a divine right. Altering that perception is not an easy task but the team is working with the local Community Resource Boards to ensure that the local community is part of the solution going forward, that local residents are involved and participate in the management of the park and GMA, are educated about conservation and, most importantly, can reap the benefits.

FLORA AND FAUNA Nsumbu protects populations of elephant, and a range of antelope including blue and yellow-backed duiker, roan, sable, bushbuck, waterbuck, sitatunga, the occasional zebra and a large number of puku; there are also reports of eland in the hills. Buffalo herds range up to about 400 individuals, and move around between Nsumbu and the neighbouring GMA. The park's main

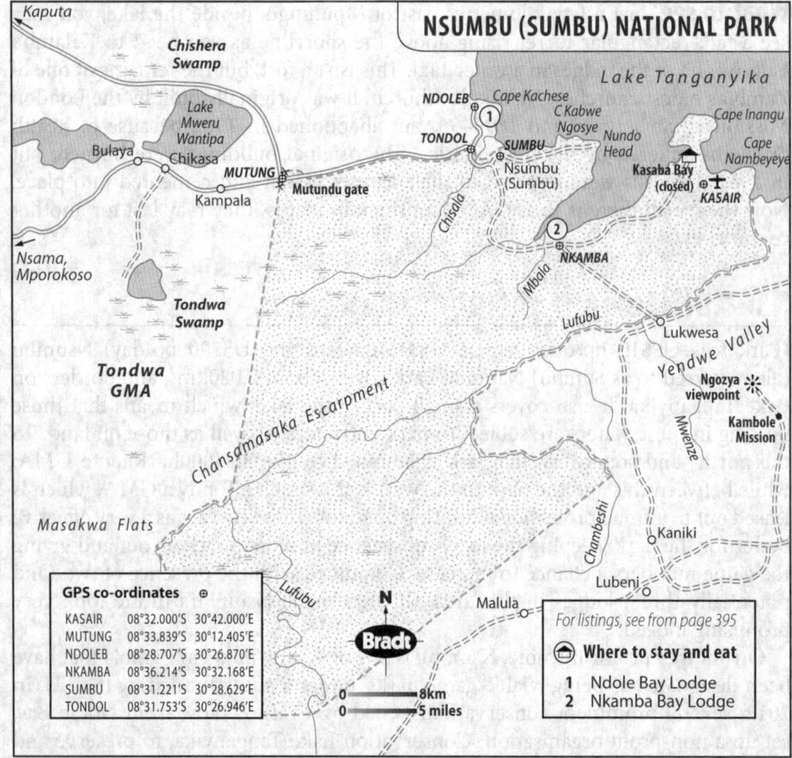

natural predators are lion and leopard, though numbers are uncertain. Although poachers continue to kill occasionally, the animal populations are increasing.

A study in the 1990s concluded that there were still wild dogs in the park and its surrounding GMAs, though their continued long-term survival was in doubt and we don't know of reports of wild dog since then.

Although Nsumbu cannot yet boast huge herds of the larger antelope, elephant or buffalo, there is sufficient game to make a trip to the park worthwhile and the first major translocation of animals – 200 buffaloes and 48 zebras – to the park in 2021 is only improving the situation. Its vegetation and environment are, on the whole, in pristine condition and offer a real Zambian wilderness experience. The NTCP has concentrated significant efforts on protecting the remaining elephants in Nsumbu, with no poaching detected since 2018. Elephants now appear to be less stressed and are a much more common sight than in previous years – a measure of the success of the work being done and an indication of the resilience of these amazing animals. Breeding herds of up to 40 elephants are not uncommon now and Nsumbu remains the only place along Lake Tanganyika where elephants survive. In time, the team hope to reintroduce black rhino and lion to the park.

The birding is good, with 295 species recorded in the park and the adjacent Tondwa GMA. A number of East African species occur here that you won't find in the rest of southern Africa. Look out especially for the bare-faced go-away bird, common on the open floodplain areas; also a waxbill known as the red-cheeked cordon bleu, occasional ospreys, palmnut vultures and red-faced crombecs. Pel's fishing owl and bat hawks also occur, though not more commonly than elsewhere.

In the lake itself, there are plenty of hippos and a very healthy population of crocodile – including both Nile crocodile (*Crocodylus niloticus*) and its smaller, endangered cousin, the slender-snouted crocodile (*Crocodylus cataphractus* or *Mecistops cataphractus*). Some are sufficiently large to dissuade you from even thinking of dipping your toe in the water. For details of fish and other reptiles in the lake, see page 385.

GETTING THERE Access has long been the main problem for visitors to the Lake Tanganyika area, and getting to Nsumbu is an added challenge. It's difficult and time-consuming or very expensive.

By air There are no scheduled flights to Nsumbu but private charters from Ndola and Lusaka can be arranged. Charter costs vary greatly based on the size of plane and duration of the trip, but as a rough guide a small plane would cost US$4,000 from Ndola and US$6,000 from Lusaka.

There is a tar airstrip at Mbala, from which lodges can organise transfers to Mpulungu and onward boat trips to Nsumba, or you can fly into the park itself. There is a new airstrip, Chisala, which opened in 2022 and cuts transfer time to Ndole Bay. The 1,500m airstrip on an isthmus at Kasaba Bay (⊕ KASAIR 08°32.00'S, 30°42.00'E) remains closed at the time of going to press. Limited amounts of AV-Gas are sometimes available from the lodges, by prior arrangement.

Both Ndole Bay and Nkamba Bay lodges will collect passengers from the airstrip by boat, taking about 30 minutes to Nkamba Bay from Kasaba, or 40 minutes to Ndole Bay. Ndole Bay charges US$150–250 per boat for return transfers from the Kasaba Bay airstrip.

By boat Though they're at least 75km across the lake, the lodges in Nsumbu most commonly arrange to transfer their guests by boat from Mpulungu, where both use the harbour facilities of Pendulum Fisheries. Each has different speeds and sizes of boat available, at different costs, but expect to pay around US$350 per boat each way. A 'banana boat' (a long, thin chug-chug motorboat with space for up to six people) will take about 4 hours to reach Nsumbu, whereas a traditional wooden dhow, although larger, can take up to 6 hours. Ndole Bay operates a range of boats, including a high-speed catamaran that covers the distance in 2 hours, taking two to ten passengers at US$750 return, with the option of snorkelling/diving (US$20 surcharge; by arrangement) en route at Cape Chaitika.

Ferry A government-operated ferry, ***Stella***, travels between Mpulungu and the township of Nsumbu (near Ndole) on most weekdays. Costing US$10 each way, and taking about 6 hours, it's a cost-effective route across the lake. Ndole Bay offers free pickups and drop-offs to the harbour in Nsumbu for guests and can arrange secure parking in Mpulungu for vehicles.

Transport boats Crowded transport boats ply up and down the lake with frequent stops, so if you don't have a transfer organised, these might be an option – though be prepared for a long wait (sometimes days). Expect to pay from about K80 for the trip, which takes between 10 and 18 hours, depending on the number of stops. Alternatively, you could negotiate to hire the whole boat for around US$150 plus about 75 litres of fuel, but make it quite clear that you wish to go direct to your destination, or you could still find yourself stopping everywhere. Either way, ask around at Ngwenya Market in Mpulungu, or by the water taxis at the main market, or – in Nsumbu town – on the beach. Remember that the lake can be rough (and thus you could get wet), you'll need to take all food and water for the journey, and do be conscious of water-safety issues if embarking on this trip in a local fishing boat.

Driving Nsumbu National Park can be approached in a 4x4 via Kaputa or Mporokoso, though neither is a fast option. There is also a 4x4 track from Mbala as far as the Lufubu River, which defines the park's eastern boundary, making it possible to ford the river in the dry season in a 4x4.

From Mporokoso For the majority of drivers, the most direct approach to the park is from Mporokoso (⊕ MPOROK 09°21.831'S, 30°07.432'E; page 407), a network of dirt roads that has been upgraded and is largely in good condition. Initially, the road heads more or less north through the village of Munyele and on towards Nsama (⊕ NSAMA 08°53.448'S, 29°56.896'E), close to the eastern shores of Lake Mweru Wantipa, where there are a few shops, a secondary school and a Catholic church. Keen birdwatchers should note that just north of Nsama there's a patch of miombo woodland where the relatively uncommon white-winged starling is easily spotted. Beyond the town, there are numerous small villages lining the road, but nowhere of note. Despite mention of Bulaya on most maps, don't expect a town here: it's nothing more than a dot on the map.

About 135km from Mporokoso, and 39km before Nsumbu, you'll reach the Mutundu gate (⊕ MUTUNG 08°33.839'S, 30°12.405'E), a game checkpoint that marks the beginning of the national park. This is also where the road from Kaputa (the area's administrative centre) joins the road from Mporokoso to Nsumbu.

From here the road runs along the northwestern edge of the park towards Nsumbu Village (page 398), with sweeping views over the bay as it descends from the plateau. Some 31km after the Mutundu gate, there's a left turn to Ndole Bay Lodge (⊕ TONDOL 08°31.753'S, 30°26.946'E). To reach the national park gate, continue along the increasingly poor main road for a further 8km or so to the turn-off to Nsumbu town. This also marks the entrance to the national park, at Nsumbu gate, and is where you'll have to pay park fees. The road then continues to Nkamba Bay Lodge and Kasaba Bay, within the national park.

From Nchelenge via Kaputa For the first stretch of this route, see page 398. Beyond Kaputa, the road widens, passing through numerous villages as it crosses the narrow strip between Lake Mweru Wantipa and the DRC border. The lake itself remains out of sight, although fishing nets laid out to dry indicate its proximity to the road. As the road descends, the land around becomes increasingly marshy, with papyrus beds and reeds, and pools dotted with purple water lilies. It's a haven for water birds, with reed cormorants, pied and malachite kingfishers, and African jacanas all easy to spot. Eventually, some 83km from Kaputa, you'll emerge onto the Mporokoso–Nsumbu road (see opposite) at the Mutundu gate (⊕ MUTUNG 08°33.839'S, 30°12.405'E), marked on some maps as Kampela, where you turn left for Nsumbu.

Note that the dirt road from Mununga to Nsama (⊕ NSAMA 08°53.448'S, 29°56.896'E) along the southern side of Lake Mweru Wantipa is very bad and becoming impassable.

Cross-country from Mbala For many years the poor track between Mbala and Nsumbu has ended abruptly at the Lufubu River, the park's southeastern boundary, with no bridge across. The road has periodically been graded and the promise that the bridge would be rebuilt over the river is a regular election promise. From the Lufubu River west to Nsumbu a gravel road covers the remaining 50km, with a particularly rough 1km climb into the park just after the river.

The reinstatement of this link between the two sides of Lake Tanganyika will offer an attractive option in the dry season for experienced drivers with a strong sense of adventure.

According to Gerard Zytkow at Ndole Bay, 'the countryside is wonderful and the drop from the escarpment into the Yendwe Valley is breathtakingly beautiful.' Follow the sign to Lunzua power station, a new hydro-electricity project about 15km outside Mpulungu on the Mbala road. Go past the hydro plant to a T-junction with the Mbala–Yendwe road.

The turn-off is just 100m or so from the Mbala T-junction on the road towards Mpulungu, with a second access road from just outside Mpulungu.

GETTING AROUND THE PARK The network of roads in the park may have been extended in the last few years but these are largely only game tracks, devised by the lodges for their own use. For practical purposes, the only passable roads in the park are between Nsumbu Town and Nkamba Bay, then on to Kasaba Bay, or east to the Lufubu River. While these are open all year, you'll still need a 4x4 at any time.

Boat trips in national-park waters can be organised through one of the lodges (see below).

WHERE TO STAY *Map, page 386*

Two lakeshore lodges, Nkamba Bay and Ndole Bay, are currently open – the first inside the national park; the second, more casual, just outside the park's northwestern boundary. A third, Kasaba Bay Lodge on the Inangu Peninsula, has been closed for several years. Historians will note that it was at the original lodge that Mozambique's president Samora Machel met regional leaders before catching his fatal flight in 1986 from the lodge's airstrip.

All three lodges have a chequered history. Originally, both those in the park were run by the government, but by the early 1990s both were in terminal decline: expensive yet poorly maintained. Eventually they were put up for tender in late 1995 and snapped up by private operators, although later fortunes have been mixed. Ndole Bay Lodge was originally privately owned, but was taken by the government in 1989, only to be closed in the early 1990s when its trade disappeared. Now it has reverted to its previous owners and is once again thriving.

Kalambo Falls Lodge (7 chalets, camping) **m** 0977 430894; **e** info@kalambolodge.com; **w** kalambolodge.com. Kalambo Falls sits just above the lakeshore, its 7 stone, thatched chalets & central area all tucked into the lush vegetation above a narrow sandy beach. The simple whitewashed interiors of the chalets are uncluttered but comfortable. Contemporary Zambian artwork & pieces of antique wooden furniture sit around a comfortable bed & each chalet has a lakeview balcony & an en-suite bathroom – there's even a claw-foot bath in the Duboisi Suite. It's a laid-back place with plenty of spots for relaxing: lie back on a converted boat sofa, grab a drink from the elevated Golden Perch bar, dip your toes in the lake from a under a palm-thatch umbrella & look forward to tasty meals from the African Women's Kitchen, where traditional Zambian cuisine using local, seasonal produce is deliciously refined. For the more active, canoeing, waterskiing and tubing are great fun, & it's possible to embark on a serious hike to the waterfall, take a boat trip to Nsumbu National Park or try your hand at fishing. Long associated with zoologists from European universities, the lodge is also a scientific research centre for the cichlids of Lake Tanganyika, & there are often researchers here exploring, recording, conserving & running breeding programmes for various fish species. The staff here will be happy to show you around the facilities.

There is also a campsite for self-drivers, including 2 simple stone chalets with bathrooms. *US$80–150 pp/dbl FB inc transfers from Mpulungu & local activities. Waterskiing & tubing US$100/hr; Kalambo Falls walk US$15 exc entrance fee.* **$$$**

Ndole Bay Lodge [also map, page 392] (11 chalets, camping) **m** 0962 036871; **e** info@ndolebaylodge.com; **w** ndolebaylodge.com. ⊕ NDOLEB 08°28.707'S, 30°26.870'E. Owned by Gerard & Barbara Zytkow, & run by their son, Craig, & his partner, Elise, Ndole Bay Lodge stands beside Lake Tanganyika in Cameron Bay, just northwest of the national park boundary, & offers the opportunity to swim, snorkel or fish from its private white-sand beach (which is considered to be perfectly safe).

Visitors usually arrive by boat, sometimes following a taxi transfer from Kasama airport. Drivers should take the well-signposted left turning as they approach Nsumbu, about 5km before the town (⊕ TONDOL 08°31.753'S, 30°26.946'E). The lodge is 7km down a partly rocky track, for which you'll need a high-clearance vehicle at all times.

It's a lovely wild spot &, despite creature comforts such as mains electricity, still feels at one with the African bush. Both the chalets & the main central building are set back from the beach, well spaced among mature gardens on a gentle slope. The main area links the dining room with the bar & a library under a grand thatched roof, all surrounded by a low stone wall. It's a practical design – cool & airy. Under a thatched shelter, hammocks swing in the breeze, just the place to relax after a dip in the small pool, while over the water is a large, shaded wooden deck with more hammocks, sunbeds & steps into the lake. On a practical note, there's a shop for essential toiletries, local crafts & fishing lures, & Wi-Fi throughout the site.

The 8 standard, en-suite chalets are built of stone with thatched roofs & are large, light & comfortable, & several have space for extra beds. 2 deluxe chalets open on to the beach from their shady veranda, while the 2-bedroom beachfront suite is perfect for families or friends travelling together, & has a great veranda shaded by sail cloth & trees. Set to one side on the beach, beneath beautiful winterthorn trees, *Faidherbia albida*, there is also a gorgeous campsite, equipped with running water, BBQ stands, & an ablution block with hot-water showers & flush toilets. Campers can book into the lodge for meals & can use its facilities, provided they do not disturb other guests, as well as purchase ice, charcoal & firewood from the bar.

There's plenty to do, but don't come expecting to be organised; this is a laid-back spot that is very much in tune with its location. You can hire various types of boat (*US$10–25/hr, or US$30–180/day plus fuel*), as well as snorkelling equipment & basic fishing tackle. There's a great house reef for snorkelling with colourful cichlids & Ndole Bay is an established PADI IRA resort – the first on the lake – offering qualified divers some excellent opportunities (all necessary equipment is available for hire) &, for groups, there's the possibility to complete PADI Discover Scuba, Open Water & Advanced Diver courses, though these must be booked in advance. If adrenalin watersports are more your thing, water-skiing, wakeboarding & tubing are all on offer too. And if you don't want to get wet at all, there are game drives, nature walks, birding trips & sunset lake cruises. Further afield, it's possible to visit some local geothermal springs, a traditional village (the lodge funds various community projects in Ndole village) & perhaps a village healer, or to organise a night trip to watch the operation of a kapenta fishing rig. A custom-built dhow, designed both for cruising & diving, allows extended trips such as a 5-night lake safari to Nsumbu NP and Kalambo Falls, or 4 nights in the park, to include the Lufubu River Valley. There's also a 1-night trip at a fly-camp near Nundo Head, including walks to the balancing boulders & Kampasa Rainforest, or the option of multi-day hikes up the Lufubu River. *Standard US$150/90 adult/child pp sharing; deluxe US$195/115 adult/child, all FB inc snorkelling, kayaking & floating sunbeds from the lodge, guided walks, village visits, sunset paddle, laundry, exc park fees. Camping US$20/12 adult/child pp.* ⌚ *All year.* ♛

Nkamba Bay Lodge [also map, page 392] (9 rooms) m 0771 054777; e info@nkambabaylodge.net; w nkambabaylodge.net; ⊕ NKAMBA 08°36.214'S, 30°32.168'E. Situated on a low, lawned rise above the water's edge, & within the national park, Nkamba Bay is one of the area's original lakefront lodges. Renovated & rejuvenated in recent years, the lodge has a strong emphasis on fishing (boats & angling equipment for hire). About 20km from the Nsumbu Park gate, there's a signpost indicating the turn-off to the lodge. You'll need a 4x4 for this road, but most guests (& all in the rainy season) are transferred by boat from Mpulungu (2–4hrs) or arrive by air at the lodge's own airstrip.

Accommodation consists of 4 spacious rooms built in a block around a couple of old fig trees overlooking the lake, & a further 5 chalets set further back with partial lake views. All have been stylishly renovated to be modern but comfortable, combining crisp white linen softened by fabrics & paintwork in more earthy tones. Each room has a king-size bed hung with walk-in mosquito nets on a minimalist concrete plinth, smart en-suite shower, & a wooden veranda that – in the lake-view rooms – is partially enclosed, a useful extra during the rains.

At the lodge's heart is a large, airy *insaka* sheltering a bar/dining area, hung with huge wooden masks & outsize baskets. To one side, deep sofas & low *mukwa* tables are fronted by a small (but deep) pool – parents beware – & the lake beyond. Activities comprise game walks from the lodge or into the rainforest, game drives, beach dinners, boat trips, sundowner cruises, canoeing & fishing, for which tackle is available to hire. This is no place to swim, though – as attested by a quick glance at the crocodiles basking in the waters off the beach. It is possible to arrange a trip to local landmarks such as the waterfalls on the Lufubu River or a nearby beach, as well as to Chieftainess Chomba's village. *US$250/125 adult/child pp FB, inc airstrip transfers, laundry, game viewing, guided walk & sunset cruise. Boat US$150/day plus US$2 per litre of fuel. Drinks, activities & park fees extra.* ⌚ *All year.* ♛♛♛

WHAT TO SEE AND DO Ndole and Nkamba Bay can both organise a range of activities both on and off the water, but there are one or two local highlights that are worth singling out, detailed below. See also page 387. Further afield, it's possible to organise excursions to Mpulungu (page 388) or Kalambo Falls (page 383).

Balancing rocks One spot well worth an excursion is the balancing rocks (one large rock balancing on three small ones) that stand on the Nundo Head Peninsula – a favourite trail destination shrouded in local mystery. Each year around early June, a pre-fishing ceremony in honour of the spirit, Nundo, is held here to mark the beginning of the five-month period in which local fishermen can fish within a small area of national-park waters. Visitors can arrange to witness the ceremony through Ndole Bay Lodge.

Game viewing and birding As the lodges extend their influence and the number of animals increases, game viewing is increasingly drawing visitors up here. Apart from the ubiquitous puku, most antelope species are still re-establishing their populations; so although you won't see huge herds, you should see some good game here. The lodges have all worked to increase the road network for game drives, and the animals themselves are becoming much more relaxed as a result. Fortunately, with a large area and only a few lodges the roads are very quiet and other vehicles are a pleasant rarity. The birdwatching here has always been excellent: look out for Pel's fishing owl, palmnut vultures and numerous East African migrants.

Guided walks About 5km from Nkamba Bay Lodge and within the national park is the small Kampasa Rainforest, a favourite spot for guided walks. Trips usually involve a boat transfer, then a 3- to 4-hour walk from the beach, and are accompanied by an armed ZAWA scout.

The rainforest itself covers only about $300m^2$ and is centred on an underground stream that bubbles up out of the ground most of the year. Mature woodland species such as sausage trees, *Kigelia africana*, and Natal mahogany, *Trichilia emetica*, grow alongside plants that include the flame creeper, *Gloriosa superba*. Before entering the forest, the trail leads past a dense reed bed where sitatunga are often seen. The area surrounding the reed beds is also rich in puku and is a well-used route for elephant, while the forest itself is regularly traversed by a pod of hippos on their way to the plains behind it. The park's lion frequent the area, too, and can often be heard from Nkamba Bay Lodge. Among the birds that are likely to be encountered are Pel's fishing owl, African broadbill, Angolan pitta and Narina trogon; crowned cranes are often seen on the plain, and during the rainy season the reed beds are the haunt of the black coucal.

A second walk option leads to the Muzinga Falls on a small stream to the east of Nsumbu town, about an hour's walk from the lake.

NSUMBU VILLAGE On the edge of Nsumbu National Park, about 8km east of the Ndole Bay turn-off, Nsumbu has an estimated 4,404 residents, largely employed by the national parks, local civil services and in commercial fishing. Having gained an electricity supply a little over a decade ago, hope remains that one day the road will be tarred, but for now vehicle access is on gravel and far more pleasant by boat from Mpulungu.

While the town isn't nearly as cosmopolitan as Mpulungu (!), it can be fairly lively. In the town square, a short walk from the harbour, small shops and bars surround the water pump, alongside a popular pool table. It's possible to buy most things, including fresh fruit and milk, if you ask around, and simple meals such as nshima and chicken can be bought for around K25.

An open-air **market** for vegetables, dried fish and secondhand clothing spills from the square down to the harbour. There is also a government-run clinic, with a medical officer (but seldom any drugs), and a ZAWA post. **Fuel** – both petrol and diesel – is sometimes available in drums; just ask around in the square.

The Zambian military maintains a presence by the harbour, but their interest is largely in checking the ID of passengers off the transport boats from Mpulungu.

THE ROAD TO MWERU WANTIPA AND KAPUTA

The western side of this region, skirting the shores of Lake Bangweulu to Samfya then continuing up the Luapula River north to Lake Mweru, is known to only a handful of visitors, but offers plenty of rewards. The river is a draw in itself, as are the waterfalls that characterise much of this area, while the journey is enlivened by countless small villages, their square, brick houses topped with a mop of loose thatch and often decorated in striking geometric patterns.

If you're coming northeastward on the Great North Road from Kapiri Mposhi, it's wise to refuel at Serenje (see map, page 332). Then, after a further 36km, take the main left turning signposted to Samfya, Mansa and Kasanka National Park. This is the artery that runs over some 580km of very good tar to Nchelenge, in the far northwest corner of the country.

The section of road up to the T-junction just west of Samfya used to be referred to as the 'Chinese Road' because it was built, like the TAZARA railway, by the Chinese. After about 55km on this road you'll pass the entrance to Kasanka National Park (page 348), then 10km later the right turn to the Livingstone Memorial (page 358) and Bangweulu. Continuing north, the road crosses the impressive 3km-long Luapula Bridge, on the border with the DRC. During and after the rainy season, from around December to July, the river overflows onto the surrounding plain, which is dotted with miniature islands topped with palm trees. In the flooded fields, water lilies flower and water birds brighten the landscape. Permanent villages are augmented by temporary fishing camps, their inhabitants making the most of the months of plenty, and along the roadside fishermen tout their catch of bream or kasepa for sale.

Beyond the Luapula Bridge, watch out for the occasional pot-hole, although generally the road remains very good. About 350km from the Great North Road turn-off, or 115km from the Luapula Bridge, you'll reach a T-junction (⊕ SAMTJN 11°21.126'S, 29°29.453'E). Turn right here and a further 9km will bring you to the small town of Samfya.

SAMFYA With its location beside the powder-fine, white-sand beaches of Lake Bangweulu, Samfya seems to have the potential for a top resort. However, on closer inspection it's less tempting than it looks: accommodation could do with a serious shake up, strong winds blowing off the lake can be decidedly disruptive, and for the most part the lake is full of crocodiles, so this is really more of a stopover than a destination in its own right. (Note that while people do bathe in the clear waters by the hotels, local advice is mixed; think very carefully before wading in.)

On a more practical note, the town has a rather unpromising-looking **fuel station**, as well as a Finance **Bank**, a **post office**, a small **market** and a range of basic **shops**.

Getting there Several **buses** a day run between Lusaka and Kashikishi via Kabwe, Kapiri Mposhi, Serenje, Samfya, Mansa and Nchelenge. Those heading north stop at the market in Samfya at around 08.00, but southbound buses must be boarded at the T-junction 9km west of town, at a similar time.

Regular **postboats** used to ply Lake Bangweulu, collecting and delivering mail to the island communities on the lake. Like the postbuses, these would happily take paying passengers, but in recent years the service has been contracted out to private concerns, and information is patchy. Even in Samfya itself it is difficult to ascertain any form of timetable, but the boat used to depart every Thursday at 10.00, calling at Mbabala Island, Chisi Island and Muchinshi among others. To get to the port, turn left at the crossroads as you enter the town and follow this dirt road, with shops on either side, for about 300m to the end.

Where to stay and eat Samfya's accommodation options seem to come and go, but the addition of a new lakeside lodge broadens the choice for visitors.

Chita Lodge Samfya (21 chalets, 10 s/c homes) m 0979 562176; e reservations@chita.co.zm. The best place in Samfya, Chita offers neat thatched chalets & self-catering accommodation with a pool and lakeside location. **$$–$$$**

Samfya Waterfront Lodge (16 rooms) m 0977 419675. Basic en-suite rooms with a view of the lake. **$**

LUBWE It would be worth exploring the road north of Samfya towards Lubwe, on the western side of the lake. Lubwe itself is home to a Catholic mission hospital built in 1926 and now run by the Sisters of Mercy.

MANSA About 72km from the T-junction, or 81km from Samfya, Mansa is the capital of Luapula Province. It's a thriving provincial town, with tree-lined roads and an appealing air of prosperity.

Getting there and away Mansa's links to the rest of the region are enhanced by its position close to the Luapula River and the DRC border (50km). A tarred road leads southwest to the border town of Chembe, where the 350m Chembe bridge has now been built over the river connecting to the Congo Pedicle road, a dirt highway across the DRC to Mufulira in the Copperbelt. Some of the Pedicle road has now been paved but reconstruction is ongoing.

By bus Long-distance buses are operated by several companies, including the reputable Juldan Motors. Most leave from Mulenshi Road in the centre of town, with regular buses connecting Mansa with Lusaka, Kashikishi on Lake Mweru and Kawambwa. Buses to Lusaka leave in the morning, taking about 9 hours to

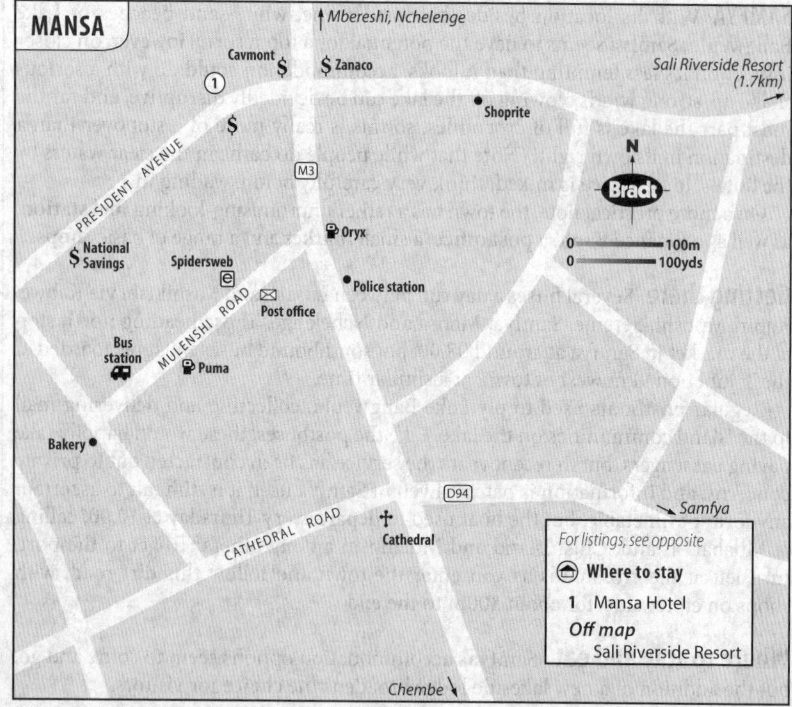

complete the journey. Typically, northbound buses load in the early hours (buy a ticket the day before) or mid afternoon.

Where to stay *Map, opposite*

Sali Riverside Resort Chabalamuwe Rd; m 0964 315131; e saliriversideresort@gmail.com. Opened in 2020, this is one of Mansa's better options: clean rooms, a nice view & a pool. **$$–$$$**

Mansa Hotel (30 rooms) President Av; 0212 821607 m 0976 051571. Central & well established, the Mansa's brick-built rooms, arranged round a series of courtyards, are simply furnished but clean. The hotel also has a bars & simple restaurant. **$$**

Other practicalities As you might expect in a regional capital, there are three all-important **fuel** stations (the last reliable source of fuel for several hundred kilometres if you're going north; Oxyx also refills gas bottles), four **banks**, a general **hospital** and two **pharmacies** (Chipamapwe Rd & Chembe Rd). There's a branch of Shoprite (08.00–19.00 Mon–Fri, 08.00–17.00 Sat, 09.00–13.00 Sun) and several roadside stalls selling seasonal fruit and vegetables. If you're heading north and camping or self-catering, this is the last chance to stock up on anything other than the basics.

NORTH OF MANSA Some 9km north of Mansa the road splits. The left turn leads to Mwense, Mbereshi and Nchelenge, while the road straight ahead is for Kawambwa. Both appear beautifully tarred, but don't be fooled; after the first 25km or so the Kawambwa road deteriorates rapidly into a bad dirt road, which is well worth avoiding, while the road to Nchelenge is pretty good tar for most of the way. Thus, if you're heading towards Kawambwa, take the road towards Nchelenge via Mwense, then turn right at Mbereshi for Kawambwa. It's both easier and quicker.

The Nchelenge road follows the verdant valley of the Luapula River as it flows north into Lake Mweru, forming the border with the DRC and widening all the way to the lake. A succession of villages lines the road, which crosses several rivers, all flowing west towards the Luapula from Zambia's higher ground in the east. It's an easy but interesting drive, particularly after the rainy season when the flooded plains attract temporary fishing camps, as further south. The route is further enhanced by views across the river to the DRC and the lure of several attractive waterfalls (see below), many of which offer a good spot for a picnic or to camp.

There are two fuel spots along this stretch: at Mwense, 111km north of Mansa, and 18km further north in the village of Chiluba, but neither is reliable, so do fill up in Mansa.

The Luapula waterfalls Along this route are numerous lovely waterfalls, many virtually unmarked, including the following:

Mumbuluma Falls (⊕ MUMBUL 10°55.801'S, 28°44.178'E; US$10/5 adult/child; vehicle US$5/day; camping US$15 pp inc entry) About 32km north of Mansa (167km from Mbereshi) there's a signposted left turn (⊕ TOMUMB 10°55.536'S, 28°47.945'E). After about 8.4km of rather bad track, you'll reach the falls.

Here, the Luamfuma River drops 5–10m over a wide, two-stage drop, about 30m across, with attractive rapids in between and a deep pool at the bottom, making for a good swimming spot. It's popular with local villagers and offers camping for visitors, with a small shelter and toilet block about 100m from the falls.

MUTOMBOKO 'DANCE OF VICTORY' CEREMONY *Thomas Morrow*

During the last week of July, the people of the lower Luapula Valley in northern Zambia gather in the village of Mwansabombwe to celebrate their Lunda traditions and their paramount chief, Mwata Kazembe. For days prior to the main event, bars serve bottled beer, much of it imported from the DRC, to quench the thirst of guests who have arrived in the hot, dusty village; women from different village sections deliver pots of millet beer to Mwata Kazembe's palace; and the youth organise special sports competitions and cultural events. Towards the weekend when the main festivities are to take place, provincial, and on occasion national, political and military dignitaries dressed in their suits and ties arrive. On Saturday afternoon, following the performance of certain rituals in the morning, chiefs, headmen, state dignitaries and the villagers crowd together in a stadium on the outskirts of Mwansabombwe. A dignitary delivers a speech that highlights the importance of culture and tradition for progress, development and national well-being. Listening to the national leadership's calls for the preservation of these traditions, the chiefs and headmen appear in the traditional Lunda garb of long *imikonso* skirts (singular, *umukonso*), leather *inshipo* belts and *ututasa* crowns (singular, *akatasa*). After the speeches, on the instruction of Mwata Kazembe, selected aristocrats and members of the royal family dance. The day's events culminate in Mwata Kazembe performing the Lunda dance of conquest, the Mutomboko.

Mambilima Falls (US$10/5 adult/child; vehicle US$5/day; camping US$15 pp inc entry) About 90km north of Mansa (111km from Mbereshi) there's a set of lovely rapids on the Luapula River which make a very pleasant spot for lunch. These used to be called the Johnstone Falls and the series of rapids run over a 5km stretch of the river. Turn off the main road about 5km south of Mambilima village, at a sign to the Christian Brethren Church Conference Centre (⊛ TUMAMB 10°32.260'S, 28°40.037'E). From here, follow the track for about 3km to the centre, where you can gaze over at the DRC or walk along the river for close-ups of some of the larger rapids.

MWANSABOMBWE The village of Mwansabombwe (⊛ MWANSA 09°49.25'S, 28°45.35'E), 13km south of Mbereshi, is the focus of the colourful Mutomboko Ceremony – the Dance of Victory – that takes place every year on the last Friday and Saturday of July (page 26). Visitors are welcome to watch, but photographers will need a pass costing about K150 for the day. A statue at the entrance to the village commemorates the event.

If you're heading east to Kawambwa, don't be tempted to take a 'short cut' before Mbereshi by turning off the road at Mwansabombwe; this may look promising at first, but quickly disappears into a series of tracks that aren't the easiest to follow; stick to the main road unless you've time to explore!

MBERESHI Mbereshi (⊛ MBERES 09°44.078'S, 28°47.350'E) has a useful **fuel** station, at the junction where you turn off for Kawambwa, Lumangwe Falls and Mporokoso, and is notable for having one of Zambia's earliest churches. Built in the early 1900s by the London Missionary Society, which was responsible for several other buildings in the vicinity (the rest of which are now in varying states of disrepair), it's worth a glance.

There are some serious speed humps at each end of the village; if you're self-driving, be warned.

NCHELENGE This small town near the shores of Lake Mweru is the base for an occasional ferry service out to the two populated islands in the lake: Kilwa and Isokwe. In addition to a **post office** and small **market**, there is usually **fuel** available. The fishing is (apparently) excellent in the area but bear in mind that there is also an abundance of crocodiles.

BEYOND KASHIKISHI TO MWERU WANTIPA NATIONAL PARK Some 3km beyond Nchelenge, at Kashikishi, the tar road comes to an end and the road deteriorates dramatically, so if you're aiming to get to Kaputa, allow plenty of time. Continue north along the edge of Lake Mweru for a scenic 30km or so, towards the village of Mununga then follow the road as it veers away from the lake until you reach the Kalungwishi River.

At the village of Mununga, there are often market traders at the junction, so it's a good place to pick up whatever produce is in season. The stretch of road from this junction through Mweru Wantipa National Park to Kaputa is stony but reasonably level, though you'll still need to drive with care. After 44km you'll come to a barrier, which marks the entrance to the national park (⊕ MWERUP 08°53.572'S, 29°28.878'E). From here, continue straight through the national park and across the top of Lake Mweru Wantipa to Kaputa (see below).

Mweru Wantipa National Park

(Park fees US$5 pp/day; vehicle US$15/day) Once a thriving national park, renowned for large elephant, black rhino and crocodile populations, poaching has decimated numbers, with most species wiped out entirely here. In addition, there are no visitor facilities. Claims are made that sitatunga can be found among the dense papyrus beds on the lakeshore, but sadly, to the casual observer, the impenetrable thicket covering the park appears to be singularly devoid of life.

That said, the whole area, including the lake, was designated a Ramsar site (Wetlands of International Importance) in 2007. The diversity of habitats along the lake, featuring riverine forest, wetlands and miombo woodland, are an attraction to numerous water birds, including the wattled crane, black stork and Goliath's heron.

On the western side of sedimentary, seasonal Lake Mweru Wantip – meaning 'muddy lake' – which itself forms part of the national park, the park's single road goes straight to Kaputa. Along this road, you'll come to a ZAWA scout post (⊕ MWSCOP 08°47.807'S, 29°30.519'E). If you anticipate camping here, or even exploring away from the road, then ask if one of the scouts can accompany you.

KAPUTA Despite being the district capital, Kaputa is a rather unattractive place, with the dejected air of a border town. There's a bank, a few local shops and a market where you can pick up basic foodstuffs but most visitors will be keen to press on towards Lake Tanganyika (page 385).

FROM MBERESHI TO KASAMA

MBERESHI TO MPOROKOSO Turning east at Mbereshi, the tar road continues as far as Kawambwa before continuing on a reasonable gravel road across the Kalungwishi River bridge at Chimpembe, finally reaching Mporokoso after 185km. A number of lovely waterfalls can be accessed from this road.

Ntumbachushi Falls (⊕ NTUMBA 09°51.167'S, 28°56.652'E; US$15/7 adult/child; vehicle US$5/day; camping US$15 pp inc entry) Created by the Ngona River tumbling over the Luapula plateau edge, these lovely falls are clearly signposted from Mbereshi (23km east), Kawambwa (18km west) and the valley turn-off (⊕ 09°50.666'S, 28°56.450'E). They are just 1.2km south of the road along a good track, and surrounded by some beautiful thick *mishitu* forest, making them well worth a detour.

The main bridal-veil falls drop about 40m into a dark pool, with a second cataract alongside. Don't swim in the main pool, as there are strong currents and undertows that can pull you under the falls themselves. However, both the pool at the foot of the second cataract and the gentle rapids above the first falls offer perfect places for a cooling dip or a proper swim. Clear footpaths lead from the car park in both directions.

In the rainy season, there is a further set of falls, the Witch Doctor's Falls a short walk upstream, so called because there used to be *ng'anga* 'medicine' shrines at its base, one containing millet, the other a model canoe carved from bone. If you'd like to visit, ask the caretaker to guide you there, and remember to offer him a tip.

Where to stay This has long been an idyllic spot to camp, with a toilet block and occasional bar-restaurant about 100m from the campsite. It can be busy, and noisy, over the weekends, but is otherwise serene. Alternatively, the new Kasuba Exclusive Lodge in Kawambwa (see below) is probably the most promising place to stay nearby.

Kawambwa Rather smaller than most maps of Zambia might suggest, Kawambwa sits on a plateau above the Luapula Valley. It's a pleasant backwater, 18.6km from Ntumbachushi Falls, widely known for the large Kawambwa Tea Estate, east of the town. Initiated in 1969 as a state pilot project in tea growing, the company was mandated in 2015 to 'rehabilitate, modernise and expand' and in 2020 doubled its processing capacity, bringing with it local job creation, especially for women who are favoured as being careful pickers of delicate tea leaves.

Chanda Wesu operate a daily bus service between Lusaka and Kawambwa, and there's a fuel station at the junction with the Mbereshi road. The town itself has a small market, a bank and a range of local shops. There is a new hotel, Kasuba Exclusive Lodge (**m** 0969 112106; **e** gdagempire1986@yahoo.com; **$–$$**), a handful of guesthouses and a DNPW office next to the fuel station issuing permits for Lusenga Plain National Park, though little really to detain the visitor here.

Lusenga Plain National Park (US$12 pp/day; vehicle US$15/day; bush camping US$30. Fees payable at DNPW office in Kawambwa) Lusenga Plain was originally designated as a park in 1972 to protect a large open plain, fringed by swamp and dry evergreen forest and surrounded by ridges of hills. On its northeastern side, it is bordered by the wide Kalungwishi River, which passes over three beautiful waterfalls: Lumangwe, Kabwelume and Kundabwika.

For many years, Lusenga was a national park in name alone. With little financial or practical support, poaching reduced wildlife considerably and with no roads in the park, there were few reasons to visit. The park was largely forgotten. Encouragingly, the tide may be turning for the park. A small road network has now been graded, the local chief has publicly condemned poaching, wildlife policing has been increased and the translocation of wildlife back into the park has been steadily increasing over the last decade. Initially, wildebeest, impala and zebra were moved from across Zambia. They were followed by 160 elephants from South Africa's Kruger and more recently, the arrival of some black lechwe from Bangweulu, thanks to the support and success of African Parks with the latter. Hopefully, with better protection, Lusenga's once-abundant wildlife will flourish again but this will take time.

Getting there The park is usually approached from the Kawambwa–Mporokoso road, and it's advisable to take a game scout as a guide from the DNPW office in Kawambwa. You should be well equipped for any visit or overnight camping stop as no facilities or support are available in the park.

Kalungwishi River Waterfalls The Kalungwishi River forms the boundary between the Luapula and northern regions of Zambia, and also the eastern boundary of Lusenga Plain National Park. Along the river are three spectacular waterfalls in relatively close succession: Lumangwe, Kabwelume and Kundabwika. The entrance fee gives you access to both Lumangwe and Kabwelume.

In addition to the falls themselves, there are miles of pleasant walking upstream, so consider staying overnight to give time to explore the other falls further downstream.

Lumangwe Falls (US$15/7 adult/child inc entry to Lumangwe & Kabwelume falls; vehicle US$5/day; camping inc in entry) Lumangwe Falls is a strikingly beautiful waterfall: a solid white-and-green wall of water, 100m across and 30m high. It's perhaps the most spectacular of the waterfalls in this region and is sometimes referred to as 'mini Mosi-oa-Tunya' on account of its resemblance to Victoria Falls from the first viewpoint. The noise is deafening, and the air is filled with fine mist and rainbows. There are two viewing points, one overlooking the main falls from the front, and a second – much drier! – from the brink of the falls where you can see how a large island splits the river's flow and it drops over the sharp rock face. The energetic might want to climb to the bottom of the falls in order to reach the end of the rainbow that's seen at this point on most days. While there are some interesting photographic angles, there are no pots of gold here, and the climb comes with a warning: instead of steps, you'll be making your way down (and then up) using a rope and the cliff side for balance. As a National Heritage Commission Site, there are guides available (guides included in entrance fee but worthy of a tip) to show you the way, and they'll happily talk about the mythical snake spirit who legend says once dwelt here too or walk the forest path 6km to Kabwelume Falls with you.

Although clearly signposted from the main road, the 9km track from the turn-off to Lumangwe is extremely rutted and pot-holed and requires a 4x4 and patience. About 2km east of the Chimpempe bridge, there's a clear signpost to Lumangwe and Kabwelume Falls (⊕ FALLST 09°32.239'S, 29°27.874'E). The falls are 300m from the small information centre at the end of the gravel.

Kabwelume Falls (US$15/7 adult/child; vehicle US$5/day; camping US$15 pp inc entry; fee includes access to Lumangwe) This trio of cascades are 6km downstream from Lumangwe, which makes a pleasant, 2–3 hour walk through the forest – alternatively, you can drive yourself (30mins), provided you have a good 4x4 and solid off-road experience: the track is very poor and it's slow going. Guides at Lumangwe information centre can help with directions by foot or road.

Kabwelume is wonderfully wild. The landscape has been left to grow untamed, with vibrant palm fronds enhancing the approach to the falls. Come prepared with good footwear as the increasingly overgrown path takes you across the river on stepping stones (probably inaccessible in the rainy season), then through thick vegetation dotted with bright flowers and alive with butterflies, and finally down a steep, slippery slope. You'll emerge after 300m or so to a most magnificent waterfall – a curving curtain of water 25m high and 100m across. It's a breathtaking spot, making it absolutely worthy of the onwards trip from Lumangwe. Below is a deep pool, which itself flows over a second fall of 20m. On the left are two cataracts falling the whole 40m; on the right water pours down the cliff face. Look about you and this makes 180° of water – with the cataract, the main waterfall and the waterspout. It's a truly beautiful sight, worth savouring.

Pressure for electricity in Zambia means that permits have been granted for two multi-million dollar, 'run of the river' hydro-electric power stations at Kabwelume and Kundabwika falls. Although actual construction has been woefully slow, being first anticipated a decade ago, the project may well come to fruition in time. As and when this does happen, it's unlikely to restrict visitor access to the falls, though it may make for a less natural vista.

Kundabwika Falls (⊕ KUNDAB 9°13.058'S, 29°18.258'E; US$10/5 adult/child; vehicle US$5/day; camping US$15 pp inc entry) These are the last major falls on the Kalungwishi River before it flows into Lake Mweru. Despite that, they are accessed from a different road, which may be impassable after rain; ask for advice locally, perhaps from the caretaker at Ntumbachushi.

There are two routes to the falls, both requiring a 4x4. The normal route is from the Kawambwa–Mporokoso road. About 21km east of the Chimpempe Bridge (⊕ KUNDTO 09°27.945'S, 29°36.447'E), or 63km west of Mporokoso, turn northwest onto a narrow, very poor track; it's just west of a road barrier and signposted to Chikwanda Basic School; some maps mark this as a place called Mukunsa. Continue along this track, which is deeply rutted and pot-holed, for about 50km. It passes through villages for about 30km, then descends into less populous woodlands. It's very slow going so allow around 2 hours to the turn-off. The turning towards the falls (⊕ TOKUND 09°11.397'S, 29°19.890'E) is into woodland, and almost invisible when the grass is high, so ask one of the villagers to point it out. From here, there's a straightforward 5km track that leads to the river.

Approaching from the opposite direction, drive 65km north of Nchelenge to the village of Mununga, on the banks of Lake Mweru. From there it's 35km to the falls on a reasonable dirt road, turning south at ⊕ TOKUND, as above.

The woodland track brings you out by a series of gentle rapids, known as the upper falls. An expanse of open grassland offers plenty of room to camp, with no villages nearby, and just the occasional fisherman for company. To reach the main falls, a further 1km downstream, involves clambering over boulders along the riverbank.

Kundabwika itself is a geometric waterfall, a 25m-wide rectangular block of green-and-white water. It's not possible to get very close to the falls, but there are good long-distance views from the top of the rock outcrop.

As you approach the falls, about 3km from the road and to the left of the woodland track, there's a rocky outcrop where rock paintings can clearly be seen. You can explore yourself or, if you have time, ask if one of the villagers can take you to see them. A basic campsite at the site, with flush toilets, is a bonus after the long drive in.

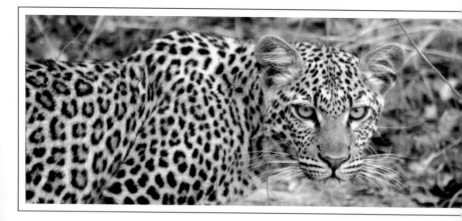

MPOROKOSO Mporokoso (⊕ MPOROK 09°21.831'S, 30°07.402'E) is a useful small town in the heart of northern Zambia. It lies at a T-junction on the Kawambwa–Kasama road, and is also the main access point for Nsumbu National Park (page 391 for directions to the park). The centre is to the west of the T-junction, along a wide, tree-lined avenue. Here you'll find a branch of the National Savings and Credit Bank, a police station, post office, shops and a small market.

During the 1999 war in DRC, a number of refugees and loyalist Congolese troops fled across the border to Zambia and were looked after by the UNHCR, the Red Cross, Oxfam and other agencies at Mwange Camp, about 60km outside Mporokoso. Many of the aid agencies retain a presence here and there's also a fairly large government hospital (with doctors but generally poor medicines and equipment), serving a large area of the country.

Getting there and away Most people coming to Mporokoso will be on the main Kawambwa–Kasama road, which is in reasonable shape having been tarred in large parts in late 2017.

If you're approaching from Mpulungu or Mbala, there is a right turn after Senga Hill on to a road that avoids Kasama, although it's over 70km long, and rough going even in the dry season (you'll need a 4x4) – so it's hardly a 'short cut'.

Where to stay If you wish to break your journey here, there are a few very simple guesthouses.

Kutemwa Lodge m 0973 004610. Signposted on the south side of the D19, on the western approach to town, Kutemwa is probably Mporokoso's best bet, offering simple, en-suite rooms with secure parking. Camping isn't allowed but travellers with a rooftent can stay in them if they pay the room rate of US$10–15. **$**

Waterfall excursions from Mporokoso

Kapuma Falls (⊕ KAPUM 09°23.235'S, 30°05.675'E) These small but delightful falls, cascading over scattered wall-like rocks, make a pleasant half-day trip from town and are a great picnic spot. Around 7km southwest of Mporokoso, past the district hospital, turn left just before the Agricultural Training Centre, from where it's around 2km to the falls. The road ends on a private farm, so if somebody is home, do ask permission to see the falls.

Pule Falls (⊕ PULEF 09°30.573'S, 30°17.001'E) Also known as Chipulwe Falls, these pretty, if not very deep (15m drop), falls lie 2 hours from Mporokoso, just off the road to the (other) Luangwa River. Just east after the Luangwa bridge, there's a motorable path for 1km before you'll need to take to the footpath through cassava fields and banana plantations for the last 500m.

Mumbuluma Falls III (⊕ MUMIII 09°33.211'S, 29°44.736'E) A curtain of water spanning the width of the Luangwa River (not the same one as in the national park of the same name), these falls are little known and surprisingly impressive. From Angelo village (⊕ ANGELO 9°26.771'S, 29°49.511'E), turn south for 14km, then west for 4km, where there's a footpath to the falls across the clearing.

Lupupa Falls (⊕ LUPUPA 9°16.441'S, 29°46.910'E) On the Mukubwe River, these fine bridal-veil falls make for a pleasant outing, and easily combine with

Mumbuluma Falls III. There are wonderful views from the falls along the sinuous Mukubwe River valley and down into the gorge pool 90m below.

To reach the falls, head 28km west from Mporokoso to Njalamimba, drive 10km to Chandalala, and continue along the 3km footpath before finally crossing the bridge on foot.

NYIKA PLATEAU NATIONAL PARK Nyika Plateau is a marvellous area for hiking, and has some unusual wildlife. It lies mostly in Malawi, with just a slim Zambian national park hugging the border, but it is best approached from the Malawian side. If you plan an extended visit to Malawi, then get hold of a copy of the excellent *Malawi: The Bradt Guide* by Philip Briggs before you travel – it's the standard reference on travel in Malawi.

14

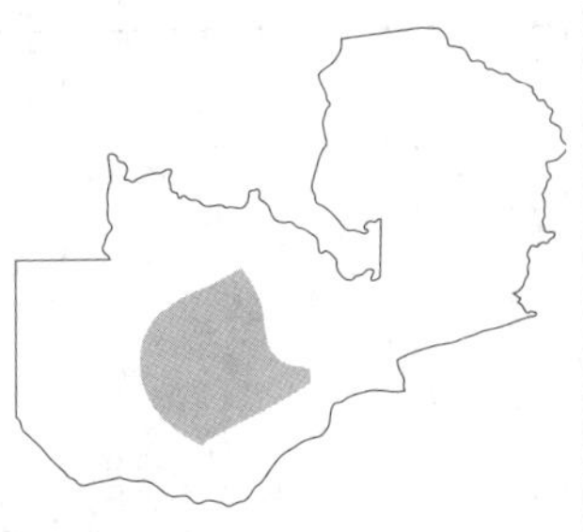

The Kafue River Basin

Southwest of the Copperbelt, the Kafue River Basin covers a large swathe of central Zambia stretching almost from the DRC to the west of Lusaka. It encompasses large areas of very sparsely populated bush as well as the Kafue, Blue Lagoon and Lochinvar national parks.

Much of this region of Zambia is difficult to visit, consisting of endless seasonal bush tracks which link occasional farming settlements. At its heart lies the huge Kafue National Park, which has some superb game-viewing areas within its boundaries. The best of these, the Busanga Plains, is not the most accessible, but at times it ranks with the subcontinent's most impressive game areas.

East of the park, there are seasonal floodplains that sustain game and attract a rich variety of birdlife – like the Lukanga Swamps and the Kafue Flats. Part of the latter is in theory protected by two small national parks – Blue Lagoon and Lochinvar – but most such areas remain outside the parks. The Kafue River Basin is a wild area, with some excellent game, endless possibilities for exploring and an increasingly enticing array of safari options.

TOWNS AROUND KAFUE NATIONAL PARK

Southern Kafue is relatively near to Livingstone, and usually accessed from Kalomo or one of the other towns on the Livingstone–Lusaka road (page 233). Northern Kafue has three towns around it which aren't usually destinations in their own right, but may be useful jumping-off points for the northern side of the park: Kasempa in the north, Mumbwa to the east, and Kaoma in the west.

KASEMPA The small town of Kasempa is set in the midst of rolling, hilly country. Although there are many villages in the surrounding bush, the overall population density doesn't feel very high, as much of the area seems to be miombo woodland. There is a **fuel** station but availability of petrol and diesel is erratic at best, leaving Kasempa without fuel for days at a time. Questionable, black-market fuel is available here – for a price. Better is to head southeast for 5km to the Mukinge Hospital (page 412), which offers both petrol and diesel for sale to the public.

Getting there and away Three roads run into Kasempa, meeting at a T-junction. To the north is an excellent, tarred road from Solwezi. That meets two reasonably good gravel roads: one just north of town (⊕ TUKAOM 13°27.388'S, 25°49.771'E), heading southwest to Kaoma; the other heading southeast towards Mumbwa, with a turn-off to the Kafue National Park's Kabanga gate. For detailed directions on this route, see page 411. There's a direct **bus** between Kasempa and Lusaka, via Solwezi. Buses stop in the square.

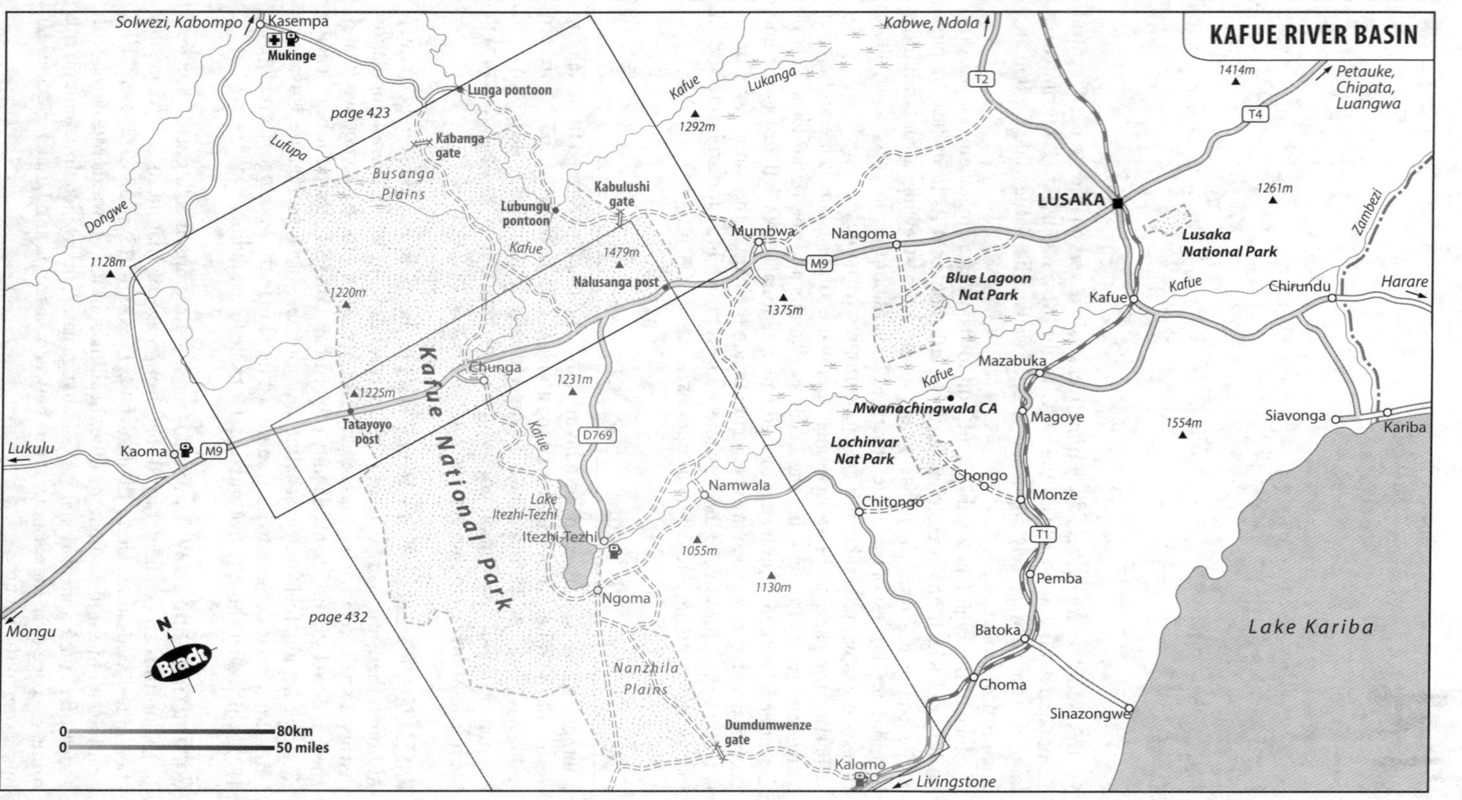
KAFUE RIVER BASIN
Solwezi, Kabompo
Kasempa
Mukinge
Kabwe, Ndola
T2
1414m
Petauke, Chipata, Luangwa
T4
Lunga pontoon
page 423
Kafue
Lukanga
1292m
Lufupa
Kabanga gate
Busanga Plains
Kabulushi gate
Lubungu pontoon
LUSAKA
1261m
Zambezi
Lusaka National Park
Dongwe
Mumbwa
Nangoma
Kafue
1479m
M9
1128m
Nalusanga post
1220m
Blue Lagoon Nat Park
1375m
Kafue
Chirundu
Harare
Kafue
Chunga
Kafue National Park
1231m
Mazabuka
1225m
Kafue
Mwanachingwala CA
Tatayoyo post
Kafue
D769
Magoye
1554m
Siavonga
Kariba
Lukulu
Kaoma
M9
Lochinvar Nat Park
Chongo
Namwala
Monze
Chitongo
Lake Itezhi-Tezhi
Itezhi-Tezhi
T1
1055m
1130m
Pemba
Ngoma
Mongu
page 432
Lake Kariba
N
Bradt
Batoka
Nanzhila Plains
Choma
Sinazongwe
0 80km
0 50 miles
Dumdumwenze gate
Kalomo
Livingstone

From Solwezi The good tar road southwest from Solwezi passes the airport then continues in a more southerly direction towards Kasempa, passing close to the Mutanda Falls. After some 140km, at ⊕ TUKALU 13°3.302'S, 25°59.199'E, the M11 from Kalulushi joins this road from the west, then a few kilometres further on there's another junction (⊕ TUKASE 13°6.226'S, 25°52.252'E). The road straight on, heading west, is the good M8 to Kabompo. For Kasempa, turn left and follow the tarred D181 for 43km to the small town (⊕ KASEMP 13°27.404'S, 25°49.779'E). Solwezi is the last reliable fuelling point, as fuel is not always available in Kasempa, so it's advisable to fill up before you depart.

Where to stay There are a few basic guesthouses in town, most of which tend to be fairly rundown, but the quality does tend to improve as you move away from the centre.

Other practicalities Most of the town's shops and other facilities form a square just off the main road. There is a **bank**, a **post office**, a Catholic church and a few very **basic shops**.

Driving from Kasempa to Mumbwa This dirt road has been graded over the years, but is still in relatively poor condition with some large pot-holes, and marked deterioration towards Mumbwa. It's easily navigable though, skirting round the eastern edge of the national park. Along the way, the road is lined with a few small rural settlements and a lot of open areas. After 4km, you'll pass the turning to Mukinge Mission, then a further 75km brings you to a right-hand fork signposted to the Kabanga gate (⊕ TUKABA 13°57.930'S, 26°11.858'E), on the northern border of Kafue National Park. The gate itself (⊕ KABANG 14°5.808'S, 26°7.036'E) is some 19km along a bumpy, sandy track. For Mumbwa, however, continue straight along the graded road, passing through lush green woodland and the occasional village, and keeping right where there's a fork in the road after 11km (⊕ KAFORK 13°57.905'S, 26°17.459'E). A total of almost 28km will bring you to the Lunga pontoon (⊕ FERRYL 13°58.984'S, 26°20.784'E; ⊙ 06.00–18.00 daily; K75 per vehicle).

About 3km before the pontoon is a turning (⊕ TULUNG 13°58.626'S, 26°20.076'E). This is the start of a very bumpy, black-cotton soil track that shadows the east bank of the Lunga River for around 25km along the boundary of the park. At a closed hunting lodge, a continuation of the road then heads northwest to the Kabanga gate (⊕ KABANG 14°5.808'S, 26°7.036'E). Most drivers, however, cross the Lunga River, then continue for another 70km along a good, but winding road to the Lubungu River (⊕ LUBUNG 14°33.750'S, 26°27.250'E); watch out for fallen trees and other debris en route. Note that the pontoon here (⊙ 06.00–18.00 daily; K75 per vehicle) is smaller than its counterpart over the Lunga, so not capable of taking large vehicles.

From the Lubungu River, it's another 75km or so to Mumbwa, the first 10km of which are in good condition, but rapidly deteriorates into large pot-holes and loose dirt after passing through the Kabulushi gate. Until this road is improved this journey will take 2½ to 3 hours.

For directions in reverse on this section, see page 422.

Note that the southern parts of this route, from around the Lunga pontoon, are within a GMA, so you are not free to camp – or indeed to do anything other than simply pass through.

MUMBWA Mumbwa's proximity to Lusaka gives it a palpable urban buzz, entirely different from the rural feel of small towns further west. The presence of a large mosque with a dominant minaret only serves to enhance this feel.

MUKINGE MISSION HOSPITAL

Mukinge Mission (w mukinge.com) started around 1925 when the Rev C S Foster came to this area as an evangelical missionary. His son, Bob, was born here, studied medicine in Toronto, and then returned in 1950 to found a mission hospital – even supervising its construction.

Today, Mukinge Hospital serves a huge area that can result in patients travelling on foot or by bike for up to five days. With about 200 beds, it cares for around 140 in-patients a day (including three or four births on average) as well as 160–180 outpatients. The seven in-patient wards include one for malnutrition and another for isolation. There are also two operating theatres, a new eye clinic, a laboratory, a range of X-ray equipment, a physiotherapy department, a training school for nurses and a pharmacy with basic drug supplies. In short, it's the best hospital for a very long way.

Mukinge is supported by the World Medical Mission, a wing of the missionary organisation Samaritan's Purse, as well as the Evangelical Church in Zambia, and the government. However funds for day-to-day expenses such as food and equipment are tight. To this end, the hospital has its own **fuel station**, with both diesel and petrol sold from large drums. Prices are on a par with black-market outlets, around K10 per litre in 2011, but there are no issues about the quality here, and you have the added feel-good factor of knowing that you have contributed to a worthy cause.

To get to the hospital (⊕ MUKING 13°28.894's, 25°51.409'E), head south of Kasempa for about 4km, and then turn right (⊕ TUMUKI 13°28.264'S, 25°51.902'E), following the signs for a further 1km. There are buses between here and Kasempa.

The town is 4km north of the main tar road between Lusaka and Mongu, and is the last place for anyone heading into the Kafue National Park to visit a bank or stock up on fuel.

Getting there

By bus Between the town's two roundabouts, in the bustling market area, is the local bus station, where buses between Mongu and Lusaka stop in both directions. It's a relatively busy route, with arrivals and departures at all times of day, though the highest frequency is the middle of the day, when buses that left from Lusaka or Mongu in the morning pass through the town.

Driving from Lusaka About 3 hours' drive from Lusaka (148km), on the Great West Road towards Mongu, a large modern factory looms next to the road, and orderly warehouses stand behind well-watered lawns. This is perhaps the country's biggest cotton ginnery. A few kilometres further west is a turning off the road to the north, which leads – after about 4km of pot-holed tar – to the thriving town of Mumbwa.

Where to stay
There are a couple of basic overnight choices in Mumbwa, of which the best is Lelesha Lodge.

La Hacienda (7 rooms, 6 chalets) 211 800288. ⊕ HACIEN 14°59.041'S, 27°03.720'E. In the centre of town, this old hotel has a quiet location set in gardens with a pool. Somewhat run down now but rooms are en suite & there's a bar with TV, & a restaurant ($). **$$**

Lelesha Lodge (11 rooms) Off M9; 260 771879980; e leleshalodge@gmail.com; f leleshalodge. Mumbwa's newest & smartest option is just off the M9 near the Oil Bay fuel station at the south of town. Neat accommodation with bright, modern interiors, a good restaurant & even a children's playground. **$**

Other practicalities Be sure to fill up with fuel here as it is the last place to fill up before heading into the park. There are now three fuel stations – Mt Meru and Total fuel stations (⊕ TOTALM 14°59.451'S, 27°03.642'E) on the main roundabout into town and at OilBay on the M9 as you turn into Mumbwa. Opportunities to buy black-market fuel for a higher price are plentiful. Ask around plainly but politely, and you should be directed to a suitable source, though it's wise to check with other buyers to ensure you are purchasing from an untampered supply. Using this fuel in your vehicle is always a risk, though. In addition to the town's **market**, located between the two roundabouts, there are endless small local **shops**. Opposite the market is a branch of Barclays Bank (⏲ 08.30–14.30 Mon–Fri) with a useful **ATM**. Again, it's not entirely reliable, so don't run your cash too low.

Driving north from Mumbwa

To the Lubungu pontoon From the tarred Great West Road, there is a road of variable quality along the eastern side of the park to the Lubungu pontoon via the Kabulushi gate, and on to Kasempa. A high-clearance vehicle remains advisable, however, and if you're heading for Hippo Lodge or McBrides' Camp (page 430), then a 4x4 is essential in the rainy season. Note that it is no longer possible to drive due north into the park from the Nalusanga scout post.

To access this eastern road from the Great West Road, turn north into Mumbwa, then left at the first roundabout by the Total garage (⊕ TOTALM 14°59.457'S, 27°03.617'E). Continue through a market and after about 1.1km, at the top of the next rise, take a right turn onto the Kasempa road, a bumpy dirt road that goes to Lubungu pontoon. The 66km stretch from here to the Kabulushi gate (⊕ KABULU 15°07.947'S, 27°21.881'E) passes through wooded areas and some farmland. The surface here is incredibly bumpy and slow going, and you can expect it to take approximately 2 hours to get to the gate. No fees are payable at the gate by those just driving through; if you're staying at Hippo Lodge or McBrides' Camp, park fees should be paid at the lodges themselves.

After passing through the gate the road improves to a more solid gravel track, which passes through forested areas with huge rounded boulders. A fork (⊕ TUHIPP 14°37.866'S, 26°29.659'E) to the left, clearly signposted from the south (but not from the north), leads to Hippo Lodge and McBrides' Camp – and also the old Hippo Mine (page 429). For the Lubungu pontoon (⊕ LUBUNG 14°33.750'S, 26°27.250'E; ⏲ 06.00–18.00 daily; K75 per vehicle or US$30 if foreign registered; 12 ton limit; payment in kwacha is usually necessary) continue on the main road for a further 10km – and note that this pontoon is smaller than its Lunga counterpart.

If you're driving to Lunga (which very few people do) you could alternatively take the longer route through the park which, although significantly slower than this one, is likely to offer some good game sightings.

From the Lubungu pontoon to the Lunga pontoon See page 422, for directions along this route.

KAOMA Kaoma is a small district town about 3km north of the Great West Road between Kafue and Mongu, and about 76km west of Kafue National Park. Though not close to Kafue, it's on the edge of the Western Province, so is very much a gateway to the area. Whichever way you're travelling, it's wise to fill your fuel tank (and spare fuel drums) here.

If you have space in your vehicle, you'll find no shortage of people wanting to share the journey. Given the shortage of transport, and the insight that hitchhikers can give to visitors, don't appear rude to the locals by refusing a lift.

Getting there and away

By bus All the buses stop at the bus station behind the Total filling station in the centre of town. Buses to/from Lusaka take about 5½ hours; those to/from Mongu about 2 hours.

Driving

From Kaoma to Lukulu If you're heading west to Lukulu, take the tar road towards Mongu for about 25km, then there's a gravel road on the right, signposted as 195km to Lukulu. After 16km on this road it forks: keep to the right. Later there's a sign heralding a turn to the right, to the M8, which leads to the Watopa pontoon (⊕ FERRY4 14°2.338'S, 23°37.744'E).

Lining this road are small villages, each consisting of thatched huts built in varying sizes. Oxcarts are also a frequent sight, straight out of a biblical scene.

From Kaoma to Kasempa From the Great West Road at Kaoma, there's a reasonable gravel road that heads north and then northeast to Kasempa.

Where to stay and eat There's a choice of small local guesthouses in Kaoma, all of which are fairly clean and may be able to arrange simple meals. The best is the Kaoma Cheshire Orphanage, which assists in raising funds for Zambia's AIDS orphans. There are also several places to eat, drink and chat along the main street, typically serving local dishes such as nshima, chips or rice, with beef, chicken or occasionally fish.

Other practicalities Kaoma has a **post office**, a Finance **Bank**, numerous **shops** (of which the best stocked is Cheap & Best along the main road) and local eateries, and three **fuel** stations: vital to anyone travelling west. The Puma and Engen stations are pretty reliable, but as always, don't run your supplies too low.

KAFUE NATIONAL PARK

(Park fees US$20 pp/day; vehicle US$15/day or K25.50 if Zambian registered; fees payable at Hook Bridge, Dumdumwenze, Kabanga & Musa gates, & at some lodges; ⏲ 06.00–18.00; **e** kafue@africanparks.org; **w** africanparks.org/the-parks/kafue, kafue-nationalpark.com; f kafuenationalparkzambia) Kafue is a huge national park, two-and-a-half times the size of South Luangwa. Sadly, in the 1980s and early '90s, few resources were devoted to its upkeep and anti-poaching efforts were left to a couple of dedicated souls from the few safari lodges that remained in the park.

Now the situation is markedly better. A steady trickle of visitors, supported by improving infrastructure, access to the park and lodge investment, have added weight (and finance) to the on going effort to build the park back up to its former glory. Even the park's elephants are visibly recovering (both in number and in terms of losing some of their shyness), although it will be a while before they return to their former strength. It is very heartening to see that the rest of the game is thriving, and occurring in a volume and variety that bodes well for the future. While the game viewing may not rival that of the South Luangwa or Lower Zambezi, the wilderness experience in the Kafue is greatly heightened when compared to these comparatively busy parks. That said, in Kafue's best areas the game can be very good. In particular, game viewing on and around the Busanga Plains can be stunning, so don't visit the park without at least a side trip into this remarkable area.

In 2022, Kafue's long-term success was enormously enhanced when the Department of National Parks and Wildlife signed a long-term management partnership with African Parks. Aiming to restore the park's vast landscape into a globally significant wildlife sanctuary, with improved community involvement and development, infrastructure initiatives and plans to boost conservation tourism, this is a game-changing venture for the park.

While a number of camps in Kafue have remained low-key, owner-run operations, giving each an individual character, recent years have seen the arrival of some well-known safari operators on to the park's safari scene. Introducing some unusual and luxury offerings into the park, especially at Busanga Plains, their arrival is beneficial both reputationally, financially and in terms of protection for Kafue as a whole.

GEOGRAPHY Established in 1924, the Kafue National Park covers some 22,400km^2 (about the size of Wales, or Massachusetts) of very varied terrain and is one of the world's largest national parks. Naturally, its geography varies considerably. Throughout the park, the permanent Kafue River follows a well-defined course, and widens in a few places where barriers of harder rocks near the surface force it into shallow, rocky rapids – Kafwala and the area beside KaingU Safari Lodge being the obvious examples.

The Hook granite massif provides dramatic granite extrusions that run from the southwest through the park in a north/northeasterly direction. This provides wonderful granite outcrops, the most prominent being Kaindabaila and Mutmbwe Hills.

Bordering the eastern side of southern Kafue is Lake Itezhi-Tezhi – a large, manmade lake that was created in 1977. The primary function of its dam is to regulate the water levels experienced by the Kafue Gorge Hydro-electric Dam, further downstream, although it also generates some electricity.

The map clearly shows that the tarred Great West Road between Lusaka and Mongu bisects the park. This road provides the easiest route into the park, and also a convenient split that allows me to refer to 'northern' and 'southern' Kafue as simply meaning the areas to the north and the south of the road. These have slightly different habitats and species, and also very different access routes. As far as casual visitors are concerned, they could almost be two separate parks.

Surrounding the whole are no fewer than eight game management areas (GMAs), which provide a valuable buffer zone for the park's wildlife.

FLORA AND FAUNA

Flora Most of Kafue is an undulating mosaic of miombo woodlands and dambos, within which you'll find smaller patches of munga woodland, and bands of riparian forest and thickets along the larger rivers.

In the extreme northwest of the park are the permanently wet **Busanga Swamps**, surrounded by adjacent floodplains and now a designated Ramsar site. These are dotted with raised 'tree islands' (a stand of trees rising above an expanse of lower-level vegetation), notable for some mammoth specimens of sycamore figs (*Ficus* *sycomorus*) among other vegetation. The floodplains are ringed by a 'termitaria zone' of grasslands.

Northern Kafue receives slightly more rain than the south, resulting in richer, taller vegetation. In many areas such woodland is dominated by the large-leafed munondo tree (*Julbernardia paniculata*), though you'll also find 'Prince of Wales feathers' (*Brachystegia boehmii*) and the odd mobola plum (*Parinari curatellifolia*).

Southern Kafue is dominated by areas of Kalahari sand, and also has a slightly lower rainfall than the north. Large stretches of Kalahari woodland are the norm here, typified by silver-leaf terminalia (*Terminalia sericea*), poison-pod albizia (*Albizia versicolor*), and *Combretum* species. Within this there are a few patches of mature teak forest – the Ngoma Forest being one of the most spectacular examples – while further south, on patches of alluvial clay, are some beautiful groves of cathedral mopane (*Colophospermum mopane*).

In the far south of the park, the **Nanzhila Plains** are a fascinating area. Wide expanses of grassland are dotted with islands of vegetation and large termitaria – often with baobabs (*Adansonia digitata*) or ebony trees (*Diospyros mespiliformis*) growing out of them.

The flora of the park is heavily affected by yearly burning, which is most apparent between June and October. Some of this burning, particularly early in the year, is part of a management regime by DNPW, but much of it is caused by poachers burning for better visibility, out of control agricultural fires, and general carelessness of people around the park. The debate about the necessity of burning is fierce, with touted benefits including stimulating growth of new grass to attract antelope. However, repeated fires can reduce the variety of plants in the ecosystem, and have a big impact on the aesthetics of the park.

Fauna Covering such a large area, with a variety of habitats, Kafue is rich in wildlife and many of its species seem to exhibit strong local variations in their distribution. This is a reflection of the wide variety of habitats in such a large park.

Antelope Kafue has a superb range of antelope, but you will have to travel throughout the park if you wish to see them all.

The **Busanga Swamps**, in the far north of the park, are permanently flooded and home to the secretive sitatunga, which is uniquely adapted to swamp life. These powerful swimmers will bound off with a series of leaps and plunges when disturbed, aided by their enlarged hooves which have evolved for walking around on floating papyrus islands. They will then stand motionless until the danger passes, or even submerge themselves leaving just their nostrils above the water for breathing.

The **Busanga Plains**, a little further south, is a much larger area that is seasonally inundated. This only starts to dry out around June (it's totally impassable by vehicle until then), when it's possible to visit and see large herds of red lechwe and puku, and a buffalo herd exceeding 1,000 animals. Smaller groups of zebra and blue wildebeest are also found, and though oribi are found throughout the park, they are particularly common here. You also have a good chance of seeing roan and the beautiful sable antelope.

Across the rest of the northern half of the park, there's a good range of mixed bush environments, and here kudu, bushbuck, eland, reedbuck, common duiker, grysbok and defassa waterbuck (a subspecies without the distinctive white ring on the rump) are all frequently seen. Even within this there are local differences; the Kafwala area, for example, is notable for good numbers of Lichtenstein's hartebeest and sable. Numerically, puku dominate most of the northern side of the park, though they gradually cede to impala as you move further south.

On the south side of Kafue, the game has been more patchy. Generally it thrives in areas around lodges, which provide some sanctuary from poaching, but away from these it can be scarce. However, the success of anti-poaching measures, the presence of three lodges in the GMA, and two new lodges on the western side of the river are certainly having an impact, and the game is improving as a result. The area around KaingU Safari Lodge is particularly rich in impala and bushbuck, and the game is fairly relaxed.

The area from Itezhi-Tezhi south to Ngoma has Kafue's densest elephant population, with some groups also frequenting the Chunga area. Large herds tend to congregate on the shoreline in midwinter, with over 500 animals sometimes being seen together, especially around Konkomoya. Currently, it is estimated that there are 3,500 elephants inside Kafue National Park.

In addition, there are three very large herds of buffalo along the western shore of Itezhi-Tezhi, around Chunga, where groups exceed 1,000 individuals, as well as plenty of impala and puku, family groups of Lichtenstein's hartebeest and waterbuck, and numerous bushbuck, warthog and baboons.

South of Ngoma, the picture is improving too. When we first visited in the early 2000s, the game was sparse and skittish. It was interesting that the only really good sightings that we had of large animals were around the Chilenje Pools loop and what is now Nanzhila Plains Safari Camp – so once again the animals were congregating in areas associated with visitors. Now, numbers are increasing, with species ranging from blue wildebeest and eland to roan and sable antelope, as well as waterbuck, kudu and impala.

Large predators **Lions** are Kafue's apex predator and dominate the landscape. They are relatively widespread all over the park, but the larger males are increasingly uncommon, with inevitable consequences for numbers as a whole. They are present in central and southern Kafue, though the highest densities of lion are on the Busanga Plains, where prides – including the so-called Busanga pride, notable for climbing trees – stalk through nervous herds of puku and lechwe nightly, using the natural drainage ditches for cover with deadly efficiency.

Leopard remain very common throughout the main forested areas of the park, though they are seldom seen on the open plains. They are most easily observed on night drives, and continue with their activities completely unperturbed by the presence of a spotlight trained upon them. In particular, Lufupa has long held a reputation for great leopard sightings, although this may have been as a result of a few particularly good guides. Today, there is an excellent leopard population along the Kafue River from Hippo Lodge through to Musekese Camp.

Spotted hyena are seen regularly, though not often, throughout the park. They appear to occur in smaller numbers than either lions or leopards. Cheetah are not common anywhere, but they're most frequently seen in the north of the park, and around the Nanzhila/Konkamoya area to the south. It's certainly the best place in Zambia to look for cheetah.

Wild Dog have done exceptionally well over the last few years, with Kafue National Park now being a feeder population for other parks including Liuwa Plain National Park (page 473). Researchers currently estimate the population to be around 200 strong and spread across 20 to 25 packs. It is a stronghold for the species in Zambia. In 2023, the southern shoreline of Itezhi-Tezhi was home to a pack of over 40 individuals.

Other large animals **Elephants** occur throughout Kafue, though overall their numbers are still recovering from intensive poaching during the 1970s, and their density varies hugely within the park. Just south of Lake Itezhi-Tezhi, around Chunga and, especially, Ngoma, there are large herds and a thriving population – though they're not always relaxed, so drivers there need to be very wary of getting too close to them. South of Ngoma, the situation was much gloomier, although anti-poaching measures have resulted in a resurgence in the elephant population.

On the north side of the park elephant densities are lower than around Ngoma, but they have improved a lot. When I first visited Lufupa in 1995, a few elephants spotted a kilometre from the lodge were a reason for excitement, causing us to leave dinner and jump into a vehicle. Now family groups are commonly seen in the Lufupa and Lunga areas, and are a lot less skittish than they used to be. Visiting in 2015, we saw some very relaxed elephants on the Busanga Plains.

The **buffalo** population is now strong in the park, with good sightings of sizeable herds – up to a thousand strong – from Lake Itezhi-Tezhi's shoreline to Busanga Pains. Sadly, **black rhino** were completely poached out of the park, but with the improved protection that has come with the African Parks' partnership, there are plans to reintroduce black rhino in 2025.

The Kafue River and its larger tributaries like the Lunga are fascinating tropical rivers – full of life and infested with **hippo** and **crocodile**, which occur in numbers to rival the teeming waters of the Luangwa. **Vervet monkeys** and **yellow baboons** (*not* chacma) are common almost everywhere, and you'll usually find **porcupines, mongooses, civets** and a wide variety of small mammals on night drives. One other curious but interesting fact: there seem to be more **pangolins** than aardvarks in North Kafue, which is a very unusual situation indeed!

Birds The birding in Kafue is very good. There have been about 495 species recorded here, suggesting that the park has probably the richest birdlife of any Zambian park. This reflects Kafue's wide range of habitats, because in addition to extensive miombo woodlands (quite a Zambian speciality!), Kafue has plenty of rivers, extensive wetlands and – in the north – seasonal floodplains.

The **wetlands and floodplains** have the full range of herons (including the black heron), large flocks of open-billed storks and ibises, plus crowned and wattled cranes, Denham's (or Stanley's) and kori bustards, secretary birds, and geese (spur-winged and Egyptian) by the thousand. Water birds are exceptionally prominent in the Nanzhila Plains Area.

Kafue has also proven to be a very important refuge habitat for vultures, with connectivity to the greater Kavango–Zambezi Transfrontier Conservation Area (KAZA) system. Vultures often leave the park to feed but roost and breed within the safety of it.

In the long, verdant stretches of **riverine vegetation** you're likely to spot Ross's turaco, Narina trogons, MacClounie's (black-backed) barbet, olive woodpecker, brown-headed apalis and the yellow-throated leaflove. Pel's fishing owl is also found here, with birding expert Bob Stjernstedt noting that there are pairs around Ntemwa, and African finfoot frequent the shady fringes of the slower rivers, swimming under the overhanging trees with part of their body submerged.

Kafue's extensive **miombo woodlands** have endemics such as pale-billed hornbill, miombo pied barbet, grey tit, miombo rock thrush, Sousa's shrike, chestnut-mantled sparrow-weaver, spotted creeper, three species of eremomela and the very rare and localised Chaplin's barbet. In the south, on the Nanzhila Plains, the black-cheeked lovebird – near-endemic to southern Zambia – is relatively common.

HUNTING AND POACHING During the 1980s and early '90s there were few efforts or government resources devoted to protecting Kafue, and poaching was rife. This ensured the extermination of black rhino, and a sharp reduction in elephant numbers at the hands of organised commercial poachers. Fortunately the park is massive, surrounded by GMAs, and not easily accessible. So although the smaller game was hunted for meat, this was not generally on a large enough scale to threaten their populations. Nor did it adversely affect the environment.

Organised commercial poaching is now relatively rare, and the remaining incidence of smaller-scale poaching by locals (for food) is being tackled by a number of initiatives. The DNPW team protecting the park has become much more active in recent years, having received a lot of training and more resources.

Some of these initiatives concentrate on increasing the physical policing of the park, the most obvious being anti-poaching patrols. Historically these have been funded by some of the most enlightened safari operators and lodges, but the 20-year partnership with African Parks (page 476) has significantly enhanced and improved all of these initiatives. African Parks have proven themselves highly effective in Bangweulu Wetlands and Liuwa Plain national parks already, so the future is very positive for Kafue. Significant assistance from NGO Partners, specifically Game Rangers International, Panthera and Musekese Conservation, will now also support African Parks in their long-term protection and development mandate, notably in the GMAs. Together these partners will bolster manpower, equipment, mobility and aerial assets to protect the park, its wildlife and the surrounding buffer zones.

GETTING THERE AND AROUND To get to Kafue, and to get around once there, you have three choices. First, you can fly or bus in and stay at one of the better camps or lodges – and the team from the camp will walk, drive and boat you around their area of the park. Second, you can drive yourself into and around the park in a 4x4. Or third, you can arrange for a company from outside to drive you in, and around the park.

By air or scheduled transfer This is certainly the most relaxing way to get to the park, especially if your time is relatively limited, or you like the idea of a holiday here rather than an expedition. There are various airstrips dotted around the park and some are in good repair. There are no scheduled flights into the park – although African Parks are working on introducing one in late 2023 – but several charter companies in Lusaka will fly you in or out on request and Wilderness Safaris usually transport their guests by air.

ProCharter m 0974 250110; e reservations@procharterzambia.com; w procharterzambia.com. Zambia's largest charter operator with 11 aircraft & bases in both Lusaka & Livingstone.

Sky Trails ☎ 0967 867848; e reservations@skytrailszambia.com; w skytrailszambia.com. Excellent, professional charter company operating between all of Zambia's national parks, Livingstone & Lusaka. Helicopter charters also available, & certified carbon neutral status.

United Air Charters ☎ 0213 323095; m reservations@uaczam.com; w uaczam.com. Offering helicopter & Cessna flights within Zambia.

Wilderness Safaris ☎ +27 21 702 7500; e enquiry@wilderness.co.za; w wildernessdestinations.com. Compared to Namibia & South Africa, Wilderness has a much smaller presence in Zambia, mostly confined to northern Kafue, although they do also own Toka Leya (page 195) in Livingstone. Wilderness deals only with agents, so reservations for their lodges should be made through a tour operator (page 92).

Driving If you want to drive within the park, then think of it as an expedition. You will need a 4x4 vehicle with good ground clearance, spare tyre, and enough fuel for your planned trip (bearing in mind that the fuel supplies in the towns surrounding Kafue can be unreliable). Cell phone coverage is limited across the park so taking a satellite phone for emergencies is advisable, but even so if you have problems, you must be able to solve them yourself, as you can expect little help. Although there are many camps listed in the sections below, only a handful would be able to offer aid in an emergency.

However, if you come well equipped then the park is wonderful. Several operators – especially in the east and south of the park – also have excellent campsites. If you do come, then you can be assured of seeing very few other vehicles during your stay in this stunning area.

Arrive with the best maps of the place you can find, and use them in conjunction with those in this book. We also recommend the Tracks4Africa app and a GPS – you will need one. Note that the speed limit within the body of the park is 40km/h – though in reality you'd often be hard pressed to come even close to that.

For those just bisecting the northern and southern areas along the tarred Lusaka–Mongu road, there's no need for a 4x4. However, aside from the obvious danger of colliding with an animal in this area, there are several speed bumps and these – together with the odd pot-hole – mean that sticking to the 80km/h limit is essential.

As a much cheaper, but considerably less convenient and comfortable option, you can easily catch a bus from Lusaka to Kafue. The buses depart between 09.30 and 13.30, with the safest and most reliable buses being run by Shalom and Juldan. You will need to purchase a fare to Koama (K120), but let the driver know to drop you off at Hook Bridge, which should take approximately 3 hours from Lusaka. The camps in the central area, the southern half of the park down to KaingU, and Musekese can all pick you up from Hook Bridge (you will need to arrange a time with them in advance); these transfers take a few hours on graded bush roads. You can also get on the buses from the Hook Bridge area, but it's best to purchase a ticket as you get on the bus rather than buying a return ticket in advance.

Mobile operators in Kafue Owing to its proximity to Livingstone, several safari operators and overlanders run mobile trips into Kafue. However, without a long-term presence in the park, they don't know the ground as well as the established camps. They seldom have the logistical support to solve their own problems and contribute little to the vital work of preserving the area.

If you want to get the very best from a trip to the park, and to effectively contribute to the work to preserve the area, we recommend you support the area's permanent operators. Although not mobile, many of the operators here have camps in different areas of the park to allow visitors to transfer between camps and experience the range of habitats and wildlife in Kafue. For something less plush and lodge-like, experienced local operator Classic Zambia Safaris (**m** 0974 173403; **e** info@classiczambiasafaris.com; **w** classiczambiasafaris.com) operate a very simple camp on Busanga Plains, Ntemwa Busanga, which offers good guiding with a light footprint and very much a low-key bushcamp experience, similar in vibe to mobile trips, which can be combined with their camp, Musekese.

NORTHERN KAFUE The northern section of the park is a slightly undulating plateau, veined by rivers – the Lufupa, the Lunga, the Ntemwa, the Mukombo, the Mukunashi, and the Lubuji – which are all tributaries of the main Kafue, whose basin extends to the border with DRC.

The main Kafue River is already mature by the time it reaches the park, though it has over 400km further to flow before discharging into the Zambezi. Thus within the park its permanent waters are wide, deep and slow-flowing, to the obvious pleasure of large numbers of hippo and crocodile. Tall, shady hardwoods overhang its gently curving banks, and the occasional islands in the stream are favourite feeding places for elephant and buffalo. In short, it is a typically beautiful, large African river.

Occasionally it changes, as at Kafwala. Here, there is a stretch of gentle rapids for about 7km. The river is up to about 1,000m wide and dotted with numerous islands, all supporting dense riverine vegetation – making a particularly good spot for birdwatching.

Most of the park's northern section, between the rivers, is a mosaic of miombo and mopane woodlands, with occasional open grassy pans known as dambos. The edges of the main rivers are lined with tall hardwood trees. Raintrees (*Lonchocarpus capassa*), knobthorns (*Acacia nigrescens*), jackalberries (*Diospyros mespiliformis*), leadwoods (*Combretum imberbe*), and especially sausage trees (*Kigelia africana*) are all very common.

The Kafue's tributaries are smaller, but the larger of these are still wide and permanent. The Lufupa is probably the most important. It enters the park from the Kasonso-Busanga GMA in the north, and immediately feeds into a permanent wetland in the far north of the park: the Busanga Swamps. In the wet season these waters flood out over a much larger area, across the whole Busanga Plains, before finally draining back into the river, which then continues its journey on the south side of the plains.

The swamp and seasonal floodplain together cover about 750km^2, and are a superb area for game. The seasonal floodwaters on the plains are shallow, but enough to sustain a healthy growth of grasses throughout the year on the mineral-rich black-cotton soil. These open plains are dotted with numerous small 'islands' of wild date palms (*Phoenix reclinata*), and wild fig trees (various *Ficus* species).

The area is perfect for huge herds of water-loving lechwe and puku, which are joined by large numbers of zebra, wildebeest and other plains grazers as the waters recede at the end of the wet season. However, the Busanga Plains are very remote, and normally impossible to reach by vehicle until about July. Until relatively recently, few people (even in the safari industry) had heard about them, let alone visited them, but now this remarkable area is firmly on the map.

4x4 routes within and around northern Kafue You really need a high-clearance 4x4 for any of the routes within the park. Despite that, you'll have problems on all of them during the rains, and anything close to the Busanga Plains is impassable between about November and July.

From the north via the Kabanga gate The Kabanga gate (⊕ KABANG 14°5.808'S, 26°7.036'E) is the park's most northerly entrance point, affording access for those coming from Kasempa and the Copperbelt. For directions to the gate, see page 411.

From the gate, the clear, largely sandy track that proceeds southwards into the park is considerably better than the approach road to the gate from Kasempa. The track keeps east of the Ntemwa River, passing the site of the old Moshi Camp (⊕ MOSHI 14°24.348'S, 26°09.474'E), until – after almost 39km, or roughly three-quarters of an hour's drive – it reaches a couple of bridges at the confluence of the Ntemwa and Lufupa rivers (⊕ BRIDG1 14°24.687'S, 26°09.180'E).

From here, the road continues south towards Lufupa, Kafwala and the Hook Bridge.

NORTHERN KAFUE

For listings, see from page 424, unless otherwise stated

Where to stay

1 Busanga Bush Camp
2 Chisa Busanga
3 Hippo Lodge
4 Kafue River Lodge
5 Kafwala Camp
6 Kasonso Busanga Camp
7 Lufupa River Camp
8 Lufupa Tented Camp
9 Lunga Kikuji Camp
10 Mayukuyuku Bush Camp
11 McBrides' Camp
12 Mukambi Plains Camp
13 Mukambi Safari Lodge *p439*
14 Musanza Tented Camp
15 Musekese Camp
16 Ntemwa-Busanga Camp
17 Shumba Camp

To the Busanga Plains Just south of the second of these bridges there used to be a turning west towards Treetops and the Busanga Plains, but despite the signpost this is now completely impassable. If you're heading for Busanga, continue south for a further 2.5km, where there's a sharp turn to the right (⊕ TUBUSA 14°25.806'S, 26°08.967'E). Note, however, that the signpost (to Treetops) is visible only if you're coming from the south. From this junction, it's a further 50km northwest to Shumba on the Busanga Plains. During the dry season, it's a relatively good track, despite the inevitable bumps, pot-holes and sand patches. Due to yearly flooding, the roads on the plains themselves are rather ephemeral, so if you are planning on driving to the camps up here it's best to contact them individually (page 424) for up-to-date directions in advance.

From the south: Lusaka–Mongu road The last fuel stations you'll find before you reach the park are at Mumbwa (coming from Lusaka) or Kaoma (if you're coming from Mongu). Either way, if you are driving north into the park from here, to Lufupa or the Busanga Plains, simply turn north off the main road at the Hook Bridge gate beside the Kafue's west bank, just west of the Hook Bridge itself (⊕ HOOKBR 14°56.477'S, 25°54.384'E). From here the track (⊕ KAFTUR 14°46.126'S, 26°4.393'E) heads northeast through the heart of the park for about 44km, where a right turn leads east to Kafwala Camp. Continuing roughly northeast for about a further 26km will lead you to Lufupa (⊕ LUFUPA 14°37.080'S, 26°11.626'E). In the dry season it's basically a good track, fine for a 2WD with high clearance, though designed more for game viewing than speed. In the wet it is impassable due to the toffee-like consistency of the black-cotton soil.

This track is the main vehicular artery through northern Kafue, and continues north over the Lufupa and Ntemwa rivers to the Kabanga gate (⊕ KABANG 14°5.808'S, 26°7.036'E). About 82km from the Hook Bridge, you'll pass a clear turning to the left (⊕ TUBUSA 14°25.806'S, 26°08.967'E) signposted to Treetops and leading to the Busanga Plains. For details of this route, see above.

From the M9 Lusaka–Mongu road to the Lubungu pontoon See page 413 for more details of this route around the northeast side of the park.

North from the Lubungu pontoon to the Lunga pontoon Once dubbed the 'road of death' by one very experienced old hand, this 75km stretch of road has been transformed into a good, graded road that makes for pleasant, relatively straightforward driving. That said, it remains quite narrow, and fallen trees can be a hazard, while pot-holes could well materialise in the rainy season.

Starting at the Lubungu pontoon (⊕ LUBUNG 14°33.750'S, 26°27.250'E), it's about 3.5km north to the right turning (⊕ TULEOP 14°32.426'S, 26°28.597'E)

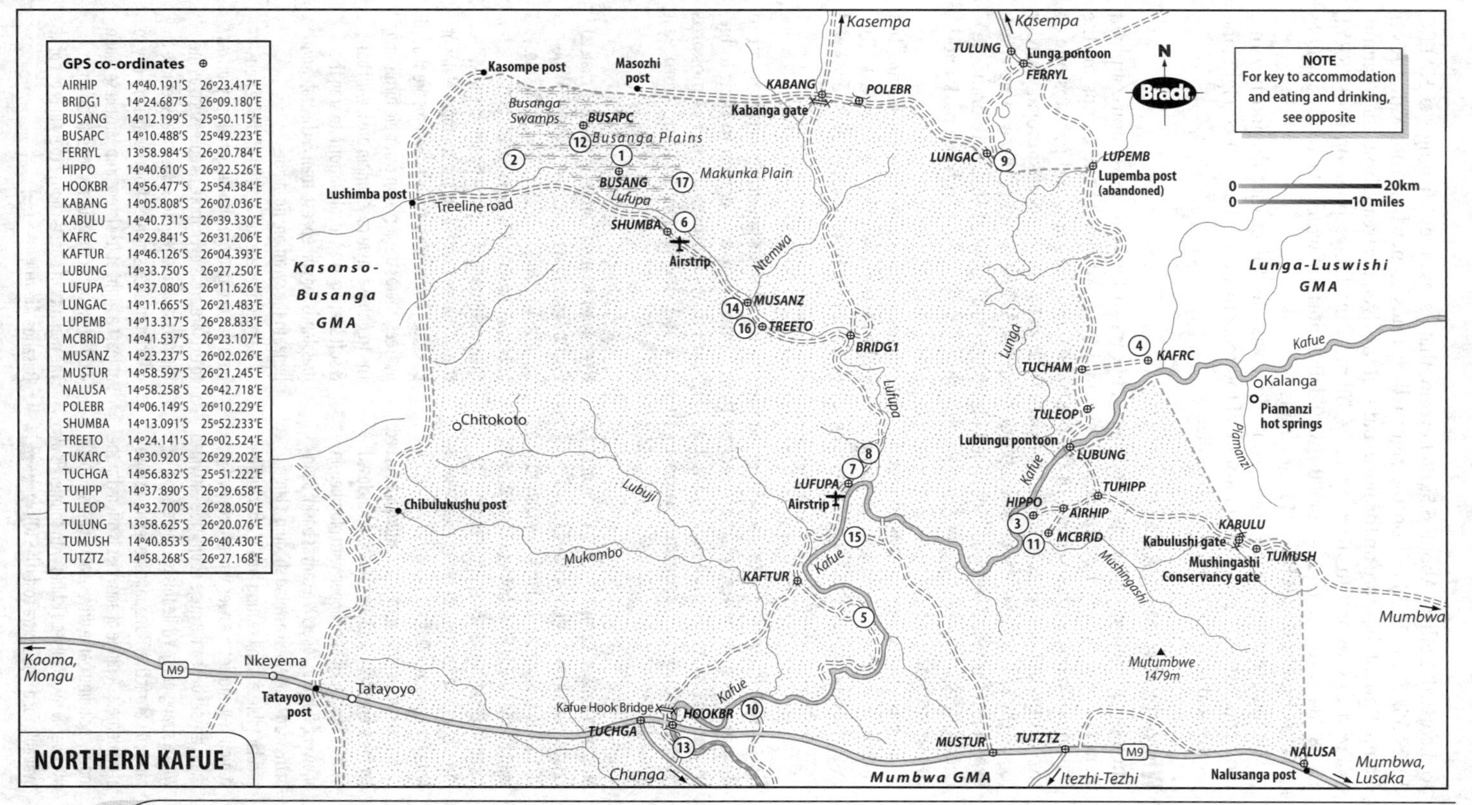

GPS co-ordinates ⊕

AIRHIP	14º40.191'S	26º23.417'E
BRIDG1	14º24.687'S	26º09.180'E
BUSANG	14º12.199'S	25º50.115'E
BUSAPC	14º10.488'S	25º49.223'E
FERRYL	13º58.984'S	26º20.784'E
HIPPO	14º40.610'S	26º22.526'E
HOOKBR	14º56.477'S	25º54.384'E
KABANG	14º05.808'S	26º07.036'E
KABULU	14º40.731'S	26º39.330'E
KAFRC	14º29.841'S	26º31.206'E
KAFTUR	14º46.126'S	26º04.393'E
LUBUNG	14º33.750'S	26º27.250'E
LUFUPA	14º37.080'S	26º11.626'E
LUNGAC	14º11.665'S	26º21.483'E
LUPEMB	14º13.317'S	26º28.833'E
MCBRID	14º41.537'S	26º23.107'E
MUSANZ	14º23.237'S	26º02.026'E
MUSTUR	14º58.597'S	26º21.245'E
NALUSA	14º58.258'S	26º42.718'E
POLEBR	14º06.149'S	26º10.229'E
SHUMBA	14º13.091'S	25º52.233'E
TREETO	14º24.141'S	26º02.524'E
TUKARC	14º30.920'S	26º29.202'E
TUCHGA	14º56.832'S	25º51.222'E
TUHIPP	14º37.890'S	26º29.658'E
TULEOP	14º32.700'S	26º28.050'E
TULUNG	13º58.625'S	26º20.076'E
TUMUSH	14º40.853'S	26º40.430'E
TUTZTZ	14º58.268'S	26º27.168'E

to Leopard Lodge. About 6.5km beyond that is another turning (⊕ KAFRC 14°29.367'S, 26°28.583'E) on the right which leads to newly rebuilt Kafue River Camp. Both of these are on the north bank of the river, upstream from the pontoon.

From this second turning, it's some 70km to the Lunga pontoon (⊕ FERRYL 13°58.984'S, 26°20.784'E; ⏲ 06.00–18.00 daily), north of which the road continues as far as Kasempa (see page 411 for details).

As you cross on the pontoon, you might wish to reflect that the journey that took you just a couple of hours would all too recently have taken at least eight, and required at least two very sturdy vehicles.

Where to stay *Map, page 423*

Though the range of camps listed here appears to be long, most non-Zambian visitors are probably best to choose a combination of one of the camps on the Busanga Plains, with a second in the central area of the park, and perhaps one or two camps in the southern half of the park such as KaingU or Konkamoya, in order to see the changing scenery throughout the park. While many of these camps have been here for years, several have been completely rebuilt and some are brand new. Each offers a different experience, yet all are closely involved with the park and its conservation.

You are not allowed to wild camp – that is just camp anywhere – in Kafue, but camping is easily arranged at camps throughout the majority of the park. The exception is on the Busanga Plains where there are no campsites and no lodges will permit you to camp on site.

Busanga Plains Guests at lodges on the Busanga Plains generally arrive by air to Busanga airstrip, where they are met by their camp guide and driven to their lodge. In wetter years this final part of the transfer sometimes requires the use of mokoros (dugout canoes). Accommodation in this area is listed largely heading from east to west.

Musanza Tented Camp (9 tents) Wilderness Safaris, page 419. ⊕ MUSANZ 14°23.237'S, 26°02.026'E. Musanza sits in a lovely leafy spot right on the Lufupa River, beloved of kingfishers, paradise flycatchers & the resident hippos. The camp is reserved for groups on set tours with the American operator OAT.

Green canvas tents with coir matting & twin beds set the scene, with outdoor bathrooms enclosed by thatching grass & equipped with plumbed-in showers, flushing toilets & a canvas basin. Sand paths lead to a tented awning shading a large circular table, a small seating area & a bar/coffee station. Beyond lies the river, where directors' chairs are set beneath a huge ebony tree entwined with a strangler fig. While this is a more basic camp, it's attractive, & manages to retain a sense of wilderness. A range of activities is offered at the lodge, including game drives, safari walks across the river, & river cruises. Fishing with spinners is also available for a small extra cost (US$10). ♛♛♛

Ntemwa-Busanga Camp (4 thatched chalets) Classic Zambia Safaris, page 420. ⊕ NTEMWA-BUSANGA 14°20'17.5"S 25°58'56.6"E. The most affordable camp in this region of the park, Ntemwa-Busanga has just 4 traditional, reed-&-thatch chalets overlooking the southern plains of Busanga. Open-air en-suite bathrooms are shaded by trees, there's a solar lamp & simple furnishings. The treehouse-style raised main area, with bar & soft seating, is an ideal platform to scan the grasslands for wildebeest, roan & cheetah from beneath the sycamore fig shade.

Game drives are the activity of choice here, both day & night, but also longer 'all-day' drives to explore areas even more remote, such as the Papyrus swamps. Ntemwa-Busanga is remote & difficult to access by road from Lusaka in 1 day so at least a night at its sister camp Musekese (page 427) helps break the journey for self-drivers. The majority of guests choose to fly in & out of Busanga Airstrip.

US$650 pp sharing/sgl FBA, inc local drinks, park fees, laundry; exc transfers. ⌚ *Jul–Oct.* 👑👑👑

Shumba Camp (6 tented chalets) Wilderness Safaris, page 419. ⊕ SHUMBA 14°13.091'S, 25°52.233'E. Set in the middle of the plains on an 'island' of large fig trees, some 15–20 mins' drive south of the permanent swamps, Shumba is 1 of the smartest camps in northern Kafue.

The camp is arranged in a wide semi-circle, with both its wide, rectangular chalets & the tiered main area looking out over the plains' panorama. The contemporary chalets are constructed from canvas walls & full-height gauze panels topped with a mop of golden thatch. The larger family room also has a set of large glazed sliding doors. Inside, all is space & light, the wooden floors offset by white linen & neutral décor. As well as twin 4-poster beds enveloped in white mosquito netting, there's a sofa or armchairs, a writing desk & ample storage space with a safe – not to mention a sherry decanter & glasses. The bathroom area, with twin basins, shower & separate toilet, leads through to an outdoor shower. Solar panels heat the water & there's 24hr electricity. Running the length of each chalet is a split-level wooden deck with a table & chairs, & cushioned seating. All wooden decks & walkways are raised some 2m off the ground, making the camp relatively safe for older children & providing some interesting wildlife viewing opportunities too: serval cats in particular seem to favour the longer grass around the camp.

Central to Shumba's main area is an open bar fronted by high stools, around which several 'rooms' are kitted out with comfy seating & a long dining table. There's also a small shop stocking safari clothes & a few curios. Large glass panels mostly surround the whole area to offer protection from the wind that whistles across the plains, without obstructing the panoramic view. Outside, an extensive split-level deck incorporates a sunken outdoor eating area with a fire & a small infinity pool. Meals can be taken as a group or at individual tables – the food is very good & there's an impressive selection of drinks on offer.

Activities revolve around day & night game drives, & boat trips (May–Sep, water permitting). Guests who stay at least 3 nights are treated to a hot-air balloon flight, offering a wholly different perspective on the plains & the animals that make it home. *US$1,353 pp sharing/sgl FBA, inc local drinks, park fees, laundry, exc transfers. No children under 8.* ⌚ *Jun–Oct.* 👑👑👑👑

Busanga Bush Camp (4 tents) Wilderness Safaris, page 419. ⊕ BUSANG 14°12.199'S, 25°50.115'E. This deceptively simple camp is on a small tree island in the middle of the plains, & offers a more rustic, low-key alternative to its sister camp Shumba, just a short distance away. The camp lacks the elevated walkways of Shumba, with sand paths winding around giant sycamore figs & palm trees connecting the rooms & the main area instead. As such it feels more like a traditional safari bushcamp tucked into its natural surroundings.

Accommodation is in walk-in tents on polished concrete floors, each with comfortable twin beds, a wooden storage trunk & a writer's desk also furnish the room, which is lit with solar-power lights. A shaded wooden deck extends from the front of the tent with a couple of directors' chairs & a hammock. Curtains separate the bedroom from an en-suite hot shower & flush toilet, plus a dressing area. It's well equipped, but not luxurious.

An open-sided main area is shaded by a canvas roof, which covers comfortable leather & wicker furniture, a reasonably stocked bar, & several wooden tables where lunch is served, allowing you to eat while looking over the plains. Evening meals are usually served in a boma nearby, where an impressive chandelier made from storm lanterns is suspended from the overhanging trees. An isolated wooden deck, a short walk from the main area, faces east, so is a great spot to have a morning coffee & watch the sun rise, or watch herds of antelope in the afternoon.

Activities offered from the camp are game drives, boat trips during wetter years, & balloon flights for guests staying at least 3 nights. *US$1,100 pp sharing/sgl FBA, inc local drinks, laundry, park fee, exc transfers.* ⌚ *Jun–Oct.* 👑👑👑

Chisa Busanga (4 rooms) Green Safaris (page 292) **w** greensafaris.com; ⊕ CHISA 14°12.203"S; 25°48.130"E. Chisa has a terrific location on a fig-tree island, overlooking the expansive floodplains & dambo close to the centre of the Busanga Plains. Opened in 2021, it makes a safari design statement unlike any other Kafue camp. The camp itself is small, smart & innovative – both in its architecture & activity options. Luxurious woven pods built to resemble giant weaver birds' nests replace traditional safari tents here, electric vehicles &

mountain bikes offer 'silent safaris' & the whole camp is solar powered.

A gorgeous, ivory tented main area houses a comfortable lounge, with fishing basket lanterns & deep cushioned sofas, a wooden table for shared meals, & a well-stocked drinks' dresser. Long views across the plains, a campfire circle in the sand & a welcoming plunge pool make this a lovely spot to hang out in camp, but it's the unique accommodation that really marks Chisa apart.

On the edge of the treeline, its four treehouse 'nests' stand on tall stilts. A touch space-age, they are deeply rooted in the local birdlife & refined basketry of the local community. The intimate open-fronted rooms are comfortable & quirky, filled with creature comforts & benefitting from terrific views. From super power showers to traditional pulleys drawing up your daybreak coffee, the rooms have an array of modern conveniences & a good dose of fun. 1 tent, located closer to the main area, has a lift, making it better suited for those with limited mobility.

For all that Chisa has carefully curated in the best of modern eco-technology & original design, it has not lost sight of the essence of great safaris: super guiding in a prime wilderness area. Guides are experienced & activities range from game drives to walking safaris & e-mountain biking. In line with Green Safaris' environmentally conscious ethos, Chisa's 4x4 game-drive vehicles are electric, allowing for an almost 'silent safari' experience. This makes for great guide interaction on the move & is particularly good for photographers as animals, & especially birds, are minimally disturbed, allowing you to get especially close to the wildlife.

Time at Chisa combines well with one or both of its sister camps, Ila Safari Lodge, located towards the centre of the Kafue, or Shawa Camp in the South Luangwa National Park, especially if, like us, you're hooked on safari by electric vehicles.

US$790 pp Jun & Nov, US$980 pp sharing Jul–Oct, all FBA inc transfers, laundry, local drink, park fees & conservation levies. ♛♛♛

Kasonso Busanga Camp (4 chalets) **m** 0978 016191; **e** res@kafueriverlodge.com; **w** northernkafuesafaris.com. KASONS 14°17.340"S 25°53.490"E. Part of Northern Kafue Safari's trio of camps in the park (Kafue River Lodge & Kikuji being the others), Kasonso is run by an experienced local team, with a super birding guide. Raised on a wooden deck, its low-key central area serves as a dining, lounge & bar area, with picture windows & a panoramic view across the plains from its terrace. To the rear sits a pole-edged campfire boma, & its 4, well-spaced tents run along the edge of the plains. Accessed along crazy-paving paths & raised on concrete platforms, the golden thatched rooms are formed of low-level green canvas, topped with mesh picture-windows offering a cooling breeze & great views. Stone-tiled flooring, neat pole ceilings & crisp white linen on the beds make for pleasant, practical rooms in a clean, simple style. There are en-suite bathrooms to the back & a small terrace with a couple of wicker armchairs. *US$272 pp sharing FB inc 1 daily activity, laundry, local drinks, park fees & conservation levies, exc transfers. Additional activities US$50 pp. Children 12+.* ◷ *Jul–mid-Nov.* ♛♛

✷ **Mukambi Plains Camp** (4 tents) Contact via Mukambi, page 439. ⊕ BUSAPC 14°10.488'S, 25°49.223'E. This intimate tented camp is also known as Busanga Plains Camp, & is not to be confused with Busanga Bush Camp. It lies on the eastern side of the Lufupa River & is the northernmost camp in the park, relatively close to the permanent papyrus swamps at the northern end of the plains, making this one of the best camps to spot the incredibly shy sitatunga antelope. To reach the camp itself you must cross a wooden walkway over a plain of floating grass, before finding the camp hidden among wild date palms on a photogenic tree island. It's a relaxed, welcoming place, a shady oasis with its main living area set beneath an extensive mobola tree (*Parinari curatellifolia*) overlooking the plains. Here, red lechwe are in their element & regularly seen from the open deck.

The 4 tented rooms are scattered around the island, hidden behind fig trees & fan palms, & feel incredibly private. The rooms aren't overly large, but they can comfortably accommodate twin or dbl beds, a couple of bedside tables & a small canvas wardrobe. The front of the tents can be rolled up to provide views of the plains, & there are also a couple of wooden chairs under a canopy at the front. Bathrooms are surrounded by reed & canvas screens, but are otherwise completely open & are just a couple of steps from the tents. Each is equipped with flush toilets, basins & bucket showers. There is solar lighting in the rooms, while paraffin storm lanterns along the paths & in the main area lend the camp a back-to-nature-feel.

With no more than 8 guests at a time, activities can be flexible – with both game drives & walks around Kapinga Island an option. Mukambi Plains Camp combines well with either of its sister camps, Mukambi Safari Lodge or Fig Tree, both just south of the Lusaka–Mongu road. The camps can arrange transfers either along the eastern boundary road (approx 4hrs), or the more scenic but slightly longer road through the park (approx 6hrs). *US$825/1,073 pp sharing/sgl FBA, inc drinks, inter-camp transfers, laundry.* ⌚ *15 Jul–Oct.* ♛♛♛♛

Centre of the park and northeast Access to this area of the park is simplest from the Hook Bridge gate: simply turn north from the Great West Road to the west of the bridge, then follow the road north. Camps are listed here from south to north, with road distances given from the gate.

Mayukuyuku Bush Camp For details of this camp, which lies in the northern Kafue but within easy reach of the main Lusaka–Mongu road, see page 438. ♛♛♛

Kafwala Camp (2 chalets, 2 rondavels) **e** wescz@coppernet.zm; **w** conservationzambia.org. ⊕ KAFWAL 14°48.090'S, 26°11.177'E. This camp is built on the bank of the Kafue River in a stunning location, about 700m below the start of the Kafwala Rapids. To get there, follow the road through the park northeast for about 44km, then take the right turn to Kafwala.

The camp is only open to WECSZ members (page 98), so if you're thinking of staying here then join the society: it does a lot of good & is deserving of more support. As the camp is popular among society members it would need to be booked reasonably well in advance. Accommodation comprises 2 simple 3-bed chalets that are linked by a walkway with 2 more beds, & 2 rondavels, 1 with a dbl bed, & 1 twin. Toilets, shower & bathroom are communal, as are the lounge, dining & BBQ area. Deep freezes, fridges, lamps, crockery, cutlery & bedding are provided – but you must bring all your own food & drink. In addition, you'll need a decent torch. The staff will also service the rooms, do the washing, & help with anything else that is reasonable. (You should tip them at the end of your stay.)

The area around camp is good for birdlife, & there are some productive game loops, & if you bring your own tackle, fishing from boats on the river is possible. However, guided activities from camp are limited. *US$300 up to 12 guests.* ⌚ *Jun–Oct.* **$**

✷ **Musekese Camp** (5 tents) Classic Zambia Safaris, page 420. ⊕ MUSEKE 14°39'14.4"S, 26°09'13.3"E. A small, intimate camp, Musekese is isolated in its own section of northern Kafue & is one of the few camps on the eastern side of the Kafue in this area of the park. To drive here, continue along the M9 from Mumbwa until you reach a lay-by 10.5km from the Itezhi–Tezhi road (⊕ MUSTUR 14°58.597.S, 26°21.245'E). Drive north along the winding dirt road, keeping left at the fork at 40km, & taking a sharp left after another 3.2km. Continue for 5km before turning right at a T-junction, & follow the track to camp. From the M9 the drive to camp should take around 2hrs. To fly in you can land at Lufupa airstrip, followed by a 25-min boat transfer & 10-min drive to camp.

The camp takes its name from the local Kaonde name for the monkey bread tree, which is particularly common in the area. Run by owners Phil Jeffery & Tyrone McKeith, both of whom have been visiting & working in the park since they were teenagers, Musekese has a personal, characterful atmosphere, where excellent guiding skills & a genuine passion for the conservation of the area & its wildlife shines though.

The camp itself is small. There are just 5 new, canvas tents, each with an open-air bathroom, equipped with a flush toilet, enamel sinks & hot-water showers, & surrounded by neat reed screens. The welcoming main area is open-sided & shaded by canvas, with a small lounge, reference library, bar & a sandy firepit nearby. All of this overlooks a large, seasonal lagoon that attracts large amounts of birdlife & game, allowing for some excellent wildlife viewing from camp.

A variety of activities are on offer, from some lovely walking in this remote area to rewarding day & night game drives. With a team of both highly qualified & trainee guides, there's a good deal of flexibility. This is one of the few areas with little-to-no burning, so the scenery is beautiful, with large swathes of tall golden grass. Boat trips are on offer too, along both the Kafue & Lufupa rivers, allowing for views of an island breeding colony of African skimmers & swimming elephants in the hotter months. Fishing is possible but this is a true safari camp & that is the emphasis here. The camp is some 60km from the Busanga Plains area so you could consider combining Musekese with its sister camp, Ntemwa-Busanga (page 424) on the southern reaches of the plains to get a feel for Kafue's diversity.

As with all of the Classic Zambia camps, a proportion of company profits go towards Musekese Conservation (**w** musekeseconservation.com), the camp's conservation fund, supporting environmental protection, wildlife research & community engagement within Kafue.

US$600 pp sharing May–Jun & Nov, US$800 pp sharing Jul–Oct, all FBA, inc local drinks, park fees, laundry; inter-camp transfers. ⌚ *May–Dec.* ♛♛♛

Lufupa River Camp (9 tents) Wilderness Safaris, page 419. ⊕ LUFUPA 14°37.080'S, 26°11.626'E. Overlooking the confluence of the Lufupa & Kafue rivers, Lufupa River Camp is in an isolated area of miombo woodland with good wildlife, about halfway between the main road & the Busanga Plains. Since 2011, like Musanza (page 424), the camp has been reserved for groups travelling with OAT, who fly guests into the airstrip only a few km from camp. There is currently no way to book this camp on an individual basis.

Accommodation is in spacious safari tents that face the Kafue River, each with en-suite shower, toilet & washbasin. Meals are served in the central dining area & there's a comfortable bar where you can always help yourself to tea & coffee. There is also a swimming pool, disappointingly set behind the camp without views of the river. The atmosphere is friendly, casual & very unpretentious. Most activities from the camp are game drives & boat trips, though walks can be organised on request. ♛♛♛

Lufupa Tented Camp (9 tents) Wilderness Safaris, page 419. ⊕ LUFUTC 14°36.832'S, 26°11.285'E. Located right next door to Lufupa River Camp, Lufupa Tented Camp is similar in design, with identical rooms, but a slightly more exclusive air. However, like its neighbour & Musanza to the north, it is also reserved for groups on set tours. ♛♛♛

Lunga Kikuji Camp (4 tents) **m** 0978 016191; **e** res@kafueriverlodge.com; **w** northernkafuesafaris.com; ⊕ KIKUJI 14°32.913'S 26°37.795'E. Kikuji, as it's known, is raised on the high banks of the Lunga River & is the newest of Northern Kafue Safari's trio of camps – Kafue River Lodge (page 430) & Kasonso Busanga (page 426) completing the group. It's an intimate bushcamp with only 4 thatched, en-suite rooms spread along the riverine forest, each with a private, cantilevered deck over the water – perfect for catching glimpses of iridescent kingfishers – & simple but comfortable interiors. As with Kasonso, there are large, gauze picture-windows affording great views of passing wildlife & a welcome breeze. An array of activities is on offer, from game drives & walks to peaceful boat cruises (we've seen both lions & elephants swimming across the river in this area), though perhaps the camp is suited best to keen anglers – the bream fishing is superb – & birdwatchers, who will enjoy the solitude & wilderness. The wildlife in this area is far less habituated that in more established areas of Kafue so expect animals to be more shy & skittish, however, it's fair to say that this is improving year-on-year. *From US$360 pp sharing FBA, inc local drinks, laundry, park fees & conservation levies, exc transfers. Children all ages.* ⌚ *Mar–Dec.* ♛♛♛

The Lubungu pontoon area Of the lodges and camps in this area, two – Hippo Lodge and McBrides' – are south of the pontoon, near the old Hippo Mine, and most of the others just to the north, outside the park boundary.

Getting to Hippo and McBrides' From the main road between Mumbwa and Kasempa, about 10km south of the Lubungu pontoon, take the fork to the west (⊕ TUHIPP 14°37.866'S, 26°29.659'E). Although this is clearly signposted from the south, it's easy to miss if you're coming from the north. For Hippo Lodge, follow this road, passing through a gate (⊕ MINEGT 14°39.169'S, 26°25.025'E) after 5km, and later turning left at the remains of the whitewashed buildings of the old Hippo

HIPPO MINE

Zambia's first commercial copper mine was discovered in 1903 by Jacob Elliott – though how he got here, in an area infested with tsetse flies and therefore inaccessible on horseback, remains a mystery. Elliott died only a couple of years later, killed by a hippo, it is said – hence the name of the mine. His grave at the site is marked by a marble gravestone.

Operations at the mine itself commenced in 1911, and it remained active until 1971. The mine acts as an interesting monument to Zambia's mining history, although all that's left is old machinery, rusting vehicles, and the ruins of the white buildings that marked the entrance to the mine on the track leading to Hippo Lodge (⊕ HIPMIN 14°39.169.S, 26°25.025'E), which can arrange visits.

Mine (⊕ HIPMIN 14°39.169.S, 26°25.025'E; see opposite). Continue for a further 4km to the airstrip (⊕ AIRHIP 14°40.191'S, 26°23.417'E). From here, it's barely 2km to Hippo Lodge (⊕ HIPPO 14°40.610'S, 26°22.526'E) – or 3km to McBrides'.

For the more direct route to McBrides', take the same fork off the main road, but after 4.5km turn left (⊕ TUMCBR 14°39.158'S, 26°27.871'E), as signposted. Follow the yellow arrows both here and after a further 5.2km (⊕ T2MCBR 14°41.512'S, 26°26.775'E), then continue for another 7km or so until you reach the camp (⊕ MCBRID 14°41.537'S, 26°23.107'E).

Hippo Lodge (6 cottages, 2 tents) **m** 0972 080115; **e** hippolodgeinfo@gmail.com; **w** hippolodge.com. ⊕ HIPPO 14°40.610'S, 26°22.526'E. This well-established lodge is located along a tranquil stretch of the Kafue River, and while it started as more of a traditional, basic bushcamp, it has grown over the years into a more substantial lodge. Hippo airstrip is less than 2km away from the lodge, making flying in on a chartered flight a very easy option, but the lodge also caters well to self-drives. Access directions for the more adventurous are above.

Quirky stone-&-thatch cottages are scattered along the riverbank, & have large unconventional baths & en-suite showers & toilets, yet each is different. Nestled between large riverine trees are 3 dbl chalets with A-frame designs, 2 of which have good views of the river, while a more conventional family chalet has a lower roof & both dbl & twin rooms. The largest, Stony House, comes with a dbl room, a twin loft room, & a spacious kitchen/living area with bunk beds. 2 of the houses are fully set up for self-catering with the added benefit of a staff member to assist guests with cleaning, cooking & laundry. Set slightly back from the river, simpler are twin-bedded safari tents under thatch, each with a small veranda &, at the back, a large stone-walled bathroom that's partially open to the sky. The main lounge/dining area overlooks the river, with a separate bar to one side, & is the focus for leisurely, home-cooked meals. Alongside the deck, sunloungers are set around an attractive stone pool for afternoon dips. There is no electricity, but a combination of solar lights & paraffin lamps light the lodge, & there is a charging point in the main area for batteries.

Just 1km from camp is a marvellous natural hot spring, where hot air bubbles up from the sandy bottom, giving the water the appearance of champagne. A rough stone wall has been built to create a swimming area, although this is always carefully checked for hippos before anyone gets in. This is just one of several possible guided walks, either close to camp or across the river, while the energetic can arrange a rendezvous with one of the lodge's boats. While the game isn't quite as prolific or varied as further west, what's around is becoming increasingly relaxed, with elephant regularly seen in & around camp, & the shy sitatunga occasionally spotted. With 70km of navigable waterways, boat trips are a major feature, where fishing & birdwatching from the river can be combined with an island b/fast or lunch. Also on offer are guided day & night drives, & for self-drivers, there's a 40km network of game-viewing loops. *US$150 pp FB, exc park fees, levies & bar drinks; Stony House US$55 pp self-catering, exc park fees, levies & bar drinks (6 people).* ⌚ *Mar–Nov.* ♛♛–♛♛♛

McBrides' Camp (7 chalets, camping) **m** 0972 909999; **e** bookings@mcbridescamp.com; **w** mcbridescamp.com. ⊕ MCBRID 14°41.537'S, 26°23.107'E. Informality sets the tone at this personal & isolated camp (to get here, see page 428), which has an incredibly rustic & eccentric feel to it. The basic camp was started in 2002 by Chris & Charlotte McBride, who have spent most of their lives in the bush, often with an academic focus; indeed, Chris's MSc thesis was on lions, & he went on to write 3 books on the subject, including *The White Lions of Timbavati.* They are knowledgeable & engaging hosts, who know the area incredibly well, even down to the individual animals frequently seen in camp.

Dotted around the grassy site are some rather quirky reed-&-thatch chalets; they have none of the 'design' element that is common to many safari lodges, but they are comfortable, & the large open windows allow you to experience the sights & sounds of the bush while lying in bed. 6 have a dbl & a sgl bed, while the others are smaller, with just a dbl or twin beds. All have mosi nets over the beds, skins or rugs on the floor, a solid wooden chest of drawers, & chairs & a table on a small veranda. Attached to each is a large bathroom, with hot shower, basin, & flush toilet, partially sheltered under a strip of thatch. Lighting is a mix of candlelight, paraffin lanterns & solar power, & batteries can be charged in the main area. There's also a simple campsite, with toilets, basins & hot showers in 3 open-air ablution blocks, but no marked pitches or river views. Campers are welcome to eat at the main camp (brunch US$20; dinner US$25 pp), & to take part in activities (boat 1-2hrs US$15 pp; game walk US$20 pp).

Set back from the Kafue River is an open-fronted lounge & dining room. While this couldn't be described as stylish, it's certainly homely with throws & cushions on the old squashy sofas, & slightly cluttered with plenty of books & artefacts.

Moored close by are the camp's boats, including a 2-storey aluminium craft, which are used for river cruises, fishing, & transfers to the western bank of the river so that guests can walk in a pristine area with no roads. Game drives on the eastern side are also possible. Alternatively you can make a trip to their fly-camp, 14km downstream. *From US$300 pp sharing FBA, inc laundry, exc transfers, bar, park fees, conservation levies. Camping US$5 pp, exc park fees. Children 14+.* ⌚ *All year.* ♛♛♛

Kafue River Lodge (4 cottages) **m** 0978 016191; **e** res@kafueriverlodge.com; **w** kafueriver.com. ⊕ KAFRC 14°29.841'S, 26°31.206'E. In the GMA on the northeastern border of the park, Kafue River Lodge is a small, comfortable, laid-back camp overlooking several small islands & large granite boulders in the Kafue River. The 4 new chalets are well spaced & all take advantage of the views along this picturesque stretch of the Kafue River. Inside, their soaring roofs keep the rooms cool in the heat & fireplaces ensure they're cosy during the winter months. They all have 2 queen-sized beds, patterned rugs & large, lockable wooden trunks for valuables – especially useful if you carry large camera kit. Indoor en-suite bathrooms, complete with claw-foot bath, outdoor shower, & private deck extending towards the river, make these chalets nice places to relax between & after activities.

The open-sided main area, known as the *lapa*, also takes full advantage of its location, with a wooden deck raised high over the river's edge. Meals are held here & there's a nearby campfire for after-dinner drinks under the stars.

The camp focuses on game drives & walking safaris, in the GMA, Mushingashi Conservancy & in the park to the south of the Kafue River. The water-based activities, however, including boat cruises & fishing, make a peaceful & beautiful way to take in the river scene, birdlife & animals coming to drink at sundown, especially in Sep/Oct. If you feel the need to get active, there are some super 'fat-tyre bikes' & guided cycling trips available to the hot springs.

To get to the lodge from the south, cross over the Lubungu pontoon & continue along the main road for about 20km before taking the left turn to camp (⊕ KRCTUR 14°31.039'S, 26°29.144'E), although the camp will easily be able to arrange transfers from Lusaka, or onwards to their camp in Busanga, Kasonso.

US$360 pp sharing FBA inc local drinks, laundry, park fees & conservation levies, exc transfers. Children all ages. ⌚ Mar–Dec. ♛♛♛

SOUTHERN KAFUE Stretching about 190km southwards from the main road, the southern part of the park is long and thin, only about 85km wide at its broadest point. On its eastern boundary are the Kafue River and the Itezhi-Tezhi Dam: 300km² of water. Itezhi-Tezhi differs from many dams as, apparently, it is not made of continuous concrete, but instead is filled with earth, in order to render it less vulnerable to tremors and minor earthquakes.

The vegetation and geography are broadly similar to the north – see *Geography* and *Flora and fauna*, page 415 – although there's more Kalahari sand in the south. Other noticeable differences are landmarks such as the impressive granite hills rising from the miombo forest as you drive south past KaingU, and a few really beautiful teak forests to the south of the lake.

Southern Kafue driving routes Mukambi and Mayukuyuku are very close to the main road and don't require a 4x4 vehicle. They are clearly signposted around the main Hook Bridge across the Kafue River in the centre of the park. All other routes will require a high-clearance vehicle, with 4x4s only outside the dry season.

The easiest approach to the southern section of Kafue is from the M9 (Lusaka to Mongu), and there are now two good access routes. About 51km east of the Hook Bridge, the Itezhi-Tezhi Road (D769) is a good tar road heading towards the eastern lakeshore and Itezhi-Tezhi village. Alternatively, the new Spinal Road down the western side of the Kafue River was graded in 2021 and is now a good-quality gravel route negating the need for a 4x4 during the dry season.

If you're approaching from Monze, Choma or Kalomo through the Namwala GMA or Dumdumwenze, the routes are much more challenging. Roads are much poorer quality and you'll need a high-clearance 4x4 and off-road driving experience at all times of year.

The Itezhi-Tezhi Road (D769) Heading west from Lusaka, the road bypasses Mumbwa after some 150km, then another 37km brings you to the Nalusanga scout post (⊕ NALUSA 14°58.258'S, 26°42.718'E) at the entrance to the Kafue National Park. The road then bisects the park before exiting on the western side, and there are several opportunities to turn south into the park along the way.

The turning left onto the southbound D769 (⊕ TUTZTZ 14°58.268'S, 26°27.168'E) is approximately 28km from the Nalusanga scout post. If you're approaching from the west, that's a fraction more than 51km from the main Hook Bridge over the Kafue River. It is clearly signposted to Itezhi-Tezhi and, in the rainy season, it's the only viable road south on the eastern side of the river.

About 45km after the turning, you will pass the DNPW Mweengwa Wildlife Checkpoint (⊕ MWEENG 15°16.539'S, 26°14.950'E), where you must stop to sign in. From here, the tar road becomes a well-maintained gravel road. About 3km south of that, there's a turning clearly marked for KaingU Safari Lodge on the right (⊕ TUKNGU 15°17.901'S, 26°14.159'E).

About 39km from the scout post you'll stop at a veterinary control post; then a further 22km and you reach Itezhi-Tezhi village (⊕ ITEZHI 15°44.252'S, 26°2.202'E). This is about 106km from the main Lusaka–Mongu road. Continue for about 2km, bearing left and uphill until you reach a ZESCO checkpoint. At this point, a right turning takes you into the village (page 434) where you can organise fuel and take in some commanding views of the lake. To continue straight to the southern section of the park then drive on, below the dam wall (⊕ ITZDAM 15°45.544'S, 26°1.302'E). You'll pass three lodges, which are well signposted on the right-hand side of the road, then it's just a couple of kilometres further to the Musa

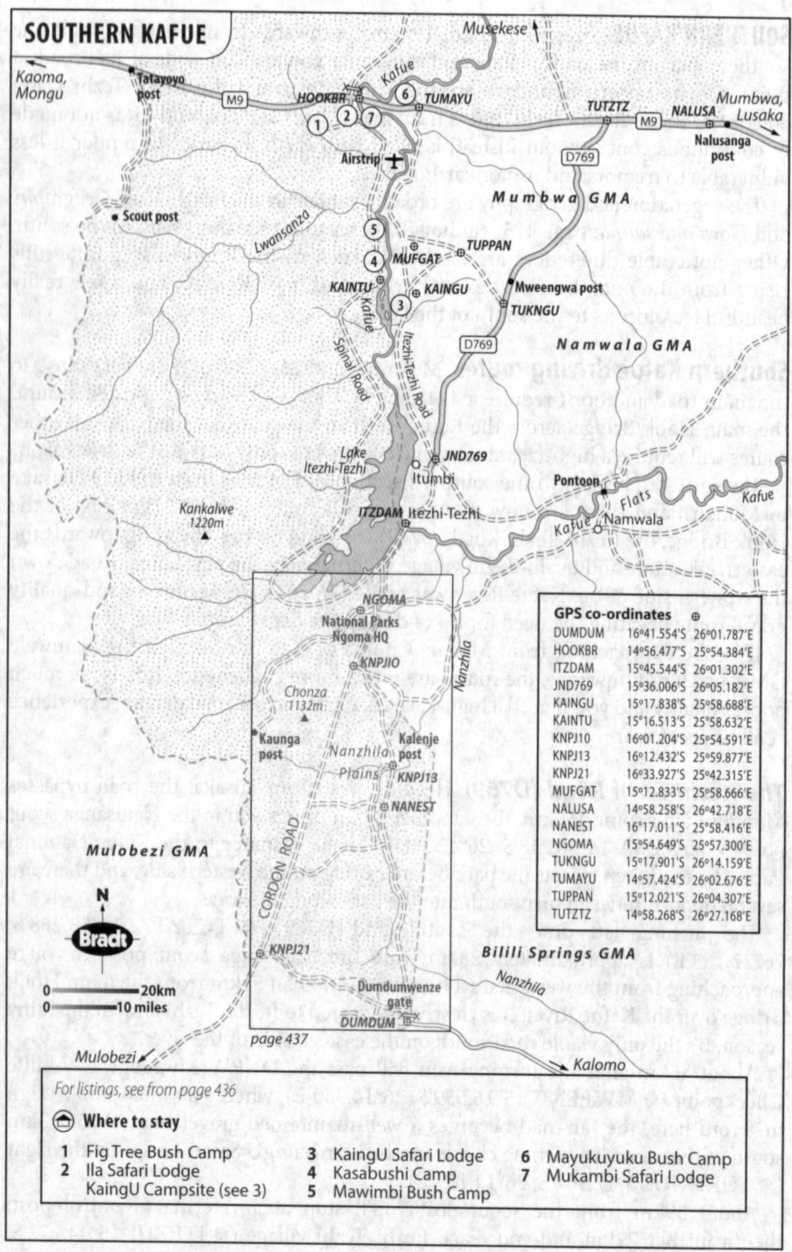

GPS co-ordinates	⊕	
DUMDUM	16°41.554'S	26°01.787'E
HOOKBR	14°56.477'S	25°54.384'E
ITZDAM	15°45.544'S	26°01.302'E
JND769	15°36.006'S	26°05.182'E
KAINGU	15°17.838'S	25°58.688'E
KAINTU	15°16.513'S	25°58.632'E
KNPJ10	16°01.204'S	25°54.591'E
KNPJ13	16°12.432'S	25°59.877'E
KNPJ21	16°33.927'S	25°42.315'E
MUFGAT	15°12.833'S	25°58.666'E
NALUSA	14°58.258'S	26°42.718'E
NANEST	16°17.011'S	25°58.416'E
NGOMA	15°54.649'S	25°57.300'E
TUKNGU	15°17.901'S	26°14.159'E
TUMAYU	14°57.424'S	26°02.676'E
TUPPAN	15°12.021'S	26°04.307'E
TUTZTZ	14°58.268'S	26°27.168'E

For listings, see from page 436

Where to stay

1 Fig Tree Bush Camp
2 Ila Safari Lodge
KaingU Campsite (see 3)
3 KaingU Safari Lodge
4 Kasabushi Camp
5 Mawimbi Bush Camp
6 Mayukuyuku Bush Camp
7 Mukambi Safari Lodge

gate (⊕ MUSAGA 15°47.802'S, 25°59.938'E). This is where you pay your park fees into the southern section of Kafue National Park, and connect onto the southern tip of the spinal road. Interestingly, the gate itself is located outside the park boundary, which you'll cross (albeit without any sign) just before Lake View Drive.

Be aware, that whole sections of this route are popular with tsetse flies, making air conditioning a valuable accessory for your vehicle.

The Spinal Road to Itezhi-Tezhi As its name suggests, the Spinal Road runs through the national park, from the north to southern point of Lake Itezhi-Tezhi. In this southern region, it tracks along the western bank of the Kafue River and down the western side of Lake Itezhi-Tezhi. After decades of disrepair, this portion of the road became near impassable and even disappeared from many paper and online maps. However, in mid-2021, the route was graded and is now a good, gravel road that links the M9 (Lusaka-Mongu) tar road with the southernmost tip of the lake (if you're self-driving, this route is marked on the latest version of Tracks4Africa's GPS map). The road is navigable year-round, with seasonal water crossings necessitating a high-clearance vehicle during the rains (in extreme rains, be sure to check locally for flash-flooding reports before embarking on this drive). The speed limit on the road, as in all of the national park, is 40km/h, but the winding nature of this route has caught out some drivers so do be careful and watch out for wildlife on the road.

Mumbwa GMA river route Between June and November, there's an altogether more scenic, albeit longer alternative to the D769, following a series of tracks along the Kafue River and passing close to KaingU safari lodges. The route crosses the Mumbwa GMA, and is absolutely legal, but note that this is also a hunting concession – so safari-goers may not always be welcome. That said, when we asked directions of a hunter, we were treated with absolute courtesy and shown the right turning without any fuss.

To find the river route, leave the M9 Lusaka–Mongu road opposite the turning to Mayukuyuku (⊕ TUMAYU 14°57.424'S, 26°02.676'E), signposted to Kafumbakwale (a very underused community campsite). Follow this narrow but good gravel track more or less southwest for about 5km, keeping an eye out for a track to your left into the bush (⊕ RR1 14°59.603'S, 26°01.020'E). There's no signpost, and it's not terribly clear, but if you overshoot it you'll soon get to the river so just retrace your steps. The correct, sandy track winds southeast through the bush for about 4km until, at ⊕ RR2 14°59.584'S, 26°01.031'E, you come to a confusing medley of tracks in a rough clearing. It's easy to become disorientated here, but continue broadly south, bearing slightly left in the clearing, then right into a steep gully at ⊕ RR3 15°00.604'S, 26°02.666'E, and emerging into a thick patch of sand. From here, the track continues roughly south, through bush and across open plains, crossing several riverbeds, and sometimes with glimpses of the river to your right. Precise route directions are of little help, but the following GPS co-ordinates mark some of the riverbeds and other landmarks en route to KaingU Safari Lodge:

RR4	15°01.884'S, 26°02.283'E	Riverbed; graveyard termitaria both sides; river on right
RR5	15°03.934'S, 26°01.525'E	Riverbed
RR6	15°05.394'S, 25°59.764'E	Riverbed
RR7	15°05.997'S, 25°59.302'E	Ignore track to left
RR8	15°06.788'S, 25°58.971'E	Ignore track to right along river
RR9	15°07.905'S, 25°58.488'E	Hunting camp to right on river
RR10	15°10.734'S, 25°58.973'E	Take right fork
RR11	15°12.199'S, 25°58.748'E	Keep right at fork
TUPPN2	15°12.389'S, 25°58.708'E	T-junction; turn right for Puku Pan and south
TUKAI2	15°13.877'S, 25°59.484'E	Take right fork to KaingU and south
POLEBR	15°17.306'S, 25°59.130'E	Cross the pole bridge and turn immediately left (continue straight on for KaingU Safari Lodge)

Continuing south from the pole bridge (and the turning to KaingU), you'll cross several more riverbeds and – after around 21km – you will pass the palace of Chief Kaingu to your left, followed 7km later by Bushinga village. From the pole bridge to the junction with the D769 (⊕ JND769 15°36.006'S, 26°05.182'E) is around 43km. From here, you turn right towards Itezhi-Tezhi village. Useful GPS co-ordinates along this stretch include:

RR12	15°21.495'S, 25°59.695'E	Dip, and pool to left
RR13	15°22.469'S, 25°59.866'E	Double river crossing
RR14	15°25.006'S, 26°00.286'E	Take left fork
RR15	15°25.760'S, 26°00.064'E	Deep river crossing
RR16	15°29.762'S, 26°00.436'E	Stone bridge
RR16	15°34.815'S, 26°03.240'E	Bear left at fork

Itezhi-Tezhi village For those heading into the park, the village is an invaluable source of both fuel and supplies. Instead of following the main road south, turn right and you'll pass a police station immediately on your left, followed by a **post office** and a bank. Pass the school and you'll get to the ZESCO offices (⌚ 08.00–12.30 & 14.00–16.30), by which point you'll be high up and overlooking the lake. Fuel is paid for and arranged at the ZESCO offices, but collected back on the main road, on the way towards the dam wall. Be aware though that the fuel station is closed at lunch (noon–14.00) and on Sundays, even though you can still pay at the ZESCO offices.

From the south

Kalomo to Dumdumwenze gate The small town of Kalomo (page 233) is about 126km from Livingstone on the way to Lusaka, and marks the turning towards the southern section of the Kafue. There's a **fuel** station here (⊕ KAFUEL 17°01.673'S, 26°29.259'E) which can be useful for a top-up, though it would be wise to have all the fuel required before you leave Livingstone or Lusaka. Just north of this, a clear sign points west to the Dumdumwenze gate. Almost immediately the road becomes a dirt track, passing through a busy **market** (a good place for supplies) to a T-junction. Turn right here and follow the road as it curves left (ignoring right-hand turn-off).

Continue over a railway bridge, followed shortly afterwards by a river bridge (⊕ KALBRI 17°0.915'S, 26°29.468'E), then take the next left fork. Continue following the main track, ignoring any turnings and keeping left at forks. After a few kilometres you should cross another river bridge

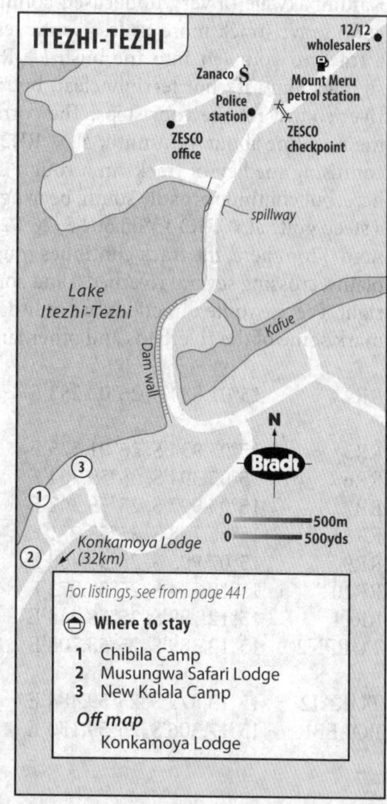

(⊕ KLOBRI 16°59.331'S, 26°27.876'E) before travelling northwest, passing through the occasional village. About 40km from the main road, you will start leaving the villages behind to climb through some hills. Eventually, after about 74km, the road drops down gradually to Dumdumwenze gate (⊕ DUMDUM 16°41.554'S, 26°1.787'E), where the game scouts will sign you into the park. (Note that Dumdumwezi is the local spelling and pronunciation.)

The road is generally good with some rough patches, but watch out for some particularly vicious speed bumps which materialise before and after both villages and river bridges, often with no warning signposts. Watch out, too, for goats, cattle and hens along the road.

North from Dumdumwenze There are two main routes leading north from the gate, both of which are affected by the yearly rains and sporadically graded, meaning the easiest route switches regularly. You should check with your planned camp when booking for advice, and let them know which route you plan to take – they aren't tricky routes, but they are long and see little traffic. Alternatively ask the scouts at the gate for advice. Whichever route you take, drive north into the park for 2.3km to the first junction (⊕ KNPJ20 16°40.332'S, 26°1.722'E).

Between about December and June, there's little choice: you will have to take the **Cordon route**, which skirts around the southwest side of the park through woodlands. This gets to Ngoma without crossing any substantial rivers, and so while it does have the odd sticky dambo, an experienced driver with a 4x4 should be able to get through even in the rains. Note, however, that high sand can pile up in the centre of the road, so a high-clearance 4x4 is as essential for this route as for any other within the park.

For this route you go into the park, heading north for about 2.3km, then take a left turn at your first junction (⊕ KNPJ20 16°40.332'S, 26°1.722'E). From here you proceed about 40km, through fairly thick forest, heading slightly north of west, until you reach a junction (⊕ KAFU01 16°33.927'S, 25°42.314'E), which indicates the southwestern tip of the park. There you turn right, to head north and slightly east on a basically straight road that passes through the heart of the southern end of the park. This ultimately meets other roads near Ngoma at a junction ⊕ KNPJ10 16°1.204'S, 25°54.591'E.

During the dry season, consider taking the **Nanzhila River route**, which is much more interesting. This shadows the river north, crossing it several times and skirting around the eastern edge of the Nanzhila Plains. From ⊕ KNPJ20 16°40.332'S, 26°1.722'E, continue straight ahead. The vegetation along this route can be exceedingly thick even in June, so it's best to wait until at least July to drive along here.

From that first junction it's about 19km until you cross to the east bank of the Nanzhila River at ⊕ NANRV2 16°30.905'S, 26°0.164'E. Although the river isn't very deep, its banks are steep and can be slippery, so if there's any danger of you getting stuck, make sure that you have a back-up plan. Continue north, and after about 29km there's a concrete marker on a junction at ⊕ NANEST 16°17.011'S, 25°58.416'E. Turn left, and in about 2km you'll reach a river crossing which is usually dry from June. About 100m afterwards there's a crossroads (⊕ KNPJ16 16°16.497'S, 25°57.318'E) where you'll need to turn right (straight on takes you to Nanzhila Plains Safari Camp, page 442). This takes you onto a really lovely road north. It passes the Nanzhila Plains, and bends east at the Chilenje Pools, and then leads to Kalenje scout post. If you didn't go west at NANEST, then continuing straight would also bring you to Kalenje.

At the junction in Kalenje (⊕ KLJJNC 16°12.430'S, 25°59.878'E) you can turn left through the park, or go straight on to take the eastern boundary road. Head straight along either, and these roads will meet up with the cordon road at the airstrip. There are deep patches of sand along both routes, so take extra care.

From Monze on the Lusaka–Livingstone road From Monze take a turning on the north side of town towards Chongo, heading northwest towards Lochinvar National Park. You may need to ask local directions to get on the right track, but it passes through waypoint ⊕ TULOCH 16°15.465'S, 27°28.632'E. After 7–8km you will pass Chongo – keep left there as the track divides after the village. About 8km after Chongo the road forks (⊕ T2LOCH 16°10.054'S, 27°23.610'E): right leads to Lochinvar National Park; left leads to Namwala and thence the Ngoma area of Kafue.

About 35km later, on a dusty (or, if wet, muddy) and rather pot-holed track, you will reach Chitongo, and a T-junction. Here you find an implausibly good tarred road! (If you turned left onto this, you would find that the tar turned into poor gravel about 60km before Choma.) For the Kafue turn right at Chitongo, and follow this heading slightly west of north, then due west. About 50km after Chitongo you will reach the larger village of Namwala, on the southern edge of the Kafue's floodplain (where, incidentally, there's a pontoon over the Kafue). From Namwala, the track leads about 60km southwest, into the park. This is bumpy and pot-holed gravel, but is passable during the rains. It enters the park past the site of the old Nkala Mission, joining the road network at ⊕ TUNAMW 15°53.894'S, 25°57.854'E, about 2km north of Ngoma.

Where to stay *Map, page 432, unless otherwise stated*

If you're just passing through the park on the main Lusaka–Mongu road, consider stopping for a night or two in the area around Mukambi – but if you have more time, it's well worth penetrating deeper into the park. The southern Itezhi-Tezhi area, and around Ngoma, has impressive game and the most spectacular scenery in this part of the park, while KaingU Safari Lodge is built beside a unique and very lovely part of the river.

If you're driving and taking camping kit, there is plenty of choice, even though both the national parks' campsites in the southern Kafue have closed. You can probably afford to turn up at the lodges along the Lusaka road and those around Lake Itezhi-Tezhi, and even at Hippo Bay, but would be advised to book the smaller, more remote campsites at KaingU and Kasabushi. For those on a fly-in trip, on a flexible budget, the options in this area include KaingU, Nanzhila Plains Safari Camp and Konkamoya.

For ease of reference, the southern Kafue's camps are split into three distinct areas: 'Near the M9 Lusaka–Mongu road', 'Further south in the Namwala GMA' and 'Around Itezhi-Tezhi Dam and south, and are listed alphabetically in each section.

Near the M9 Lusaka–Mongu road There are several places to stay very near the M9 road, but for most people those listed here are likely to be the best bet. All are on the river, and either in or opposite the national park – with Mayukuyuku just inside the northern Kafue.

Fig Tree Bush Camp (4 tents) Contact via Mukambi (see above). ⊕ FIGTRE 15°00.045'S, 25°49.062'E. Owned by Mukambi Safaris, Fig Tree is located west of the Kafue River in the national park; it's just 6km south of the main Lusaka–Mongu road. It's sister camp to Mukambi Plains

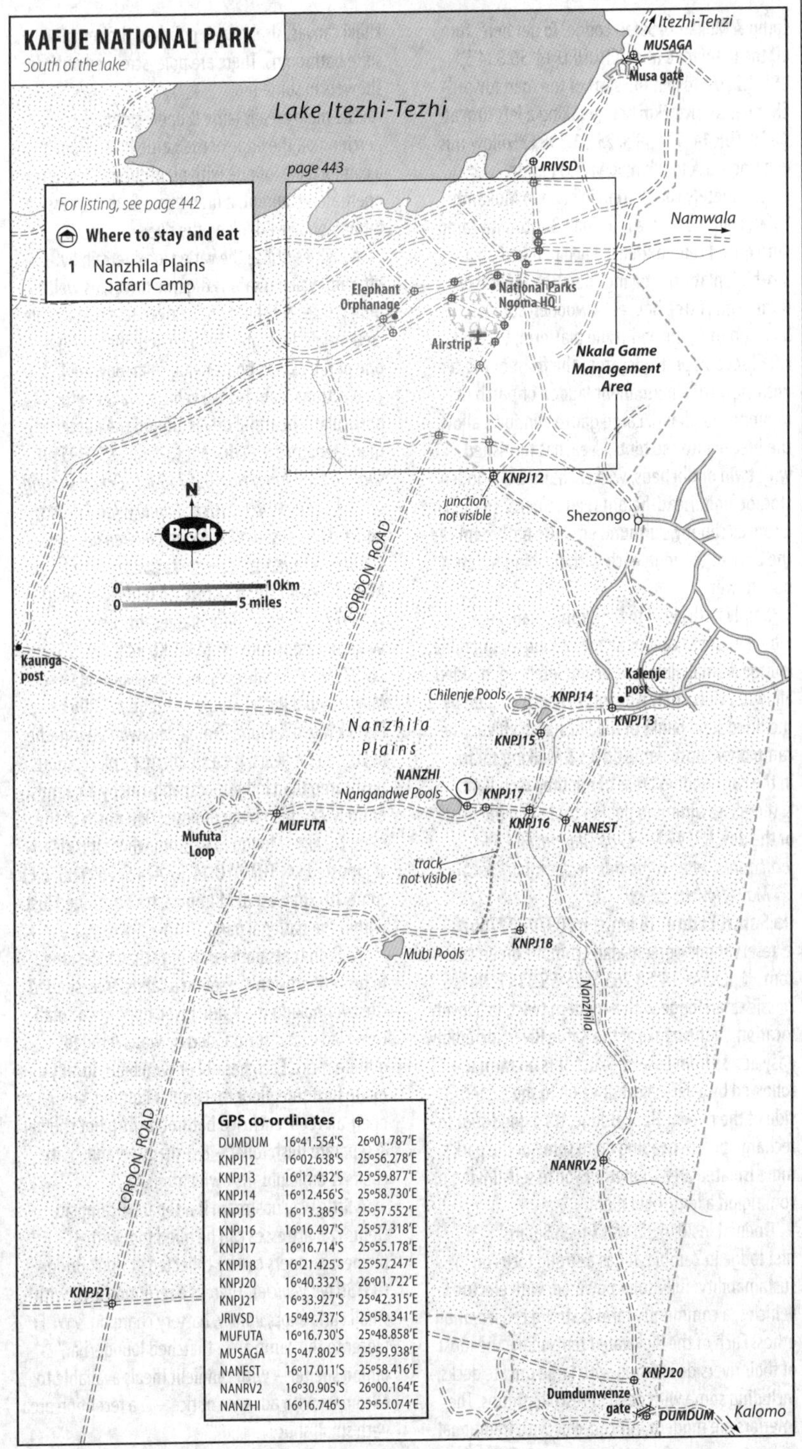

GPS co-ordinates

DUMDUM	16°41.554'S	26°01.787'E
KNPJ12	16°02.638'S	25°56.278'E
KNPJ13	16°12.432'S	25°59.877'E
KNPJ14	16°12.456'S	25°58.730'E
KNPJ15	16°13.385'S	25°57.552'E
KNPJ16	16°16.497'S	25°57.318'E
KNPJ17	16°16.714'S	25°55.178'E
KNPJ18	16°21.425'S	25°57.247'E
KNPJ20	16°40.332'S	26°01.722'E
KNPJ21	16°33.927'S	25°42.315'E
JRIVSD	15°49.737'S	25°58.341'E
MUFUTA	16°16.730'S	25°48.858'E
MUSAGA	15°47.802'S	25°59.938'E
NANEST	16°17.011'S	25°58.416'E
NANRV2	16°30.905'S	26°00.164'E
NANZHI	16°16.746'S	25°55.074'E

Camp & Mukambi Safari Lodge. To get here, turn off the main road at ⊕ CHUNRD 14°56.834'S, 25°51.220'E to join the start of the road towards Chunga, & drive 2km before taking a left turn at ⊕ FIGTUR 14°57.848'S, 25°51.398'E. Follow this winding track for 8km down to Fig Tree.

Completely contrasting in style to Mukambi Safari Lodge, Fig Tree is a small & intimate camp with only 4 tented rooms, each perched on a 3m-high platform, giving them the feeling of rather smart tree houses. A wooden staircase leads up to a polished stone platform, where a small section protrudes from the front of the tent with views of a permanent lagoon or patch of miombo woodland. Large gauze windows allow the breeze into the tents, & each is furnished with twin or dbl beds, wicker chairs & a wooden storage unit. Head-height reed screens, shaded by a canvas canopy, surround en-suite bathrooms at the back of the tent, each with flushing toilets & hot showers.

Sandy paths lead to the simple main area, where a canvas canopy shades a long dining table, lounge & small library. It's completely open-sided, allowing views of the beautiful beach created by the dried sand banks of the Shishamba River. The camp offers both game drives & walking safaris in the surrounding areas of miombo woodland, & there's a swimming pool to cool off in the heat of the day. *US$440–535 pp sharing; FBA, inc local drinks, inter-camp transfers; exc park fees.* ⌚ *May–Nov.* ♛♛♛

Ila Safari Lodge (8 tents) **m** 0979 312766; **e** reservations@greensafaris.com; **w** greensafaris.com. ⊕ ILASAF 14°58.265'S, 25°55.318'E. Ila is a classic safari lodge with a modern twist, in a lovely location on the banks of the Kafue River. Incredibly easy access from Lusaka – just 3hrs on tarmac followed by a very short drive on to the eastern side of the river at Hook Bridge. It's a good spot to recharge before heading on to some of the park's more isolated areas, whether you're self-driving or coming off a long-haul flight.

Opened in 2016, Ila was Green Safaris' first lodge in Zambia. It has a strong focus on sustainability: fully solar powered, with electric vehicles, a community farm & strong conservation ethos. Each of the 8 elevated tents make the most of their riverside location with large private decks, including some with deep alfresco bathtubs. The interiors are modern, African-chic with traditional khaki canvas, sisal rugs & polished timber en-suite bathrooms. There are pole-screened outside showers in some too.

The main area is large & open-sided, perching on the edge of the Kafue River. There's a comfortable lounge with plentiful seating, an open-air restaurant, a firepit area & an impressive infinity pool overlooking the river.

Activities utilise the varied local terrain by offering walking safaris & game drives, as well as boat cruises & fishing on the river. Ila's sustainable credentials are highlighted on activities, with one of the camp's boats being solar-powered, & an electronic game-drive vehicle available for particularly peaceful drives around the game management area adjacent to camp. *US$495 pp sharing Jan–Jun & Nov, US$745 Jul–Oct pp sharing, all FBA, inc airstrip transfers, laundry, local drinks, park fees & conservation levies. Children all ages.* ⌚ *Jun–Nov.* ♛♛♛–♛♛♛♛

Mayukuyuku Bush Camp (4 tents, camping) **m** 0972 179266; **e** info@kafuecamps.com; **w** kafuecamps.com. ⊕ MAYUKU 14°54.975'S, 26°03.925'E. Small, personal & welcoming, Mayukuyuku Bush Camp was set up in 2006 by Patrick Moyo & Pippa Turner, who worked together at Lufupa for years. It's a small, rustic place, more bushcamp than lodge, & capably run by an almost entirely Zambian team. It lies 5.7km north of the main Lusaka–Mongu road, from where it is clearly signposted (⊕ TUMAYU 14°57.424'S, 26°02.676'E), some 107km west of Mumbwa. It's positioned just within the national park.

Walk-in tents under a shaggy thatch designed to prevent erosion are set on a sandy, tree-shaded site overlooking the Kafue River, opposite a small tree-clad island surrounded by water-eroded granite rocks. Each has dbl or twin beds, locally made furniture, floor mats, solar lighting, an open-air reed-enclosed bathroom with hot shower & separate flush toilet – & a shady veranda with chairs & table plus its own hammock.

A little way upstream is a separate campsite (tents & mattresses can be hired too) with 4 pitches; campers can be collected at Hook Bridge (*US$30 per vehicle*). There is a reception area with small curio shop, library, battery charging & Wi-Fi. Closer to the camp are a thatched lounge/bar/dining shelter – with candlelit meals available to allcomers with advance notice – & a reception area with small shop.

As well as offering fully inclusive packages, both guests & day visitors can book activities like boat cruises, fishing, walking safaris & game drives on an individual basis (*all US$45 pp*). The camp also caters well to self-drivers with a good map of local game drive loops. It's also possible to hire a guide to accompany you in your own vehicle (*from US$30/3hrs*). *US$550 pp FBA inc 2 activities/ day, park fees & bed levy; US$400 FB; no sgl suppt. Camping US$30 pp; Transfers extra. Green season rates available.* ⌚ *All year.* ♛♛♛

Mukambi Safari Lodge (9 chalets, 4 tents, 1 villa) **m** 0974 424013; **e** info@mukambi.com; **w** mukambi.com. ⊕ MUKAMB 14°58.656'S, 25°59.599'E. In the capable hands of Linda & Jacques van Heerden, Mukambi is a well-built, comfortable lodge in the GMA, with consistently high standards. It is clearly signposted from the main Lusaka–Mongu tar road (⊕ TUMUKA 14°57.584'S, 25°59.721'E), about 9km east of the Hook Bridge over the Kafue. The camp is 2km from the main road – easily accessed in a 2WD.

Thatched, cream-painted rondavels (8 dbl & 1 family) are solidly built with beautifully carved wooden doors. There's no AC or fan, but the circular shape, tree shade & netted windows help to keep them cool, & each has a small veranda with chairs. Inside are 4-poster beds under mosquito nets, the neutral décor enlivened by soft rugs & wood carvings. Stone-tiled showers in the bathrooms are solar-heated, with a geyser in the 2-bedroomed villa.

The 4 riverside tents have glazed sliding doors to their deck – complete with alfresco claw-foot bath – & contemporary interiors & furniture carved form Indian Ocean dhows.

The multi-level central area, overlooking the Kafue River to the national park, brings an open & relaxed feeling to the lodge. A resident hippo often spends his afternoons sleeping in this area, although a member of staff is always present to keep an eye on him when he's about. The food, from a set menu, is good, served in the substantial restaurant area, while lower down is a relaxed seating area over the river. There's a large swimming pool surrounded by sunloungers & a cosy lounge/bar with a fire for the winter months. Day visitors are welcome & can join in activities subject to availability.

A range of boating & 4x4 game-viewing trips is available, with no more than 8 guests in each safari vehicle. Overall game densities in the Chunga area (where they usually drive) have improved considerably since the camp was opened in 1997 & anti-poaching measures were put in place. In addition to some lovely herds of elephant & buffalo, there are now regular sightings of lion, leopard, cheetah & wild dog. Guests may also visit the local primary school, which is supported by the lodge. *Chalets US$370-455 pp sharing FBA, exc park fees; Villa $60 pp/day supplement. Sgl suppt applies.* ⌚ *All year.* ♛♛♛

Further south in the Namwala GMA There are four more southerly lodges on the eastern and western banks of the river, which are too far from the Lusaka–Mongu road to be mere stopovers. Several have campsites, which are best booked in advance. The camps on the eastern bank are accessible from the spinal road, but you will have to leave any vehicles on the western side of the river, so if you're camping it's advisable to approach these camps using the D769. There has long been game in this area, effectively protected from poaching by the presence of the lodges. That said, although the game is building up, it isn't as good as in the park's best corners – but the river here is stunning!

KaingU Safari Lodge (6 tented chalets, 1 family chalet) **e** info@kaingu-lodge.com, reservations@kaingu-lodge.com; **w** kaingu-lodge.com. ⊕ KAINGU 15°17.838'S, 25°58.688'E. KaingU stands in an idyllic setting on the east bank of the Kafue; as the bee-eater flies it's about 40km from the M9. To get here from the D769 (page 431) turn west at the signpost to KaingU ⊕ TUKNGU 15°17.901'S, 26°14.159'E. This bush track twists & winds through dense miombo woodland for about 23.5km until you fork left at ⊕ TUPPAN 15°12.021'S, 26°4.307'E. From there it's just under 18km to the lodge, during which you cross a small pole bridge (⊕ POLEBR 15°17.306'S, 25°59.130'E). An alternative approach is to drive down the spinal road for 33km before turning right (⊕ KAINTU

15°16.513'S, 25°58.632'E). Follow this track towards the river for 700m until you reach a small grass car park. You will need to arrange with the lodge a time to meet you here in advance so that they can boat you the rest of the way to camp.

The lodge is broadly traditional in design, & finished with a high degree of care. 2 of its large, cream Meru-style tents are raised on polished wooden decking under thatch, with a proper wood & gauze door leading to a large veranda facing the river. Large, high-quality beds stand on hand-woven rugs, & it's possible to open up the whole of the front of the tent to be one big mesh window. At the back, an attractive stone bathroom, with green bottles cleverly built into the walls, has an indoor & outdoor shower (or bath), & individual touches like a towel rail of knurled wood. There's hot water aplenty & small 12V solar-powered lights. The 4 older rooms are broadly similar but are slightly larger, the beds face sideways rather than towards the river, & the bathrooms are at the back without a view. Finfoot cottage is a properly constructed house rather than a tent, & works well for families. It has 2 en-suite rooms, each with outdoor showers, either side of a central living area.

The lodge is owner-run by a small group of incredibly passionate & personable individuals, virtues that are shared by the camp's knowledgeable guides. Activities at the camp include game drives on either side of the river, walking safaris – walking up some of the large granite hills in the area is particularly enjoyable – fishing excursions, & visits to one of their photographic hides overlooking a waterhole & on an island in the river. For the more adventurous, it's possible to go on overnight camping trips in basic dome tents. With such a small lodge, & a high degree of enthusiasm, there's plenty of flexibility.

The river beside the lodge is as lovely as any stretch of African river that we know: it's worth coming here just to spend a few days afloat. KaingU stands beside an area where the river broadens to accommodate a scattering of small islands, each consisting of vegetated sandy banks & huge granite rocks interspersed with rapids. Imagine someone throwing half of Zimbabwe's Matobo Hills into a wide, shallow river & you'll get the picture. So to potter round here in a boat, inflatable canoe or even just to go fishing is a real journey of discovery. With endless side channels & islands to explore, there's something different around every corner, plenty of vegetation everywhere – & birds all around. When the water's low it's even possible to swim in the pools above the rapids. It's a real gem of an area. *US$490 pp sharing Apr–Jun & Nov, US$660 pp sharing Jul–Oct; Sleep-out option US$75 pp sharing; all FBA inc laundry, local drinks, park fees & conservation levies. Group bookings considered in March & Dec.* ⏲ *Apr–Nov.* ♛♛♛

KaingU Campsite (3 private campsites) Contact KaingU Safari Lodge, page 439. KaingU has 3, really lovely private riverside pitches next to the rapids with space for 6 people (2 cars max). Each has its own spotless & creatively designed 'brick & bottle' built ablutions (flush toilet, hot shower & washbasin), a cooking grid, a fireplace, a tap & a table for washing up. All the sites are pleasant & grassy, under trees, & firewood is provided. However, you must bring all your food, as meals are available at the lodge only if you've arranged them well in advance. The communal facilities at the lodge are generally off limits to campers. You must bring all your own equipment, so you must approach from the eastern side of the river along the D769. *US$25 pp.* ⏲ *Mar–Dec.* **$$**

Kasabushi Camp (2 chalets, camping) **e** info@undiscoveredafrica.com; **w** kasabushi.wordpress.com. ⊕ KASABU 15°15.475'S, 25°58.493'E. One of the few camps on the western bank of the Kafue River within the park itself, creating Kasabushi has been a labour of love for its owners Andy & Lib Wilson. Their hand-built, wood-framed, tented chalets – or 'kasas' – are perched on a steep section of the riverbank, with wooden decks extending out over the river. Simply furnished with quality bed linen, solar lighting & outdoor showers overlooking the water.

The main area is unusual: a red-brick roundhouse made using mud from termite mounds, with an ingenious self-supported roof made from twisted local timber & canvas sails. A lounge area nearby will also be shaded by canvas sails, but will otherwise be completely open, with lovely views of a rocky section of the river filled with tree-clad islands. **$$**

Kasabushi also has a well-maintained, year-round campsite a short distance from camp. With 4 shady pitches, private picnic seating & tables, BBQ areas, hot-water waterfall showers, flush toilets & washing up facilities, it's a great option for self-drivers. To get here, drive along the spinal road until you reach the turning at ⊕ KASCTU 15°16.059'S, 25°58.114'E. To get to the main lodge, take the signposted turning at ⊕ KASLTU 15°16.059'S, 25°58.396'E. *US$240 pp FBA, inc park fees & local drinks. Camping US$30 pp (pre-booking pitches advisable Jun–Nov).* ⏲ *Mar–Nov.* ♛♛♛

Mawimbi Bush Camp (4 tents) +263 242 861286; e res@mawimbibushcamp.com; w mawimbibushcamp.com. ⊕ MAWIMB 15°09.937'S, 25°57.630'E. Originally a small fly-camp associated with KaingU Safari Lodge, Mawimbi is now its own independent operation, with a permanent camp constructed in 2014. Located on the western bank of the Kafue River, Mawimbi can be reached via the spinal road. Take the signposted turning at ⊕ MAWITU 15°10.598'S, 25°57.062'E & drive approximately 1km to camp.

Accommodation, inside the national park, is in 4 large canvas tents with concrete bases, each with twin or dbl beds & decorated in subtle African themes. Each has an en-suite bathroom at the back, surrounded by reed screens & completely open to the sky. They are equipped with hot-water bucket showers & flushing toilets. A veranda at the front, with a couple of armchairs, has views over a picturesque section of the river. Meals are typically served outside, or under the basic, open-sided main area.

Activities focus on canoeing here, led by the camp manager. Several stretches of the river offer peaceful wildlife viewing & some stunning scenery, as well as a few technical rapids (although these can easily be avoided with alternate routes). There are several trails, & it's possible to paddle the inflatable canoes as far as the Itezhi-Tezhi Dam. Safari walks are also available, but the canoeing is the real highlight at this camp. *US$490 pp sharing FBA. No children under 12.* ♛♛–♛♛♛

Around Itezhi-Tezhi Dam and south Grouped in the GMA to the southeast of Lake Itezhi-Tezhi, and just south of the dam wall, are three fairly old-style camps catering more to Zambian tastes than to overseas visitors. They're relatively inexpensive – and some would regard them as good value. There's also the option of a small new lodge in Itezhi-Tezhi village.

In the national park itself, Konkamoya offers a unique setting right on the lake, while further south, Nanzhila Plains Safari Camp has made this remote area of the park accessible once again to adventurous visitors. Although both national parks' campsites have been closed, most of the lodges offer camping, and there's also the simple Shiluwe Hill site near the Musa gate.

Chibila Camp [map, page 434] (3 chalets, 2 tents, camping) 0211 251 630; m 0954 192660; e wecsz@microlink.zm, wecszzam@gmail.com; w conservationzambia.org. ⊕ CHIBIL 15°46.638'S, 26°00.407'E. Almost next door to New Kalala, Chibila (or Chibala – formerly the David Shepherd Camp) stands between large granite boulders on the shores of the lake. It was built for members of the Wildlife Conservation Society of Zambia (the present WECSZ, page 98), although unlike their other camps in the park it's available for independent booking, on the condition that you join once you reach the camp. Each chalet has 4 beds (dbl & twins), en-suite shower & toilet & a private veranda. There are also 2 simple safari tents with a shared ablution block or the option to camp if you are fully equipped. At heart it's a self-catering camp, but staff are on hand to help cook in the fully equipped kitchen & BBQ area, & rates are available for FB and HB. *Chalet US$45/50/75 pp SC/B&B/FB; tent US$35/40/65 pp SC/B&B/FB; Camping US$10 pp.* ⏲ *All year.* **$$$$**

Hippo Bay Campsite [map, page 443] Contact via Konkamoya, see below. Well away from the lodge, Konkamoya's no-frills campsite is set back from the lake & comfortably has space for 12 people. There's a good solid ablution block with hot water, plus a supply of firewood & – a real bonus – drinking water, but otherwise campers need to be entirely self-sufficient. They can, however, join in with lodge activities. *Camping US$25 pp.* **$$**

Konkamoya Lodge [map, page 443] (4 tents) 0211 213362; m 0969 806957; e info@konkamoya.com; w konkamoya.com. ⊕ KONKAM

15°52.040'S, 25°52.976'E. With a prime position on the lakeshore, Konkamoya has a truly unique & picturesque location in the park. Many visitors fly in to Ngoma, a ½-hr game drive to the south. If you're driving yourself, follow the main track from the Musa gate, turning right after 5km on to Lake View Drive. From here, keep to the lakeshore until after 18km you come to a crossroads (⊕ TUKONK 15°53.061'S, 25°52.671'E). Turn right & the lodge is within 2.5km.

Konkamoya sits at the end of a grassy peninsula, fronted by drowned trees & a small island rising from the lake. With such excellent views, improving levels of game & stunning birdlife in the area it remains a surprise that this is still the only lodge right on the lake. The lodge is run by Andrea Porro, an eccentric Italian expat who brings a good deal of character to the camp, as well as a few Italian home comforts such as excellent coffee, & jars of biscotti in the rooms.

A major refurbishment of the lodge began in 2019, replacing their tents & rebuilding the main area. A large tent serves as the central meeting point, in the shade of which the dining room, bar & communal lounge are located. This area was built over a large termite mound, allowing for a magnificent panorama & gentle breeze. A swimming pool has also been added for cooling dips during the warmer months of the year. The 4 elegant en-suite tents are huge & tastefully furnished. Discretely tucked into the riparian vegetation, each enjoys a wooden deck facing the lake.

Activities focus on game drives around the lake area. As the lake waters recede towards the dry season mud flats are exposed that are quickly grassed over, providing ample grazing. The waters also leave residual pools that are prolific breeding grounds for fish, amphibians & invertebrates, which in turn attracts a plethora of birdlife. A drive around this section of the lake bed is fascinating both in terms of the scenery & diversity of wildlife, & at the end of the dry season you can see herds of elephants numbering in their hundreds coming down to drink at the lake. Andrea is intensely passionate about the area & its wildlife. Safari walks are also available, but unfortunately activities on the lake itself aren't currently offered. *From US$850 pp FBA, inc park fees & airstrip transfers, exc bar.* ⏲ *Apr–Dec.* ♛♛♛

Musungwa Safari Lodge [map, page 434] (24 chalets, camping) ☎ 0964 791585; **e** musungwasafarilodge@gmail.com; **w** musungwalodge.co.za. ⊕ MUSUNG 15°46.987'S, 26°00.329'E. On the shore of Lake Itezhi-Tezhi, Musungwa is about 7km south of the dam wall, & just 1km north of the Musa gate. With 24 chalets, this is the largest lodge in the area & is more like a small hotel than a safari lodge. Twin & 3-bed en-suite chalets have tiny private verandas overlooking the lake. Housed in 4 large rondavels are the reception, bar, restaurant & conference centre, open to day visitors. Just below is a swimming pool commanding a stunning view of the lake & surrounded by pleasant gardens, complete with grass, bamboo, bougainvillea & the odd palm. There are tennis & squash courts, too. Activities include boat cruises, game drives &, of course, fishing, with the lodge being a popular base for local fishing competitions. *Chalet US$80–140 pp sharing FB, exc activities; camping US$20 pp.* **$$$**

Nanzhila Plains Safari Camp [map, page 437] (3 chalets; 3 tents) ☎ +27 799 799681; **e** info@nanzhila.com; **w** nanzhila.com. ⊕ NANZHI 16°16.746'S, 25°55.074'E. In the remote south of the park, this comfortable family-run camp is surrounded by woodland & plains. To the front, the large, grass-fringed Nangandwe Pool attracts good herds of game, including roan & sable antelope, defassa waterbuck, Lichtenstein's hartebeest & eland – which in turn draw predators such as wild dog & cheetah. Birdlife is good year round; look out in camp for paradise flycatchers & red-headed weaver birds, while the near-endemic black-cheeked lovebird is regularly spotted on game drives.

Most visitors arrive by air at Ngoma, followed by a 2-hr game drive. A new airstrip is being constructed a short distance from camp, but this is work in progress & unlikely to be finished soon. To drive in you'll need a 4x4, & plenty of time. From the Musa gate, continue 22km to the park HQ at Ngoma, then bear left & follow the Cordon Rd to the airstrip. Here you can carry straight on down the Cordon Rd, before turning left at the junction at MUFUTA 16°16.730'S, 25°48.858'E. Alternatively, you can turn left just after the airstrip for a further 35km to the Kalenji scout post, then right for a further 15km to camp. The conditions of these sandy bush tracks change rapidly, so it's best to check with the camp which is currently in the best condition. From the Dumdumwenze gate, follow the track for 3km to a fork; if it's dry, continue straight ahead to the east of the river, but when wet you *must* turn left & head north for 65km on the Cordon Rd, before turning right to the camp.

Facing the pool is an open-fronted thatched boma, raised up beneath a mature ebony tree (*Diospyros mespiliformisi*). With a lounge, dining area & extensive wooden deck, this is the focal point of the camp, its largely wicker furniture offset by comfy cushions & a selection of books. In the evenings, guests congregate by the firepit, before adjourning to a communal table for dinner.

To one side of the pool are 3 solidly built thatched chalets, each with an en-suite shower, toilet & twin washbasins, & a combination of netted windows & doors to allow a through breeze. Although not very spacious, they're furnished with care, to include dbl or twin hardwood beds & matching bedside tables under wraparound mosi nets, & good storage space. Opposite, 3 twin Meru-style tents under shadecloths offer a simpler alternative, with partially open en-suite facilities at the back, & the bonus of a small veranda overlooking the pool. Donkey boilers heat the water, & paraffin lamps add a slightly romantic touch, with a solar-powered generator useful for charging camera batteries etc – usually when guests are out of camp.

Flexibility is the key here, with a series of loops for day & night drives, plus guided walks, & trips to Lake Itezhi-Tezhi or – by arrangement – to Shezongo village, the Elephant Orphanage or Ngoma Forest. In the winter months, Jul–Sep, bush b/fasts can also be organised. *US$400 15 May–Jun & Nov, US$540 Jul–Oct pp sharing FBA, inc local drinks, laundry & internal road transfers; exc park fees.* 🕘 *May–Nov.* ♛♛♛

New Kalala Camp [map, page 434] (13 chalets, camping) 📞 0213 263179, 0211 290914; **e** newkalala@gmail.com; info@newkalala.com; **w** newkalala.com. ⊕ NEWKAL 15°46.583'S, 26°00.538'E. Well signposted south of the dam wall, New Kalala overlooks the lake from a stunning perch on a granite kopje where you'll

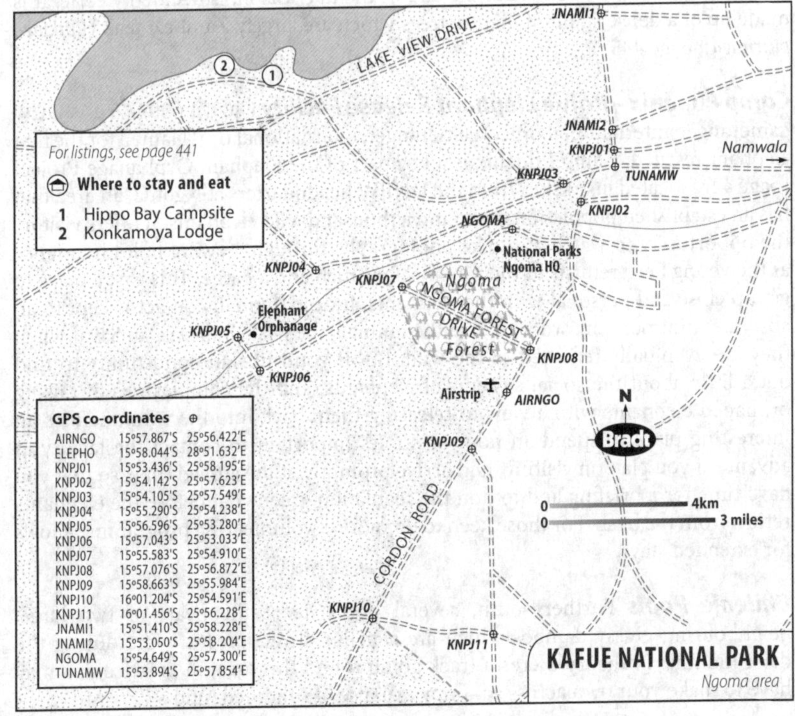

AIRNGO	15°57.867'S	25°56.422'E
ELEPHO	15°58.044'S	28°51.632'E
KNPJ01	15°53.436'S	25°58.195'E
KNPJ02	15°54.142'S	25°57.623'E
KNPJ03	15°54.105'S	25°57.549'E
KNPJ04	15°55.290'S	25°54.238'E
KNPJ05	15°56.596'S	25°53.280'E
KNPJ06	15°57.043'S	25°53.033'E
KNPJ07	15°55.583'S	25°54.910'E
KNPJ08	15°57.076'S	25°56.872'E
KNPJ09	15°58.663'S	25°55.984'E
KNPJ10	16°01.204'S	25°54.591'E
KNPJ11	16°01.456'S	25°56.228'E
JNAMI1	15°51.410'S	25°58.228'E
JNAMI2	15°53.050'S	25°58.204'E
NGOMA	15°54.649'S	25°57.300'E
TUNAMW	15°53.894'S	25°57.854'E

see the odd rock dassie scurrying about. The large chalets, dotted around well-tended gardens above the lake, are clean & well maintained, although they remain rather stark. All have en-suite bathrooms, fridge & AC. It is also possible to camp on the lakeshore. Overlooking the lake, the restaurant/bar serves lunch (US$15) & dinner (US$20). Guests can take part in game drives (US$45 & park fees); boat cruises (US$30 pp, or boat hire from US$160/½ day, plus fuel); & a hot-springs tour (US$15 pp), & there's a nice pool here, too. *Chalet US$180/200 dbl HB/FB. Camping US$15 pp.* **$$$$–$$$$$**

Places to visit in Southern Kafue Southern Kafue suits exploration in your own 4x4 well, so to concentrate on a few places to visit is really to miss the point. However, a few notable highlights are:

Lake View Drive This area is home to some of the best game in the south, enticed in the dry season by lush grassy plains next to the lake. Protection of the game is afforded both by the presence of Konkamoya, and the proximity of the national park's Ngoma headquarters (⊕ NGOMA 15°54.649'S, 25°57.300'E), about 20km from the Itezhi-Tezhi Dam wall. At Ngoma itself, there are various offices and houses for the park's staff, and you can drop in, but it's not in great condition, and isn't really set up for visitors. About 5km south of here is an all-weather airstrip (⊕ AIRNGO 15°57.867'S, 25°56.422'E).

Ngoma Forest In the Ngoma area of the park's southern section, between two junctions (⊕ KNPJ07 15°55.583'S, 25°54.910'E and ⊕ KNPJ08 15°57.076'S, 25°56.872'E), is a fairly clearly signposted track that is seldom driven. This is a shame, as it weaves its way through the beautiful and intriguing Ngoma Forest which, when devoid of leaves at the end of the dry season, is decidedly eerie. It is made up of a dense stand of mature trees which are largely Zambezi teak (*Baikiaea plurijuga*); page 445.

Camp Phoenix – Kafue Elephant Release Facility (☎ 0971 609777; **e** WDC@gamerangersinternational.org; **w** gamerangersinternational.org) Named for the first elephant rescued, Camp Phoenix is a key part of the Elephant Orphanage Project (page 446) located just 12km from the DNPW headquarters at Ngoma, an area that has an established population of around a thousand wild elephants. It offers visitors the opportunity to watch and take photographs through viewing holes in a fence as the young herd returns to their 'boma' for lunch and a bathe. This isn't a place to get up close and personal with the elephants. Indeed, human contact is kept to an absolute minimum, in order to give the animals the best chance of survival when they are eventually returned to the wild. But if you'd like an opportunity to find out a little about the social systems of elephants, and the complexities of raising orphaned elephants with a view to releasing them back into the wild, then it's an interesting place to spend an hour or so. It's important to contact the facility in advance if you plan on visiting, and arrive promptly at the agreed time, so that you have time for a briefing and to don the regulation green coat before the elephants return from the bush. For those keen to do more, a volunteering programme allows for extended stays.

Chilenje Pools Further south, several pools lie at the heart of two large, neighbouring grassy dambos which are a major attraction for game during the drier months. In theory there's a track going round this area; in practice you may have to make your own across a bumpy expanse of solidified mud.

THE DEMISE OF THE TEAK FORESTS

In the past, stands of teak forest probably covered fairly large areas of the Kalahari, and certainly of southwestern Zambia. They are comprised largely of Zambezi teak (*Baikiaea plurijuga*), previously called Rhodesian teak – a tree that occurs only in undisturbed areas of Kalahari sand in northern Botswana, northern Namibia, southern Angola and western Zambia. Now, however, this tree is severely threatened, its demise typical of that of several other hardwood species that were once common here, like *mukwa* (*Pterocarpus angolensis*), and rosewood (*Guibourtia coleosperma*).

Zambezi teak trees reach up to 20m in height, with a dense, spreading crown of leaves, and smooth, grey-brown bark. The trees flower from December to March, bearing lovely pinky-mauve flowers. Seedpods follow, from June to September, cracking open explosively to catapult their seeds a distance to the ground.

The tree's wood is dense and hard, but also very even-grained and strong. Although it has never had many traditional uses, as it was too hard to cut, it was a sought-after timber that was (and sadly is) commercially very valuable. It's been widely used for bridge-building and railway sleepers, and Coates Palgrave (page 512) reports that 'when the London corn exchange was rebuilt in 1952 a special grooved floor was designed to take the grain thrown down by the merchants, and *B. plurijuga* was selected for the parquet blocks because of its ability to withstand abrasion without splintering'.

Baikiaea plurijuga has been commercially logged in Zambia since around the start of the 20th century. Zambian timber production probably peaked in the 1930s, but by the 1960s huge tracts of teak forest had been lost. Now, although the export of *Baikiaea* logs is banned, export licences are still being issued for *Baikiaea* timber, predicated on (difficult-to-enforce) promises to leave a minimum number of the trees, and then not log the same area for 20 years.

Meanwhile, experts suggest that a 300-year cycle would be needed to allow the forests to regenerate. They note that fire is often used as a tool by loggers, to open up the dense under-storey of vegetation (known as *mutemwa*) in *B. plurijuga* forests, and that the debris left behind after logging will often lead to fires. *B. plurijuga* is particularly sensitive because its thin bark renders it very susceptible to fire; once burnt, these forests degrade forever and don't recover.

In recent years the poverty in the area, combined with major commercial pressures, has led to many of Zambia's remaining 'forest reserves' being degazetted, which then opens them up for commercial logging. So, sadly, a beautiful teak forest like Ngoma is an increasingly rare sight.

Mufuta Loop West of Nanzhila Plains Safari Camp, this is another interesting game-drive loop that takes in more undulating terrain, fringed by woodland and dotted with pools that attract numerous water birds. Keep an eye out in particular for the magnificent sable antelope.

Nanzhila Plains If you're travelling through the south of the park, then two tracks run east–west. Take these towards the start of the dry season, and you'll often find yourself in plains with grass several metres tall, which is lovely but doesn't

ELEPHANT ORPHANAGE PROJECT

Established in 2001 with the aim to 'rescue, rehabilitate and release' elephants orphaned as a result of human actions, such as poaching, the Elephant Orphanage Project is based on a similar model in Kenya run by Daphne Sheldrick. Under the auspices of the Zambian NGO Game Rangers International, and with the support of the David Shepherd Foundation, it is one aspect of three elephant-focused projects, which also include park protection and training, plus – crucially – education and awareness. In the long term, it is hoped to extend the remit to include both research and community development.

By mid 2015, the unit comprised ten elephants, from the youngest, three-year-old Mphamvu, to the oldest, 11-year-old Chodoba. They, like the others, were traumatised on arrival, having lost not just their mothers but also their social bonds within the herd, but with time and care they adapt to both their new companions and the strange environment. The little ones in particular receive protection from Chamilandu, who until recently was the only female here before she was joined by Kavalamanja. Their keepers – ten of them working on a 24-hour rota – form part of a wider 'family' network, bottle-feeding the babies every 3 hours until they are weaned at around two–three years.

The elephants are split into two groups, with six still living within the facility, sleeping within a boma where an electric fence keeps them safe from lions. These elephants are up early, heading out into the bush at 06.00 with two keepers and a DNPW scout, and returning only at lunchtime. The afternoon routine is similar, leaving at around 14.30 and returning at 18.00, which allows time for regular monitoring, ranging from measuring the orphans to checking the colour of their tongues as a guide to appetite.

The rest of the herd are currently in the release phase, and while they do return to visit the orphan herd, they largely live away from the facility and the keepers. Already, they are interacting with the wild population, although it is not until they reach maturity – and full independence – that they have a hope of being accepted into the herd. With an average maturation of around 15 years for males, and from nine to 15 for the females, this is a long-haul project, with each elephant expected to stay at the orphanage for at least ten years.

For those interested in helping, there's a programme through which volunteers spend a month working in pairs in the areas of community development, education, research, and may be required to assist with the elephant husbandry including feedings and support during rescues. The project runs during the dry season only, between April and November.

make for good game viewing. It's also surprisingly easy to get lost here! (Beware of inflammable seeds in your radiator; page 143.) Later in the year, when the grass dies back, visibility is excellent.

Within this area you'll also find woodland sections, tree-islands and even the odd lone baobab tree (*Adansonia digitata*). There are several pools here, too, which attract relatively large herds of game and some wonderful birdlife.

South of Nanzhila, however, the lack of wildlife tells a sorrier tale, with just the odd reedbuck putting in an appearance among the tree squirrels and hornbills; poaching in this area of the Kafue is a serious problem.

FURTHER INFORMATION The Kafue Trust sponsored publication of *The Kafue National Park, Zambia,* by Ashley Nikki; page 514.

LOCHINVAR AND BLUE LAGOON NATIONAL PARKS

Further down the Kafue's course, east of Ngoma, are two small national parks that encompass opposite sides of the Kafue River's floodplain. Their geography and ecosystems are very similar, but despite continuing efforts to rejuvenate both parks, their infrastructure has all but collapsed and wildlife has suffered heavily from poaching in the last few years.

Historically, both Blue Lagoon and Lochinvar have had populations of people living and farming around their borders, and often inside the park. Most are poor cattle herders, and probably aren't averse to supplementing their diets with (technically illegal) subsistence hunting. Their ancestors probably hunted here before these areas were either taken over as farms, or declared national parks; hence it could easily be argued that these lands belong more to these people than they do to ZAWA. Clearly any long-term solution needs to include these people – which is not an easy task.

Neither park receives many visitors, and those who do visit should arrive with their own supplies; there is currently no lodge accommodation or camping facilities here.

GEOGRAPHY Both parks are very flat, and the sections nearer the river are seasonally flooded. The resulting watery grassland reflects the sky like a mirror, for as far as you can see. It is quite a sight, and a remarkable environment for both animals and waterfowl.

In both parks you'll find a variety of quite clearly defined environments, as you move away from the waterways to the dry, permanent woodlands. Immediately beside the water, you'll find very large areas of open grassland which are seasonally flooded – a classic **floodplain** environment. On the drier side of this, where the grassland does not receive a regular annual flooding, termitaria can exist – with high solid mounds (often looking like chimneys) to keep their occupants safe from drowning in the occasional exceptional flood. This is a very distinct area in the grasslands, known as the **termitaria zone**.

Further away still, where there's absolutely no risk of flooding, you'll find a variety of trees in the woodlands which extend across the south of Lochinvar and the north of Blue Lagoon.

FLORA AND FAUNA

Flora The landscapes in both parks change with proximity to the river, especially above the 'high flood' line. Within parts of the termitaria zone you'll find some low bushes like the paperbark acacias (*Acacia sieberana*), zebrawoods (*Dalbergia melanoxylon*), fever trees (*Acacia xanthophloea*) and rough-leaved raisin bushes (*Grewia flavescens*). Drier patches here, such as the area around the tented camp, often have pretty acacia glades with large and shady white thorns (*Acacia polyocantha*) and smaller blue thorns (*Acacia erubescens*).

As the plains gradually merge into woodland, you'll find some of the typical species from munga woodlands (page 31) including sickle-leafed albezias (*Albezi harveyi*), pepper-leafed commiphoras (*Commiphora mossambicensis*) and the distinctive woolly caper-bushes (*Caparis tormentosa*).

Slightly higher and further from the water, the tree-belt becomes more established and varied, containing different bands of mixed woodlands. The belts of mopane woodland are particularly distinctive, dominated by *Colophospermum mopane*, but also including leadwoods (*Combretum imberbe*), raintrees (*Lonchocarpus capassa*), and even the occasional knobthorn (*Acacia negrescens*).

Finally, well away from the water, you find stands of classic miombo woodland becoming the dominant environment – for example, as you travel south out of Lochinvar. (As an aside, it was interesting to see some notable specimens of Natal mahogany, *Trichilia emetica*, in this particular woodland.)

Fauna The very different bands of vegetation in these parks give rise to a wide variety of birds and animals – although this also means that some of the species found here are restricted to fairly small areas of the parks and so you need to move around if you're to have a chance of seeing a good range of them.

Animals Traditionally, the parks have been home to huge herds of Kafue lechwe – a little-known subspecies of the red lechwe, endemic to the Kafue's floodplain. The Kafue lechwe used to occur here in enormous numbers, with population estimates in the 1930s suggesting about 250,000 lived across the whole Kafue Flats area. By the 1950s an aerial survey put the population at about 95,000 lechwe, which continued to decline to 38,000 in 2005. Little data has been collected on their populations since, but they remain threatened by poaching, and increasing pressure from cattle grazing by local communities; we have to move swiftly to conserve them, and their habitat.

Alongside the Kafue lechwe, many other species occur here – although all have reduced in numbers drastically over the last few decades. Typical of this area are buffalo, eland, roan, plains zebra, Lichtenstein's hartebeest, blue wildebeest, puku, reedbuck and the delightful, diminutive oribi antelope; while in the thickets on the edge of the plains you'll find kudu, baboon and vervet monkeys. That said, last reports were that reedbuck had disappeared from Blue Lagoon, and that bushbuck numbers were in single digits.

Birds The best season for birds on the Kafue's floodplain is probably around April/May, when the waters are at their highest levels. Then the resulting lagoons attract a great variety of migrant birds – giving a staggering spectacle of waterfowl. Often you'll find large numbers of just a couple of species in one area. This may be dominated by fulvous ducks, pratincoles, sandgrouse, or waders like sandpipers, avocets, ruff, Kittlitz's plovers, little stints and black-winged stilts. In the last ten years, Lochinvar has become a major wintering ground for black-tailed godwits, 3,000 or more of them. Lapwings – or plovers – are usually plentiful, including long-toed, crowned, white-crowned and the ubiquitous blacksmith.

Pelicans are always around, both white and pink backed, and sometimes so are small numbers of flamingos. Cranes, both wattled and crowned, are there, usually in flocks of a hundred or more, plus spoonbills and a variety of storks and ibises (notably sacred and glossy). In both parks the best areas for watching water birds are unpredictable. They depend on the water levels, which in turn depend on the flood regime of the Itezhi-Tezhi Dam upstream.

However, during the early rains, the grasslands are always full of harlequin quails, Luapula cisticolas, Ethiopian snipe, yellow-crowned bishops and a sprinkling of streaky-breasted flufftails. Later in the season when the plains are dry, secretary birds pace around in pairs, while in the air are plenty of raptors – bateleur, martial and African hawk eagles, plus brown and black-breasted snake eagles. Among the thousands of lechwe there are always recent deaths, so there are four species of vulture present, plus large numbers of marabou storks.

LOCHINVAR NATIONAL PARK (Park fees US$10 pp/day; vehicle US$15/day) Lochinvar's northern boundary is the Kafue River. The land on which the park stands was originally obtained from the local Chief Hamusende in around 1908 by a Mr Horne, a man known locally as 'the Major'. Horne was a Scottish cattle farmer from Botswana who registered the land on behalf of the British South Africa Company, and built the old Lochinvar Lodge as his farmhouse.

Previously little of this land had been used for farming because of the game here, including lion and leopard. To convert the land into a cattle ranch, Horne set about exterminating these. In a ruthless programme of annihilation, populations of sable, roan, eland, warthog and wildebeest were wiped out, as well as lion – the last of which is thought to have been killed in 1947.

However, in 1966 Lochinvar Ranch (as it was then called) was bought by the Zambian government with the help of a grant from the WWF, and converted into a GMA; but the extra protection afforded to the wildlife by this designation was not enough to prevent its numbers from diminishing further, and so in 1972 Lochinvar was upgraded to a national park.

Subsequently the park has been designated as a 'wetland of international importance', and at one point a WWF team was working with the local people to help manage the park on a sustainable basis.

There are a lot of settlements around Lochinvar, and local people still come into the park – as they have done for centuries. Many were unhappy with Lochinvar Ranch – and have always felt that this is their land. They come to gather wild foods and fish, and even to drive their cattle from one side to the other; so although major conservation efforts are being made in Lochinvar, building up the diversity and number of game species here is not an easy task.

Getting there Lochinvar is easiest to approach from Monze, on the Livingstone–Lusaka road – about 287km from Livingstone and 186km from Lusaka. The road that heads northwest from Monze, signposted for Namwala, is just north of the grain silos on the Lusaka side of town. From town head for the point ⊕ TULOCH 16°15.465'S, 27°28.632'E.

It passes Chongo village and forks (⊕ T2LOCH 16°10.054'S, 27°23.610'E) about 8km afterwards. Ask local advice to find this junction if necessary. Take the right fork, or you will end up in Kafue. Follow this road for about 10km and then turn left at another sign (⊕ TULV14 16°3.718'S, 27°22'E). It is then about 14km to the park gate. This last section of the track twists and turns, but all the tracks that split off eventually rejoin each other and lead to the park. There are also a few more signs so, if you become unsure, ask a local person and they'll show you the way. The gate to Lochinvar (⊕ LOGATE 16°0.737'S, 27°15.569'E) is about 48km from Monze.

Where to stay There have been no safari lodges or camps in Lochinvar for over 15 years now and, in spite of occasional mumblings about reinvigorating the old Lechwe Plains Tented Camp, the reality of poor park infrastructure makes the economic viability of even a simple safari camp here economically questionable.

With no camps or lodges, your only option for staying in the park is camping, for which you will need all your own supplies. There have been several sites here, but it's best to ask the scouts at the gate for the latest news. To reach what was the official

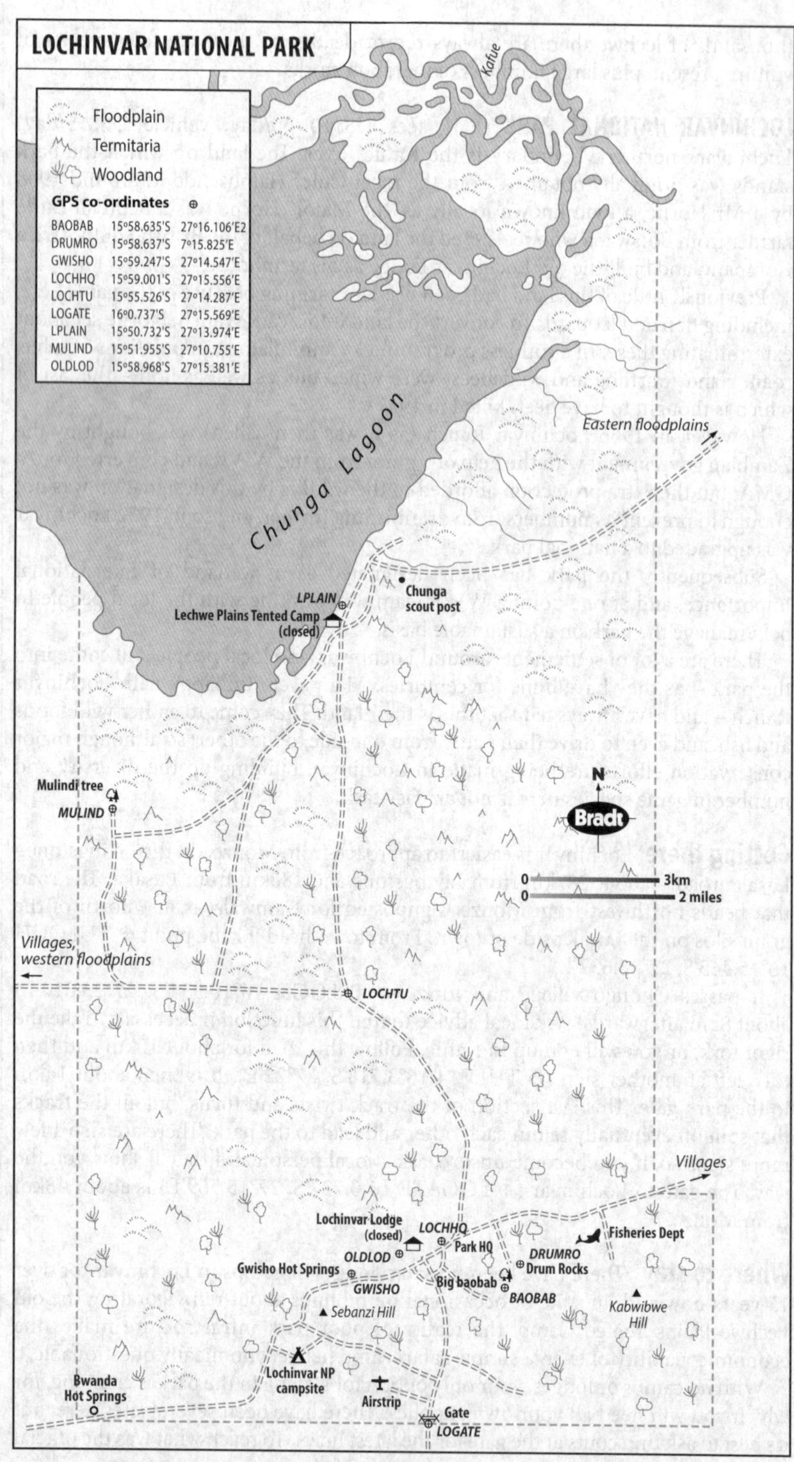

LOCHINVAR NATIONAL PARK
Floodplain
Termitaria
Woodland
GPS co-ordinates
BAOBAB 15º58.635'S 27º16.106'E2
DRUMRO 15º58.637'S 7º15.825'E
GWISHO 15º59.247'S 27º14.547'E
LOCHHQ 15º59.001'S 27º15.556'E
LOCHTU 15º55.526'S 27º14.287'E
LOGATE 16º0.737'S 27º15.569'E
LPLAIN 15º50.732'S 27º13.974'E
MULIND 15º51.955'S 27º10.755'E
OLDLOD 15º58.968'S 27º15.381'E
Kafue
Chunga Lagoon
Eastern floodplains
Chunga scout post
LPLAIN
Lechwe Plains Tented Camp (closed)
Mulindi tree
MULIND
N
Bradt
0 3km
0 2 miles
Villages, western floodplains
LOCHTU
Villages
Lochinvar Lodge (closed)
LOCHHQ
Park HQ
Fisheries Dept
OLDLOD
DRUMRO
Drum Rocks
Gwisho Hot Springs
GWISHO
Big baobab
BAOBAB
Sebanzi Hill
Kabwibwe Hill
Lochinvar NP campsite
Airstrip
Bwanda Hot Springs
Gate
LOGATE

campsite, drive about 2km past the gate into the park, and take the second left turning. Continue for about 5km. This site in theory has water, a long-drop toilet and a simple cold shower, with firewood and a barbecue provided. It is close to the hot springs at Bwanda, near the old Lupanda Wildlife Camp. If you wish to pick up a scout from the gate to guide you, then it's advisable to arrange this in advance.

What to see and do With the rapid depletion of the game, the birds are the main attraction at Lochinvar. The best birding is generally close to the water, on the floodplain. For this it's probably best to walk north and east from Mulindi Tree or north of Chunga towards Hippo Corner. It's vital to avoid driving anywhere that's even vaguely damp on the floodplain as your vehicle will just slip through the crust and into the black-cotton soil – which will probably spoil and extend your stay in equal measure. A few sites to note include:

Gwisho Hot Springs (⊕ GWISHO 15°59.247'S, 27°14.547'E) Gwisho Hot Springs are near the southern edge of the park. To get here drive from the main gate to the old lodge, and then turn sharp left immediately in front of the old lodge's gates. From the campsite, drive north out of the camp and turn right towards Sebanzi Hill, following the edge of the plain. After about 2.5km turn left at a stone cairn and palms. The springs are signposted, and just a few kilometres further on, about 2km west of the old lodge.

The springs were formed by a geological fault which stretches along the southern end of the park, on the edge of the Kafue Flats Basin. Associated with this is a deposit of gypsum, the mineral used to make plaster of Paris, which was mined at Gwisho from 1973 to 1978. You can follow the white rocks which mark this fault from Bwanda Hot Springs past the old campsite and Sebanzi Hill through Gwisho Hot Springs to the lodge, and past Drum Rocks.

The water which wells up into these springs has been heated far below the surface, and thus is independent of the rainfall or local surface water conditions. It varies from about 60°C to 94°C, and contains a high concentration of sodium, chlorine, calcium and sulphates.

The thick vegetation around the springs is surrounded by a picturesque stand of real fan palms (*Hyphaene petersiana*), whose small fruits, when opened, are seen to have a hard kernel known as 'vegetable ivory'. In the thick, wet vegetation here keep a lookout for birding 'specials' including black coucal and Fülleborn's longclaw. Also look out for the stand of gnarled old trees on the rocks at the top of the small rise beside the springs. These may look a little like deformed baobabs, but they are in fact African star-chestnut trees (*Sterculia africana*).

In the early 1960s, when the remains of late Stone-Age settlements were excavated here, it was described as one of the best-preserved and oldest sites in southern Africa. Among the findings were Arab-style trading beads, suggesting that the local inhabitants had traded the salt collected here far and wide, possibly as far as east Africa. Some artefacts discovered here are on display at Livingstone Museum.

Talk to the local people and they will tell you that the Gwisho area was the location of several fierce battles between the Tonga/Ila people and the Batwa, with hundreds of men being killed at a time – hence the existence of several mass burial sites nearby.

Bwanda Hot Springs Bwanda Hot Springs lie in the southwest of the park, surrounded by a large area of reed beds. They're quite close to Limpanda scout camp, and so are often used for bathing and washing by the local people – and even sometimes as a place to water their cattle.

KAFUE RIVER FLOODS

The Kafue River was dammed in two stages. Initially, in 1971, a dam was built in the Kafue Gorge, just south of Lusaka, which permanently flooded 800–1,100km² of land on the eastern side of the Kafue Flats. However, the gradient of the river above this point had always been very low (about 8m drop in over 200km of river), so the result was a huge, shallow reservoir with a relatively low volume (785 million cubic metres). The Kafue Dam's primary purpose was to provide hydro-electric power: it supplies up to 75% of Zambia's electricity. To guarantee this it needed a reservoir which was effectively larger than this.

Thus a second dam was built and closed in 1977: the Itezhi-Tezhi Dam. This is about 450km upstream of the Kafue Dam, and flooded only 300km² of land with a much deeper lake – holding about 4,925 million cubic metres of water. Hence the flow from Itezhi-Tezhi could be regulated to provide the constant flow needed by the Kafue Dam to generate electricity. When the dams were constructed, ZESCO (Zambia Electricity Supply Corporation) was obliged to ensure that there was a continuous flow out of Itezhi-Tezhi, in order to preserve the Kafue Flats habitat, and service the other users of the water. (The largest of these are the sugar industry around Mazabuka, and the municipality of Lusaka, which extracts water for the city.) However, this was a very difficult task – made all the more complex because the flood takes about six weeks to get from Itezhi-Tezhi to the Kafue Dam.

Before the dams, the river's flow varied enormously with the season: the Kafue Flats flooded every year and the floodplains experienced a long dry season. Since

Sebanzi Hill This national monument marks the position of an Iron-Age village on the top of the hill, which was excavated during the 1960s. Archaeologists say it has been inhabited for most of the last millennium. Originally known as Ko-Banza, the village continued to exist right up to the first half of the 20th century when the villagers were evicted, presumably by the ranch owners. Looking out from this site you have an excellent view over the park and the springs, and hence realise why it was a strategically important site in times of turmoil.

The giant baobab on Sebanzi is said to be 2,500 years old, and is often used by nesting white-backed vultures. There are also said to be some caves in the side of the hill, though these are now hidden behind deep, impenetrable thicket. The hill is still probably home to some threatened southern African species, including pangolin and aardvark, as well as hyenas, jackals, bush pig, bushbuck and small wildcats. Notable birds often seen here include the African broadbill.

Drum Rocks Close to the lodge, in the south of the park, is an outcrop of rocks (⊕ DRUMRO 15°58.635'S, 27°16.106'E) that echo when tapped, producing a curious, resonant, almost metallic sound. These are the Drum Rocks, or Ibbwe Lyoombwa in the local language. Ask the scouts to direct you to these: they are fascinating. (Similar rocks, on the farm called Immenhof, in Namibia, were originally discovered by San/Bushmen and are now known locally as the 'singing rocks'.)

Considered sacred by the locals, these rocks are actually just the remnants of much larger boulders that were dynamited by the ranch's owners, curious to know the secret of their sound. They play an important part in the local religious calendar. As part of an elaborate rite of passage, it is traditional for a young man to come with his cattle to the rocks, chant '*Ibbwe Lyoombwa*' and then perform a dance the dams, ZESCO has released a four-week artificial 'flood' in March, but clearly it has failed to simulate the natural situation. The UK's Department for International Development (DFID) reported in 2001 on *Managed Flood Releases from the Itezhi-Tezhi Reservoir*, and within that noted:

> Since the dams, the flooding pattern has changed considerably. There has been a reduction in the seasonal fluctuations. The annual minimum flood area has increased from about 300km² to approximately 1,500km². In places permanent lagoons have formed where ephemeral aquatic habits had existed before. In broad terms, the western half of the Flats is drier, while the eastern half is wetter than they were prior to dam construction.

This altered flood pattern has knock-on effects to the whole ecosystem. Old-time visitors to Lochinvar will tell you that the vegetation there has changed enormously over the last 30 years, and not for the better. With the change in vegetation come changes in the grazing – for both wildlife and cattle. Then, of course, the breeding cycles of the fish are affected and there's no longer any movement of fish upriver past the dams. When fish populations change, so do those of many bird species.

There is much further research to be done, and the WWF is involved in a project to simulate the river's old flood regime using new computer models to control the Itezhi-Tezhi Dam outflow. Many people are now starting to make strenuous efforts to ensure that while maximising the benefits provided by these dams, they also minimise the inevitable environmental problems caused by them.

and various rituals designed to prove his manliness. At the end, he should leave with his cattle without turning back, for fear of seeing his dead ancestors, and then stay away from his village until the beginning of the rains. If he has proved himself sufficiently, he will then be considered an adult and will be able to take a bride on his return. Even today, visitors are supposed to chant '*Ibbwe Lyoombwa*' to prevent bad luck befalling them.

Nearby is a large baobab (⊕ BAOBAB 15°58.637'S, 27°15.825'E) with a completely hollow trunk that can be entered from a crack in the side (which is the size of a small doorway). According to Chief Hamusende, the hollow was formed by an old man who, given a magic club, decided to try it out by bashing it against a nearby baobab; a broken tree and the formation of the hollow were the result of his experiment. It was actually used as a shelter by the district commissioner during the 1800s, and local legend has it that anybody who refuses to believe in the customs and beliefs of the villagers will enter into the hollow and never return, the tree sealing up and closing behind them.

Mwanachingwala Conservation Area Although east of the national park boundary, Mwanachingwala lies in a similar environment to Lochinvar National Park, but is normally accessed from Mazabuka (page 237).

BLUE LAGOON NATIONAL PARK (US$10 pp/day; vehicle US$15/day) Blue Lagoon is on the north side of the Kafue River. It was originally owned by a farming couple turned conservationists, the Critchleys, but more recently, especially during KK's reign, the Ministry of Defence restricted access to the military, plus a few privileged politicians and generals who used the old

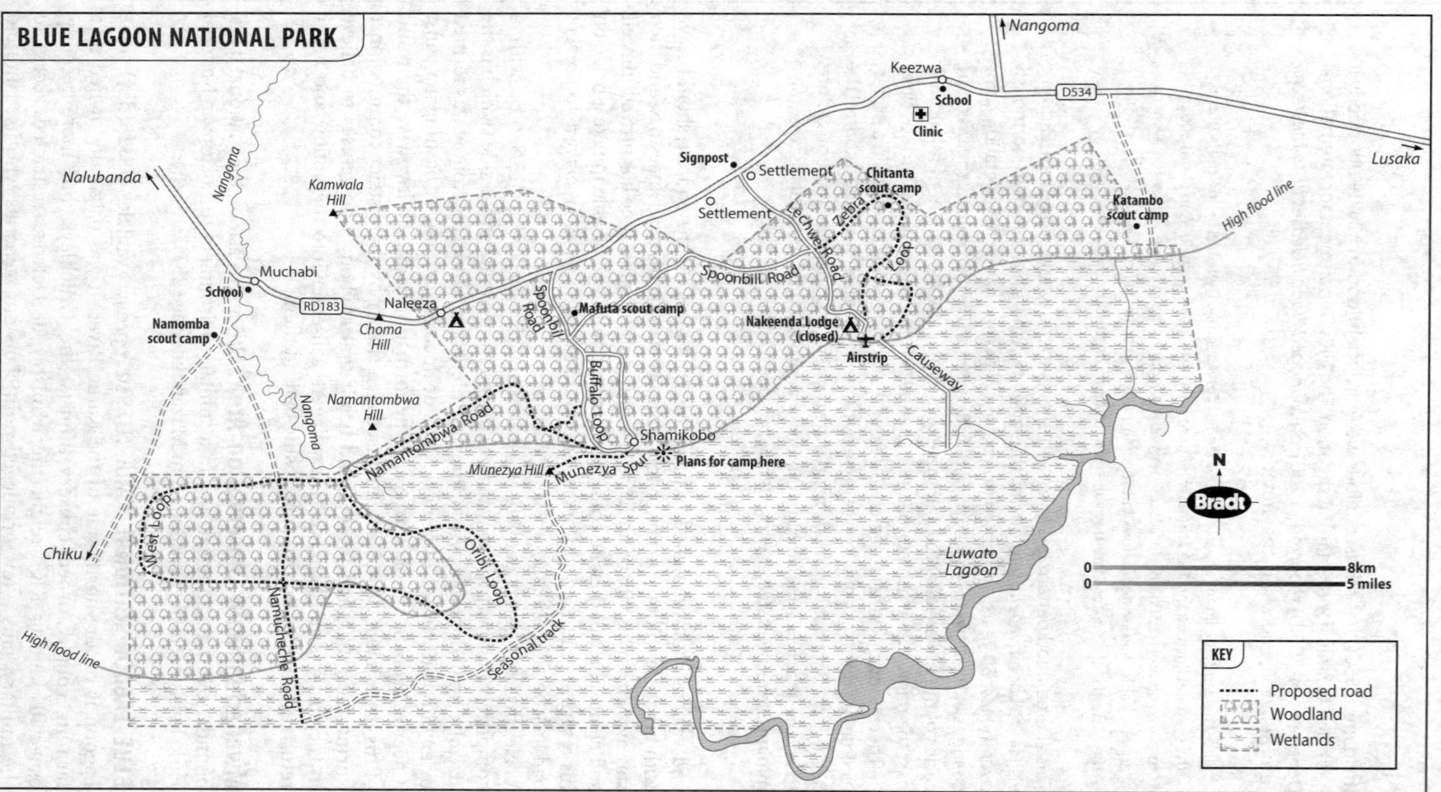
BLUE LAGOON NATIONAL PARK
Nangoma
Keezwa
School
D534
Clinic
Lusaka
Signpost
Settlement
Settlement
Chitanta scout camp
Katambo scout camp
High flood line
Nalubanda
Nangoma
Kamwala Hill
Zebra Loop
Lechwe Road
Spoonbill Road
Muchabi
School
RD183
Naleeza
Spoonbill Road
Mafuta scout camp
Nakeenda Lodge (closed)
Airstrip
Causeway
Namomba scout camp
Choma Hill
Buffalo Loop
Namantombwa Hill
Nangoma
Namantombwa Road
Shamikobo
Plans for camp here
Munezya Hill
Munezya Spur
N
Bradt
West Loop
Chiku
Oribi Loop
Luwato Lagoon
0
8km
0
5 miles
Namucheche Road
High flood line
Seasonal track
KEY
Proposed road
Woodland
Wetlands

farmhouse intermittently as a hunting retreat – with predictable impact on the local wildlife.

Despite being declared a Ramsar site, along with Lochinvar, and the WWF drawing up conservation plans for the area, nothing was ever finalised, and no practical management takes place. While it's feasible that the area could be rejuvenated, it would require significant private investment, which is not forthcoming. The park's Nakeenda Lodge has been closed since 2007, so the future remains uncertain. Reports suggest that many of the park's trails are very overgrown and that, while the birding is excellent, and antelope are to be seen near the lagoons, other wildlife is little in evidence.

Getting there Blue Lagoon is reasonably well signposted, and there are several ways to reach it. Note, however, that it's not possible to reach it from the south, unless you're arriving by boat during the floods!

From Lusaka The easiest route from Lusaka is to take the Great West Road towards Mumbwa, then turn left after about 22km, opposite the filling station. There is a faded sign for the park here, but a much clearer one for Nampundwe Mine. This all-weather gravel road leads to the national park's scout camp at Naleeza. If you're heading for Nakeenda Lodge (currently closed) then follow the sign left.

From the west From the west, pass through Kafue's Nalusanga scout post and about 81km from here, beyond Mumbwa, look for a Lushomo garage near Nangoma. Fill up here if they have fuel, then continue towards Lusaka for a few hundred metres, before taking the first right turn after the filling station, following the power lines. In less than a kilometre, turn right at the crossroads and keep following those power lines! (This junction is on a local bus route, so if you ask directions you will probably end up with a guide and their luggage; a fair deal all round!) Continuing for 9km brings you to Myooye village, where you should take the left fork that passes the clinic on the right-hand side.

Follow this track for 31km to a T-junction, ignoring smaller side tracks. (If the group of huts on the left, halfway along this road, has a flag flying, it means that the Tonga chief who lives here is in residence.) Turn right at the T-junction, and continue for 22km, ignoring a right-hand turn, passing through the first gate and finally reaching the scout post. Sign in here, pay the park and camping fees, and check the current camping rules with the scouts.

Where to stay The old-style self-catering Nakeenda Lodge has long been abandoned but there are still four basic chalets nearby available (e info@bluelagoon.co.zm; **$$**). The better option is probably to bring all your equipment with you and ask one of the scouts at the gate if you can camp at one of the old national park sites.

What to see and do The park is dominated by the Kafue Flats, which are flooded in the rainy season. This is certainly the best time for birdwatching here, and the park is generally at its best. In the dry season the view is not as stunning but still worth a visit.

The Critchleys built a causeway that extends for about 5km over the marshy flats, which although overgrown still enables vehicles to drive out onto the flats for a wonderful view of the stunning birdlife; there's even a turning circle at the end. Along the causeway are several memorial stones, one reading:

Erica Critchley 1910–1976
To the memory of the
one who loved Zambia
so much she cared for
human and natural resources.
Let what she stood for
not be forgotten by Zambians
especially by its youth.

Kenneth Kaunda
President of Zambia
March 30 1976

In the dry season, when the end of the causeway doesn't usually reach the water, a ranger from the scout post will take you on walks around the flats. Aside from the wildlife, do visit the old farmhouse that used to be owned by the Critchleys. It's fascinating.

15

Western Zambia

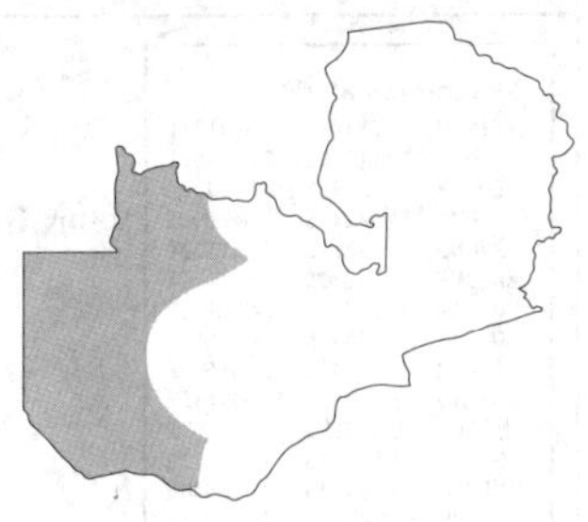

Western Zambia is remote; it can be difficult to visit but rewards intrepid travellers with some of the country's most culturally fascinating experiences, superb tiger fishing and the wonder of Liuwa Plain National Park. The star in Western Zambia's safari crown, Liuwa Plain is the venue for one of Africa's last great wildlife migrations, or 'gatherings', but has remained largely unknown because of the challenges of getting into the area. It was not so long ago that expedition-style self-drive trips were the only way to visit the park and the visitor book on the entrance gate was only just hitting double-digits. Now, with significantly improved access, good safari operations, some great campsites and a reliable network of roads, it makes a terrific destination for experienced safari-goers keen to see excellent game alongside few visitors.

The other parks in the region, Sioma Ngwezi and West Lunga, do not have the same reputation for wildlife, but Sioma Ngwezi at least is still a very wild place to explore with a well-prepared group of 4x4 vehicles. The Barotse floodplains, near Mongu, offer a glimpse of rural Zambian life that is still largely untouched by the 21st century and are home to one of the country's most flamboyant festivals: **Kuomboka**.

Common to almost the whole area are the related problems of supplies and transport. Much of the region stands on deep Kalahari sand where vehicles need a high-clearance 4x4 capability. If you are going off the main roads, then a small expedition convoy is needed consisting of several vehicles, in case one runs into problems. During the rainy season, many of the roads are completely impassable, and even the pontoons (ferries) across the rivers will often stop working. Being stranded is a very real possibility. Thus the area's paucity of visitors is largely explained by the sheer difficulty of getting around.

The Christian missions have a very well-established network here. On the whole, these do remarkable work for the communities in the area, being involved with schools, hospitals, churches, development projects and many other aspects of local life. The courteous traveller can learn a lot about the region from these missions, and they are also good places to find English-speaking guides to accompany you on your travels – who will prove invaluable for just a few dollars per day.

For convenient travel planning, this chapter is divided into three sections: southwestern Zambia, Barotseland and northwestern Zambia. These don't slavishly follow provincial divisions; rather they reflect the differences between the areas as we understand them and a practical way to explore the region. The first section, through southwestern Zambia, is detailed as a tour, starting from the border towns of Kazungula and Sesheke, and continuing north up the Zambezi to Mongu. This is how you'd approach the region from Livingstone, where reliable, fully kitted out 4x4 vehicles can be hired and supplies easily acquired.

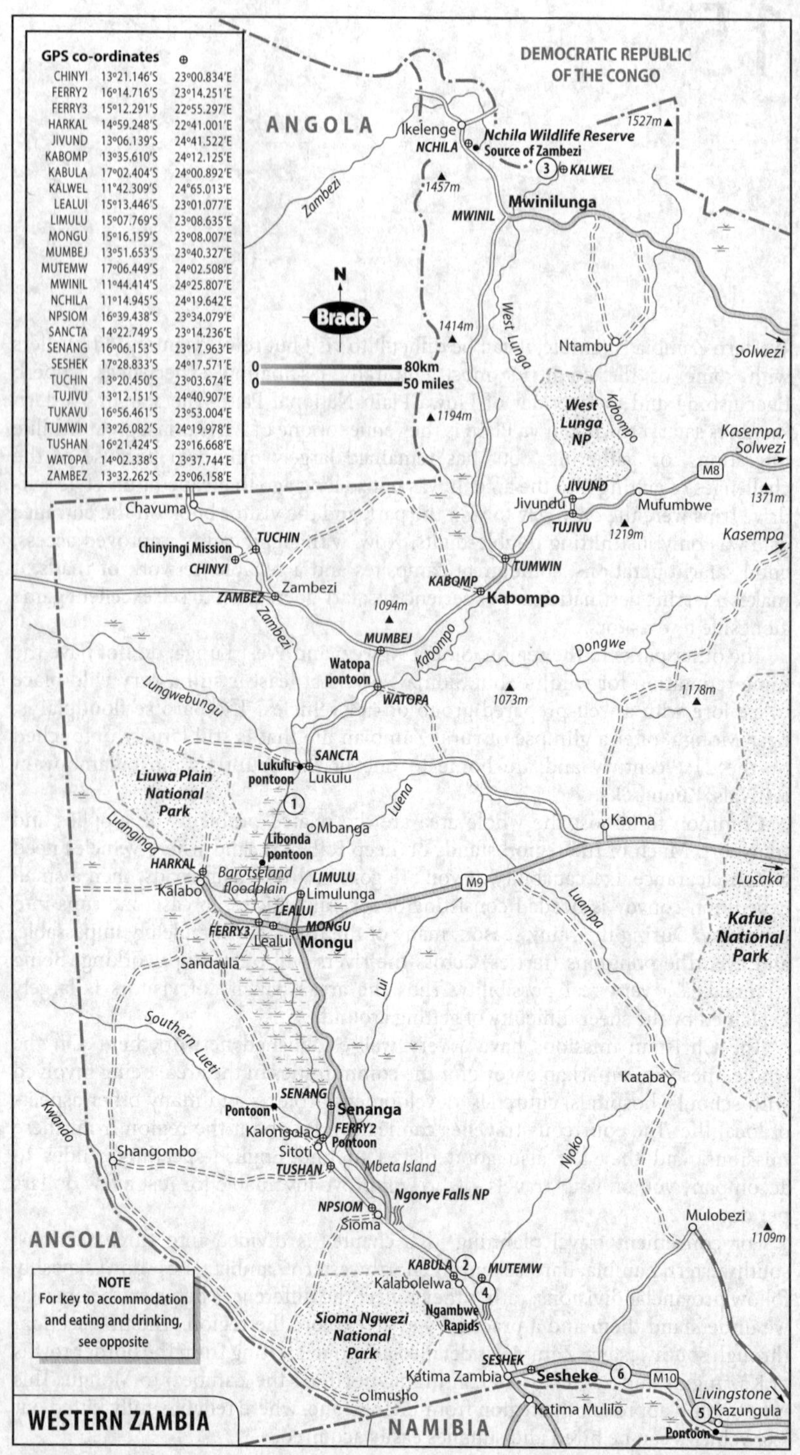
GPS co-ordinates
CHINYI 13°21.146'S 23°00.834'E
FERRY2 16°14.716'S 23°14.251'E
FERRY3 15°12.291'S 22°55.297'E
HARKAL 14°59.248'S 22°41.001'E
JIVUND 13°06.139'S 24°41.522'E
KABOMP 13°35.610'S 24°12.125'E
KABULA 17°02.404'S 24°00.892'E
KALWEL 11°42.309'S 24°65.013'E
LEALUI 15°13.446'S 23°01.077'E
LIMULU 15°07.769'S 23°08.635'E
MONGU 15°16.159'S 23°08.007'E
MUMBEJ 13°51.653'S 23°40.327'E
MUTEMW 17°06.449'S 24°02.508'E
MWINIL 11°44.414'S 24°25.807'E
NCHILA 11°14.945'S 24°19.642'E
NPSIOM 16°39.438'S 23°34.079'E
SANCTA 14°22.749'S 23°14.236'E
SENANG 16°06.153'S 23°17.963'E
SESHEK 17°28.833'S 24°17.571'E
TUCHIN 13°20.450'S 23°03.674'E
TUJIVU 13°12.151'S 24°40.907'E
TUKAVU 16°56.461'S 23°53.004'E
TUMWIN 13°26.082'S 24°19.978'E
TUSHAN 16°21.424'S 23°16.668'E
WATOPA 14°02.338'S 23°37.744'E
ZAMBEZ 13°32.262'S 23°06.158'E
DEMOCRATIC REPUBLIC OF THE CONGO
ANGOLA
Ikelenge
Nchila Wildlife Reserve
NCHILA
Source of Zambezi
KALWEL
1527m
1457m
Zambezi
MWINIL
Mwinilunga
N
Bradt
1414m
0 80km
0 50 miles
West Lunga
Ntambu
Solwezi
1194m
West Lunga NP
Kabompo
Kasempa, Solwezi
M8
JIVUND
Jivundu
Mufumbwe
1371m
TUJIVU
1219m
Kasempa
Chavuma
TUCHIN
Chinyingi Mission
CHINYI
TUMWIN
KABOMP
Kabompo
ZAMBEZ
Zambezi
1094m
MUMBEJ
Dongwe
Watopa pontoon
WATOPA
1073m
1178m
Lungwebungu
SANCTA
Lukulu pontoon
Lukulu
Liuwa Plain National Park
Luena
Luanginga
Libonda pontoon
Mbanga
Kaoma
HARKAL
Kalabo
Barotseland floodplain
LIMULU
Limulunga
M9
Lusaka
LEALUI
FERRY3
Lealui
MONGU
Mongu
Luampa
Kafue National Park
Sandaula
Lui
Southern Lueti
Kataba
SENANG
Pontoon
Senanga
Kwando
Kalongola
FERRY2
Pontoon
Njoko
Shangombo
Sitoti
TUSHAN
Mbeta Island
Ngonye Falls NP
NPSIOM
Sioma
Mulobezi
1109m
ANGOLA
KABULA
MUTEMW
Kalabolelwa
NOTE
For key to accommodation and eating and drinking, see opposite
Ngambwe Rapids
Sioma Ngwezi National Park
SESHEK
Katima Zambia
Sesheke
M10
Livingstone
Imusho
Katima Mulilo
Kazungula
Pontoon
WESTERN ZAMBIA
NAMIBIA

Compared with the rest of Zambia, the southwest of the country has been largely neglected, with few roads and no major towns. For the wilderness-seeking visitor, this has the benefit that its sights, like the marvellous Ngonye Falls, are very quiet.

The big draw of the Upper Zambezi, and the *raison d'être* of the camps along the river, has always been fishing – for bream and tiger fish. While an increasing number of visitors are coming for Ngonye Falls, the excellent birdlife and onward trips to Liuwa, it is fishing that retains the greatest appeal.

HIGHLIGHTS

Fishing on the Upper Zambezi The Zambezi River here is generally wide, although in parts of its course between Sesheke and Senanga it becomes shallow, broken by forested islands and rocky outcrops, and you'll also find waterfalls and rapids. So there are conditions suitable for challenging fly-fishing and spinning.

Tiger fish are the most sought-after challenge, while various bream species, particularly the predatory yellow-belly and the thin-face breams, make good sport fishing in the faster sections. In the slower sections, fishermen find the more sedentary three-spot, red-breast and greenhead bream.

Birdlife For a more gentle interaction with some of the wildlife, this area offers some excellent, undisturbed birdwatching – with various species frequenting different areas of the river and the surrounding vegetation. A few of the river's 'specials' include rock pratincoles, seen darting about the rocks of many sections of rapids; African finfoots, which lurk at the water's edge in areas of thick, overhanging vegetation; African skimmers, which nest on some of the river's exposed sandbanks; and Pel's fishing owls resting in some of the old riverine trees. You'll also have the chance to spot Schalow's and Lady Ross's turacos, yellow-spotted nicator, narina trogon and wood owls (the Mutemwa Lodge area is particularly good for these; page 462).

WEST TO SESHEKE The M10 road, running parallel to the Zambezi from Livingstone to Sesheke, is in astonishingly poor condition: from Kazungula to Sesheke its more pot-hole than road in many places. In its current state it is fairly dangerous and certainly unpleasant to drive (even trucks are taking the long route via Mongu to Lusaka!). There are plans to repair the road but infrastructure projects rarely happen quickly so do be aware and check for updates locally.

After 63km, a turning left leads to the small border town of Kazungula, with its swish new bridge to Botswana. Continuing past this turning brings you to Sesheke, where there's another bridge over the Zambezi to Katima Mulilo, and a border post with Namibia. The 190km journey from Livingstone to Sesheke takes about 4 hours on account of the driving speed required.

Kazungula This small town marks the location of an old **pontoon ferry** and a dramatic new **bridge** over the Zambezi into Botswana.

WESTERN ZAMBIA

Where to stay

1. Barotse Tiger Camp *p486*
2. Kabula Tiger Lodge *p462*
3. Kalwelwa Bushcamp *p496*
4. Mutemwa Lodge *p462*
5. Sekoma Island Lodge *p460*
6. Shackletons Lodge *p460*

On the main M10 road, just before the turn-off, the Kazungula Reststop offers snacks and more substantial dishes to passing travellers. Then, just before the ferry itself, there are a few shops, a small market (⏲ early–18.00 daily) and a simple restaurant. This is also where local buses stop.

Getting there and away The much anticipated, US$259 million **Kazungula bridge** is a road, rail and pedestrian bridge that opened in May 2021 to relieve pressure from the ferry and enhance trade routes in the region. At just under 1km in span and with a curious curve to avoid crossing into Nambia or Zimbabwe at this border quadripoint, the bridge and improved border-crossing facilities have transformed this once chaotic and slow crossing point.

If you are **crossing the border** here with a vehicle, there is a raft of paperwork (and payment) required – insurance, immigration, car import permit, carbon and road tax and police levy. It's often worth enlisting the help of one of the many 'agents' who are likely to hassle you at the border. Come prepared with plenty of cash (US$ and Kwacha) and a good deal of patience. As is often the case at busy border crossings, it's worth keeping a close eye on your belongings, ideally leaving someone with your vehicle while another deals with the paperwork. Fees vary by vehicle size but expect to pay around US$15 for a car and US$20 for a 4x4 vehicle.

The old floating **pontoon ferry** still operates (though it's hard to imagine why you might choose this route) and can take just one truck and two or three cars at a time.

A regular **bus** service run by Mazhandu Family Bus links Livingstone with Sesheke. If you're heading for Botswana, then hop on one of these and get off at Kazungula.

Where to stay *Map, page 458*

Kazungula itself has nowhere of note to stay, but there are a couple of fishing lodges to the west that welcome visitors:

Sekoma Island Lodge (9 tents) m +27 83 708 3787; e info@sekoma.co.za, sekoma.island@gmail.com; w sekoma.co.za. ⊕ SEKOMA 17°44.900'S, 25°10.533'E. Set on an island of the Zambezi near the Mambova Rapids, Sekoma is well placed for the angler in search of tiger fish or Zambezi catfish (all catch & release), while outside the fishing season it attracts keen birders, with walks & boat trips available. The lodge is accessible only by boat from Mambova village jetty. Safari-style tents sleep 2–4 guests, each with a small, decked porch right on the river's edge. During the fishing season (May–Sep) each is allocated a speedboat & guide. There's a riverside deck, too, & a boma with bar & large, cool dining room. ⏲ *mid–May–mid–Jan.* ♛♛

Shackletons Lodge (6 chalets); ☎ +27 83 251 7257; e info@shackletons.co.za; w shackletons.co.za. ⊕ SOKACA 17°29.793'S, 24°46.519'E. 55km east of Sesheke, Shackletons lies 3.5km down an easily navigable sandy track (turn-off ⊕ TUSOKA 17°28.010'S, 24°46.948'E), overlooking an island beside the Zambezi. Beyond are wide floodplains, typical of the seasonally flooded eastern end of Namibia's Caprivi Strip.

En-suite, thatched chalets overlook the river from wooden verandas. At the heart of the lodge, the split-level main building incorporates a lounge, dining area & riverside bar, with a firepit & small pool nearby & a deck over the river shaded by an ebony tree. It's a relaxed, unpretentious place, with the emphasis firmly on fishing, albeit river cruises & birding opportunities abound. ♛♛

Sesheke Sesheke sits on the eastern side of the Zambezi River, linked by a 900m bridge to a smaller town on the other side, known locally as Katima Zambia. The bridge, financed largely by Germany, was opened in 2004 by the presidents of

Zambia and Namibia. It lies about 5km inside Zambian territory, and was only the fifth bridge constructed to span the width of the Zambezi.

Sesheke itself (⊕ 17°28.599'S, 24°17.208'E) is an underwhelming, if strategically important, border village. It has a few **stores**, a small branch of the Finance **Bank**, a simple hospital, a police station (listen for their early-morning marching songs if you're staying overnight!), a **post office** and a few small **guesthouses**. There's also a **fuel** station here – although fuel is considerably cheaper across the border in Namibia's Katima Mulilo. Supplies are more plentiful there, too, so Sesheke can be very quiet.

The smaller Katima Zambia, right next to the border with Namibia, has just a police post, a small market and a few local stores.

Getting there and away Sesheke is easily reached from either Livingstone or Katima Mulilo, in Namibia. Heavy traffic has left the section of road from Kazungula to Sesheke in very poor condition though, with frequent and sizeable pot-holes making the road slow going (page 111).

There's a twice-daily bus service from Livingstone to Mongu that stops at the Sesheke border, and an InterCape bus to/from Namibia's capital Windhoek (w intercape.co.za) that leaves from the Namibian side of the border.

Where to stay Sesheke's limited accommodation options are both unsophisticated and correspondingly inexpensive, with the best being Brenda's. If you're driving yourself, you'll find several lodges along the river, both to the east of town (see below) and on the way north to Ngonye Falls (page 462).

Brenda's Best Baobab Lodge (4 chalets, camping) Mulambwe St; m 0766 793572. ⊕ SESHES 17°28.833'S, 24°17.571'E. Popular with backpackers & independent overlanders, this unexpected waterfront gem is just over 1km east of the town centre, accessed down a drive between the civic centre & St Kizito Roman Catholic Church. It's owned by friendly Brenda & her husband Harry, a Dutch GP. Their en-suite chalets under high thatch have a fridge, TV & fan & a small campsite is a convenient stopover near the border. There are basic toilets & showers, & down by the river are grassy lawns dotted with shady picnic tables, as well as wooden decking around a large central baobab. Food, drinks & an eclectic range of beers drawn from Namibia, Zambia & South Africa are available. **$$**

Sisheke Lodge (9 rooms) 0211 481086. On the left as you drive into Sesheke from Kazungula, this functional place has simple but clean en-suite rooms. There's a lounge, porch area & self-catering kitchen. **$**

DRIVING NORTH FROM SESHEKE TO NGONYE FALLS The tarred road northwest from Sesheke follows the western bank of the river for 139km to Ngonye/Sioma. If you've travelled this far from Livingstone, you'll be relieved to know the road's in excellent condition, although the rise in trucks using this stretch has increased somewhat since the Sioma Bridge opened in late 2016. From this bridge, just south of Ngonye Falls, the road crosses to the eastern bank of the Zambezi, before continuing north to Senanga.

Aside from the perennial appeal of the fishing, and other river-based excursions, the main reasons for visiting this area of southwest Zambia are the Ngonye Falls (often referred to as the Sioma Falls; page 464) and the Sioma Ngwezi National Park, which lies to the west of the river, and is encompassed within the transfrontier KAZA park (page 462). With travel further north often being very slow, this is also a good area to break the journey for a few days on your way north or south.

Where to stay *Map, page 458*

Along the Upper Zambezi, between Sesheke and Ngonye Falls, you'll pass signposts to several places to stay – primarily fishing camps, the best of which we've included here (listed south to north).

Mutemwa Lodge (6 tents) (Namibia) +27 (72) 536 1337; **e** james@hiddengemstravelco.com; **w** mutemwa.co.za. ⊕ MUTEMW 17°6.449'S, 24°2.508'E. About 55km north of Sesheke is a neatly signposted turn-off (⊕ TUMUTE 17°7.056'S, 24°1.861'E), from where it's just 2km to the lodge.

Although the best lodge in the area, it retains an appealing simplicity: tents are simple, food is wholesome fare & lighting comes from paraffin lamps (no mains electricity). The twin-bed tents have a small deck overlooking a channel of the Zambezi, shaded by the tall pale-bark waterberry trees of the riverine forest. A large central thatched roof shelters a bar, lounge & dining area, & there's a small pool nearby.

Guests, from independent self-drivers to fly-in groups (the lodge has its own landing strip), come primarily for the fishing; the camp has 6 good motorboats & several guides. More broadly, birding trips & sundowner cruises, canoeing excursions & guided walks on a 1km-long island opposite the lodge are available. During the winter months, keen anglers can choose between 3 Barotse rivers in Mutemwa's annual Barotse Floodplain Fishing Safaris: the Lungwebungu, the Zambezi & the Kwamashi floodplain. *Closed during heavy rains (Jan–Feb).*

Kabula Tiger Lodge (7 chalets, camping) +27 82 550 8642, +27 82 672 5168, +27 82 569 2998; **e** info@kabulalodge.com; **w** kabulalodge.com. ⊕ KABULA 17°02.404'S, 24°00.892'E. This self-catering lodge & campsite is primarily geared to those coming in search of fishing & birding. Simple, en-suite reed chalets have solar lighting & decks overlooking the river. Two communal kitchens are equipped with gas fridges, a cooker & basic utensils. For campers, there's a tree-shaded campsite with 6 pitches, ablution facilities, a washing-up area, & a thatched *lapa* with tables & benches beneath a venerable pod mahogany.

Guided fishing trips & walking & birding on Kabula Island, just upstream of the lodge, are possible. *All year.*

SIOMA NGWEZI NATIONAL PARK (US$5 pp/day, vehicle US$15/day) Of all Zambia's remote and seldom-visited parks, Sioma Ngwezi should probably be one of the easiest to regenerate. It is really very close to the Victoria Falls/Livingstone area, which has a huge reservoir of visitors keen to do short safari trips. Tourism to Namibia's Caprivi Strip is growing, and with a tarred main road between Sesheke and Senanga, access to the vicinity of the park is very good.

Against this background, the park was incorporated into a transfrontier 'Peace Park' (**w** peaceparks.org) in 2012: the Kavango-Zambezi Transfrontier Conservation Area, known locally as KAZA. The area covers around 287,132km², connecting Sioma Ngwezi and the surrounding GMAs with protected areas in neighbouring Botswana, Zimbabwe, Angola and northern Namibia – and notably including the Okavango Delta and Victoria Falls. As with all the Peace Parks, the primary aim is to create a corridor to allow migratory animals to move freely between the various reserves, unencumbered by manmade boundaries. In particular, this would be a step towards ending the absurd situation where Chobe has too many elephants… yet this corner of Zambia, just over the border, has too few!

Although Sioma Ngwezi's tourist infrastructure is still very rudimentary, rough tracks are being cut so that self-drive visitors can explore the park, provided that they take a game scout to show the way and are fully self-sufficient.

Geography Positioned in the far southwestern corner of Zambia, Sioma Ngwezi National Park covers 5,000km², making it the third largest of Zambia's national parks. It shares a long border with Angola, along the Kwando (or Cuando) River, and a short border with Namibia in the south. This corner is less than 50km from northern Botswana, and its vegetation and landscape owe much to the Kalahari sand that lies beneath it.

Most of the park is flat, dry and quite densely wooded – covered with a mosaic of miombo and acacia woodland, with the occasional area of teak forest. There are a few open dambos and sometimes these surround the occasional pool in the bush – but surface water is rare here during the dry season.

Geographical problems Bordering both Angola and Namibia's Caprivi Strip, Sioma Ngwezi was always going to be a difficult park to keep secure and well managed. Following years of civil war, Angola is very much still on the long road back to peace, and is far from prosperous for many. Namibia's Caprivi Strip has historically had security problems too, though these are now thankfully resolved. Sioma Ngwezi itself was a stronghold of Namibia's SWAPO fighters in the early years – and later of the Angolan rebels.

While cross-border poaching is rarely as prevalent as many in Africa will claim (people from 'over there' always make easy scapegoats for crimes the world over), it certainly is a problem in this area.

Looking at the park's geography, you'll realise that most of the animals must either survive entirely without surface water, or need to drink from one of the two rivers nearby: the Kwando on the western border, or the Zambezi which is east, outside of the park. Study a detailed map and you'll realise that what settlements there are in this area are strung out on the banks of these same rivers. So after around July, by which time the park's few dambos have dried out, much of the game needs to run a daily (or more likely, nightly) gauntlet of the riverside villages to drink.

A further problem is the logging. The practice has decimated the oldest hardwood trees in most of Zambia's western provinces, and certainly encroached illegally into this park.

Flora and fauna Sioma Ngwezi is the only Zambian park, outside the Luangwa Valley and the Mosi-oa-Tunya National Park, where giraffe have historically been found. It is claimed that rather than being the same subspecies as those in Luangwa (Thornicroft's giraffe), these are an 'Angolan' subspecies, which is different again from the more common 'southern' variety found throughout the subcontinent. Native antelope species include roan, sable, eland, tsessebe, blue wildebeest, zebra, reedbuck, kudu, steenbok, oribi and possibly lechwe on the Kwando River. The major predators are lion, leopard and spotted hyena, and there have been occasional sightings of wild dog, although these are quite possibly packs visiting from the strong population in northern Botswana. Small numbers of elephant, too, frequent the park, especially in the dry season.

Current game populations Sioma Ngwezi's game populations have taken a battering over the years. Poaching (aka subsistence hunting) is common, and made much easier by the trek to water that much of the game makes – thus bringing it into close contact with the settlements beside the two main rivers. The predators have also suffered, as they're attracted to the easy meat of grazing cattle from nearby local villages, which then bring them into direct conflict with the local people.

Thus, although small populations of most of the main game species still occur here, it is both scarce and skittish. That said, indications are that the wildlife is recovering slowly and that species like sable, roan, tsessebe, eland and reticulated giraffe are increasingly being spotted. Elephants too are returning and are visible, having re-established an old migration route in the southeast border of the park.

When to go The best time to visit Sioma Ngwezi is probably just after the end of the rains, between May and November, when the dambos inside the park still have a little water and are attracting game. Alternatively, spend time beside the Kwando later in the year, when it's the only water source around.

Getting there and getting organised There is a track leading to the eastern corner of the park and around the boundary from the Sesheke–Ngonye Falls road, about 16km south of Mutemwa Lodge. A second, 51km further north at Silumbu (⊕ TUSNNP 16°54.674'S, 23°51.117'E), close to Sioma, is clearly signposted. This heads southwest around the perimeter of the park to the Kwando River. Here it joins up with a track that runs parallel to the river from Shangombo in the northwest almost to the park's southern boundary. A new border post with Angola opened at Shangombo in 2022, crossing a 10km stretch of water along the Kwando River and likely paving the way for an improved road network to the area.

Driving is difficult and requires the backing of a couple of 4x4s. The Kalahari sand can be slow going, and is also very heavy on fuel – so remember that this is available only at Sesheke or Katima Mulilo in the south, or Senanga and Mongu to the north.

Permits for the park are available from the national park office at Ngonye Falls (⊕ NGOFNP 16°39.820'S, 23°34.264'E). If you intend to explore this area independently, then get a scout from the office to guide you, and perhaps show you to a good spot for camping. There are, as yet, no designated campsites within the park. Alternatively, you can take a two-night guided trip to the park with Mutemwa Lodge (page 462).

Security note Note that there is some question over the precise location of the border, as pre-1970s it used to be the eastern edge of the Kwando floodplain. Then Zambia 'moved' it to the middle of the river. Wherever it is, you don't want to stray over it accidentally.

NGONYE FALLS COMMUNITY PARTNERSHIP PARK (US$5 pp; vehicle US$15; ⌚ 06.00–18.00) One of the newest of Zambia's national parks, Ngonye Falls was gazetted in December 2009 and officially opened in August 2012. Conceived in partnership with the local community and traditional leaders, it lies about 127km north of Sesheke and covers just 200ha on each side of the river, although it is envisaged that it will eventually encompass a total of 1,760ha. The park is centred on the spectacular Ngonye Falls (often referred to as the Sioma Falls), and the surrounding land has been fenced off in order to start restocking it with game.

Livingstone passed this way, having come north through what is now Botswana. He noted:

> 30th November, 1853 – At Gonye Falls. No rain has fallen here, so it is excessively hot. The trees have put on their gayest dress, and many flowers adorn the landscape, yet the heat makes all the leaves droop at mid-day and look languid for want of rain. If the country increases as much in beauty in front, as it has done within the last four degrees of latitude, it will indeed be a lovely land.

> For many miles below, the river is confined in a narrow space of not more than one hundred yards wide. The water goes boiling along, and gives the idea of great masses of it rolling over and over, so that even the most expert swimmer would find it difficult to keep on the surface. Here it is that the river when in flood rises fifty or sixty feet in perpendicular height. The islands above the falls are covered with foliage as beautiful as can be seen anywhere. Viewed from the mass of rock which overhangs the fall, the scenery was the loveliest I had seen.

This was about two years before Livingstone journeyed further down the Zambezi and saw the Victoria Falls for the first time.

Flora and fauna Now that the fences are in place, initial plans to stock the park with the introduction of both zebra and several species of antelope – impala, kudu, bushbuck and sitatunga – as well as warthog and bushpig have started. As the park boundaries are widened, so the number of species will be increased.

Back on the river, one of the wildlife highlights is the presence of cape clawless otters, which cavort in the fast-running waters and rest on the sandbanks.

Getting there and away The park entrance (⊕ NGOFNP 16°39.820'S, 23°34.264'E) is about 127km north of Sesheke, or 57km southeast of the Sitoti pontoon, and is clearly signposted to the east of the road. Here you can pay your entry fees, leave your vehicle safely, and find a guide to take you down to the falls themselves.

Where to stay

Ngonye River Camp (4 rooms) **m** 0973 222549; **e** ngonyecamp@yahoo.com; **w** ngonyerivercamp.com. Serene grassy campsite (US$10–15/night) overlooking the river & sandy beaches (camping allowed on sand too; no swimming). Friendly service, elevated firepit, simple chalets available (*US$50*) & walking distance to Ngonye Falls. **$–$$**

What to see and do Although nothing like as high as Victoria Falls, the Ngonye Falls are still impressive, and if the former didn't exist then they would certainly draw more visitors. The geology of the area is the same as that of Victoria Falls, and these falls were formed by a similar process, with erosion taking advantage of cracks in the area's basalt rock.

Ngonye's main falls form a rather spectacular semicircle of water, with lots of smaller streams and falls around the edges. Some of these create little pools, ideal for bathing, though be careful to remain at this point as the main river has too many crocodiles to be safe. The falls are at their most beautiful during the dry season, from July to December, when the drop is at its greatest. Earlier in the year, the Zambezi floods, so the drop between the falls and the next stage of the river can all but disappear.

Seeing the falls from the western bank is easy – it's a 15-minute walk from the park gate, just beyond the campsite. However, most of the main falls cannot be seen from the bank, and you certainly won't appreciate them fully. To get a really good view, you must cross onto an island in the river in front of the falls. At low water, the park scouts can organise a mokoro to take you across (US$5 pp, inc guide), although when the river is in flood, this becomes too dangerous.

Nearby, Sioma River Camp has a number of motorboats that they use for trips to the falls.

For notes on birdwatching in this area, see page 459.

DRIVING NORTH FROM NGONYE TO SENANGA From the park's office at Ngonye Falls it's about 61km northwest on the M10 to the road bridge at Kalongola. The tarmac road on the eastern side of the Zambezi makes it an easy drive to Senanga and on to Mongu. The village of Sioma, where the presence of a tyre repair place could well prove welcome, is also where you turn off for Sioma Ngwezi National Park.

SENANGA Coming from the south, Senanga is the first 'proper' town after Sesheke. On the eastern bank of the Zambezi, it's a pleasant place, linear in layout with trees lining the main road and a tall radio mast near the centre. Here you'll find a vital Puma **fuel** station (which usually even has fuel), a **hospital** (almost opposite the Puma garage), a **post office**, a **market** and a handful of **shops** and small bottle stores – but you still can't shake off the feeling that it's out on a limb. That said, thanks to the new road bridge at Sioma, the town, and Barotesland as a whole, is accessible year-round.

Getting there and away The 104km stretch of road from Senanga to Mongu east of the Zambezi is good tarmac all the way. Heading south, you have to cross to the west bank of the Zambezi on the M10 bridge at Kalongola or on the old Sioma pontoon ferry (15km south of Senanga.)

Kashuwa and Oasis operate buses to Mongu from Senanga (and onwards to Lusaka). There is also a daily Oasis bus from Mongu to Livingstone, taking around 12 hours on good roads until the final Sesheke–Livingstone section.

Where to stay and eat There are several basic guesthouses and restaurants in town. The best is currently Kashuwa Lodge (16 rooms; m 0979 314979; **$**), which offers basic, clean, en-suite rooms around a lush courtyard on Zanaco Road in the centre of town.

BAROTSELAND

The heartland of the former British protectorate of Barotseland, now the Western Province, covers the floodplains which surround some of the upper reaches of the Zambezi. It is the homeland of the Lozi king, the Litunga, and his people – a group who have retained much of their cultural heritage despite the ravages of the past century. They were granted more autonomy by the colonial authorities than most of the ethnic groups in Zambia's other regions, and perhaps this has helped them to preserve more of their culture. The Litunga has winter and summer palaces nearby, and a hunting lodge in Liuwa Plain. (Chapter 47 of John Reader's excellent *Africa: A Biography of the Continent* covers some of the history of this area in fascinating detail; page 511.)

For the traveller this means that some aspects of life here have altered relatively little since pre-colonial times. Most of the local people still follow lifestyles of subsistence farming, hunting and gathering, and when rains are good they must still move to higher ground to escape the floodwaters. Be aware, though, that political feelings occasionally run high over the level of autonomy that is permitted by the government.

BAROTSE FLOODPLAINS The area bordering the Zambezi River as it runs west of Mongu represents the second-largest wetland in Zambia, and was designated as a Ramsar site in 2007. After the rains, the Barotse or Zambezi floodplains are transformed with small islands of vegetation dotted through the expanse of water. Ramsar (**w** ramsar.org) notes that 'there is sparse riparian vegetation, small stands of *Acacia albida* in the floodplains, *Syzygium guineens* along the main river channel and patches of *Diplorhynchus* scrub and *Borassus* forest in the northern areas. Semi-evergreen woodlands found on the Kalahari sands have economically important species like *Baikiaea plurijuga* and *Pterocarpus angolensis*'.

MONGU Perched high on a ridge overlooking the eastern edge of the Barotse Plains, Mongu is the provincial centre for western Zambia – and the only large town this side of Livingstone or Lusaka. In the past, very few visitors came here, so there are few people who aren't Zambian, and almost all of those who are work for the fairly permanent contingent of NGO personnel in town. The areas around Mongu are among Zambia's poorest and many are still isolated by seasonal floods, so there is often need for relief workers in the region. However, the new causeway crossing the floodplain means that Mongu is expanding rapidly, not only as a hub for NGOs, but as a rudimentary tourist destination.

The town is easily reached from Lusaka and Senanga, and is the best place in the region to get **fuel** or **supplies**. The town is also one of the best places in Zambia to buy beautiful, **high-quality basketry** – we say this as people who travelled for a month with two large laundry baskets on the roof of our Land Rover! Take time to visit the **Mumwa Craft Association** on the Lusaka Road (**m** 0977 810160; **e** mundiakeke@gmail.com; **w** mcazambia.weebly.com) to purchase fair-trade crafts from the region's Lozi, Mbunda and Luvale artisans.

There are precious few amenities on the road north or west of Mongu, so stock up on all essentials here (page 471).

Geography Mongu is about 25km from the dry-season course of the Zambezi, or immediately adjacent to the water when the river is in full flood. The town is spread out on a ridge above the plains, with no real centre but several quite different busy areas. Small villages and cattle dot the dusty plains during the dry season, but when wet it is all transformed into a haze of green grass on a mirror of water that reflects the sky. Then, when the water is fairly high, the views west over the floodplain are spectacular: myriad channels snaking through apparently endless flat plains.

Orientation The tarred M9 from Lusaka meets the tar road heading south to Senanga at a central roundabout. The Barotse Shopping Mall sits at this key junction. North of this is a vibrant, packed old town area with shops, a heaving market, a bus station and an army barracks; if you pass these, then ultimately you'll find a tar road north to Limulunga. West of the roundabout lies a small hill, upon which you'll find most of the government buildings. Beyond, on the other side of this hill, you drop down to the harbour, and to the road across the floodplain which leads to the Zambezi, Kalabo and Liuwa Plain.

Getting there and away Good tar roads link Mongu to Lusaka (638km) and Senanga (103km) and the new causeway to Kalabo to the northwest has meant that Liuwa Plain National Park has become more accessible, but vehicular access to the north is seriously challenging.

By air There is an airport 2km northeast of Mongu, though currently no scheduled flights operate here. It is possible to charter from Livingstone or Lusaka, though this is very expensive.

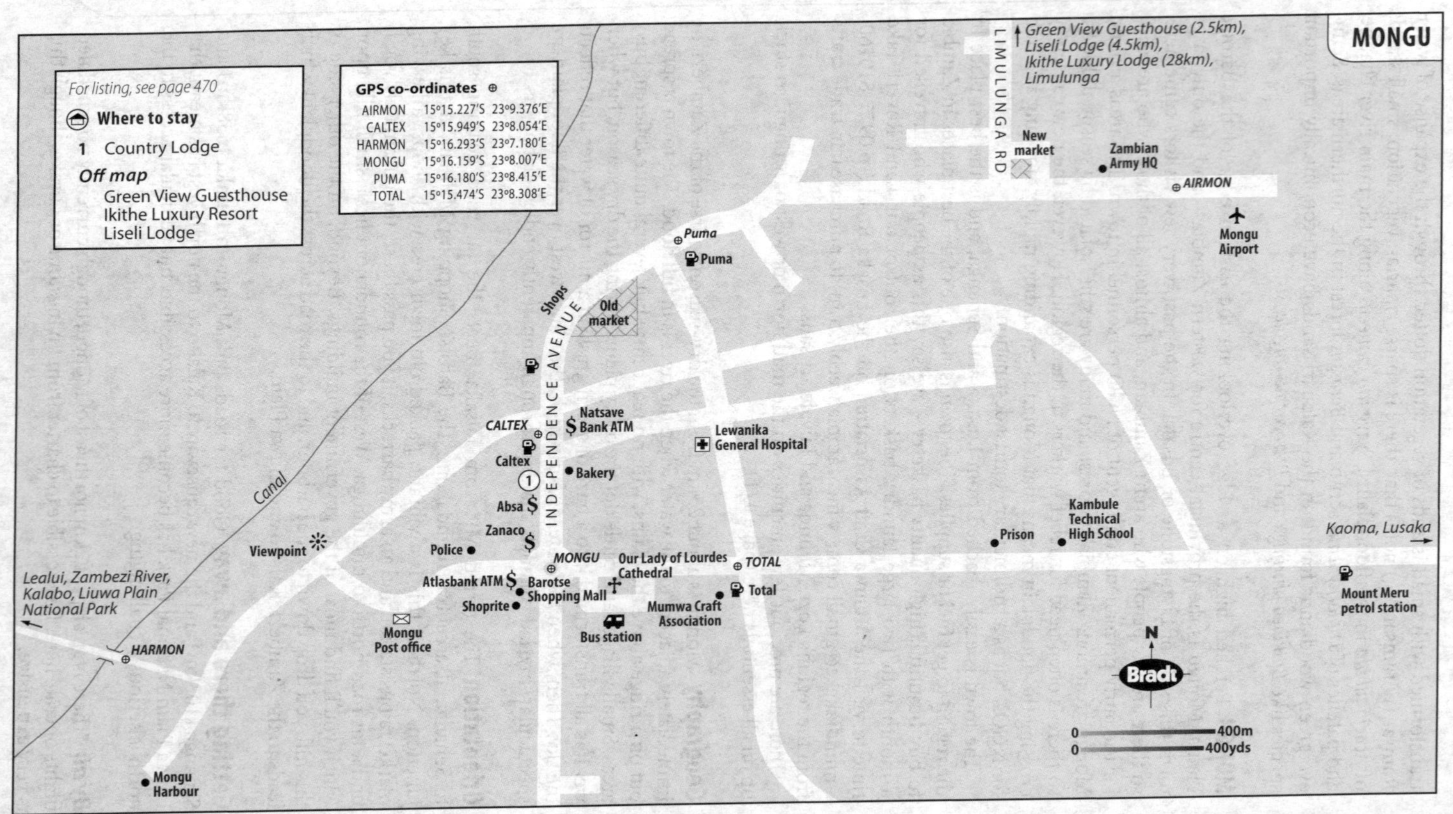
MONGU
For listing, see page 470
Where to stay
1 Country Lodge
Off map
Green View Guesthouse
Ikithe Luxury Resort
Liseli Lodge
GPS co-ordinates
AIRMON 15°15.227'S 23°9.376'E
CALTEX 15°15.949'S 23°8.054'E
HARMON 15°16.293'S 23°7.180'E
MONGU 15°16.159'S 23°8.007'E
PUMA 15°16.180'S 23°8.415'E
TOTAL 15°15.474'S 23°8.308'E
Green View Guesthouse (2.5km), Liseli Lodge (4.5km), Ikithe Luxury Lodge (28km), Limulunga
LIMULUNGA RD
New market
Zambian Army HQ
AIRMON
Mongu Airport
Puma
Puma
Shops
Old market
INDEPENDENCE AVENUE
Canal
CALTEX
Caltex
Natsave Bank ATM
Lewanika General Hospital
Bakery
Absa
Zanaco
Viewpoint
Police
MONGU
Our Lady of Lourdes Cathedral
TOTAL
Total
Atlasbank ATM
Barotse Shopping Mall
Shoprite
Mumwa Craft Association
Bus station
Mongu Post office
Prison
Kambule Technical High School
Kaoma, Lusaka
Mount Meru petrol station
Lealui, Zambezi River, Kalabo, Liuwa Plain National Park
HARMON
Mongu Harbour
N
Bradt
0 400m
0 400yds

By bus Several buses link Lusaka to Mongu and Senanga every day. The bus station is beside the old market, while long-distance coaches stop behind the Catholic church on the main road.

Driving west to Kalabo After several failed attempts (the bridges kept failing in the floods!), an impressive, 34km long, causeway bridge is now fully operational across the floodplain between Mongu and Kalabo. It was a major project in difficult terrain that required 26 bridges (see below). The causeway has transformed the lives of these remote fishing communities, giving them year-round road access to services and markets, and providing easy access to Liuwa Plain National Park.

To get to the causeway, head west over the hill from the main Mongu roundabout at the Barotse Shopping Mall and drop down onto the Barotse floodplain. Remember to fill up with fuel in Mongu before you leave; there are currently no fuel stations west of here.

About 14km from Mongu's harbour, you'll reach the village of Lealui (⊕ LEALUI 15°13.446'S, 23°1.077'E; page 472). Lealui itself is the location of the isolated summer palace of the Litunga, the Lozi king, and a centre for the Lozi administration. Visitors are advised to show courtesy and respect, even if it doesn't appear to be different from any other small African village.

A little over 10km northwest of Lealui, you'll cross the Zambezi, at Sandaula. See page 472 for details of the route continuing to the west.

Driving north to Lukulu There's a good tarred road for 15km north of Mongu, basically as far as the Litunga's winter palace at Limulunga. Then there's nothing more than vanishing local tracks across the Barotse floodplains between there

NYAMINYAMI AND THE MONGU–KALABO CAUSEWAY

Contracts signed in March 2002 started the construction of a 74km tar road from Mongu, via Kalabo, to the Angolan border which, it was envisaged, would completely open up wet-season access to impoverished areas west of the Zambezi and a new trade route into Angola.

The project planned to connect Mongu and Kalabo, and ultimately Lusaka, with Angola – spanning not only the Zambezi River, but also the width of the Zambezi floodplain. This entailed 35km of raised causeway above low-lying plains that are seasonally inundated when the river breaks its banks. Initially it was scheduled for completion in 2004, but exceptional flooding washed away part of the structure, prompting a major reassessment of the design. By then, funds for the project were starting to run seriously short, and a hydrologist's report suggested that the section of causeway east of the Zambezi River (from the Zambezi to the canal at Mongu) wasn't strong enough to support a road.

For a while after, only the 22km section of tar road running from the western edge of the floodplain to Kalabo was opened, and the rest of the original project was abandoned. But finally, in 2016, despite all the challenges, the road was completed, including the bridge across the Zambezi, and the impressive tar road across the entire Barotse floodplain was opened. And what a beautiful drive across lush, green floodplains and remote fishing communities it is! Perhaps Nyaminyami, the old river god of the Zambezi Valley's Tonga people, has finally mellowed since the days of building Kariba Dam.

and Lukulu. These are passable in the dry season (page 87) but otherwise consider driving to Lukulu on all-weather (albeit relatively poor) roads via Kaoma.

Getting around The Mongu police appear to be vigilant, and there are often roadblocks around town where they will check your vehicle and its papers. If you're driving, make sure that you're wearing your seatbelt and moving slowly. The taxi rank and bus station are located between the market and the garage.

Driving Apart from the main tar roads to Lusaka, Senanga and the new causeway to Kalabo, most of the area's roads are little more than vehicle tracks, and they degenerate into patches of deep sand quite frequently. A 4x4 is essential here, even in the dry season, and the worst of these tracks will require almost constant low-range driving through long sections of Kalahari sand.

During the wet season, from around December to July, the whole area north of Ngonye Falls is subject to flooding and the Barotse floodplain becomes a large, shallow lake. Much of the population moves to higher ground to live, and boats are the only option for getting around. Don't even think about trying to drive anywhere off the tarred roads then. The new causeway does make it easier to cross the floodplain, even in high water, and you can now drive year-round to villages such as Lealui (page 469) which could formerly only be reached by boat during the floods.

By boat For much of the year, boat transport has always been the best way to see the immediate area around Mongu, and used to be the only way if the flood was high. The causeway has changed this. The best way to find a suitable boat is to ask at the harbour office in Mongu.

For a few dollars you can hire a mokoro to take you out on the waterways, and – except at the end of the dry season – perhaps down towards Lealui and the main channel. Spend a few hours like this, on the water, and you will appreciate how most of the locals transport themselves around. You will see everything from people to household goods, supplies, live animals and even the occasional bicycle loaded onto boats and paddled or poled (punted) from place to place.

For rather more, there are two larger ferries with outboard motors that will take 20 or so people on longer journeys; once the floods start, there's typically at least one of these per day between Mongu and Kalabo. This may change now the causeway across the Barotse floodplain has been completed.

There is also a privately run postboat on the Zambezi that carries passengers, the mail and cargo, including the occasional vehicle – but note that ferrying a vehicle is likely to be a very expensive option.

Where to stay *Map, page 468*

There's a choice of accommodation in Mongu, much of it of fairly poor quality; the best option by far is Liseli Lodge. There are a couple of large, old-style hotels and a rash of small guesthouses catering to local businesspeople, foreign aid workers and expats, so standards of accommodation and security among the best are reasonable, if nothing special. Note that price is seldom a useful guide to quality here – and as new places spring up they will often be better than the older establishments. Try to book accommodation in advance, especially around the time of the Kuomboka ceremony (page 25).

Country Lodge (20 rooms) 3066 Independence Av; **m** 0977 222216; **e** mongu@countrtylodgezambia.com; **w** countrylodgezambia.com. In the centre of town, this well-placed lodge offers en-suite rooms with TV, Wi-Fi, fridge & AC, plus secure parking. **$–$$$**

Green View Guesthouse (23 rooms, camping) Limulunga Rd; t 0217 221029; m 0967 405551; ⊕ GREENV 15°13.960'S, 23°8.721'E. Some 2.5km north of Mongu on the tarred Limulunga Rd, behind the New Apostolic Church, this quiet guesthouse is a 15min drive from the Litunga's winter palace. En-suite chalets with AC, older rondavels, & camping (limited facilities) available; *b*/fast & dinner on request. **$–$$**

Ikithe Luxury Resort (6 chalets; camping) t 07675 56599; e reservations@leelementos.com. Ikithe sits on the white-sand shore of Lake Makapaela, 32km north of Mongu – accessed via a challenging road (4x4 only). Sadly, the once tastefully decorated rooms have suffered from poor maintenance. It's a good lakeside location for self-sufficient campers though & they do have tents available for hire. *Chalet US$125; Camping US$40–55.* **$–$$$**

Liseli Lodge (19 rooms) Limulunga Rd; m 0964 409805 (WhatsApp), 0974 303102; e liselilodge3@gmail.com; w liselilodge.com. By far the best place to stay in Mongu. 4.5km north of the centre on the Limulunga Rd, Liseli Lodge is in a peaceful spot offering self-catering chalets & well-equipped en-suite rooms with AC & Wi-Fi. There's a restaurant, bar, plenty of parking & friendly team on hand to help. **$$**

Where to eat and drink Some of the hotels have restaurants and others serve meals on request. Alternatively, you could put together a picnic from Shoprite or grab some fast food from Hungry Lion at Barotse Shopping Mall.

Other practicalities

Shopping Mongu is the obvious place in the Western Province to buy **supplies** and get organised. The best place to head for is the large and well-stocked Shoprite **supermarket** (⏲ 08.00–18.00 Mon–Fri, 08.00–17.00 Sat, 09.00–13.00 Sun & public holidays) in the Barotse Shopping Mall, by far the biggest and best store in town.

There are myriad other small shops, several banks with **ATMs**, **fuel stations** and **fast food outlets**. Several mechanics can be found to tune up any vehicle issues – especially tyre or batteries – and some camping kit is available at Shoprite and various hardware stores.

The huge old **market** in town is a good place to buy locally produced fresh fruit and vegetables. Be sure to also buy firewood if you are self-driving and camping in Liuwa Plain – it is illegal to collect wood in the park and firewood is not always available in Kalabo or at the campsites.

For **crafts**, do visit the excellent Mumwa Craft Association (m 0977 810160; e mundiakeke@gmail.com; w mcazambia.weebly.com). This non-profit-making society was established in 1994 to improve the economic, social and cultural well-being of the local communities by representing a network of several hundred local producers throughout the Western Province. They concentrate on good basket weaving, as well as woodcarvings, pottery and metalwork. Items on sale vary according to the season but may include the large and very beautiful linen baskets that are woven using skills developed over the centuries by the Lozi people in making their fishing traps. You won't find better baskets supporting a more worthy cause, or at lower prices. During and after the rains, when many of the craftsmen gather here during the day, you can also watch them at work.

What to see and do Aside from wandering around the old market or visiting the craft association (see above), there are no specific sights in Mongu. You may, though, like to visit the lively and very traditional **harbour**. The two main attractions, however – the Litunga's summer and winter palaces – are both excursions from town.

The greatest of Zambia's cultural festivals, the **Kuomboka** (page 25), is the tradition of moving the Litunga, the Lozi king, plus his court and his people, away from the floodwaters and onto higher ground. If the rains have been good and the floodwaters are rising, this spectacular ceremony takes place around February or March, often on a Thursday, just before full moon. It involves a flotilla of boats for most of the day, plus an impromptu orchestra of local musicians and much celebration. Don't miss it if you are travelling in western Zambia at the time.

The Litunga's summer palace at Lealui About 13km west of Mongu, amid the floodplains, the Litunga's summer palace (⊕ LEALUI 15°13.637'S, 23°01.107'E) is set in a large grove of trees that is easily seen from the escarpment on which Mongu stands.

Don't expect a Western-style palace; this appears to be a normal small African village with thatched huts. However, it is not only the king's summer residence, but also the main Lozi administration centre. Visitors are warmly welcomed, and are strongly advised to show the utmost courtesy and respect to their hosts. Indeed, until very recently it was normal to introduce yourself to the Kuta (the traditional court) as a courtesy, especially if you planned to continue on to Liuwa. See page 469 for directions of how to get here from Mongu.

The Litunga's winter palace and the Nayuma Museum and Heritage Centre (m 0955 985750; ⏲ 08.00–17.00 Mon–Fri) North of Mongu, next to the Litunga's main winter palace, this museum houses some interesting exhibits on the history and culture of the Lozi people, with a strong focus on conserving and promoting the region's heritage. A small craft shop sells some really beautiful basketwork from the area, at very reasonable prices.

This royal palace complex is all fairly grand and impressive, complete with keen security guards from about March to June, when the Litunga is in residence.

KALABO This small, rambling town by the Luanginga River is the gateway to Liuwa Plain National Park. The name is derived from the Lozi word *silambo*, meaning 'paddling stick'.

Coming from Mongu, you'll arrive at a T-junction where you turn right into a wide main street lined by grand old buildings with verandas, most in various states of decay.

Continue down this main road to reach the **harbour**, where there is a small, hand-operated pontoon ferry (⊕ HARKAL 14°59.248'S, 22°41.001'E) over the Luanginga. It is a good idea to reduce your tyre pressure here before you hit the deep sand on the other side of the river.

Getting there and away With the opening of the tarred causeway, Kalabo has become much easier to reach. From Mongu, the drive is around 45 minutes. Off the causeway, however, anywhere west of the Zambezi remains expedition territory at any time. 'Roads' here are usually just tracks in often deep Kalahari sand, which need days of low-range driving. They require not only a 4x4 (preferably several, in case of emergency), but also large quantities of fuel. This can be replenished only in Mongu, so long-range fuel tanks and lots of jerrycans are vital. See page 139 for more advice – and note especially the points on higher fuel consumption and misleading milometer readings.

Water is also a problem, as it tends to seep through the Kalahari sand rather than forming pans on the surface. Hence no potable water can be relied upon, even in Kalabo, so if you're heading west, take some good containers and fill up in Mongu.

Kalabo has its own airstrip (⊕ KALAIR 14°59.501'S, 22°38.484'E), so it is possible – albeit very expensive – to charter a plane into the area.

Driving to Liuwa See page 469 for details.

Other practicalities There is **no fuel** available in Kalabo – and although you can get the basics in the market or in local shops, it's sensible to buy all your **supplies** in Mongu before you arrive. There are, though, often people selling fish along the roadside, and there are a few general stores close to the harbour. There's also a basic **café** there – ideal if you have to wait for someone to fetch the pontoon for you! And if you've longer to spare, the **market** is well worth a visit in its own right.

Kalabo has a mission with a large **hospital** (⊕ HOSPKA 14°59.111'S, 22°40.654'E), and a basic government **resthouse.**

The **immigration** office is just beside the harbour and hand-operated Luanginga pontoon.

Liuwa Plain National Park Headquarters (☎0964 168394; e liuwatourism@african-parks.org) Of vital importance to most visitors is the tourism reception centre for Liuwa Plain National Park, which is located 12km after the river crossing, next to the park's headquarters. This is where you get permits for Liuwa Plain National Park, check in for campsites, and get directions for the park. It's also the place where you can organise a guide to accompany you, if required. It is essential that you contact the team here well in advance to book accommodation and discuss any guiding options.

LIUWA PLAIN NATIONAL PARK (m 0964 168394; reservations e liuwatourism@african-parks.org, information e liuwa@african-parks.org; w african-parks.org; park fees US$40 pp/day; camping US$15/7 adult/child/day; guide fee US$20/day; ⏲ Self-drive 06.00–18.00 May/Jun–Dec) Liuwa Plain is as wild and remote as virtually any park in Africa; at the right time of year, its game is also as good as most of the best. The cliché 'best-kept secret' is applied with nauseating frequency to many places in Africa by copywriters who can't think of anything original; this is perhaps one of the few places that would deserve it.

Liuwa Plain has long been a very special place. It was declared a 'game reserve' as early as the 19th century by the king of Barotseland, and subsequently administered by the Litunga, or Lozi king. Traditionally, the park was the Litunga's private hunting ground, and the people whose villages were located around the land were charged with looking after the animals for him. Then in 1972 it became a national park, and its management was taken over by central government. Although the local people retained utilisation rights of the park, grazing their animals, fishing in the rivers and pools, and harvesting plants for use in traditional crafts, their cultural connection with the land was broken, and poaching became rife. It was not until 2003, when the park was taken over by African Parks and the link with the Litunga reinstated, that the villagers regained stewardship. Now, in addition to their utilisation rights, they run campsites for visitors, and once more have an interest in the preservation of the wildlife.

The word *liuwa* means 'plain' in the local Lozi language. Legend relates how one Litunga planted his walking stick here on the plain, where it grew into a large *mutata* tree. The tree in question can still be seen from the track which leads from

Minde to Luula: after leaving the first tree belt, look in the distance on your left side when you are halfway to the next tree belt.

Liuwa Plain is certainly the most fascinating park in the region, but getting here almost always requires an expedition. For this reason, visitor numbers are tiny but increasing due to improved facilities and infrastructure: in 2014 fewer than 800 visitors entered the park. Yet even these figures dwarf those in some of the previous years: only 50 tourists visited in the whole of 2000.

Geography Although a network of sand game-viewing tracks has been established in the 3,662km² park, it remains largely untouched. Most of it is a vast honey-coloured grass plain, stretching about 70km long and 30km wide. Within this there's just the occasional open pan, cluster of raffia palms, or small tree-island interrupting the flatness. In places you can look 360° around you and see nothing but a flat expanse. The environment is unlike any other park in Zambia – the most similar places are probably Katavi, in western Tanzania, and, possibly, the much smaller Kazuma Pan in Zimbabwe.

Large areas of this plain are totally flooded from around December to April, with the waters rising in the northwest and spreading southeastwards. It's this flooding which drives the wildebeest migration, or 'gathering', as the herds move in search of new, fresh grazing.

In the centre, and especially the southern side, of this enormous grassy plain, you'll find a scattering of open pans, many of which hold their water well into the dry season. These are well worth investigating. Although in the dry season some will appear almost lifeless, others will have great concentrations of birds or antelope.

Flora and fauna

Flora Liuwa Plain's main plant life, on first glance, appears to be vast areas of grasslands, within which species like *Vossia cuspidate* and *Echinocloa stagnina* are among the most important for the herds of grazing herbivores. On tree-islands, and around the edges of the plain, you'll find the small false mopane, or copalwood (*Guibourtia coleosperma*); the silver cluster-leaf (*Terminalia sericea*), which is so typical of the Kalahari; stands of Zambezi teak (*Baikiaea plurijuga*) and weeping wattle (*Peltophorum africanum*), while around the pans are occasional stands of palms including the odd tall *Hyphaene*.

Mammals and reptiles As is common in vast open areas, many of Liuwa's larger mammals tend to group together into great herds when on the plain – and these are much of the park's attraction. The 2013 aerial wildlife census estimated populations at 46,000 blue wildebeest, 8,000 tsessebe, 5,800 zebra and thousands of other large mammals, including herds of buffalo, sitatunga, red lechwe, eland, Lichtenstein's hartebeest and roan antelope, duiker and bush pigs as well as assorted pairs of reedbuck and the delightful, diminutive oribi which are so common here.

Active protection within the park has shown clear evidence that wildlife numbers are increasing across all herbivore species. Both roan antelope and wild dogs have returned to the park, and the population of red lechwe is recovering well. Eland, buffalo and wild dogs have been reintroduced, and the sitatunga are still found in some of the rivers on the edge of the park.

The largest herds currently seen in the park are the blue wildebeest which mass here in their thousands during the rains. Among them, you'll find zebra and tsessebe. Though widely regarded as a 'migration', some suggest that it may in fact

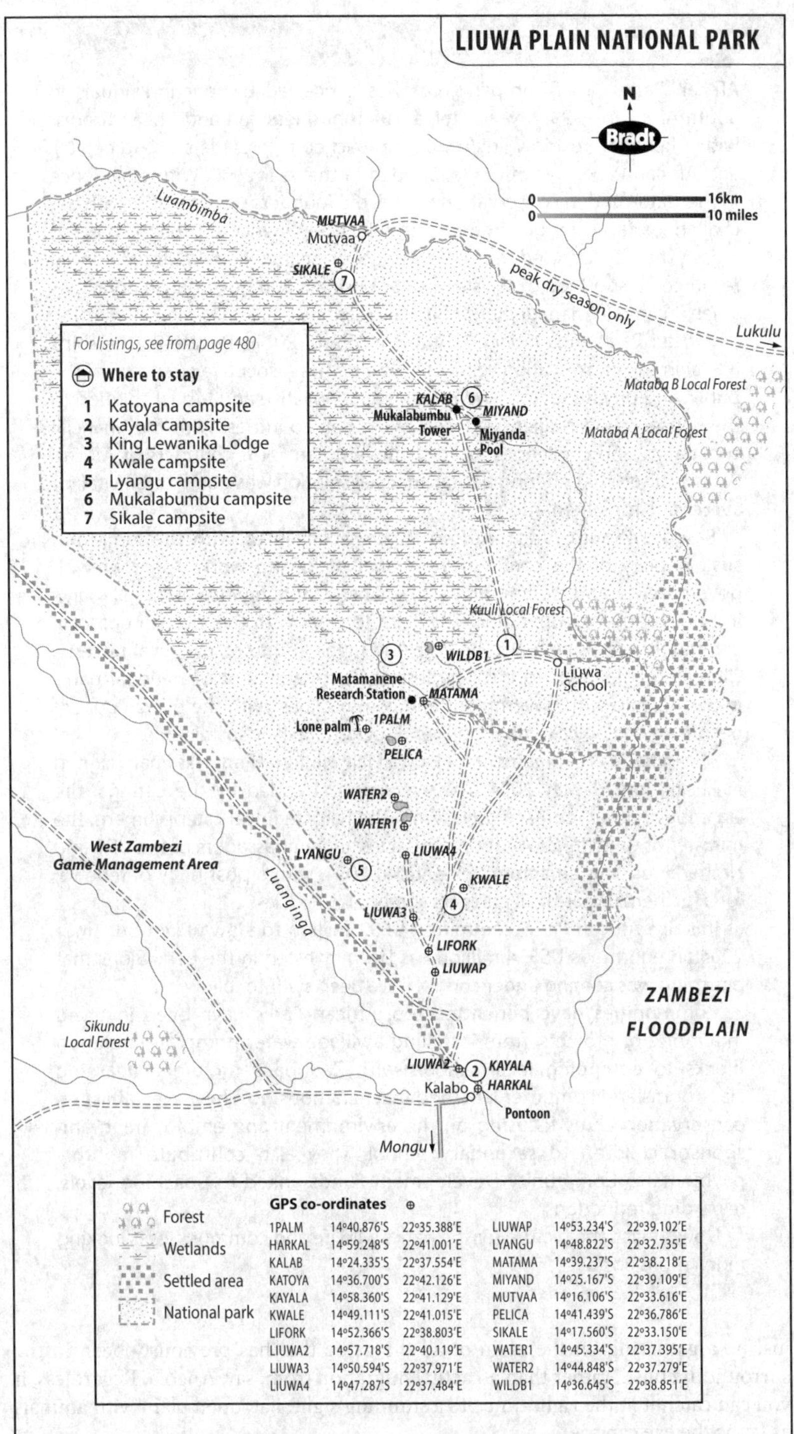

GPS co-ordinates ⊕

1PALM	14°40.876'S	22°35.388'E	LIUWAP	14°53.234'S	22°39.102'E
HARKAL	14°59.248'S	22°41.001'E	LYANGU	14°48.822'S	22°32.735'E
KALAB	14°24.335'S	22°37.554'E	MATAMA	14°39.237'S	22°38.218'E
KATOYA	14°36.700'S	22°42.126'E	MIYAND	14°25.167'S	22°39.109'E
KAYALA	14°58.360'S	22°41.129'E	MUTVAA	14°16.106'S	22°33.616'E
KWALE	14°49.111'S	22°41.015'E	PELICA	14°41.439'S	22°36.786'E
LIFORK	14°52.366'S	22°38.803'E	SIKALE	14°17.560'S	22°33.150'E
LIUWA2	14°57.718'S	22°40.119'E	WATER1	14°45.334'S	22°37.395'E
LIUWA3	14°50.594'S	22°37.971'E	WATER2	14°44.848'S	22°37.279'E
LIUWA4	14°47.287'S	22°37.484'E	WILDB1	14°36.645'S	22°38.851'E

A PERFECT PARTNERSHIP: AFRICAN PARKS AND LIUWA PLAIN

African Parks (w african-parks.org) was conceived by four individuals in South Africa in 1999. A year later, a Dutch businessman and philanthropist with a keen interest in wildlife was approached to provide start-up capital, and African Parks was officially founded in the year 2000. With experience in the state-funded conservation model, the founders were familiar with the challenges faced by governments in effectively managing their protected areas. They recognised that African governments had limited financial resources, a shortage of skills and poor business and governance principles when it came to management of these areas.

African Parks thus pioneered the concept of Public Private Partnerships (PPPs) in the conservation sector, leveraging the respective strengths of the public and private sectors and offering an innovative and robust solution to the conservation challenges faced by African countries. With the financial constraints and challenges faced by governments, the founders of African Parks realised that offering a total financial solution was going to be vital for successful implementation.

Based in South Africa, African Parks is concerned with the long-term sustainability of the continent's national parks and works together with governments and communities to manage and finance national parks in the countries of operation. They aim to work with the inclusion of local communities, to safeguard the flora and fauna and to relieve local poverty. Ultimately, they aim to instil professional management of national parks in partnership with government and communities, with the overall goal of becoming ecologically, financially and socio-politically sustainable.

The initial lease agreement for Liuwa Plain National Park was finally signed in Lusaka on 31 May 2004. The event was attended by the Litunga, the Ngambela, other representatives from the Barotse Royal Establishment, the minister of tourism, ZAWA representatives and ambassadors of the USA and Netherlands. This agreement extends to 2024, with a possibility of renewal for a further 20 years if all partners agree.

Initially, African Parks committed US$2 million to Liuwa Plain but since 2004 an enormous US$34 million has been invested in the park. Signs that poaching was coming under control have been swift to follow.

Communities have benefitted too. African Parks have been involved in a range of projects, from installing a village water pump and ablution blocks to equipping local schools with Zedupads for digital learning classrooms and computer labs, and teachers' housing. They've established conservation clubs focusing on the environment and employment; and sponsor children to secondary school. They also contribute monthly payments to Community Development Funds linked to poaching levels, rewarding reductions.

Now, at last, the picture for the park's wildlife and communities is looking much more positive.

just be a gathering on the plain of all the game that has previously been in the surrounding bush, rather than an actual migration from, say, Angola. Regardless, if you can catch it at the right time, it's a stunning sight: flat, open plain with animals as far as the eye can see.

That said, it's quite wrong to concentrate on the sights in November and, in effect, dismiss the rest of the year. We've visited in September and seen plenty of wildebeest on the plain, including one herd of over a thousand; several smaller herds of zebra, tsessebe and red lechwe, one of the last numbering over 120 individuals; and some of the most spectacular birding we've seen in southern Africa.

Predators have also been well represented in Liuwa, with lion, leopard, cheetah, wild dog, side-striped jackal and spotted hyena all occurring here.

Unusually, thanks to sheer numbers (around 350 individuals), hyenas are the apex predators here, rather than scavengers. They are fairly commonly seen skulking around the plains, and can be cheeky enough to come to the edge of your firelight's glow. The Zambian Carnivore Programme is currently monitoring the movements of two clans to better understand their range and behaviour within Liuwa.

Lion have had a more challenging time in Liuwa. In 2007, there was just one remaining lioness in the park, popularly known as Lady Liuwa, whose story of lonely survival was made famous by a National Geographic documentary in 2010. Two male lions were brought in to join her in 2009, though one was killed in Angola. In 2011, two females were reintroduced from Kafue National Park only for one of them to die in a snare. The surviving lioness, Sepo, formed a partnership with Lady, who took the young lioness under her wing and they remained together throughout their lives. Sepo had three cubs in December 2013 – a male and two females – though their father sadly died a year later in a suspected poisoning. Lady and Sepo both died in 2017, the former of natural causes and the latter in a fight with a translocated male lion as she protected her second litter of cubs – two males. Her cubs survived, were raised by their older sisters and thankfully new cubs are still being born in the park, with three new arrivals in 2021. Hopefully pride stability and the park's protection will ensure the survival of Liuwa's most recent lions.

As with lions, wild dogs have had a turbulent time in the park. For a while there were two different packs breeding successfully in Liuwa, although sightings are very erratic, varying from 20 wild dogs being seen at Makalabumbu in the northeast of the park in mid 2015 to the belief that no wild dogs remained in the park at all. However, in 2021, 11 wild dogs were translocated to Liuwa from South Africa and Kafue National Park to form a new pack and, so far, the pack has gelled well and hopes are high for their future on the plains.

Leopard do occur within the national park, though the surrounding forest is a better habitat for them than the plain itself. As of 2019, there were two groups of cheetah (20 individuals).

With sharp eyes you're likely to spot smaller, curious omnivores like side-striped jackal, troops of banded mongooses, and possibly porcupines. We've had reports of some particularly large snakes living here – though have been unable to verify these ourselves.

Birds Liuwa boasts a total of about 334 bird species which, even when I visited during a dry month like September, were amazing: spectacular groups of crowned cranes often numbered several hundred birds; wattled cranes, so endangered in many places, thrive here with numerous pairs and smaller groups of up to 30 individuals; while one particular flock of pelicans included several hundred birds. I saw all of these in just a few days in early September – and so when it rains, the park's birding must be quite unbelievable.

Then, when the pans fill up, open-billed, yellow-billed, marabou and saddle-billed storks arrive, with spoonbills, grey herons, egrets, three-banded and lots of blacksmith's plovers, pygmy and spur-winged geese, and many other water birds. Slaty egrets are seen in groups, a rare occurrence elsewhere.

The late Bob Stjernstedt, a Zambian birding expert, commented that Liuwa is relatively rarely visited, and so many more birds are sure to be added to this list. Secretary birds and Denham's and white-bellied bustards are common; and the park is famous for thousands of the migrant black-winged pratincoles, a finely marked swift-like bird which is rare further east. Other 'specials' here include the pink-billed and clapper larks, rosy-breasted longclaw, swamp boubou, long-tailed widow, sharp-tailed starling and white-cheeked bee-eater. The plain is also a great area for raptors from the greater kestrel to bateleur and martial eagles, fish eagles and palmnut vultures. Pel's fishing owl is found along the rivers, the Luanginga to the south and the Luambimba to the north.

When to go With the exception of guided fly-in trips, the park is open to independent visitors only between May/June and December, depending on the rains: if you want to travel during May/June, contact the park *beforehand* to check on conditions and opening dates. For many people, Liuwa is at its best during November, when the gathering of wildebeest on the plains reaches its peak. That said, the park is worth visiting whenever you can get there – there's always some amazing wildlife to be seen!

Before you visit it's important to understand the weather and the usual game movements in the park.

From **January to about May**, a large area of the plain is covered in shallow water, and all the pans in the south of the park are full. Although the park is closed to visitors until mid-April, these conditions are perfect for the large herds of herbivores which gather there, and the large numbers of birds which also arrive. However, **around June/July** the plains dry up, the waters recede northwards, and gradually the herds move that way also. They desert the waterholes of the southern side of the plain, and move back northwest, eventually melting back into the woodlands which surround the park. Plenty of resident wildlife remains, relying on a scattering of pans which retain their water for most of the year.

From **August to October** the herds start drifting southwards again. At first, in September, you'll find just a few herds, typically just a few hundred wildebeest, venturing south onto the northern areas of the plain – but gradually as the rains approach these increase in number and move further south into the park.

In **November and December** the first rains are falling, and the plains are teeming with game, including young animals, for this is also the calving period. November is classically the best time to visit the park – a balance between catching the best of the game, and ensuring that you can get out rather than getting stuck.

Getting there and away Access via the new Mongu–Kalabo causeway has transformed park access for everyone. Specific route guidance is given opposite.

Self-driving For independent drivers (4x4 only), access to the park is technically from May/June to 15 December only; either side of this and you would stand a strong chance of getting completely stuck in deep mud. Contact the park for information if you plan to come early in the season. A GPS is essential and note that there is no mobile phone signal within the park. If you would like some additional reassurance or local knowledge, it would be advisable to contact the local African Parks team in advance (0964 168394; e liuwatourism@africanparks.org; f LiuwaPlainNationalPark).

From Kalabo First head to the new park headquarters and reception, 12km after the Kalabo pontoon ferry, to get your permits. As you leave the pontoon, there are clear African Parks signs to direct you. This stretch of road is likely to be the most challenging you'll encounter on your Liuwa adventure. It is deep Kalahari sand, and the driving is a very steady, slow plod in a low-range gear, with an average speed of about 15km/h. There are a few small villages, but little game along the early part of the drive, although here and there lilac-breasted rollers brighten up the tops of trees along the roadside with dazzling flashes of blue as they fly.

As you get further into the park the trees start to spread out, grouping themselves into small, slightly raised islands, surrounded by a sea of knee-to-thigh-deep golden grass. Carry on for a further 10km or so after ⊕ LIUWAP to ⊕ LIUWA4 14°47.287'S, 22°37.484'E, by which time you're basically out of the trees, and onto the southern edge of the plain. Here, the track into the park starts to become much less distinct – and ultimately vanishes. (If you're coming back out of the park, then head for this point to pick up the track out.)

You should expect 2 or 3 hours of rough, sandy driving after you leave the Kalabo pontoon before you are well into the park. The good news is that although getting into the park is a slow slog through deep sand, most of the tracks within the park are generally much firmer, easier and more pleasant to drive. Do keep to these tracks – and enjoy!

North and east to Lukulu While almost all visitors to Liuwa enter and leave via Kalabo, it is nevertheless possible in the peak of the dry season to drive out of the north of the park, crossing the Luambimba River before turning east towards Lukulu. Note that it can't be done in reverse, since both entry permits and campsite bookings for the national park can only be organised at the park headquarters outside Kalabo (page 473).

If you're considering this route, you'll need at least one self-contained 4x4 vehicle (and preferably two), and the services of a local guide (ask at Sikale campsite) in order to negotiate the Luambimba River, since it's a tortuous route that changes according to the level of the river and the time of year. A GPS is also essential.

From Sikale (⊕ SIKALE 14°17.933'S, 22°33.226'E), head due north to Mutvaa village (⊕ MUTVAA 14°16.106'S, 22°33.616'E). Just after the village, turn right at ⊕ MUTVA2 14°15.884'S, 22°33.437'E onto a narrow track through the trees, emerging after 0.5km back on to the plain. Shortly after this, at ⊕ MUTVA3 14°15.761'S, 22°33.655'E, take the left fork towards the woodland, following a sandy track with the trees on your right. At ⊕ LUAMBI 14°15.524'S, 22°33.842'E, descend through the trees to wind your way through deep sand across a series of channels that make up the Luambimba River. At ⊕ LUAMB2 14°15.380'S, 22°34.068'E, emerge from the wood and cross to two wooden stakes; go left, keeping the stakes on your right, into more woods. At ⊕ LUAMB3 14°15.027'S, 22°34.322'E, there's a junction; turn right here, still in the woodland, on to a good track – well used by oxcarts – with the plain on your right. About 10km from Sikale (40 minutes' drive), or 4.6km from the river, you'll come to the village of Silange (⊕ SILANG 14°15.201'S, 22°35.951'E). Bear left into the woodland once more, then follow this track eastwards for close on 77km to the Zambezi River, opposite Lukulu (⊕ LUKZAM 14°22.410'S, 23°13.933'E). For details of crossing the river, see page 364. Approaching the river, the woodlands thin out, the number of villages increases, and isolated fan palms dot the plains. Significant landmarks along the way include:

⊕ TOLUK1 14°14.166'S, 22°43.125'E	Village on right; bear left just after village, keeping in woodland
⊕ TOLUK2 14°14.896'S, 22°46.927'E	Take right fork
⊕ TOLUK3 14°15.130'S, 22°47.949'E	Continue straight on at crossroads in small village, across a riverbed, then into woodland
⊕ TOLUK4 14°16.912'S, 23°00.060'E	Track diverts around a pool then returns on other side across the plain, keeping village on right
⊕ TOLUK5 14°19.045'S, 23°03.899'E	Take left fork

Getting around The only means to explore the park, unless you're on an organised safari (page 481), is by private 4x4. Game-drive loops have been designated for independent visitors, who are provided with a simple map of the park and route advice from the park headquarters. A 30km/h speed limit is largely self-policing; you'd rarely be in a position to drive faster than this anyway.

There's no real need to take a scout as a guide – provided that you're fully equipped with a reliable GPS and have a back-up plan in case of an emergency (see below). However, if you do take a guide (US$20 per day, inc food), then you may learn quite a bit from him or her, as well as helping the park with a valuable extra source of employment. The scout also carries a radio that can be used to communicate with the park headquarters in case of emergency.

Safety precautions A GPS system is essential for anyone planning to visit the park as landmarks are few and the tall grass can obscure views. Early in the season it's essential to have netting on your vehicle to stop grass seeds which will clog up your radiator and may combust (page 143). It's also wise in a park that's this remote to travel in convoy, with a reliable satphone in case of emergency – there is no mobile phone signal in the park. Should an emergency arise, African Parks may be able to help, either by supplying fuel, or with the rescue of a vehicle (US$215 exc fuel). Do note, however, that availability of fuel cannot be relied on; this is absolutely a last resort.

Where to stay *Map, page 475*

There has been a radical shift in Liuwa's accommodation options since the arrival of African Parks, and a range of safari styles and budgets are now on offer. The old Matamanene Camp is now purely a scientific research camp (no visitors) but in its place, visitors can now choose between the park's first luxury safari camp – King Lewanika Lodge – some high-quality guided mobile trips and, for those in a position to self-drive a small expedition, five great campsites.

Lodges

King Lewanika Lodge ☎ +27 60 6424004; e travel@timeandtideafrica.com; w timeandtideafrica.com. In 2017, King Lewanika Lodge opened as the first permanent safari camp on Liuwa Plain. Tucked into the woodland & surrounded by grasslands reaching for the curving horizon, it's a magical wilderness setting, shared by only 6 luxury tents (1 is a 2-bed family suite), making exclusivity a given. Open-fronted, canvas villas offer chic, understated luxury, focusing attention on the plains' impressive panorama. The laid-back leather & linen main area has swinging chairs, a great selection of reference books & a well-stocked bar – all of which encourage you to put your feet up, slow down & relax. There's a nightly campfire for superb stargazing, & great food. Activities centre on game drives (day & night), boat & canoe excursions when the waters start to rise on the pans (Nov/Dec & Mar), & walking safaris. Access is either a 3hr drive from Kalabo or a 2½hr flight from Lusaka to nearby Matamanene Airstrip. ♕♕♕♕♕

Guided mobile safaris Genuine Zambian safari operators and private guides are able to book Liuwa's campsites on an exclusive-use basis for private-guided trips. If this is something that appeals, the knowledgeable and enthusiastic owners of **Reel Nature** (**e** info@reel-nature.com; **w** reel-nature.com), Phil and Tyrone, and their guiding team, have been guiding filmmakers (they helped with the incredible *BBC Dynasties 2: Hyena & Cheetah*) in this park for years and now operate regular private-guided trips into Liuwa, alongside running their Kafue camps (Musekese and Ntemwa Busanga), and joining forces with two others in Lower Zambezi (Kutali and Chula Island). They are expert at navigating the grasslands, informing about the park's wildlife and landscape, and are thoroughly entertaining with it.

Campsites (**m** 0977 758603; **e** liuwatourism@african-parks.org; US$15 pp) In a joint venture between the community and African Parks, there are five neat, clean community campsites in the national park, most along the wildebeest migration route, and one in the north of the park. A sixth site, Kayala, is located 2km from Kalabo, south of the park entrance, and so is ideal if you arrive late. All camping fees go to the Liuwa Community Development Fund, administered by African Parks and the area chiefs. Some of this revenue goes towards running the camps; the rest is used for community projects, such as schools and teachers' housing.

The campsites are simple but well maintained, and all have a helpful campsite manager on site. Each site has five smooth sand pitches, complete with a simple thatched shelter to shade tents. A maximum of one vehicle and four people are allowed per pitch. With the exception of Sikale, where facilities are more basic, each of the sites also has two showers (not always hot), flush toilets, a washbasin and water from a well (not recommended for drinking unless treated).

Remember that **you must be *totally* self-sufficient**. You are not allowed to collect firewood in the park, and although it can sometimes be supplied for a small fee by the attendant at each campsite, do not count on being able to purchase fuel in the park. It is best to buy firewood in Mongu and bring it with you.

It is sometimes possible to arrange with the campsite manager to be shown a range of local crafts, or for traditional dances to take place at the campsites or to be invited to a nearby village. Similarly, for those interested in fishing, traditional techniques can be demonstrated or even taught, while other options may include boat trips or guided walks, the latter with an armed scout.

Outside the national park

Kayala ⊕ KAYALA 14°58.360'S, 22°41.129'E. Kayala is just 2km north of Kalabo, so ideally placed for those arriving later in the day or travelling with a trailer or caravan.

Inside the national park

Katoyana ⊕ KATOYA 14°36.700'S, 22°42.126'E. With a central location in the park, about 42km (2½hrs) from Kalabo, Katoyana occupies a peaceful, wooded site on the edge of the plain, not far from Liuwa School. The eastern area of the park is easily accessible from here. Hyenas den nearby & walk through camp frequently; birdlife is superb, & you might be lucky to see cheetah in the vicinity.

Kwale ⊕ KWALE 14°49.111'S, 22°41.015'E. Situated in the southeast of the park, 19km (1hr) from Kalabo, Kwale is a shady site bordering open grassland. Buffalo are seen here throughout the year, wildlife is at its best from the end of Oct & there's great local birdwatching.

Lyangu ⊕ LYANGU 14°46.822'S, 22°32.735'E. 26.4km (1½hrs) from Kalabo, in the southwest of the park, this is a woodland site with plenty of indigenous flora on the edge of a large pan. It is within easy distance of the Lone Palm & several self-drive loops affording excellent birding & game viewing.

Mukalabumbu ⊕ SIKALE 14°17.560'S, 22°33.150'E. In the northern section of the park, 75km north of Kalabo (3½hrs), Mukalabumbu's 5 shaded pitches are within easy striking distance of the incredible birdlife at Miyanda Pools (5km southeast). There are 4 flush toilets & 2 showers (hot water available).

Sikale ⊕ SIKALE 14°17.560'S, 22°33.150'E. Just 78km (3½hrs) from Kalabo, the most isolated of the park's campsites – & consequently less frequented – Sikale is in a wooded glade overlooking the plain at the northern edge of the park, close to the route taken by local fishermen as they return with their evening catch. Immaculately maintained, it has a long-drop toilet & 2 washing enclosures, with water drawn from a waterhole & heated by the camp attendant.

Places to visit Liuwa is all about exploring on your own, although there are a few spots worth noting, some of which are highlighted below. Wherever you go, it's important to stick to the existing roads; the vegetation is extremely fragile and easily damaged. Note, too, that drivers found off road could well incur a fine. You should receive a very simple park map at the entrance, on the back of which is a list of key waypoints with GPS co-ordinates to assist your planning and navigation. Some highlights from our last research trip:

- ⊕ WATER1 14°45.334'S, 22°37.395'E This great waterhole seemed to be a magnet for cranes, with a huge flock of crowned cranes always around it, augmented by parties of wattled cranes.
- ⊕ WATER2 14°44.848'S, 22°37.279'E Another lovely spot which was generally quieter, though did seem to be visited daily by a herd of red lechwe.
- ⊕ 1PALM 14°40.876'S, 22°35.388'E This is the spot known as 'Lone Palm', for obvious reasons. There's also a huge waterhole here where the general birding was excellent.
- ⊕ MIYAND 14°25.167'S, 22°39.109'E Miyanda Pool, one of the park's larger pools, close to the Mukalabumbu Tower. Even when devoid of water in mid-October, a thousand or so wildebeest formed a cordon around the lake, interspersed with up to a hundred zebra, numerous waders, and a fair few scavengers – vultures and marabou storks – anticipating their dinner.

LUKULU

The riverside town of Lukulu, at the northern reach of the Barotse floodplain, is the main town in the district, with a collection of government and local council offices in the boma, or central area. Supplies of **fuel**, from a drum rather than a pump, are both expensive and not terribly reliable, although at least the quality is considered to be acceptable. As always in outlying areas, you'd be wise not to run your tank too low.

The town, with its primary school, two high schools and a district hospital (now with very limited facilities), was founded as a Catholic mission, and remains typical of rural Zambia; visitors – especially those with fair skins – are still something of a novelty. It has a public water pumping and distribution system, which means running (drinkable) water most of the time, but despite the presence of a ZESCO plant (Zambia's electricity supply company), supplies of electricity are erratic. Lukulu is also notable for having a **post office** but no vehicle, so post to or from Lukulu is often transported by one of the Catholic nuns who work at the mission!

Getting there and away There are graded all-weather roads linking Lukulu (⊕ SANCTA 14°22.749'S, 23°14.236'E) with Kaoma, which is just off the Lusaka–Mongu road, Kabompo and Zambezi. Despite the proximity of Mongu, the route between the two towns is nothing but a series of inter-village footpaths across the Barotse floodplain; it is usually faster to travel via Kaoma. There are no reliable roads on the west side of the Zambezi, though crossing the river and finding a route through to Liuwa Plain is possible in the height of the dry season.

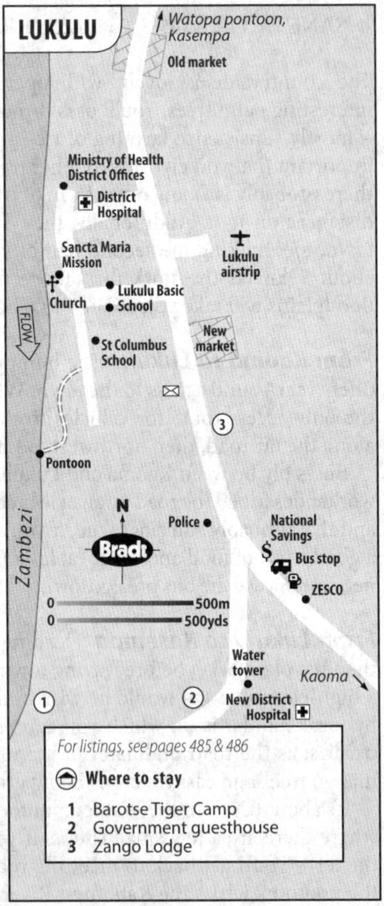

From Mongu across the Barotse floodplain By far the quickest and best route to Lukulu starts near the Kaoma turn-off, on the Lusaka–Mongu road. However, if it is well into the dry season, then there is another possibility described here: heading cross country across the floodplains.

Leaving Mongu past the new market, the tar ends after the shops at Limulunga (⊕ LIMULU 15°7.769'S, 23°8.635'E) and shortly the track forks. Head down the hill, towards the small river. Fording the first shallow channel of this, take a hard right onto a motorable track and follow this. There are lots of people down here, and if you can pick up a hitchhiker to guide you, then do so. It is very rural here and you'll probably give lifts to several before the day is out!

As you head north the tracks split and fork, getting smaller all the time, until about midway to Lukulu. Then there appear to be no good tracks. However, gradually, as you continue, they get clearer again as you approach Lukulu. Think about it and you'll realise that they are all made by the local people, travelling from village to village, and (crucially) to their nearest town – so they radiate out from the towns. This is the typical pattern made by the smallest thoroughfares in most rural areas.

There's little point in trying to describe the precise route here, as every vehicle will end up on a slightly different track – which is half the fun! Instead, here are a few waypoints, south to north, so that those travelling with a GPS can keep track that they're heading in the right general direction:

- ⊕ NANGIL 14°52.659'S, 23°4.478'E Nangili School where an engaging headteacher presides over about 350 children, from grades one to nine.
- ⊕ AIRNGU 14°36.687'S, 23°6.977'E Ngulwana Airstrip, which is occasionally used by fishermen coming on private trips up to this corner of the Zambezi.
- ⊕ KAWYA 14°28.827'S, 23°13.999'E Near the school at Kawaya. If coming south towards Mongu, this point marks where you deviate from the track to Mbanga, turning right down a steep bank. Coming north, you join a better track here.
- ⊕ TUMONG 14°24.515'S, 23°15.588'E Where the bush track from Mongu/Mbanga meets the reasonable Kaoma–Lukulu road.

LUKULU

For listings, see pages 485 & 486

Where to stay

1 Barotse Tiger Camp
2 Government guesthouse
3 Zango Lodge

⊕ SANCTA 14°22.749'S, 23°14.236'E The Sancta Maria Mission at Lukulu.

The countryside is lovely, with open fields and plenty of patches of various interesting palm trees. You'll pass through a variety of tiny villages and settlements – mostly subsistence farming of rice and maize. On very rural routes like this it's important that you give lifts to other travellers; they're often poor people for whom there probably isn't any other form of transport, and they'll likely be travelling long distances on foot. Additionally, they'll often be able to direct you to the nearest town, too, making the second half of your journey much easier than the first. It's about 99km as the stork flies between Mongu and Lukulu, and going over the floodplains will take you about 5 to 6 hours.

From Kaoma to Lukulu The bumpy gravel road between Kaoma and Lukulu offers year-round access to the town. When the Barotse Plains are flooded, it is also the only access route for vehicles from Mongu, which must head east to Kaoma along the tar road, then northwest to Lukulu; the alternative is to go by boat.

Buses ply between Kaoma and Lukulu a couple of times a week. Years ago a VSO worker described the road as 'an axle breaker…the buses creak and groan from abuse' and that probably still rings true. If you're braving this way on public transport, take a good stock of food and water (at least for two days), a sleeping bag and a mosquito net, just in case the bus breaks down.

From Lukulu to Kasempa Heading north-northwest you pass the school and then the old market before leaving town. This is a reasonable gravel road for which a high-clearance 4x4 would be wise in the rains – but otherwise it is a main artery by local standards on which you can reach 50–60km/h. Traffic is light, primarily oxcarts, as the road undulates past a mix of bush and settlements, with plenty of mango trees and cassava crops being grown.

It's about 63km to the Watopa pontoon (⊕ WATOPA 14°02.338'S, 23°37.744'E), where there are a few small shops. If you were to follow the road southeast from the ferry you'd get back to meet the road to Kaoma. For Kasempa, however, take the pontoon across the Kabompo River and follow the similarly good gravel road for almost 22km until you come to a T-junction with the east–west M8. This is Mumbeji (⊕ MUMBEJ 13°51.653'S, 23°40.327'E), notable only for a range of small stalls and intriguingly named grocery shops: 'God's Chance' and 'Work like a Slave'.

From here the good all-weather M8 gravel road (50–60km/h when dry!) goes west to the town of Zambezi (⊕ ZAMBEZ 13°32.262'S, 23°06.158'E), and east about 67km to Kabompo (⊕ KABOMP 13°35.610'S, 24°12.125'E). Although there has clearly been some logging here, much of this road goes through thick woodland with very few settlements.

From the west There is a pontoon crossing at Lukulu, but it's by no means regular, and there are no real roads on the other side – just a series of paths that link the small villages there.

Crossing here and then driving south to Liuwa and/or Kalabo is possible in the height of the dry season, but a GPS and a local guide are essential. Kalabo is much easier to reach by crossing the river further south.

If you do want to use the pontoon at Lukulu, you'll need both plenty of time and, quite possibly, some local help as the chances of it being manned are slim. The fare is a matter of local negotiation with the pontoon operator and you will be charged each way – if the pontoon is on the 'wrong' side of the river and has to cross to fetch you. There's room for only one car on the pontoon and as the riverbanks are steep and sandy on both sides, you'll need to reverse onto it in order to be in a position to drive off in forward gear.

Where to stay *Map, page 483*

Until 2019, Lukulu's only accommodation option was the very basic **government guesthouse** near the post office. Now, **Zango Lodge** (0979 173322; e zangolodges@gmail.com), on the main road, offers clean, en-suite rooms in whitewashed terraces around a tidy lawn with secure parking and a simple restaurant.

There are no campsites, but if you ask permission you may be able to **camp** in front of the Sancta Maria Mission. The mission itself has rooms, although these are usually occupied by local people working in the town. Either way, the sound of children singing at the local school is likely to be balanced by that of late-night revelry from across the river! If you'd prefer to camp out of town, there are many lovely spots along the river, especially just across from Lukulu on the far bank, where a well-equipped traveller can camp in peace in the dry season. Ask whoever owns the nearest homestead for permission.

For details of fishing camps in the area, see page 486.

Where to eat and drink There are several basic restaurants, mostly in the markets. All offer rather meagre fare of nshima and some form of relish ($).

If you're self catering, it's wise to arrive with a good stock of food and drink. The shops in the old and new markets have only the most basic essentials, and the chances of finding even canned food are not great. Both soft drinks and beer depend on a truck supplying them from Lusaka; news of its arrival spreads like wildfire through the town.

SANCTA MARIA MISSION

The peaceful Sancta Maria Catholic Mission (⊕ SANCTA 14°22.749'S, 23°14.236'E) at Lukulu was founded in the 1930s by Father Phelem O'Shea, later Bishop of Livingstone. Painted a dark pink, it has a stunning setting high on one bank of the Zambezi, overlooking palm-fringed woodlands opposite, and is a beautiful place from which to watch the sunset.

Over the years, several different Catholic missionaries have worked here, including the Sisters of the Holy Cross, who established the girls' school. The sisters tell of one day, in the 1950s, when the bell in the tower started ringing wildly. On investigation the bell ringer proved to be a spotted hyena – probably from Liuwa – which had seized the rawhide rope in its jaws, and was trying to pull it off and eat it.

The building served as a treatment centre for leprosy patients in the early 1960s and continues to care for those disabled by the condition. It now also functions as a community guesthouse and home for the elderly. The mission continues its community and social work, particularly in the areas of schools, welfare and health. There is a dedicated 'Mother's Milk' programme, providing formula milk for babies who cannot be breastfed because their mothers have died or are unwell and/or unable to feed their children. School lunches, fees and scholarships are provided for the poorest families.

There is a Sunday service in Lozi that offers a fascinating blend of Catholicism and Lozi culture – with lots of singing and dancing.

The local people live by subsistence farming and fishing, eating just what they cultivate or catch, so not much fresh produce reaches the market either. That said, you'll probably find one or two varieties of seasonal fruits and vegetables, plus dried fish, eggs and roller meal for nshima and a butcher in the old market for meat. Bread supplies are erratic, but scones are sometimes available as an alternative.

What to see and do Lukulu doesn't have many obvious attractions, though the nearby Zambezi River and floodplains are very scenic, with excellent views from the Sancta Maria Mission (page 485). As in many of the area's smaller places, privacy can be a problem as an outsider is regarded as a source of free entertainment by some of the local community. Karun, a VSO volunteer living here, commented, 'If the visitor is willing to offer to the local people the same right to watch that s/he has assumed, then we have a happy relationship; if not, we have an unhappy visitor but content locals. Except for an occasional visit by a group of Makishi dancers, there are no other festivals that take place in Lukulu.'

Fishing camps around Lukulu In the early 1990s several fishing camps started up between Mongu and Lukulu, focusing on the superb tiger fishing in the area. However, it proved a difficult and expensive place to run a camp and several failed.

During July and August, there are fully catered five-night fishing camps on the Lungwebungu River, northwest of Lukulu on the western side of the Zambezi River, run by Mutemwa Lodge (page 462).

Barotse Tiger Camp [map, page 458] (6 tents) ☎ 0213 327489; **m** 0977 707829; **e** info@anglezam.co.zm; **w** zambezifishing.com. Some 20km south of Lukulu, this classy fishing lodge, under the ownership of the Livingstone-based Angle Zambia, is on a stretch of river where numerous fishing world records have been attained over the years. Guests fly in to Lukulu airport & are transferred to the camp by vehicle & boat. There is no vehicular access to the camp itself. A traditional tented camp, spread out along the river with a swimming pool & 2 large mess tents: 1 with a bar & lounge, comfortably kitted out with sofas & armchairs; the other the dining area (gourmet picnic lunches are on offer, too). As for the fishing, with waters teeming with fish & 18ft aluminium boats with GPS fish-finding technology, anglers will be in their element trying to join the camp's '20lb+ Club' for landing giant tigers. 👑👑👑

NORTHWESTERN ZAMBIA

West of the Copperbelt, squeezed between Angola and DRC, this area is distant from most of Zambia. This is reflected in its flora and fauna which, in parts, are much more like those of the wet tropical forests which occur to the north than those of the drier areas of the Kalahari to the south.

Despite being out on a limb, the road access is pretty good, though travel to the region does require some planning and confident self-sufficiency.

MUFUMBWE Once little more than a dot on the map, the linear town of Mufumbwe (⊕ MUFUMB 13°08.212'S, 25°00.251'E), 108km west of the turn-off to Kasempa and 121km east of Kabompo, is growing rapidly. There are two **fuel stations** (though neither offer 100% fuel reliability) and a **tyre-repair** place. These, as well as a **bakery** and a small **market**, are invaluable if you're planning a detour into West Lunga National Park.

WEST LUNGA NATIONAL PARK (Park fees US$10 pp/day; vehicle US$15/day or K17 if Zambian registered; ◷ Jun–Oct) Some 150km northwest of Kafue, as the pied crow flies, West Lunga is another of Zambia's parks which is both very wild and little visited. It was originally gazetted as a game reserve in the late 1940s, mainly to preserve its population of yellow-backed duiker. Then elephants were also abundant, along with a multitude of antelope species including sable and Lichtenstein's hartebeest. There was big game here – including buffalo, lion and leopard – but probably never in the volumes found in the Luangwa or Kafue. However, in the last few decades, it's been used very little, except for hunting and fishing by the local communities. As a result, the game was seriously depleted.

That said, it's important to note that the park's spectacular forests have remained intact and over the last decade there has been a dedicated effort to restore this ecosystem and increase park protection, with the specific aim of facilitating wildlife recovery. The formation of the West Lunga Trust, to try to conserve some of this pristine corner of Zambia, was a hugely positive step.

The surrounding population density here is relatively low, and almost entirely adjacent to the main roads. Thus, with the help and drive of the local chiefs, the Trust has been able to mobilise many of the local communities to help engage with and support the environmental conservation project. Community Resource Boards (CRBs) have been introduced with a view to managing the natural resources in each of the surrounding areas, and derive a financial benefit from any operations there. It is to be hoped that the willingness of the park's staff, which is considerable, plus their consistent anti-poaching efforts and the introduction of an alternative livelihoods program in the areas surrounding the park by the West Lunga Conservation Project will in time translate into improvements in both the infrastructure and environment within the park itself. Certainly the biannual wildlife monitoring over the last five years has shown some exciting signs of recovery.

Geography, flora and fauna West Lunga National Park covers 1,684km^2 of forests, dambos, open grasslands and papyrus swamps. It is bounded by the Kabompo River to the east and south (adjacent to which are most of the park's swamps) and by the West Lunga River to the west. The environment is still pristine miombo, interspersed with large grassland plains, flooded dambos and some particularly attractive *Cryptosepalum* forests. It's very beautiful and wild, but the grass and vegetation are thick and difficult even to walk through. The rivers that bound through the park are great for canoeing and boating – with some sections of rapids, and some where you canoe beside rock walls.

Buk's 1993–94 survey (page 512) reported two sightings of wild dog in West Lunga, although noted that poaching remained heavy and the species was probably declining here. Rob Munro reports that he saw buffalo, impala, puku and warthog in the park on a trip in mid-1999.

Ten years later, Dorian Tilbury (a first-class guide with a long history in Zambia's more remote areas) confirmed sightings of puku, hippo, crocodile, vervet monkey, yellow baboon and numerous excellent sightings of samango monkey, plus spoor of bushbuck, bush pig, cane rat, thick-tailed bushbaby, civet and genet.

Today, the wildlife populations in West Lunga are certainly continuing to recover, albeit very slowly. The most evident signs of recovery are for puku, bushbuck, bushpig and meso-carnivores such as caracal and side-striped jackal. Remnant populations of sable antelope, buffalo and elephant exist, however their numbers are still critically low. There are a number of species that are likely locally extinct: defassa waterbuck, Lichtenstein's hartebeest, eland, roan antelope and the large carnivores such as lion and wild dogs. One active hyena midden was recorded in early 2023 and there are certainly still vervet monkey, baboon, hippo and crocodile here.

In terms of distribution and spotting opportunities, you are very likely to see oribi and reedbuck on the park's large central Kamanya plains. Bushpig are common throughout the park and even in areas surrounding the park and you have a very good chance of seeing them in the early hours of the morning. Sable sightings are not uncommon on the finger dambos in the east section of the park and blue duiker are commonly seen throughout. Both thick-tailed and lesser bush baby are very common and often seen and heard at night. Tree hyrax are also often heard at night but very rarely seen. Sitatunga are likely common and have even been seen in the communal land to the south of the park around Jivundu, although they can be hard to spot due to their shy nature and preference for a dense papyrus swamp habitat.

Of course with an untouched environment, the birding remains excellent – and even a short visit along the rivers should yield sightings of half-collared kingfishers and large numbers of black saw-wing swallows, Pel's fishing owl and crowned

CRYPTOSEPALUM FORESTS AND THE WHITE-CHESTED TINKERBIRD

Almost exclusive to Zambia, *Cryptosepalum* forests are distinctive dry evergreen forests which occur in the area of the Kabompo River. They are regarded by botanists as forming the largest area of tropical evergreen forest in Africa outside the equatorial zone.

Dominating these forests is the mukwe tree (*Cryptosepalum pseudotaxus*), which grows on relatively infertile Kalahari sand where there is no permanent surface water. This lack of water means that these areas remain relatively uninhabited. Other trees often found here include the much-exploited rosewood (*Guibourtia coleosperma*). Further south, the character of these forests gradually changes and they become dominated by Zambezi teak trees (*Baikiaea plurijuga*; page 445). Hence logging is a serious threat to them.

The under-storey in *Cryptosepalum* forests is usually dense and tangled, including *Liana* and *Combretum* species which form impenetrable thickets. Epiphytic lichens are common, and the forest floor is mainly covered in mosses. It's very difficult to walk through unless a path has already been cleared.

The avifauna is usually particularly rich, with a mixture of bird species which frequent moist evergreen forests, woodlands and riverine forests. Among specials found in these forests are gorgeous bush shrikes, crested guineafowls, purple-throated cuckoo-shrikes, Margaret's batises and square-tailed drongos. However, the area is famous among ornithologists for the controversy surrounding its one and only endemic species: the white-chested tinkerbird. Just one of these birds has ever been found, and that was the 'type specimen' netted in 1964. Numerous subsequent attempts to find more have failed.

Some feel that they have simply been defeated by the dense foliage, and that a population of these birds exists deep within the thickets. Others argue that the one specimen found was probably an aberrant individual of the similar golden-rumped tinkerbird, which also occurs in these forests. Whatever the truth, it makes these forests a magnet for birdwatchers, all keen to catch a glimpse of the world's second white-chested tinkerbird!

eagles, among many more common species. Zambia's turacos do well here, with Schalow's and Ross's more common than the grey lourie or go-away bird. The area also boasts some highly sought after 'specials' in abundance: Nerina trogon, African finfoot, African broadbill to name a few.

Getting there West Lunga is still exceptionally wild – so you will require an independent streak both to get here, and to get around.

The park's main entrance, near the Department of National Parks and Wildlife compound and HQ at Jivundu (⊕ JIVUND 13°06.139'S, 24°41.522'E), is accessed from the main M8 road, 64km east of Kabompo, and 41km west of Mufumbwe. There is a relatively obscure signpost here, so it's easy to miss the turning (⊕ TUJIVU 13°12.151'S,' 24°40.907'E). This leads on to a sandy track, which runs through woodland for 11.5km to the ZAWA scout post on the south bank of the Kabompo River. Here you pay your entrance and campsite fees, and can arrange for a scout to accompany you across the river into the park. Do remember that from mid-December to June the pontoon is not able to cross the river.

The easiest ways to get to West Lunga are either from the Copperbelt or from Kafue National Park's eastern boundary, via Kasempa. Approaching from Lukulu is straightforward, and from Mongu it's best to take the road between Kaoma and Kasempa, which is currently good and well maintained by the mines, which use this route to reach Namibia. It's usually an easy and reliable route at any time of year, though a good 4x4 is advised.

From the Copperbelt Take the tar road through Kitwe and Chingola to Solwezi (⊕ SOLWEZ 12°10.931'S, 26°23.960'E), from where it turns south until crossing the Mutanda River at Mwelemu (⊕ MWELEM 12°23.661'S, 26°14.276'E). On the other side of the river, there's a tar road on the right, which heads west to Mwinilunga. For West Lunga, continue on the road south, towards Kabompo and Kasempa, and be on the lookout for pot-holes as the road has deteriorated in recent years. After almost 90km it is joined from the east by a road from Kitwe (which would have made a shorter, but more time-consuming, approach), via the village of Ingwe.

About 16km later there is a road left to Kasempa, and one straight on to Kabompo (⊕ KABOMP 13°35.610'S,' 24°12.125'E). Take the road going straight. This is a super tarred road – though you still need to watch out for pedestrians and animals. After 140km you'll come to the turning off the M8, above. Allow 4 hours' driving time between Solwezi and West Lunga.

From Kafue Follow the directions on page 422, to approach Kasempa from Mumbwa via the Lubungu and Lunga pontoons, stopping at Mukinge Hospital for fuel, then head north from Kasempa onto the road from Mwelemu to Kabompo. Alternatively, take the tar road to Kitwe and Solwezi, and then cut southwest; this is likely to be easier and probably faster.

Where to stay

Kabompo River Lodge & Campsite m 0955 441567, 0966 441567; e info@kitebesafaris.com. The lodge has 7 chalets with verandas overlooking the park across the Kabompo River (max 14 guests) & a campsite with ablutions blocks & showers; the generator is on in the evenings & tents can be hired if needed. Boat trips can be organised but are dependent on fuel availability so if this is something you're keen to do, make sure you contact them well in advance to make this clear. *Chalet K400/500 sgl/sharing; camping K150 pp.* **$**

Kafunfula Community Camp m 0963 362657, 0965 058769, 0763 317800; e kafunfulanatltd@gmail.com; w westlunga.org/kafunfula. About

2½hrs' drive from Kalumbila town, this lovely community-run campsite to the north of the park is supported by the West Lunga Conservation Project & is a great accommodation option for those driving through the park. With beautiful views across the Kabompo River & neat facilities, it's possible to stay in pre-erected tents or book a pitch for your own.

The 4, good-quality dome tents, each with 2 beds, sit on concrete platforms under shady trees, alongside separate pitches with BBQ facilities. All enjoy riverside vistas & help from the committed team here. Hot showers & flush toilets are in a separate, clean ablution building & there's a communal washing area & picnic tables under thatch. A boat launch can be used by anyone who would like to fish or go for a relaxing river cruise, though boats are not provided by the camp. Launch your own boats here or ask the team if someone local is able to take you out on the water. Excellent driving directions are provided on their website. *Pitch US$5.50 pp; tent US$26/tent; boat launch US$10.* ⌚ *Apr–Dec.* **$**

What to see and do A vehicle pontoon across the river was installed a few years ago and there is now a well-developed road network in the park that can be accessed between June and December, making park exploration easily possible. The roads have been maintained annually for the last four years now as commitment to protecting and promoting West Lunga's beauty grows. It's possible to take a scout/guide from DNPW Jivundu to drive or walk with you in the park, returning to camp in the evening.

If you'd like to go out on the river, boat trips can be arranged by Kabompo River Camp (provided that fuel is available) to Mabongo Hot Springs or Mulongwanyimu Swamp. Thus these are best booked in advance. Similarly, fishing – with your own kit (or hiring) – is another option. Boats and mokoros can be launched from the campsite. Note that DNPW collects park entry fees and/or angling fees from anyone who goes boat cruising, canoeing or fishing in addition to the hire costs.

KABOMPO This small town beside the surging Kabompo River, in the sparsely populated northwest, is at the centre of Zambia's remaining teak forests – and 121km from Mufumbwe. There is a long-established Catholic mission here, as well as a **market**, a hospital, a **post office**, a branch of the Finance **Bank**, several small **shops** and a handful of guesthouses. There is a **fuel station** but supplies are not guaranteed.

Getting there and away Navigating to and from Kabompo (⊕ KABOMP 13°35.610'S; 24°12.125'E) is very easy, as it's on the main M8 road.

From Mwinilunga The turning northwards to Mwinilunga (⊕ TUMWIN 13°26.082'S; 24°19.978'E) is 25km east of Kabompo, and although it's signposted, is easily missed. After about 4.5km this road splits; the road to Mwinilunga takes the right fork over the tributary, and then bends back to the left, heading roughly north-northwest with the Manyinga River on its left. See the section on getting to Mwinilunga, page 496, for more about this road.

Just 2km east of the turning is the busy roadside town of **Manyinga** (⊕ MANYIN 13°25.095'S; 24°19.901'E), spread out between two bridges – over the Kabompo River on the east side, and the scenic Manyinga River to the west.

By bus Buses to and from Zambezi stop every day except Sunday outside the Big Tree Restaurant on the main road, almost opposite the water tower. There are also three buses a week between Chavuma and Solwezi, and on to Kitwe all stopping in Kabompo.

Where to stay and eat A clutch of simple guesthouses (**$**) is signposted off the main road towards the river. To get there, turn off the main road at ⊕ TUGSTH 13°35.618'S, 24°12.156'E, continue over a rather incongruous but neatly planted roundabout, and you will find them on the left-hand side.

ZAMBEZI Like many regional centres in Zambia, Zambezi is referred to locally as 'the boma'. It's a small town with a few very basic **shops**, a **post office**, a Catholic mission and a small local **market**. Most of its amenity buildings, including the

NATURE'S NECTAR HONEY

Driving around the Kabompo area, you'll often see what look like hollow logs, suspended high in the trees. These are beehives, and beekeeping has long been a tradition in these forests, with fathers handing down to their sons not only the skills, but also traditional hives of grass, bark and hollow tree trunks.

Now this traditional process has developed into a thriving industry with global reach. This started as a Zambian government initiative, initially supported by funding from the German Technical Development Agency, to improve the marketing of the local honey that was produced here, and thus increase the income of the rural population. Then there were only a few hundred local producers, but in 1979 North Western Bee Products was established. By 2016, the company bought honey and beeswax from about 3,000 traditional bark-hive beekeepers in Zambia, which was sold globally.

However, while traditional bark-hives do enable easy and low-cost participation in the honey industry, there are real concerns about the environmental impact of bark-hive production.

The cylindrical hives are hollow timber and are produced by ring-barking, or removing the bark, of trees. This resulted in the loss of one indigenous tree for a hive that may only last two to three years. With the honey market growing 700% in the last five years alone, increasingly large numbers of trees were being ring-barked annually for this purpose, significantly contributing to deforestation. Additionally, bark-hive production was putting pressure on the very nectar-producing forest species that provided much of the desirable honey flow, notably mutondo trees (*Julbernardia paniculate*).

Fortunately, there are now companies engaged in more sustainable community beekeeping initiatives, such' as Nature's Nectar (w naturesnectarzambia.com). They do not source any wood from Zambia's native forests but instead distribute 'top bar beehives' to communities. These hives are made from fast-growing pine or other sustainably grown timber, last five times as long as traditional hives, and are provided with an agreement that the indigenous forest around the hives must be conserved. Thus, the valuable knowledge of traditional beekeepers is harnessed but the forests are also protected. This is considered to be a more scalable and sustainable option, given the currently insatiable global demand for honey and rapid growth of the industry in Zambia.

To date, Nature's Nectar have distributed over 20,000 beehives, trained 2,000 beekeepers (44% of whom are women) and increased the income of its beekeepers by 22% annually. If you'd like to support them with this initiative, you can donate a top bar beehive to the community for US$25 from their website.

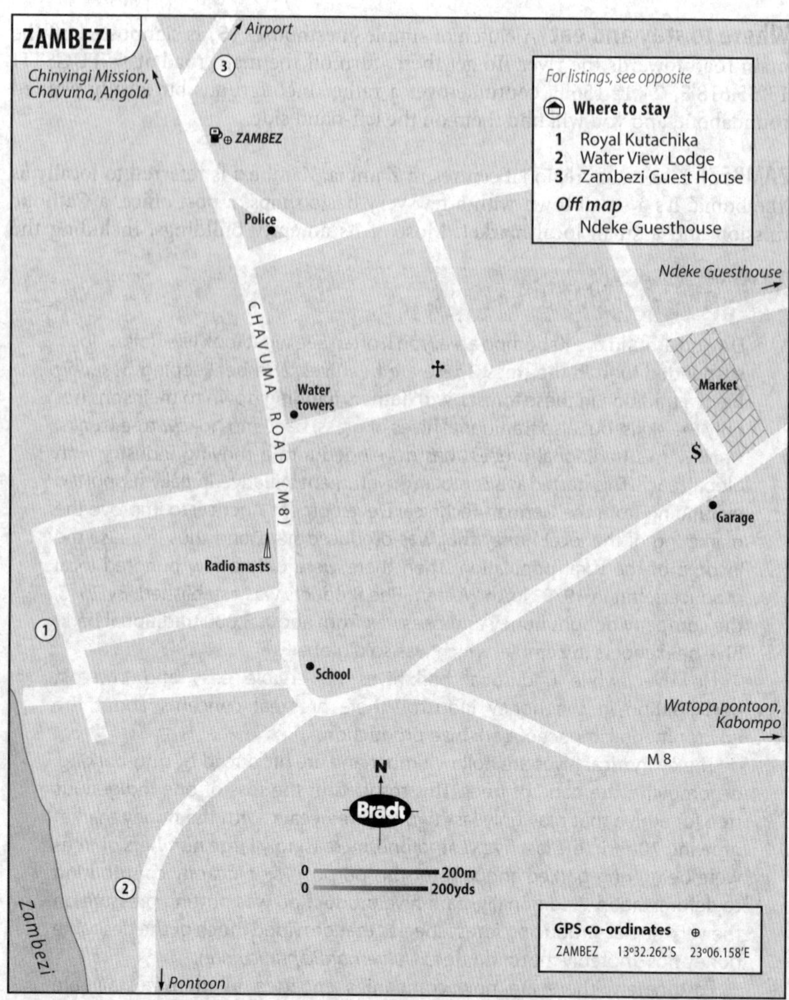

police station and government offices, are situated just off the main road, behind the 'new' **fuel** station (⊕ ZAMBEZ 13°32.262'S,' 23°06.158'E), which when we visited was showing no signs of opening. In fact, if you're driving into this area, do so with very large reserves of fuel as supplies are erratic at best. Do be aware that watered-down petrol from illicit sources – known as 'bush fuel' – is sometimes sold to unsuspecting travellers, so ask locally for a reliable source.

Getting there and away The road west from Kabompo, the M8, is a remarkably good tar road that continues north to the Angolan border at Chavuma. Along the road are relatively few villages and lots of thick teak forests. In the dry season the smoke from occasional bush fires will be seen drifting in the sky, above areas of scorched and blackened ground. It's a measure of the improvements in the road infrastructure that the journey to Lusaka that used to take five days can now be completed, via Lukulu and Kaoma, in around 12–14 hours depending on the road conditions.

There's a pontoon across the river just below Water View Lodge, although most people pay just to be ferried over the water by mokoro. Few visitors have any reason to cross here, though it's worth noting that there is talk of prospecting for oil to the west.

From Lukulu See page 484 for the road to Watopa pontoon (⊕ FERRY4 14°02.338'S, 23°37.744'E), and note that this pontoon is incorrectly marked on the ITM map of Zambia. Then it is nearly 22km north to Mumbeji (⊕ MUMBEJ 13°51.653'S, 23°40.327'E), where you turn left on to the good M8 for a further 75km west and northwest to Zambezi (⊕ ZAMBEZ 13°32.262'S, 23°06.158'E).

Where to stay and eat *Map, opposite*

Perhaps unexpectedly, Zambezi has a handful of guesthouses, including **Ndeke Guesthouse**, and those below – all of which have restaurants.

Royal Kutachika (25 rooms) m 0969 657441; e info@kutachika.com; w kutachika.com. Pleasant en-suite rooms in very neat, thatched buildings. Great views from a high bank towards the Zambezi & floodplains beyond. Well-maintained gardens, a swimming pool & restaurant. **$$–$$$**

Water View Lodge (14 rooms) m 0979 379449. Perched high above the Zambezi, & clearly signposted from the main road, this pleasant guesthouse has 3 types of room, with en-suite shower, TV, fridge, fan & b/fast included. Meals of nshima with chicken or fish are served in a thatched restaurant overlooking the river, where there's also an open rondavel, ideal for sunset drinks. **$**

Zambezi Guest House (25 rooms, camping) off Chavuma Rd; t 0218 371124; m 0978 642882; e zambezi@limagarden.com; w limagarden.com. En-suite brick-&-thatch chalets with TV, fridge, AC & dbl/twin beds. **$**

What to see and do

Traditional dancing The palaces of the Lunda and the Luvale senior chiefs are about 17km north of town, on the east and west sides of the road respectively – as you might predict from the rough distribution of languages mapped out on page 21. The Luvale chief's palace is the venue for the popular Likumbi Lya Mize ceremony in late August (page 26), as well as for traditional dancing, which is held here several times a week.

Chinyingi Mission About 23km north of Zambezi, just after the Makondu River, is a sandy track heading west (⊕ TUCHIN 13°20.450'S, 23°03.674'E). It's signposted to Chinyingi Mission, which is a further 8km along this track, for which a high-clearance 4x4 is essential.

The mission (⊕ CHINYI 13°21.146'S, 23°00.834'E), which stands on the western bank of the Zambezi, was founded in 1953 by a group of Capuchin brothers. It is perhaps most famous for the Chinyingi suspension bridge – one of only four bridges to span the width of the Zambezi at the time of its construction (page 495), though now bridges at Sesheke, Ngonye Falls and Kazungula have since been built, or are currently being constructed. If you walk across the bridge to the mission (you can park by the bridge), you get a real feel for its 300m span, and some beautiful views along the river, too.

Although the mission is not currently inhabited, the school and a rural health centre are still operational, as is the mission church, and visitors are welcome to look around. It's a tranquil spot, lit up by frangipani and flame trees. The church itself is simple but light and spacious, drums at the ready for the next service, and notable for its cross of scaffolding bars.

MAKISHI DANCERS *Judi Helmholz*

Sometimes in Mongu, or while travelling in the north of the western provinces, you will encounter colourfully clad characters adorned with fearsome costumes – Makishi dancers. For the uninitiated (defined as women and children in Luvale society), these are traditionally believed to be female spirits from the dead, and most will talk in high voices and even have 'breasts' made of wire.

The creative and artistic skills of the Luvale people are reflected in the wide variety of mask styles worn by the Makishi. These are huge constructions, often made of bark and wood and frequently coloured with red, white and black. Even helicopter blades are sometimes spotted in the designs – a memory of the war in Angola.

Each Likishi (the singular of Makishi) dancer is distinctive and plays a specific role within the various ceremonies and festivals. For example, the Mungali, or hyena, depicts menacing villains, while the Chikishikishi, a monster with a boiling pot, represents discipline – and will consume mischievous members of society.

Apart from their occasional appearances throughout the land, the Makishi dancers play central roles during two of the most important ceremonies of Luvale culture: the Mukanda and the Wali. These are the initiation rites for boys and girls respectively.

The Mukanda, also known as circumcision camps, are traditional 'schools' for local boys, normally aged from 12 to 17, but sometimes as young as five. Here, they are introduced to adult life and circumcised. The dancer known as Chileya cha Mukanda, which literally means 'the fool of the school', serves as a jester by mimicking the participants so as to relieve tension and anxiety before the circumcision ceremony. The girls attend a similar ceremony, though there is no physical clitoridectomy operation, as occurs in other cultures.

CHAVUMA Some 80km north of Zambezi, or 6km south of the Angolan border, Chavuma lies at the point where the Zambezi re-enters Zambia. The land around here is arid, and the soil mostly grey in colour, which makes villages in this area look dull compared with those further south. Proximity to the border means that the town has attracted a number of illegal Angolan diamond sellers.

The Brethren Missionaries, who live in a large compound up on the hill by the town, have their own camping spot by the river, which they may allow you to use, or they may be able to direct you to other suitable places to stay.

Fuel supplies are very intermittent, so it's important not to rely on filling up here.

Getting there The M8 here from Solwezi via Kabompo and Zambezi is a decent tar road. If you're approaching from the south via Lukulu then it's best to cross the Kabompo River at the Watopa pontoon (⊕ FERRY4 14°02.338'S, 23°37.744'E), then join this road from there (page 484).

What to see and do

Chavuma Falls This is not nearly as spectacular as the Zambezi's drops at Ngonye and Victoria Falls, but makes a good picnic site for an afternoon. The falls are found by taking the footpath near the pontoon.

No-man's-land Every morning there is a small market in no-man's-land, between the territories of Zambia and Angola. Both Zambians and Angolans come to barter for goods, under the watchful eyes of the armed border guards. It is a fascinating occurrence. As a foreigner, make sure you have very clear permission from the border guards before you even consider joining in, and don't take any photographs without permission.

MWINILUNGA Mwinilunga is a large, thriving outpost of a town, raised up in the remote northwest corner of Zambia. Although the town isn't on the national grid, there's now two fuel stations (though they can't be 100% relied upon) about 500m

CHINYINGI SUSPENSION BRIDGE

With thanks to Richard Miller, Cheshire, Connecticut, USA

The Chinyingi Mission was founded in 1953 to minister to villagers on both sides of the Zambezi, bringing them education and health care. However, at this point the river is over 210m wide, very deep, and subject to annual flooding, yet the only means of crossing it in the early days of the mission was by dugout canoe.

When he first arrived at the mission, Brother Crispin was responsible for transport, maintenance and cooking, and in order to help bring heavy supplies as well as people over the river he introduced a pontoon ferry. However, in 1971 four people were drowned while bringing a woman to hospital in a dug out canoe, and he vowed to prevent any further accident by building a bridge over the river. While his was an unlikely background for the engineering feat he had undertaken, Brother Crispin didn't lack faith. From a picture of a suspension bridge in Nepal that he had seen in *National Geographic*, he set to work, identifying people who could help him in the design of the bridge, sourcing the materials, and securing funds to pay for the project. He pulled together a team of just five young labourers, then spent all his free time working alongside them; for safety reasons, no work was undertaken unless he was present.

The project was not without significant setbacks. At just 6m high, the original towers at each end of the bridge proved to be too low for the cables to span the river at the right height, and had to be rebuilt twice to reach the necessary 18m. The suspension cables, when first hung, swung wildly, until Brother Crispin was advised to install guy wires to hold them in place. And every element of the supplies had to be trucked up to 800km across unforgiving terrain in all weathers. Little wonder that it took over five years for the bridge to be completed.

The result, though, has stood the test of time. Since its opening in 1977, the 300m bridge has continued to provide a lifeline to people on the opposite side of the river to the mission, and a supply line for the mission itself. While Brother Crispin has now returned to his native Italy, as many as 500 people a day continue to cross the 1m-wide metal walkway (the original wood was replaced by Brother Crispin before he left), that he and his team suspended some 13m above the waters. They come on foot, on bicycles, and even on mopeds, up to 60 at a time, taking for granted the work of a Capuchin monk who built their bridge on faith.

after the bridge, shops with basic supplies, a sizeable local **market**, a bank, a large **post office** and a small Franciscan mission.

Getting there and away By far the easiest way to get to Mwinilunga from Lusaka is via the Copperbelt, Chingola and Solwezi – be aware that there are seven tolls along the route, each costing K20. The route from Chingola to Solwezi is on a great tarmac road. About 28km after Solwezi, there's a junction at Mwelemu (⊕ MWELEM 12°23.661'S, 26°14.276'E) on to the Mwinilunga road. Sadly, from just after the Kalumbila Mine, it's around 160km of very poor road that will take around 3½ hours of tough driving to reach Mwinilunga. It is also possible to take a longer, more adventurous route from Lusaka, heading to Kaoma, through Kafue National Park and on to the Mutanda turn-off via Kasempa. It's a longer route by about 2 hours and much more offbeat, but more a scenic drive through the park.

From Kabompo See page 490 to locate the turn-off for Mwinilunga from the M8 (⊕ TUMWIN 13°26.082'S, 24°19.978'E). Then after 4.5km, take the right fork, and bend around left. It's a beautiful drive along a good but narrow road on which you can average about 30–40km/h in the dry season. On either side are occasional subsistence farming communities, and large areas of forest. It does cross one or two large dambos, which could be very sticky during the rainy season. Note that this route goes relatively close to Angola, and you'd be well advised to check the security situation locally before coming this way. Equally, don't be tempted to divert off to the west of the road unless you know exactly where you're going.

After about 49km you'll pass the village of Lunsongwe (⊕ LUNSON 13°02.068'S, 24°13.385'E) – spelled 'Lusongwa' on some maps – where there's a school and a small grocery shop. Around 54km later, you pass the very spread-out village of Kanyilambi, notable mainly for its church and beautiful silvery fields of rice – and then you're almost halfway to Mwinilunga.

Continuing north, the forests and other vegetation start to get thicker while the atmosphere becomes perceptibly warmer and more humid – despite the slight but steady rise in altitude. In places the forest is thick enough for the canopy of trees over the track to interlock – and for some of the birding 'specials' found in Mwinilunga to occur here too.

Eventually you reach a T-junction (⊕ TUKABO 11°45.158'S, 24°26.114'E) with the main Mwinilunga–Solwezi tar road, and the centre of town is a few kilometres west. In the dry season it takes about 5 hours to cover the 219km from Kabompo.

Where to stay Mwinilunga has an assortment of largely unremarkable places to sleep and eat, all fairly inexpensive, of which Kakuwahi is the best bet. There are some interesting options a little further afield, though: a super bushcamp, Kalwelwa, owned by one of Zambia's top ornithologists, and Hillwood Farm (see opposite) on the Nchila Reserve.

Kakuwahi Lodge (3 rooms) In an attractive setting on the banks of the Lunga River, this lodge is owned by a Christian husband-&-wife team, Roma & Catherine Nyukambumba. Its neat chalets are backed by manicured lawns dotted with trees & shrubs. Inside, clean en-suite rooms come with queen or dbl beds, AC, DSTV, radio & fridge – & (very welcome) hot water. There's a modern lounge & the food is reasonable. **$$**

Kalwelwa Bushcamp [map, page 458] (5 tents, camping) **m** 0978 430655; **e** BirdingZambia@gmail.com; **w** birdingzambia.com/kalwelwabushcamp. ⊕ KALWEL 11°42.309'S, 24°65.013'E. An hour east of the source of the Zambezi, Kalwelwa Bushcamp opened in 2020 in an untouched area of wet & dry grasslands & evergreen 'Congo forest'. Owned by Zambia's leading ornithologist, Frank Willems, & Inge Akerboom, the 5 simple, en-suite safari tents offer self-catering (a fully kitted-out camp kitchen & assistants are available) or FB (booking essential) accommodation; camping is also possible here.

Not surprisingly it's a splendid spot for birdwatching with 350 species already recorded & many of the area's 'specials' to be found in & around camp. From wattled cranes to Denham's Bustard & vermiculated fishing owl, there are birds from a diverse range of habitats here. Not to mention, a variety of antelope, palm civets & dwarf galago are among notable mammals. Frank & Inge are working hard to create a large Conservancy area in partnership with local communities to protect the area's rich biodiversity, reintroduce indigenous animal species & create sustainable incomes for local people.

4x4 drives & walks to the grassland plains & rainforest are available, you can enjoy a cooling dip in the dam, & – for an extra charge – you can enjoy Frank guiding you around this beautiful region & sharing his extensive knowledge.

To reach Kalwelwa, turn off the Ikelenge Rd 25km north of Mwinilunga. From there, it's 38km on dirt roads making a high-clearance vehicle necessary & a 4x4 essential in the wet season. Note: there is limited power supply & mobile phone reception. 🕘 *1 Jun–30 Nov; Dec–May on request. US$190pp/dbl FBA, US45pp/dbl SC; US$250/day Frank Willems specialist guiding, US$50 for additional pax (min 2 pax, 4 days). Advance booking essential. Self-catering* **$$$**, *FBA* 👑

HILLWOOD FARM AND NCHILA WILDLIFE RESERVE Hillwood Farm is an improbable place. It's an oasis of peace and order in a corner of Zambia which the world's media might expect, given its position between Angola and the DRC, to be under permanent siege. What's more, within its bounds, Hillwood has a very special reserve, Nchila, which has flora and fauna that are unique to Zambia: it contains a slice of equatorial forest that's been preserved and nurtured. The family who own this farm, the Fishers, have been working in close partnership with the local communities here for generations.

In recent years the family has placed an increasing emphasis on hunting, and – since hunting and photographic guests don't mix – there are very few weeks of the year that are available for other guests. That said, they still welcome campers, ornithologists and photographers whenever they can.

So while it's exceedingly 'out of the way' by anyone's standards, and there are restrictions on the times when non-hunting guests can stay, Hillwood remains a totally fascinating place that's delightful to visit and contains some amazing wildlife. If you're anywhere near here, do contact them to see if you can stay.

Getting there and away To reach here from Mwinilunga, continue through town on the main road, past the turn-off to the airport. After about 7km, the road changes from tar to well-maintained gravel road. Over its course it then crosses a series of rivers, and you'll drive over four bridges. (While you don't need a 4x4 for this in the dry season, there are several steep sections that could become tricky in the wet season.) In sequence, the rivers include Luakela, the Chitunta and the Kaseki.

About 47km from Mwinilunga there's a right turn that is clearly marked (⊕ TUZAMB 11°23.321'S, 24°16.632'E). After about 4.6km, this leads to the source of the Zambezi (page 501). Then about 3km after that turning, you cross the final river, the Sakeji. About 9km after this there is a clear signpost to the right (⊕ TUHILL 11°17.040'S, 24°16.663'E) proclaiming that Hillwood Farm and Nchila Wildlife Reserve are about 7km away. This final road felt a little like a local footpath through a village to us, but eventually you do reach Hillwood Farm (⊕ HILLWO 11°14.989'S, 24°18.852'E) – an oasis of order.

Note that on the way from Mwinilunga to Hillwood you pass (although may not notice) the Luakela Forest Reserve and later Chitunta Plain, both of which have some of the birds which attract ornithologists to this corner of the country. Luakela Forest Reserve is noted for lots of bar-winged weavers, while Chitunta Plain is very important for many species, including the Angola lark, Grimwood's longclaw, the dambo (black-tailed) cisticola, the black and rufous swallows and short-tailed pipits. Venture several kilometres up the stream there, and you've a good chance of seeing another very uncommon bird, Bocage's weaver.

Hillwood is about 68km from Mwinilunga and, if you don't stop for any birdwatching, will take a bit less than 2 hours to drive. Alternatively, Nchila can be reached by a short (though not very cheap) charter flight from Lusaka or (marginally less costly) from Lunga River Lodge in northern Kafue.

Where to stay Both the bushcamp and the campsite are on the Nchila reserve, and reservations for both are essential, since hunters are never mixed with other guests. In addition, they may not otherwise have the space, staff or supplies to accommodate you. Clients are now also flown by helicopter to a remote second tented camp on Nkwaji Reserve high on the bank of the Lunga river for specific hunts.

Nchila Camp (3 chalets) e nchila@nchilawildlifereserve.com, nchilawildlife@iwayafrica.com. ⊕ NCHILA 11°14.945'S, 24°19.642'E. Nchila's small bushcamp overlooks a large plain & dambo from the edge of riverine forest & miombo woodland. It can take a max of 6 people (8 if squeezed!) in well-furnished chalets with solid wooden furniture, stylish fabrics & imaginative touches & you can relax in a swimming pool & jacuzzi a short walk away. 1 stunning chalet has a king-size bed & a big en-suite bathroom, incorporating a large, slightly sunken bath beside the window, & a good shower. A good 2nd chalet has 2 twin rooms which share a flush toilet, shower & a bath with another shower over it. Both are spacious, built of stone with thatched roofs, & with water heated by wood-fired boilers. A smaller chalet (comfortable for 1 person, or 'cosy' for 2) has its own en-suite shower & toilet.

At the camp's heart is a thatched dining & lounge area, the 2 separated by a large log fire. With a lovely view over the dambo, it makes a pleasant place to sit & watch the wildlife. The food is good but simple: very fresh wholesome farm fare. ◷ *15 May–15 Nov.* ♛♛♛♛

Nchila Campsite Nchila's campsite, in a lovely shady spot next to the Sakeji River, has an ablution block with showers & flush toilets. There's also a dining area & a kitchen with a small wood stove & hot water. Lighting is courtesy of a connection to your car battery. Firewood is provided & a staff member is available to draw & heat water for showers. You'll need to come with all your own camping kit & most of your food, although limited amounts of fresh produce may sometimes be available from the farm. It's best to agree this in advance with Nchila. *US$25 pp plus entry fee US$10 pp.* ◷ *15 May–15 Nov.* **$$$**

What to see and do

Although most people will stay on the reserve (page 497), there is lots to see around the farm. Most people will also detour to the source of the Zambezi, and keen ornithologists will frequently head into the surrounding area in search of the 'specials' found in this corner of Zambia.

Hillwood Farm Zambian farms don't come much more remote or well established than Hillwood. Relatively speaking, it's had a lot of time to build up a very self-sufficient yet interdependent community of people.

Of interest here is the farm itself, which these days relies on beef and dairy cows, cereal and, increasingly, tourism to generate income. The orphanage and the school are also fascinating; the boarding school is used by some of Zambia's more affluent residents, so it's not at all impoverished by local standards.

If you have the opportunity to chat with Pete, Lynn or Chris – do so. You'll get an intriguing insight into the area's past and present. They have always worked

THE FISHER FAMILY

Pete Fisher is Zambian – part of the fourth generation of Fishers in Zambia. He lives in the oldest house on Hillwood Farm with his Californian wife Lynn. For much of the year, his son, Chris, is also based on the farm and his wife Sarah runs the newly built primary school for locals and orphans from the Hillwood Orphanage.

The history of the Fisher family is an interesting one, and inextricably linked with the development of the local area. The story begins in the late 19th century. Inspired by David Livingstone's and Fred Arnott's aspirations to end the slave trade in Africa by establishing Christianity and legitimate commerce in its place, Walter Fisher was a willing recruit to the missionary quest. In 1889, freshly qualified as a doctor and with a gold medal for surgery at Guy's Hospital, Walter Fisher left the UK with a party of seven other men and women, bound for the Angolan coast. Suffering from various hardships on arrival, the party moved out of Portuguese territory to Kalene Hill in Northern Rhodesia. Indeed, the ruins of the houses and storerooms they built in the Angolan style, with bricks made of baked anthill, can still be found there.

Kalene Hill eventually became the home of a mission hospital and an orphanage after Walter's wife, Anna Fisher, rescued a newborn baby. She found the child after it had been lying on its mother's grave for two days – where it had been placed as it was believed to have caused her death (the mother had died in childbirth). The orphanage is now on Hillwood Farm and its emphasis is on keeping a traditional African way of life so that the children can return to their village at about six years old. Until then, they are taught, fed and clothed to give them a good start. As has always been the case here, each baby comes with a female family member to assist with its care. There are currently 30 orphans and visitors are warmly welcomed.

In addition to the orphanage, Anna Fisher was also responsible for establishing the Nyamuweji village for old ladies, where they cultivated the land and were protected by the Fishers from customary witch-hunts. Such women, too old to work hard, often came for refuge. There remain six to eight women at Kalene, and they are more or less self-supporting.

Sakeji School started in 1925, next to Hillwood. It has a very wide catchment area for its size, made possible by road links and the well-maintained Sakeji airstrip. The school teaches Grades 1 to 7 (Junior) and is funded and staffed by mainly Canadian and American missionary workers from an organisation called 'Christian Churches in Many Lands' (CCML). In 1962 the Bible was translated into Lunda by Singleton Fisher and was subsequently updated by Paul Fisher, the third-generation patriarch of the family, before his death in 2014.

closely with the surrounding communities – Pete meets with the local village headmen once a month to inform, involve and share out the maintenance and development work on the reserve fairly between the villages. Roads, bridges, fences and shelters are all built and maintained with local labour and materials wherever possible. This 'Nchila Committee' also helps a great deal to prevent poaching, kept to a minimum thanks to the excellent rapport within the community as a whole. This is built on many years of talking together, mutual trust and help.

Nchila Wildlife Reserve (**w** nchilawildlifereserve.com; ⌚ 15 May–15 Nov; entrance US$10 pp; camping US$25 pp/night) Nchila Wildlife Reserve is a 40km² area of virgin bush within the boundaries of Hillwood Farm. It's a great area for game drives and walks, always accompanied by a guide from Nchila (hence the need to book in advance). See below for more on the flora and fauna, but note that even if you're not a keen 'twitcher', the rolling country is very pleasant walking, with patches of evergreen forests adding a welcome touch of shade.

The prime time to visit is August to end-October for the birding.

Flora and fauna Nchila attracts a steady stream of ornithologists, herpetologists, zoologists and other keen observers of the natural world. Most come for the reserve's pockets of pristine wet, evergreen forest (rainforest). These are typical of large areas of its neighbouring countries – so you'll find species here which you can't see anywhere else, unless you're prepared to brave the instability of either Angola or the DRC.

Note that you'll find some exceedingly comprehensive details of Nchila's flora and fauna on the reserve's website so here I'll just mention a few of the more obvious highlights.

Flora This beautiful, rolling and hilly area has large areas of moist open plains dotted with termitaria. These are veined by miombo woodland and, in the lower areas, patches of wet, evergreen (mishutu) forest which surround many permanent streams.

Animals The larger wildlife here includes possibly Zambia's largest herd of sable antelope (some of which appear to have some genes in common with Angolan giant sables, given their appearance), and very good numbers of roan and eland that are generally very relaxed and approachable. In addition, there are plains zebra, defassa waterbuck, impala, Kafue lechwe, puku and kudu. Oribi are abundant on the plains and warthog are sometimes seen grubbing around.

Sitatunga frequent the denser, wetter patches of forest – and, like the bushbuck which are found here, sometimes venture out along the edge of the open plains; it's here that I had one of the clearest sightings of these shy antelope that I've ever experienced. The sitatunga here are all an Angolan subspecies, similar to the forest sitatunga. There are also East-Angolan bush duiker, making this one of the few places that they can be seen in their endemic habitat. In the forest patches you'll find vervet and blue monkeys, as well as common and blue duiker. (With some luck and much skill, the guides can sometimes call the curious blue duiker in to approach you.)

Birdlife The birdlife here is a real draw; it's a very special place. The forests contain 30 species not found anywhere outside of the DRC, Angola and this area – most of which do not even occur around Mwinilunga (only 70km south of Nchila). However, for some of this area's 'specials' you may have to go a further 50km north to the very tip of Zambia – around the source of the Salujinga and the Jimbe. The borders with Angola and the DRC are very sensitive – so take local advice before you venture that far.

The source of the Zambezi and the Sakeji River, which runs through Hillwood, is a microcosm of the DRC forests. Many of the birds which occupy ecological niches south of here are replaced by different, but closely related, species. The area's 'specials' often need work to spot, and a fair amount of searching with one of Nchila's guides who knows where to look. They include afep and bronze-naped pigeons; black-collared bulbuls; grey-winged robins; rufous ant thrushes; Fülleborne's and rosy-breasted longclaws; honeyguide greenbuls; shining blue, white-bellied and blue-breasted kingfishers; olive long-tailed cuckoos; orange-tufted, green-throated and Bates' sunbirds; buff-throated apalises; Laura's and bamboo warblers; white-cheeked bee-eaters; red-bellied paradise flycatchers; and splendid glossy starlings.

Excursions from Hillwood and Nchila The **Zambezi rapids** near to Hillwood are a very popular day trip – as a lovely spot to play in the water and float down on inflatable inner tubes. This is a particularly good place for birdwatchers to search for the rare Forbes plover, which hunts for insects on the bare rocks.

Further north, around the **source of the Jimbe River**, is the best place to look for the compact weaver and white-spotted flufftails; a recent sighting of the shrike flycatcher was a new discovery for Zambia.

Source of the Zambezi About 12km south of the entrance road to Nchila is a turn-off (⊕ TUZAMB 11°23.321'S, 24°16.632'E) to the official spot at Kalene Hill where the mighty Zambezi begins its 2,700km journey to the Indian Ocean. Protected both as a national monument and a World Heritage Site, the site itself is unexceptional, but the surrounding dense forest canopy, part of a 36.8ha reserve, is impressive.

A copper plaque, unveiled in 1964 to celebrate Zambia's independence, marks the site, at an altitude of about 1,500m. There's a good thatched shelter here, ideal for picnics, and it takes about half an hour to walk to the source. Note that the short access road is, in part, the boundary between Zambia and the DRC.

Appendix 1: Tracks and Signs

An extract from Southern African Wildlife: A Visitor's Guide *by Mike Unwin*

Animals seldom parade across the bush the way they do across a TV screen. In fact, the untamed wilderness, far from teeming with wall-to-wall wildlife, can sometimes seem a disappointingly empty place. But there is much more to see than simply the animals themselves, and the trained eye will find the land littered with evidence of their presence or passing: tracks and trails, pellets and droppings, diggings and rubbings, torn branches, flattened grass, feathers, nests and bones. These clues, often known by the Afrikaans word spoor, tell the story of what happened when nobody was looking.

Some awareness of tracks and signs will greatly enrich your own understanding of wildlife. Trackers, like forensic detectives, combine acute eyesight and vigilance with great patience, a photographic memory and the imagination to reconstruct a complete picture from a few scattered fragments. It is a humbling experience to watch an expert in action: a mere scratch in the soil can not only identify the animal responsible, but also reveal its age, sex, size, where it was heading, how it was moving, when it passed by and why.

MAKING TRACKS

Every animal that touches the ground leaves tracks. Some are easily recognised; others are more puzzling. Most small creatures, such as lizards, can only be identified to a broad generic level, but many larger mammal species have unique signatures. No two individuals of any species are identical, and the tracks of many show marked differences of size and shape between forefeet and hindfeet or between male and female. Conditions underfoot are critical to tracking. The clearest tracks are laid on surfaces that hold an impression, such as firm mud or damp sand. Hard, baked soil is too resistant, while soft sand allows slippage that distorts the shape.

Weather is also important: wind and rain can help to date tracks, but may erode or completely obliterate them. Neither overcast weather nor a midday sun are very helpful to trackers. Early morning is the best time to look – partly because tracks are still fresh, but also because the low light and slanting shadows throw any imprint into sharper relief.

THE HEAVY BRIGADE The bigger the animal, the harder its footfall. Elephants leave huge, round tracks, up to half a metre across, with the hindfeet smaller and more oval than the forefeet. In soft mud they create knee-deep craters that become sunbaked into a treacherous pitted moonscape. On hard ground, the latticework of cracks on their soles leaves a distinct, mosaic-like impression, even though the circular track outline may be invisible. A small heap of soil in front of each print indicates the elephant's direction (the rear of each track shows a clean edge). Rhino tracks have a cloverleaf shape, with each foot showing three distinct toes. On hard ground only the curved outer rim of each toenail may be visible. White rhinos have larger tracks (up to 30cm long) than black rhinos (about 24cm), with relatively broader toe marks. Hippos leave tracks of a similar size, but spaced more closely together and showing four clear toes on each foot. Their regular trails to and from water leave two, deep, parallel ruts either side of a central ridge.

ON THE HOOF Most ungulates leave symmetrical cloven-hoofed tracks. Those of antelope differ in little other than size, though some, like an impala's, are pointed, while others, like a kudu's, are more rounded. Identification often depends upon other clues: for example, an impala's tracks are likely to be in a herd and unlikely to be on a hillside. A few antelope show more unusual tracks: a sitatunga's are very long (over 15cm in the male) and widely splayed for bounding over marshy terrain, while klipspringers drill neat round holes with their cylindrical tip-toed hooves. A giraffe's enormous hooves (up to 20cm long) leave imprints like a steam iron, spaced far apart by its great stride. A buffalo has tracks like a cow's – larger and rounder than any antelope's except an eland. A warthog's are also quite rounded, with the two halves clearly separated. Zebra, with only a single big hoof on each foot, leave horseshoe tracks, the size of a donkey's.

PADS, PAWS AND CLAWS Most predator tracks show the typical pad and toes arrangement of domestic cats and dogs. The crucial things to look for are size, shape, number of toes and whether or not claws are visible. The male lion's are the biggest (up to 15cm long) and, like all cats, each shows four well-spaced, rounded toes and two small indentations in the back of the pad. Except for the cheetah, whose claws are permanently extended, cats do not leave claw marks. Conversely, all dog tracks show claws, and most have a longer, narrower shape than a cat's, with all four toes set in front of the pad. A hyena's tracks also show claws, but the curved toes are tucked closer together and the back of the pad slopes at a distinct diagonal. Spotted hyena tracks are about 10cm long, similar in size to a leopard's, and are commonly found around campsites. Mustelid tracks have five toes: an otter's show the hand-like spread of its dextrous fingers; a honey badger's show the furrows of its long claws, set well ahead of the toes. A genet's neat tracks resemble a tiny cat's – four-toed, clawless and rounded – but spaced close together by its short-legged gait. Most mongooses leave small, clawed tracks, some showing a fifth hind toe set back behind the four in front.

MAMMAL VARIATIONS An aardvark's tracks show only three toes on each foot, each one capped with a heavy claw mark, and its meandering trail is scattered with freshly excavated soil. Monkeys leave five-toed hand prints, with the opposable thumb or big toe clearly visible on each. A baboon's look particularly human, and are often confusingly overlaid where a whole troop has been active. A lesser bushbaby hops upright between trees, so leaves only the prints of its hindfeet. Squirrel tracks show longer hind feet than forefeet, and usually lead to and from a burrow or tree. A hare leaves tracks in sets of four, each of which shows the two front feet placed in line, one ahead of the other, and the overlapping back feet placed side-by-side in front. Rat and mice tracks are tiny and show four front toes, five hind toes and sometimes the drag mark of the tail.

BIRDS Bird tracks can be roughly classified by the shape and arrangement of the toes. Most have three toes pointing forward and one back. In some, such as starlings or hornbills, the hind toe points straight back, while in others, such as doves, it is set at a slight angle. Korhaans and dikkops show no hind toe at all, while an ostrich show only two toes in each of its enormous (20cm long) tracks and at least a metre's stride between them. The pattern of a bird's tracks reflects the way in which it moves: robins place both feet together in a series of well-spaced hops; doves follow a winding trail in which the feet move alternately in quick, short steps.

SCALE TRAILS The undulating motion of a typical snake leaves a series of S-shaped ripples, where each curve has pushed against surface irregularities to propel the body forward. A few heavy-bodied snakes, such as pythons and puff adders, can also grip the ground with their belly to push themselves along caterpillar-fashion, leaving a broad, straight furrow,

ANIMAL TRACKS (DRAWN TO SCALE)

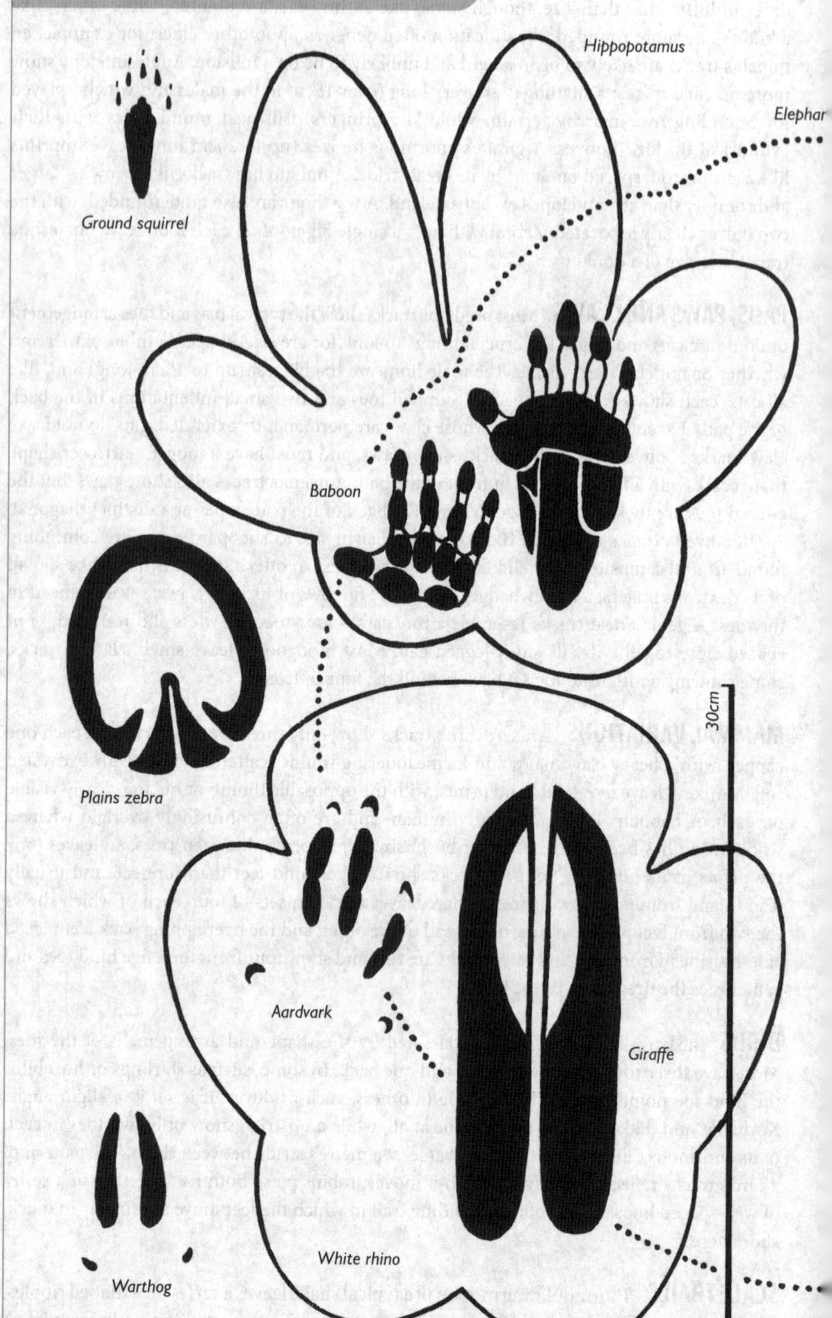

Hippopotamus

Elephar

Ground squirrel

Baboon

Plains zebra

30cm

Aardvark

Giraffe

White rhino

Warthog

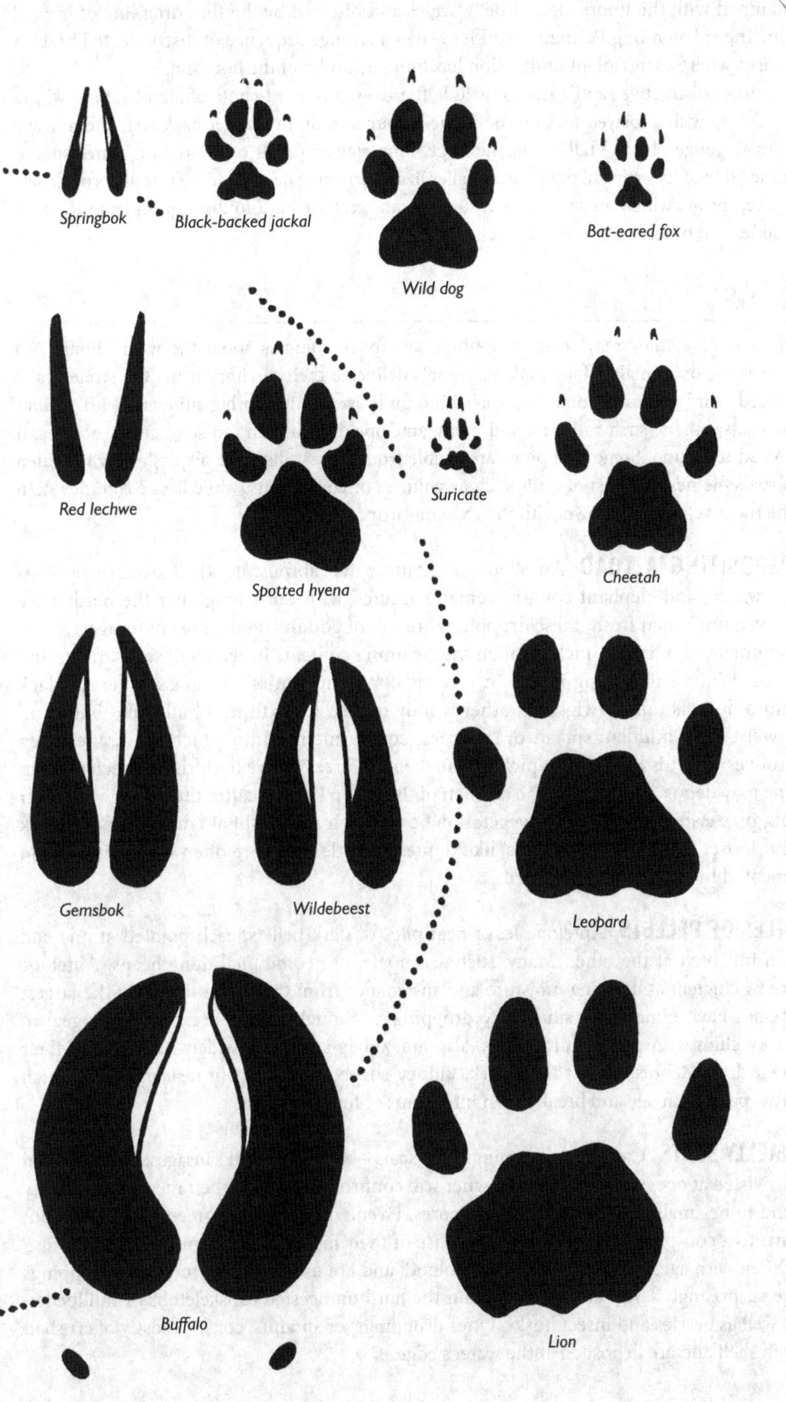
Springbok
Black-backed jackal
Wild dog
Bat-eared fox
Red lechwe
Spotted hyena
Suricate
Cheetah
Gemsbok
Wildebeest
Leopard
Buffalo
Lion

stamped with the impression of belly scales and bisected by the thin drag-line of the tail tip. The sidewinding Peringuey's adder leaves a strange sequence of disconnected bracket marks where each violent undulation has flung its body off the hot sand.

Other distinctive reptile tracks include the riverbank mud-chute of a crocodile – whose tracks show five splayed toes on the forefeet, four toes on the longer back feet, and a heavy furrow gouged by the tail – and the large, long-clawed prints of a monitor lizard, spaced either side of its wavy tail drag line. Smaller lizards inscribe neat, winding tramlines of closely spaced prints which, in soft surfaces such as sand, can be hard to distinguish from those of beetles and other larger invertebrates.

DROPPINGS

Unsavoury as they may seem, droppings can speak volumes about the whereabouts and behaviour of animals. Many male mammals delineate their territory using the strategically placed whiff of dung. Some, such as rhino and civet, build up big middens with regular deposits; others, such as hyena and many antelope, roll in theirs to soak up the scent and spread it around. Some droppings are visible from a great distance: a splash of white often reveals the nest or roost of birds such as vultures or cormorants, while dassie colonies stain the rocks yellow and brown with their viscous urine.

DEPOSITING A LOAD An elephant scatters its fibrous, football-sized droppings anywhere, and elephant country remains littered with dung long after the herds have moved on. When fresh, these droppings are full of goodies, and a host of foragers, from baboons to francolins, pick through the steaming contents in search of seeds, fruits and pods. White rhino dung is fine in texture, consisting entirely of grass, whereas black rhino dung is full of twigs and other woody matter. Over time, a bull rhino builds up a waist-deep midden, spread over several square metres, into which he scrapes deep grooves with his hind feet to pick up the scent. In areas where both rhino species occur, one may deposit its dung on the midden of the other. Hippo scatter their dung with their tail, plastering it messily over vegetation beside their trails. Buffalo droppings are black and loose, falling in folded 'pats' like domestic cattle's, and are often left trampled and smeared by the traffic of the herd.

PILES OF PELLETS Antelope leave neat piles of dark pellets, each pointed at one end and indented at the other. Many, such as impala, use communal dung heaps. Antelope are so efficient at deriving moisture and sustenance from their food that even the largest species have remarkably small, dry droppings – though a wildebeest's may congeal in sticky clumps. A giraffe's droppings, also amazingly small, are widely scattered by their great drop. Zebras deposit their dark, kidney-shaped droppings in neat mounds, which grow paler with age and break down into heaps of fine, dry grass.

SMELLY SCATS Carnivore droppings – or scats – are cylindrical sausages, often pointed or twisted at one end – as any dog-owner will confirm. Because of their meat content, they tend to be smellier than those of herbivores. Hyena droppings are green when fresh, but turn to a conspicuous chalky white because of their high bone content. A lion's may also whiten with age, but can be black with blood, and are usually full of fur. Civet droppings are surprisingly large, and often contain the hard undigested exoskeletons of millipedes, as well as berries and insect husks. Otter droppings, or spraints, consist mostly of crushed crab shell and are deposited at the water's edge.

WHO'S AT HOME?

Many animals can be detected by the homes they build. Bird nests are the best known, and some, such as the enormous thatches of sociable weavers or hammerkops often provide shelter for a whole community of other animals. Tree holes offer a desirable residence to anything from hornbills and hoopoes to bushbabies and squirrels, and a promising-looking cavity is always worth watching during the breeding season. Burrows should be checked for signs of life: a complex of small holes may indicate a mongoose or ground squirrel colony, while a big burrow may house either the aardvark that dug it, or more recent tenants such as warthogs, wildcats or porcupines – so look out for signs of occupation, such as a snake skin or porcupine quill.

The state of an area's vegetation can also betray local residents with no permanent home. A flattened depression in long grass might be where a waterbuck bedded down for the night, while tattered bushes could be the work of a territorial bull sable, who thrashes them with his horns. Deep parallel gashes gouged into a tree trunk are the calling card of the local leopard, and a shiny tree stump beside a mud wallow is a 'rubbing post', polished to a smooth finish by generations of itchy rhinos.

FEEDING SIGNS

A good look at the landscape soon reveals who had what for dinner. Elephant are the messiest of eaters: freshly broken branches, peeled strips of bark and tussocks of grass tossed across the track are all sure signs of their presence, as are deep holes dug in sandy riverbeds for fresh water. Big grazers such as hippo or rhino trim clearly defined and well-managed lawns. Giraffe prune thorn trees up to a height of six metres, creating a visible browse line, and leave glistening strings of saliva in overhead branches. Kudu leave bushes frayed and nibbled at head height, while black rhino will even munch thorny, poisonous euphorbias, sometimes demolishing them entirely. Many smaller animals also refashion the landscape in their search for food: bark stripped from the foot of a tree trunk is probably the work of porcupines; excavations at the base of an anthill show where an aardvark dug for termites; a hillside littered with overturned stones shows the methodical foraging of baboons for lizards and scorpions.

Predators usually leave evidence of their kills, though even a large carcass quickly disappears beneath an army of scavengers, as hyenas scatter the bones, vultures strip the skin, blowfly maggots consume the final shreds of flesh and ants clean the last drops of blood from the soil. Even the keratin of an antelope horn is food for the larvae of the horn-boring moth, which leaves strange tubular casts along its length. Leopards often cheat scavengers, at least for a while, by hoisting their kill into a tree, so look out for hooves overhead. A scattering of feathers may reveal the regular plucking post of a raptor – which tears out tough flight feathers individually, leaving small, V-shaped punctures on the shafts, whereas a mammalian predator rips them out in clumps, shearing right through the quills with its teeth. Owls and other birds of prey regurgitate pellets of undigested bones and fur, often found beneath their roosts, while some shrikes impale prey such as lizards and grasshoppers on acacia thorns and barbed-wire fences.

Appendix 2

LANGUAGES

Zambia's main language groups are briefly outlined from page 20. This section will try to note down just a few useful phrases, and give their local translations in six of the most frequently encountered languages: Nyanja, Bemba, Lozi, Lunda, Tonga and Luvale. The visitor will probably find Nyanja or Bemba the most useful of these: Nyanja is the language that visitors are most likely to hear in the parks, while Bemba is more widely spoken countrywide. However, in the more remote areas – like the Western Province – where Nyanja and Bemba are not spoken, the other languages will prove invaluable.

Space is too short here, and my knowledge too limited, to give a detailed pronunciation guide to these six languages. However, all are basically phonetic and by far the best way to learn the finer nuances of pronouncing these phrases is to find some Zambians to help you as soon as you arrive. Asking a Zambian to help you with a local language is also an excellent way to break the ice with a new local acquaintance, as it involves them talking about a subject that they know well, and in which they are usually confident.

There may be several ways of saying goodbye, depending on the circumstances. In Nyanja, for example, one form may be said by the person leaving, and the other by the person staying behind – translating as 'go well' and 'stay well'. An alternative is to use the more informal 'see you later'.

Note that there is no specific word for 'please'; rather the meaning is incorporated into the word structure, so in Lozi, for example, 'please' is expressed by adding an 'a' to the subjunctive of the verb.

As noted on page 123, learning a few simple phrases in the local language will go a long way towards helping the independent traveller to have an easy and enjoyable time in Zambia. Just remember to laugh at yourself, and have fun. Most Zambians will be very impressed and applaud your efforts to speak their language, no matter how hard they may laugh!

	Nyanja	**Bemba**	**Lozi**
Good morning;	*Muli bwanji?* (formal)	*Mwashibukeni?* (formal)	*Muzuhile cwani?* (formal)
How are you?	*Muli shani?* (informal)	*Muzuhile?* (informal)	*Mucwani?* (informal)
I am fine	*Nile bwino* (formal) *Bwino* (informal)	*Eyamukwayi, Ndifye bwino* (formal) *Bwino* (informal)	*Lu zuhile hande* (formal) *Hande* (informal)
Goodbye	*Salani bwino*	*Shaaleenipo*	*Muzamave hande*
See you later (*ciao*)	*Tisau onana*	*Twalaamonana*	*Lukabonana*
yes	*inde*	*eya ye*	*kimona*
no	*iyayi*	*awe*	*baatili*
thank you	*zikomo*	*twa to te la*	*nitumezi*

NAMES

Judi Helmholz

During your travels you may have the good fortune to meet a Wireless, a Handbrake or an Engine. If you are really lucky, you may encounter a Cabbage. These are names of people I have met in Zambia.

Looking for Fame and Fortune? Look no further than twin boys living in the Western Province. Beware of Temptation though, he is a money-changer known for calculating exchanges solely to his advantage.

Working with Sunday and Friday got rather amusing, 'Sunday, can you work on Saturday with Friday?' Working with Trouble was another matter entirely, as we had frequently to enquire, 'Where can I find Trouble?' Gift, true to his namesake, felt compelled to ask for one, while Lunch took on a whole new meaning and Clever is a friend who is true to his name.

Unusual names aren't limited solely to English. For example, there is Mwana Uta which literally means 'son of a gun', and Saka Tutu meaning 'father of an insect'. Pity the local man named Mwana Ngombe or 'child of a cow'!

	Nyanja	**Bemba**	**Lozi**
hey you!	*iwe!*	*iwe!*	*wena!*
I want	*ndifuna*	*ndefwaya*	*nabata*
there	*kunja*	*kulya* (also 'food')	*kwale*
here	*apa*	*hapa* (silent 'h')	*faa*
stop	*imilira*	*yema*	*iminina*
let's go	*tiyeni or tye*	*aluye*	*natuleya*
help me	*niyetizipita*	*ngafweniko*	*nituse kwteni*
how much?	*zingati?*	*shinga?*	*kibukayi?*
it is too much!	*yadula!*	*fingi!*	*kihahulu!*
where can I find…?	*alikuti…?*	*kwisa…?*	*uinzi kai…?*
the doctor	*sing'ang'a doctoro*	*shinganga*	*mualafi*
the police	*kapokola*	*kapokola*	*mupokola*
the market	*kumusika*	*ekobashita fyakulya*	*kwamusika*
drinking water	*mazi akumwa*	*amenshi ayakunwa*	*mezi a kunwa*
some food	*chakudya*	*ichakulya*	*sakuca*

	Lunda	**Tonga**	**Luvale**
Good morning;	*Mudi nahi?*	*Mwabuka buti?*	*Ngacili?*
How are you?		*Muli buti?*	
I am fine	*Cha chiwahi*	*Kabotu*	*Kanawa*
Goodbye	*Shalenuhu*	*Muchale kabotu*	*Salenuho mwane*
See you later (*ciao*)	*Tuualimona*	*Tulabonana*	*Natulimona*
yes	*ena*	*inzya*	*eawa*
no	*inehi*	*pepe*	*kagute*
thank you	*kusakililaku*	*twalumba*	*gunasakulila*
hey, you!	*enu!*	*yebo!*	*enu!*
I want	*nakukena*	*ndiyanda*	*gikutonda*
there	*kuna*	*okuya*	*haaze*
here	*kunu*	*aano or awa*	*kuno*
stop	*imanaku*	*koyima or ima*	*imana*

	Lunda	Tonga	Luvale
let's go	*tuyena*	*atwende*	*tuyenga*
help me	*kwashiku*	*ndigwashe*	*gukafweko*
how much?	*anahi?*	*ongaye?*	*jingayi?*
it is too much!	*yayivulu!*	*chadula! or zinji!*	*yayivulu!*
where can I find…?	*kudihi….?*	*ulikuli…?*	*ali kuli…?*
the doctor	*ndotolu*	*mun'ganga*	*ndotolo*
the police	*kapokola*	*kappokola*	*kapokola*
the market	*chisakanu*	*musika*	*mushika*
drinking water	*meji akunwa*	*maanzi akunywa*	*meya a kunwa*
some food	*chakuda*	*chakulya*	*kulya*

Appendix 3

FURTHER INFORMATION

BOOKS
History, politics and economy

Bigland, Eileen *The Lake of the Royal Crocodiles* Hodder and Stoughton, London, 1939.

Clark, John *Zambia: Debt & Poverty* Oxfam, Oxford, 1989. This slim volume looks with clarity at Zambia's international debt, its causes and its consequences.

Hobson, Dick *Tales of Zambia* Zambia Society Trust, London, 1996. This is a lovely book, cataloguing big moments in Zambia's history, as well as some of its quirkier incidents and characters. It has sections on legends, mining and the country's flora and fauna and is very readable. Dick Hobson's knowledge and love of Zambia shine through.

Lamb, Christine *The Africa House* Viking, London, 2nd edition 2004. This fascinating book pieces together the life and times of Sir Stewart Gore-Browne from diaries, correspondence and memories. It's a spellbinding tale, eloquently told. If this can't convey the fascination of Shiwa, and make you want to see it, then nothing can.

Livingstone, David *Missionary Travels and Researches in Southern Africa* 1857. Over a century after it was written, this classic still makes fascinating reading.

Macmillan, Hugh *An African Trading Empire: the story of Susman Brothers & Wulfsohn, 1901–2005* I B Tauris, London, 2005.

Macmillan, Hugh, and Shapiro, Frank *Zion In Africa: the Jews of Zambia* I B Tauris and the Council for Zambia Jewry, London and Lusaka, 1999.

Reader, John *Africa: A Biography of the Continent* Penguin Books, London, 1997. Over 700 pages of highly readable history, interwoven with facts and statistics, make a remarkable overview of Africa's past. Given that Zambia's boundaries were imposed from Europe, its history must be looked at from a pan-African context to be understood. This book can show you that wider view; it is compelling and essential reading. Chapter 47 is largely devoted to the Lozi people.

Roberts, Andrew *A History of Zambia* Africana Publishing, New York, 1976. A detailed and complete history of Zambia, from prehistory to 1974.

Rotberg, Robert I *Black Heart: Gore-Browne and the Politics of Multiracial Zambia* University of California Press, Berkeley, 1977.

Scott, Guy *Adventures in Zambian Politics: A Story in Black & White* Lynne Rienner Publishers, 2021. Guy Scott's memoir of his political career and time as acting president of Zambia.

Williams, Geoffrey J (ed) *Lusaka and its Environs* ZGA Handbooks, Lusaka.

David Livingstone and the Victorian Encounter with Africa National Portrait Gallery, London, 1996. Six essays on Livingstone's life, concentrating on not only what he did, but also on how he was perceived in the UK.

Zambia: Condemned to Debt World Development Movement (**w** wdm.org.uk), London, May 2004. The WDM is a charity which researches into global trade and debt trends, and campaigns for policies to reduce injustice and tackle poverty.

Wildlife and natural history Books published by the Wildlife and Environmental Conservation Society of Zambia (WECSZ) and the Zambian Ornithological Society (ZOS), are usually obtainable from bookshops and the National Museum in Lusaka, or direct from the WECSZ office (page 98).

Aspinwall, Dylan, and Beel, Carl *A Field Guide to Zambian Birds not found in Southern Africa* Zambian Ornithological Society, Lusaka, 1998. This excellent small guide is designed to complement a book covering Africa south of the Zambezi, such as Newman's guide, by describing only the birds occurring in Zambia which aren't included in Newman's guide. It's available in Zambia, but difficult to find elsewhere.

Bolnick, Doreen *A Guide to the Common Wild Flowers of Zambia and Neighbouring Regions* Macmillan Educational, London, 1995. This is a good small field guide to the more common species. A revised edition was published in 2007 by WECSZ.

Buk, Kenneth (Zoological Museum, University of Copenhagen) 'African Wild Dog Survey in Zambia', *Canid News*, vol 3, 1995. This piece of academic research looked at the distribution of wild dogs in Zambia in 1994, the reasons for their decline, and their possibilities for long-term survival.

Carr, Norman *A Guide to the Wildlife of the Luangwa Valley* Montford Press, Malawi, 3rd edition 1997. This small paperback (70 pages) was written by the valley's most famous guide and conservationist. It's not comprehensive, but is fascinating for the author's personal insights into the Luangwa area and its wildlife.

Coates Palgrave, Keith and Meg (eds) *Trees of Southern Africa* Struik, South Africa, 2003.

Cooray, Gerald, and Lane, Andrew *Minerals of Zambia* Nchanga Consolidated Copper Mines Ltd.

Hide, Phil *Birds of the Luangwa Valley* Zambian Ornithological Society, Lusaka, 2008.

Jackman, Brian, Scott, Jonathan & Angela *The Marsh Lions: The Story of an African Pride* Bradt Travel Guides, 2012

Jackman, Brian *Savannah Diaries* Bradt Travel Guides, 2014

Konings, Ad *Tanganyika Cichlids in their Natural Habitat* Cichlid Press (**w** cichlidpress.com), El Paso, 1998.

Leonard, Peter *Important Bird Areas in Zambia* Zambian Ornithological Society, Lusaka, 2005. The most comprehensive survey of the country's top birding areas – complete with a lot of other useful detail about Zambia's ecology, flora and fauna.

Newman, Kenneth *Newman's Birds of Southern Africa* Southern Books, South Africa, 1st edition 1988. This has been republished numerous times since its first edition and has become the standard field guide to birds in southern Africa, south of the Kunene and Zambezi rivers. It also covers most species found in Zambia.

Nyerenda, Patrick *A Guide to the Snakes of the Luangwa Valley* WECSZ, reprint 2007.

Pietersen, D et al. *Snakes and Other Reptiles of Zambia and Malawi* Penguin Random House, South Africa, 2021

Van Driel, Marcel *Snakes and First Aid in Snakebite in Zambia* Pensulo Publishers Limited, Zambia, 2022

Scott, Jonathan & Angela *The Leopard's Tale* Bradt Travel Guides, 2013

Sinclair, Ian, and Ryan, Peter *Birds of Africa south of the Sahara* Struik, Cape Town, 2003. The field guide used by many of Zambia's birders as it incorporates both central African and southern African species, though it's a hefty tome to cart around.

Sinclair, Ian, Hockey, Phil, Tarboton, Warwick, and Ryan, Peter *Sasol Birds of Southern Africa* Penguin Random House, South Africa 5th edition, 2020. Although it doesn't cover Zambia, it includes all species found in the country, bar a few endemics. Used by many of the camps, guides.

Smith, P P *Common Trees, Shrubs and Grasses of the Luangwa Valley* Trendrine Press, Cornwall, 1995. This small, practical field guide has pictures to aid identification at the back, and includes a small section on the value to wildlife of the various plants.

Solomon, Derek *Animals in Action: a guide to the common mammals of South Luangwa National Park* 2005.

van Perlo, Ber *Birds of Southern Africa* Collins Illustrated Checklist, 1999. The only concise field guide that covers both Zambia and the rest of the region.

A Guide to Common Wild Mammals of Zambia WECSZ, 1991. A small field guide to the more common species.

A Guide to Reptiles, Amphibians & Fishes of Zambia Wildlife Conservation Society of Zambia, Lusaka, 1993. Another good guide to the more common species.

Common Birds of Zambia Zambian Ornithological Society, Lusaka, revised 1993. A good small field guide to the more common species.

Art and culture

Jordan, Manuel *Makishi: Mask Characters of Zambia* Fowler Museum of Cultural History, Los Angeles, 2007.

Phillipson, D W, revised by Katanekwa, N M *National Monuments of Zambia* National Heritage Conservation Commission, Livingstone, 1972 (4th printing 1992). Look for this small, green paperback around Lusaka, and buy it if you see one as they're quite scarce. It describes all of Zambia's national monuments, including many historical monuments, archaeological sites and even places of great scenic beauty – with some great old black-and-white photos.

Smith, Benjamin W *Zambia's Ancient Rock Art: The Paintings of Kasama* National Heritage Conservation Commission, Livingstone, 1997.

Coffee-table books

d'Elbée, François *Bush and Eye* Editions de la Martinière, Paris, 2002, and *Busanga: The Northern Plains of the Kafue National Park* 2004. D'Elbée's illuminating photographs focused first on the Lower Zambezi National Park, and then on the northern Kafue – with stunning results.

Travelogues and biography

Carr, Norman *Kakuli: A Story about Wild Animals* CBC Publishing, Harare, 1996. A collection of Norman Carr's tales from his time in the Luangwa Valley. Excellent light reading while on safari.

Owens, Mark and Delia *Survivor's Song: Life and Death in an African Wilderness* HarperCollins, London, 1993. Published as *The Eye of the Elephant* in the USA. This relates the authors' struggles to protect the wildlife of North Luangwa National Park from poachers, and their efforts to develop viable alternatives to poaching for the local people. It is excellent reading, though insiders complain of sensationalism, and that it ignores valuable contributions made by others.

Palin, Michael *Pole to Pole* BBC Consumer Publishing, London, 1999. This has an excellent section on Zambia, and Shiwa Ng'andu in particular is covered well.

Quarmby, C A *Just Driving Around in the North* Health Rescue International, Zambia.

Siddle, Sheila, with Cress, Doug *In My Family Tree: A Life with Chimpanzees* Grove/Atlantic, New York, 2002, and Double Storey, Cape Town, 2004. Sheila Siddle's story of the establishment of Chimfunshi Wildlife Orphanage.

Guidebooks

Allen, Quentin, Mwanza, Ilse and Chalcraft, Heather *A Guide to Little-Known Waterfalls of Zambia* Published privately, Lusaka, 2005. A mine of useful information, this detailed guide offers an excuse to head off the beaten track as well as detailed information relating to Zambia's innumerable waterfalls. Illustrated with line drawings, paintings and photographs, it also has plenty of practical information, including GPS co-ordinates. There's a frequently updated Facebook page managed by the group which posts reliable updates on access and the waterfalls themselves.

Ashley, Nikki *The Kafue National Park, Zambia* CBC Publishing, Harare, 2012. This detailed guide to the national park is written by a biologist but also incorporates visitor information and a species list, with photographs by Ian Murphy.

Atlas of the National Parks of Zambia ZAWA, Chilanga, 2009. Available only at ZAWA's Chilanga HQ, near Lusaka, this useful atlas presents the country's national parks through a series of helpful maps.

Johnson, Sigrid Anna *A Visitor's Guide to Nyika National Park, Malawi* Nyika Vwaza Trust, 2017. A detailed historical and ecological background to Nyika, including special-interest sites and notes on recommended walks and hikes, as well as complete checklists of all mammals, birds, butterflies and orchids that are known to occur in the park.

Rattray, Gordon *Access Africa: Safaris for People with Limited Mobility* Bradt Travel Guides, UK, 2009. This is an invaluable guide to taking a safari for travellers with limited mobility, and includes a section on Livingstone.

Welcome to Lusaka – A Guide for Newcomers Diplomatic Spouses Association, Lusaka, 2011

Health

Wilson-Howarth, Dr Jane *The Essential Guide to Travel Health: Don't Let Bugs, Bites and Bowels Spoil Your Trip* Cadogan Books, London, 2009. An amusing and erudite overview of the hazards of tropical travel which is small enough to take with you.

Wilson-Howarth, Dr Jane, and Ellis, Dr Matthew *Your Child Abroad: A Travel Health Guide* Bradt Travel Guides, 3rd edition (eBook) 2014. An invaluable resource for all those travelling with children.

Novels

Banda-Aaku, Ellen *Patchwork* Penguin, South Africa, 2011. Banda-Aaku's award-winning novel of a child growing up in Lusaka gives an insight into Zambian life in the late 1970s. In so doing, it touches on issues as wide ranging as wealth and poverty, cultural evolution and post-independence politics.

Serpell, Namwali *The Old Drift* Hogarth Press, 2019. Written by an American-Zambian author and English professor at Harvard University, well known for her essays and short story writing, this is Serpell's award-winning debut novel. Part historical fiction, part science fiction fable, it's an epic spanning three Zambian families over three generations, from colonial Northern Rhodesia to the modern day.

Smith, Wilbur *Elephant Song* Zaffre, UK, 2018. Zambian-born British author Wilbur Smith was a prolific historical fiction writer whose 41 books span multiple African countries. *Elephant Song* is a gripping adventure centred on elephant and rhino poaching in Zimbabwe, Zambia and Malawi.

Children's books

Apps, Peter *My First Book of Southern African Mammals* Penguin Random House – Struik, 2008. Excellent first field guide for young children covering 58 mammals with clear, factual information on their appearance, size, diet and tracks. For ages 4–8.

Cuthbert, Erroll *My First Book of Southern African Birds* (2 volumes) Penguin Random House – Struik, 2009. Clear bird guide with good colour illustrations and facts. For ages 4–8.

Griffiths, Meg *Wonky Tusk* Muddy Boots, Zambia, 2008. A children's story about a naughty elephant whose mother has a wonky tusk. The 'Wonky Tusk' of the title refers to the elephant matriarch who annually leads her family through Mfuwe Lodge in the South Luangwa in search of ripe mangoes.

Stuart, Chris and Stuart, Mathilde *My First Book of Southern African Animal Tracks* Penguin Random House – Struik, 2014. Well-presented, full-colour-illustrated guide showing life-sized tracks of 55 different species. For ages 4–8.

WEBSITES Website addresses seem to change frequently, especially in Zambia, but some of the more interesting ones include the following.

Tourist information

w **zambia.co.zm** Called 'The National Homepage of Zambia', with some useful links.
w **zambiatourism.com** The official website of the Zambia National Tourist Board.

Media

w **lusakatimes.com** Online news site focused on politics, economy, sport and nationwide news, with the ability for readers to post opinion articles.
w **times.co.zm** The site of the state-owned *Times of Zambia* newspaper featuring the main stories of the day.

Appendix 3 FURTHER INFORMATION

A3

Acknowledgements

The seventh edition of this book has been built on the foundations of the first six, and, like those before, it has been inspired, influenced and improved by the knowledge and kindness of many in Zambia. Many of those who've provided valuable insights and support during the research and writing of this guide have been a part of every edition we've written, helping to shape the content and ensuring we're always abreast of change. For this edition, we would particularly like to thank Jess Salmon and Ade Coley at Flatdogs; John and Carol Coppinger, Jennifer Coppinger, Nick Riddin and all of the Remote Africa team; Derek and Jules Shenton from Shenton Safaris; Grant and Lynsey Cumings of Chiawa Safaris.

Several people took time to answer questions on their corner of the country, checking details of the text, or kindly providing missing pieces of the overall jigsaw. Thanks for this are due to Ian Pollard at African Parks in Kafue; Anél Joubert at African Parks in Liuwa Plain; Xanthe Zytkow at African Parks Bangweulu; Christine Coppinger, Bruce Ellender and Dorian Tilbury in West Lunga and Chris Fisher at Nchila.

Many others went out of their way to help with the research for earlier books, including Tricia and Bob Hayne, who worked extensively on the previous three editions; Sue Wat and Will Witford for their past research on the Bangweulu Wetlands Area chapter; Judi Helmholz and Arthur Sonnenberg in Livingstone; Christina (Gid), Abraham and the NCS crew; Jo and Robin Pope at RPS; Babette and Phil Berry at Kuyenda; Bryan Jackson for great walking, and pulling my Land Rover through a few rivers; Charlie and Jo Harvey at Shiwa Lynn; Pete and Paul Fisher; Charlie Rae; Pete Leonard, who kindly shared information from his encyclopedic Zambian bird atlas; Philip Briggs, for the kind use of his writings as the basis for the wildlife chapter, and Heather Chalcraft, for kindly allowing us to reprint articles from *The Lowdown*.

Zambia's top birding expert, the late Bob Stjernstedt, kindly reviewed the birding comments, making a number of very helpful additions and contributions. Anna Weyher of the Kasanka Baboon Project made similarly valuable comments on the baboon text. And I still owe huge thanks to John Coppinger, not only for unstinting hospitality over the years, but also for his time and many emails about the Luangwa's history, wildlife and environment.

Many readers of earlier editions have helped with their news and views, and countless Expert Africa travellers have generously provided valuable feedback on their trips. These have given us hundreds of extra pairs of eyes and ears in Zambia every year – constantly updating us on the latest news and views of the various camps, lodges and offbeat corners. We couldn't list everyone here if we tried, but we are eternally grateful.

Fantastic colleagues at Expert Africa, all of whom possess incredible knowledge, have contributed much – Megan Green, Lucy Copson, Maruska Adye-Rowe and

Amanda Bond stand out here – while working tirelessly on their day jobs of creating super safaris for travellers. Without their considerable abilities and understanding, this guide would be less accurate and detailed.

Bradt's whole team have, as ever, been superb, with special thanks due to Emma Gibbs and Susannah Lord for their care and attention throughout the editorial process.

And, finally, to Mike and Margaret Shand, who ventured to Zambia from Scotland when it seemed like the end of the Earth and filled Susie's childhood with wild African adventures, and to our children, James and Charlotte, who now make those adventures so joyful. Thank you!

Seventh edition published August 2023
First published 1996
Bradt Guides Ltd
31a High Street, Chesham, Buckinghamshire, HP5 1BW, England
www.bradtguides.com
Print edition published in the USA by The Globe Pequot Press Inc, PO Box 480, Guilford, Connecticut 06437-0480

Project Manager: Susannah Lord
Copy editor: Emma Gibbs
Cover research: Pepi Bluck, Perfect Picture

ISBN: 9781804690154

British Library Cataloguing in Publication Data
A catalogue record for this book is available from the British Library

Photographs AWL images: John Warburton-Lee (JWL/AWL); Chiawa Safaris (CS); Collective (C); Dreamstime.com: Christianef (C/D), Ecophoto (E/D), Andrey Gudkov (AG/D), Irishkoala (I/D), Paula Joyce (PJ/D), Robert Khafizov (RK/D), Milosk50 (M50/D), Smellme (S/D), Whpics (WH/D), Wrangel (WR/D); Steve Lorenz Fischer (SLF); Tricia Hayne (TH); Peter W. Hills (PWH); Charlotte McIntyre (CEM); Chris McIntyre (CM); James McIntyre (JM); Susie McIntyre (SM); Mana Meadows (MM); Mulberry Mongoose (MMG); Nature Picture Library: Will Burrard-Lucas (WBL/NPL); Remote Africa Safaris (RAS): Francois d'Elbee (FdE/RAS); Shenton Safaris (SHS); Shutterstock.com: 2630ben (2630/S), Tristan Barrington (TB/S), Braam Collins (BC/S), COULANGES (C/S), CreativeWILD - CS (CW/S), Daniel Danckwerts (DD/S), Dr Livingstone Supongo (DLS/S), EcoPrint (EP/S), Matt Elliott (ME/S), Kelly Ermis (KE/S), Erni (E/S), Chris Fourie (CF/S), paula french (PF/S), GTW (GTW/S), Roger de la Harpe (RH/S), clayton harrison (CH/S), David Havel (DH/S), Jukka Jantunen (JJ/S), Daniel Loncarevic (DL/S), Boris Mayer (BM/S), Martin Mecnarowski (MM/S), Katarina Medger (KM/S), Christian Nuebling (CN/S), nwdph (NWD/S), Hansie Oosthuizen (HO/S), Martin Pelanek (MP/S), Stu Porter (SP/S), Ondrej Prosicky (OP/S), Thomas Retterath (TR/S), Dr Ajay Kumar Singh (AKS/S), Michal Sloviak (MS/S), Eugene Troskie (ET/S), Willem Van Zyl (WVZ/S), Tyrone Winfield (TW/S); SuperStock (SS); Time+Tide (TT); Marcel Van Driel, Helping Hands in Snake Safety (MVD/HHISS); Ariadne Van Zandbergen (www.africaimagelibrary.com) (AVZ).
Front cover Leopard (*Panthera pardus*), South Luangwa National Park (WBL/NPL)
Back cover, clockwise from top left Victoria Falls in morning light (2630/S), shoebill stork (*Balaeniceps rex*) in flight (SLF), African elephants (*Loxodonta africana*), South Luangwa National Park (PF/S)
Title page, clockwise from left African wild dog (*Lycaon pictus*) (SHS), game drive with young lions (CS), southern carmine bee-eaters (*Merops nubicoides*) (TR/S)

Maps David McCutcheon FBCart.S; colour map relief base by Nick Rowland FRGS

Typeset by Ian Spick, Bradt Guides; and Geethik Technologies, India
Production managed by Page Bros Ltd; printed in the UK
Digital conversion by www.dataworks.co.in

NOTES

Index

Page numbers in **bold** indicate main entries; those in *italic* indicate maps

INDEX OF ADVERTISERS

In the beginning

It all began in 1974 on an Amazon river barge. During an 18-month trip through South America, two adventurous young backpackers – Hilary Bradt and her then husband, George – decided to write about the hiking trails they had discovered through the Andes. *Backpacking Along Ancient Ways in Peru and Bolivia* included the very first descriptions of the Inca Trail. It was the start of a colourful journey to becoming one of the best-loved travel publishers in the world; you can read the full story on our website (bradtguides.com/ourstory).

Getting there first

Hilary quickly gained a reputation for being a true travel pioneer, and in the 1980s she started to focus on guides to places overlooked by other publishers. The Bradt Guides list became a roll call of guidebook 'firsts'. We published the first guide to Madagascar, followed by Mauritius, Czechoslovakia and Vietnam. The 1990s saw the beginning of our extensive coverage of Africa: Tanzania, Uganda, South Africa, and Eritrea. Later, post-conflict guides became a feature: Rwanda, Mozambique, Angola, and Sierra Leone, as well as the first standalone guides to the Baltic States following the fall of the Iron Curtain, and the first post-war guides to Bosnia, Kosovo and Albania.

Comprehensive – and with a conscience

Today, we are the world's largest independently owned travel publisher, with more than 200 titles. However, our ethos remains unchanged. Hilary is still keenly involved, and **we still get there first**: two-thirds of Bradt guides have no direct competition.

But we don't just get there first. Our guides are also known for being **more comprehensive** than any other series. We avoid templates and tick-lists. Each guide is a one-of-a-kind expression of an expert author's interests, knowledge and enthusiasm for telling it how it really is.

And a commitment to wildlife, conservation and respect for local communities has always been at the heart of our books. Bradt Guides was **championing sustainable travel** before any other guidebook publisher. We even have a series dedicated to Slow Travel in the UK, award-winning books that explore the country with a passion and depth you'll find nowhere else.

Thank you!

We can only do what we do because of the support of readers like you – people who value less-obvious experiences, less-visited places and a more thoughtful approach to travel. Those who, like us, take travel seriously.